Republics Ancient and Modern

Republics

Ancient and

Modern

VOLUME III

Inventions of Prudence:

Constituting the American

Regime

PAUL A. RAHE

The University of North Carolina Press

Chapel Hill and London

Republics Ancient and Modern was originally published in hardcover in one volume by the University of North Carolina Press in 1992. Both the initial research and the publication of this work were made possible in part through grants from the Division of Research Programs of the National Endowment for the Humanities, an independent federal agency whose mission is to award grants to support education, scholarship, media programming, libraries, and museums in order to bring the results of cultural activities to a broad, general public.

Publication of this book was also aided by grants from the Lynde and Harry Bradley Foundation, the Earhart Foundation, and the John M. Olin Foundation.

Library of Congress
Cataloging-in-Publication Data
Rahe, Paul Anthony.
Republics ancient and modern / by Paul A. Rahe.
p.   cm.
Includes bibliographical references and index.
Contents: v. 1. The Ancien régime in classical
Greece—v. 2. New modes and orders in Early
Modern political thought—v. 3. Inventions of
prudence: constituting the American regime.
1. United States—Politics and government—
1775–1783.   2. Political science—United States—
History—18th century.   3. Republicanism—
History.   4. Political science—Greece—History.
I. Title.
E210.R335   1994
321.8'6—dc20   94-5728
                                                      CIP

ISBN 0-8078-4473-x (pbk. : alk. paper) (v. 1)
ISBN 0-8078-4474-8 (pbk. : alk. paper) (v. 2)
ISBN 0-8078-4475-6 (pbk. : alk. paper) (v. 3)

98   97   96   95   94
5   4   3   2   1

JOSEPH WRIGHT ALSOP, JR.

I. F. STONE

In Memoriam

Contents

Preface

More than ten years ago, I set out to transform my dissertation into a publishable monograph. In the course of making the attempt, I paused in my work, unhappy with the conceptual framework into which I was trying to fit the pieces of the puzzle constituted by late fifth-century Sparta and Athens. I then thought that I would better be able to deal with those scattered fragments of information if I first clarified my own thinking about the character of ancient politics by composing a brief article comparing the constitution of ancient Lacedaemon with that of the modern United States. Had I had any notion at the time of the enormity of the task that I was then taking on, I would no doubt have jettisoned the project right then and there.

When I began that essay in comparative politics, I presumed that I knew virtually all that I needed to know about modern republicanism. I had been born in such a republic. I had grown up there, and I had spent three glorious years in Great Britain, studying ancient history and observing the politics of that remarkable polity at close hand. But, as I pursued my new project, I lost my way—or, rather, discovered that I had never had a very good grasp of where I was—and gradually I came to find strange and mysterious that which had always seemed familiar and obvious. The more I learned about the foundations of modern politics, the less I found that I could depend upon that which I had been taught and had always been inclined to take for granted. And so what began as an attempt to elucidate the character of ancient politics became as much, if not more, a study of modernity.

So, let the reader be warned. This three-volume work is not a summary of the received wisdom concerning the republics of ancient Greece, the political speculation of early modern Europe, and the character of the American founding. Moreover, it is unlikely that the arbiters of intellectual fashion will ever find my thinking congenial. In the three spheres discussed, I have not only broken with the orthodoxy currently reigning in the academy; I have also eschewed the latest trends; and I suspect that many, both in and outside our universities, will find what I have to say unsettling. Thus, for example, where present-minded ancient historians are inclined to place emphasis on the institutions or to stress the sociology of the ancient Greek city and to treat Athens as an exemplar, I present the world of the *pólis* in the light cast by the regime-analysis of Thucydides, Plato, Aristotle, and the like, and I try to show that the ancient tendency to prefer Sparta to Athens made considerable sense. Similarly, where students of early modern political thought now stress the continuity between the ancients and the moderns, I contend that there was a decisive break, disguised somewhat by the need of the latter to circumvent censorship and to make the new thinking more persuasive by presenting it in a fashion designed to soothe rather than shock, and I argue, therefore, that Machiavelli, Harrington, the radical Whigs, and Lord Bolingbroke were as much opposed to classical republicanism as Hobbes, Locke, Hume, and Montesquieu. And finally, where American historians debate whether the regime produced by the American Revolution was republican or liberal, ancient or modern, or simply confused, I argue that it was a deliberately contrived mixed regime of sorts—liberal and modern, first of all, but in its insistence that to vindicate human dignity one must demonstrate man's capacity for self-government, republican and classical as well. In short, it is my contention that we cannot understand our own situation without thinking a great deal about the politics of antiquity and the speculation of early modern times. Moreover, if I am correct, the modern social science that customarily guides our reflections with regard to this question is itself the chief obstacle to our understanding that which we most need to know. To put it bluntly, these volumes are intended solely for those willing to pause and rethink.

Because I address in these pages questions of permanent public interest, I have tried to make my argument and the evidence on which it is based as accessible as possible to the general reader. To that end, I have cited, where available, English translations of the secondary works which I have found useful, and I have in every case provided translations of the pertinent primary source material. Moreover, where the inclusion of a critical word or phrase in the original language may alert readers familiar with that language to my particular interpretation of the passage or to something going on in the text cited that I have been unable to capture fully in translation, I have provided such information as well. All of the translations, unless otherwise indicated, are my own. In quoting works published in English, I have nearly always retained the original spelling, punctuation, and emphasis. Exceptions are specified in the notes or marked by brackets in the text. In the last note to the introduction to each volume, I have listed books and articles, pertinent to the themes of that volume, which have appeared or come to my attention since the original edition went to press.

Washington, D.C.
18 December 1993

Acknowledgments

En route to publishing these three volumes, I have accumulated a great many debts. Some are exclusively professional. As anyone who peruses my notes will discover, I have read widely in the secondary literature of the three fields covered in this work, and I have learned a great deal from those who have preceded me—not least, let me add, from those whose opinions I challenge here. As will be evident, I owe much to the late M. I. Finley and Louis Gernet, to G. E. M. de Ste. Croix, Jean-Pierre Vernant, Pierre Vidal-Naquet, Marcel Détienne, and to their many students and associates; to John Dunn, Quentin Skinner, J. G. A. Pocock, and those who have succumbed to their influence; to the late Leo Strauss and his many, intrepid admirers; and to the late Hannah Arendt, to Bernard Bailyn, Gordon S. Wood, Joyce Appleby, Lance Banning, and to those who have further elaborated their various arguments.

Many of my debts are personal as well. Donald Kagan first introduced me to ancient history when I was a freshman at Cornell University, and a decade later he directed my dissertation at Yale University. Though rightly inclined to think that I should turn my thesis into a book before embarking on a project as ambitious as this one, he was always generous in his support and encouraging. At one time or another, he read every word printed below. From the outset, he has been my model of what a scholar should be. Allan Bloom first introduced me to the study of political theory and, while tolerating a sophomore's stubborn resistance to his arguments, he taught me how to read. At Oxford's Wadham College, I profited from the tuition of W. G. G. Forrest and I. M. Crombie, and I learned a great deal as well the term I was shipped out to Oswyn Murray of Balliol. Not the least of my Oxford acquisitions was my friendship with Peter Simpson, once my tutorial partner in philosophy, then a boon companion, and a generous reader of everything that I have written since, always ready to make a suggestion, to supply a reference, and to dig up an article. I was always fortunate in my colleagues while a student: Jonathan Erichsen, Julius Grey, and Gibson Kamau Kuria have all been a great help. In graduate school at Yale, I learned at least as much from my colleagues Barry Strauss, Brook Manville, Peter Krentz, Michael Cadden, Williamson Murray, and Stephen Holmes as I learned in class; and in one fashion or another, they have all been helpful since. To Douglas and Roseline Crowley, I owe more than I can say.

I began this work while a fellow at the Center for Hellenic Studies in Washington, D.C. I owe much to Bernard Knox, who was the first to suspect that the story now told here might be well worth telling, and I gained greatly from exchanges with Nicholas Richardson, Peter Burian, Maria Dzielska, Richard Kraut, Jan Bremmer, and Tessa Rajak. That year saw the beginning of the many pleasant conversations that I have had with my former student William Connell on this subject. He has been very generous with his time, reading drafts of various chapters and sending me articles and references that he has come across.

While teaching at Franklin and Marshall College, I encountered Joel Farber, who never denied me his time and advice, and met James W. Muller, who has gone over every word I have written since, sharing with me his deep knowledge of political theory, correcting me when I am wrong, pointing out errors in spelling and grammar, and encouraging me to get on with the task and finish my work. To no contemporary do I owe a greater debt; from no friend have I learned more. In some ways, this is his work as much as it is mine.

I learned something as well from a National Endowment for the Humanities Summer Seminar on slavery which I took with Orlando Patterson at Harvard University before trekking out West to the University of Tulsa. My colleagues at that institution have always been free with their time and advice and tolerant of my frequent absences. I am particularly indebted to Lawrence Cress, Robert Rutland, David Epstein, Marvin Lomax, Thomas Buckley, Patrick Blessing, Joseph C. Bradley, Mary Lee Townsend, Thomas Horne, Michael Mosher, Eldon Eisenach, and Jacob Howland, and I have mercilessly exploited the generous leave policy pioneered by Thomas Staley and reaffirmed by Susan Parr.

While a fellow at the National Humanities Center, I profited from conversations with Charles Blitzer, J. H. Hexter, Timothy Breen, John Shelton Reed, Donald Horowitz, Marc Plattner, Michael Alexander, Josiah Ober, and Shaul Bakhash, who read and commented on divers chapters. Thanks to Charles Blitzer and Kent Mullikin, I was later able to return to the center for three summers running to test my ideas in a national institute for high school teachers on ancient and modern republicanism taught with Christine Heyrman and Peter Riesenberg, who saved me from many a blunder.

While pondering the questions addressed here, I spent two years in Istanbul as a fellow of the Institute of Current World Affairs, thinking and writing about contemporary politics in Greece, Turkey, and Cyprus, and often wondering whether the hypotheses advanced in this work accurately describe contemporary republics in the eastern Mediterranean. While abroad, I drew on the wisdom of Peter Bird Martin, Dennison Rusinow, Nicholas

Rauh, Charles and Marie Henriette Gates, Joan and Patrick Leigh Fermor, and Antony Greenwood.

I finished the initial draft of this work while a fellow of the John M. Olin Foundation, and I revised much of the manuscript while a fellow at Washington University's Center for the History of Freedom. There I was saved from errors by criticism and suggestions advanced by Richard Davis, David Wootton, Blair Worden, Maurice Goldsmith, and Herbert Rowen. Along the way, I became acquainted with Hiram Caton and Lance Banning, who looked over the entire manuscript and gave me detailed and helpful advice, and with Alvin H. Bernstein, Carnes Lord, William and Susan Kristol, Eugene D. Genovese, Elizabeth Fox-Genovese, Bertram Wyatt Brown, Harvey C. Mansfield, Jr., Mark Golden, Kurt Raaflaub, and Father Ernest Fortin—who read and commented on particular chapters.

In writing this volume, I have drawn freely on the following, previously published work: "Church and State: Jefferson, Madison, and 200 Years of Religious Freedom," *The American Spectator* 19, no. 1 (January 1986): 18–23; and "Slavery, Section, and Progress in the Arts," in *The Revival of Constitutionalism*, ed. James W. Muller (Lincoln: University of Nebraska Press, 1988) 123–50. I am grateful to the University of Nebraska Press for permission to reprint the material used here.

My research and the writing of these volumes were aided greatly by generous support from the Center for Hellenic Studies, Franklin and Marshall College, the National Endowment for the Humanities, the National Humanities Center, the University of Tulsa, the Oklahoma Foundation for the Humanities, the John M. Olin Foundation, and Washington University's Center for the History of Freedom. Publication was made possible by subventions from the John M. Olin Foundation, the Earhart Foundation, the Lynde and Harry Bradley Foundation, and the National Endowment for the Humanities. The introductions to the three volumes were written while I was a fellow of the National Endowment for the Humanities and of the Woodrow Wilson International Center for Scholars. To these institutions and their officers, I owe a great debt.

It is with pleasure that I thank Lewis Bateman, of the University of North Carolina Press, and my three readers for suggestions and encouragement, as well as Alice Kauble, Gail Newman, and David Pettyjohn, all students at the University of Tulsa, who helped me check the notes.

In the fall of 1980, when I first set out to deal with the issues treated here, I met in Washington, D.C., two elderly journalists who, in retirement, were devoting much of the enthusiasm that they had once reserved for contemporary affairs to the study of ancient connoisseurship, literature, philosophy, and politics. They were not friends, but, as luck would have it, both be-friended me. That year, I saw a great deal of each; and in subsequent years, as circumstances brought me to the nation's capital, I always found time to stop by for lunch, tea, drinks, or dinner. Many of the arguments now presented here were first tried out on them. Both died in the summer of 1989, at about the time I finished the initial draft of the work, and I greatly regret not ever having had the opportunity to present them with copies and give them my thanks. It is with the peculiar generosity of the old to the young in mind that I dedicate this volume to the memory of these two very different men.

Suppose that we were to define what it means to be a people (populus) *not in the usual way, but in a different fashion—such as the following: a people is a multitudinous assemblage of rational beings united by concord regarding loved things held in common. Then, if we wished to discern the character of any given people, we would have to investigate what it loves. And no matter what an entity loves, if it is a multitudinous assemblage not of cattle but of rational creatures and if these are united by concord regarding loved things held in common, then it is not absurd to call it a people; and, surely, it is a better or worse people as it is united in loving things that are better or worse. By this definition, the Roman people is a people, and its estate* (res) *is without doubt a commonwealth* (res publica). *What this people loved in early times and what it loved in the ages that followed, the practices by which it passed into bloody sedition and then into social and civil wars, tearing apart and destroying that concord which is, in a certain manner, the health and welfare* (salus) *of a people—to this history bears witness. . . . And what I have said concerning this people and concerning its commonwealth, this also I should be understood to have said and thought concerning the Athenians, the rest of the Greeks, . . . and the other nations as well.*

AUGUSTINE

Introduction

No man can be a Polititian, except he be first an Historian or a Traveller; for except he can see what Must be, or what May be, he is no Polititian: Now, if he have no knowledge in story, he cannot tell what hath been; and if he hath not been a Traveller, he cannot tell what is: but he that neither knoweth what hath been, nor what is; can never tell what must be, or what may be.
—James Harrington

On the fifth of October 1938, Winston Churchill rose to address the House of Commons. It was not, in his estimation, an auspicious occasion. Four days before, Neville Chamberlain had returned from the Munich Conference to announce to nearly everyone's applause and relief that he had brought "peace in our time." To the consternation and annoyance of many within his own party and many without, Churchill insisted on throwing cold water on the prime minister's claim. He started off in an almost apologetic tone. "If I do not begin this afternoon," he said, "by paying the usual, and indeed almost invariable tributes to the prime minister for his handling of this crisis, it is certainly not from any lack of personal regard. We have always, over a great many years, had very pleasant relations, and I have deeply understood from personal experiences of my own in a similar crisis the stress and strain he has had to bear." Churchill then drew attention to the candor of others, and having fortified himself from their example, he came to the point: "I will, therefore, begin by saying the most unpopular and most unwelcome thing. I will begin by saying what everybody would like to ignore or forget but which must nevertheless be stated, namely, that we have sustained a total and unmitigated defeat, and that France has suffered even more than we have." Initially, he claimed, "One pound was demanded at the pistol's point. When it was given, £2 were demanded at the pistol's point. Finally, the dictator consented to take £1 17s. 6d. and the rest in promises of good will for the future." As for Czechoslovakia, "All is over. Silent, mournful, abandoned, broken, [she] recedes into the darkness."

More important from Churchill's perspective was his own country's descent in the brief span of time that had passed since Adolf Hitler had come to power. Czechoslovakia's disappearance was merely, he insisted,

the most grievous consequence of what we have done and of what we have left undone in the last five years—five years of futile good intentions, five years of eager search for the line of least resistance, five years of uninterrupted retreat of British power, five years of neglect of our air defenses. Those are the features which I stand here to expose and which marked an improvident stewardship for which Great Britain and France have dearly to pay. We have been reduced in those five years from a position of security so overwhelming and so unchallengeable that we never cared to think about it. We have been reduced from a position where the very word "war" was considered one which could be used only by persons qualifying for a lunatic asylum. We have been reduced from a position of safety and power—power to do good, power to be generous to a beaten foe, power to make terms with Germany, power to give her proper redress for her grievances, power to stop her arming if we chose, power to take any step in strength or mercy or justice which we thought right—reduced in five years from a position safe and unchallenged to where we stand now.

He could not believe "that a parallel exists in the whole course of history" for such a squandering and neglect of combinations and resources. By allowing the remilitarization of the Rhineland, by standing idly by while Austria was seized, by giving away Czechoslovakia, by opening the way for a Nazi domination of Eastern Europe, "we shall find that we have deeply compromised, and perhaps fatally endangered, the safety and even the independence of Great Britain and France." He feared that his own country would fall "into the power, into the orbit and influence of Nazi Germany" and that its "existence" would become "dependent upon their good will or pleasure." He predicted that there would be additional demands. He foretold that a "policy of submission" would "carry with it restrictions upon the freedom of speech and debate in Parliament, on public platforms, and discussions in the Press, for it will be said—indeed, I hear it said sometimes now—that we cannot allow the Nazi system of dictatorship to be criticized by ordinary, common English politicians. Then, with a Press under control, in part direct but more potently indirect, with every organ of public opinion doped and chloroformed into acquiescence, we shall be conducted along further stages of our journey."

He concluded his oration by saying that he did not grudge "our loyal, brave people . . . the natural spontaneous outburst of joy and relief when they learned that the hard ordeal would no longer be required of them at the moment." But he added that "they should know the truth." Above all else, they should know "that there has been gross neglect and deficiency in our defenses; they should know that we have sustained a defeat without a war, the consequences of which will travel far with us along our road; they should know that we have passed an awful milestone in our history, when the whole equilibrium of Europe has been deranged, and that the terrible words have for the time being been pronounced against the Western democracies: 'Thou art weighed in the balance and found wanting.' "[1]

Churchill's greatest speech makes strange reading today. Fifty years before he delivered it, liberal democracy appeared to be the wave of the future, its victory inevitable, its triumph almost at hand. In the first half-century that passed after the Munich crisis, the western democracies were time and again weighed in the balance; and though they were not ultimately found wanting, they were generally on the defensive. Indeed, for a long time, it seemed by no means certain that the future would be theirs. Then, suddenly, in the wake of Mikhail Gorbachev's rise to power in the Soviet Union, events took a new turn in that country and in Poland, in Hungary and Czechoslovakia, in East Germany and Bulgaria, in Romania, Yugoslavia, and ultimately even in Albania. The totalitarian regimes in Europe collapsed; the long, twilight struggle dubbed the Cold War came to an end; and it became evident that the patient postwar American policy of containment had actually worked. There were even grounds for the hope that communism would someday soon be regarded as a stage on the way to liberal democracy—not just in Europe, but in Asia and in the Caribbean as well.[2]

At a moment so fraught with hope for the future, it may seem untimely to resurrect past failures and to remind readers that the welcome events which have transpired need not have taken place. But I would submit that a certain sobriety is in order on our part and that it is not entirely fortuitous that the West has greeted the transformation of the East with a comparative lack of euphoria. It is essential to remember that it is in large part an accident that at the end of the Second World War liberal democracy was not in effect restricted to the continent of North America. Churchill's fears for his country no doubt seemed overly dramatic when he expressed them; they may seem so as well today. But this was not the case during the Battle of Britain, for, in truth, he was right in every particular. As a consequence of what Churchill called "an improvident stewardship," Western Europe fell to Nazi aggression and Britain was left all but defenseless. If Hitler had staked everything on an invasion of the British Isles, or if he had simply been content to consolidate his hold on Western and Central Europe, build submarines, and await his opportunity, there can be little doubt that he would eventually have prevailed, and Churchill's worst suppositions would have been translated into fact. One can, of course, imagine Hitler succumbing to Stalin. But a Soviet domination of the continent would hardly have improved Britain's prospects for survival as an independent, liberal democracy. It took direct

American intervention in the war to change the fundamental situation, and that intervention was entirely due to the Japanese attack on Pearl Harbor and the German declaration of war. Had the Japanese high command chosen to avoid a confrontation with the United States, the war would have had a different outcome—and not just in the Pacific. Indeed, if Hitler had held back from declaring war on the United States, there would have been no obvious occasion for an American military intervention in Europe, and one may wonder whether the United States would ever have involved itself directly in the conflict raging on that continent. The grave blunders of democracy's enemies obscure the fact that the world's first and most firmly settled liberal democracy was also then weighed in the balance and found very much wanting.[3]

The events of the 1930s and the 1940s proved to be a sobering experience for many of those who lived through them, and that costly education served them well when the time came for forging the postwar world. But that generation has now all but passed from the scene, and it is not difficult to imagine that liberal democracy in Europe, in North America, and elsewhere might once again suffer from "an improvident stewardship"—especially if faced with a challenge as unexpected, as formidable, and as terrifying as the one mounted some fifty years ago. This may seem unlikely in the wake of communism's collapse, but it is by no means impossible: modern military technology is dynamic; and where inattention, complacency, and wishful thinking are the rule, unforeseen developments can quickly and decisively alter the balance of power. In the 1930s, five years made all the difference. Nothing prevents such an eventuality in our own time. Indeed, as Saddam Hussein's abortive lunge for power should serve to remind us, the proliferation of nuclear, biological, and chemical weapons may well render the coming decades much more unstable than those in the recent past. There is every reason to suspect that, in one fashion or another, we will continue to be weighed in the balance.

But even if my misgivings prove unjustified, even if now, for the first time in more than half a century, we have nothing to fear from the appeasement of evil, there is little to justify self-satisfaction on our part, for there are clouds of another sort forming on our horizon. As Alexis de Tocqueville warned us long ago, the prosperity engendered by the modern republic and its remarkable success do not in any way preclude a fall: if the "decent materialism," which he found regnant in America, was unlikely to corrupt those exposed to it, it could nonetheless "soften the soul and without noise unbend its springs of action," and it could thereby prepare the way for a species of tyranny all the more horrifying because welcome and unremarked.[4] Something of the sort may be in wait for us, for over the last few decades a noiseless revolution has been under way; and as countless commentators on both left and right have repeatedly pointed out, domestic developments in all of the modern republics have been disheartening in one critical regard. There is a drift toward a species of soft, administrative despotism evident nearly everywhere—not least in the United States, the oldest, the least centralized, and most democratic republic in the world.

This point needs particular emphasis, for one can hardly think a liberal democracy in good health that acknowledges no limits to the expansion of public "entitlements," government services, and controls; that eats up an ever increasing proportion of the national income; that effectively relegates all severely contentious political decisions to a court of men and women appointed to office for life; and that leaves much of public policy to be determined by a dialogue between tenured bureaucrats and judges who never have to justify to the voters or even to one another in a public forum the decisions they have made. Nor can one be heartened to discover that those elected to the polity's most popular branch have so effectively entrenched themselves in office that death and retirement account for virtually all changes in personnel. These are straws in the wind. Like the gradual disappearance of the state and local autonomy that Thomas Jefferson and Alexis de Tocqueville thought so important for the maintenance of political freedom, they are indicative of a decline in democratic vigor, and this is a phenomenon which should give us pause.

There is, then, reason to ask what has gone wrong, what accounts for the modern republic's long period of vulnerability in the international sphere, and what explains the malaise now besetting it at home, for one must wonder whether modern republicanism suffers somehow from a debilitating, genetic disorder. These are, however, questions that it is far easier to pose than to answer, for the very character of modern republicanism is cast into the shadows by its brilliant, initial success when pitted against the old order. The men who made the American Revolution were arguably the most self-conscious legislators in human history. They claimed that they were initiating "a new order of the ages," and subsequent events in France and throughout the world suggest that they knew whereof they spoke. One consequence of their remarkable accomplishment is that the ancien régime is no longer with us, and that makes it extremely hard for us to adequately understand the political options that were open to them and the reasoned choices that they made. In past ages, one could gain perspective on one's own regime and come to discern its peculiarities by traveling, as Herodotus, Machiavelli, and James Harrington did, and thereby one could attain an awareness of the very considerable range of human possibilities. But when we travel today, we encounter polities by and large constructed in our own image and peoples uncannily eager to imitate our ways. Those polities which are not like ours are with the rarest of exceptions decidedly, if to our way of thinking, strangely, modern; and they are, in nearly every instance, tyrannies. For the comparative study of republicanism, historical inquiry is our only recourse. In no other way can we liberate ourselves from the tyranny of the familiar. In no other way can we come to see our own world with the discerning eye of a visitor from abroad.[5]

Here, however, we encounter another difficulty. The way that human beings tend to read the past is for the most part decisively shaped by the regime in which they live. In our case, this penchant is strengthened and fortified by a phenomenon peculiar to the modern age. The republicanism and the tyranny familiar to us.are unique in human history in that they are explicitly grounded on a species of political science; and, as I try to show in the chapters of this three-volume work, that political science is, despite its pretensions, quite partial to those very regimes. Like all peoples, then, we warm to what is familiar and we instinctively tend to prefer that which is our own. What distinguishes us is the partisan character of our political science, which serves chiefly to reinforce our prejudice in our own favor and which cannot, therefore, emancipate us from our natural sense of our own superiority. In sum, our status as children of the Enlightenment provides us with an elaborate and highly plausible rationalization of our own way of life— which tends to prevent us from seeing the polities of the past as their citizens saw them, and which in turn virtually rules out our seeing ourselves and our own regime as they would have seen us. Above all else, we lack a sense of our own peculiarity, and the most obvious sign of this fact is that the species of servitude which we think of as the peculiar institution our more distant ancestors considered a perfectly normal state of affairs.

The extended essay that stretches through this volume and its two predecessors is not intended as a thoroughgoing diagnosis of the strengths and weaknesses of modern republicanism. Its goals are more modest and perhaps more easily achieved. It is designed to make the present discontents more comprehensible by making visible their roots. It is aimed at preparing the way for the requisite diagnosis by bringing the ancient Greek republic back on stage, by doing justice to the legitimate appeal and moral purchase of the way of life which it fostered, and by setting the modern republic alongside it so that the elements of continuity and discontinuity in the history of republicanism can become visible. In this regard, this three-volume work is an essay in comparative politics. But it is something else as well: for in the process of trying to lay bare the fundamental principles of self-government in antiquity and today, it seeks to clarify and weigh the reasoning that led the Founders of the first and paradigmatic modern republic to deliberately turn their backs on the ancient model and to reject, or at least transform, classical politics; and it aims, therefore, at casting new light on the peculiar foundations on which they purposed to construct modern political life. In this regard, it is an attempt to study the influence of one epoch on another, and it is an appreciative examination of the thinking of a remarkable group of men.

Students of American history and politics have long felt the need for such a study. In a review published nearly seventy years ago, Carl Becker issued a challenge. "Will not someone write a book showing how the revolutionary state of mind of the eighteenth century was also nourished on an ideal conception of classical republicanism and Roman virtue?" he asked. "Just why did Madame Roland often weep to think that she was not born a Spartan? Just why did John Adams ask himself if Demosthenes, had he been a deputy to the first Continental Congress, would have been satisfied with non-importation and non-exportation agreements? To know the answers . . . would help much to understand both the French and American Revolutions."[6] Three years later, when Gilbert Chinard published Thomas Jefferson's *Commonplace Book,* he was driven to observe that the study of the classics "was an essential part in the moral foundations of many of the men who framed the American institutions. It contributed to give a Stoic tone to their characters and a clearer ring to their utterances." As he put it, "We can hardly realize the power exerted by the classics at a time and in a land where only a few books were available."[7]

In the first few decades that followed, remarkably little was done in American history along the lines that Becker had in mind. In 1942, Chinard could accurately write that "our ignorance and neglect of this classical background vitiates most of our studies in eighteenth-century thought."[8] In an article first published in 1955, Douglass Adair could still mourn the fact that "there is not even a beginning on the classics in Revolutionary America."[9] He could, in truth, have written something similar, though milder, at almost any time within the last ten years with almost equal justification. To be sure, considerable progress has been made. Charles F. Mullett, Robert Middlekauff, Gordon S. Wood, J. G. A. Pocock, and Meyer Reinhold have all drawn attention to the influence exerted on the founding generation by the example of the ancient republics.[10] If Vernon Parrington were now alive, he could hardly manage to rewrite the first volume of his monumental *Main Currents in American Thought* without adding some reference to the classical curriculum of America's colleges and the manner in which it influenced American rhetoric and thought. But he would find it difficult even now to reach a just assessment of its relative weight.

Forty-one years ago, Clinton Rossiter concluded that "the Americans would have believed just as vigorously in public morality had Cato and the Gracchi never lived."[11] Fourteen years thereafter, Bernard Bailyn examined in detail the pamphlet literature occasioned by the Stamp Act crisis and the pertinent public debates leading up to the American Revolution. He found "the classics of the ancient world . . . everywhere in the literature of the Revolution," but he concluded that "they are everywhere illustrative, not determinative, of thought. They contributed a vivid vocabulary but not the logic or grammar of thought, a universally respected personification but not the source of political and social beliefs. They heightened the colonists' sensitivity to ideas and attitudes otherwise derived."[12]

In the interim, Hannah Arendt argued an entirely different case. "Without the classical example shining through the centuries," she wrote, "none of the men of the revolutions on either side of the Atlantic would have possessed the courage for what then turned out to be unprecedented action," and she therefore averred that the American Revolution's "ultimate end" was public, participatory "freedom" of the sort exemplified in the Greek *pólis* "and the constitution of a public space where freedom would appear."[13] Twenty-five years ago, Gordon Wood took up her suggestion, contending that "for Americans the mid-eighteenth century was truly a neo-classical age" and that their "compulsive interest in the ancient republics was in fact crucial to their attempt to understand the moral and social basis of politics." As he put it, "The sacrifice of individual interests to the greater good of the whole formed the essence of republicanism and comprehended for Americans the idealistic goal of their Revolution. From this goal flowed all of the Americans' exhortatory literature and all that made their ideology truly revolutionary."

Wood denied that this "common interest" was, "as we might today think of it, simply the sum or consensus of the particular interests that made up the community," and he insisted that it "was rather an entity in itself prior to and distinct from the various private interests of groups and individuals." He identified this entity as "the one supreme moral good to which all parts of the body politic must surrender"; he contended that, "in the minds of most Whigs in 1776, individual rights, even the basic civil liberties that we consider so crucial, possessed little of their modern theoretical relevance when set against the will of the people"; and he argued that "the important liberty in the Whig ideology was public or political liberty." "Ideally," he wrote, "republicanism obliterated the individual," for in a republic "each man must somehow be persuaded to submerge his personal wants into the greater good of the whole." Not surprisingly, then, he ultimately concluded that the republican ideology of the Revolution was "essentially anti-capitalistic."[14]

Still more recently, J. G. A. Pocock reconsidered the vast literary output of the American revolutionaries and surveyed the writings of the British commonwealth tradition that they drew on. He suggested that "the American Revolution" be considered "less as the first political act of revolutionary enlightenment than as the last great act of the Renaissance." He concluded that it was "a flight from modernity"; he described it as the "last great premodern efflorescence" of a species of thinking "anchored" in a continuous and relatively coherent tradition of political speculation stretching from Aristotle through Guicciardini, Machiavelli, Harrington, the radical Whigs, and Bolingbroke on to Jefferson; and he attempted a magisterial history of what he dubbed "the civic humanist paradigm." "In terms borrowed from or suggested by the language of Hannah Arendt," his book purports to tell "part of the story of the revival in the early modern West of the ancient ideal of *homo politicus* (the *zōon politikon* of Aristotle), who affirms his being and his virtue by the medium of political action, whose closest kinsman is *homo rhetor* and whose antithesis is the *homo credens* of Christian faith." He conceded that "not all Americans were schooled in this tradition," but he insisted that "there was (it would almost appear) no alternative tradition in which to be schooled."[15]

In the last few years, the neoclassical depiction of the American intellectual milieu has come under sustained attack on the part of historians and political scientists who have resurrected an older view, attributing great and even preponderant influence to the liberal political philosophy of John Locke and his various disciples.[16] A number of scholars have even suggested the presence within American thought of a plurality of opposed and competing political visions or even "a profusion and confusion of political tongues."[17] Pocock is himself now inclined to acknowledge the presence of "alternative paradigms" and even to concede that his earlier work may have taken the form of what J. H. Hexter has criticized as "tunnel history."[18] But he persists in denying any great importance to the thinking of Locke. He still insists that the "civic humanist paradigm" remains "irreplaceable as a means of explaining why" the United States of America possesses "the only political culture which recurrently laments the corruption of its virtue, the loss of its innocence and the end of its dream, and then sets about renewing them." And he continues to assert that the pertinent species of "virtue" is inseparable from "the practice of citizenship in the classical or Graeco-Roman sense of that term" and that it presupposes the view "that the human personality" is "that of a *zōon politikon*" and is "fully expressed only in the practice of citizenship as an active virtue."[19] On this matter, his opinion and that of Gordon Wood still carry great weight.[20]

If we are to understand the origins of the world's first modern republic and to discern its character, we will have to take a fresh look at classical republicanism, at the political thought of the early modern period, and at the work of the American founders, and we will have to ponder which of the opinions cited above, if any, is right and to what degree. It is more than merely possible that the "confusion" which many now attribute to the revolutionary generation is really our own—rooted in our remarkable confidence that we can actually reconstruct all the *mentalités*, paradigms, traditions, ideologies, and languages of discourse available at a given time and place, and grounded in our unwarranted presumption that all those who lived in the past, even those far more brilliant and penetrating than we can ever hope to be, were somehow the prisoners of the crude interpretive models which we so blithely now build.[21] If the debate concerning the ideological character of the American Revolution seems increasingly sterile, it is largely because of our inclination to underestimate the intellectual discernment of the Founding Fathers and because of the long-standing tendency to divorce intellectual history from the study of practical politics.[22] To understand the thinking of the American founders and their early modern predecessors, we must set aside our fashionable, modernist notion that reality is somehow constructed by linguistic or social convention, and we must jettison the vain supposition that the greatest of our predecessors were the witless captives of inherited institutions and conceptual frameworks.[23] Then, we must read their pronouncements with something like the care, attention, and respect that the pious ordinarily reserve for Holy Writ; and while doing so, we must never for a moment forget that the formidable practical task assigned philosophical statesmanship is the prudent reconciliation of political wisdom with popular consent by means of noble deeds and persuasive speech.[24]

Only when we ponder the enormity of this endeavor are we likely to recognize the paradox that the popular enlightenment now taken for granted could not have been instituted without a considerable measure of dissimulation. Circumstance and the climate of opinion no doubt limited in certain respects what could be accomplished by philosophical statesmen in ages gone by, and they certainly circumscribed what such men could openly and publicly say. But there is no compelling reason to suppose that these meaningfully restricted what the greatest of our early modern predecessors could think. In viewing most of what has happened in the past, we should perhaps be impressed by "the latent limitations within which everyone involved was obliged to act; the inescapable boundaries of action; the blindness of the actors—in a word, the tragedy of the event." But one may justly wonder whether the emergence of modern republicanism was not an exception to Bernard Bailyn's generally sensible rule. If there was ever a moment in history when the principal actors attained "heroic" stature by recognizing "the inescapable boundaries of action," if there was ever a time when "individuals" counted "overwhelmingly" and when "their personal qualities" actually made "the difference between victory and defeat," this was surely it.[25]

The great oracle of those Americans who labored long and hard in the late eighteenth century to establish just and workable political constitutions was the French philosophe the baron de Montesquieu. "To comprehend modern times well," he warned his readers, "it is necessary to comprehend ancient times well; it is necessary to follow each law in the spirit of all the ages."[26] That piece of advice they took to heart, and so, I would suggest, must anyone who really desires to understand their remarkable achievement. If at least some of the readers of this volume and its two predecessors emerge from pondering my long and labyrinthine argument with a new sense of detachment from their own world and with an inkling of what it is that makes modern republicanism so wondrous, so vulnerable, and so very strange, I will have achieved my goal. Wonder is, as Plato suggests, a very philosophical passion[27]—and until we are in its grip, we cannot even begin to understand. In the words of the greatest of the American poets,

> We shall not cease from exploration
> And the end of all our exploring
> Will be to arrive where we started
> And know the place for the first time.[28]

Such is the task that we have undertaken. But before embarking on this, the third and final stage of our long voyage of self-discovery, we must pause briefly to look back, review the distance thus far traversed, and equip ourselves for the difficult journey ahead.

We might have begun our journey by seeking a premodern exemplar for self-government outside classical Hellas, in ancient Rome or in medieval and Renaissance Europe. A case can no doubt be made for according priority to each. I would not want to suggest that one can make full sense of the history of the struggle for self-government in early modern Europe without referring to the influence of Roman institutions and law or that one can do so without considering the medieval heritage of corporate liberty. Nor would I argue that little or nothing can be learned from an extended comparison between modern republicanism and these earlier forms of self-government.[29] I would merely contend that classical Greece has a special claim on our attention. It was in Hellas that the first republics known to the West appeared and flourished. There is reason to suppose that it was their example that inspired the subsequent appearance of republicanism in ancient Italy; and Roman institutions provided, in turn, the impetus for medieval corporatism and, thereby, for the development of representative assemblies and for the emergence of the medieval commune in the Latin West. In Greece, one encounters premodern republicanism in its pristine and purest form. Moreover, there survives from ancient Hellas a sophisticated body of theoretical writing concerning politics that knows no equal in any subsequent time and place. To the extent that modern political reflection draws on and responds to the political thought of the ancient Greeks, Hellas must be accorded primacy.

With this last point in mind, I began the initial volume of this trilogy by asking my readers to consider the case for a revival of the species of regime-analysis pioneered by Herodotus and Thucydides, developed by Plato and Xenophon, and fully articulated by Aristotle and his disciples. Arguing that the modern distinction between materialism and idealism makes little practical, political sense, I invited my readers to join me in adopting and testing an alternative hypothesis. It was and is my contention that what really matters most with regard to political understanding is this: to decide who is to rule or what sorts of human beings are to share in rule and function as a community's political class (*políteuma*) is to determine which of the various and competing titles to rule is to be authoritative; in turn, this is to decide what qualities are to be admired and honored in the city, what is to be considered advantageous and just, and how happiness and success (*eudaimonía*) are to be pursued; and this decision—more than any other—determines the moral education (*paideía*) which constitutes a political regime (*politeía*) as "the one way of life of a whole city (*pólis*)." As a consequence of entertaining this hypothesis, we took to heart Aristotle's claim that it is chiefly the distribution and disposition of offices and honors (*táxis tôn archôn*) that determines the *paideía* which constitutes the *politeía* of a particular city and makes of its citizens a single political community.[30] And we then considered what it was that the citizens of an ancient Greek *pólis* embraced when they treated political liberty and political participation, in John Stuart Mill's phrase, as "*something . . . settled, . . . permanent, and not to be called in question*," as a "fixed point: something which men agreed in holding sacred; which, wherever freedom of discussion was a recognised principle, it was of course lawful to contest in theory, but which no one could either fear or hope to see shaken in practice; which, in short (except perhaps during some temporary crisis), was in the common estimation placed beyond discussion."[31] It was our purpose to provide a general survey of the consequences of their making political liberty and active participation central to the "concord regarding loved things held in common" which transformed them from "a multitudinous assemblage of rational beings" into what Augustine described as "a people" possessed of "a commonwealth."[32]

In the chapters that followed, we explored a single principle found to be fundamental to classical republicanism: the presumption that human beings are political animals possessed of a capacity for *lógos*—reason, speech, and argument—which enables them to deliberate in common concerning the advantageous, the just, and the good. To the consequences of that presumption, and of the political practices and institutions embodying it, we traced the Greeks' obsession with honor and glory, with virtue, and magnanimity or greatness of soul (*megalopsuchía*)—as well as their subordination of the concerns of the household (*oîkos*) to those of the *pólis*, their subjection of women, and the readiness with which they embraced the institution of slavery. To this same principle we traced the propensity of the ancient republics to be always at war, their vulnerability to civil strife (*stásis*), their desperate need to encourage civic solidarity and likemindedness (*homónoia*), and the measures they took to give their citizens the same opinions, passions, and interests, as well as the role played in the promotion of *homónoia* by a piety indistinguishable from patriotism, by the exaggerated respect accorded ancestral customs and laws (*pátrioi nómoi*), and by the institutionalization of pederasty as part of a young man's *paideía*. It was in light of this same presumption that we explained the suspicion with which the Greeks regarded commerce, the stagnation of technology in antiquity, and both the emergence of philosophy and the efforts made to eliminate it or at least confine it to the margins of public life.

In the epilogue to that volume, we noted the disappearance of public liberty as a consequence of Macedonian and Roman imperialism, and we studied Christianity's denial of primacy to political life. Then, we pondered Christianity's status as a religion of faith and Christian theology's dependence on philosophy, the resulting survival within the Christian *ecclesia* of the rancorous spirit animating the classical Greek public assembly (*ekklēsía*), the persistence within Christendom of the presumption that human beings possess *lógos* and are capable of reasoning together concerning common concerns, and the ultimate revival of public liberty in the Latin West under the aegis of the Roman law of private corporations. Finally, we contemplated the unavoidable and unresolvable tension between the demands of a dogmatic faith and those of the philosophic quest for the truth; and we anticipated one of the themes of the subsequent volumes by noting the praise that the radical Whig leader Robert Molesworth lavished on those countries which commit "the Government of their Youth to *Philosophers* instead of *Priests*" and by quoting his suggestion that "the Character of *Priest*" must "give place to that of true *Patriot*."[33]

We began the second volume of this trilogy by considering modern philosophy's rebellion against clerical tutelage. Then, we examined in detail a phenomenon closely related to that rebellion and, in the event, inseparable from it—the elaboration of a critique of classical republicanism and of the theoretical principle of *lógos* that it embodied. Niccolò Machiavelli presented himself as the progenitor of this critique, which was then rearticulated in the name of the new moral principle of humanity by Michel de Montaigne, Sir Francis Bacon, René Descartes, John Locke, and their successors among the enlightened in Italy, England, and France before being taken up by the American Founding Fathers. Having explored the assault that these figures launched against moral reason, the moral imagination, and classical and Christian virtue, we contemplated the willingness of Americans in the founding generation to abandon the Greek presumption that man is a political animal, to entertain Benjamin Franklin's suggestion that man is "a tool-making animal," and to commit themselves to the modern, scientific project of conquering nature that was espoused by Sir Francis Bacon, René Descartes, and their successors in Europe; and we explored the new understanding of the human capacity to reason and of man's place within the universe that this extraordinarily ambitious project presupposed. We then turned to Thomas Hobbes and the new science of politics that he attempted to build on the crucial modern presumption that human reason is the slave of the passions; that human beings lack the capacity to deliberate together concerning the advantageous, the just, and the good; and that they possess in its stead an admirable ability to make calculations concerning cause and effect.

In the second volume's later chapters, we reviewed the attempts made by figures such as Niccolò Machiavelli, Thomas Hobbes, James Harrington, John Locke, the baron de Montesquieu, the radical Whigs, Lord Bolingbroke, David Hume, and Jean Louis de Lolme to find in what came to be called "political architecture" an antidote to sedition and the other diseases that had afflicted self-government in antiquity; and we traced the emergence and development of two tendencies within modern republican speculation—one that looked to constitutional machinery as a cure for all ills, and another which sought to harness the ambition of those within the "natural aristocracy" and to discourage tyranny and abuse on their part by promoting within the "natural democracy" a spirit of vigilance and jealous distrust. Then, we contemplated the manner in which John Locke managed to make the modern understanding of human reason, of man's place within the cosmos, and of first principles and political architecture accessible and palatable to a people still inclined to think of itself as Christian. Finally, in the volume's epilogue, we surveyed the English polity as it came to be articulated in the wake of the Glorious Revolution, treating it as a species of mixed regime, composed of elements hearkening back to its premodern origins and of elements portending the upheaval and transformation that were to take place across the seas in America.

Here, in the third and final volume of the trilogy, we come to "the end of all our exploring" and "arrive where we started," hoping to "know the place for the first time." To this end, we will focus our attention on the American Revolution, on the constitution of liberty within the United States, and on the struggles and debates that took place within that polity—initially concerning the ratification of the Constitution and then, after that event, concerning the manner in which it should be interpreted. This we will do with an eye to Aristotle's claim that it is chiefly the distribution and disposition of offices and honors (*táxis tôn archôn*) that determines the *paideía* which constitutes the political regime and makes of the citizens a single political community. Consequently, in attempting to define the American regime, we are looking for that in America which, in the course of the Revolution, came to be "*something . . .* settled, . . . permanent, and not to be called in question." We are searching for America's "fixed point: something which men agreed in holding sacred; which," since "freedom of discussion was a recognised principle, it was of course lawful to contest in theory, but which no one could either fear or hope to see shaken in practice; which, in short (except perhaps during some temporary crisis), was in the common estimation placed beyond discussion." It is therefore our task to discover and display that "concord regarding loved things held in common" which transformed the Americans from "a multitudinous assemblage of rational beings" into what Augustine described as "a people" possessed of "a commonwealth."[34]

VOLUME III

Inventions of Prudence: Constituting the American Regime

Pythagoras, as well as Socrates, Plato, and Xenophon, was persuaded that the happiness of nations depended chiefly on the form of their government. They were fully sensible of the real misery, as well as dangerous tendency, both of democratical licentiousness and monarchical tyranny; they preferred a well-tempered aristocracy to all other governments. Pythagoras and Socrates . . . both thought, that the laws could neither prevent the arbitrary oppressions of magistrates, nor turbulent insolence of the people, until mankind were habituated, by education and discipline, to regard the great duties of life, and to consider a reverence of themselves, and the esteem of their fellow-citizens, as the principal source of their enjoyment. In small communities, especially where the slaves were many, and the citizens few, this might be plausible; but the education of a great nation can never accomplish so great an end. Millions must be brought up, whom no principles, no sentiments derived from education, can restrain from trampling on the laws. Orders of men, watching and balancing each other, are the only security; power must be opposed to power, and interest to interest. . . . Experience has ever shown, that education, as well as religion, aristocracy, as well as democracy and monarchy, are, singly, totally inadequate to the business of restraining the passions of men, of preserving a steady government, and protecting the lives, liberties, and properties of the people. . . . Religion, superstition, oaths, education, laws, all give way before passions, interest, and power, which can be resisted only by passions, interest, and power.

JOHN ADAMS

Could we convert a city into a kind of fortified camp, and infuse into each breast so martial a genius, and such a passion for public good, as to make every one willing to undergo the greatest hardships for the sake of the public; these affections might now, as in ancient times, prove alone a sufficient spur to industry and support the community. It would then be advantageous, as in camps, to banish all arts and luxury; and, by restrictions on equipage and tables, make the provisions and forage last longer than if the army were loaded with a number of superfluous retainers. But as these principles are too disinterested and too difficult to support, it is requisite to govern men by other passions, and animate them with a spirit of avarice and industry, art and luxury.—David Hume

Jefferson is one of the great men whom this country has produced, one of the men who has contributed largely to the formation of our national character—to much that is good and to not a little that is evil in our sentiments and manners. His Declaration of Independence is an abridged Alcoran of political doctrine, laying open the first foundations of civil society; but he does not appear to have been aware that it also laid open a precipice into which the slave-holding planters of his country sooner or later must fall. With the Declaration of Independence on their lips, and the merciless scourge of slavery in their hands, a more flagrant image of human inconsistency can scarcely be conceived than one of our Southern slave-holding republicans. Jefferson has been himself all his life a slave-holder, but he has published opinions so blasting to the very existence of slavery, that, however creditable they may be to his candor and humanity, they speak not much for his prudence or his forecast as a Virginian planter. The seeds of the Declaration of Independence are yet maturing. The harvest will be what West, the painter, calls the terrible sublime.—John Quincy Adams

Old religious factions are volcanoes burnt out; on the lava and ashes and squalid scoriæ of old eruptions grow the peaceful olive, the cheering vine, and the sustaining corn. Such was the first, such the second condition of Vesuvius. But when a new fire bursts out, a face of desolations comes on, not to be rectified in ages. Therefore, when men come before us, and rise up like an exhalation from the ground, they come in a questionable shape, and we must exorcise them, and try whether their intents be wicked or charitable, whether they bring airs from heaven or blasts from hell.—Edmund Burke

PROLOGUE

Novus Ordo Seclorum

[The American colonists] are extreamly proud of their Country, and they have reason to be so. . . . They have a pious Horror, of consenting to any Thing, which may intail slavery on their Posterity. They think that the Liberties of Mankind and the Glory of human Nature is in their Keeping.—John Adams

Aristotle's definition is really this—that man is by nature the citizen of a city (Stadtbürger). This definition is just as characteristic for classical antiquity as is Franklin's definition for Yankee civilization (das Yankeetum)—that man is by nature a maker of instruments.—Karl Marx

In 1755, when Francis Hutcheson raised the possibility that there might be just occasion for rebellion in a misgoverned province or colony, the Scots-Irish professor added an observation suggesting that his remarks might be more than merely hypothetical. "There is something so unnatural," he wrote,

> in supposing a large society, sufficient for all the good purposes of an independent political union, remaining subject to the direction and government of a distant body of men who know not sufficiently the circumstances and exigencies of this society; or in supposing this society obliged to be governed solely for the benefit of a distant country; that it is not easy to imagine there can be any foundation for it in justice or equity. The insisting on old claims and tacit conventions to extend civil power over distant nations, and form grand unwieldy empires, without regard to the obvious maxims of humanity, has been one great source of human misery.[1]

Hutcheson was not the first to foresee that Britain's transatlantic empire would become vulnerable to dissolution with the passage of time. Almost precisely one hundred years before, James Harrington had observed with regard to the European "Colonies in the *Indies*" that "they are yet babes that cannot live without sucking the breasts of their mother-Cities, but such as, I mistake, if when they come of age they do not wean themselves: which causeth me to wonder at Princes that delight to be exhausted in that way."[2]

John Trenchard and Thomas Gordon had similarly addressed the question in *Cato's Letters* and had even borrowed Harrington's earthy metaphor. "I would not suggest so distant a Thought," they wrote in 1722, "as that any of our Colonies, when they grow stronger, should ever attempt to wean them-

selves from us; however, I think too much Care cannot be taken to prevent
it, and to preserve their Dependences upon their Mother-Country."

It is not to be hoped, in the corrupt State of human Nature, that any
Nation will be subject to another any longer than it finds its own Account
in it, and cannot help itself. Every Man's first Thought will be for himself, and his own Interest; and he will not be long to seek for Arguments
to justify his being so, when he knows how to attain what he proposes.
Men will think it hard to work, toil, and run Hazards, for the Advantage of others, any longer than they find their own Interest in it, and
especially for those who use them ill: All Nature points out that Course.
No Creatures suck the Teats of their Dams longer than they can draw
Milk from thence, or can provide themselves with better Food: Nor will
any Country continue their Subjection to another, only because their
Great-Grandmothers were acquainted.

There were, they averred, but two ways for Britain to hold on to her colonies: "one to keep" independence "out of their Power, and the other out of
their Will." Force they deemed counterproductive: the cost of denying colonists located some three months' voyage from Britain the power to assert
their independence would be prohibitive. And so the two could only suggest that the British "take all the Precautions in our Power, that it shall never
be their Interest to act against that of their native Country." Ultimately, they
concluded, when a colony has become "too powerful to be treated only as
a Colony," one must, if one wishes to maintain the ties, "imitate the Example of Merchants and Shopkeepers; that is, when their Apprentices are
acquainted with their Trade and their Customers, and are out of their Time,
to take them into Partnership, rather than let them set up for themselves in
their Neighbourhood." [3]

On the whole, Britain's empire was managed fairly and well. One consequence was that, by 1763, the thirteen British colonies on the eastern
seaboard of North America had very nearly come of age. In population, resources, and developed wealth, they had the potential to be self-sufficient,
and they were advancing rapidly.[4] The Seven Years War had eliminated the
French from nearby Quebec, and there was no other power in their vicinity in
the New World capable of posing a serious military threat. In Massachusetts,
New York, Pennsylvania, Virginia, and South Carolina, and quite possibly in
the other colonies as well, there was a faction or party of wealthy and ambitious men persuaded that British North America formed the nucleus of what
would eventually become a mighty empire; and when the crisis presented
itself, these men were more than ready to take the lead.[5]

The continued subjection of the colonies to the mother country was partly a consequence of sentiment and habit, partly caused by their distrust of one another, and partly due to the absence of any serious occasion for rebellion. In many respects, the colonies were already independent states. They had their own representative assemblies, and by and large they managed their own affairs. All were ultimately subject to the purview of the Board of Trade and the Privy Council, and all but Connecticut and Rhode Island had royal or proprietary governors armed with a prerogative considerably more impressive on paper than the powers wielded in Britain by the king. But apart from enacting navigation acts to regulate trade between America, Britain, and Europe, the authorities in London rarely had any compelling reason to insist on meddling in local affairs; and when they did intervene, they could often be persuaded to side with the assembly against the governor, especially since the latter usually occupied his office for a brief period of time before returning to Britain, while the former represented interests not likely to disappear. Moreover, whatever their expectations may at first have been, the appointed governors soon discovered that in America the legislature really was supreme. In part as a consequence of the program of reform pressed on the Board of Trade in the late 1690s by John Locke, in part as a result of local initiative and legislation, the appointed governors had very little in the way of patronage with which to influence the deliberations of the colonial assemblies. In addition, there were no rotten boroughs in the New World and no prospect that they would ever emerge, and those who represented a given locality in the colonial assembly paid close attention, even when not under instruction, to the sentiments of their constituents. America was in many respects a radical Whig paradise.[6]

This was true in more ways than one.[7] In the colonies, the trappings of the ancien régime were for the most part lacking. There were no lords and no bishops; there was no royal court; and where there were religious establishments, these were far more tolerant of dissent than the national churches in England, Scotland, and Ireland. Dependency among whites was by no means unknown: there were tenant farmers in New York's Hudson Valley and in New Jersey, and a great many immigrants first came to America as indentured servants or became such soon after their arrival. But in most of the colonies there was an abundance of unworked land; so tenant farmers were an anomaly, and indentured servitude was a temporary state that served to impress upon those subject to it the value and importance of the freedom they had thereby earned. In this respect, Negro slavery was a lesson to all white men.

Colonial families were patriarchal to a considerable degree. This circum-

stance, together with the Americans' inherited and unquestioned allegiance
to England's king, nourished in some quarters the confusion between pater-
nal and political authority that childhood experience nearly always instills.
But, of course, the king was far away and never to be seen; the economic
opportunities widely available in the colonies encouraged an independence
in young adults rarely to be found in the mother country; and, as one might
therefore expect, by the late eighteenth century, patriarchy's hold on the
American political imagination was, at least by European standards, quite
tenuous.[8] Moreover, though religion had played a prominent and even pre-
eminent role in the founding of the colonies, most had been from the start
entrepreneurial enterprises as well. In fact, the legal instrument that made
it possible for the crown to reward inventors with a limited monopoly had
also been employed by the English government to promote voyages of discovery and merchant ventures. The establishment and development of the
colonies had been very much a part of Sir Francis Bacon's overall scheme
for the promotion of commerce and progress in the arts,[9] and through much
of the seventeenth and eighteenth centuries, the colonial system was managed by men such as John Locke who shared that great statesman's vision of
economic and technological development. In part as a consequence of their
efforts to encourage immigration, the American population grew at far too
fast a rate to be compatible with the maintenance of traditional, comparatively uniform religious communities.[10]

In practice, subsistence farming was quite common and perhaps even predominant in the Northeast, but the same cannot be said for the South. Well
before the Revolution, the colonies had become in both spirit and fact pretty
much what they were meant to be from the start: dynamic, commercial societies intimately tied by trade to their common metropolis.[11] Daniel Defoe
would have been perfectly comfortable in the New World, as he advertised
in *Moll Flanders* and elsewhere. His great admirer Benjamin Franklin made a
remarkable success of himself, and Franklin was by no means unusual: in the
colonies, self-made men were more plentiful than they had been anywhere
in the world at any previous time in human history; and as was only natural, these entrepreneurs found the new economic thinking and the political
outlook that went with it thoroughly congenial.[12] Where visitors from the
continent of Europe were inclined to suppose that they had seen in England
the future of the human race, well-to-do Americans who crossed the Atlantic were prone to think that they had made a journey into the distant past.
More often than not, they evidenced alongside pride in their heritage and a
certain jealousy of the English a distinct dislike for the vestigial remains of
the ancien régime.[13] Most human beings instinctively prefer their own, and

self-made men who are proud of their own accomplishments are rarely inclined to warm to those among the wellborn who manifestly hold them in contempt.

Of course, religious faith continued to play a prominent role in colonial life—but not in a fashion likely to encourage political deference and permanent subordination or to reinforce belief in the divine right of kings or even in the supremacy of an ancient assembly some three thousand miles away. When Edmund Burke tried to persuade Parliament to conciliate the colonies in 1775, he made much of the fact that in the "character of the Americans a love of freedom is the predominating feature which marks and distinguishes the whole," and he traced "this fierce love of liberty" not just to the fact that "the people of the colonies are descendants of Englishmen," that "their governments are popular in an high degree," and that their heritage and their local experience had made them devoted "to liberty according to English ideas and on English principles." He emphasized as well that "the people are Protestants, and of that kind which is the most adverse to all implicit submission of mind and opinion." Theirs, he contended, "is a persuasion not only favorable to liberty, but built upon it." The very history of "the dissenting interests" reinforced the natural tendency of Protestantism, for they had "sprung up in direct opposition to the ordinary powers of the world, and could justify that opposition only on a strong claim to natural liberty." "All Protestantism," he observed, "even the most cold and passive, is a sort of dissent. But the religion most prevalent in our northern colonies is a refinement on the principle of resistance: it is the dissidence of dissent, and the protestantism of the Protestant religion."[14]

In the South, Burke conceded, the Church of England was predominant. But he observed "a circumstance attending these colonies" that "fully counterbalances this difference, and makes the spirit of liberty still more high and haughty than in those to the northward": the presence, especially in Virginia and the Carolinas, of "a vast multitude of slaves." "Where this is the case in any part of the world," Burke explained,

those who are free are by far the most proud and jealous of their freedom. Freedom is to them not only an enjoyment, but a kind of rank and privilege. Not seeing there, that freedom, as in countries where it is a common blessing, and as broad and general as the air, may be united with much abject toil, with great misery, with all the exterior of servitude, liberty looks, amongst them, like something that is more noble and liberal. I do not mean, Sir, to commend the superior morality of this sentiment, which has at least as much pride as virtue in it; but I cannot alter the nature of man. The fact is so; and these people of the southern colonies are much more strongly, and with an higher and more stubborn spirit, attached to liberty, than those to the northward. Such were all the ancient commonwealths; such were our Gothic ancestors; such in our days were the Poles; and such will be all masters of slaves, who are not slaves themselves. In such a people, the haughtiness of domination combines with the spirit of freedom, fortifies it, and renders it invincible.[15]

To this observation, he might have added that, in the absence of bishops, effective power in the Anglican church fell into the hands of slave-owning vestrymen in no way eager to surrender control. Colonial Anglicanism was, in consequence, predominantly a low church manned by parsons who knew their place, and American Anglicans were therefore very rarely, if ever, treated to political theology of the traditional sort.[16]

The religious situation was complicated by another fact. The Great Awakening, occasioned by George Whitfield's triumphal tour of America, had had a profound and lasting effect on religious sensibilities in every colony, and in the aftermath it gave rise to an unexpected result: the splintering of the traditional sects. By the time of the Revolution, the colonies which had religious establishments found those establishments under sustained assault. Moreover, the religious revival had had another surprising consequence. Ordinarily, one would not think religious enthusiasm conducive to the spread of a reasonable Christianity like that espoused by Locke, and the first Great Awakening can hardly be said to have been friendly to coldly rational religion. But, as David Hume had pointed out, there is a considerable difference between superstition and enthusiasm in this regard. The former, he asserted, *"is favourable to priestly power,"* while the latter is *"not less"* but *"rather more contrary to it than sound reason and philosophy."* Because "superstition is founded on fear, sorrow, and a depression of spirits, it represents man to himself in such despicable colours, that he appears unworthy, in his own eyes, of approaching the divine presence, and naturally has recourse to any other person, whose sanctity of life, or, perhaps, impudence and cunning, have made him be supposed more favoured by the Divinity." Enthusiasm, on the other hand, inspires self-confidence, and it renders its supporters "free from the yoke of ecclesiastics" and inclined to "great independence in their devotion" and even to "a contempt of forms, ceremonies, and traditions." Hume acknowledged that *"religions, which partake of enthusiasm are, on their first rise, more furious and violent than those which partake of superstition."* But he insisted that *"in a little time,"* when the novelty wears off, they *"become more gentle and moderate.*" Indeed, he added, when "the first fire of enthusiasm is spent, men naturally, in all fanatical sects, sink into the greatest remissness and coolness in sacred matters; there being no body of men among them, endowed with sufficient authority, whose interest is concerned to support the religious spirit." In these circumstances, the independence of mind initially fostered by enthusiasm opens the way for enlightenment: England's "sectaries, who were formerly such dangerous bigots, are now become very free reasoners," and this has had political repercussions, for "the leaders of the *whigs* have either been *deists* or profest *latitudinarians* in their principles; that is friends to toleration, and indifferent to any particular sect of *christians*." [17] Something of the sort took place in America. Initially, disgust at the excesses of Whitfield's admirers drove more conventional Anglicans and Dissenters in the direction of rational religion; later, as the ardor of the enthusiasts cooled, some of them stumbled onto the same path. A remarkably high proportion of those prominent in the Revolution were heterodox Christians, if not Deists outright.[18] In political affairs, American ministers and laymen evidenced the self-confidence; the independence of mind; the contempt for forms, ceremonies, and traditions; and something of the sense of mission and destiny that had distinguished the enthusiasts in days gone by.[19]

In accounting for the Americans' "fierce spirit of liberty," Burke also placed emphasis on "their education." He knew of no country in which "the law" was "so general a study." Not only was that profession "numerous and powerful"; in most of the colonies, it took "the lead." Lawyers dominated the Continental Congress, and nearly everyone in America who could read, "and most do read," endeavored "to obtain some smattering in that science." Many legal tracts were exported to the colonies, and more were printed there. "I hear," he wrote, "that they have sold nearly as many of Blackstone's 'Commentaries' in America as in England." The consequences deserved attention, for the study of law "renders men acute, inquisitive, dexterous, prompt in attack, ready in defence, full of resources. In other countries, the people, more simple, and of a less mercurial cast, judge of an ill principle in government only by an actual grievance; here they anticipate the evil and judge of the pressure of the grievance by the badness of the principle. They augur misgovernment at a distance, and snuff the approach of tyranny in every tainted breeze."[20]

In surveying American education, Burke made no mention of John Locke. But he might well have done so: for the ethos of jealous anticipation and political distrust that the British statesman correctly identified as so typically American is grounded on the conviction that the people have the right to alter their constitution and government when they see fit; and as James

Wilson was wont to remark, the celebrated Whig philosopher was the most important intellectual fountainhead for that unsettling political persuasion. At the Pennsylvania Ratifying Convention in 1787, Wilson insisted on the principle that "the supreme, absolute, and uncontrollable authority *remains* with the people," and he gloried in the fact that the "practical recognition of this truth was reserved for the honor of this country." America's claim to fame was restricted solely by the accomplishments of one great man, for "the great and penetrating mind of Locke seems to be the only one that pointed towards even the theory of this great truth."[21] Three years later, in his inaugural lecture as professor of law in the College of Philadelphia, the recently appointed Supreme Court justice paused once again to spell out in detail the principles of the Revolution and the debt which his compatriots owed the renowned author of the *Two Treatises of Government*.[22]

That debt was profound. Like their cousins on the other side of the Atlantic, especially the Dissenters and low church Anglicans, educated Americans tended to be familiar with *An Essay Concerning Human Understanding, Some Thoughts Concerning Education, A Letter Concerning Toleration*, and *A Paraphrase and Notes on the Epistles of St Paul*, and these works confirmed their inclination toward an independence of mind in matters religious, moral, and political. Many purchased Locke's collected works; and a remarkable number of clerics and laymen, especially the critical few with an abiding interest in public affairs, embraced the defense of religious freedom and limited government found in *A Letter Concerning Toleration* and went on to peruse the *Two Treatises of Government* and to imbibe and, in some cases, even digest its doctrine. No political work was to be found in more colonial libraries; and in the sermons, pamphlets, and newspapers published in America during the decisive period stretching from 1760 to 1776, none was as often cited, quoted, paraphrased, plagiarized, and applied to the crisis that arose. Locke's sly exploitation of religious rhetoric in that book and the Socinian biblical hermeneutics which he employed there and outlined in greater detail elsewhere enabled unsuspecting clergymen throughout the colonies to present his novel political doctrine to their parishioners as the teaching of St. Paul.[23]

Of course, there was a host of literate individuals in America who never bothered to read Locke's tract. Of these, however, a great many imbibed his teaching concerning the natural rights of man and his doctrine of anticipation, resistance, and revolution from other, more entertaining sources. Some encountered a virtually indistinguishable doctrine while reading Algernon Sidney's spirited *Discourses Concerning Government*.[24] A goodly number, especially among churchmen, were familiar with the sermons and pamphlets of the Whig Bishop Benjamin Hoadly. Many more, if we are to judge by the holdings in American libraries, absorbed their Locke while enjoying the rhetorical flourishes that make perusing *The Independent Whig* and *Cato's Letters* a great pleasure even today. Others read Bolingbroke or Francis Hutcheson or pored over the annotated edition of Pufendorf's *De officio hominis et civis* published by Gershom Carmichael; and of course, after 1765, the lawyers and those who dabbled in the law had at their disposal the first volume of William Blackstone's *Commentaries on the Laws of England.* Moreover, on the eve of the Revolution, James Burgh's three-volume *Political Disquisitions* appeared. If self-respect and a sense of their own dignity as Englishmen gave the colonists a powerful motive for resenting Parliament's attempt to tax them without securing their consent, the Lockean first principles so visible in the political books they read provided them with a theoretical framework justifying by a universalist appeal to nature and nature's God their conviction that the self-government and effective autonomy accorded them in the past were theirs, not by custom, charter, or royal grace, but simply and solely by right.

In reading these works, the Americans also came across the political architecture pioneered by Harrington and Neville, inspirited by the Machiavellian political dynamics espoused in John Wildman, Sidney, and Locke, and further elaborated as a critique of the machinations of the Court party by John Toland, Walter Moyle, John Trenchard, Robert Molesworth, Thomas Gordon, Lord Bolingbroke, and their successors in Scotland and among the English radicals of George III's reign. This aspect of the colonists' Whig heritage had a profound impact on the conduct of public affairs within the colonial assemblies, and it shaped the rhetoric of conspiracy and corruption that had already come to characterize American public debate decades before the Stamp Act was passed. In the midst of the American crisis, the influence of the Whig canon was powerfully reinforced by the controversy that erupted in England over Parliament's treatment of John Wilkes, whose repeated expulsion served to confirm the colonists' worst suspicions regarding the defective character of the representative institutions in the mother country. Consequently, if Lockean first principles added force to the Americans' instinctive annoyance at Parliament's clumsy attempts at an encroachment on their traditional rights, the political architecture that they had also imbibed encouraged them to renounce the authority of the succeeding British administrations on the grounds that Parliament was a corrupt and, even with regard to England, an unrepresentative body almost entirely lacking in political legitimacy.[25]

The movement for independence could perhaps have been headed off, and it would certainly have been delayed, if Britain had followed the advice of Trenchard and Gordon and offered the colonies a species of partnership

as each came of age.[26] Had the more prosperous colonies been given representation in Parliament, had the colonial elite been given reason to entertain
the prospect of ennoblement, had care been taken to entwine the interests
and aspirations of the Americans more closely with those of the crown,
events might have taken a rather different turn. But the empire's success
bred arrogance; Britain's political class looked down on the upstarts who
dominated the colonial assemblies; and at Whitehall and Westminster, the
requisite statesmanship was lacking. At the very moment when the colonies
had ceased to depend upon Britain for protection, the authorities in London
decided to assert a prerogative that, when challenged in the past, had prudently been allowed to fall into abeyance: the right to tax the colonists.[27] At
the time, nearly every colony was wracked with faction: those out of favor
with the royal or proprietary governors were quick to avail themselves of the
opportunity to humiliate their rivals; those who foresaw the establishment
of a continental empire were not about to sit idly by; and in most respects
the opponents of the stamp tax were able to have their way.[28] Edmund Burke
was right: the Americans really were inclined to "augur misgovernment at
a distance, and snuff the approach of tyranny in every tainted breeze." As
one evidently prominent, but anonymous, American admirer of the Revolution summed up the situation in 1783, "The principles . . . of political liberty,
deeply rooted in the first establishments of the colonies, had flourished with
such unrestrained luxuriance, that the anticipation of distant tyranny gave
birth to opposition more firm and unanimous, than the iron rod of despotism, wielded with unrelenting fury, had ever roused mankind to, in other
climes."[29]

Burke was right as well when he traced the prickliness of Britain's colonists
with regard to the Stamp Act and the Townshend duties to the fact that "the
great contests for freedom in this country were from the earliest times chiefly
upon the question of taxing."[30] Moreover, when George Grenville's ministry
fell, when William Pitt denounced the Stamp Act and praised the colonists
for resisting its implementation, and when the marquis of Rockingham and
his supporters rallied the tax's opponents and secured its repeal, the colonists
could easily ignore the Declaratory Act then passed to assert that the king in
Parliament "had, hath, and of right ought to have, full power and authority
to make laws and statutes of sufficient force and validity to bind the colonies and people of *America*, subjects of the crown of *Great Britain*, in all cases
whatsoever."[31] To the inattentive, Parliament seemed in effect to concede the
justice of the resolutions presented by the Stamp Act Congress and the various colonial assemblies, and it appeared to sanction the extralegal resistance
organized by the Sons of Liberty and to testify to its effectiveness. In the

end, England's initial retreat served only to heighten American bitterness at the subsequent passage of the Townshend duties and to encourage renewed resistance against the measures undertaken to enforce the new laws.

Psychological stress and social strain no doubt had something to do with the outbreak of the Revolution.[32] The conspiratorial frame of mind endemic within radical Whig circles certainly contributed to American sensitivities.[33] And James Otis, Patrick Henry, John Dickinson, Samuel Adams, John Adams, Thomas Jefferson, and their colleagues clearly exaggerated the seriousness of their compatriots' plight.[34] But it would be a blunder to depict the revolutionary generation as victims of psycho- or sociopathology or even to ascribe their behavior to the prevalence of a quasi-paranoid way of looking at the world. After all, events justified the suspicions of those most inclined to "augur misgovernment at a distance, and snuff the approach of tyranny in every tainted breeze," for they, and they alone, accurately diagnosed the logic of the mother country's policy and the ultimate consequences for the colonists' freedom to manage their own affairs.[35] "Leave America to tax herself," pleaded Edmund Burke.

> I am not here going into the distinctions of rights, nor attempting to mark their boundaries. I do not enter into these metaphysical distinctions; I hate the very sound of them. . . . Leave the rest to the schools; for there only may they be discussed with safety. But if, intemperately, unwisely, fatally, you sophisticate and poison the very source of government, by urging subtle deductions, and consequences odious to those you govern, from the unlimited and illimitable nature of supreme sovereignty, you will teach them by these means to call that sovereignty itself in question. When you drive him hard, the boar will surely turn upon the hunters. If that sovereignty and their freedom cannot be reconciled, which will they take? They will cast your sovereignty in your face. Nobody will be argued into slavery.[36]

But that great orator was wasting his breath: in the 1770s the authorities in London were in no mood to listen; and so, in the end, by passing and implementing the Coercive Acts, they forced the colonists to choose between their allegiance to Britain and the privilege of self-government which they had long enjoyed.[37]

In the beginning, at the time of the Stamp Act crisis, the colonists were inclined to take their stand as Englishmen defending their traditional rights.[38] But even then there were those, such as James Otis and Richard Bland, who did not hesitate to make an appeal to the dictates of nature and nature's God.[39] As it gradually became evident that Parliament was prepared to use force to collect the tax on tea, and as it became apparent that the logic of resistance would soon require independence as well,[40] the colonists increasingly turned for guidance to the theory of anticipation, resistance, and revolution espoused by John Locke.[41] Alexander Hamilton is a case in point. In 1774, when he first entered the lists against the Loyalist Samuel Seabury, Hamilton grounded his vindication of the Continental Congress on the supposition that "all men have one common original: they participate in one common nature, and consequently have one common right. No reason can be assigned why one man should exercise any power, or pre-eminence over his fellow creatures more than another; unless they have voluntarily vested him with it." A year later, when he returned to the fray, he asserted that "the sacred rights of mankind are not to be rummaged for, among old parchments, or musty records. They are written, as with a sun beam, in the whole *volume* of human nature, by the hand of divinity itself; and can never be erased or obscured by mortal power." Hamilton defended his position by drawing attention to "the *natural rights* of mankind" and by urging his opponent to apply himself "to the study of the law of nature" as expounded by Locke and the other students of natural jurisprudence; and to clarify what he had in mind, he reiterated the Whig philosopher's argument. He began by asserting that, "in a state of nature, no man had any *moral* power to deprive another of his life, limbs, property or liberty; nor the least authority to command, or exact obedience from him; except that which arose from the ties of consanguinity." From this premise, he concluded that "the origin of all civil government, justly established, must be a voluntary compact, between the rulers and the ruled; and must be liable to such limitations, as are necessary for the security of the *absolute rights* of the latter; for what original title can any man or set of men have, to govern others, except their own consent? To usurp dominion over a people, in their own despite, or to grasp at a more extensive power than they are willing to entrust, is to violate that law of nature, which gives every man a right to his personal liberty; and can, therefore confer no obligation to obedience." In his judgment, Parliament was guilty of just such an usurpation of dominion.[42]

In restating Locke's argument, Hamilton was typical.[43] Indeed, so influential was the thinking of the Whig philosopher that not even the Loyalists could escape his grasp. After all, with rare exceptions, they were Whigs themselves.[44] In 1768, when Thomas Hutchinson drafted a dialogue designed to counter the influence of John Dickinson's celebrated *Letters from a Farmer in Pennsylvania*, his spokesman made a point of insisting that Locke's doctrine favored his cause.[45] In similar fashion, seven years later, Joseph Galloway made a desperate and mendacious attempt to ground his case against inde-

pendence on the authority of Locke[46]—while, in Massachusetts, the debate
that took place between the Loyalist Daniel Leonard's Massachusettensis and
John Adams's Novanglus turned not on first principles but on whether a long
train of abuses could legitimately be said to have caused British oppression
to be "seen or felt" in America. In espousing "the revolution principles" of
figures such as "Sydney, Harrington and Locke" and in defending the role
played by the "few" who had "foretold" quite early on "the horrible calamities" that the many now "see and feel," Adams appealed to "experience,
and to universal history" and asked whether "it has ever been in the power
of popular leaders, uninvested with other authority than what is conferred
by the popular suffrage, to persuade a large people, for any length of time
together, to think themselves wronged, injured, and oppressed, unless they
really were, and saw and felt it to be so."[47] That one could readily discern
such "a long train of abuses and usurpations" was, of course, the assertion
that Thomas Jefferson made when he drafted the Declaration of Independence; and more important, it was the argument that the representatives of
the various colonies formally endorsed when they appended their names to
that celebrated document.[48] This assertion was precisely what the Loyalists
most emphatically denied.[49] And it was with an eye to this issue that many
Americans made up their minds when the great crisis came.

Peter Van Schaack is a case in point. To settle his own tender conscience,
this prominent New Yorker studied the situation and read Locke with particular care. By the end of January 1776, he had persuaded himself that the
errors made by the authorities in London could "fairly be imputed to human
frailty, and the difficulty" inseparable from the administration of an inter-
continental empire. Most of their objectionable acts seemed to him "to have
sprung out of particular occasions," and he thought them "unconnected with
each other." Since he judged that they had been "passed without a precon-
certed plan of enslaving us," he concluded that it made no sense to "think
the government *dissolved*," and he decided that he could not in good conscience join John Jay and his other friends in "taking up arms." Not long
after reaching this conclusion, Van Schaack withdrew to England in search of
medical help. There, he observed the debates in the House of Commons, and
he once again studied "the American controversy," trying to determine just
what were "the designs" of those in charge of Britain's "government." There,
on better information, he came to doubt "the sincerity of their avowed disposition to peace, to redress the American grievances, and to remove the causes
of their uneasiness." And by the end of 1780, he realized that the authorities
really had evidenced "an intention to destroy the liberties of the Colonies." "I
see," he sadly concluded, "the British constitution in its most essential prin-

ciples totally lost. I find the British spirit extinct. I see luxury its predominant character, and power in almost every department centered in those who are most abandoned, and that class of people, who might have virtue to rescue the government from its abuses, excluded from office because they have not the means of corruption." And so, after the war had come to an end, Van Schaack returned to America to pledge allegiance to the new nation, insisting that his vacillation provided no grounds for an "impeachment of his firmness, or of the rectitude of his principles."[50]

In justifying their right to independence on the basis of Locke's argument, revolutionary Americans made a profound and lasting decision of untold importance concerning the legitimate purpose and limits of government in the fledgling United States. As early as 1764, James Otis cited "the great law of *self-preservation*" and contended that the "*end* of government" is "the *good* of mankind" and that "above all things" it exists "to provide for the security, the quiet, and happy enjoyment of life, liberty, and property." Indeed, he insisted that "there is no one act which a government can have a *right* to make that does not tend to the advancement of the security, tranquillity, and prosperity of the people," and he added that "if life, liberty, and property could be enjoyed in as great perfection in *solitude* as in *society* there would be no need of government."[51] Four years later, in a letter to Britain's secretary of state penned by Samuel Adams, the Massachusetts House of Representatives traced the principle of representation to the fact that it "is acknowledged to be an unalterable law in nature that a man should have the free use and sole disposal of the fruit of his honest industry, subject to no controul."[52] In 1775, when Alexander Hamilton condemned "the pretensions of parliament," he did so not just because "they are subversive of our natural liberty, because an authority is assumed over us, which we by no means assent to." He gave even greater emphasis to the fact that those pretensions "divest us of that moral security, for our lives and properties, which we are intitled to, and which it is the primary end of society to bestow. For such security can never exist, while we have no part in making the laws, that are to bind us; and while it may be the interest of our uncontroled legislators to oppress us as much as possible."[53]

In similar fashion, when George Mason drafted the Virginia Declaration of Rights, he began by asserting that "all men are by nature equally free and independent and have certain inherent rights, of which, when they enter into a state of society, they cannot by any compact, deprive or divest their posterity; namely, the enjoyment of life and liberty, with the means of acquiring and possessing property, and pursuing and obtaining happiness and safety."[54] John Adams sounded precisely the same theme in the bill of rights attached to the Massachusetts Constitution of 1780: "All men are born free and equal, and have certain natural, essential, and unalienable rights; among which may be reckoned the right of enjoying and defending their lives and liberties; that of acquiring, possessing, and protecting property; in fine, that of seeking and obtaining happiness."[55] Similar wording can be found in the bills of rights adopted in Pennsylvania, Vermont, and New Hampshire,[56] and there are provisions in the constitutions of Maryland and of North and South Carolina presupposing much the same point of view.[57] Moreover, in the Declaration of Independence, Thomas Jefferson and the other signatories asserted on behalf of all their countrymen that "all men are created equal, that they are endowed by their Creator with certain unalienable Rights, that among these are Life, Liberty and the pursuit of Happiness," and that "to secure these rights, Governments are instituted among Men, deriving their just powers from the consent of the governed" so that "whenever any Form of Government becomes destructive of these ends, it is the Right of the People to alter or to abolish it, and to institute new Government, laying its foundation on such principles and organizing its powers in such form, as to them shall seem most likely to effect their Safety and Happiness."[58] From the outset of the Revolution, constitutionalism was conceived of primarily as a formal, legal instrument to limit legislative discretion, contain the populist impulse, and thereby safeguard the natural rights of man.[59]

In dropping the traditional reference to property, Jefferson and his colleagues did not intend to deny that its acquisition and possession are among man's inalienable rights.[60] After all, just three years later, in his revisal of Virginia's laws, Jefferson drew attention to the penchant of "wicked and dissolute men" for committing "violations on the lives, liberties and property of others" and then noted that what "principally induced men to enter into society" and what accounts therefore for government's "principal purpose" is the desire for "the secure enjoyment of these."[61] As one would expect, the delegates to the Constitutional Convention placed a similar emphasis on natural rights and the preservation of property.[62] Like the great majority of their compatriots, they recognized that, where human beings are denied a right to the fruits of their labor, their lives and liberties (both public and private) are similarly at risk.[63] In framing and approving the Declaration of Independence, their predecessors in the Continental Congress merely shifted the focus from the possession of property to something less tangible but much more fundamental—for, like Bacon, Hobbes, and Locke, they recognized three critical facts: that man's "pursuit of happiness" nearly always includes a quest for "comfortable Preservation," that the latter dictates and thereby justifies human acquisitiveness by means of labor, and that the protection of labor requires the protection of property as well.[64]

No one spoke more eloquently on the subject than Thomas Jefferson. In his second inaugural address, he insisted on the maintenance of "that state of property, equal or unequal, which results to every man from his own industry, or that of his fathers."[65] And in a letter written some years later, he elaborated on the point, specifying that "to take from one, because it is thought his own industry and that of his fathers has acquired too much, in order to spare to others, who, or whose fathers have not exercised equal industry and skill, is to violate arbitrarily the first principle of association, 'the *guarantee* to everyone of a free exercise of his industry, and the fruits acquired by it.'"[66] It was his conviction "that a right to property is founded in our natural wants, in the means with which we are endowed to satisfy these wants, and [in] the right to what we acquire by those means without violating the similar rights of other sensible beings."[67]

On the very same principle, Jefferson was no less horrified than had been John Locke at unemployment accompanied by a concentration of unworked lands in the hands of the idle rich. To head this off before the event or to obviate it after the fact, he was prepared to recommend the abolition of primogeniture and entails as well as positive laws encouraging partitive inheritance and other "devices for subdividing property, only taking care to let their subdivisions go hand in hand with the natural affections of the human mind." In general, he shared James Madison's predilection for "the silent operation of laws, which, without violating the rights of property, reduce extreme wealth towards a state of mediocrity, and raise extreme indigence towards a state of comfort." As he put it, "the best corrective is the law of equal inheritance to all in equal degree; and the better, as this enforces a law of nature, while extra-taxation violates it." And yet, at times, Jefferson spoke favorably of duties on items of luxury, and at one point he even toyed with the notion of progressive taxation aimed at "silently lessening the inequality of property." Moreover, in 1785, with regard to prerevolutionary France, he remarked, "Whenever there is in any country, uncultivated lands and unemployed poor, it is clear that the laws of property have been so far extended as to violate natural right. The earth is given as a common stock for man to labour & live on. If for the encouragement of industry we allow it to be appropriated, we must take care that other employment be provided to those excluded from the appropriation. If we do not, the fundamental right to labour the earth returns to the unemployed."[68] It should not be surprising that this great advocate of industry should soon thereafter, in a fashion recalling Bacon, celebrate the fact that "it is part of the American character to consider nothing as desperate; to surmount every difficulty by resolution and contrivance. . . . Remote from all other aid, we are obliged to invent and to execute; to find means within ourselves."[69]

The emphasis placed by Jefferson on industry and labor and on invention and execution deserves special attention. For it would appear that, in *The Federalist*, when James Madison traced "the rights of property" to "the diversity in the faculties of men" and grounded his defense of America's novel regime on the premise that "the first object of Government" is "the protection" of the "different and unequal faculties of acquiring property," he was simply drawing out the implications of the fundamental doctrine so elegantly laid out by his fellow Virginian.[70] With a candor elsewhere unequaled, James Wilson made much the same point at the federal convention when he interrupted a debate concerning slavery and representation, alluded to the question of *"personal* rights," denied "that property was the sole or primary object of Govert. & Society," and asserted, instead, that the "cultivation & improvement of the human mind was the most noble object."[71] In 1789, when Madison drafted a series of amendments to the new federal constitution designed to placate the Anti-Federalists, he initially included in their number a declaration, requested by the ratifying conventions of Virginia and North Carolina and soon to be endorsed by Rhode Island, to the effect that "government is instituted, and ought to be exercised for the benefit of the people; which consists in the enjoyment of life and liberty, with the right of acquiring and using property, and generally of pursuing and obtaining happiness and safety."[72] In his first inaugural address, Jefferson spoke of "a wise and frugal Government, which shall restrain men from injuring one another, shall leave them otherwise free to regulate their own pursuits of industry and improvement, and shall not take from the mouth of labor the bread it has earned" as "the sum of good government."[73] Few, if any Americans thought that it was the task of the government to define and provide for human happiness. But it was universally agreed that it is the government's duty to protect and promote its pursuit, and the acquisition and use of property were deemed central to that.

In this spirit, when Alexander Hamilton presented to Congress his famous *Report on the Subject of Manufactures*, he paid particular attention to the fact that the promotion of that branch of human endeavor would furnish "greater scope for the diversity of talents and dispositions, which discriminate men from each other." "It is a just observation," he explained, that minds of the strongest and most active powers for their proper objects fall below mediocrity and labour without effect, if confined to uncongenial pursuits. And it is thence to be inferred that the results of human exertion may be immensely increased by diversifying its objects. When all the different kinds of industry obtain in a community, each individual can find his proper element, and can call into activity the whole vigour of his nature. And the community is benefited by the services of its respective members, in the manner, in which each can serve it with most effect.

In Hamilton's judgment, it was the task of the government to "cherish and stimulate the activity of the human mind, by multiplying the objects of enterprise." "Even things in themselves not positively advantageous," he contended, "sometimes become so, by their tendency to provoke exertion. Every new scene, which is opened to the busy nature of man to rouse and exert itself, is the addition of a new energy to the general stock of effort."[74] Hamilton was evidently no less inclined than Jefferson, Madison, and Wilson to suppose that Benjamin Franklin was right when he remarked in passing one evening that man is by nature "a tool-making animal."[75] The teleology that Bacon, Descartes, and Hobbes had tried to keep at least partially concealed was to be even more visible in American thought than it had been in the works of John Locke.[76] In the modern republic, the hopes voiced by Robert Viscount Molesworth were fulfilled; and as a consequence of the populist rhetoric of Baconian science and Lockean politics, the character of priest gave way to that of patriot and philosopher.

Not surprisingly, then, the Americans tended to treat politics as an instrument for the protection of inherent human rights and not as an end in itself.[77] Gouverneur Morris confronted the question directly in 1776 when he observed that "Political Liberty considered separately from civil Liberty can have no other Effect than to gratify Pride" and when he added by way of explanation,

If we consider political in Connection with civil Liberty we place the former as the Guard and Security to the latter. But if the latter be given up for the former we sacrifice the End to the Means. We have seen that the Progress of Society tends to Encrease civil and diminish political Liberty. We shall find on Reflection that civil Liberty itself restricts political. Every Right of the Subject with Respect to the Government must derogate from its Authority or be thereby destroyed. The Authority of Magistrates is taken from that Mass of Power which in rude Societies and unballanced Democracies is wielded by the Majority. Every Separation of the executive and judicial Authority from the Legislature is a Diminution of political and Encrease of civil Liberty. Every Check and Ballance of that Legislature has a like Effect.[78]

The suspicion that Morris directed at politics was fundamental to the humanitarianism that distinguished the epoch. It was widely, if perhaps not quite universally, shared, and it led even the greatest statesmen of the age to speak of participation in public affairs as a burden rather than a joy.

In the last will and testament that he drew up some three years before drafting the Virginia Declaration of Rights, George Mason recommended to his sons "from my own Experience in Life, to prefer the happiness of independance & a private Station to the troubles and Vexations of Public Business."[79] Thomas Jefferson evidenced a similar reluctance. "If we are made in some degree for others," he explained to James Monroe in 1782, "yet in a greater are we made for ourselves. It were contrary to feeling and indeed ridiculous to suppose a man has less right in himself than one of his neighbors or all of them put together. This would be slavery and not that liberty . . . for the preservation of which our government has been changed."[80] A decade later, he sounded the same theme in a letter to James Madison. He did not deny that everyone owes his fellow citizens a "debt of service," but his, he insisted, had long ago been paid. "It is not easy perhaps to say of what length exactly this tour should be. But we may safely say of what length it should not be. Not of our whole life, for instance, for that would be to be born a slave. Not even of a very large portion of it." And so he announced his "uniform determination to retire from" public office as secretary of state "at an early day." Jefferson conceded, to be sure, that there was a time when his feelings

> were very different from what they are now: when perhaps the esteem of the world was of higher value in my eye than every thing in it. But age, experience & reflection, preserving to that only it's due value, have set a higher on tranquility. The motion of my blood no longer keeps time with the tumult of the world. It leads me to seek for happiness in the lap and love of my family, in the society of my neighbors & my books, in the wholesome occupations of my farm & my affairs, in an interest or affection in every bud that opens, in every breath that blows around me, in an entire freedom of rest or motion, of thought or incogitancy, owing account to myself alone of my hours & actions.[81]

John Adams similarly treated political life as a burden. In a letter written to his wife, Abigail, from Paris in 1780, he described his gambols about the town. "I could fill Volumes with Descriptions of Temples and Palaces, Paintings, Sculptures, Tapestry, Porcelaine, &c. &c. &c.—if I could have time," he wrote. "But I could not do this without neglecting my duty.—The Science of Government it is my Duty to study, more than all other Sciences: the Art of Legislation and Administration and Negotiation, ought to take Place, indeed to exclude in a manner all other Arts.—I must study Politicks and War that my sons may have liberty to study Mathematicks and Philosophy. My sons ought to study Mathematicks and Philosophy, Geography, natural History, Naval Architecture, navigation, Commerce and Agriculture, in order to give their Children a right to study Painting, Poetry, Musick, Architecture, Statuary, Tapestry and Porcelaine."[82]

Something of the same spirit is evident in the inaugural lecture on the study of law that James Wilson delivered in 1790 to an audience including President George Washington, Vice-President John Adams, Secretary of State Thomas Jefferson, and a host of lesser worthies. When he had completed his preliminary discussion of American principles and institutions and of the role to be played in the new polity by the law and legal education, Wilson raised a question largely ignored by his fellow Founding Fathers.[83] "Methinks," he said, "I hear one of the female part of my audience exclaim— What is all this to us? We have heard much of societies, of states, of governments, of laws, and of a law education. Is every thing made for your sex? Why should not we have a share? Is our sex less honest, or less virtuous, or less wise than yours?" In his reply, Wilson made no assertion of male superiority in honesty, virtue, or wisdom. In fact, he pointedly denied that such an assertion could be supported; and in the process, he tacitly conceded that, in signing the Declaration of Independence, he and his colleagues in the Continental Congress had opened a can of worms. For one cannot assert the natural equality and freedom of all human beings and impose strict conditions for judging the legitimacy of virtual representation, as Wilson and the most distinguished of his fellow revolutionaries all did, without at the same time casting grave doubt on the arguments once thought compelling for the denial to women of the right to vote, hold office, and otherwise participate in political life.

Of course, James Wilson did deny the propriety of women undertaking "the management of publick affairs," and he defended in rough outline the traditional division of responsibilities between the two sexes. But he did so in a characteristically modern fashion, which set him in opposition to the ancient Greeks, for he was inspired by Jean-Jacques Rousseau's celebration of domesticity as a bulwark against the psychologically debilitating effects of the corrosive individualism at the core of modern life. "You have, indeed," he admitted to the women in his audience,

> heard much of publick government and publick law: but these things were not made for themselves: they were made for something better; and of that something better, you form the better part—I mean society— I mean particularly domestick society: there the lovely and accomplished woman shines with superiour lustre.
>
> By some politicians, society has been considered as only the scaffolding of government; very improperly, in my judgment. In the just order of things, government is the scaffolding of society: and if society could be built and kept entire without government, the scaffolding might be thrown down, without the least inconvenience or cause of regret.
>
> Government is, indeed, highly necessary; but it is highly necessary to a fallen state. Had man continued innocent, society, without the aids of government, would have shed its benign influence even over the bowers of Paradise.

After waxing eloquent on the subject of female beauty and after suggesting that women "were destined to embellish, to refine, and to exalt the pleasures and virtues of social life," Wilson concluded that "the end of government and law" is "to protect and to improve social life." "If therefore," he told his female listeners, "you have no share in the formation, you have a most intimate connection with the effects of a good system of law and government." If Wilson thought it proper to exalt the status of women in a fashion utterly foreign to classical antiquity, and if he inadvertently prepared the way for their admission to public life by underlining the fact that they had as legitimate a stake in good government as their fathers, brothers, and husbands, it was ultimately because, like George Mason, Thomas Jefferson, and John Adams, he insisted on according primacy to the household and to private affairs.[84]

It would be tempting to suppose that there were exceptions to the rule. In singling out "the love of fame," in identifying it, respectively, as "the great spring to noble & illustrious actions" and as "the ruling passion of the noblest minds," Gouverneur Morris and Alexander Hamilton might seem to have set themselves apart from their compatriots. The sentiment they voiced was classical; the language in which it was expressed owed a great deal to Tacitus. But in describing that love as a spring or passion in the manner of David Hume, the two Americans conceded its irrationality and deprived it of the dignity accorded it by the ancients. In that important regard, they remained within the horizon drawn by Machiavelli, Montaigne, and Montesquieu. Nowhere did either insist that the love of fame is a spur to the pursuit of virtue or an echo of the universal human longing for true excellence.[85] In fact, nowhere in the fledgling United States did anyone persistently and unambiguously assert the primacy of political life in the manner of the ancient Greeks. Thomas Paine summed up what was to be the quasi-official American view in the first two paragraphs of *Common Sense* when he told his readers, "Society is produced by our wants and government by our wickedness; the former promotes our happiness *positively* by uniting our affections, the latter *negatively* by restraining our vices. . . . Society in every state is a blessing, but government, even in its best state, is but a necessary evil."[86] It is, then, in no way surprising that John Adams should castigate Aristotle for proposing the exclusion of merchants, artisans, and the like from the body politic.[87] As he put it in his *Defence of the Constitutions of Government of the United States of America*, "It is of infinitely more importance to the national happiness, to abound in good merchants, farmers, and manufacturers, good lawyers, priests, and physicians, and great philosophers, than it is to multiply what are called great statesmen and great generals."[88]

It would, nonetheless, be a mistake to take what the American Founding Fathers have to say in denigrating political life simply at face value. If men like Washington, Mason, Jefferson, Adams, and Wilson rarely had a good word to say for political ambition, they were nonetheless clearly influenced, if not driven, by something of the sort. And their aspirations were even grander than those of Pericles, Demosthenes, Cicero, Cato, and Caesar.[89] When John Adams celebrated the fact that his generation had "been sent into life at a time when the greatest lawgivers of antiquity would have wished to live," he tipped not just his own but everyone's hand.[90] A student called upon to illustrate what Aristotle had in mind when he spoke of the man of great soul (*megalópsuchos*) or what the Greeks meant when they singled a gentleman out as noble, beautiful, or fine and good (*kalokagathós*) could hardly do better than to direct attention to the men most responsible for America's conduct in the course of the Revolution. As the historian David Ramsay had occasion to observe firsthand while a member of the Continental Congress, that event

> called forth many virtues, and gave occasion for the display of abilities which, but for that event, would have been lost to the world. When the war began, the Americans were a mass of husbandmen, merchants, mechanics, and fishermen; but the necessities of the country gave a spring to the active powers of the inhabitants, and set them on thinking, speaking, and acting, in a line far beyond that to which they had been accustomed. . . . In the years 1775 and 1776, the country, being sud-

denly thrown into a situation that needed the ability of all its sons, these generally took their places, each according to the bent of his inclination. As they generally pursued their objects with ardour, a vast expansion of the human mind speedily followed. . . . It seemed as if the war not only required, but created talents. Men whose minds were warmed with the love of liberty, and whose abilities were improved by daily exercise, and sharpened with a laudable ambition to serve their distressed country, spoke, wrote, and acted, with an energy far surpassing all expectations which could be reasonably founded on their previous acquirements.[91]

When Philip Freneau predicted in 1771 that his compatriots would soon be able to boast of their own "Scipio's, Solon's, Cato's, sages, chiefs," he was, if anything, understating his case.[92] In light of the ancient Greek practice of worshiping the founders of cities as heroes after they had died, it was entirely appropriate that Thomas Jefferson speak of the federal convention as "an assembly of demigods."[93]

The Founding Fathers were by no means blind to their own potential stature. Alexander Hamilton disclosed something of their spirit in 1778 when he remarked,

The station of a member of C———ss, is the most illustrious and important of any I am able to conceive. He is to be regarded not only as a legislator, but as the founder of an empire. A man of virtue and ability, dignified with so precious a trust, would rejoice that fortune had given him birth at a time, and placed him in circumstances so favourable for promoting human happiness. He would esteem it not more the duty, than the privilege and ornament of his office, to do good to mankind; from this commanding eminence, he would look down with contempt upon every mean or interested pursuit.[94]

Five years later, when the anonymous North American who caught James Madison's attention exhorted his compatriots to reform the defective constitutions hastily adopted in the various states in the wake of the Declaration of Independence, he was even more direct. "Let them," he wrote, "by a government adequate to the ends of society, secure those blessings to which the virtues, sacrifices and sufferings of America have an undeniable claim.—Let them do this—and then, when corroding time, shall separate pure and immortal virtues from attendant frailties, which at first obscure their lustre— when envy and jealousy shall be no more—a just and grateful fame will rank them amidst those idolized patriots of Greece and Rome, whose names antiquity has already consecrated at her venerable shrine."[95]

Even James Wilson was prepared to compare the American states favorably with "the most illustrious commonwealths, which adorn the records of fame." "When some future Xenophon or Thucydides shall arise to do justice to their virtues and their actions," he told those present for his inaugural lecture, "the glory of America will rival—it will outshine the glory of Greece." Wilson could make so extravagant an assertion because, like many American patriots, he was persuaded that the humane, commercial, democratic brand of republicanism established in the United States was decisively superior to the cruel, martial, aristocratic republicanism of ancient times. Israel Evans touched on the central issue in an election sermon that he delivered in Concord, New Hampshire, in June 1791. He could remember "no aera since the creation of the world, so favourable to the rights of mankind as the present." For though he entertained considerable respect for the "imperfect civilization" of "the Grecian and Roman nations" with "their boasted love of Liberty," he denied that they were "acquainted with the true principles of original, equal, and sentimental liberty." As he put it,

> They neither understood the nature, nor practised the duties, of humanity. They who are acquainted with the true history of Greece and Rome, need not be informed, that the cruelty they exercised upon their slaves, and those taken in war, is almost beyond the power of credibility. The proud and selfish passions have always endeavoured to suppress the spirit of Freedom. Even Rome herself, while she pretended to glory in being free, endeavoured to subject and enslave the rest of mankind.— But no longer shall we look to antient histories for principles and systems of pure freedom. The close of the eighteenth century, in which we live, shall teach mankind to be truly free.

Two years later, in New York, DeWitt Clinton sounded the same theme in language that he lifted from John Locke. He was persuaded that the "important truth" of *the natural equality of mankind*," if it "had been properly understood and practised upon," would have eliminated "all the despotisms of the antient and modern world." But, unfortunately, that truth must be "considered as hidden from the antients, and as one of the wonderful discoveries of modern times." As James Wilson put it, the polities of ancient Hellas might be "gilded with the gay decorations of fable and mythology," but the American states "are clothed in the neater and more simple garb of freedom and truth."[96]

James Madison, normally the most sober of the Founders, gave similar testimony with regard to the intoxicating influence of the spirit of rivalry aroused by reflection on the ancient exemplars. In the midst of the struggle to ratify the Constitution, he paused to wonder at the fact "that in every case reported by antient history, in which government has been established with deliberation and consent, the task of framing it has not been committed to an assembly of men; but has been performed by some individual citizen of pre-eminent wisdom and approved integrity." After considering the tales told of Minos, Zaleucus, Theseus, Draco, Solon, Lycurgus, Romulus, Numa, Tullus Hostilius, Servius Tullius, and Brutus, he could only "admire the improvement made by America on the ancient mode of preparing and establishing regular plans of government."[97]

There can be little doubt that a great many members of the revolutionary generation were swept away by the longing to accomplish something brilliant and worthy of remembrance. Looking back on the event some fifty years after the ratification of the Constitution, the young Abraham Lincoln remarked that the American republic was then "felt, by all to be an undecided experiment."

> Then, all that sought celebrity and fame, and distinction expected to find them in the success of that experiment. Their *all* was staked upon it:— their destiny was *inseparably* linked with it. Their ambition aspired to display before an admiring world, a practical demonstration of the truth of a proposition, which had hitherto been considered, at best not better, than problematical; namely, *the capability of a people to govern themselves.* If they succeeded, they were to be immortalized; their names were to be transferred to counties and cities, and rivers and mountains; and to be revered and sung, and toasted through all time. If they failed, they were to be called knaves and fools, and fanatics for a fleeting hour; then to sink and be forgotten. They succeeded. The experiment is successful; and thousands have won their deathless names in making it so.[98]

If John Adams and Thomas Jefferson seem to suggest that the American regime somehow involved a mixture of ancient and modern, if the former identified the "revolution principles" as "the principles of Aristotle and Plato, of Livy and Cicero, and Sidney, Harrington, and Locke," and if the latter traced the "authority" of the Declaration of Independence to "the harmonizing sentiments of the day, whether expressed in conversation, in letters, printed essays, or in the elementary books of public right, [such] as Aristotle, Cicero, Locke, Sidney, etc.," it was at least in part because the institution of a modern republic designed as a decided improvement on its ancient predecessors was a profoundly political act.[99]

It would be a mistake to interpret the American Revolution in the manner of J. G. A. Pocock as "a flight from modernity" and to describe it as simply or even chiefly a "part of the story of the revival in the early modern West of the ancient ideal of *homo politicus*." In most respects, as should now be clear, the very opposite is the case. The "civic humanism" which some purport to find in seventeenth- and eighteenth-century Britain and America is by and large a figment of the scholarly imagination. In this age, Adam Ferguson apart, few, if any, British subjects or Americans were prepared to publicly affirm "that the human personality" is "that of a *zōon politikon*" and is "fully expressed only in the practice of citizenship as an active virtue." It would, however, be almost equally wrong to run to the other extreme and join Clinton Rossiter in supposing that "the Americans would have believed just as vigorously in public morality had Cato and the Gracchi never lived," for there is no reason to judge Bernard Bailyn correct in arguing that the ancient classics were "everywhere" merely "illustrative, not determinative, of thought." The study of antiquity contributed much more than "a vivid vocabulary" to the thinking of the Americans. By stirring ambition and by teaching men what it meant to aspire to true political greatness, Plutarch and the other ancient writers contributed powerfully to the "logic" and "grammar" of the thinking that animated the revolutionary generation.

Gordon Wood was undoubtedly wrong when he described American republicanism as "essentially anti-capitalistic," when he insisted that the revolutionaries gave priority to "public or political liberty" over "individual rights," and when he asserted that "the sacrifice of individual interests to the greater good of the whole formed the essence of republicanism and comprehended for Americans the idealistic goal of their Revolution." In similar fashion, Hannah Arendt erred when she asserted that the American Revolution's "ultimate end" was public, participatory "freedom" of the sort exemplified in the Greek *pólis* "and the constitution of a public space where freedom would appear." But Wood was arguably correct when he contended that the Americans' "compulsive interest in the ancient republics was in fact crucial to their attempt to understand the moral and social basis of politics"; Arendt was surely right when she argued that, "without the classical example shining through the centuries, none of the men of the revolutions on either side of the Atlantic would have possessed the courage for what then turned out to be unprecedented action"; and there is no reason to attribute the Americans' restricted appropriation of the classical heritage to any "confusion" on their part.[100] The very act of founding the world's first modern republic was a tacit assertion that some men really are political animals endowed with a capacity for *lógos* enabling them to discern and make clear to one another what is advantageous, just, and good. The words that John Adams penned concerning the federal convention when he came to conclude his *Defence of the*

Constitutions of Government of the United States of America in late December 1787 could be applied with equal justice to the revolutionary generation's overall struggle to devise and establish political institutions appropriate to the new nation's needs: "The conception of such an idea, and the deliberate union of so great and various a people in such a plan, is, without all partiality or prejudice, if not the greatest exertion of human understanding, the greatest single effort of national deliberation that the world has ever seen."[101]

The American founders were in a position comparable to James Harrington's Lord Archon. They were themselves political men through and through; they longed to be remembered forever, and to that end they tried to accomplish the most noble of deeds. But they were also acutely, even painfully aware of the dangers that would arise from an opening up of what the Greeks had called "middle ground." And so, for the sake of domestic tranquillity and the general welfare, they tried to establish stable political institutions that would limit the scope of American statesmanship and effectively deny future generations the opportunity to achieve lasting glory that they had themselves enjoyed; and by way of consolation, they sought, in the manner suggested by Bacon, Hobbes, and Locke, to provide a substitute for politics in the socioeconomic sphere constituted by labor, commerce, and technology. In order that "no manner of Food might be left unto ambition," most of them even tried what George Washington, like Harrington's Lord Archon, actually accomplished: to contrive affairs so that "the minds of men were firme in the opinion, that he could be no seeker of himselfe, in the way of earthly Pompe and Glory."[102] In reading the Founders' public statements and private correspondence, one must sometimes wonder whether by and large they even succeeded in deluding themselves.

The problem that the American founders set for themselves was an inordinately difficult one. They acknowledged the force of the humanitarian assault on ancient republicanism, and they conceded that of Hobbes's trenchant critique of politics. They deemed it essential that the American regime give primacy to protecting life, liberty, and property and to fostering man's conquest of nature; and as Gouverneur Morris's testimony suggests, they were therefore generally prepared to treat political freedom as a constitutional instrument devised for that end.[103] But, as we have already had occasion to observe,[104] they were steeped in the classics, and they felt the force of the ancient example. In consequence, they were of the opinion that freedom is valuable in and of itself and that human dignity is somehow bound up with man's capacity for self-governance;[105] and so, while they sought the establishment of a polity that would give first place to man's capacity as a tool-making animal, they tried to allow for and even foster within limits political liberty as well. If forced to choose between the protection of life, civil liberty, and property on the one hand and political freedom on the other, their choice would be clear. But they were hopeful that such a choice could be avoided and that the protection of life, personal liberty, and property could be achieved within a new kind of republic. It was with this goal in mind that, in the Declaration of Independence, they cited not just their fellow colonists' "right" to "throw off" a government that, by means of "a long train of abuses and usurpations, . . . evinces a design to reduce them under absolute Despotism" but "their duty" to do so; and this is why they concluded that document by pledging to one another not just their "Lives" and their "Fortunes" but also their "sacred Honor." For their duty and honor as men were inextricably linked with the quest to reconcile justice with political liberty and wisdom with consent.[106]

The endeavor to found a regime that would concede primacy to man's capacity as a tool-making animal while paying tribute as well to his questionable and apparently restricted capacity for self-governance drove the American founders to launch a republican experiment that reached the limits of Lockean first principles and then silently passed beyond their narrow confines, and it forced them in the process to reassess the dictates of traditional Whig political architecture in light of the conviction, voiced by John Adams, that by indirect, institutional means "a regular, well-ordered constitution" can "bring forth men capable of conducting the national councils and arms."[107] In 1790, in devising a reading list for his new son-in-law, Thomas Jefferson remarked that "Locke's little book on government is perfect as far as it goes." Then, he added an observation that deserves our attention: "Descending from theory to practice there is no better book than the Federalist."[108] In our endeavor to understand what the American founders set out to do, we could begin at no better place.[109]

CHAPTER 1

James Madison and the New Science of Politics

We may appeal to every page of history we have hitherto turned over, for proofs irrefragable, that the people, when they have been unchecked, have been as unjust, tyrannical, brutal, barbarous, and cruel, as any king or senate possessed of uncontrollable power. The majority has eternally, and without one exception, usurped over the rights of the minority.—John Adams

III.i.1

Despite its lasting fame, *The Federalist* is less a treatise in political philosophy composed for the ages than a work of political rhetoric aimed at a particular audience.[1] All but the last eight numbers were written in extreme haste and first appeared in the popular press of New York City as a series of brief articles designed to explain and defend the new constitution devised for the United States of America at the federal convention held in Philadelphia from May to September 1787. The various numbers were then collected, corrected, and republished in two volumes in time for the New York Ratifying Convention.[2]

Precisely two decades before the delegates from Britain's former colonies gathered for the federal convention, Adam Ferguson had published in Edinburgh *An Essay on the History of Civil Society*. The twenty years separating the publication of Ferguson's book and the framing of the American Constitution mark a watershed in human history. Before we can begin to understand what Hamilton, Madison, and Jay have to say, we must ponder the events of those two decades. We must consider their import as understood by the men of that age, and we must pause to reflect on the character of the audience which the authors of *The Federalist* addressed.

Though virtually forgotten today, Ferguson was much esteemed at the time. A Gaelic-speaking Highlander, educated in the Lowlands and closely associated with David Hume and Adam Smith, he held in succession the chairs in natural philosophy, moral philosophy, and mathematics at Edinburgh in a period in which that university was generally regarded as the greatest in all of Europe. In the decades after its publication, his essay was to exercise a profound influence on economists and political theorists alike. Ferguson was no less aware of the unprecedented nature of the emerging new order than his two better-known friends. But unlike them, as we have already remarked, he had grave reservations concerning the consequences, for the experience of living in the Highlands and his years as chaplain to

the Black Watch had left him with a deep and abiding appreciation for the
virtues of the world soon to be lost.[3] The sharpness of his moral sense and
the breadth of experience that he brought to bear on the issues which he confronted in his book make it a work of seminal importance for understanding
the differences which separate modern from ancient times.

And yet, for all his perspicacity, not even Adam Ferguson fully grasped the
radical character of the change that was to come. He had occasion to weigh
the claims made on behalf of the great legislators of antiquity—Lycurgus
and Solon, Romulus, Numa, and Moses—and like those among his fellow
Scots who had followed Samuel Pufendorf and Bernard Mandeville in transforming Hobbes's notion of man's asocial sociability into an elaborate theory
of the gradual and spontaneous evolution of economy, society, and polity,
he found the evidence for ancient statesmanship sadly wanting. "Nations
stumble upon establishments which are indeed the result of human action,
but not the execution of any human design," he argued. "No constitution is
formed by concern, no government copied from a plan."[4] So it must have
seemed to many, if not to most, of his contemporaries.

But they were wrong. Ferguson had blundered—and badly. Within his
lifetime, the men who made the American Revolution were to demonstrate
that he and his fellow Scots had underestimated the dignity and scope of
statesmanship; and as a consequence of their action, the world has never
since been the same. Consciously and deliberately, after a period of sustained experimentation in the states and after a time of intensive preparation
and learned discussion, the framers of the American Constitution set out to
institute a government and to shape a people as well.[5] The radically novel
character and the epoch-making importance of the experiment they brought
to completion was perfectly evident to many at the time.

In the initial chapter of his *Second Treatise*, John Locke had denied the generally held supposition that "all Government in the World is the product
only of Force and Violence, and that Men live together by no other Rules
but that of Beasts, where the strongest carries it." Instead, he had sought
to demonstrate the truth of the novel proposition that there was "another
rise of Government, another Original of Political Power, and another way of
designing and knowing the Persons that have it." In his view, all legitimate
government actually rested on the consent of the governed.[6] David Hume
was skeptical: he was perfectly prepared to acknowledge "that government
in its earliest infancy arose from consent or rather the voluntary acquiescence
of the people." But he deemed absurd Locke's contention that "at present,
when it has attained its full maturity, it rests on no other foundation." To
make his case against these "philosophical notions," Hume simply appeals

to "fact and reality." Almost without exception, "usurpation or conquest" has been the origin of dominion; "force and violence" are, therefore, the true foundations of government. Even "where consent may seem to have taken place, it was commonly so irregular, so confined, or so much intermixed either with fraud or violence, that it cannot have any great authority." Locke's doctrine is attractive for the reason that it is dangerous—because it flatters human pretension: "When we assert, that all lawful government arises from the consent of the people, we certainly do them a great deal more honour than they deserve, or even expect and desire from us." In truth, there is "not a more terrible event, than a total dissolution of government." In such a situation, "every wise man" looks for solace not to the wisdom and good sense of the people, but to the power and discipline of an obedient army headed by a general "who may seize the prize, and give to the people a master, which they are so unfit to chuse for themselves." Some years after the publication of Hume's critique of Locke, when the American framers set out to fashion a government for themselves that would both rest on and operate through consent, they arguably had "reason, history, and experience" against them.[7]

This they fully recognized. The unprecedented character of their endeavor both buoyed them up and weighed upon them. Prior to January 1776, when Thomas Paine launched a furious assault on monarchy in *Common Sense*,[8] neither republicanism nor democracy had been in good odor.[9] Of this fact the Framers were all too painfully aware. And yet they could not deny what James Madison openly proclaimed: that "no other form would be reconcileable with the genius of the people of America; with the fundamental principles of the revolution; or with that honorable determination, which animates every votary of freedom, to rest all our political experiments on the capacity of mankind for self-government."[10] Nor could they ignore the fact that the science of government was then "almost in its state of infancy." As James Wilson reminded the delegates to the Pennsylvania Ratifying Convention, "governments, in general, have been the result of force, of fraud, and of accident." That simple fact set America apart. "A period of six thousand years has elapsed since the Creation," he observed, and now "the United States exhibit to the world, the first instance, as far as we can learn, of a nation, unattacked by external force, unconvulsed by domestic insurrections, assembling voluntarily, deliberating fully, and deciding calmly, concerning that system of government, under which they would wish that they and their posterity should live." The scene which America exhibited to the world was "hitherto unparalleled."[11]

James Wilson was by no means alone in his conviction. Even before the federal convention met, John Adams openly celebrated the fact that the individual American states had "exhibited, perhaps, the first examples of governments erected on the simple principles of nature." He even contended that, "if men are now sufficiently enlightened to disabuse themselves of artifice, imposture, hypocrisy, and superstition, they will consider this event as an era in their history," for it "will never be pretended that any persons employed" in establishing the American governments "had interviews with the gods, or were in any degree under the inspiration of Heaven, more than those at work upon ships or houses, or laboring in merchandise or agriculture." Instead, he added, "it will forever be acknowledged that these governments were contrived merely by the use of reason and the senses." In Adams's estimation, "Thirteen governments thus founded on the natural authority of the people alone, without a pretence of miracle or mystery, and . . . destined to spread over the northern part of that whole quarter of the globe, are a great point gained in favor of the rights of mankind." [12]

In New York, by the time that James Wilson rose to address the Pennsylvania Ratifying Convention, his colleague and collaborator Alexander Hamilton had already introduced the first number of *The Federalist* with a similar assessment of the importance of the American experiment. "It has been frequently remarked," he argued,

> that it seems to have been reserved to the people of this country, by their conduct and example, to decide the important question, whether societies of men are really capable or not, of establishing good government from reflection and choice, or whether they are forever destined to depend, for their political constitutions, on accident and force. If there be any truth in the remark, the crisis, at which we are arrived, may with propriety be regarded as the æra in which that decision is to be made; and a wrong election of the part we shall act, may, in this view, deserve to be considered as the general misfortune of mankind. [13]

Hamilton's reading of the situation differs in but one respect from that to which James Wilson would soon after give voice. When the New Yorker spoke of a crisis, he had in mind the prospect of domestic insurrection—and eventualities even more dire. The delegates to the federal convention had met in the shadow of Shays's Rebellion. [14] In 1787, despite John Adams's sanguine observations, success was by no means a foregone conclusion.

III.i.2

Eleven years had passed since the united colonies had declared their independence from Britain, and for the makers of the American Revolution, those eleven years had been a sobering experience.[15] Already in 1783, George Washington had expressed grave misgivings. In early June, on the eve of his retirement as general of the armies, he addressed a circular to the governors of the states. It was intended to be his last official communication, his farewell address. In this open letter, Washington congratulated his compatriots on their great victory, but reminded them that there was much left to do. They had won the war, but they could lose the peace. "It is yet to be decided," he noted, "whether the Revolution must ultimately be considered as a blessing or a curse: a blessing or a curse, not to the present age alone, for with our fate will the destiny of unborn Millions be involved." This great question remained to be decided in part because there was a serious danger that the end of the war would bring a relaxation of the Union, "annihilating the cement of the Confederation" and allowing the United States "to become the sport of European politics."[16]

Washington had written because this seemed to be taking place before his very eyes. While coordinating American resistance to the Coercive Acts, the delegates to the Continental Congress had gradually assumed many of the powers traditionally accorded the king;[17] and under the pressures of initiating a difficult and often chaotic struggle for independence, they had stitched together the Articles of Confederation in a haphazard fashion without much discussion. The resulting document was mute testimony to the power of what Hamilton would call "accident and force" and to the debility of human "reflection and choice." Thus, for example, in response to the need to foster cooperation and achieve unanimity among the states, Congress denied itself the right to impose and collect taxes on its own; accordingly, the finances of the confederation were never placed on a proper foundation.[18] The consequences had nearly crippled the war effort.[19] This Washington knew only too well. "No man in the United States is, or can be more deeply impressed with the necessity of a reform in our present Confederation than myself," he wrote in a letter to Hamilton. "No man perhaps has felt the bad efects of it more sensibly; for to the defects thereof, & want of Powers in Congress may justly be ascribed the prolongation of the War, & consequently the Expences occasioned by it. More than half the perplexities I have experienced in the course of my command, and almost the whole of the difficulties & distress of the Army, have there origin here."[20]

Victory had reduced the urgency but not the need for reform. As the war drew near its end, the public creditors openly wondered whether they would ever receive recompense, and they were not alone. After the victory at Yorktown, Washington's troops had been left unpaid for months, and the legitimate fear that the confederation would renege on its pledge to provide some sort of pension for the officers of the Continental Line had eventually occasioned worrisome disturbances within the army.[21] In truth, however, the insolvency of the confederacy and the fact that there were murmurs of mutiny among the soldiers at Newburgh were only symptoms. As Washington recognized, there were other, more serious problems confronting the Union. In matters pertaining to the nation as a whole, Congress lacked the power to force cooperation on the states, and voluntary compliance with its decisions (though required by the Articles of Confederation) was but rarely forthcoming. There was, already in 1783, good reason to fear the dissolution of the Union itself.

There were grounds for hope as well. During the colonial period, Americans had become accustomed to relying on Britain to serve as an impartial umpire in settling the jurisdictional disputes that grew up between the various colonies. When the newly independent states ratified the Articles of Confederation, they quite naturally conferred this power of superintendence on the Continental Congress;[22] and though their boundary disputes were many, the states did manage to muddle through the Revolutionary War and its immediate aftermath without ever coming to blows. Moreover, while in the midst of war and revolution, the states that had claims to vast tracts of unsettled land in the West had found it difficult, if not impossible, to police those claims, and they had been so pestered by separatist movements on the frontier that, over time, the leaders of the various states became increasingly eager to negotiate a general settlement to all territorial disputes that would render each state secure in all its remaining possessions. Thus, Pennsylvania found it remarkably easy to settle its quarrels with Virginia and Connecticut; and when the Continental Congress called on the landed states to cede their western territories to the confederation as a prelude to the formation of new states, New York and Virginia quickly displayed a willingness to comply. There was every reason to expect Massachusetts, Connecticut, and North Carolina to follow suit. No one seriously believed that the individual states could go it alone.[23]

Thus, when Washington sent out his circular, he had reasons for thinking that it was still possible to set things right by strengthening the confederation. That is why he took the time to remark on the favorable circumstances attending the establishment of republican government in the new nation.

The foundation of our Empire was not laid in the gloomy age of Ignorance and Superstition; but at an Epocha when the rights of mankind were better understood and more clearly defined, than at any other period. The researches of the human mind after social happiness have been carried to a great extent; the Treasures of knowledge acquired by the labors of Philosophers, Sages and Legislators, through a long succession of years, are laid open for our use, and their collected wisdom may be happily applied in the Establishment of our forms of Government. . . . At this auspicious period, the United States came into existence as a Nation; and, if their Citizens should not be completely free and happy, the fault will be intirely their own.[24]

Four years would pass before Washington's call received an answer, and that answer was made manifest only when civil strife between rich and poor, between creditors and debtors, and between frontier separatists and defenders of the former colonies' territorial integrity threatened to spawn anarchy in each and every one of the states. Indeed, had it not been for Shays's Rebellion in western Massachusetts, the state legislatures and the Continental Congress might have ignored the request of Alexander Hamilton, James Madison, and the other delegates to the abortive Annapolis Commercial Convention that a federal convention be called to amend the Articles of Confederation.[25] It is not fortuitous that the constitution which that federal convention eventually produced explicitly guarantees to each of the states a republican government and includes, in addition, provisions denying to these subordinate polities the right to issue money and to impair the obligation of contracts.[26] Experience had demonstrated that the legislatures sitting in the various state capitols were not to be trusted,[27] and men like John Jay and John Marshall were beginning to wonder whether human beings are really "incapable of governing" themselves after all.[28]

For those who shared Washington's fears from the start, this incontrovertible evidence that the states were insufficient on their own was a godsend. To recover a sense of what happened, one need only peruse the correspondence of James Madison. Shortly after the close of the federal convention, this acute observer wrote to Thomas Jefferson that "the mutability of the laws of the States is found to be a serious evil. The injustice of them has been so frequent and so flagrant as to alarm the most steadfast friends of republicanism. I am persuaded I do not err in saying that the evils issuing from these sources contributed more to that uneasiness which produced the Convention, and prepared the public mind for a general reform, than those which accrued to our national character and interest from the inadequacy of the Confederation to its immediate objects."[29] According to the preamble of the constitution they devised, the delegates who gathered for the federal con-

vention in Philadelphia sought "to form a more perfect union" in order to
"establish justice, insure domestic tranquillity, provide for the common defense, promote the general welfare, and secure the blessings of liberty" for
themselves and for their posterity. They came to Philadelphia because they
believed that the states alone or linked by the Articles of Confederation were
an instrument inadequate to the purpose.

The framing of the Constitution was an occasion for debate, for discussion,
and even for discord.[30] And yet, when the hall fell silent and the document
was presented in its final form, there was near unanimity. All but a handful
of the delegates were prepared to endorse and defend the proposed constitution. To facilitate candor, they had conducted their deliberations in secret,
behind closed doors, beyond the purview of the general public.[31] And there,
on the floor of the convention, some had expressed doubts and even grave
misgivings regarding their handiwork. But nearly all of these were nonetheless persuaded that the new constitution would far better meet the needs of
the Union than the Articles of Confederation.[32]

This consensus among the delegates was of the greatest importance. It was
a precondition absolutely necessary for the establishment of the new constitutional order. But, though necessary, it was not sufficient. It was not enough
to compose a document well suited to the nation's requirements. It would
be essential as well to secure that document's ratification. And to do that,
the proponents of the new constitution would have to persuade their fellow
citizens in the states and those elected to the various ratifying conventions
of the efficacy of their proposal. That was the task undertaken in New York
by the authors of *The Federalist*.

Victory would not come easily. Within the various states, there were many
who had a personal stake in maintaining the existing order; and in their
eagerness to repudiate the work of the convention, these men could appeal to
long-established and powerful prejudices in favor of the various localities.[33]
There was every reason to suppose that the defenders of local supremacy
would be well organized in many of the states,[34] and they had arguments—
long thought decisive—at their disposal.[35] Those expert in the science of
government—the "philosophers, sages, and legislators" whom Washington
had so lavishly praised—taught that a pure republic of the sort which the
Framers envisaged would have to be constructed on the model of the direct
democracies of classical antiquity. But, in the vast reaches of the New World,
such an enterprise was wildly impracticable. Thus, the Framers (Washington
included) had been forced by experience to modify their own presuppositions and to disregard in one crucial respect the "collected wisdom" of the

ages.[36] That is why Alexander Hamilton, James Madison, and John Jay found it necessary to address the problem of classical republicanism in their defense of the Constitution. To secure support for what Madison candidly termed "the experiment of an extended republic," the authors of *The Federalist* had to encourage in their compatriots the "manly spirit" which the Constitution's framers had shown. They had to dissuade their countrymen from evidencing "a blind veneration for antiquity, for custom, or for names." And, most important of all, they had to teach the citizens of the various states to ignore the voices telling them that the proposed government "is a novelty in the political world; that it has never yet had a place in the theories of the wildest projectors; that it rashly attempts what it is impossible to accomplish."[37]

Not long after the various numbers of the newspaper series had been gathered and published in two volumes, George Washington wrote to Alexander Hamilton to express his "great satisfaction" in perusing "the political papers" which the New Yorker's "Triumvirate" had published "under the signature of Publius." "When the transient circumstances & fugitive performances which attended this *crisis* shall have disappeared," Washington remarked, "that work will merit the notice of Posterity; because in it are candidly discussed the principles of freedom & the topics of government, which will be always interesting to mankind so long as they shall be connected in Civil Society."[38] Thomas Jefferson was even less sparing in his praise. To James Madison, he described the fruits of the threesome's efforts as "the best commentary on the principles of government which ever was written." In later years, when the Virginian sought edification on the subject of politics, when he pondered personal liberty and "the structure of government best calculated to preserve it," he could console himself over the loss of many of the great works of classical antiquity precisely because he was in possession of *The Federalist*.[39]

III.i.3

To present the case for the modern alternative to classical republicanism, Hamilton, Madison, and Jay wrapped themselves in the toga of Plutarch's Publius Valerius Publicola[40]—but despite the aura of republican virtue they assumed, they rejected outright any great veneration for the far distant past. Samuel Adams had once expressed the pious hope that his beloved Boston would become "a *Christian* Sparta." Such thoughts were far from the minds of the men who framed the American Constitution.[41] Alexander Hamilton even suggested that it would be imprudent for his contemporaries to look to classical antiquity for a solution of their political difficulties. In modern times, he contended, there had been "great improvement" in "the science of politics."

> The efficacy of various principles is now well understood, which were either not known at all, or imperfectly known to the ancients. The regular distribution of power into distinct departments—the introduction of legislative ballances and checks—the institution of courts composed of judges, holding their offices during good behaviour—the representation of the people in the legislature by deputies of their own election— these are wholly new discoveries, or have made their principal progress towards perfection in modern times. They are means, and powerful means, by which the excellencies of republican government may be retained and its imperfections lessened or avoided. To this catalogue of circumstances, that tend to the amelioration of popular systems of civil government, I shall venture, however novel it may appear to some, to add one more, on a principle, which has been made the foundation of an objection to the New Constitution, I mean the ENLARGEMENT of the ORBIT within which such systems are to revolve either in respect to the dimensions of a single State, or to the consolidation of several smaller States into one great confederacy.

This last addition to Hamilton's catalogue was to be America's greatest and most revolutionary contribution to the cause of modern republicanism.[42]

Though first announced by Hamilton, this discovery was the work of his colleague James Madison, who had been chief among the many architects of the American Constitution. The young statesman from Virginia was quite often on the losing side in Philadelphia.[43] But he was the first to recognize that strengthening the Union and granting it more extensive responsibilities might do much to prevent injustice and to reduce class strife within the various states, and as the instigator and principal author of the Virginia Plan, he managed to set the agenda for the convention. It was his eloquence and erudition that persuaded the delegates to take the bold step of ignoring their limited mandate and of proposing the establishment of an entirely new central government supreme in its restricted sphere and indebted for its authority not to the individual states but rather to the citizens of the entire nation.[44] To convince his fellow delegates and then his fellow citizens that such a regime was consistent with the principles of republican liberty, Madison had to confront the celebrated Montesquieu.

The French philosophe towered over the latter half of the eighteenth century like a colossus. In matters pertaining to the constitution of liberty, his authority exceeded even that of John Locke. It was only natural that American patriots, who had cited the latter more often than any other writer in the years when they saw need to justify their revolution, should confer similar primacy on the former when America's independence was established and recognized and constitution making had become their principal concern.[45] In *The Spirit of the Laws*, Montesquieu had argued that it was impossible to construct a viable republic on an extended territory,[46] and many of the more thoughtful contemporaries of Hamilton and Madison were inclined to agree.[47] In their view, the supreme obstacle to the survival of such a republic was faction: the predilection of men to form groups "united or actuated by some common impulse of passion, or of interest, adverse to the rights of other citizens, or to the permanent and aggregate interests of the community." They believed that this proclivity was rooted in a selfishness which could be overcome only within the confines of a small civic community modeled on those of ancient Greece and early republican Rome. Madison accepted part of their argument but rejected the conclusion. To secure ratification of the constitution he had done so much to shape, he had to expose once and for all "the error which limits Republican Government to a narrow district." In doing so, he found it necessary to lay bare the structural differences which would distinguish the new American republic from its classical predecessors.[48]

In the most famous of his numerous contributions to *The Federalist*, Madison responded to the most serious objection to his new constitution by directly addressing the problem of faction. He argued that it was "impracticable" to remove "the causes of faction" without sacrificing political liberty and suggested that one could cure "the mischiefs of faction" by regulating its effects. Even within the confines of a small civic community, Madison writes, it is impossible to eradicate factions altogether because "the latent causes of faction are . . . sown in the nature of man."

> As long as the reason of man continues fallible, and he is at liberty to exercise it, different opinions will be formed. As long as the connection subsists between his reason and his self-love, his opinions and his passions will have a reciprocal influence on each other; and the former will be the objects to which the latter attach themselves. . . . So strong is this propensity of mankind to fall into mutual animosities, that where no substantial occasion presents itself, the most frivolous and fanciful distinctions have been sufficient to kindle their unfriendly passions, and excite their most violent conflicts. But the most common and durable source of factions, has been the various and unequal distribution of

property. Those who hold, and those who are without property, have
ever formed distinct interests in society.

Opinions, passions, and interests—these are the notions that lie at the heart
of Madison's analysis. As long as men are men, they will form different opinions and have different interests; and as long as this is the case, their passions
will be engaged and they will quarrel with bitterness. "Neither moral nor religious motives," writes Madison, "can be relied on as an adequate control."
Men will always be at odds, particularly where the landed and the landless
coexist.[49]

Madison was not the first to fathom the human propensity to quarrel. As
we have already had ample opportunity to observe, the ancients were no less
conscious of the clash of interests dividing the rich from the poor, and they
were acutely aware that the heightened political rivalry innate to republics
tends to give rise to disorder and incessant civil strife. Aristotle, nonetheless,
considered it possible to blunt, if not resolve, class tension by establishing
a mixed regime and to restrain and channel the love of glory by giving first
place to an aristocracy of true gentlemen (*kaloì kagathoî*) educated in prudence, moderation, and virtue and dedicated to cultural as well as to martial
pursuits.[50] James Madison and his colleagues harbored no such convictions.
Whigs rarely if ever praised Thomas Hobbes, but virtually all of them tacitly
acknowledged the force of the critique which that great advocate of enlightened despotism launched against classical republicanism and its Aristotelian defenders; and like Hobbes and his chief disciples Harrington, Locke,
Montesquieu, Hume, Blackstone, and Lolme, they embraced the principle of
representation as a corrective and, with it, the strategy of indirect rule.[51]

In one of the first Federalist pamphlets, Noah Webster sketched out the
logic of the American Whig stance. He readily conceded the attractiveness
of the notion that "all the members of a society should be present, and each
give his suffrage in acts of legislation." But this did not prevent him from
restating Montesquieu's critique of participatory democracy. As he put it,
direct, popular exercise of the legislative power is "impracticable in all large
states," and it is "very questionable" in any case "whether it would be the
best mode of legislation." After all, direct democracy had been "practised in
the free states of antiquity; and was the cause of innumerable evils." "To
avoid these evils," he asserted, "the moderns have invented the doctrine
of *representation*, which seems to be the perfection of human government."
The Romans' ignorance of that doctrine "exposed their government to frequent convulsions, and to capricious measures," and much the same could
be said for the Greeks—for "pure democracy" is utterly "inconsistent with

the peace of society, and the rights of freemen."[52] James Wilson made much the same point in the celebrated speech which he delivered at the opening of the Pennsylvania Ratifying Convention.[53]

Like Webster and Wilson, the authors of *The Federalist* shared Montesquieu's opinion concerning the defects of classical republicanism. Alexander Hamilton prefaced his eulogy for the new "science of politics" by restating the case made by Hobbes and the other defenders of enlightened despotism. "It is impossible to read the history of the petty Republics of Greece and Italy," he noted, "without feeling sensations of horror and disgust at the distractions with which they were continually agitated, and at the rapid succession of revolutions, by which they were kept in a state of perpetual vibration, between the extremes of tyranny and anarchy." The ancient republics he described as "little jealous, clashing, tumultuous commonwealths, the wretched nurseries of unceasing discord and the miserable objects of universal pity or contempt." They had given political freedom a bad name: "From the disorders that disfigure the annals of those republics, the advocates of despotism have drawn arguments, not only against the forms of republican government, but against the very principles of civil liberty. They have decried all free government, as inconsistent with the order of society."[54]

Of course, Hamilton was no more ready to accept Hobbes's conclusions than Montesquieu had been. To refute the "gloomy sophisms" of the English philosopher concerning "free government," he could point to states, such as England and perhaps the Netherlands as well, where "stupendous fabrics reared on the basis of liberty . . . have flourished for ages." He had hopes also for the purely republican governments recently established in the New World. For, though the author of *The Spirit of the Laws* had reserved his greatest admiration for the English constitution, he had also drawn attention to the principle of federalism as an "expedient" not only "for extending the sphere of popular government" but also for "reconciling the advantages of monarchy with those of republicanism." But if Hamilton was hopeful, he was not entirely sanguine concerning the prospects of purely republican government. In 1777, he had been willing to suppose that what he was the first to call "a representative democracy" would be more workable than direct democracy on the classical model. "When the deliberative or judicial powers are vested wholly or partly in the collective body of the people," he admitted, "you must expect error, confusion and instability. But . . . where the right of election is well secured and regulated & the exercise of the legislative, executive and judiciary authorities, is vested in select persons, chosen *really* and not *nominally* by the people," the government is quite "likely to be happy, regular and durable." In the intervening decade, however, experience had robbed him of his confidence. If it proved "impracticable" to devise "models of a more perfect structure" than those hitherto employed in America, he warned in 1787, "the enlightened friends to liberty" would be "obliged to abandon the cause of that species of government as indefensible."[55]

Madison was no less unhappy than Hamilton with all forms of direct rule and no less attached to what he called "the great principle of representation." Direct democracies, he told his readers, provide an arena for sycophants and demagogues: they "have ever been spectacles of turbulence and contention; have ever been found incompatible with personal security, or the rights of property." In rejecting Aristotle's antidote to the diseases incident to self-government, he charged that direct aristocratic rule was similarly flawed. As he put it, "in all very numerous assemblies, of whatever characters composed, passion never fails to wrest the sceptre from reason. Had every Athenian citizen been a Socrates; every Athenian assembly would still have been a mob."[56]

The authors of *The Federalist* believed that, if republican government was on the verge of collapse in the various states, it was largely because the state constitutions were too faithful to the classical models. They had discovered that modern representative government can reconcile the advantages of monarchy with those of republicanism and effectively promote the subordination of passion to reason only in federal republics situated on an extended territory.[57]

III.i.4

Madison hoped that, in a superintending role, the new national government would perform the function reserved for the monarch in the English regime and serve as a "disinterested and dispassionate umpire in disputes" between the factions that would inevitably arise.[58] To this, he and his colleagues thought the new nation's ablest citizens could make a special contribution. Along with David Hume,[59] Madison was prepared to believe that the substitution of representative government for direct democracy might enable a republic "to refine and enlarge the public views, by passing them through the medium of a chosen body of citizens, whose wisdom may best discern the true interest of their country, and whose patriotism and love of justice, will be least likely to sacrifice it to temporary or partial considerations." But, at the same time, he conceded that the effect might be the reverse. He was sensitive to the increasingly populist tenor of American politics, and he was aware that "men of factious tempers, of local prejudices, or of sinister designs, may by intrigue, by corruption or by other means, first obtain the suffrages, and then betray the interests of the people." Madison was convinced that the magnitude of the constituencies to be established in the American republic would make it "more difficult for unworthy candidates to practice with success the vicious arts, by which elections are too often carried," and he hoped that this would encourage the election of "men who possess the most attractive merit, and the most diffusive and established characters." But he did not deem this inevitable. Prudence and virtue are great advantages. They are evidently required for the foundation of a just regime; and Madison would no doubt have been willing to concede that wise and public-spirited statesmanship would be needed from time to time for the perpetuation of such a regime—but, in his estimation, it would be folly to depend too much on its permanent presence. In a world marked by tension between the rich and the poor, the obstacles are simply too great. Practical wisdom is rare and virtue exceedingly fragile: "It is in vain to say, that enlightened statesmen will be able to adjust these clashing interests, and render them all subservient to the public good. Enlightened statesmen will not always be at the helm: Nor, in many cases, can such an adjustment be made at all, without taking into view indirect and remote considerations, which will rarely prevail over the immediate interest which one party may find in disregarding the rights of another, or the good of the whole." The founders of the American regime would have to settle for something more modest than that to which the ancients had aspired. By lowering their sights, they hoped to discover firmer ground on which to erect the edifice of republican liberty.[60]

Montesquieu and Hume showed the framers of the American Constitution where to look.[61] They acknowledged the greater nobility of public-spiritedness but suggested that baser motives would provide a more solid foundation. "Every man who possesses power," Montesquieu explained, "is driven to abuse it; he goes forward until he discovers the limits."[62] On this subject, Hume was characteristically blunt. In a passage echoing Machiavelli and much admired by Alexander Hamilton, John Adams, and like-minded Americans, he acknowledged that it might appear "somewhat strange, that a maxim should be true in *politics*, which is false in *fact*." But he asserted, nonetheless, that it was "a just *political* maxim, *that every man must be supposed a knave*."[63] This conviction, shared by nearly all of the political theorists of the early modern age, was the foundation for Madison's discussion as well.[64] "If men were angels," he observed, "no government would be necessary. If angels were to govern men, neither external nor internal controuls on government would be necessary. In framing a government which is to be administered by men over men, the great difficulty lies in this: You must first enable the government to controul the governed; and in the next place, oblige

it to controul itself." That statement—so elegant in its simplicity—summed
up the political problem with admirable brevity.[65]

Montesquieu employed Hume's principle to differentiate political regimes.
He had read Hobbes's assertion that "no great Popular Common-wealth was
ever kept up; but either by a forraign Enemy that united them; or by the reputation of some one eminent Man amongst them; or by the secret Counsell of
a few; or by the mutuall feare of equall factions; and not by the open Con-
sultations of the Assembly," and he was among the first to grasp the political
possibilities opened up by the deliberate employment of "the mutuall feare
of equall factions."[66] Thus, in *The Spirit of the Laws*, the French philosophe
distinguished two types of republicanism—the sort represented by ancient
Athens, Sparta, and Rome; and the kind exemplified by eighteenth-century
Great Britain. The classical city was a republic of virtue: it could not long
survive *on* an extended territory because the dispersion of its citizens undermined the force of the moral and religious motives which sustained the
public-spiritedness it required. In contrast, Great Britain is a "republic which
disguises itself (*se cache*) under the form of a monarchy"; it is a "democracy
founded on commerce": such a regime cannot survive *without* an extended
territory because, in the absence of genuine civic virtue, its stability depends
on a balancing of factions of the sort possible only in a complex society.[67] In
the course of this discussion, Montesquieu only intimated his preference—
but not so discreetly that Madison mistook his intention. "The British Constitution was to Montesquieu," he observed, "what Homer has been to the
didactic writers on epic poetry."[68]

Hume used much the same scheme of classification as Montesquieu and
shared his preference as well. "The chief support of the BRITISH government is the opposition of interests," he wrote, "but that, though in the main
serviceable, breeds endless factions." Hume even agreed with the philosophe
that the paramount task of statesmanship is to arrange matters so that this
breeding of factions "does all of the good without any of the harm." He
broke with his French correspondent on only one fundamental issue: with
the proper institutions, he thought it possible to do without the monarchical disguise; he believed that, even in a large sphere, one might establish a
pure republic—lacking king and aristocracy alike. In a seminal essay read by
James Madison, Hume asserted

> the falsehood of the common opinion, that no large state, such as FRANCE
> or GREAT BRITAIN, could ever be modelled into a commonwealth, but
> that such a form of government can only take place in a city or small
> territory. The contrary seems probable. Though it is more difficult to

form a republican government in an extensive country than in a city; there is more facility, when once it is formed, of preserving it steady and uniform without tumult and faction. . . . The parts are so distant and remote, that it is very difficult, either by intrigue, prejudice, or passion, to hurry them into any measures against the public interest.

Here, paradoxically, in the ruminations of an author persuaded that "societies of men . . . are forever destined to depend, for their political constitutions, on accident and force," lay the inspiration for the course of "reflection" on Madison's part that explains his and his fellow framers' "choice."[69]

As the framers of the American Constitution conceived it, the modern alternative to ancient republicanism involves neither the direct, systematic promotion of genuine civic virtue nor the outright suppression of factions but, rather, an indirect assault on "the mischiefs of faction." The establishment of representative institutions makes possible what Hamilton had called "the ENLARGEMENT of the ORBIT" of the republic "either in respect to the dimensions of a single State, or to the consolidation of several smaller States into one great confederacy." The most controversial element in the new constitution turns out to be its mainstay. "Extend the sphere," Madison argues, "and you take in a greater variety of parties and interests; you make it less probable that a majority of the whole will have a common motive to invade the rights of other citizens; or if such a common motive exists, it will be more difficult for all who feel it to discover their own strength, and to act in unison with each other."[70]

Convinced that it is impossible to uproot the selfishness that is the source of faction, and fearful that a concerted attempt to do so would give occasion to tyranny, Madison proposes using selfishness to check selfishness itself. As he would put it some months later,

The society itself will be broken into so many parts, interests and classes of citizens, that the rights of individuals or of the minority, will be in little danger from interested combinations of the majority. In a free government, the security for civil rights must be the same as for religious rights. It consists in the one case in the multiplicity of interests, and in the other, in the multiplicity of sects. The degree of security in both cases will depend on the number of interests and sects; and this may be presumed to depend on the extent of country and number of people comprehended under the same government.

Madison's solution is not so much an extension of the territory encompassed by the republic as a multiplication of the factions composing it. If the new federal government could be made a dispassionate and impartial umpire, it was paradoxically because of the great number and variety of petty parties and factions clamoring for its favor and maneuvering to gain political leverage.[71]

III.i.5

The precise character of Madison's reasoning concerning the problem of faction may not be evident at first reading. Indeed, this eminently practical politician's rhetorical strategy and his desire to refute the particular objections raised by the opponents of the new constitution caused him to compress much of his argument and to give an emphasis to the strictly geographical dimension of his discussion that could easily mislead the unwary.

That is one difficulty, but there is another—the second even more troubling than the first. Here, Jefferson is an invaluable guide. In praising Madison's contributions to *The Federalist*, he noted that "in some parts it is discoverable that the author means only to say what may best be said in defence of opinions in which he did not concur."[72] Madison's lack of complete frankness is a serious obstacle to understanding, for a man who finds it necessary to say what he does not believe may also discover that prudence dictates his silence or near-silence on matters of great import and even greater delicacy. To begin to comprehend fully Madison's intention, we must turn to one such subject and ponder the danger posed to the modern republic by religious enthusiasm.

In fact, Madison does touch on the problem of sectarian strife in *The Federalist*, but only in passing. He openly acknowledges that "the most frivolous and fanciful distinctions" can generate faction, and he specifically mentions that "a zeal for different opinions concerning religion" has at times "divided mankind into parties, inflamed them with mutual animosity, and rendered them much more disposed to vex and oppress each other, than to co-operate for their common good."[73] This much he says, but he lays little stress on the point and quickly moves on. One might be tempted to suppose that for Madison the religious issue was of minor concern.

That would be an error. On the floor of the Constitutional Convention, where the delegates conducted their discussions in private, the Virginian could afford to be a bit more frank than in a newspaper series specifically designed to promote the Constitution's ratification in a state dominated by its opponents. When contemplating the role played by "conscience" in restraining men from injustice, he observed that it "is known to be inadequate in individuals" and that "in large numbers little is to be expected from it." "Besides," he added, "Religion itself may become a motive to persecution &

oppression."[74] This remark, though telling, might still lead one to underestimate the depths of Madison's concern. Fortunately for us, he could afford
to be perfectly blunt in a letter to his close friend and longtime political ally
Thomas Jefferson. In that missive, Madison rehearsed once again the arguments he had made in the convention, emphasizing the weakness of religious
conscience as a restraint. "Enthusiasm" might sometimes give to conscience
greater strength, he noted, but this was "only a temporary state of Religion."
And in any case, he concluded, such enthusiasm "will hardly be seen with
pleasure at the helm. Even in its coolest state, it has been much oftener a
motive to oppression than a restraint from it."[75]

Regarding a matter this delicate, prudence generally dictated reticence in
public, but not always. Just two years before the federal convention, under
circumstances demanding candor, Madison had found occasion to confront
the problem posed by religious enthusiasm without much need for indirection. At that time, he had penned a petition advocating the disestablishment
of the Episcopalian church and an end to religious establishments altogether.
While keeping his authorship of the petition a secret, he had then arranged to
have it circulated throughout his native Virginia. That petition spoke boldly
of the "torrents of blood" that had been "spilt in the old world, by the vain
attempts of the secular arm, to extinguish religious discords, by proscrib-
ing all difference in religious opinion."[76] Without question, Madison was as
fully aware and as deeply concerned as the best-informed of his contemporaries regarding the wars of religion that had convulsed both England and
the continent less than a century before. And yet, by the time of the federal
convention (if not well before), the chief architect of the American Constitution had reached the conclusion that there was little ground for worry and
that the United States would be relatively free from the travails of sectarian strife. In this subject, John Locke, Voltaire, Montesquieu, David Hume,
Adam Smith, and the citizens of Virginia had been among his instructors.[77]

Like many of his contemporaries, Madison was well aware that America
was destined to be a commercial republic. Such a regime, if Voltaire and
Montesquieu are to be trusted, has comparatively little to fear from religious
zeal. In the view of the former, "the *Royal-Exchange* in *London*" was "a place
more venerable than many courts of justice"; it was the place "where the
representatives of all nations meet for the benefit of mankind."

There the Jew, the Mahometan, and the Christian transact together as
tho' they all profess'd the same religion, and give the name of Infidel to
none but bankrupts. There the Presbyterian confides in the Anabaptist,
and the Churchman depends on the Quaker's word. At the breaking

up of this pacific and free assembly, some withdraw to the synagogue and others to take a glass. This man goes and is baptiz'd in a great tub, and in the name of the Father, Son, and Holy Ghost: That man has his son's foreskin cut off, whilst a sett of *Hebrew* words (quite unintelligible to him) are mumbled over his child. Others retire to their churchs, and there wait for the inspiration of heaven with their hats on, and all are satisfied.[78]

Montesquieu makes much the same point when he writes that the best way "to attack a religion is by favor, by the commodities of life, by the hope of wealth; not by what turns away, but by what makes one forget; not by what arouses indignation, but by what renders men lukewarm—so that other passions act on our souls, and those which religion inspires are silent."[79] The *philosophe* could be confident that an indirect assault of this type would eventually succeed because something of the sort had gradually taken place in the "democracy founded on commerce" that was located just across the channel from France.

In canvassing the same development, as we have already seen, Hume placed particular emphasis on political institutions. He pointed out that "parties from *principle*, especially abstract speculative principle, are known only to modern times," and he traced that "extraordinary and unaccountable *phenomenon*" to the peculiar character of the Christian faith: to the independent authority which it vested in the clergy and to the systematic theology— born of the awkward marriage of revelation with philosophy—that distinguished it from all other religions.[80] Throughout much of Europe, factions of this sort might still pose the gravest of difficulties. But fortunately, in England, the force of sectarian zeal had gradually abated. In that happy island, Hume was pleased to report, time had all but eliminated what he called the "ecclesiastical parties." As he put it, "Liberty of thinking, and of expressing our thoughts, is always fatal to priestly power, and to those pious frauds, on which it is always founded."[81] As a consequence, "the progress of learning and liberty" in the first half-century following the Glorious Revolution had brought "a sudden and sensible change in the opinions of men." Most British subjects had "divested themselves of all superstitious reverence to names and authority." The clergy were in disrepute, and "the mere name of *king* commands little respect." At the "least shock or convulsion," Hume believed, "the royal power, being no longer supported by the settled principles and opinions of men, will immediately dissolve." Indeed, "had men been in the same disposition at the *revolution*, as they are at present, monarchy would have run a great risque of being entirely lost in this island."[82]

At the time when the Revolution took place in America, the citizens of the thirteen colonies were in the very disposition which Hume had mentioned, and that fact (as much as any other) helped account for their adoption of republican government—and for Madison's sanguine outlook regarding religious convulsions as well. Just three weeks before the Continental Congress approved Thomas Jefferson's Declaration of Independence, James Madison (already an intellectual force at the tender age of twenty-five) had succeeded in persuading the Virginia convention to add to its bill of rights a clause acknowledging that "all men are equally entitled to the free exercise of religion, according to the dictates of conscience."[83] With regard to sectarian conflict, he had reason to be hopeful.

Madison even had grounds for optimism of a sort that Hume might well have disputed. In his magisterial *History of England*, the Scottish philosopher had argued that "the interested diligence of the clergy" was a condition which "every wise legislator will study to prevent." Where the civil magistrate was absolutely neutral in sectarian matters, the competition of the preachers would inevitably infuse into religion "a strong mixture of superstition, folly, and delusion. Each ghostly practitioner, in order to render himself more precious and sacred in the eyes of his retainers, will inspire them with the most violent abhorrence of all other sects, and continually endeavor, by some novelty to excite the languid devotion of his audience. No regard will be paid to truth, morals, or decency, in the doctrines inculcated. Every tenet will be adopted that best suits the disorderly affections of the human frame." Only where there was an official religious establishment would the zeal of the clergy be greatly reduced. "The most decent and advantageous composition" which the authorities can make "with the spiritual guides is to bribe their indolence, by assigning stated salaries to their profession."[84]

Madison disagreed. As a recent Princeton graduate, still very much under the influence of the pious Dr. Witherspoon, he had distrusted "encourage[r]s of free enquiry." In a letter to a close friend, he had called them destroyers of "the most essential Truths" and "Enemies to serious religion." Yet, even then, Madison had openly wondered whether the support of civil society required "an Ecclesiastical Establishment" or whether this might not in fact be "hurtful to a dependant State." Within a matter of weeks, he wrote back to that same friend to suggest that if his own sect "the Church of England had been the established and general Religion in all the Northern Colonies . . . , slavery and Subjection might and would have been gradually insinuated among us. Union of Religious Sentiments begets a surprising confidence and Ecclesiastical Establishments tend to great ignorance and Corruption[—]all of which facilitate the Execution of mischievous Projects."[85] This conviction, firmly held and vigorously defended, explains why Madison expended great effort at the Virginia convention in a futile attempt to write disestablishment into that fledgling state's declaration of rights.[86] A decade later, he would finally succeed, by steering Jefferson's Bill for Establishing Religious Freedom through the Virginia legislature;[87] and in 1788, he was prepared to argue that the very presence of a great "multiplicity of sects" was "the best and only security for religious liberty in any society."[88] This argument Madison owed to Hume's close friend and disciple Adam Smith.[89]

In *A Letter Concerning Toleration*, John Locke had made the wry observation that, where religious sects "have not the power to carry on persecution and to become masters, there they desire to live upon fair terms, and preach up toleration." Indeed, he added, "when they are not strengthened with the civil power, they can bear most patiently and unmovedly the contagion of idolatry, superstition, and heresy in their neighborhood; of which in other occasions the interest of religion makes them to be extremely apprehensive."[90] Smith drew the obvious conclusion. In *The Wealth of Nations*, he quoted Hume's discussion of the problem at length. He readily confessed that "the interested and active zeal of religious teachers can be dangerous and troublesome," but he argued that this condition would obtain "only where there is, either but one sect tolerated in the society, or where the whole of a large society is divided into two or three great sects."

> That zeal must be altogether innocent where the society is divided into two or three hundred, or perhaps into as many [as a] thousand sects, of which no one could be considerable enough to disturb the publick tranquillity. The teachers of each sect, seeing themselves surrounded on all sides with more adversaries than friends, would be obliged to learn that candour and moderation which is so seldom to be found among the teachers of those great sects, whose tenets being supported by the civil magistrate, are held in veneration by almost all the inhabitants of extensive kingdoms and empires, and who therefore see nothing round them but followers, disciples, and humble admirers. The teachers of each little sect, finding themselves almost alone, would be obliged to respect those of almost every other sect, and the concessions which they would mutually find it both convenient and agreeable to make to one another, might in time probably reduce the doctrine of the greater part of them to that pure and rational religion, free from every mixture of absurdity, imposture, or fanaticism, such as wise men have in all ages of the world wished to see established.

To support his argument, Smith pointed to Pennsylvania, where the establishment of full religious freedom had been "productive of this philosophical good temper and moderation."[91]

If Smith's argument came to have a considerable effect on the young American statesman, it was largely because it accorded with his experience. What Edmund Randolph would later write of Thomas Jefferson could have been said of James Madison with equal justice: "His opinions against restraints on conscience ingratiated him with the enemies of the establishment, who did not stop to inquire how far those opinions might border on skepticism or infidelity."[92] Of this fact, Madison was acutely, even painfully, aware. He knew that he owed his success in promoting religious freedom within Virginia less to the force of the Lockean arguments he presented in his celebrated "Memorial and Remonstrance against Religious Assessments" than to the large number of Baptists and Presbyterians resident within the state.[93] According to his neighbor and biographer William Cabell Rives, the great statesman was accustomed in his later years to quoting often and "with great approbation" Voltaire's claim that "if one religion only were allowed in England, the government would possibly be arbitrary; if there were but two, the people would cut each other's throats; but, as there are a multitude, they all live happy and in peace."[94]

In 1787, prudence dictated that the Virginian be more reticent than Hume, Smith, and Voltaire. By that time, Madison had already himself become an encourager "of free inquiry" and an enemy to what the majority of his contemporaries would have considered "serious religion." Political action required discretion. The divines influential in the various states would not have looked kindly on the proposed constitution had they recognized that it embodied a strategy for reducing the various sects to a "pure and rational religion" of the sort favored by "wise men"—even in wholly pagan times. His reticence notwithstanding, Madison's purpose and that evidenced by Hume, Smith, and Voltaire were one and the same. As he conceded some three decades later in a letter to a prominent American Jew, the Virginian had not only long been inclined to consider "the freedom of religious opinions & worship as equally belonging to every sect." He had "ever regarded . . . the secure enjoyment of" that freedom "as the best human provision for bringing all either into the same way of thinking, or into that mutual charity which is the only substitute."[95] For Madison and for Jefferson, freedom of conscience was as much a matter of policy as a matter of principle. Like the author of the Declaration of Independence, the father of the American Constitution was a Deist who looked for moral and political guidance, not to the Holy

Scriptures, but to the "law of nature and of nature's God."[96] If his stratagem was successful, his fellow citizens would someday be unable to distinguish the God of Abraham, Isaac, and Jacob from the God of the philosophers; and when that day came, the danger posed by parties of principle would disappear altogether.[97]

Madison could take it for granted that religious factions were entirely artificial because in antiquity there had been no parties of abstract, speculative principle apart from the completely powerless philosophical sects. Had it not been for the peculiar character of Christianity, circumstances in modern times would have been much the same. And even then, where good fortune and good policy combined to disarm superstition, civil strife was most likely to arise in a fashion perfectly familiar to the ancients.

In Madison's view, factions should normally spring into existence because men (and the rich and the poor in particular) have conflicting material interests. It was with this in mind that he developed the most controversial and original aspect of his argument for the extended republic. Alexander Hamilton had remarked on the scope given to "commercial enterprise" in America by "the diversity in the productions of different States."[98] Madison's sanguine experience with religious diversity in Virginia enabled him to see that the economic diversity noted by Hamilton could be politically advantageous as well.[99] In Europe, where aristocratic hauteur added insult to the injuries of class, it might be impossible to obviate the tension between the rich and the poor. But, in a large and prosperous society unencumbered with the tradition of juridically defined orders, the *various* distribution of property would greatly outweigh in importance its *unequal* distribution. In the New World, if perhaps not in the Old, it would be possible to substitute the healthy competition of divers parochial interests for the internecine strife that had so plagued the republics of antiquity.[100]

In short, once artificial factions had been disposed of, the real import of geographical extension was economic diversity, and this is the goal that was Madison's primary concern. His argument is essentially an economic argument and only tangentially a geographical argument. Because of the dissimilarity in climate and in terrain, because of the disparity in soil quality and in natural resources, and because of the discrepancy in the conditions of security, in the ease of communication, and in the means of transport available, the myriad of distinct localities composing the nascent republic were suited for different modes of subsistence: for the growing of different crops, for the procurement and export of different raw materials, and for the manufacture of different finished goods. This geographically dictated division of labor would pit town against country, seaport against hinterland, and frontier region against settled district; it would set mountain against plain, swamp against forest, and thin soil against rich.[101]

Distressed by the dreary record of the state legislatures and persuaded that the Articles of Confederation were unworkable, Madison and his colleagues longed for a more perfect union. If they thought it possible to improve on the ancients and to avoid class struggle altogether, it was because they believed that the economic diversity characteristic of an extended republic and the social fragmentation that went with that diversity would undercut the fundamental antagonism between the rich and the poor by generating a host of petty and easily reconcilable antagonisms. The Framers did not establish a corporate state, but they did devise institutions intended to have something of the same effect: as they well knew, the representatives elected from the various territorial districts would inevitably take to heart, at least in some measure, the parochial interests and affections of their constituents.[102]

III.i.6

To supplement and fully exploit the advantages which accrued from geographical extension, Madison applied the principle of the multiplication of factions to the framework of government itself. The Anti-Federalists had expressed fear that the new constitution would give rise to the misrule of irresponsible magistrates. Because of the new nation's magnitude, the citizens would be unable to govern in person, and this would require conceding great and dangerous power to distant officials. Madison shared this concern. In a letter written to Thomas Jefferson shortly after the Constitutional Convention, he noted that, "in too extensive" and fragmented a society, "a defensive concert may be rendered too difficult against the oppression of those entrusted with the administration."[103] He nonetheless urged his fellow citizens to ratify the proposed constitution.

If, in his public pronouncements, Madison was less than fully candid about the perils that he thought the growing republic someday might face, it was because he was far more deeply distressed by the immediate danger. Indeed, he was willing to go much further than his fellow delegates in strengthening the central administration. From the outset, he urged that the federal government be given a veto over all state legislation, and when he lost out on the issue, he wrote to Jefferson of his apprehension that "the *plan should* it *be adopted* will neither effectually *answer* its *national object* nor prevent the local *mischiefs* which every where *excite disgusts* against the *state governments*." Six weeks later, when the convention had completed its work, he wrote again to reiterate his fears. In his view, the judicial review of state legislation by federal courts was an inadequate substitute for the federal veto. "Without such a check in the whole over the parts," he contended, "our system involves the evil of imperia in imperio." He acknowledged that, under the proposed constitution, the United States would be more than "a Confederacy of independent States." It presented "the aspect rather of a feudal system of republics." As a partial consolidation, this reform was welcome but insufficient. In the fall of 1787, Madison still supposed excessive centralization to be the least of the dangers faced by the infant republic.[104]

Madison had his reasons for holding this position. Although he privately voiced his concern that the republic not be extended too far, he did not believe that the power conceded to the elected representatives of the people would pose a great threat in the near future. "By a judicious modification and mixture of the *federal principle*," he argued, it would prove possible to carry the "practicable sphere" of self-government "to a very great extent."[105] Moreover, in the individual states, American statesmen had gained invaluable experience in the framing of constitutions.[106] Though these states were riven by feuds, they had already shown how the worst might be avoided, and they, it must be remembered, were denied the full advantage of geographical extension and were unable to profit from the vital addition of the federal principle. To Europe, Madison acknowledged, America owed "the great principle of representation," but his compatriots in the states could themselves "claim the merit of making the discovery the basis of unmixed and extensive republics. . . . They accomplished a revolution which has no parallel in the annals of human society. They reared fabrics of government which have no model on the face of the globe." The American contribution was the deliberate and systematic employment within a wholly popular government of "auxiliary precautions" akin to those which the British had devised piecemeal over a great span of years to restrain the men who ruled over them.

The principle underlying these precautions was simple, and, by now, it should seem familiar: just as interest could be used to check interest, so "ambition must be made to counteract ambition." As we have already had occasion to note, James Harrington had made this principle the foundation of his new science of political architecture; Locke had employed it when he explained the manner in which a separation of powers between an elected body, which devised the laws, and an independent, hereditary executive, capable of enforcing those same laws against their makers themselves, would encourage the latter to exercise prudence and to adhere to justice in performing their legislative function; and Bolingbroke and the radical Whigs had used it in arguing the case for constitutional balance. In the years subsequent to the implementation of Robert Harley's Act of Settlement, David Hume had in the same spirit suggested that "the particular checks and controuls" provided in a republican constitution could make it "the interest, even of bad men, to act for the public good," while Montesquieu had illuminated the manner in which a division of privileges and responsibilities between an hereditary monarch, an aristocratic assembly, a congress elected by the people, an independent judiciary, and local juries made up of the defendant's peers contributed to fostering among the English a salutary sense of security and tranquillity. Such was the vision that informed William Blackstone's *Commentaries on the Laws of England* and Jean Louis de Lolme's *Constitution de l'Angleterre*. "The true excellence of the English government," Blackstone told his readers, "consists" in the fact "that all the parts of it form a mutual check upon each other" so that "they jointly impel the machine of government in a direction different from what either, acting by themselves, would have done; but at the same time in a direction partaking of each, and formed out of all; a direction which constitutes the true line of the liberty and happiness of the community." Having profited from the partial success and the more evident failures of their predecessors in the states, the framers of the American Constitution sought to improve on the governmental machinery described by Harrington, Locke, the radical Whigs, Bolingbroke, Hume, Montesquieu, Blackstone, and Lolme and to institute an impartial regime of indirect rule without the benefit of the social underpinnings provided by an hierarchy of juridically defined orders.[107]

Madison and his colleagues tried to do this "by so contriving the interior structure of the government . . . that its constituent parts may, by their mutual relations, be the means of keeping each other in their proper places." As a check against usurpation, they divided the power of amending the Constitution and allocated the responsibilities of government between the states and the Union; to curb the dangers of centralizing administration, they arranged that the president and the senators be chosen in a manner that would ensure their responsiveness to the diversity of state and local concerns; to safeguard constitutionalism and the rule of law, they established an independent, federal judiciary and conferred on it the power of judicial review; and to prevent the national government from falling into the hands of a single faction, they instituted a separation of powers and a system of checks and balances. The result was, "in strictness, neither a national nor a federal Constitution, but a composition of both."[108]

The least federal of the elements that made up Madison's "judicious modification and mixture" was by far the most important. Though influenced by Montesquieu, those states with constitutions calling for a separation of powers had not fared particularly well. In state after state, the legislature,

usually by the legitimate exercise of its constitutional prerogatives, had managed to overawe and dominate both the executive and the judiciary. Montesquieu had denied that the resulting concentration of power was compatible
with liberty, and James Madison and Alexander Hamilton both agreed.[109]
As Thomas Jefferson had argued, the consequence was "an *elective despotism*." The absence of an effective barrier between the various branches left
"the judiciary and the executive members . . . dependent on the legislative for their subsistence in office—and some of them for their continuance
in it." As a result, where the legislature encroached on the executive and
judicial functions, "no opposition" was "likely to be made; nor, if made,"
could "it be effectual." If the regime was to "be founded on free principles,"
Jefferson argued, the Constitution would have to ensure that "the powers
of government" were "so divided and balanced among several bodies of
magistracy . . . that no one could transcend their legal limits, without being
effectually checked and restrained by the others."[110] The Framers took this
warning to heart.[111] That is why they supplemented the separation of powers
with an extraordinarily complex system of balances and checks.

Here, as elsewhere, Madison and his colleagues practiced indirection and
followed "a policy of supplying by opposite and rival interests, the defect of
better motives." As he put it, "The interest of the man must be connected
with the constitutional rights of the place. . . . The constant aim is to divide
and arrange the several offices in such a manner as that each may be a check
on the other; that the private interest of every individual, may be a sentinel
over the public rights." To this end, those serving in each of the various
branches of the government were to be given "the necessary constitutional
means, and personal motives, to resist the encroachments of the others."[112]
Hamilton noted that "the dissimilar modes of constituting the several com-
ponent parts of the government" would be such that "there would be little
probability of a common interest to cement these different branches in a
predilection for any particular class of electors."[113] Madison added that the
elected official's "pride and vanity" would "attach him to a form of government which favors his pretensions and gives him a share in its honors and
distinctions." Because he and his colleagues represented "the dignity of their
country in the eyes of other nations," they would "be particularly sensible to
every prospect of public danger, or of a dishonorable stagnation in public affairs." The congressmen, the senators, the president, and the federal judges
would not always be men of virtue, but the exalted character of their separate
and distinct stations would have on them the effect which Montesquieu had
attributed to the articulation of a monarchy into its various, graded orders
and ranks: it would inspire in them a passion for what he resolutely refused

to dignify as more than "false honor," and this artificially induced longing would tend to summon forth from these officials something in its effects indistinguishable from public-spiritedness. In most cases, their sense of their own stature would be a spur adequate to insure the proper performance of their duties, and it would nearly always be a sufficient deterrent to the sacrifice of their rightful prerogatives to the ambitions and material interests of their rivals. Within each branch of government a collegial spirit would develop: each branch could be trusted to exercise a jealous oversight with regard to the others.[114]

As should be evident, the American separation of powers is two-dimensional: for it seems to deny what it asserts, and it seeks to vindicate man's capacity for self-government by teaching him to acknowledge the limits of that capacity and to conduct his affairs accordingly. On the one hand, it is egalitarian and distinctively modern: for it presupposes grave doubts as to man's ability to ascend from a passion for private advantage to a dedication to justice and the transcendent good, and it therefore embodies the spirit of jealous distrust propagated by Locke, Sidney, the radical Whigs, and Bolingbroke; it mimics the constitutional machinery variously depicted by Harrington, Locke, Bolingbroke, Hume, Montesquieu, Blackstone, and Lolme; and it considerably restricts the scope of American statesmanship thereby. On the other hand, it is self-consciously aristocratic and classical in character: for it presupposes a capacity for *lógos* on the part of some men, and it deliberately opens up for these few a public space comparable to what the ancient Greeks had called the middle ground; it provides them with a field for the exercise of virtue; and it harnesses the pride of the country's most ambitious men in service to the public good. It even seeks by an indirect process, similar in its purpose to the civic *paideía* of the classical republics, to transform that pride and that ambition into something considerably more exalted; and to the extent that it succeeds in eliciting a simulacrum of virtue from the nation's highest officials, it educates the general public in the most effectual way: by the shining examples it holds up for emulation.[115]

The new American republic was not what the ancients would have called a democracy. Nor can it be accurately described as an aristocracy, an oligarchy, or even a limited monarchy. It certainly was not a republic of virtue. And yet its framers doubted whether it could survive if its citizens were utterly bereft of that quality. The American republic was, as James Madison would later insist, "a system without a precedent ancient or modern."[116] It claimed to be unmixed. In a sense, it was.[117] And yet, in its own, strange, convoluted way, it bore a certain, undeniable resemblance to what the ancients chose to refer to as a mixed regime.[118] It occupied an intermediate status between the

enlightened despotism of Thomas Hobbes and the classical republicanism of
the ancient Greeks, and in assessing the degree to which man could justly be
termed a political animal, its advocates tried to strike an appropriate balance.

James Madison and his colleagues paid careful attention to the weakness of
human reason and to its propensity to fall under passion's sway.[119] But, just
as they rejected enlightened despotism and a slavish dependence on political
architecture and on man's unreasoning spirit of resistance, so they stopped
well short of endorsing the presumption, fundamental to the proponents of
these mechanical principles, that reason is simply the slave of the passions.[120]
They considered government "a reflection on human nature," and, as we
have already remarked, they were acutely sensitive to the fact that men are
not angelic. The defects in human nature that render government necessary
render it rightly suspect as well. Here, again, Madison's observation is apt:
"In framing a government which is to be administered by men over men, the
great difficulty lies in this: You must first enable the government to controul
the governed; and in the next place, oblige it to controul itself." Madison and
his colleagues sought to solve this quandary by restoring, within a carefully
defined and limited sphere, the autonomy of moral and political reason. By
means of the extended sphere, federalism, the separation of powers, and
the other "inventions of prudence" built into the constitutional frame, they
hoped that "the passions" of the citizens could "be controuled and regulated
by the government" so that "the reason of the public," liberated from bondage, might serve "to controul and regulate the government" in turn.[121] In
this regard, their description of the American regime bears a certain resemblance to Polybius's depiction of Rome, for the American Constitution de-
ploys institutional checks not only as a substitute but also as a reinforcement
and inspiration for a virtue of sorts.[122]

In their judgment of the human capacity for transcendence, the authors of
The Federalist staked out a position intermediate between Hobbes and the ancient republicans. Thus, for example, James Madison readily acknowledged
that "there is a degree of depravity in mankind which requires a certain degree of circumspection and distrust." But he insisted as well that "there are
other qualities in human nature, which justify a certain portion of esteem
and confidence," and he contended that "republican government presupposes the existence of these qualities in a higher degree than any other form."
"Were the pictures," he observed, "which have been drawn by the political jealousy of some among us, faithful likenesses of the human character,
the inference would be that there is not sufficient virtue among men for
self-government; and that nothing less than the chains of despotism can restrain them from destroying and devouring one another." In much the same

spirit, Alexander Hamilton remarked in one passage that "the history of human conduct does not warrant" an "exalted opinion of human virtue" and then added, almost immediately thereafter, that "the supposition of universal venality in human nature is little less an error in political reasoning than the supposition of universal rectitude. The institution of delegated power implies that there is a portion of virtue and honor among mankind, which may be a reasonable foundation of confidence." The New Yorker would certainly not have queried the claim advanced by the Virginian that "the aim of every political Constitution is or ought to be first to obtain for rulers, men who possess most wisdom to discern, and most virtue to pursue the common good of the society; and in the next place, to take the most effectual precautions for keeping them virtuous, whilst they continue to hold their public trust."[123]

The establishment of the American republic was a bold experiment in the reconciliation of wisdom and virtue with popular consent. That regime was to be, first and foremost, a constitutional polity. It made no provision for the direct rule of reason, for its founders knew better than to suppose the United States "a nation of philosophers." Instead, it embodied the next best expedient: the rule of law. And so it was guided less by popular whimsy than by "reverence" and "veneration" for a document which presented itself to the people as an instrument for the implementation of their Declaration of Independence and thereby as a surrogate for the higher law of reason proclaimed therein. As John Quincy Adams put it in a work published some fifty years after the Constitution's ratification, "Its VIRTUES, its republican character, consisted in its conformity to the principles proclaimed in the Declaration of Independence, and as its administration must necessarily be always pliable to the fluctuating varieties of public opinion; its stability and duration by a like overruling and irresistible necessity, was to depend upon the stability and duration in the hearts and minds of the people of that *virtue*, or in other words, of those principles proclaimed in the Declaration of Independence, and embodied in the Constitution of the United States."[124]

To describe the character of that constitution, Abraham Lincoln would later borrow a famous biblical metaphor. The Declaration of Independence is worthy of reverence, he argued, above all else because it embodies "the principle of 'Liberty to all'—the principle that clears the *path* for all—gives *hope* to all—and, by consequence, *enterprize*, and *industry* to all. . . . The assertion of that *principle*, at *that time*, was *the* word, '*fitly spoken*' which has proved an 'apple of gold' to us. The *Union*, and the *Constitution*, are the *picture* of *silver*, subsequently framed around it. The picture was made, not to *conceal*, or *destroy* the apple; but to *adorn*, and *preserve* it. The *picture* was made *for* the apple—*not* the apple for the picture." To be precise, for the purpose of

putting flesh on that "word, '*fitly spoken*,'" the American republic conferred
on a constitution, ultimately derivative from the people but placed for the
most part beyond their reach, a sacred authority limiting their prerogatives,
directing their common activities, and forming their character as citizens.[125]
In this fashion, it reminded them that man's capacity for self-government can
be vindicated only if it can be shown to serve a higher purpose. "Justice is
the end of government," James Madison observed in concluding his defense
of the separation of powers. "It is the end of civil society. It ever has been,
and ever will be pursued, until it be obtained, or until liberty be lost in the
pursuit."[126]

To make sense of American constitutionalism and its central doctrine the
separation of powers, one must initially pay careful attention to the critique
of classical republicanism developed by the founders of modern political science, and one must thoroughly assimilate the first principles of John Locke
and the political architecture of James Harrington and his many heirs. But
then one must pause, turn back, and rethink the political science of ancient
times.[127] One must ponder anew Aristotle's claim that nothing other than the
provision of a common education (*paideía*) can turn a multitude (*plêthos*) into
a unit and constitute it as a *pólis*, and one must reconsider his contention that
the distribution and disposition of a given community's offices and honors
(*táxis tôn archôn*) is the most important determinant of the *paideía* that gives
it its character as a regime (*politeía*). One must think through the implications of Augustine's assertion that "a people is a multitudinous assemblage
of rational beings united by concord regarding loved things held in common"; one must weigh in the balance Goethe's contention that "the soul" of
a great dramatic poet's plays can become "the soul of the people"; and one
must remind oneself of the authority which the Greeks and Romans conferred on what they respectively called the *pátrioi nómoi* and the *mos maiorum*.
For, to the extent that the federal charter was the Declaration's "word" made
flesh, it was to provide that *paideía*, to embody "that concord," to make manifest that "soul," to serve as the nation's ancestral constitution (*pátrios politeía*)
and to exemplify its *mos maiorum*. For Americans, the Constitution was to
become what Madison and his fellow framers intended it to be: an object of
"allegiance or loyalty" fulfilling what John Stuart Mill took to be one of the
conditions of "permanent political society." It was that "*something* which is
settled, something permanent, and not to be called in question; something
which, by general agreement, has a right to be where it is, and to be secure
against disturbance, whatever else may change." As such, it has enabled
Americans "to weather" many "storms, and pass through turbulent times"
unscathed—confident that, "however important the interests about which

men fell out, the conflict did not affect the fundamental principle of the system of social union which happened to exist; nor threaten large portions of the community with the subversion of that on which they had built their calculations and with which their hopes and aims had become identified." [128]

III.i.7

To enable the Constitution to serve this exalted function, the American republic exacted from the individual elected to its highest office an oath or affirmation not just to "faithfully execute the Office of President of the United States" but to act "to the best" of his "Ability" to "preserve, protect and defend" the nation's constitution;[129] and by the agency of that constitution, it gave itself a structure designed to enable all of its magistrates to honor the spirit underlying that oath. Thus, to sustain its constitutional integrity, it sought to prevent "an unqualified complaisance to every sudden breese of passion, or to every transient impulse which the people may receive from the arts of men, who flatter their prejudices to betray their interests"; and to this end, it did what no ancient democracy had ever even contemplated: it provided for "*the total exclusion of the people in their collective capacity* from any share" in the public administration. Moreover, lest the people be led by demagoguery to forcibly seize a share, it deliberately subverted *homónoia* by promoting in the citizenry a diversity in interests, passions, and even opinions—contained only by the "veneration" which they were to reserve for the "word, '*fitly spoken*,'" and its constitutional incarnation.[130]

For similar reasons, the new republic denied unmitigated supremacy to the branch of government most closely associated with the people. To this end, it weakened the force of popular opinion by parceling out political responsibilities between the state and federal governments and by dividing the legislative power of the national government between two distinct representative assemblies—one filled with deputies chosen at frequent intervals by popular election, the other made up of individuals selected for extended terms by the state legislatures. To the same end, it gave a limited legislative veto to an executive chosen by an elected panel of notables, permanently eligible for reelection, and charged with the conduct of foreign policy and the enforcement of the laws. And finally, to obviate the need for a frequent and unsettling return to first principles, it conferred on courts composed of men appointed by the executive in effect for life not just the duty of interpreting the laws but a sacred responsibility hitherto unknown: the right of judicial review.

Within the constitutional frame, each branch of government had a special role to play. The Framers could be confident that, in America, "the citizens understand their rights and are disposed to defend them," and they did not doubt that "the people commonly *intend* the PUBLIC GOOD." But they were aware that the latter claim cannot always be made on behalf of their public servants. In consequence, they looked to a house of representatives, directly elected by the people at frequent intervals and entrusted with the power of the purse, as a safeguard for their rights. The Framers conceded that it would prove impossible to "combine the interests and feelings of every part of the community, and to produce a due sympathy between the representative body and its constituents" of the sort advocated by the partisans of "an actual representation of all classes of the people." But this they regarded as an advantage: for, within limits, there was a case to be made for virtual representation. The electorate was, for the most part, made up of "discerning citizens" aware of their own limitations. "They know from experience, that they sometimes err"; and if given encouragement by the creation of electoral districts of a sufficient size, they will choose from among their "natural" patrons and friends those "land-holders, merchants, and men of the learned professions" who combine "natural abilities" with "acquired endowments" and can be expected to look out for "the different branches of industry" or to serve as "an impartial arbiter between them." These men, "as they will have been distinguished by the preference of their fellow citizens," will generally "be somewhat distinguished also, by those qualities which entitle them to it." But this distinction will not be their primary virtue. They are chiefly to be valued because they are very unlikely to betray their trust: they "will be bound to fidelity and sympathy with the great mass of people" by "chords" of "duty, gratitude, interest, ambition itself." The congressman's electoral "dependence" on the people, of which he has biennial reminders, "and the necessity of being bound himself and his posterity by the laws to which he gives his assent, are the true, and they are the strong chords of sympathy between the representatives and the constituent." [131]

The particular excellence assigned the American congressman was inextricably related to a peculiar vice. His short term of office left him little opportunity to become expert, and the "dependence" which ensured his "fidelity" would all too often prevent him from exercising his better judgment. It was the task of the senator to make good on what he lacked. The men elected to the Senate by the state legislators would presumably be those "most distinguished by their abilities and virtue." They would serve six-year terms, and they would consequently "continue in place a sufficient time to become perfectly acquainted with our national concerns" and to secure "a knowledge of the means" by which "the object of government, which is the happiness of the people," is to "be best attained." Moreover, they would be few in number, and this would make them sensitive to "the want of a due sense of national character." This last point needs emphasis. For, in pondering the manner in which public offices shape the character of their occupants, the authors of *The Federalist* paid careful attention to what they dubbed *responsibility*. In their judgment, anonymity renders large assemblies irresponsible: "The more numerous any assembly may be, of whatever characters composed," wrote Madison, "the greater is known to be the ascendancy of passion over reason." In such a setting, "ignorance will be the dupe of cunning; and passion the slave of sophistry and declamation," as was the case in ancient Athens where "popular liberty" bore "the indelible reproach of decreeing to the same citizens, the hemlock on one day, and statues on the next." In contrast, he insisted, "the smaller the number and the more permanent and conspicuous the station of men in power, the stronger must be the interest which they will individually feel in whatever concerns the government." The requisite sensitivity to questions of "national character" is only to be found in a body composed of "a number so small, that a sensible degree of the praise and blame of public measures may be the portion of each individual; or in an assembly so durably invested with public trust, that the pride and consequence of its members may be sensibly incorporated with the reputation and prosperity of the community." Such was to be the character of the deliberative assembly entrusted with the responsibility for approving treaties and legislation and for passing on presidential appointments.[132]

In discussing the presidency, the authors of *The Federalist* faced a difficulty. With the equivocal exception of the Roman dictatorship, the unitary executive was unknown to the republican tradition, and it was widely believed in America "that a vigorous executive is inconsistent with the genius of republican government." This supposition Alexander Hamilton elected to meet head on:

> The enlightened well wishers to this species of government must at least hope that the supposition is destitute of foundation; since they can never admit its truth, without at the same time admitting the condemnation of their own principles. Energy in the executive is a leading character in the definition of good government. It is essential to the protection of the community against foreign attacks: It is not less essential to the steady administration of the laws, to the protection of property against those irregular and high handed combinations, which sometimes interrupt the ordinary course of justice, to the security of liberty against the enterprises and assaults of ambition, of faction and of anarchy.

As had been intimated by Machiavelli, Hobbes, Locke, Montesquieu, Blackstone, and Lolme, necessity dictates, even within a republic, the presence of a prince capable of meeting the emergencies forever incident to human affairs, and the distinction between a workable republic and one incapable of providing for domestic tranquillity and the common defense turns largely on the provisions made to ensure the "decision, activity, secrecy, and dispatch" necessary to this end. "A feeble executive implies a feeble execution of the government," wrote Hamilton. "A feeble execution is but another phrase for a bad execution: And a government ill executed, whatever it may be in theory, must be in practice a bad government." [133]

Of course, energy and dispatch are virtues only when subordinate to the public good. The real question to be posed was whether the American prince might not be tempted to abuse his power. To justify entrusting an individual with prerogatives so extensive, Hamilton had to address the question of executive character. In his judgment, what was true for the senator was doubly true for the occupant of the presidency. His selection by an electoral college of notables directly elected by the people "affords a moral certainty that the office of president, will seldom fall to the lot of any man, who is not in an eminent degree endowed with the requisite qualifications." Indeed, there will be "a constant probability of seeing the station filled by characters pre-eminent for ability" and for a more than merely Machiavellian "virtue." Moreover, the fact that the office was to be held by a single individual would leave its occupant little choice but to take "responsibility" for all that transpired and would beget within him "a livelier sense of duty and a more exact regard to reputation" than one could expect from those within the two bodies of the legislature. In similar fashion, his extended term of office would encourage a "personal firmness . . . in the employment of his constitutional powers," and one could hope that what presents itself initially as Machiavellian *virtù* would in the end manifest itself as Aristotelian *megalopsuchía*, for the president's extended term of office would enable a man of genuine virtue "to expose himself" when necessary, to save "the people from very fatal consequences of their own mistakes," and to procure for himself "lasting monuments of their gratitude" for having had "courage and magnanimity enough to serve them at the peril of their displeasure." Even if his use of the executive veto to check a legislature "sufficiently numerous to feel all the passions which actuate a multitude" merely served to slow the pace of legislation, that would be all to the good, for "the oftener a measure is brought under examination, the greater the diversity in the situation of those who are to examine it, the less must be the danger of those errors which flow from want of due deliberation, or of those missteps which proceed from the contagion of some common passions or interest."[134]

There was also, Hamilton emphasized, an "intimate connection between the duration of the executive magistrate in office, and the stability of the system of administration." In his judgment, this fact was critical, for the executive was to play the central role in the conduct of administration, and "the true test of a good government is its aptitude and tendency to produce a good administration." At the federal convention, when Gouverneur Morris singled out "the love of fame" and identified it as "the great spring to noble & illustrious actions," he was speaking of the unitary executive, the eligibility of the American president for reelection, and the role to be played by his lieutenants. Similarly, in *The Federalist*, it was with the president's conduct of administration in mind that Hamilton spoke of "the love of fame" as "the ruling passion of the noblest minds." For the fact that the president was eligible for reappointment and "could flatter himself with the prospect of being allowed to finish what he had begun" would "prompt" him "to plan and undertake extensive and arduous enterprises for the public benefit, requiring considerable time to mature and perfect them."[135]

If the creation of a unitary executive presupposes that there is something to be said for the argument made on behalf of the prince by Machiavelli, Hobbes, Locke, Montesquieu, Blackstone, and Lolme, the establishment of the Supreme Court points in the opposite direction. Staffed by experts who are trained in jurisprudence, blessed with permanent tenure, and entrusted with the power to interpret the law and judge the constitutionality of state and federal legislation, that body occupies a position within the American constitutional structure more restricted than the one allocated to the Nocturnal Council in Plato's Cretan city Magnesia but in one critical regard analogous. It helps fulfill a condition which the Socrates of Plato's *Republic* thought necessary for good government: it arises from an attempt to ensure that within the polity there be always something possessing the same understanding (*lógos*) of the regime that the lawgiver possessed when he framed its laws; and in elaborating that understanding as it expounds the law, it contributes powerfully to the political education of the nation's citizenry.[136] The federal judiciary can hardly be termed a democratic or even a strictly republican institution. It more nearly resembles what James Madison called "a will in the community independent of the majority," for, as he readily acknowledged, the judges "are too far removed from the people to share much in their prepossessions."[137] The shrewdest of the Anti-Federalists recognized and deplored this fact. They were aware that the Constitution makes no mention of judicial review, but they perceived the implications of the stipulation that "the judicial Power shall extend to all Cases, in Law and Equity, arising under this Constitution, the Laws of the United States, and Treaties made, or which shall be made, under their Authority."[138]

The Federal Farmer worried that the courts might "have a very extensive influence for preserving or destroying liberty, and for changing the nature of the government," and he suspected that his compatriots were "more in danger of sowing the seeds of arbitrary government in this department than in any other." He recognized that the courts would decide the constitutionality of state and federal laws not only with regard to "the letter of the constitution" but also with regard to its "spirit and true meaning . . . , as collected from what must appear to have been the intentions of the people when they made it," and he feared that the judges would take their charge as an opportunity "to decide as their conscience, their opinions, their caprice, or their politics might dictate." In his estimation, the judges would be effectively unchecked, for their "proceedings" are "intricate, complex, and out of [the] immediate view" of the public. In the best of circumstances, when the courts are restricted to the exposition of ordinary law, the "judicial power is of such a nature, that when we have ascertained and fixed its limits, with all the caution and precision we can, it will yet be formidable, somewhat arbitrary and despotic—that is, after all our cares, we must leave a vast deal to the discretion and interpretation—to the wisdom, integrity, and politics of the judges." To place the Constitution itself within the scope of judicial interpretation would be tantamount to abandoning the cause of self-government.[139]

In New York, Brutus sounded the same theme. He argued that the pertinent clause of the Constitution would place Americans "in a situation altogether unprecedented in a free country." He, too, saw that, in their "construction of the constitution," the judges would explain it "according to the reasoning spirit of it, without being confined to the words or letter." And mindful that "there is no power provided in the constitution, that can correct their errors, or controul their adjudications," he feared that "the opinions of the supreme court, whatever they may be, will have the force of law." "From this court," as he put it, "there is no appeal." Certainly, the legislature "cannot set aside a judgment of this court," for the people's elected representatives are to "be controuled by the constitution, and not the constitution by them." Moreover, the judicial power would operate in a manner "silent and imperceptible," and the preamble of the Constitution and the clause conferring on Congress the right "to make all Laws necessary and proper for carrying into Execution" its enumerated powers offered the court an extraordinary "latitude of interpretation." Brutus warned his compatriots that "every body of men invested with office are tenacious of power; they feel interested, and hence it has become a kind of maxim, to hand down their offices, with all its rights and privileges, unimpaired to their successors; the same principle will influence them to extend their power, and increase their rights; this of itself will operate strongly upon the courts to give such a meaning to the constitution in all cases where it can possibly be done, as will enlarge the sphere of their own authority." In one passage, he remarked, "I question whether the world ever saw, in any period of it, a court of justice invested with such immense powers, and yet placed in a situation so little responsible." In another, he elaborated on the range of discretion allowed the judges: "There is no power above them, to controul any of their decisions. There is no authority that can remove them, and they cannot be controuled by the laws of the legislature. In short, they are independent of the people, of the legislature, and of every power under heaven." This species of independence Brutus thought intolerable, for it was his conviction that "men placed in this situation will generally soon feel themselves independent of heaven itself." [140]

Much of what the Federal Farmer and Brutus took to be a vice, Alexander Hamilton treated as an advantage. [141] In particular, he argued, judicial independence is a prerequisite for the maintenance of "a limited constitution." Just as an independent judiciary is "an excellent barrier to the despotism of the prince" in a limited monarchy, so also in a limited republic it is "a no less excellent barrier to the encroachments and oppressions of the representative body. And it is the best expedient which can be devised in any government, to secure a steady, upright and impartial administration of the laws." In a republic, the real danger to be feared is that "the representatives of the people" may "substitute their *will*" for "that of their constituents." Only an independent judiciary, armed with the power of judicial review, can act "to keep the latter within the limits assigned to their authority." Indeed, if the judges are "to guard the constitution and the rights of individuals from the effects of those ill humours which the arts of designing men, or the influence of particular conjunctures, sometimes disseminate among the people themselves," they will have to be graced with an "independent spirit" and "an uncommon portion of fortitude" unlikely to be found in men denied "permanent tenure." In his estimation, that same "firmness" would be "of vast importance in mitigating the severity and confining the operation" of "partial laws." [142]

In reply to the charge leveled by Brutus and the Federal Farmer, Hamilton presented two arguments. To begin with, he contended, in a government of separated powers, "the judiciary, from the nature of its functions, will always be the least dangerous to the political rights of the constitution." It will neither dispense "the honors" nor bear "the sword of the community." It will neither command "the purse" nor prescribe "the rules by which the duties and rights of every citizen are to be regulated." For these are the prerogatives of the executive and the legislature. Of the judiciary, "it may truly be said to have neither Force nor Will, but merely judgment." Though the courts might err from time to time, "the general liberty of the people can never be endangered from that quarter." In practice, the nature of the judicial power, its objects, its manner of exercise, its weakness, and "its total incapacity to support its usurpations by force" render "the supposed danger of judiciary encroachments on the legislative authority . . . in reality a phantom."[143]

After making this point, Hamilton readily confessed that it could be said "that the courts on the pretence of a repugnancy, may substitute their own pleasure to the constitutional intentions of the legislature." But he denied that such a claim could bear any "weight" as an objection against judicial review. Even where that doctrine was not accepted, it was the duty of the courts to "declare the sense of the law; and if they should be disposed to exercise WILL instead of JUDGMENT, the consequence would equally be the substitution of their pleasure to that of the legislative body." If the objection were judged valid, it would render nugatory the only available means for insuring the supremacy of the federal government within its sphere, and it would constitute a refutation of Montesquieu's argument for the separation of powers.[144]

In the end, Hamilton implied, the Framers had little choice. To sustain a government of enumerated powers limited to a specified end, one has to confer a guardianship of the Constitution on some body effectively independent of the people and their elected representatives, and the courts are a far safer and far better expedient than the executive: for one can hardly expect a man who has had "even a partial agency in passing bad laws" to exhibit the requisite impartiality, and the courts will be staffed by experts trained in the law and accustomed to a peculiar kind of reasoning. "To avoid an arbitrary discretion in the courts," he argued, "it is indispensable that they should be bound down by strict rules and precedents, which serve to define and point out their duty in every particular case that comes before them." Very few men will have devoted the time to "long and laborious study" necessary "to acquire a competent knowledge" of those "rules and precedents," and very few "will have sufficient skill in the laws to qualify them for the stations of judges." As a consequence, Madison insists that "in the constitution of the judiciary department . . . , it might be inexpedient to insist rigorously on the principle" that "all appointments" to high federal office "should be drawn from the same fountain of authority, the people, through channels, having no communication whatever with one another." Here, in fact, "the primary consideration ought to be to select that mode of choice, which best secures" the "peculiar qualifications . . . essential in the members."[145] The federal courts may be "the least dangerous" branch of the government, but—as Hamilton's cautious defense allows his reader to see for himself—Brutus and the Federal Farmer had identified an unavoidable danger which is apparently coincident with constitutional government. As the Supreme Court's adjudication of the Dred Scott case would eventually demonstrate, "the least dangerous branch" of the American government is capable of doing untold harm.[146] Certainly, no other branch presupposes in its members greater virtue and wisdom, more self-restraint, and a fuller dedication to democratic constitutionalism and the separation of powers.

The Federal Farmer and Brutus were convinced that the Constitution's provisions for the judicial power violate what James Madison called the "fundamental maxim of republican government which requires that the sense of the majority should prevail," and one must confess that they had a case. But one must also admit that the vindication of man's capacity for self-government requires something comparable to the political architecture which the Framers devised, for they were certainly right to follow Montesquieu in supposing the separation of powers "a sacred maxim of free government." To repudiate the judicial power as an antirepublican innovation would be to concede that the republican "form" is incompatible with the only "structure" capable of providing for the sense of security and the tranquillity of spirit which are the distinctive features of what Montesquieu had called "free government."[147] Thus, if the delegates to the Philadelphia convention were prepared to check the democratic impulse and to employ institutions exhibiting in some measure an aristocratic and even monarchical spirit, it was ultimately for the purpose of fortifying, refining, and justifying government by the people. As James Wilson pointed out to his colleagues in the Pennsylvania Ratifying Convention, "in its principle," the new government "is purely democratical. But that principle is applied in different forms, in order to obtain the advantages, and exclude the inconveniences of the simple modes of government."[148]

The aim of the Framers was less to thwart than to inform the popular will; their goal was to frustrate passion by preventing precipitous and potentially dangerous action; their purpose was to minimize the influence of what Hamilton had termed "accident and force" while giving maximum play to the human capacity for rational "choice" grounded in mature "reflection on human nature" and the natural necessities beyond reason's control. "Occasions present themselves in which the interests of the people are at variance with their inclinations," Hamilton observed. A representative government set at a distance from the people and endowed with the proper safeguards would enable "the guardians of those interests to withstand the temporary delusion" of the populace and take the "time and opportunity for more cool and sedate reflection." The separation of powers and the system of checks and balances were instituted in the hope that the decisions reached by the American government would emerge from thoughtful discussion and prudent debate guided by a dedication to the principles proclaimed by the Declaration of Independence and embodied in the Constitution. In this fashion, these decisions would mirror not the fickleness and inconstancy of public opinion but, rather, what both Hamilton and Madison called the "deliberate sense of the community." [149]

III.i.8

Madison acknowledged the import of such "auxiliary precautions." He regarded them as a "necessity," and he considered "no political truth" to be "of greater instrinsic value" than the argument advanced on behalf of the separation of powers.[150] But he did not deem the Constitution's various "auxiliary precautions" adequate in and of themselves, for he believed that there are limits to the trust one can and should confide in any government. Constitutional machinery cannot be rendered infallible, and human frailty dictates that those given power are likely to abuse it. "There are," Hamilton conceded, "men who could neither be distressed nor won into a sacrifice of their duty; but this stern virtue is the growth of few soils." [151] In consequence, Madison insisted, "all these securities . . . would be found very insufficient without the restraint of frequent elections." If these "auxiliary precautions" were to provide effective support for good government in an otherwise unmixed, undisguisedly democratic republic, it was in part because of a consequence of the second and more important of the two principles for whose inspiration Madison was indebted to David Hume: the efficacy of geographical extension. Because of its vast scope, the national government would be much more free from the sway of the passions and the mischiefs of faction than the individual states. To govern so large a republic, ambitious men would have to negotiate alliances between "the parts, interests, and classes of citizens," and the variety would be so great that "a coalition of a majority of the whole society could seldom take place on any other principles than those of justice and the general good." [152]

Madison nowhere asserts that the good of the whole is simply the sum of the advantages sought by the parts. In fact, by implication, he denies any such claim. The Virginian was fully aware that public safety, and the need for national defense in particular, often requires the sacrifice of one or more parts for the sake of the whole. That is the chief reason why, in the tenth number of *The Federalist*, he consistently distinguishes "the public good" and "the permanent and aggregate interests of the community" from the dictates of what he calls "justice" or "private rights."[153] In the long run, respect for the rights of other citizens is generally a prerequisite for the avoidance of civil strife that would threaten the general good. In that sense, justice is one of the permanent and aggregate interests of the community. But, in the short run, war—whether present or merely anticipated—can and often must override all other priorities and render even the achievement of justice a matter of secondary concern. Only in a polity that survives and achieves a certain prosperity can one effectively pursue justice and protect private rights.

In *The Federalist*, Madison only hints at the tension between justice and the public good. He can pass over the matter quickly because of the protection afforded Britain's former colonies by their relative isolation. Barring the dissolution of the Union, the various states could expect to be generally free, at least for a time, from threats originating in countries abroad. Thus, with these reservations acknowledged, Madison appears to assume that a compromise negotiated between the various parts will, most of the time, be as reasonable an approximation of the general good as practical men are likely to achieve. Frequent elections guaranteed that this system would work: on the one hand, they stirred in officials "an habitual recollection of their dependence on the people"; on the other, they forced at regular intervals a renegotiation of the social contract by which that "coalition of a majority of the whole society" was called into existence.[154]

The modern republic was to have a much narrower scope than the one assigned to government in antiquity and the Middle Ages. American statesmen were not inclined to echo the contention of Plato's Athenian Stranger that politics is "the art whose task is caring for souls" or to repeat Aristotle's assertion that the political community exists less for the sake of mere life than to encourage human beings to live nobly and well. None of any importance was ever to restate Richard Hooker's claim that "pure and unstayned religion ought to be the highest of all cares apperteyninge to publique regiment"— for they feared that to do so would be to open the door to the presumption that "the mass of mankind" had somehow "been born with saddles on their backs" and "a favored few booted and spurred, ready to ride them legitimately, by the grace of" nature and nature's "God." If the American regime was to promote the perfection of the soul, it was to do so stealthily and solely by indirection while ostensibly pursuing less exalted ends. Like the polity imagined by John Locke, the modern republic was to be a government explicitly limited with regard to the ends it could openly pursue.[155] The framers of the American Constitution were therefore eager to avoid flattering the pretensions of their compatriots to political and moral rationality, and as a consequence, they were reluctant to reopen questions affecting what John Stuart Mill would call "the fundamental principle of the system of social union."[156] There was, however, one firmly entrenched, American interest which could not be defended in the long run without recourse to and a reconsideration of the fundamental principles of the regime. From the very beginning of the republic, disputes concerning that peculiar interest threatened to make the requisite political compromises impossible and thereby to divide the Union. It is to the attempts made by the framers of the Constitution to paper over those disputes and grapple with the difficulties they posed that we will now turn.

CHAPTER 2

Slavery, Section, and Progress in the Arts

Suppose this business of religion were let alone, and that there were some other distinction made between men and men upon account of their different complexions, shapes, and features, so that those who have black hair (for example) or grey eyes should not enjoy the same privileges as other citizens; that they should not be permitted either to buy or sell, or live by their callings; that parents should not have the government and education of their own children; that they should either be excluded from the benefit of the laws, or meet with partial judges; can it be doubted but these persons, thus distinguished from others by the colour of their hair and eyes, and united together by one common persecution, would be as dangerous to the magistrate as any others that had associated themselves merely upon the account of religion?—John Locke

III.ii.1

On the eve of the Virginia Ratifying Convention, the young James Monroe circulated a brief pamphlet summing up his own observations on the virtues and vices of the Constitution designed by the delegates to the Philadelphia convention. The future president was fully prepared to acknowledge that it was "an idea not only elevated and sublime, but equally benevolent and humane" that "the citizens of America, who have fought and bled together," be united, made "one people," and taught "to lay aside those jarring interests and discordant principles, which state legislatures if they do not create, certainly foment and increase." But he sincerely doubted whether such a project was "practicable." In particular, he openly questioned whether "a legislature"—containing "within it all the vital parts of a democracy, and those provisions which the wisdom of ages has pointed out as the best security of liberty"—could actually "be organized upon such principles as to comprehend the territory lying between the Mississippi, the St. Lawrence, the Lakes, and the Atlantic ocean, with such a variety of soil and climate, . . . and be at the same time a strong, efficient, and energetic government."[1]

Monroe was by no means alone in his fears. In New York, the unnamed author of *The Letters of Cato* made much the same point in an even more striking and memorable fashion: "Whoever seriously considers the immense extent of territory comprehended within the limits of the United States, together with the variety of its climates, productions, and commerce, the difference of extent, and number of inhabitants in all; the dissimilitude of interest, morals, and policies, in almost every one, will receive it as an intuitive truth, that a consolidated republican form of government therein, can never *form a perfect union, establish justice, insure domestic tranquility, promote the general welfare, and secure the blessings of liberty to you and your posterity.*" Such a consolidation would produce an "unkindred legislature . . . composed of interests opposite and dissimilar in their nature." Such a government would "in its exercise, emphatically be, like a house divided against itself."[2]

These were typical of the arguments against which James Madison directed the tenth number of *The Federalist*. Though dismayed by the rejection of his proposal that the federal government be given a veto over the legislation of the states, the Virginian had reason to contemplate the Constitution with pleasure. On the whole, that document promised to fashion, from the various disadvantages pointed out by James Monroe, by the pseudonymous Cato, and by the other Anti-Federalists, firm supports for the new regime. Madison was prepared to demonstrate to the world not only that "a house divided against itself" could actually stand but also that the very divisions which appeared to augur its collapse were the proper foundations for its long-term stability. Unfortunately, one great obstacle remained. The turbulence and class strife within the individual states was Madison's most immediate, but not his only (and perhaps not even his primary, long-range) concern. The Virginian had learned much from his years of service in Congress.[3]

In the principle of the multiplication of factions, Madison believed that he had found a way to obviate the danger of sectarian zeal and the perils of class struggle as well. But if geographical extension promised to solve these two problems, it posed a third, perhaps even greater. On the eve of the Constitutional Convention, Madison wrote to a fellow delegate from Virginia of his apprehension that there would be a "partition of the Empire into rival & hostile confederacies" if the Union were not "organized efficiently & on Republican Principles."[4] On the floor of the convention, he discreetly pointed to the roots of the peril. While arguing against the efficacy of conscience as a restraint against evildoing, Madison sadly noted that "we have seen the mere distinction of colour made in the most enlightened period of time, a ground for the most oppressive dominion ever exercised by man over man."[5] Here— in an institution firmly established in his native Virginia—lay the source of the trouble which James Madison foresaw.

In 1776, when the American Revolution began, slavery had been an universal phenomenon legal in each and every one of the American colonies.[6] Before that event, even in the North, John Jay later remembered, "the great majority or rather the great body of our people had been so long accustomed to the practice and convenience of having slaves, that very few among them even doubted the propriety and rectitude of it." Jay's observation should give us pause, for what he wrote concerning the English colonists was then true for all the peoples of the world, and it had always been so. In solemnly calling into question the propriety and rectitude of all involuntary servitude, the Revolution marked a watershed in human history. Eleven years after the final break with Britain, when the delegates met at Philadelphia to frame a constitution for the fledgling republic, all of the northern states except New York and New Jersey had already outlawed slavery or established programs of gradual emancipation. The spirit of the Revolution and the principles enunciated within the Declaration of Independence had had a profound effect on the states least economically dependent on what soon came to be called the peculiar institution; within these communities, the populace had quickly recognized that the enslavement of blacks involved an unjustifiable denial to them of the very inalienable rights which, in the course of launching their rebellion, whites had claimed for themselves and the entire human race. In 1787, abolition on the part of the last two northern states could easily be foreseen; Madison apparently expected Delaware to follow suit; and many supposed that Maryland would do so as well. As Jay put it not long after the Philadelphia convention, the doctrine of the abolitionists "prevailed by almost insensible degrees, and was like the little lump of leaven which was put into three measures of meal." Even in 1788, he acknowledged, "the whole mass is far from being leavened, though we have good reason to hope and to believe that if the natural operations of truth are constantly watched and assisted, but not forced and precipitated, that end we all aim at will finally be attained in this country."[7] In principle, Madison can only have welcomed this trend as a proper working out in practice of what was already clear from the principles elaborated in the Declaration of Independence. In practice, however, developments in the Northeast and in the mid-Atlantic states posed a problem: nothing of the sort could be foreseen in the immediate future for Virginia and for the states farther south.

III.ii.2

Late in 1776, Thomas Jefferson, George Wythe, and Edmund Pendleton had been named by the Virginia House of Delegates to a committee charged with the responsibility of making the statute and common law of the commonwealth compatible with its recently acquired status. Even then, Jefferson favored emancipation, but he was also persuaded that the racial prejudice of the whites and the justifiable resentment of the blacks would render impossible the maintenance of domestic tranquillity within any society that included both races.[8] In keeping with his convictions, he took his new appointment as an opportunity to write a program of gradual emancipation and colonization into the law code of Virginia. But that attempt quickly foundered, and Jefferson found himself forced to abandon the quest as ill-timed. In the fall of 1785, James Madison renewed the effort in the state assembly, but to no avail.[9] Although the slaveholders of Virginia generally regarded the institution as an evil, they were not at that time prepared to do what would have been necessary to eliminate it altogether.

In his attitude toward slavery, Patrick Henry may have been a typical Virginian. It left him dumbfounded that an age which could "boast of high Improvements in the Arts and Sciences & refined Morality" should also "have brought into general Use, & guarded by many Laws, a Species of Violence & Tyranny, which our more rude barbarous, but more honest Ancestors detested." He found it "amazing, that at a time when the rights of Humanity are defined & understood with precision in a Country above all others fond of Liberty: that in such an Age and such a Country, we find Men . . . adopting a Principle as repugnant to humanity, as it is inconsistant with the Bible & destructive to Liberty." Of course, he remarked, "every thinking honest Man rejects it in Speculation." But, he asked, "how few in Practice from conscientious Motives?" In juxtaposing theory and practice, Henry knew only too well whereof he spoke. "Would any one believe," he exclaimed in dismay, "that I am Master of Slaves of my own purchase! I am drawn along by ye general Inconvenience of living without them; I will not, I cannot justify it." He could only affirm his belief that "a time will come when an oppertunity will be offered to abolish this lamentable Evil." In the interim, it was his duty and that of his compatriots to "transmit to our descendants together with our Slaves a pity for their unhappy Lot, and an abhorrence for Slavery." In the short run, one could not reasonably hope for a greater consummation.[10]

Farther south, particularly in South Carolina and in Georgia, circumstances were even less propitious than in Virginia: for, there, slavery was but rarely perceived as a great embarrassment, and abolition was hardly mooted. The Founding Fathers were acutely aware of this fact. In late June 1776, when Thomas Jefferson drafted the Declaration of Independence, he included within the list of grievances the charge that George III had "waged cruel war against human nature itself, violating it's most sacred rights of life and liberty in the persons of a distant people who never offended him, captivating and carrying them into slavery in another hemisphere, or to incur miserable death in their transportation thither." In due course, the clause was struck out. This was, in part, due to embarrassment—and rightly so, for the slaves brought in from Africa could hardly be said to have been forced on an unwilling populace, and many of them had been transported in American bottoms. According to Jefferson, however, the clause was dropped chiefly "in complaisance to S. Carolina and Georgia, who had never attempted to restrain the importation of slaves, and who on the contrary still wished to continue it."[11]

Of course, even in the Deep South, there were exceptions to the rule, and some were prominent and highly influential men. Preeminent among these were Henry Laurens of Charleston, South Carolina, and his son John. The elder Laurens was a man of considerable importance. He represented his state in the Continental Congress from very early in 1777 almost to the end of 1779; from November 1777 to December 1778 he served as that body's presiding officer; and later he helped negotiate the Peace of Paris. During much of the period of his father's service in the Continental Congress, the younger Laurens was an aide to George Washington. In the process, he became a close friend of Alexander Hamilton, and with enthusiastic support from the New Yorker, he began agitating for the adoption of a program that, he hoped, would prepare the way for a general emancipation.

During the Revolutionary War, the South proved far more vulnerable to British attack than did the North. The rivers running inland made it easy to land troops in the interior, and the slave population was a potential fifth column. Nowhere was the danger greater than in the Deep South. There, white manpower was particularly scanty. Moreover, in South Carolina the blacks were the majority, and in Georgia they exceeded two-fifths of the total population. In this situation, John Laurens managed to persuade his father of the propriety of the federal government's purchasing slaves from their masters and promising full emancipation to those willing to enlist as soldiers in the revolutionary struggle. Early in 1779, when the desperate weakness of the Deep South had become evident to all, Henry Laurens succeeded in convincing not just a few, but all of the delegates to the Continental Congress that his son's proposal had merit; and in due course, John Laurens was commissioned as a lieutenant colonel and dispatched to Charleston to persuade the state assembly to adopt Congress's recommendation and to empower him to raise a corps of slave soldiers.

The younger Laurens made two concerted attempts to persuade his fellow South Carolinians—one in 1779 and the other in 1782. On each occasion, he enjoyed the vigorous support of the Pennsylvania-born physician and future historian David Ramsay. But, though the military crisis grew more severe with every passing day, Washington's former aide was never able to get as many as twenty of the more than one hundred state assemblymen to vote for enlisting even those slaves that had already become public property with the confiscation of the Loyalists' estates.[12] In a letter recommending Laurens and his project to John Jay, Alexander Hamilton had warned that "prejudice and self-interest" would probably prove an insuperable obstacle. "The contempt we have been taught to entertain for the blacks," he remarked, "makes us fancy many things that are founded neither in reason nor experience; and an unwillingness to part with property of so valuable a kind will furnish a thousand arguments to show the impracticability or pernicious tendency of a scheme which requires such a sacrifice." And so it transpired: the abject failure of Laurens's mission says much about "the baneful influence" exerted in the Deep South at this time by what he called "Avarice, prejudice, and pusillanimity."[13]

It is just possible that John Laurens would have had better luck farther south. Until 1751, slavery had been banned in Georgia.[14] The colony's militia act, adopted in 1755 and revised in 1773, not only authorized slaveholders and overseers to enroll slaves in the militia in time of emergency; it provided as well for the emancipation of those slaves "who shall actually engage the Enemy, in times of Invasion of this Province, and Shall Couragiously behave themselves in Battle so as to kill any one of the Enemy, or take a prisoner alive or Shall take any of their Colours."[15] During the Revolutionary War, the new nation's southernmost state was in even more desperate straits than South Carolina, and there Laurens would have encountered a good many more like-minded men—at least if one is to judge the situation by two remarkable documents: a petition sent the Georgia trustees in January 1739 by the Highland Scots who had settled Darien in St. Andrew's Parish, and a resolution passed in January 1775 when their descendants and successors met under the leadership of Henry Laurens's longtime friend and business partner Lachlan McIntosh to pledge their wholehearted support to the Continental Congress. The two documents deserve careful attention.

In 1738, a group of malcontents resident in Savannah had petitioned the Georgia trustees to sanction the introduction of slavery into the colony. At the instigation of the one trustee actually resident in Georgia, the Scots responded in a fashion foreshadowing the moral, humanitarian critique of slavery pioneered by Montesquieu and eventually taken up by Thomas Jefferson. To begin with, they argued that the peculiar institution would endanger the settlement and corrupt the manners of its free inhabitants; and then, by way of conclusion, they added, "It is shocking to human Nature, that any Race of Mankind and their Posterity should be sentenc'd to perpetual Slavery; nor in Justice can we think otherwise of it, than that they are thrown amongst us to be our Scourge one Day or other for our Sins: And as Freedom must be as dear to them as to us, what a Scene of Horror must it bring about! And the longer it is unexecuted, the bloody Scene must be the greater."[16]

Thirty-seven years later, embarrassed at the prospect of launching a revolution that could be justified only on principles which they were themselves breaching in practice, chastened by a minor slave uprising in their own parish, and eager to justify themselves in their own eyes and in the eyes of the world, the citizens of Darien restated the antislavery case in terms even more striking. "To show the world that we are not influenced by any contracted or interested motives, but a general philanthropy for all mankind of whatever climate, language, or complexion," they wrote,

> we hereby declare our disapprobation and abhorrence of the unnatural practice of Slavery in America, (however, the uncultivated state of our country, or other specious argument may plead for it,) a practice founded in injustice and cruelty, and highly dangerous to our liberties, (as well as lives,) debasing part of our fellow creatures below men, and corrupting the virtues and morals of the rest, and . . . laying the basis for the liberty we contend for . . . upon a very wrong foundation. We therefore resolve, at all times to use our utmost endeavours for the manumission of our Slaves in this Colony, for the most safe and equitable footing for the masters and themselves.[17]

It would be hard to find a more eloquent contemporary critique of chattel slavery, but it would nonetheless be an error to treat this resolution as a faithful indicator of attitudes throughout Georgia. Its adoption was an isolated occurrence; when confronted with a choice between doing injustice to Africans and condemning his own family to insolvency, Lachlan McIntosh demonstrated that he was in no great hurry to see slavery abolished; and on this subject the citizens of Darien were never heard from again.[18] In truth, by the time of the Revolutionary War, slavery was so firmly established in Georgia that very few of the state's citizens were less fully persuaded than their immediate neighbors to the north that slave labor was a prerequisite for economic development in the lower South.[19]

Opinion in that region did not alter much, if at all, in the war's immediate aftermath. In 1785, not long after receiving a copy of *Notes on the State of Virginia*, the well-known statistician, political radical, and Presbyterian divine Richard Price wrote to Jefferson from England to express his admiration of the man's "Sentiments and character." "How happy would the united States be were all of them under the direction of Such wisdom and liberality as yours," he exclaimed. But he knew better than to suppose that this was the case. Price had learned from a correspondent in South Carolina that the leading men of the state were "agree'd in reprobating" the *Observations on the Importance of the American Revolution, and the Means of Making it a Benefit to the World* which he had recently published. They objected to Price's

> pamphlet on the American Revolution because it recommends measures for preventing too great an inequality of property and for gradually abolishing the Negro trade and Slavery; these being measures which . . . will never find encouragement in that State. . . . Should Such a disposition prevail in the other United States, I shall have reason to fear that I have made myself ridiculous by Speaking of the American Revolution in the manner I have done; it will appear that the people who have been Struggling so earnestly to save *themselves* from Slavery are very ready to enslave *others*; the friends of liberty and humanity in Europe will be mortify'd, and an event which had raised their hopes will prove only an introduction to a new Scene of aristocratic tyranny and human debasement.

A few weeks later, Jefferson wrote back from Paris that he could easily predict the fashion in which Price's pamphlet will have been received and that the little information he had been able to glean from his American correspondents and visitors had confirmed his expectations. "Southward of the Chesapeak it will find but few readers concurring with it on the subject of slavery," he acknowledged.

> From the mouth to the head of the Chesapeak, the bulk of the people will approve it in theory, and it will find a respectable minority ready to adopt it in practice, a minority which for weight and worth of character preponderates against the greater number, who have not the courage to divest their families of a property which however keeps their consciences inquiet. Northward of the Chesapeak you may find here and there an opponent to your doctrine as you may find here and there a robber and a murderer, but in no greater number. In that part of America, there being but few slaves, they can easily disencumber themselves of them, and emancipation is put into such a train that in a few years there will be no slaves Northward of Maryland.[20]

In most respects, Jefferson's expectations were fully borne out.[21] In particular, we know that Jefferson's open advocacy of the cause of abolition in his essay on Virginia occasioned "general alarm" among the citizens of South Carolina. As one of his correspondents from that state explained, "It is not easy to get rid of old prejudices, and the word 'emancipation' operates like an apparition upon a South Carolina planter."[22] James Madison understood the consequences of all this only too well. For some time to come, the new nation was destined to be half-slave and half-free, and if dissolution was to be avoided, its institutions would have to be fashioned to meet the needs of such a hybrid union.

The young statesman from Virginia took the tension between the small states and the large states, so visible to the delegates attending the Constitutional Convention, to be but a chimera.[23] "The States were divided into different interests not by their difference of size," he told his colleagues in Philadelphia, "but by other circumstances; the most material of which resulted partly from climate, but principally from ‹the effects of› their having or not having slaves." The greatest danger was that the Union would itself disintegrate, and "the institution of slavery & its consequences formed the line of discrimination."[24] The same geographically dictated division of labor that promised to shield the federal administration from class strife by pitting one locality against another would at the same time inevitably set the North against the South.

III.ii.3

Madison made his brief remarks regarding the importance of slavery and section in late June and in mid-July 1787, at a time when his fellow delegates were busy negotiating the compromise between the large and the small states which granted each of the former colonies equal representation in the Senate and determined representation in the House of Representatives on the basis of population.[25] While they were engaged in this discussion, the Virginian pondered the merits of another plan, "casting about in his mind for some expedient that would answer the purpose" which he deemed most pressing. Madison believed that the maintenance of internal harmony and the survival of the Union would not be possible unless the Constitution embodied safeguards capable of preventing each of the nation's two great regions from enforcing its will on the other. To achieve this end, he contemplated allocating representation to the states in one of the two houses of the federal congress in proportion to the number of residents (both free and slave) while allocating representation in the other house in proportion to the number of those in the free population alone. In 1787, the two regions were very nearly equal in overall population, and Madison believed that, as more and more Americans settled in the nation's warmer climes, this constitutional arrangement would give "the Southern Scale . . . the advantage in one House, and the Northern in the other."

Two considerations restrained the Virginian from actually pressing for such a scheme of apportionment. At the time, his fellow delegates seemed relatively unperturbed, and he was unwilling "to urge any diversity of interests on an occasion when it is but too apt to arise of itself." In addition, he recognized that an "inequality of powers . . . must be vested in the two branches" of Congress and that this inequality would, in any case, "destroy the equilibrium of interests" which he sought. Madison supposed—wrongly, as it turned out—that the great compromise between the small and the large states would relegate the Senate to the North. This expectation was but one of the many considerations that caused the Virginian to oppose a concession of equal representation in the Senate to the smaller states. If Madison was later willing to put aside his misgivings regarding this particular consequence of the compromise, it was because he could take consolation from the arrangement through which direct taxation in the South by the federal government as well as southern representation in the House of Representatives would be augmented substantially by computing each on the basis of a figure secured through adding three-fifths of the slave population to the number of those who were free. Like nearly everyone else, James Madison believed that, in population, the South would soon outstrip the North.[26]

The three-fifths rule stirred grumbling and a desultory debate but no serious and sustained opposition.[27] At the time, the Framers were far more deeply agitated about another question. Almost no one foresaw the flood of immigrants into the northern cities, western Pennsylvania and New York, and the Northwest Territory. For more than a quarter-century, the population of North America had been shifting to the South and West. While the delegates from the northeastern states feared that their region would soon become a backwater—underpopulated and lacking the political influence to protect its interests in fishing, manufacturing, and the carrying trade—their southern colleagues looked forward with full confidence to continued growth and, in time, political predominance. In 1787, Virginia was the nation's most populous state; the citizens of North Carolina outnumbered those of New York; those of South Carolina outnumbered those of New Jersey; and Georgia's population had been increasing by leaps and bounds. If the Union could only secure control of the Mississippi or at least ensure that American farmers living in the transmontane region of the Southwest could freely export their produce down that great river, all would be well. If not, however, those migrating to the West might turn for protection to a foreign power. Here lay a difficulty. In the conduct of foreign relations, the northerners predominant in the national councils were inclined to make concessions on the Mississippi question for the sake of protecting the interests of their fishermen and merchants. The matter had already occasioned disputes, and neither region trusted the other to look after its interests. Some of the delegates representing the North at the convention hoped that the apportionment of seats in the House of Representatives would be left to the discretion of Congress, while their southern colleagues, rightly fearful that this would merely prolong their subordination to the North, insisted that there be a strict rule linking apportionment with population as determined by a regular census.[28]

The three-fifths rule drew fire from William Paterson of New Jersey, from James Wilson and Gouverneur Morris of Pennsylvania, and from Rufus King of Massachusetts. Paterson was the first to object and the only one to argue the case in detail. Apart from noting that the three-fifths rule might make the Constitution seem obnoxious in Pennsylvania and elsewhere in the North where antislavery feeling was strong, the others had little to add. Paterson began by observing that slaves are not "free agents" and that they "have no personal liberty, no faculty of acquiring property, but on the contrary are themselves property, & like other property entirely at the will of the Master." Nowhere in the southern states, he noted, did slaves figure in the scheme of representation—and for good reason. Representation is nothing but "an expedient by which an assembly of certain individls. chosen by the people is substituted in place of the inconvenient meeting of the people themselves." If slaves were not allowed to vote at such a general assembly, there was no reason why they should be counted when it came to apportioning representation. To do so would be to reward slave ownership and to encourage the slave trade.[29]

Paterson was poorly situated to advance this understanding of representation. At the convention, he was the preeminent champion of the claims and interests of the smaller states. When James Madison reminded the New Jerseyan that his theory of representation would be fatal to the pretensions of the small states, Paterson quickly retired from the fray.[30] If the other opponents of slavery failed to take up the banner, it was largely because they, too, had doubts as to the propriety of Paterson's understanding of the representative principle.

Like their brethren from across the waters, America's Whigs were inclined to suppose that the apportionment of representation should somehow reflect the distribution of wealth as well as that of population. Thus, Gouverneur Morris unwittingly provided a rationale for a mode of measurement he profoundly disliked when he reminded his fellow delegates of the Lockean contention that "property was the main object of Society. The savage State was more favorable to liberty than the Civilized; and sufficiently so to life. It was preferred by all men who had not acquired a taste for property; it was only renounced for the sake of property which could only be secured by the restraints of regular Government. . . . If property then was the main object of Govt. certainly it ought to be one measure of the influence due to those who were to be affected by the Governmt."[31] In replying to Morris, James Madison elaborated an understanding of the sources of wealth in a modern republic that showed just how deeply the American Founding Fathers were indebted to Locke's mentor Sir Francis Bacon. "It was said that Representation & taxation were to go together; that taxation & wealth ought to go together, that population and wealth were not measures of each other," he observed.

> He admitted that in different climates, under different forms of Govt. and in different stages of civilization the inference was perfectly just. He would admit that in no situation numbers of inhabitants were an accurate measure of wealth. He contended however that in the U. States it was sufficiently so for the object in contemplation. Altho' their climate varied considerably, yet as the Govts. the laws, and the manners of all were nearly the same, and intercourse between different parts perfectly free, population, industry, arts, and the value of labour, would constantly tend to equalize themselves. The value of labour, might be considered as the principal criterion of wealth and ability to support taxes; and this would find its level in different places where the intercourse should be easy & free, with as much certainty as the value of money or any other thing. Wherever labour would yield most, people would resort, till the competition should destroy the inequality. Hence it is that the people are constantly swarming from the more to the less populous places—from Europe to Am[eric]a from the Northn. & middle parts of the U.S. to the Southern & Western. They go where land is cheaper, because there labour is dearer.[32]

Madison's argument was effective because it reflected what had long since become the common opinion.

In late July 1776, when the Continental Congress first set out to frame a constitution for the newly independent nation, there had been a consensus that the size of the laboring population is a rough and ready measure of a community's wealth and therefore a useful yardstick for apportioning assessments. If the delegates eventually decided to base requisitions on an estimate of the value of the land, buildings, and improvements in each state, it was only because they could not agree on an equitable formula for counting slaves. Those representing the southern states insisted that free men were far more productive. Benjamin Harrison of Virginia suggested a compromise

grounded on the supposition that the labor of two slaves was roughly equal
to that of one free man, but the northern delegates thought his claim exaggerated and objected in principle to any arrangement that might encourage
the further importation of slaves.[33]

The three-fifths rule emerged in the Continental Congress years later, in
1783, as part of a compromise initially devised by James Madison, rejected
by the delegates, and then successfully revived by Alexander Hamilton. In
due course, it was presented to the nation as part of a proposed amendment
to the Articles of Confederation designed to provide the federal government
with a more dependable income. According to the notes kept by Madison,
even the opponents of the compromise were willing to concede that the "industry & ingenuity" of slaves "were below those of free men." Its proponents
contended that, because slaves had "no interest in their labor, they did as
little as possible, & omitted every exertion of thought requisite to facilitate &
expedite it."[34]

It says much about eighteenth-century American assumptions regarding
representation that, when southern delegates to the Philadelphia convention sought to have slaves counted as if free men for the apportionment of
representation, they deemed it necessary to ground their argument on the
premise, long denied by their fellow southerners in the Continental Congress, that America's black slaves were no less productive than her free white
laborers.[35] To make sense of the formula adopted by the convention for determining representation, one must pay careful attention to estimates of what
General Charles Cotesworth Pinckney of South Carolina later termed "the
productive labor of the inhabitants" of the various states.[36]

Were it not for subsequent developments, the ease with which the delegates to the federal convention initially reached a consensus regarding the
three-fifths rule would be decisive against Madison's contention that slavery
would be the root of sectional strife. Unfortunately, as events at the convention quickly demonstrated, the Virginian's worries were entirely justified.

III.ii.4

Not long after Madison first voiced his fears, the delegates from the lower
South made it clear that they would exact a high price for their adherence
to the proposed union. By that time, the first flush of revolutionary idealism
had passed. The citizens of Darien, Georgia, had fallen silent; Henry and
John Laurens had died; and though David Ramsay commanded considerable
respect in Charleston, South Carolina, he was far too closely linked with the
antislavery struggle to be elected a delegate to the convention.[37]

The first inkling of trouble came on 12 and 13 July 1787, when General Pinckney expressed alarm at the antislavery utterances of Paterson, Wilson, Morris, and King, and when Pinckney's fellow South Carolinian Pierce Butler muttered darkly that "the security the Southn. States want is that their negroes may not be taken from them which some gentlemen within or without doors, have a very good mind to do."[38] Ten days later, when the Committee of Detail was appointed, General Pinckney took up Butler's suggestion. At that time, he rose to remind "the Convention that if the Committee should fail to insert some security to the Southern States agst. an emancipation of slaves . . . he shd. be bound by duty to his State to vote agst. their Report." A little over a month later, he raised the issue again and reportedly pressed for the inclusion of "some provision" in the Constitution "in favor of property in slaves." The result was the so-called fugitive-slave clause which committed the free-soil states to the odious task of seizing and returning blacks who had escaped from bondage in the South.[39]

In late August, General Pinckney was finally able to extract this particular concession as a consequence of a compromise already reached regarding a related concern. On the sixth day of that month, when Pinckney's fellow South Carolinian John Rutledge presented the report of the Committee of Detail, the members of the convention had learned that security against emancipation was not the only and not the most troubling demand being made. The proposal placed before them included a provision stipulating that "no tax or duty shall be laid by the Legislature . . . on the migration or importation of such persons as the several States shall think proper to admit; nor shall such migration or importation be prohibited."[40] It is a sign of the general embarrassment which slavery occasioned that Rutledge and the other committee members deemed it prudent to resort to circumlocution. Within the confines of South Carolina's House of Representatives, Charles Cotesworth Pinckney might dismiss antislavery sentiment as "the religious and political prejudices of the Eastern and Middle States," and an opponent of the Constitution might—without fear of incurring contempt—even try to justify the slave "trade . . . on the principles of religion, humanity and justice," contending that "to translate a set of human beings from a bad country to a better, was fulfilling every part of these principles."[41] But in 1787 and for a long time thereafter, such sentiments were rarely voiced anywhere in America. Certainly, no one was prepared to argue in a national forum that slavery was actually a positive good. In fact, James Madison spoke for nearly everyone present at the federal convention and for their immediate successors in the generation of statesmen that followed when he indicated that he for one "thought it wrong to admit in the Constitution the idea that there could be property in men."[42] But, of course, though shame affected the language of the report prepared by the Committee of Detail, it did nothing to alter its substance. Despite the committee's reliance on euphemism in wording the pertinent clause, its purpose was clear to everyone present: the national government was to be prevented from outlawing and even taxing the importation of slaves from abroad.[43]

Two days after Rutledge presented the committee's report, the time came for discussing the proposed mode of determining representation in the lower house. It is our good fortune that James Madison kept careful and extensive notes of the convention debates.[44] Soon after the issue came up, Rufus King of Massachusetts renewed his objections to "the admission of slaves into the rule of Representation." He made it clear that "he never could agree to let them be imported without limitation & then be represented in the Natl. Legislature." Later in the discussion, Gouverneur Morris of Pennsylvania moved that only the free inhabitants of the states be counted in determining representation and then explained his reasoning in some detail.

> He never would concur in upholding domestic slavery. It was a nefarious institution. . . . The admission of slaves into the Representation when fairly explained comes to this: that the inhabitant of Georgia and S. C. who goes to the Coast of Africa, and in defiance of the most sacred laws of humanity tears away his fellow creatures from their dearest connections & dam‹n›s them to the most cruel bondages, shall have more votes in a Govt. instituted for protection of the rights of mankind, than the Citizen of Pa or N. Jersey who views with a laudable horror, so nefarious a practice. He would add that Domestic slavery is the most prominent feature in the aristocratic countenance of the proposed Constitution. The vassalage of the poor has ever been the favorite offspring of Aristocracy. And What is the proposed compensation to the Northern States for a sacrifice of every principle of right, of every impulse of humanity. They are to bind themselves to march their militia for the defence of the S. States; for their defence agst those very slaves of whom they complain.

Morris's motion was easily defeated. No one was eager to reopen the vexed question of representation, and not even Pennsylvania was prepared to fight the issue posed by slavery on the ground chosen by Morris.[45] There was, however, other ground on which to dispute, and the initial setback to the opponents of slavery did nothing to end the debate.

On 21 August, when the particular provision protecting the slave trade came up for discussion, the dispute erupted once again. Luther Martin of Maryland promptly rose to argue for deleting the clause, first contending that the slave trade was prejudicial to the interests of the free states and then adding that "it was inconsistent with the principles of the revolution and dishonorable to the American character to have such a feature in the Constitution."[46] The next day, George Mason, author of the Virginia Declaration of Rights and a slaveowner himself, reaffirmed Martin's objections, pointing first to the increased danger of insurrection and then drawing attention to what might transpire in the long run. James Madison summarized his intervention as follows:

> Maryland and Virginia . . . had already prohibited the importation of slaves expressly. N. Carolina had done the same in substance. All this would be in vain if S. Carolina & Georgia be at liberty to import. The Western people are already calling out for slaves for their new lands; and will fill that Country with slaves if they can be got thro' S. Carolina & Georgia. Slavery discourages arts & manufactures. The poor despise labor when performed by slaves. They prevent the immigration of Whites, who really enrich & strengthen a Country. They produce the most pernicious effect on manners. Every master of slaves is born a petty tyrant. They bring the judgment of heaven on a Country. As nations can not be rewarded or punished in the next world they must be in this. By an inevitable chain of causes & effects providence punishes national sins, by national calamities. . . . He held it essential in every point of view, that the Genl. Govt. should have power to prevent the increase of slavery.[47]

As both Martin and Mason were well aware, the logic of their arguments pointed beyond curbing importation from abroad to something far more radical: to outlawing the interstate traffic in slaves and to emancipation itself.[48]

On these matters, however, the two men said nothing at the time—and probably for good reason. Though they themselves would have preferred that slavery be placed on the road to ultimate extinction, they both represented states that possessed an overabundance of slaves, that had stopped short of granting these slaves their freedom, and that allowed the slaves' masters to sell them to men from outside the state. The slaveholders of Maryland and Virginia may well have approved of closing the African slave trade on moral grounds, but this gesture cost them nothing: suppressing the transatlantic traffic was, in fact, very much in their interest. Those who had more slaves than they needed and who were prepared to sell them to men from Georgia, South Carolina, or the territories in the West were perfectly happy to see the rise in price which the elimination of competition would make inevitable. Abolition was another matter. There is every reason to suppose that the citizens of Maryland and Virginia would have refused to ratify a constitution that committed the central administration to depriving them of a species of property which they had thus far been unwilling to give up themselves. Not even George Mason was prepared to accept federal interference in that delicate matter. In fact, he thought the fugitive-slave clause insufficient. Later, at the Virginia Ratifying Convention, when he rehearsed his reasons for opposing the Constitution, Mason included the fact that there was no provision within the document explicitly barring an emancipation effected by the intervention of the national government.[49] One can hardly suppose that slaveholders so protective of their legal rights to property in human beings would have been ready to accept severe limitations on their capacity to market their chattels of a sort that would cause these to decline precipitously in value.[50]

The objections to the transatlantic slave trade raised by Luther Martin and George Mason drew a particularly spirited response from the delegates representing South Carolina. These representatives not only drew attention to the manner in which closing that traffic favored the less than palatable economic interests of their neighbors in the upper South; they resorted to threats. To the evident horror of many of those from the other states, the South Carolinians made their adherence to the cause of the Union conditional upon acceptance of their demand that the slave trade be kept open. Rutledge was the most belligerent. He contended that "religion & humanity had nothing to do with this question—Interest alone is the governing principle with Nations—The true question at present is whether the Southn. States shall or shall not be parties to the Union." Charles Pinckney agreed. "South Carolina can never receive the plan if it prohibits the slave trade," he explained to his fellow delegates. "In every proposed extension of the powers of Congress, that State has expressly & watchfully excepted that of meddling with the importation of negroes."[51]

Though more vehement than the other delegates from the lower South, the South Carolinians were not alone. Hugh Williamson of North Carolina was on record as a "principled" opponent of slavery.[52] He represented a state that imposed a substantial, almost punitive tax on the importation of slaves from abroad and then multiplied that tax tenfold when applying it to slaves brought in from American states that allowed manumission.[53] But, this notwithstanding, he too chimed in: "He thought that the S. States could not be members of the Union if the clause should be rejected." Abraham Baldwin of Georgia agreed. His state had always been suspicious of the centralizing tendencies of the federal government. "From this it might be understood in what light she would view an attempt to abridge one of her favorite prerogatives." With characteristic bluntness, Rutledge summed up the situation when he concluded that "if the Convention thinks that N. C; S. C. & Georgia will ever agree to the plan, unless their right to import slaves be untouched, the expectation is vain. The people of those States will never be such fools as to give up so important an interest." [54]

In the end, of course, the delegates from the lower South were prepared to compromise—particularly after Edmund Randolph of Virginia explained to them "the dilemma to which the Convention was exposed." He could himself "never agree to the clause as it stands. He wd. sooner risk the constitution." And he was by no means alone. If the passage was left untouched, he insisted, "it would revolt the Quakers, the Methodists, and many others in the States having no slaves." But if the clause was deleted, he acknowledged, "two States might be lost to the Union." If, then, there was to be an Union at all, it would be necessary to find "some middle ground." Eventually, the delegates from Georgia and South Carolina agreed to what Gouverneur Morris accurately described as "a bargain among the Northern & Southern States." [55] In return for a clause stipulating that the federal government could not close the slave trade for twenty years, the states of the lower South agreed to accept a moderate tariff on the import of slaves and to allow Congress to enact by majority vote navigation acts and other commercial regulations favorable to the merchants of the Northeast.[56]

To make this compromise palatable, its advocates employed the carrot as well as the stick. Two of the men from the Lower South even made attempts to pacify those who found slavery utterly offensive. Baldwin indicated that it was probable that Georgia would herself "put a stop to the evil" traffic in human flesh, and Charles Pinckney suggested that South Carolina also, if left alone, would eventually outlaw importation on her own. He even expressed a willingness to vote for such a measure himself. To the more perceptive, however, these claims must have seemed disingenuous. When pressed, General Pinckney was forced to admit that South Carolina would not close the trade "in any short time" and even then would do so "only . . . occasionally as she now does." And Baldwin supported his conjecture in a bizarre fashion—by pointing to the existence of a religious sect "which he said was a respectable class of people, who carryed their ethics beyond the mere *equality of men*, extending their humanity to the claims of the whole animal creation." In any case, earlier in the debate that day, Charles Pinckney had defended the institution of slavery itself. "If slavery be wrong," the South Carolinian argued, "it is justified by the example of all the world." Madison reports that "he cited the case of Greece Rome & other antient States; the sanction given by France England, Holland & other modern States." "In all ages," Pinckney claimed, "one half of mankind have been slaves." He even "contended that the importation of slaves would be for the interest of the whole Union. The more slaves, the more produce to employ the carrying trade; The more consumption also, and the more of this, the more of revenue for the common treasury."[57]

The discussion of the slave trade opened a wound. Madison's notes suggest that the debate became quite heated. At one point, Oliver Ellsworth of Connecticut intervened in the discussion to urge caution. In the process, he took occasion to remind his fellow delegates that there were many abroad within the various states who were vigorously opposed to the project of consolidation which they were themselves engaged in. "This widening of opinions has a threatening aspect," he told the convention. Failure to "agree on this middle & moderate ground" would cause the loss of "two States with such others as may be disposed to stand aloof," and the states which did remain outside the Union would "fly into a variety of shapes & directions, and most probably into several confederations and not without bloodshed." Ellsworth feared that the dispute would provoke a dissolution of the Union, and he depicted a future fraught with dire consequences if that came to pass.[58]

He may well have been right. When the convention finally adjourned, ratification was by no means a foregone conclusion. Even as things stood, in Virginia and in the Carolinas, the Constitution's opponents were numerous and highly influential.[59] Moreover, in their enthusiasm for slavery and for the slave trade in particular, upcountry South Carolinians were considerably more vehement than the tidewater aristocrats who represented them at the federal convention.[60] Of course, Rutledge and his colleagues may have been bluffing. British attacks during the Revolutionary War had made them acutely aware of the military weakness of the southern states, and men like General Pinckney feared that, without help from the North, they would not be able to defend themselves.[61] But in judging what they said at the convention, one must also keep in mind that Rutledge and his supporters were southerners bound by a code of honor. On the question of the slave trade, they had thrown down the gauntlet, and they could be expected to make good on their threats.[62] In these circumstances, it is not hard to imagine the delegates from South Carolina, from Georgia, and even from North Carolina walking out of the convention; and it is not difficult to reconstruct the various arguments by which they might have persuaded their fellow citizens, and in time those of Virginia and Maryland as well, that—despite all the risks—the interests of the South would best be served by forming a separate confederation. What Supreme Court Justice Joseph Story would later assert concerning the fugitive-slave clause was arguably true also for the provision which delayed the abolition of the transatlantic slave trade: it may well have "constituted a fundamental article, without the adoption of which the Union could not have been formed." [63]

III.ii.5

Of course, not all of the delegates to the federal convention feared that slavery would increase in strength and spread to the West. Roger Sherman of Connecticut thought it "expedient to have as few objections as possible to the proposed scheme of Government" and therefore urged that the necessary concessions be made to South Carolina and Georgia. He could be conciliatory because he expected slavery, if left alone, to wither away. At one point, "he observed that the abolition of slavery seemed to be going on in the U. S. & that the good sense of the several States would probably by degrees compleat it." Oliver Ellsworth agreed. Like nearly all of his countrymen, he thought slavery economically inefficient. "As population increases," he contended, "poor laborers will be so plenty as to render slaves useless. Slavery in time will not be a speck in our Country." [64]

It is hard not to sympathize with the awkward attempt of the Framers to finesse a question that no one knew how to address. [65] In just a few short years, the Revolution had wrought a profound transformation of sentiment on the question of slavery. Few of the Americans who had witnessed the change were prepared to quarrel with the anonymous advocate of ratification who counseled patience, writing that the Constitution "provides for the interest of the Southern States, and, at the same time, manifests to the world that slavery is inconsistent with the views and sentiments of this country, which error will be reformed as soon as it can be done consistent with the interest of the people." [66] In New England, where there had never been many slaves, abolition had been easy. But, in the South, as everyone realized, the situation was far more complicated.

To describe that situation, Thomas Jefferson would later turn to the rhetoric of ancient Greece and Rome, appropriating Pericles' description of Athens's plight as the tyrannical ruler over an Aegean empire and adding as spice a proverb that the emperor Tiberius is said to have employed in venting his frustration at his inability to give up power and restore the Roman republic. "We have the wolf by the ears," the Virginian observed, "and we can neither hold him, nor safely let him go. Justice is in one scale, and self-preservation in the other." [67] Hardly anyone in America believed that it would be possible for a multiracial polity to long endure. It was taken for granted that the deep-seated racial prejudices of the white citizens, coupled with the legitimate resentment of the recently emancipated slaves, would, where the latter were sufficiently numerous, inevitably give rise to armed conflict between the two. And though the principles of the American Revolution ruled out the proposition that one might legitimately hold property in another human being, they placed no limits on what one might do when one's own preservation hung in the balance. The Virginian St. George Tucker spoke for Jefferson, Madison, and nearly all of the southern opponents of slavery when, in the mid-1790s, he observed, "The calamities which have lately spread like a contagion through the West India Islands afford a solemn warning to us of the dangerous predicament in which we stand, whether we persist in the now perhaps unavoidable course entailed upon us by our ancestors, or, copying after the liberal sentiments of the national convention of France, endeavour to do justice to the rights of human nature, and to banish deep-rooted, nay, almost innate, prejudices." And Tucker articulated their unspoken fears when he added that "the latter is a task, perhaps, beyond the power of human nature to accomplish."[68]

Of course, arguments of the sort advanced by Tucker, Jefferson, Madison, and the others who supported gradual emancipation only in conjunction with a program of colonization are rendered suspect by the fact that they were so obviously self-serving.[69] When joined with the fact that very few freedmen were willing to leave the only country that they had ever known, these arguments allowed southern planters to give lip service to the rights of man without having to incur the inconveniences that would have been occasioned by an immediate emancipation of their own slaves. And yet it is striking just how rarely the charge of hypocrisy was leveled. The Bostonian James Sullivan found Tucker's case "unanswerable," and John Adams agreed. "What is justice?" he asked. "Justice to the negroes would require that they should not be abandoned by their masters and turned loose upon a world in which they have no capacity to procure even a subsistence. What would become of the old? the young? the infirm? Justice to the world, too, would forbid that such numbers should be turn'd out to live by violence, by theft, or fraud." Adams could think of "no better expedient . . . than to prohibit the importation of new negroes, and soften the severity of the condition of old ones, as much as possible, until the increasing population of the country shall have multiplied the whites to such a superiority of numbers that the blacks may be liberated by degrees, with the consent both of master and servant."[70] No one quibbled with Noah Webster in 1787 when, in the guise of "A Citizen of America," he reminded his compatriots that "an immediate abolition of slavery would bring ruin upon the whites, and misery upon the blacks, in the southern states."[71] At that time, and for some while thereafter, nearly all Americans were willing to make allowances for their southern brethren, and few saw any point in risking the Union over a dispute concerning what was, after all, a dying institution.

Thomas Dawes was typical. "What could the Convention do more?" he asked the delegates to the Massachusetts Ratifying Convention. "The members of the Southern States, like ourselves, have *their* prejudices. It would not do to abolish slavery by an act of Congress, in a moment, and so destroy what our Southern brethren consider as property. But we may say, that, although slavery is not smitten by an apoplexy, yet it has received a mortal wound, and will die of a consumption." Like nearly all of the Constitution's supporters, the Baptist leader Isaac Backus was willing to look on the bright side: he rejoiced that some provision had been made for bringing the slave trade to an end and then cited Dawes's conclusion with approval.[72]

Some of the Constitution's proponents, particularly in Pennsylvania, were even prepared to argue against the Anti-Federalists that article 1, section 9, of the Constitution actually set a term of twenty years for the institution of slavery itself.[73] At least one prominent citizen of Georgia—Lachlan McIntosh of Darien—was inclined to oppose an unconditional ratification on the supposition that they might well be right.[74] The conviction shared by these men may seem absurd on the face of it; but, as Daniel Webster pointed out in the great speech he delivered in the United States Senate on 7 March 1850, it was easy in 1787 to suppose that closing the transatlantic trade would itself stop the spread and growth of slavery and thereby prepare the way for its ultimate extinction.[75] At the time, nearly everyone assumed that no slave population could ever reproduce itself. In the absence of an accurate census, very few Americans—and almost no one outside the upper South—recognized that, well before the middle of the century, the slave population in Virginia had begun to defy reigning dogma and not only reproduce itself but also grow in size through natural increase.[76] And even those who suspected the truth failed to grasp its full import.[77] In his *Notes on the State of Virginia*, Thomas Jefferson observed that "under the mild treatment our slaves experience, and their wholesome, though coarse, food, this blot in our country increases as fast, or faster, than the whites." Yet, in the very same paragraph, he celebrated the fact that the first meeting of the Virginia assembly under republican auspices had "passed a law for the perpetual prohibition of the importation of slaves" by concluding that "this will in some measure stop the increase of this great political and moral evil."[78] Prior to 1808, the transatlantic trade brought roughly four hundred thousand slaves to the American shores. In 1787, no one even imagined that by 1860 there would be four million slaves in the South.[79]

But, while no one at the time foresaw that the natural process of reproduction would make possible an interstate traffic sufficient to allow slavery to spread and grow in importance, there were delegates who were far from confident that the institution would quickly or easily disappear. George Mason made his expectations clear during the debates in Philadelphia; Luther Martin took up the theme later, shortly after the convention had adjourned, in a speech that he delivered to the Maryland legislature at the end of November 1787. "I think there is great reason to believe," he observed, "that if the importation of slaves is permitted until the year eighteen hundred and eight, it will not be prohibited afterwards: At *this time* we do not generally hold this commerce in so *great* abhorrence as we have done—When our liberties were at stake, we *warmly* felt for the *common rights of men*—The danger being thought to be past, which threatened ourselves, we are daily growing *more insensible* to those rights." He even feared that the states which had passed laws restraining or prohibiting the traffic would reverse their policy since "the odium attending it will be greatly effaced by the sanction which is given to it in the general government."[80] A good many of the men attending the federal convention must have shared the worries voiced first by Mason and developed later by Martin.[81] In the end, to be sure, the compromise passed—but only because New England was almost desperate in its eagerness to secure a privileged position for its shipping. New Jersey, Pennsylvania, Delaware, and Virginia voted against the bargain.[82]

James Madison was torn. He shared Oliver Ellsworth's fears that failure to appease Georgia and South Carolina would have dire consequences without similarly sharing the Connecticut Yankee's confidence that slavery would soon die out on its own. At Philadelphia, Madison may have been prepared to see the slave trade kept open until 1800, but he vigorously opposed the extension to 1808. On the one hand, there were principles at stake. "So long a term," he told the delegates, "will be more dishonorable to the National character than to say nothing about it in the Constitution."[83] On the other hand, one had to ponder the consequences for the consolidation of the slave interest in the lower South and for its extension to the West.

In 1784, the Continental Congress had come within an ace of adopting an ordinance, proposed by Thomas Jefferson, that would have banned slavery from the entire national domain. At that time, as Madison knew, the North had been unanimous in favoring the ban; all but two of the southern delegates present had voted against it; and the measure had failed solely because of the absence due to illness of a single New Jersey congressman.[84] The consequences were perfectly evident at the time. "The voice of a single individual . . . would have prevented this abominable crime from spreading itself

over the country," Jefferson lamented. "Thus we see the fate of millions unborn hanging on the tongue of one man, and heaven was silent in that awful
moment!"[85] Three years after the defeat of Jefferson's proposal, while the
Philadelphia convention was meeting, Congress enacted legislation including the ban (this time with firm southern support), but the ordinance then
adopted applied only to those territories north of the Ohio River.[86] The implications were clear, and George Mason was not alone in noting the danger.
Very few of the Framers were prepared to join James Wilson in supposing
that the southern states would allow the new Congress to ban slavery in
the region to the south of that river.[87] Kentucky remained a part of Virginia,
and it was widely understood that she would enter the Union without ever
coming under national jurisdiction. North Carolina had evidenced a willingness to turn over to the nation the land she claimed in the West—but only
on condition that the federal government refrain from enacting regulations
tending to the emancipation of slaves.[88] By 1787, the servile population of the
West was no longer negligible. If the transatlantic traffic remained open, it
could be foreseen that slavery would grow rapidly not only in Virginia's Kentucky region but also in the considerable territory that North Carolina, South
Carolina, and Georgia were expected to cede to the national domain—and
eventually that would mean a great increase in the number of slave states. As
Madison put it during the convention debates, "Twenty years will produce
all the mischief that can be apprehended from the liberty to import slaves."[89]

Of course, once the bargain was sealed, the young statesman became its
defender.[90] "Great as the evil is," he later reminded the delegates to the
Virginia Ratifying Convention, "a dismemberment of the Union would be
worse. If those states should disunite from the other states for not indulg-
ing them in the temporary continuance of this traffic, they might solicit and
obtain aid from foreign powers."[91] If Madison lent his name to the cause
of the Union and remained sanguine about its future despite his conviction
that the continued existence of slavery and the likelihood of its expansion in
the West would contribute significantly to sectional strife, it was clearly not
because he supposed that the rough balance of forces existing in 1787 was
stable. Nor is it sensible to suppose that he believed that any such balance
could be adequate indefinitely as a deterrent to conflict. History had taught
him that, in the long run, "governments of dissimilar principles and forms"
have far more trouble cooperating in "a federal coalition of any sort, than
those of a kindred nature."[92] He was no stranger to the bitter character which
disputes over matters of principle could easily assume; he had lived through
the Revolutionary War. If, in 1787, Madison preserved his equanimity and
even evidenced a certain confidence, it was probably because he was con-

vinced that the means were available for reducing the tension and the danger over time. Apart from geographical extension, there was another, far more effective way to promote economic diversity and to generate petty factions; and though polemical considerations ruled out his laying great stress on it in *The Federalist*, Madison deemed it to be of greater importance in the long run than geographical extension itself. To grasp what was involved in this matter, we will need to consider the import of a clause of the American Constitution that has no obvious relation to the problem of slavery at all.

III.ii.6

In and of itself, as we have seen, the decision to embed the patent system within the organic law of the United States was of profound importance, since it was symptomatic both of the American commitment to Bacon's scientific and technological project and of the American celebration of the dignity of labor. That same decision deserves detailed discussion in this context for another reason: for it had serious implications for the actual working of the American political regime and, in particular, for the manner in which it would cope with the problem of faction. Alexander Hamilton had remarked on "the adventurous spirit, which distinguishes the commercial character of America." In keeping with his colleagues' enthusiasm for economic and technological development, he added that

> the prosperity of commerce is now perceived and acknowledged, by all enlightened statesmen to be the most useful as well as the most productive source of national wealth; and has accordingly become a primary object of their political cares. By multiplying the means of gratification, by promoting the introduction and circulation of the precious metals, those darling objects of human avarice and enterprise, it serves to vivify and invigorate the channels of industry, and to make them flow with greater activity and copiousness. The assiduous merchant, the laborious husbandman, the active mechanic, and the industrious manufacturer, all orders of men, look forward with eager expectation and growing alacrity to this pleasing reward of their toils.[93]

James Madison agreed. In one passage, he described the Union as "the guardian of our commerce and other common interests"; in another, he defined "the objects of federal legislation" as "commerce, taxation, and the militia," adding later that the second of these three objects would "consist, in a great measure, of duties which will be involved in the regulation of commerce."[94]

Far more important: Madison fully understood and welcomed the political side effects of the encouragement of commerce and technology. Years before, David Hume had argued that "progress in the arts" was "favorable to liberty" and had "a natural tendency to preserve, if not produce a free government."

> Where luxury nourishes commerce and industry, the peasants, by a proper cultivation of the land, become rich and independent; while the tradesmen and merchants acquire a share of the property, and draw authority and consideration to that middling rank of men, who are the best and firmest basis of public liberty. These submit not to slavery, like the peasants, from poverty and meanness of spirit; and having no hopes of tyrannizing over others, like the barons, they are not tempted, for the sake of that gratification, to submit to the tyranny of their sovereign. They covet equal laws, which may secure their property, and preserve them from monarchical, as well as aristocratical tyranny.

At the same time, he contended, commerce and manufactures promote "laws, order, police, discipline," soften "the tempers of men," and beget "mildness and moderation." Where the citizen is beset with concern regarding the incremental improvement of his personal well-being, "factions are then less inveterate, revolutions less tragical, authority less severe, and seditions less frequent."[95]

Madison accepted much, if not all, of this.[96] The more thoughtful among his contemporaries generally did.[97] His good friend Thomas Jefferson applauded technological progress not only because it relieved human suffering but also because "the arts and sciences" had "advanced gradually thro' all the 16th. 17th. and 18th. centuries, softening and correcting the manners and morals of man," and because "their natural effect" was, "by illuminating public opinion, to erect it into a Censor, before which the most exalted tremble for their future, as well as present fame." Even Alexander Hamilton was prepared to concede "the softening and humanizing influence of Commerce."[98] Lincoln merely carried Jefferson's arguments to their logical conclusion when he later linked "the art of invention" and the attendant "*habit* of observation and reflection" with the revolution that overthrew that "slavery of the mind" which had hitherto rendered "the great mass of men . . . utterly unconscious, that their *conditions*, or their *minds* were capable of improvement," willing to look "upon the educated few as superior beings," and persuaded that they were themselves "naturally incapable of rising to equality."[99] The heirs of the Enlightenment recognized that, by emancipating the mind, progress in the arts prepared the way for—though it did not guarantee—the emancipation of mankind.

James Madison grasped all of this, and something else besides. He discerned that trade and industry could do more than merely soften the force of religious enthusiasm and the spirited passions, and he recognized that the marriage of commerce and science might do more than simply promote the independence of condition and the freedom of thought prerequisite for the realization and defense of political equality. Behind his confidence in the new regime's capacity to withstand, in the long run, the turbulence of political storms lay the conviction that the emergence of capitalism, already visible in Britain, would engender economic specialization on a scale hitherto hardly imagined—and thereby mute the strains of sectional strife by multiplying the number of factions *within* each of the many localities.[100] "At present," he acknowledged, "some of the States are little more than a society of husbandmen. Few of them have made much progress in those branches of industry, which give a variety and complexity to the affairs of a nation." But this would change. Such economic and technological progress would eventually "in all of them be the fruits of a more advanced population." Even within a narrowly circumscribed district, the attendant variety and complexity would blunt class antipathy, and in time the divers industries borne from the marriage of trade and technology would reduce, if not entirely efface, the distinctiveness of the states and the regions.[101]

III.ii.7

In 1787, that distinctiveness was marked—and not only by the presence of slavery. Prior to the struggle for independence, the British colonies in North America had had remarkably little in common. Communications were primitive: the roads were abysmal and unguarded, and, even by sea, the direct trade between these neighboring outposts of European civilization was negligible. Most of their commerce was with their common metropolis. It should not be surprising that only a handful of the delegates who convened in September 1774 at the First Continental Congress had ever before met. Many of them had visited London; some had spent a good many years in England; but few had ever seen Philadelphia, then the second-largest city under British dominion.[102]

This state of affairs was by no means fortuitous. Divide and rule: that had been the policy of Britain, and it had had its effect. There is no clearer statement of the principles of British administration than the words penned in the 1760s by Thomas Pownall, once the royal governor of the Massachusetts Bay Colony:

Great Britain . . . must be the center of attraction to which these colonies, in the administration of every power of their government, in the
exercise of their judicial powers, in the execution of their laws, and in
every operation of their trade, must tend. . . . The different manner in
which they were settled, the different modes under which they live, the
different forms of charters, grants and frame of government which they
possess, the various principles of repulsion that these create, the different interests which they actuate, the religious interests by which they
are actuated, the rivalship and jealousies which arise from hence, and
the impracticability, if not impossibility of reconciling and accommodating these incompatible ideas and claims, will keep the several provinces
and colonies perpetually independent of, and unconnected with each
other, and dependent on the mother country.[103]

Pownall's forecast proved wrong, but his statement of the obstacles to colonial cooperation is borne out by a letter John Adams wrote from the Continental Congress. "Here," he observed, "is a diversity of religions, educations,
manners, [and] interests, such as it would seem almost impossible to unite
in one plan of conduct."[104]

It took colossal stupidity on the part of the British government to drive
the Puritans of Massachusetts, the Quakers of Pennsylvania, the Catholics
of Maryland, and the tepidly religious Anglicans of Virginia to make common cause against their royal master. In 1760, Benjamin Franklin had judged
such a "union" inconceivable unless inspired by "the most grievous tyranny
and oppression." The colonies "are not only under different governors," he
explained. They "have different forms of government, different laws, different interests, and some of them different religious persuasions and different
manners. Their jealousy of each other is so great that however necessary an
union of the colonies has long been, for their common defense and security
against their enemies, and how sensible soever each colony has been of that
necessity, yet they have never been able to effect such an union among themselves, nor even to agree in requesting the mother country to establish it for
them."[105] A quarter of a century later, Americans had occasion to ponder
anew the arguments which Franklin had advanced.[106] Though their leaders
had once pledged to each other their lives, their fortunes, and their sacred
honor in a struggle against what they took to be intolerable tyranny and oppression, the citizens of the United States still had little but the experience of
the Revolution to hold them together.[107]

In truth, the fears so eloquently expressed by James Monroe and the
pseudonymous Cato were far from foolish. The fledgling republic was "a

house divided against itself." As Madison recognized, there was a chance—and not a small chance—that the Union would collapse. The different institutions and customs inherited by states that had once been independently chartered colonies settled by misfits of various stripes, by merchant adventurers, and by mutually antagonistic sects of religious refugees spawned distrust and divided the infant nation. Because they were economically underdeveloped, James Madison observed, the former colonies, taken each alone, had "interests but little diversified." Within "a single State," the "existing laws" were "uniform throughout the State," and "the general affairs of the State," because they lay "within a small compass," exhibited relative simplicity. But this was not true of the nation as a whole. "The great theatre of the United States presents a very different scene," he noted. "The laws are so far from being uniform, that they vary in every State; whilst the public affairs of the Union are spread throughout a very extensive region, and are extremely diversified by the local affairs connected with them." As a consequence, it had not been easy to secure cooperation between the states. During the struggle with Britain, the specter of defeat had been a deterrent to division; but, in the years after, the Union had been little more than what the Articles of Confederation called "a firm league of friendship," if even that. In Congress, boundary disputes and taxation had occasioned incessant squabbling—and even when a compromise had been reached on the latter, individual states had at times refused to collect the imposts demanded.[108]

The framers of the American Constitution believed that the passage of years would greatly alter the circumstances which caused so much division. "All these difficulties," Madison wrote, "will by degrees be very much diminished. . . . The increased intercourse among those of different States will contribute not a little to diffuse a mutual knowledge of their affairs, as this again will contribute to a general assimilation of their manners and laws." The chief cause of that intercourse would be commerce; and as technological and economic development multiplied the number of factions within each of the individual states, it would render them, in their internal divisions, materially alike. "On the comparative situation of the different states," Madison observed, "the changes of time . . . will have an assimilating effect. The effect of time on the internal affairs of the states taken singly, will be just the contrary."[109]

Time would have this effect even in the South. "At the expiration of twenty-five years hence," Madison told the Virginia Ratifying Convention, "I conceive that in every part of the United States, there will be as great a population as there is now in the settled parts." That would have profound implications, for the need to support so large a population would, then, "compel" even the Virginians and their neighbors farther south "to recur to manufactures." "We see already," Madison noted, "that in the most populous parts of the union, and where there is but a medium, manufactures are beginning to be established." In judging the Constitution, the delegates should keep one fact firmly in mind: "When we are preparing a government for perpetuity, we ought to found it on permanent principles and not on those of a temporary nature."[110]

Madison hinted at, but never spelled out in precise detail, the consequences of these changes for the system of slavery. Excessive candor might have been impolitic; ratification was by no means a foregone conclusion in Virginia. For this reason, the elaboration of the argument was left to those who came after—to men like George Tucker, who was for a short time a congressman and, then, at the invitation of Jefferson and Madison, became professor of moral philosophy and political economy at the University of Virginia.[111] Madison could afford to be reticent in 1787 precisely because he thought future developments clear; decisive action on his part was not required. Step by step, as the population grew and the economy changed character, the South would free itself from its abject dependence on tobacco, cotton, and rice—crops particularly well suited to cultivation with the aid of slaves.[112] The closing of the slave trade in 1808 would force the industrious and the frugal to abandon what was, in any case, an inefficient system and to turn to free labor as it became increasingly plentiful. In this fashion, the importance of slavery would slowly decline. Then, when circumstances became more propitious, it might just be possible to effect in Virginia and North Carolina and even in South Carolina and Georgia a gradual emancipation on the lines laid out already in 1787 by many of the states in the North. Madison could take consolation from the fact that, in 1787, almost no southerners were prepared to argue that slavery was a positive good, and many, if not most, were inclined to think it a curse.[113]

In 1785, not long after the failure of his attempt to introduce gradual emancipation in his native state, Madison's close friend Thomas Jefferson published his *Notes on the State of Virginia*. There, he predicted ultimate victory. "I think a change already perceptible, since the origin of the present revolution," he wrote. "The spirit of the master is abating, that of the slave rising from the dust, his condition mollifying, the way I hope preparing, under the auspices of heaven, for a total emancipation, and that this is disposed, in the order of events, to be with the consent of the masters, rather than by their extirpation."[114] Madison shared his friend's hopes from the beginning, and he never gave up. In 1816, he joined with John Marshall and Henry Clay in founding the American Colonization Society. When he died in 1836, he was its president. For the better part of twenty years, he had been an advocate of the federal government's using the proceeds from the sale of western lands to smooth the transition by making voluntary emancipation followed by enforced colonization safe, easy, and perhaps even profitable for the slaveholders of the South.[115]

In *The Federalist*, Madison made his observations regarding the long-term social and political effects of commercial intercourse and technological development only in passing. It would have been imprudent to direct too much attention to a process of gradual assimilation likely to be profoundly disturbing to those partisans of the Union who were, at the same time, deeply attached to the peculiar character and customs of their local communities. Indeed, brief though they were, Madison's remarks may have been in danger of having precisely this effect. This would certainly help explain why Alexander Hamilton raised the issue once again, taking great care to qualify his colleague's more general claims. As the New Yorker put it, "There is sufficient diversity in the state of property, in the genius, manners, and habits of the people of the different parts of the union to occasion a material diversity of disposition in their representatives towards the different ranks and conditions in society. And though an intimate intercourse under the same government will promote a gradual assimilation, of temper and sentiment, yet there are causes as well physical as moral, which may in a greater or less degree permanently nourish different propensities and inclinations in this particular."[116] Apparently, no one was greatly worried that the ineradicable residue of the distinctiveness of the individual states would pose any insuperable problem in the long run. Once reduced, these local and regional differences would presumably contribute to that diversity required for the proper functioning of the Union without in any way threatening its continued existence. Though ultimately in tension with each other, the forces generated by inherited differences and those spawned by the new capitalist order could be made to serve the same salutary function. The world's first technologically dynamic, unabashedly modern, fully commercial, and purely republican regime was to be a nation of states.

III.ii.8

In the end, of course, the authors of *The Federalist* proved overconfident. As it turned out, the commercial spirit was inadequate fully to dissipate the force of the passions aroused by differences of opinion and fundamental disagreements of principle. Hamilton, Madison, and Jay failed to see that permanently organized political parties—operating within a party system characterized by party government and formed opposition—would be needed to mediate the never-ending clash of opinions and of interests;[117] and at the same time, they radically underestimated the recalcitrance of the tensions dividing the North from the South. Of the three men who concealed themselves under the guise of Publius, not one lived to see the great struggle which some would call the War between the States; but Hamilton and Madison, much to their mutual dismay, found themselves locked in bitter, partisan combat within a few short years of their literary collaboration,[118] and the Virginian lived long enough to recognize that the sections would not soon become similar and even to foresee that the failure of his strategy might mean the coming of civil war.[119]

When the agitation aroused by the suggestion that Missouri be admitted to the Union only on condition that it institute a program of gradual emancipation came to Madison's notice, he immediately grasped the danger that lay ahead. In April 1820, Jefferson wrote to a correspondent that "this momentous question, like a fire-bell in the night, awakened and filled me with terror. I considered it at once as the knell of the Union. It is hushed, indeed, for the moment. But this is a reprieve only, not a final sentence. A geographical line, coinciding with a marked principle, moral and political, once conceived and held up to the angry passions of men, will never be obliterated, and every new irritation will mark it deeper and deeper."[120] Jefferson's letter, because it is almost apocalyptic in tone, is often quoted. Less often do scholars note that five months before Jefferson penned these memorable words, Madison wrote to a correspondent in a less strident, but perhaps even more prophetic fashion. He first reported that the dispute filled him "with no slight anxiety." Then, he explained what it might entail: "Parties under some denominations or other must always be expected in a Gov! as free as ours. When the individuals belonging to them are intermingled in every part of the whole Country, they strengthen the Union of the Whole, while they divide every part. Should a State of parties arise, founded on geographical boundaries and other Physical & permanent distinctions which happen to coincide with them, what is to controul those great repulsive Masses from awful shocks agst each other?"[121] By 1819, for those prepared to read it, the handwriting was already visible on the wall.

More than thirty years had gone by since Madison had advanced his prediction that the passage of a quarter-century would see manufacturing spread across the land. The population had grown by leaps and bounds, but the result was not what he had expected. In the meantime, the Louisiana Purchase had opened up a vast new territory for agriculture capable of absorbing the surplus population; Eli Whitney's discovery of the cotton gin had made the cultivation of cotton less labor-intensive and more profitable than ever before; and through importation and natural increase, the slave population had kept pace with an ever-growing demand. In 1819, the southern states were still societies of husbandmen; not one among them had "made much progress in those branches of industry which give a variety and complexity to the affairs of a nation." The two Virginians recognized the failure of Madison's strategy,[122] and they both began grasping at straws, not only abandoning the policy of containment that they had pursued in the 1780s, but arguing that the best hope for abolition in the long run lay in the diffusion of the slave population throughout the Union as a whole.[123]

By the time of the Missouri crisis, it was clear that James Monroe and the anonymous Cato had, at least in some measure, been right. The Framers had left behind as their legacy an "unkindred legislature" composed of "jarring interests and discordant principles," and the new nation was gradually becoming "a house divided against itself." As John Quincy Adams confided to his diary in February 1820, the "discussion" of the Missouri question "disclosed a secret: it revealed the basis for a new organization of parties." To be precise, there was "a new party ready formed . . . terrible to the whole Union, but portentously terrible to the South—threatening in its progress the emancipation of all their slaves, threatening in its immediate effect that Southern domination which has swayed the Union for the last twenty years," and quite likely in the end to be fatal to the Union.[124] Adams was himself left with the "impression" that "the bargain between freedom and slavery contained in the Constitution of the United States is morally and politically vicious, inconsistent with the principles upon which alone our Revolution can be justified; cruel and oppressive, by riveting the chains of slavery, by pledging the faith of freedom to maintain and perpetuate the tyranny of the master; and grossly unequal and impolitic, by admitting that slaves are at once enemies to be kept in subjection, property to be secured or restored to their owners, and persons not to be represented themselves, but for whom their masters are privileged with nearly a double share of representation." "If the Union must be dissolved," he confessed, "slavery is precisely the question upon which it ought to break."[125]

In short, the three men who had masqueraded as a noble Roman redivivus had badly misjudged the future. And yet, as political prophecy goes, theirs were relatively minor errors of judgment. Though at an agonizingly slow pace, time has gradually diminished, but not erased, the distinctiveness of the states and the regions; and except at rare and particularly revealing moments, the nation's political parties have exhibited a flexibility in matters of principle sufficient to drive to distraction the ideological purists among their members.[126] More important, the vision of liberal democracy projected by Madison and his colleagues proved strikingly prescient. In its two centuries of existence, the American regime has been remarkable for turbulence, but (with a single, notable, ultimately decisive exception) it has been singularly free from the kind of civil strife that culminates in open and sustained rebellion. Madison's polity did eventually include, as he predicted, "a landed interest, a manufacturing interest, a mercantile interest, a monied interest, with many lesser interests," and he was perfectly correct when he observed that "the regulation of these various and interfering interests forms the principal task of modern Legislation, and involves the spirit of party and faction in the necessary and ordinary operations of Government."[127] Disappointment was to stalk the likes of Samuel Adams, for neither Boston nor any other American city ever became "a *Christian* Sparta." As a commercial society founded on the marriage of trade and technology, the liberal republic tended to present itself as a congeries of special interests, not as a people united by a common cause. And—at least to the unsuspecting glance—that simple fact, more than anything else, sets the modern republic apart from the regimes established by the legendary lawgivers of old.

CHAPTER 3

Alexander Hamilton and the
Conduct of Administration

Take mankind as they are, and what are they governed by? Their passions. There may be in every government a few choice spirits, who may act from more worthy motives. One great error is that we suppose mankind more honest than they are. Our prevailing passions are ambition and interest; and it will ever be the duty of a wise government to avail itself of those passions, in order to make them subservient to the public good—for these ever induce us to action.—Alexander Hamilton

We shall very soon have parties formed; a court and country party, and these parties will have names given them. One party . . . will support the President and his measures and ministers; the other will oppose them.—John Adams

III.iii.1

The critique of virtue advanced by those Americans most fully in accord with the modern advocates of Enlightenment left some dissatisfied. Among those with grave misgivings were to be found many of the Anti-Federalists. "Whatever the refinement of modern politics may inculcate," Pennsylvania's Federal Republican observed, "it still is certain that some degree of virtue must exist, or freedom cannot live." That point had to be conceded "unless Mandevill's position was to be embraced, 'that private vices are public benefits.'" He was himself satisfied that "virtue and simplicity of manners . . . create a healthy constitution" while "*vice* like a sickly air, debilitates the nerves of the political body, and withers its bloom."[1]

New York's Cato stated virtue's case with even greater force. "It is alledged," he noted, "that the opinions and manners of the people of America, are capable to resist and prevent an extension of prerogative or oppression." This he seemed prepared to acknowledge, but he openly wondered what effect a commercial regime would have on those "opinions and manners." "You must recollect," he told his readers, "that opinion and manners are mutable, and may not always be a permanent obstruction against the encroachments of government; that the progress of a commercial society begets luxury, the parent of inequality, the foe to virtue, and the enemy to restraint; and that ambition and voluptuousness aided by flattery, will teach magistrates, where limits are not explicitly fixed to have separate and distinct interests from the people, besides it will not be denied that government assimilates the manners and opinions of the community to it."[2] He was far less worried regarding the immediate impact of the new constitution than by the slow, but sure effects of the commercial principles that it was designed to inculcate.

Mercy Otis Warren took a similar stand. Even after Massachusetts had ratified the Constitution, she remained hopeful that Virginia, Maryland, and New York would repudiate the document. "An heroic love for the publick good, a profound reverence for the laws, a contempt of riches, and a noble haughtiness of soul, are the only foundations of a free government."[3] So she insisted—and she did not alter her opinion with the passage of time. Nearly two decades after the new government had been established, she looked back over those events and struck a melancholy note. "Nothing seemed to be wanting to the United States but a continuance of their union and virtue," she remarked. "It was their interest to cherish true, genuine republican virtue, in politics; and in religion, a strict adherence to a sublime code of morals, which has never been equalled by the sages of ancient time, nor can ever be abolished by the sophistical reasonings of modern philosophers." That was the prospect that had been open to her countrymen then. "Possessed of this palladium, America might bid defiance both to foreign and domestic intrigue, and stand on an eminence that would command their veneration of nations, and the respect of their monarchs: but a defalcation from these principles may leave the sapless vine of liberty to droop, or be rooted out by the hand that had been stretched to nourish it." By abandoning "the independent feelings of ancient republics," the Americans had announced "a dereliction of those principles." And the result was "a melancholy trait in the story of man," for by their own choice, the Americans had condemned themselves to "the pit of avarice." Behind "the factitious appearances of grandeur and wealth," one could discern "peculation," "usurious contracts," "illegal and dishonest projects," and "every private vice."[4]

This state of affairs caused the woman sadness, not despair. She could console herself that, "notwithstanding the apprehensions which have pervaded the minds of many, America will probably long retain a greater share of freedom than can perhaps be found in any other part of the civilized world." But she argued that this would be the consequence of good fortune and little else. It would stem from America's "local situation" rather "than from her superior policy or moderation." As the historian put it, "From the general equality of fortune, which had formerly reigned among them, it may be modestly asserted, that most of the inhabitants of America were too proud for monarchy, yet too poor for nobility, and it is to be feared, too selfish and avaricious for a virtuous republic."[5]

The misgivings expressed by the Anti-Federalists came gradually to be shared in some measure by others who had remained silent or who had even vigorously supported ratification of the proposed constitution. In the 1790s, some from among these men emerged to assert leadership over those who continued to fear that the new central government would crush all local power and impose a monarchy or a despotism on what had hitherto been the preserve of free men.[6] If the Anti-Federalists were quickly reconciled to the new constitution, it was in part because their new allies based their attack on the conduct of the new regime's first administration on an extraordinarily strict and narrow construction of that document.[7] These erstwhile Federalists were driven to this course by the conviction that there was a conspiracy afoot to subvert the new republic. The man most responsible for generating these fears was the fledgling nation's first secretary of the treasury. He had grasped the implications of Bernard Mandeville's claim "that Private Vices by the dextrous Management of a skilful Politician may be turned into Publick Benefits"; and, in his conduct of administration, he was guided by the Dutchman's conviction that "the Power and Sagacity as well as Labour and Care of the Politician in civilizing the Society, has been no where more conspicuous, than in the happy Contrivance of playing our Passions against one another."[8]

III.iii.2

Alexander Hamilton was arguably the most brilliant of the American Founding Fathers.[9] Guizot later classed him "among the men who have best known the vital principles and fundamental conditions of" government.[10] Such was also the opinion of the great majority of the distinguished figures directly acquainted with the man. To an American he encountered in Paris, Talleyrand "spoke willingly, freely, and with great admiration" for the statesman from New York: "He had known, during his life, many of the more marked men of his time, but . . . he had never, on the whole, known one equal to Hamilton."[11] Some forty years after Aaron Burr put an end to Hamilton's life, Supreme Court Justice Joseph Story recalled having heard Samuel Dexter, John Marshall, and Chancellor Livingston all say that "Hamilton's reach of thought was so far beyond theirs that by his side they were schoolboys— rush tapers before the sun at noon day."[12] Story's recollections accord well with the views expressed by the keenest observers when Hamilton was still alive. In the bitterness of old age, John Adams might dismiss the New Yorker as "a bastard brat of a Scotch pedlar,"[13] but Hamilton's most serious political antagonist was prepared to concede in the midst of their great struggle that, even when out of office, his opponent was "a colossus" to the supporters of the Washington administration and its most controversial measures. "Without numbers," the man sadly remarked, "he is an host within himself."[14] The exceptional character of Hamilton's abilities were evident from the moment he first set foot on the public stage at the tender age of seventeen.[15] Unfortunately, his shortcomings would eventually be evident as well, for, as his political opponents would ultimately demonstrate, Alexander Hamilton was not the shrewdest and the most politic of his contemporaries.

At least one observer grasped this fact quite early on. In 1788, the French ambassador reported back to his superiors that Hamilton was a rare individual—"equally distinguished on the field of battle and in court (*barreau*)." The man came from a most undistinguished background. In truth, he owed "everything to his talents." But he also had faults to match those talents. Hamilton had already suffered setbacks because of his "indiscretions." Overall, he was "a bit too pretentious," and he exhibited "too little prudence." The New Yorker was, the ambassador concluded, "too impetuous—and in wishing to manage everything, he misses his goal."[16] Twenty-three years later, after Hamilton's death, his friend and longtime associate Gouverneur Morris confirmed the ambassador's report in at least one particular. Hamilton "was of all men," he acknowledged, "the most indiscreet."[17] By revealing too much and trying to move too fast and too far, the New Yorker had squandered everything. It had all begun at the Philadelphia convention.

In the 1780s, no American had devoted more time and effort to preparing the way for a federal convention that would strengthen the central government than had Alexander Hamilton;[18] and after the meeting in Philadelphia disbanded, no one was to press harder for ratification of the federal constitution than he. And yet, both in 1787 and later, Washington's former aide-de-camp entertained grave doubts as to whether the new government which that constitution instituted would prove adequate to the infant nation's needs, and he took little care to hide those doubts.[19] Hamilton barely participated in the deliberations of the Philadelphia convention. He gave but one extended speech—a critique of both the New Jersey and Virginia plans, which culminated in an extended eulogy of the British constitution. After making his point, Hamilton withdrew, only to return near the end at Washington's urging with the purpose of affixing his signature to the document which the convention produced.[20] Before he signed his name, the New Yorker urged others to follow his example. "No man's ideas were more remote from the plan than his own were known to be," he acknowledged. But there was no viable alternative to supporting the proposed constitution—unless one deemed it "possible to deliberate between anarchy and Convulsion on one side, and the chance of good to be expected from the plan on the other."[21]

The jottings which Hamilton made in preparation for his great speech deserve careful attention, as do the notes which James Madison, Robert Yates, John Lansing, and Rufus King took as they listened to the astonishing things that he had to say.[22] The concerns which Hamilton evidenced in June 1787 were abiding concerns, and they were later decisive in shaping the controversial program he launched when he served as secretary of the treasury in the administration of George Washington.

Through nearly all of his adult life, Hamilton was haunted by the specter of the Union's dissolution; he had a keener sense than any of his contemporaries that the American experiment might end in a great and terrible civil war. On the floor of the Philadelphia convention, the New Yorker expressed the fear that the new government, like the old, would be too weak to bind the Union together. There were, he suggested, five "great & essential principles necessary for the support of Government." No regime would be successful without "an active & constant interest in supporting it." None would be effective that lacked a sense of its own "importance & self-sufficiency." And none could survive which failed to inspire "an habitual attachment of the people." Indeed, to achieve its end, a government needed "*Force* by which may be understood a *coertion of laws* or *coertion of arms*," and it required "*influence*" as well—for without "a dispensation of those regular honors & emoluments, which produce an attachment to the Govt.," no regime could survive for long. Unfortunately, Hamilton observed, "almost all the weight of these" five principles "is on the side of the States; and must continue so as long as the States continue to exist. All the passions then we see, of avarice, ambition, interest, which govern most individuals, and all public bodies, fall into the current of the States, and do not flow in the stream of the Genl. Govt. The former therefore will generally be an overmatch for the Genl. Govt. and render any confederacy, in its nature precarious." This analysis he thought borne out by an examination of the history of those confederacies, both ancient and modern, which had been composed of independent and sovereign polities. "How then are all these evils to be avoided?" he asked. "Only by such a compleat sovereignty in the general Governmt. as will turn all the strong principles & passions above mentioned on its side," he then answered. To make way for that, he was willing to contemplate the abolition of the states or, at least, their reduction to the status of subordinate jurisdictions.[23]

Even then, however, Hamilton was "discouraged" by "the extent of the Country to be governed." He was concerned that so distant a government would have difficulty "drawing" wise and virtuous "representatives from the extremes to the center of the Community," and he had other fears as well. When James Madison presented his argument regarding the problem of faction, the New Yorker had listened with great care and had taken notes summarizing the various points made and sketching his own objections to them. He acknowledged that Madison's argument possessed considerable force. But he doubted in the end that geographical extension alone would sufficiently muffle the tension between rich and poor, and he perceived that the size of the new nation was itself an obstacle to the establishment of a government vigorous enough to provide a focus for the citizens' interests and passions. In particular, he worried that strife between the sections and conflict between the commercial and the agrarian states would endanger the Union. In fact, Hamilton later confessed in his speech to the convention, "This view of the subject almost led him to despair that a Republican Govt. could be established over so great an extent."[24]

He was sensible at the same time that it would be unwise to propose one of any other form. In his private opinion he had no scruple in declaring, supported as he was by the opinions of so many of the wise & good, that the British Govt. was the best in the world: and that he doubted much whether any thing short of it would do in America. He hoped Gentlemen of different opinions would bear with him in this, and begged them to recollect the change of opinion on this subject which had taken place and was still going on. It was once thought that the power of Congs was amply sufficient to secure the end of their institution. The error was now seen by every one. The members most tenacious of republicanism, he observed, were as loud as any in declaiming agst. the vices of democracy. This progress of the public mind led him to anticipate the time, when others as well as himself would join in the praise bestowed by Mr. Neckar on the British Constitution, namely, that it is the only Govt. in the world "which unites public strength with individual security."

"In every community where industry is encouraged," Hamilton warned, "there will be a division . . . into the few & the many." That result was unavoidable, and it had consequences fatal to unmixed republics. "Give all power to the many, they will oppress the few. Give all power to the few they will oppress the many."[25] To reconcile public strength and individual security, Hamilton believed, like Jean Louis de Lolme before him, that the few and the many must each be given the means of self-defense and that there must be "a mutual check" in the form of "a monarch" endowed with "so much power, that it will not be his interest to risk much to acquire more." In sum, he wrote, "the principle chiefly intended to be established is this—that there must be a permanent *will*."[26]

Hamilton did not suggest to his fellow delegates that they should establish in America an hereditary monarchy, a House of Lords, and a House of Commons on the British model, but he did advocate going "as far in order to attain stability and permanency, as republican principles will admit." In the United States, he acknowledged, "all the Magistrates" should be "appointed" and all "vacancies . . . filled, by the people, or a process of election originating with the people." But senators, once chosen, should hold office "for life or at least during good behaviour," and the executive should be similarly established. Only a senate rendered splendid and independent in this fashion "would induce the sacrifice of private affairs which an acceptance of public trust would require, so as to ensure the services of the best Citizens." None but such a body would be "capable of resisting the popular current." Like the members of England's House of Lords, America's senators would have "nothing to hope for by a change, and a sufficient interest by means of their property, in being faithful to the National interest." As a consequence, they would not only "form a permanent barrier agst. every pernicious innovation"; they would endow the government with "a permanent will." Their very "duration" would be "the earnest of wisdom and stability." By the same token, if the president was placed—like Britain's king—"above the danger of being corrupted from abroad" and if "at the same time" he "was both sufficiently independent and sufficiently controuled," he could be made to see to the "vigorous execution" of the laws and to "intend, in respect to foreign nations, the true interest and glory of the people."[27]

The role assigned the president deserves particular notice, for in urging that the executive be strengthened, Hamilton had more in mind than life tenure during good behavior. Four days after the delivery of his great speech, he rose twice to oppose the constitutional provision barring placemen from serving in Congress. "We must take man as we find him," he explained, "and if we expect him to serve the public must interest his passions in doing so. A reliance on pure patriotism has been the source of many of our errors." In his view, the use of patronage by the king's ministers as a means of managing Parliament was essential to the strength and vitality of the admirable British regime. "It was," he remarked, "known that ‹one› of the ablest politicians (Mr Hume) had pronounced all that influence on the side of the crown, which went under the name of corruption, an essential part of the weight which maintained the equilibrium of the Constitution."[28] In making this assessment, David Hume had emphasized the fundamental weakness of the executive power. On the one hand, he noted, it is everywhere subordinate to the legislative power. On the other hand, he added, its exercise "requires an immense expence; and the commons have assumed to themselves the sole right of granting money." Indeed, the legislative body would undoubtedly have overwhelmed the crown had it not been that the latter had "so many offices at its disposal, that, when assisted by the honest and disinterested part of the house," it could "always command the resolutions of the whole so far, at least to preserve the antient constitution from danger."[29] In Hamilton's view, the American executive was destined to be endangered in much the same fashion. No government but one properly balanced and endowed with stability and vigor in the fashion outlined by Hume could at the same time display public strength and protect individual security—and thereby enlist interest, opinion, habit, force, and influence on its side.

It is easy to see why Hamilton considered inadequate the Constitution which the Philadelphia convention eventually endorsed. In his speech, he had compared the Virginia Plan with the Articles of Confederation and called it "but *pork still, with a little change of the sauce.*"[30] The same remark could be applied with even greater justice to the proposed constitution. It left the states intact as formidable rivals to the national power; it restricted the sphere of federal endeavor; and it granted little in the way of permanence and real strength to the Senate and, more important, the presidency. It is no wonder, then, that in *The Federalist* Hamilton discreetly tempered his praise for the new constitution—referring in the first number to the Union's need for *"a government at least equally energetic with the one proposed"* and then, in the last number, declaring the new system "the best that the present views and circumstances of the country will permit."[31]

Despite his misgivings, Hamilton was willing to fight—and to fight with unexcelled vigor—for what he had called *"a little change of sauce."* He feared that the states would reject the new constitution, and he was convinced that, if this happened, the Union would dissolve and civil war would soon follow. On the other hand, if the proposal were ratified, he thought that much still might be done. George Washington would almost certainly be the first president, and this would be all to the good.

In a private memorandum composed shortly after the close of the convention, Hamilton observed that Washington's election would "insure a wise choice of men to administer the government and a good administration." This development might, in turn, have a profound effect, for "a good administration will conciliate the confidence and affection of the people and perhaps enable the government to acquire more consistency than the proposed constitution seems to promise for so great a Country." Hamilton was even willing to contemplate the possibility that the federal government would "then triumph altogether over the state governments and reduce them to an intire subordination." In the process, the "*organs* of the general government" might "also acquire additional strength." But if the national government failed to achieve a decisive victory in the struggle to come, "it is probable that the contests about the boundaries of power between the particular governments and the general government and the *momentum* of the larger states in such contests will produce a dissolution of the Union. This after all seems to be the most likely result."[32] At the time, no one else saw the danger posed by states' rights with such clarity.

III.iii.3

When Hamilton remarked that the election of Washington as president would insure a wise choice of men to administer the new government, he clearly had one man above all others in mind. The old general was a firm nationalist, and in most other respects, he shared the predilections of his former aide-de-camp.[33] He seems, in addition, to have had more affection and respect for Hamilton than for any other man; the orphan from the West Indies may well have been a surrogate for the son he had never had.[34] Thus, once the Constitution was ratified, Hamilton knew that his time had come. The most important of the tasks initially confronting the new government would have to do with the levying of taxes, the collection of revenue, and the determination and payment of the national debt. All else would depend on what were seemingly mundane details—and the manner in which the difficulties were surmounted would in large part determine the relationship between the nation and the states, and might well contribute more to shaping the new regime than the framing of the Constitution itself.

Hamilton had long ago grasped this fact. By 1789, he had spent a decade or more studying political economy.[35] He had read Malachy Postlethwayt's *Universal Dictionary of Trade and Commerce*; he had wrestled with Sir James Steuart's *An Inquiry into the Principles of Political Oeconomy*; he had pondered Adam Smith's *The Wealth of Nations*; and he had studied Wyndham Beawes's *Lex Mercatoria*, Richard Price's *Schemes for raising Money by Public Loans*, and many of the other tracts written at the time. In addition, he had given careful consideration to the financial revolution carried out in Britain by the Junto Whigs just a century before, and—more clearly than any other American— he had realized the fashion in which this development had decisively altered the character of both domestic politics and international affairs.[36] In coming to understand the new relationship between politics, economics, and human psychology, Hamilton had profited greatly from the essays of "the judicious" David Hume.[37] But, perhaps even more important, the young statesman had only recently devoured the three volumes of memoirs published by "the celebrated" Jacques Necker—once and soon again to be director-general of finance in service to the king of France.[38] It would be safe to say that the man slated to be Washington's first secretary of the treasury had a just estimation of the central role played by fiduciary institutions in the modern political economy.[39]

This had not always been the case. At the beginning of the Revolutionary War, Hamilton's outlook had had much in common with that of the ancients. He then thought Britain's public debt a crippling burden, and he predicted that the Americans, superior as they were in numbers, would coast to a relatively easy victory despite Britain's advantage in discipline and military skill. "There is a certain enthusiasm in liberty, that makes human nature rise above itself, in acts of bravery and heroism," he explained. "It cannot be expected, that America would yield, without a magnanimous persevering and bloody struggle."[40] The young man's experience as a soldier soon robbed him of the illusion that one could and should depend solely or even primarily on human nature rising above itself. In fact, he initially became interested in finance when he came to recognize that victory in the Revolutionary War would depend upon a marshaling of resources impossible without the reestablishment of credit. By 1780, he was urging the establishment of a national bank modeled on the Bank of England to organize America's growing public debt and to secure the confidence of foreign governments and the new nation's monied men.[41]

Soon thereafter, Hamilton evidenced an awareness that money was much more than the sinews of war and that such an institution might be able to do far more than merely enable the Continental Congress to supply its army. In 1781, upon learning that Robert Morris had been selected to organize a department of finance, Hamilton wrote him a long letter, arguing that "the tendency of a national bank is to increase public and private credit." "The former gives power to the state for the protection of its rights and interests, and the latter facilitates and extends the operations of commerce among individuals," he contended. "Industry is increased, commodities are multiplied, agriculture and manufactures flourish, and herein consist the true wealth and prosperity of a state." The trick was to fund the debt in such a fashion that the government's promissory notes could circulate as a substitute for coin. By thus promoting an expansion of credit, by checking tendencies toward irresponsible speculation, and by channeling the capital created into productive enterprises, the national government could itself become the engine of economic growth—and that would, in turn, have important political implications. Only the passage of time could make "habitual" the "attachment of the people" to the Union which Hamilton sought to inspire, and only circumstance would enable the national government to assert itself through "a *coertion of laws* or *coertion of arms*." But, in the meantime, much might be done. Through the vigorous promotion of prosperity, the nation's financier could actively enlist interest, opinion, and influence on the side of the Union. As Hamilton put it in his letter to Morris, "A national debt if it is not excessive will be to us a national blessing; it will be powerfull cement of our union."[42] Nine years later, when the nation's first secretary of the treasury presented to Congress his famous *Report Relative to a Provision for the Support of Public Credit*, he would resort to this language once again.

Hamilton could argue in 1790 that "the proper funding of the present debt will render it a national blessing," and he could contend at the same time that "a proper provision, at the present period for the support of public credit" would "cement more closely the union of the states" because he perceived what some deemed an unmitigated disaster as a grand opportunity. By assuming the debts incurred by the states in the course of the War of Independence, he could justify imposing an excise tax. His principle was fiscally sound: "The creation of debt should always be accompanied with the means of extinguishment."[43] But his purpose was political as well. States with reduced revenues would be states less capable of what he had described to the Philadelphia convention as "a dispensation of those regular honors & emoluments, which produce an attachment to the Govt." By the same token, a national government endowed with substantial and dependable income would be able to exercise what Hamilton and the men of the time called "influence." In 1782, Hamilton had argued that the Continental Congress should be empowered "to appoint its own officers of the customs, collectors of taxes, and military officers of every rank" because this would enable it "to create in the interior of each state a mass of influence in favour of the Foederal Government." Then and later, he believed that "the great danger" was that the central government would "not have power enough to defend itself and preserve the union, not that it will ever become formidable to the general liberty." The truth was that "a mere regard to the interests of the confederacy will never be a principle sufficiently active to curb the ambition and intrigues of different members." In the end, force might be required to protect the Union, but its application was "always disagreeable" and "the issue uncertain." In the meantime, it would "be wise to obviate the necessity of it, by interesting such a number of individuals in each state in support of the

Foederal Government, as will be counterpoised to the ambition of others."
This would go far toward preventing the champions of local autonomy from
uniting "the people in opposition to the just and necessary measures of
the union."[44]

Patronage was not all that Hamilton had in mind. He knew as well that
those who invested in the national debt would have a stake in the health
of the Union, and he expected this group to include the leading figures in
virtually every locality. Indeed, assumption was designed, at least in part,
to transform the many creditors of the various states into firm supporters
of the national government.[45] To form what he had described to the federal
convention as "an active & constant interest in supporting" the Union, the
secretary of the treasury soon proposed the foundation of a national bank
virtually identical in most respects to the Bank of England—but subject to
the control of the individuals who subscribed to its stock and designed less
as an instrument of public finance than as a means for monetizing the debt so
that its circulation could facilitate commerce and private investment.[46] When
forced to defend his proposal, he prepared a memorandum for President
Washington which concluded by laying great emphasis on "the tendency of
an institution immediately connected with the national Government which
will interweave itself into the *monied* interest of every State, which will by
its notes insinuate itself into every branch of industry and will affect the
interests of all classes of the community." In his opinion, an "attentive consideration" of this tendency "ought to produce strong prepossessions in its
favor in all who consider the firm establishment of the National Government
as necessary to the safety & happiness of the Country, and who at the same
time believe that it stands in need of additional props."[47] Later, when his program came under attack, Hamilton would deny that this was "the weightiest
motive to the measure," but he would at the same time acknowledge that
he had paid close attention to "the tendency" of his program "to strengthen
our infant Government by increasing the number of ligaments between the
Government and the interests of Individuals." In that fashion, he conceded,
assumption was designed at least temporarily to serve "as a prop to the Government in the infancy of its authority while there was yet a numerous party
alive whose vanity and envy pledged them to opposition and before it had
acquired the confirmations of habit & age."[48] In the early 1790s, Hamilton's
task was nothing less than the creation of a national interest where there
had been none before. Where Robert Morris had tried and for the most part
failed, Hamilton intended to succeed.[49]

III.iii.4

To complete the task which he assigned to himself, Hamilton made yet another proposal, one which went well beyond anything suggested by the great financier of the confederation. He had long been an advocate of manufacturing; he regarded the establishment of industry in America as a prerequisite for the maintenance of the new nation's independence. When he was but seventeen, he had contended that "if by the necessity of the thing, manufactures should once be established and take root among us, they will pave the way, still more, to the future grandeur and glory of America, and by lessening its need of external commerce, will render it still securer against the encroachments of tyranny."[50] Eight years later, while serving as a member of the Continental Congress, he drafted but ultimately decided not to submit a resolution calling for a convention to amend the Articles of Confederation. It was his intention that the convention would confer on the Congress "a general superintendence of trade . . . because by general prohibitions of particular articles, by a judicious arrangment of duties, sometimes by bounties on the manufacture or exportation of certain commodities, injurious branches of commerce might be discouraged, favourable branches encouraged, useful products and manufactures promoted."[51] Thus, it should not be surprising that—when Congress requested that he devise "a proper plan or plans . . . for the encouragement and promotion of such manufactories as will tend to render the United States independent of other nations, for essential, particularly for military supplies"[52]—he took the opportunity to present a program far more grand.

One must doubt whether Congress would have made such a request had President Washington not raised the question in his address opening the second session of the First Congress.[53] In the late eighteenth century, few Americans were seriously willing to contemplate the prospect that the newborn republic would have to endure war time and again. Hamilton exaggerates only slightly when he reports that "at the close of our revolution[ary] war the phantom of perpetual peace danced before the eyes of every body."[54] In his time, there were "visionary, or designing men" abroad in the land, and they really were "ready to advocate" what the New Yorker called "the paradox of perpetual peace." The talented publicist Thomas Paine subscribed to this doctrine and had spread it far and wide first in his tract *Common Sense* and later in his two-volume work *Rights of Man*. By the 1790s, many of Hamilton's compatriots had been persuaded that "the genius of republics . . . is pacific"; few then doubted the truth of Montesquieu's assertion that "the spirit of commerce has a tendency to soften the manners of men and to extin-

guish those inflammable humours which have so often kindled into wars."
On the basis of these premises, they tended to conclude that "commercial
republics" would "never be disposed to waste themselves in ruinous contentions with each other" and that such republics would in the future "be
governed by mutual interest" and would "cultivate a spirit of mutual amity
and concord." [55]

James Madison was inclined to dismiss the establishment of perpetual
peace as one of those "events which will never exist but in the imagina-
tions of visionary philosophers," but even he was prepared to trace "the past
frequency of wars" in large measure to the existence of "a will in the government independent of the will of the people." "Whilst war," he wrote, "is to
depend on those whose ambition, whose revenge, whose avidity, or whose
caprice may contradict the sentiment of the community, and yet be uncon-
trouled by it; whilst war is to be declared by those who are to spend the
public money, not by those who are to pay it; by those who are to direct the
public forces, not by those who are to support them; by those whose power
is to be raised, not by those whose chains may be riveted the disease must
continue to be *hereditary* like the government of which it is the offspring." In
conclusion, he added that "a‹s› the first step towards a cure, the government
itself must be regenerated. Its will must be made subordinate to, or rather the
same with, the will of the community." [56] In noting that, in the past, republics
had not been particularly devoted to peace; in suggesting that commercial
rivalry could itself occasion war; and in advocating the need for a standing
army, Hamilton stood out. [57] This fact goes a long way toward explaining why
he was so exceptional in his eagerness to strengthen the Union; few others
had pondered the strains that war would inevitably bring.

Hamilton's *Report on the Subject of Manufactures* presented a plan designed
in part to reduce those strains. In accord with the spirit of Congress's request, he emphasized that it was essential that the country produce for itself
all that was necessary for the conduct of war. But he went further as well. He
vigorously denied that the true interests of the nation's farmers would be at
odds with the concerns of those engaged in manufacturing. To persuade his
compatriots that the interests of the two classes were harmonious, he drew
attention to the capricious character of the foreign demand for agricultural
products and argued that the United States would be stronger, more prosperous, more closely bound together, and more fully independent if there was a
large, utterly dependable domestic market of tradesmen and factory workers
prepared to consume the foodstuffs grown on the nation's farms. Hamilton had long recognized that agrarian polities oriented toward the export of
tobacco, cotton, grain, and the like would inevitably become dependent on

the nations engaged in manufacturing finished goods.[58] He wanted Americans to look to one another for their needs and not abroad. If they did so, then they would perhaps "never be disposed to waste themselves in ruinous contentions with each other." Instead, they might "be governed by mutual interest" and might "cultivate a spirit of mutual amity and concord." That is certainly what he hoped.

In this matter, as in others, Hamilton emphasized the role that a vigorous national government could play. He believed that the new nation was commercial, but not nearly commercial enough; he was persuaded that his fellow citizens were enterprising, but not nearly enterprising enough. Some would argue, he knew, "that Industry, if left to itself, will naturally find its way to the most useful and profitable employment." From this, they would conclude "that manufactures without the aid of government will grow up as soon and as fast, as the natural state of things and the interest of the community may require." He acknowledged the cogency of this argument but denied that economic behavior was as rational as the argument's proponents presumed. Human beings were often paralyzed by "the strong influence of habit and the spirit of imitation—the fear of want of success in untried enterprises—the intrinsic difficulties incident to first essays towards a competition with those who have previously attained to perfection in the business to be attempted."

> Experience teaches, that men are often so much governed by what they are accustomed to see and practice, that the simplest and most obvious improvements in the [most] ordinary occupations, are adopted with hesitation, reluctance and by slow gradations. The spontaneous transition to new pursuits, in a community long habituated to different ones, may be expected to be attended with proportionably greater difficulty. When former occupations ceased to yield a profit adequate to the subsistence of their followers, or when there was an absolute deficiency of employment in them, owing to the superabundance of hands, changes would ensue; but these changes would be likely to be more tardy than might consist with the interest either of individuals or of the Society. In many cases they would not happen, while a bare support could be ensured by an adherence to ancient courses; though a resort to a more profitable employment might be practicable. To produce the desireable changes, as early as may be expedient, may therefore require the incitement and patronage of the government.

The artificial capital created by funding and assumption would set things in motion, but the example set by other nations suggested the necessity of employing "bounties premiums and other artificial encouragements" as well.

Hamilton advocated the sparing use of federal revenues to subsidize domestic production and foreign exports. With that encouragement, foreign and domestic capital might be attracted to enterprises requiring a considerable outlay for machinery and facilities.[59]

In advocating this grand undertaking, Hamilton never forgot the importance of public opinion. From the outset, he recognized that credit was itself but a creature of the imagination—an illusion capable of setting men in motion, a bubble that could only too easily burst.[60] That is why he took such care to advertise the fact that he was linking the assumption of debts with provisions for paying the interest on the debt and, over time, the principal as well.[61] Some of the more passionate advocates of manufacturing sought the immediate adoption of a system of protective tariffs designed to secure a monopoly for American production. But, to their great annoyance and frustration, Hamilton resolutely refused to countenance this effort. He recognized that such a policy would invite retaliation, and, at least for the time being, he preferred bounties and premiums to protection and commercial discrimination. His own design for the promotion of manufacturing depended above all else on the establishment and maintenance of public credit, and he recognized that exclusionary tariffs would not produce the revenue required to win and sustain the confidence of those foreigners and Americans who had invested in the national debt. His first task as a financier was to justify trust. As he recognized, all else depended on that.[62]

When he spoke of opinion and pondered the problem of trust, Hamilton also had politics in mind. "The manner in which a thing is done has more influence than is commonly imagined," he once observed. "Men are governed by opinion; this opinion is as much influenced by appearances as by realities; if a Government appears to be confident of its own powers, it is the surest way to inspire the same confidence in others; if it is diffident, it may be certain, there will be a still greater diffidence in others, and that its authority will not only be distrusted, controverted, but contemned."[63] The Continental Congress had undermined its own power through diffidence; the new government would have to assert what he had described to the convention as its "importance & self-sufficiency," and it could best do so by moving firmly and decisively to set its own financial house in order. Men would look beyond the states to the national government if and only if it was more intelligently and dependably administered. Decision and consistency were prerequisite if Hamilton was to attain his goal—by making "all the passions . . . of avarice, ambition, interest, which govern most individuals, and all public bodies," and which had hitherto fallen "into the current of the States," begin to "flow in the stream of the Genl. Govt." As he had put it in *The Federalist*, "The more the operations of the national authority are intermingled in the ordinary exercise of government; the more the citizens are accustomed to meet with it in the common occurrences of their political life; the more it is familiarised to their sight and to their feelings; the further it enters into those objects which touch the most sensible cords, and put in motion the most active springs of the human heart; the greater will be the probability that it will conciliate the respect and attachment of the community." [64]

In later years, when his program, though endangered, was still partially in place, Hamilton would appeal to the voters on behalf of the national government by drawing attention to the fact that they owed their "prosperity" to more than their own "industry and . . . the blessings of Providence." Then, he could ask them,

> But has not your industry found aliment and incitement in the salutary operation of your government—in the preservation of order at home— in the cultivation of peace abroad—in the invigoration of confidence in pecuniary dealings—in the increased energies of credit and commerce, in the extension of enterprise ever incident to a good government well administered. Remember what your situation was immediately before the establishment of the present Constitution. Were you then deficient in industry more than now? If not, why were you not equally prosperous? Plainly because your industry had not at that time the vivifying influences of an efficient, and well conducted government.

It was an eloquent appeal, and, here and there, it fell on fertile soil. But there were many, perhaps even a majority, who remained deeply suspicious of what Hamilton meant by "a good government well administered." [65]

Had Hamilton been fully successful in his quest to strengthen and render more vigorous the national government and to subordinate the states to it, the Union might never have been rent asunder and the nation might have escaped the horrors of civil war. In the end, however, despite the brilliance of his initial successes, he failed, and his program was arguably the victim of the pretensions, the lack of prudence, and the impetuosity which the French ambassador had identified. Hamilton really did wish to manage everything, and, at least partially for that reason, he missed his goal.

III.iii.5

It was inevitable that Hamilton's program attract opposition. The Anti-Federalists were hostile to the new government from the outset, and many other Americans were inclined to be suspicious of all centralized power. As we have already observed, the entire generation which had made the American Revolution had been reared on the literature produced by the opponents of the Junto Whigs and the Walpole administration. These men owed their understanding of the social and institutional basis of liberty not only to works by Montesquieu and Lolme but also to books like John Locke's *Two Treatises of Government*, Algernon Sidney's *Discourses Concerning Government*, and James Burgh's *Political Disquisitions* as well as to collections of essays from England's periodical press such as *Cato's Letters* by John Trenchard and Thomas Gordon and *The Craftsman* by Henry St. John, Viscount Bolingbroke. From these and other similar sources, Americans had learned to expect and fear the encroachment of government on their liberty.[66] They had likewise been taught to link that danger with the imposition and collection of excise taxes by a national government. So it is not surprising that the prospect of the new federal government's employing its agents to collect levies of this sort had caused a stir even before the first administration was formed. Many of the state conventions which ratified the Constitution indicated their misgivings by proposing at the same time that the document be amended in one way or another; it is striking that all of the ratifying conventions which chose this path urged that the federal government be restricted to indirect taxation, that its additional needs be met by requisitions on the states, and—most important—that federal collection of taxes within a state be allowed only if that state had failed to deliver the sum levied on it.[67]

The authors who treated the excise as the harbinger of tyranny's approach were similarly critical of two developments which distinguished the new politics which emerged in the wake of England's Glorious Revolution: the ministerial corruption of Parliament through patronage, and the stockjobbing produced by the assumption and funding of a national debt through a national bank.[68] Hamilton was well acquainted with this line of thinking. In his adolescence, he, too, had fulminated against Britain's national debt, against her national bank, against her standing army, and against "ministry, ministerial tools, placemen, pensioners, parasites," and the other phenomena which the English opposition considered the instruments of tyrannical domination.[69] The coauthor of *The Federalist* was also aware of the particular objections raised to the Constitution by its Anti-Federalist opponents, and he did not fail to notice that the prospect of the new government's levying excise taxes had alarmed many of his countrymen.[70] In seeking to bolster the Union by adopting the methods initially made infamous by the Junto Whigs and later perfected by Sir Robert Walpole, the secretary of the treasury must have known that he would be opening yet another very old wound.

Despite the acute sensitivity of his countrymen regarding the type of program he sought to institute, Hamilton might well have succeeded had he continued to enjoy the confidence of James Madison. It was natural to assume, as Hamilton did, that his chief collaborator in producing *The Federalist* would become a stalwart supporter of his entire program. Of course, the New Yorker can hardly have been unaware that the Virginian was no admirer of the English constitution. At the federal convention, the latter had demonstrated a positive dislike for the British regime with its "vicious representation"; he had shown himself unfriendly to "high toned Govts" possessed of "too much energy"; and he had openly argued that "a standing military force, with an overgrown Executive will not long be safe companions to liberty."[71] Moreover, before coming to Philadelphia, Madison had expressed the hope that the convention might find "some middle ground" between the "individual independence of the States" and "a consolidation of the whole into one simple republic." While there, as one delegate pointed out, he had distinguished himself from Hamilton by intimating a desire "to leave the States in possession of a considerable, tho' a subordinate jurisdiction"; and on the floor of the convention, he had explicitly conceded that "the Genl. Govt. could not extend its care to all the minute objects which fall under the cognizance of the local jurisdictions." In a moment of exasperation, he even insisted that he meant "to preserve the state rights with the same care" as he "would trials by jury."[72] Nonetheless, Hamilton had no reason to suppose that Madison left Philadelphia a stout defender of the newly restricted state prerogatives and a principled opponent of further consolidation.

At the federal convention, the Virginian had opposed with all the considerable eloquence at his command the compromise that allowed the state legislatures to elect the Senate.[73] When defeated on this point, he was so exasperated that he tried to persuade "the side comprising the principal States, and a majority of the people of America" to act in a separate capacity and "propose" on their own "a scheme of Govt. to the States."[74] He was known to be even more unhappy that the Constitution had denied the federal government a general veto over state laws. Like Hamilton, he worried that "the *plan should* it *be adopted* will neither effectually *answer* its *national object* nor prevent the local *mischiefs* which every where excite *disgusts* ag[ain]st the *state governments.*" Like the New Yorker, he was convinced that the proposed system would involve "the evil of imperia in imperio."[75] In Philadelphia, he had tried to persuade the advocates of the New Jersey Plan that "the true policy of the small States . . . lies in promoting those principles & that form of Govt. which will most approximate the States to the condition of Counties." It was his opinion that "no fatal consequence could result" from "a tendency in the Genl. Government to absorb the State Govts."[76]

Moreover, in 1783, the Virginian had been a strong advocate of Congress's making provision for payment of the federal debt. In fact, in an address which he had drafted for the Continental Congress, he had advanced the very arguments which the secretary of the treasury would later employ against those who advocated discriminating between the original creditors and the speculators who had purchased federal notes for ten or twenty cents on the dollar at a time when the ability and willingness of the nation to pay its debts was still very much in doubt.[77] Similarly, in *The Federalist*, when Madison alluded to sectional rivalry and hinted at the danger posed to the Union by the continued existence of slavery in the South, he appeared to be willing to countenance and even welcome the growth and spread of manufacturing throughout the nation and, in particular, the agrarian states.[78] In that document, he had foreseen the day when the federal government would need to substitute bounties for tariffs on the import of "raw materials" destined to "be wrought into articles for exportation."[79]

Thus, Hamilton had good reason to suppose that the Virginian would welcome funding, assumption, the establishment of a national bank, the organized encouragement of manufactures, and all that this implied. He was understandably surprised, bewildered, and discouraged when Madison organized the opposition to his program. To a mutual friend, he wrote, "When I accepted the Office, I now hold, it was under a full persuasion, that from similarity of thinking, conspiring with personal goodwill, I should have the firm support of Mr. Madison, in the *general course* of my administration. Aware of the intrinsic difficulties of the situation and of the powers of Mr. Madison, I do not believe I should have accepted under a different supposition."[80] He had badly misjudged his former collaborator. Hamilton might have been a bit more wary had he read the French ambassador's judgment that the young congressman from Virginia was "a man whom it is necessary to study for a long time in order to form a just idea of him."[81]

Alexander Hamilton's outlook as a radical nationalist accorded well with his experience and situation. Like George Washington and most of the other officers of the Continental Line, he had become disillusioned with state sovereignty quite early on as a direct consequence of what he had undergone and had witnessed in the course of the Revolutionary War. By the beginning of the 1780s—well before it had become evident that the states were incapable of protecting private property and rights—he was already an advocate of a complete federal consolidation. It had been easy for Hamilton to reach this conclusion. Unlike most of his fellow citizens, he had been born abroad in the West Indies, not in one of the thirteen colonies, and he had barely reached New York on the eve of the Revolution. Thereafter, he had devoted his efforts and even risked his life on behalf of the new nation; by the standards of the time, he was relatively indifferent to his adopted state.

The diffidence which Hamilton felt for the state in which he resided was not a quality widely shared by the statesmen with whom he worked. James Madison, in particular, and his close friend and neighbor Thomas Jefferson—these men were Virginians through and through. They had been born into well-established families, they had grown up in the colony, and over time they had become deeply attached to it by sentiment and by interest. Furthermore, neither had done military service during the war. Despite all that he said and did at the Philadelphia convention and in its immediate aftermath, Madison was, at least in the beginning, a reluctant nationalist. Circumstances had driven him to a position superficially similar to that occupied by Hamilton, but his commitment to centralization was, in fact, far less extreme. Madison had served in the Continental Congress from 1780 to 1783, and he had recognized the dangers to the Union arising from its imbecility. That had distressed him, and he had gone to considerable lengths to bolster the Union, particularly during his last year as a congressman. Even then, however, he rarely failed to give the interests of Virginia preeminence, and as a strict constructionist of the Articles of Confederation, he had opposed Robert Morris's proposal that Congress charter a bank of North America. The years which Madison spent in the Virginia assembly after his retirement from Congress were, in fact, far more decisive in shaping his views, for there he had gained a keen appreciation of the horrors which unimpeded state sovereignty could produce. It would not be a great exaggeration to say that the Virginian became a nationalist in the first place in order to protect the political health of the state which he loved.[82] There was, then, warrant for the mistake which Hamilton later made in supposing that his opponent's attachment to the United States was "more an affair of the head than of the heart—more the result of a conviction of the necessity of Union than of cordiality to the thing itself."[83] When it came to political loyalties, Madison felt more than one tug.

Madison's devotion to the Commonwealth of Virginia rendered him much more sympathetic than Hamilton to those of his friends and neighbors who had expressed grave misgivings regarding the new constitution. Among the Anti-Federalists, he was persuaded, there were "not a few, particularly in Virginia" who were governed by "the most honorable and patriotic motives."[84] The sentiments of men like Patrick Henry, George Mason, James Monroe, and John Tyler were not to be spurned. So, in the wake of ratification and his own election to Congress, Madison took it as his own particular task to promote a reconciliation between the men of goodwill in both of the parties which had divided his state and the nation as a whole. He was acutely aware that it was in the public interest that the Constitution and, with it, the question of the regime cease to be the focus of partisan strife. If factional disputation was not to tear the fledgling nation asunder, it was in fact vital that the document come to be accepted and revered by all.

It would be an error to suppose that, in his eagerness to promote reverence for the Constitution, Madison was comparable with Edmund Burke, for the American left it unambiguous that he took as his ultimate guide man's natural rights; he emphatically asserted the right to revolution; and he never assigned to prescription anything even remotely like the elevated status conferred on it by the English statesman. Indeed, in 1787, Madison demonstrated an extraordinary capacity for revolutionary action. For, in effect, he helped stage a second American revolution when he masterminded the effort to persuade the federal convention to ignore its commission, to jettison the Articles of Confederation, and to propose an entirely new system of government—which would be ratified not in accord with the established legal procedures for amendment spelled out in the articles but by the people of the United States acting outside the bounds of law through specially elected conventions. And yet, if Madison was a revolutionary, he tended also to be extremely cautious and prudent. He had learned a great deal from reflection on the arguments presented by David Hume, and in at least one regard, he resembled his former colleague Alexander Hamilton: from the Scot, he had imbibed a healthy respect for the power of prejudice, if not for its adequacy as a substitute for moral and political rationality.[85]

In consequence, Madison rejected Thomas Jefferson's case for "a frequent reference of constitutional questions, to the decision of the whole society," and he did so on two distinct, but closely related grounds. "As every appeal to the people would carry an implication of some defect in the government," he noted, "frequent appeals would in great measure deprive the government of that veneration, which time bestows on every thing, and without which perhaps the wisest and freest governments would not possess the requisite stability." At the same time, he thought "the danger of disturbing the public tranquility by interesting too strongly the public passions . . . a still more serious objection." There was something almost miraculous about the comparative unanimity achieved in the federal convention and the success of the new constitution's supporters in securing that document's ratification, for it was always dangerous to open up the middle ground of grand politics by raising fundamental questions regarding the very nature of the regime. One could hardly do so without stirring up party strife, and then it was almost inevitable that "the *passions*" and "not *the reason*, of the public, would sit in judgment."[86] If Madison was intent on appeasing the Anti-Federalists and on enlisting them as supporters of the new constitutional order, it was because he was convinced that no other expedient could more effectively unite the country, stabilize the new regime, and prevent a frequent recurrence to first principles.

Of course, Madison had other reasons for pursuing the same immediate end. But it is no disparagement of his character to add that it was also very much in his own interest not only to regain the confidence of those in the state legislature who had chosen the Anti-Federalists Richard Henry Lee and William Grayson United States senators in his stead but also to attract the support of the considerable group from among his more immediate neighbors who had voted for his Anti-Federalist opponent James Monroe when the two men ran for Congress. No democratic statesman can afford to ignore the opinions of the people.[87]

Thus, while Hamilton was pondering the various, indirect means by which the states could be further subjected to the federal will, Madison was considering how one might most effectively mollify and win over the last-ditch defenders of state sovereignty and local control. For this reason, the latter never again suggested that the federal government be empowered with a veto over state laws. With considerable justice, he believed that the Constitution had been ratified on the understanding that the limits it imposed on federal power would be strictly enforced and on the supposition that a bill of rights would be subsequently added to the document itself. He was particularly eager that the new government honor that understanding and that supposition, and he hoped that it would be administered in such a fashion that it would attract to the Constitution an unanimous consent.[88]

Madison's first act in pursuit of these ends was to propose a series of constitutional amendments embodying a bill of rights. On this matter, he was not in agreement with Thomas Jefferson.[89] He did not consider the absence of such a declaration within the document "a material defect." In fact, he told his neighbor that he would not himself be particularly "anxious" to add a bill of rights to the Constitution "by subsequent amendment" were it not for the fact "that it is anxiously desired by others." In a monarchy, he explained, "the latent force of the nation is superior to that of the Sovereign." In such a regime, "a solemn charter of popular rights" could "have a great effect as a standard for trying the validity of public acts, and a signal for rousing and uniting the superior force of the community." But, where there is "a popular Government, the political and physical power may be considered as vested in the same hands, that is in the majority of the people, and consequently the tyrannical will of the Sovereign is not to be controuled by the dread of an appeal to any other force within the community." The "parch-ment barriers" prefixed to the various state constitutions had not served as a restraint on the state legislatures; no similar barrier could be expected to control the national legislature either. Fortunately, there was little danger to be apprehended from that quarter: the limitations imposed on "the powers of the federal Government, and the jealousy of the subordinate Governments" were a sufficient check.[90]

Madison was, nonetheless, willing to acknowledge that a declaration of rights might be of some advantage even in a popular regime. To begin with, the Anti-Federalists were right on at least one point.[91] Such a charter would inevitably have an educational effect: "The political truths declared in that solemn manner acquire by degrees the character of fundamental maxims of free Government, and as they become incorporated with the national senti-ment, counteract the impulses of interest and passion." Furthermore, though generally "the danger of oppression lies in the interested majorities of the people rather than in usurped acts of the Government," there might still be "occasions on which the evil may spring from the latter sources; and on such, a bill of rights will be a good ground for an appeal to the sense of the community." Madison was even willing to contemplate the possibility "that a succession of artful and ambitious rulers" might "by gradual and well-timed advances, finally erect an independent Government on the subversion of lib-erty." "Should this danger exist at all," he concluded, "it is prudent to guard against it, especially when the precaution can do no injury."[92]

These remarks were made in a letter written in October 1788. Eight months later, when Madison actually proposed the Bill of Rights, he evidenced a far greater sense of urgency. "Every motive of prudence," he remarked to his fellow congressmen, dictates that "some things . . . be incorporated into the Constitution, as will render it as acceptable to the whole people of the United States, as it has been found acceptable to a majority of them." In that way, "those who had been friendly to the adoption of this constitution" might prove "to those who were opposed to it, that they were as sincerely devoted to liberty and a republican government, as those who charged them with wishing the adoption of this constitution in order to lay the foundation of an aristocracy or despotism." His aim was "to extinguish from the bosom of every member of the community any apprehensions, that there are those among his countrymen who wish to deprive them of the liberty for which they valiantly fought and honorably bled." There were two states, he re-minded his listeners, which had not yet ratified the Constitution; everything should be done to encourage Rhode Island and North Carolina to rejoin the Union.

Madison had not in the intervening months changed his mind in any dramatic way. He still doubted whether there was any great danger to be apprehended from the federal government itself, and he even specified that, under the new constitution, "it is, perhaps, less necessary to guard against abuse in the executive department than in any other; because it is not the stronger branch of the system, but the weaker." In a popular republic, he asserted once again, the real danger came not from the executive nor, in fact, from the legislature; it stemmed, rather, from "abuse" by "the community" itself, that is, from injustices committed by "the body of the people, operating by the majority against the minority." Because he still supposed that such abuse was most likely to take place on the level of the states and localities, he included among his proposals a series of restrictions intended to prevent these governments from infringing on the rights of conscience, the freedom of the press, and the right to trial by jury in criminal cases. Against the popular will, he acknowledged, "paper barriers" might well have little effect—except perhaps in their "tendency to impress some degree of respect for them, to establish the public opinion in their favor, and rouse the attention of the whole community."

To these remarks, Madison added others which indicated that the debates at the convention and those which took place during the ratification struggle had caused him to do some more thinking—first, about the manner in which "a succession of artful and ambitious rulers" might "by gradual and well-timed advances finally erect an independent Government on the subversion of liberty," and, then, about the means by which such advances might most effectively be resisted. Those who thought the passage of a bill of rights unnecessary tended to argue that the enumeration of powers within the Constitution was a sufficient check on federal aggrandizement. Madison acknowledged the point but drew attention to the fact that "even if the Government keeps within those limits, it has certain discretionary powers with respect to the means, which may admit of abuse to a certain extent." There is within the Constitution, he noted, "a clause granting to Congress the power to make all laws which shall be necessary and proper for carrying into execution all the powers vested in the government of the United States, or in any department or officer thereof." Congress could easily judge certain laws "necessary and proper . . . which laws in themselves are neither necessary nor proper." There were two ways in which a bill of rights could serve to prevent encroachments of this sort. In the first place, the incorporation of such a declaration within the Constitution would enable "independent tribunals of justice" to function as "the guardians" of the popular rights by becoming "an impenetrable bulwark against every assumption of power in the legislative or executive" contrary to the rights expressly stipulated in the Constitution. "Besides this security," he added, "there is a great probability that such a declaration in the federal system would be inforced." For this advantage, one could depend on "the state legislatures." They "will jealously and closely watch the operations" of the central government; they will "be able to resist with more effect every assumption of power than any other power on earth can do." The opponents of the federal constitution themselves "admit the state legislatures to be sure guardians of the people's liberty." [93]

Already, in *The Federalist* and at the Virginia Ratifying Convention, Madison had defended the new constitution against those inclined to distrust the central government by remarking that the state legislatures would be able to rally the people against federal encroachment—but, in truth, he had not then been a particularly vigorous partisan of what he called "the *federal principle*." [94] He had long been willing to concede the possibility that, "in too extensive" and fragmented a society, "a defensive concert may be rendered too difficult against the oppression of those entrusted with the administration" of the federal government.[95] But he did not think the danger either immediate or great. At that time, his distrust was still focused on the sundry state administrations.[96] Nonetheless, as the months passed and he tried to do full justice to the objections raised by his friends and neighbors, Madison began to treat the possibility of federal encroachment and the virtues of the relative independence left to the states with increasing respect. By the summer of 1789, he had in an extremely rough and tentative fashion sketched out the grounds on which and the means by which he, Thomas Jefferson, and the many allies they enlisted from among the Anti-Federalists would later oppose and resist the system of Alexander Hamilton and the measures adopted by his allies in what would become known as the Federalist party.[97]

III.iii.6

Had anyone predicted to James Madison in June 1789 that he would soon be leading the opposition to the Washington administration, the young statesman would probably have thought the man daft. Up to that point, he had been the chief spokesman in Congress for that administration, and the work he had done in securing passage of the legislation which set the new government in motion had been absolutely essential to its well-being. It was only gradually that he came to be an opponent, and he did not begin shifting ground until after the first session of the First Congress had come to an end.

In January 1790, when Alexander Hamilton presented to Congress his *Report Relative to a Provision for the Support of Public Credit*, he made one costly error. He proposed that the new government make provision for the debts owed by the old confederation, that it assume the as yet unpaid obligations incurred by the states in the course of the Revolutionary War, and that it fund both through a system of tariffs and excise taxes—but in suggesting these measures, he failed to take into account the peculiar situation of Virginia and North Carolina. By the time that Hamilton and the other members of the initial administration assumed their responsibilities, the loan office and final settlement certificates issued by the Continental Congress had become an object of speculation; fully four-fifths, if not more, had been sold (usually for a pittance) by those to whom they had originally been issued. Some men, those who had had the capital to invest, stood to reap enormous, windfall profits from the measures proposed by the secretary of the treasury, but very few of these were to be found among the debt-ridden planters of Virginia and North Carolina.[98] There was another problem as well. By 1790, a number of states—North Carolina and Virginia among them—had managed by means generally less than admirable to eliminate or retire most, if not all, of their outstanding debts.[99] In short, for the citizens of these two states, Hamilton's plan entailed taxes but little in the way of largesse or relief.[100]

That placed James Madison in an extremely awkward and potentially embarrassing position. He had long been aware that "every new regulation concerning commerce or revenue, or in any manner affecting the value of the different species of property, represents a new harvest to those who watch the change, and can trace its consequences; a harvest reaped not by themselves, but by the toils and cares of the great body of their fellow-citizens." And, in *The Federalist*, he had announced his hostility to measures and institutions with a tendency to give "unreasonable advantage . . . to the sagacious, the enterprising, and the moneyed few over the industrious and uninformed mass of the people."[101] Moreover, James Madison was ambitious; he had been denied a seat in the Senate and had encountered formidable opposition in his campaign for election to Congress; and during the recess, he had visited Virginia and had been reminded just how many of his neighbors considered the new government suspect. It was natural and perhaps even inevitable that he find a way to vote and speak against a measure so beneficial to clever speculators and so contrary to the interests of his hardworking constituents back home. The fact that nine of the ten congressmen from his state joined him speaks volumes about the response which Hamilton's report generated there.[102] In February 1790, Madison reversed course, abandoned his earlier opposition to discrimination, and advanced two proposals that would have set a precedent fatal both to Hamilton's plan to restore the government's ability to borrow and to his program for turning the public debt into a medium able to circulate as a substitute for coin. To appease his constituents, the Virginian first advocated that Congress distinguish between the two groups in possession of the federal certificates by paying face value to the small number of original holders who still retained the paper issued them and half that or less to the speculators who had purchased theirs later; he then proposed that Congress make some provision for those original holders who had sold their certificates. Fortunately for Hamilton, North Carolina had only recently ratified the Constitution and was as yet unrepresented in New York. The proposal attracted only four votes from congressmen representing states other than Virginia.[103]

Congress's rejection of discrimination did not end Hamilton's difficulties. For Madison then attacked the assumption of the state debts, and this time he drew support from the newly arrived North Carolina delegation.[104] A number of prominent Virginians had been speculating in land located along the Potomac River near the falls that marked the limits of its navigability from the sea; their hope and expectation was that the new nation would follow George Washington's wishes and build its capital there.[105] By holding Hamilton's proposals for funding and assumption hostage, as they were able to do, Madison and his friends thought that they could force a compromise. Funding and assumption would pass—but only if two conditions were met: a way would have to be found to compensate Virginia in some measure for the debts she had retired, and the capital would have to be located in a place convenient for Virginians in general and profitable for a few Virginians in particular. The strategy worked. Not long after he had taken up his duties as Washington's secretary of state, Thomas Jefferson invited both Hamilton and Madison to dinner, and his two guests struck a deal. Mindful of the popularity which his opposition to funding and assumption had won him back home, Madison chose not to alter his own vote. But he saw to it, nonetheless, that the requisite number of congressmen did so.[106]

Unfortunately, however, the agreement reached by Jefferson's dinner companions was not in itself sufficient to guarantee that the terms of the bargain would be honored. Hamilton could himself see to it that Virginia was generously treated by the Department of the Treasury, but he could not guarantee that Congress would vote to locate the District of Columbia on the Potomac— and when it did so, he could not ensure that it would then subsequently go through with its initial decision. To enforce the terms of the deal, Madison and Jefferson later found that they had to threaten and ultimately launch a second assault, this time on the constitutionality of Hamilton's plan for the establishment of a national bank.[107] In making that attack, the two Virginians found themselves expounding principles that set them in opposition to the New Yorker's entire program.[108]

Here again, the two men had political motives as well. In the months following the approval of Hamilton's first report, the citizens of Virginia had become alarmed, and in December 1790, just as Hamilton's *Report on the National Bank* was being presented, the legislature of that state had approved a remonstrance against funding and assumption. Drafted by a committee made up of Anti-Federalists and Federalists alike, the memorial cited the constitutional clause enumerating the powers of the federal government, charged that funding and assumption were unconstitutional encroachments on powers reserved to the states, and noted that there was "a striking resemblance" between Hamilton's "system and that which was introduced into England at the Revolution—a system which has perpetuated upon that nation an enormous debt and has, moreover, insinuated into the hands of the executive an unbounded influence which, pervading every branch of the government, bears down all opposition and daily threatens the destruction of every thing that appertains to English liberty." The memorialists contended that "to erect and concentrate and perpetuate a large monied interest is a measure which . . . must, in the course of human events, produce one or other of two evils: the prostration of agriculture at the feet of commerce or a change in the present form of federal government fatal to the existence of American liberty."[109] Even if they had thought the establishment of a national bank essential, Madison and Jefferson could hardly have with impunity ignored the convictions of their fellow citizens back home.

And yet, had the location of the capital not been at stake, the two men might well have remained silent or at least muted in their criticism regarding the bank. In the event, they waited to intervene until the last possible moment. While Jefferson argued against the bank bill within the administration, Madison did so on its third reading in Congress. In the first of his two speeches on the subject, he read aloud a variety of passages from the debates at the ratifying conventions held in Pennsylvania, Virginia, and North Carolina; these speeches revealed "the grounds on which the Constitution had been vindicated by its principal advocates, against a dangerous latitude of its powers, charged by its opponents."

Madison's premise—unspoken at the time, but later made explicit—was that the principles of republican government and the doctrine of consent require that the "legitimate meaning" of the federal constitution "be derived from the text itself" as interpreted in light of "the sense in which" that instrument "was accepted and ratified by the nation"—which is to say, as

interpreted in light of "the sense attached to it by the people in their respective State Conventions where" the Constitution "rec^d all the Authority
which it possesses." In elaborating this argument, Madison would eventually expand his list of "just guides" for "interpreting the Const^n of the U.S."
to include three additional, but closely related canons: the "evils & defects"
which the Constitution was "called for and introduced" to cure, "the comments prevailing at the time it was adopted," and "the early, deliberate &
continued practice under the Constitution." By that time, he was even willing to concede that "the 'Federalist' may fairly enough be regarded as the
most authentic exposition of the text of the federal Constitution, as understood by the Body which prepared & the Authority which accepted it." But
in 1791 he had no need to recommend historical study: his point was simply
that the arguments advanced in the public debates concerning ratification
just three and four years before could give no warrant to anything other than
a narrow construction of the clause granting to Congress the right to make all
laws "necessary and proper" for carrying into execution the powers vested
in the government. "With all this evidence of the sense in which the constitution was understood and adopted," he pointedly asked, "will it not be
said, if the bill should pass, that its adoption was brought about by one set
of arguments, and that it is now administered under the influence of another
set; and this reproach will have the keener sting, because it is applicable to
so many individuals concerned in both the adoption and administration."[110]

In his second speech, Madison echoed the fears of his friends and neighbors back home. He drew the attention of the Congress to "the great and extensive influence that incorporated societies had on public affairs in Europe."
"They are," he observed, "a powerful machine, which have always been
found competent to effect objects on principles, in a great measure independent of the people." For him, this was a critical objection, for "he considered
the enlightened opinion and affection of the people, the only solid basis for
the support of this government."[111]

Madison's advocacy of discrimination and his opposition to assumption
were tactical maneuvers; his assault on the bank bill had an additional dimension as well. He really was convinced that the Constitution had been ratified
on the basis of a promise that the clauses listing the powers and responsibilities of the federal government be narrowly construed, and he shared not
only the distrust his countrymen evidenced for high-toned government but
also their distaste for the Junto Whigs' use of financial institutions to stabilize
and strengthen the English regime. On all three counts, Thomas Jefferson
was in full agreement with his friend, and the two had other grounds for dis-
satisfaction with Hamilton's scheme. They had long been persuaded that the

European states were so dependent on the import of American agricultural products that, if the United States were endowed with a vigorous national government, the country would be in a position to dictate the terms of its trade with the outside world.[112] In *The Federalist*, Hamilton had eloquently defended this view himself.[113] But, in 1791, he was no longer willing to see the new nation incur the risks which commercial warfare involved. In particular, he was firmly committed to sustaining the public credit and to the system of moderate tariffs which provided the steady income necessary to make provision for the national debt, and this inevitably set him against any immediate attempt to use commercial restrictions in an attempt to free the newborn republic from its embarrassing dependence on commerce with Britain. To the two Virginians, Hamilton's change of heart in this particular seemed inexplicable and regrettable. All three men were inclined to the view that American independence would be incomplete so long as the United States remained an economic appendage of the mother country. They differed in their estimation of the country's staying power. The two southerners were far more optimistic than their colleague from New York regarding the capacity of the infant republic to emerge victorious from a commercial struggle with Great Britain, and they had already begun to wonder whether the secretary of the treasury was willing to sacrifice essential attributes of sovereignty for the sake of bolstering the new nation's credit.[114]

Though Jefferson and Madison were less than fully satisfied, neither man was as yet bitterly opposed to the administration. Neither then alluded to Hamilton's proposals as a scheme for subjecting America to England and for subverting its republican regime.[115] Indeed, they were both far more favorable to the measures he recommended than their public demeanor would have led one to expect, and they were on polite, even amicable terms with Hamilton himself.[116] Nonetheless, each of the two Virginians evidenced a marked uneasiness regarding the direction in which the new government was tending, and the weight of the arguments which they had publicly advanced clearly demanded that they oppose with greater vigor the policies they disliked. By the spring of 1791, it may have seemed easier and more natural for the two Virginians to continue down the same path than to reverse their course.

III.iii.7

Hamilton appears not to have foreseen any danger. Consequently, he took little care to avoid offending the sensibilities of his colleagues. That spring, not long after Congress recessed, President Washington left Philadelphia to make an extended tour of the southern states. He instructed the members of his Cabinet to meet in his absence when the public business demanded decision, and he suggested that John Adams, the vice-president, be invited to join them. In April, on one such occasion, Thomas Jefferson hosted a dinner. After the meal, once the business had been dispatched, the discussion somehow drifted onto the subject of the British constitution. It was to be a conversation fraught with significance for all of those present.

According to Jefferson's subsequent report, the vice-president and the secretary of the treasury took this as an opportunity for an exchange of quips: "Mr. Adams observed 'purge that constitution of it's corruption, and give to it's popular branch equality of representation, and it would be the most perfect constitution every devised by the wit of man.' Hamilton paused and said, 'purge it of it's corruption, and give to it's popular branch equality of representation, & it would become an *impracticable* government: as it stands at present, with all it's supposed defects, it is the most perfect government which ever existed.' "[117] Jefferson cannot have been pleased by the vice-president's remarks, but he can hardly have been shocked. He had long been painfully aware that John Adams, after a brief flirtation with classical republicanism, had returned to traditional Whig doctrine—monarchy, aristocracy, and all.[118] In February 1787, when Adams sent him the first volume of his massive *Defense of the Constitutions of Government of the United States of America*, Jefferson immediately offered to arrange for its translation into French and its publication in Paris. But after perusing the work, he abandoned the attempt in apparent dismay. His old friend's representation of the various state constitutions as more or less faithful replicas of the British constitution left him appalled.[119] But, distressing though it clearly was, this news was stale long before the spring of 1791, and Adams had, in any case, just recently restated his unfortunate opinions in the *Discourses on Davila* which he published in the popular press.[120] It was Hamilton's retort that jolted the secretary of state.

From 1784 to 1789, Jefferson had been abroad in France. While his countrymen were framing, debating, and ratifying a new constitution, he had been contemplating with unbounded optimism the approach of a second great democratic revolution. He did not witness the extraordinary speech which Hamilton delivered in Philadelphia. Nor was he present four days thereafter when the New Yorker fought against the constitutional provision barring placemen from serving in Congress. And so Jefferson did not hear his future colleague and dinner companion heap praise on the British constitution and then later cite David Hume to the effect that the "influence on the side of the crown, which went under the name of corruption," was "an essential part of the weight which maintained the equilibrium of" that constitution. In short, it is just possible that it was during that fateful, after-dinner discussion in April 1791 that Thomas Jefferson first became aware of the degree to which the secretary of the treasury was an admirer of both the English constitution and the system of Walpole. It was, in any case, only thereafter that he turned against the man.

Before that event, the sentiments voiced by Adams and others had made Washington's secretary of state somewhat fearful regarding the future of the American democracy, but he had not expressed any particular alarm concerning the fiscal measures proposed by his colleague from New York. In early February, Jefferson had written to George Mason of his eagerness that the revolutionary government in France be firmly established. "I consider the establishment and success of their government," he explained, "as necessary to stay up our own, and to prevent it from falling back to that kind of Half-way house, the English constitution." He thought this necessary because he had discovered, at the seat of the American government, "a sect" persuaded that the English model contained "whatever is perfect in human institutions." He added that "the members of this sect have, many of them, names and offices which stand high in the estimation of our countrymen." Though Madison had launched his assault on the constitutionality of Hamilton's proposal for the establishment of a national bank just two days before, Jefferson seemed concerned only that Hamilton's "fiscal arrangments" might have an ill effect on "the present temper of the Southern states." "Whether these measures be right or wrong, abstractedly," he observed with evident equanimity, "more attention should be paid to the general opinion."[121] At no time prior to that evening in April did either Jefferson or Madison describe Hamilton's system as a conspiracy against the republican order. For them, the New Yorker's flippant remark seems to have caused everything to fall gradually into place. One can only guess that Jefferson's report induced Madison to look over again the notes he had taken during the Philadelphia convention; it was all too easy to find confirmation in Hamilton's great speech and his subsequent remarks for the suspicion that his bold and comprehensive program was aimed at preparing the way for a change of regime.[122]

Some time passed before Hamilton had any inkling of the degree to which his remarks and the views espoused by the vice-president had disturbed the secretary of state. By that time, it had become public knowledge that Jefferson discerned in the *Discourses on Davila* "political heresies" in need of forceful refutation; and in the midst of the ensuing controversy, Adams had written to his old friend to make it clear that the Virginian was mistaken in assuming that the vice-president had ever had "a design or desire, of attempting to introduce a Government of King, Lords and Commons [or] in other Words an hereditary Executive or hereditary Senate, either into the Government of the United States, or that of any Individual State, in this Co[untry]." [123] When Jefferson mentioned the letter, Hamilton seized the opportunity to clarify his own views as well. According to the notes which Jefferson made just after the New Yorker's departure, Hamilton acknowledged his belief that "the present govmt is not that which will answer the ends of society by giving stability & protection to it's rights, and that it will probably be found expedient to go into the British form." But he then added a disclaimer. Once the republican "experiment" was undertaken, he was "for giving it a fair course," his doubts notwithstanding. Thus far, the regime had been far more successful than he had anticipated, and he was reasonably sanguine regarding its future. Even if the new constitution proved inadequate to its purpose, he was of the view that various amendments "may be tried & ought to be tried before we give up the republican form altogether[,] for that mind must be really depraved which would not prefer the equality of political rights which is the foundn of pure republicanism, if it can be obtained consistently with order." [124]

Years later, when Hamilton was in his grave, John Marshall included in his account of the New Yorker's retirement from office an assessment of the man's career. "It was known that, in his judgment, the constitution of the United States was rather chargeable with imbecility, than censurable for its too great strength," he wrote,

> and that the real sources of danger to American happiness and liberty, were to be found in its want of the means to effect the objects of its institution;—in its being exposed to the encroachments of the states,—not in the magnitude of its powers. Without attempting to conceal these opinions, he declared his perfect acquiescence in the decision of his country; his hope that the issue would be fortunate; and his firm determination, in whatever might depend upon his exertions, to give the experiment the fairest chance for success. No part of his political conduct has been perceived, which would inspire doubts of the sincerity of these declarations. His friends may appeal with confidence to his official acts, to all his public conduct, for the refutation of those charges which were made against him while at the head of the treasury department, and were continued, without interruption, till he ceased to be the object of jealousy. [125]

Marshall's judgment deserves acceptance. [126] There is no reason to doubt the sincerity of Hamilton's remarks to Jefferson. [127] They accord well with what he said and did both before and after. [128] At the Philadelphia convention, he had not seriously sought the establishment of an American monarchy; his purpose in delivering his great speech had been to break the deadlock which had developed over the allocation of representation to the states. He merely wanted to persuade the delegates of the need "to tone their Government as high as possible." Indeed, before he had made his initial withdrawal from the convention, he had intervened one last time to indicate that "he concurred with Mr. Madison in thinking we were now to decide for ever the fate of Republican government; and if we did not give to that form due stability and wisdom, it would be disgraced & lost among ourselves, disgraced & lost to mankind for ever."[129] There was no need to speak in this way if he was not, as he later claimed, "*affectionately* attached to the Republican theory."[130]

Hamilton never budged from the position he outlined during his conversation with the secretary of state. In May 1792, in a letter meant to have a wide circulation, the New Yorker testified that he desired "*above all things* to see the *equality* of political rights exclusive of all *hereditary* distinction firmly established by a practical demonstration of its being consistent with the order and happiness of society." He still had "strong hopes" for "the success" of the republican "theory," but he conceded that he was "far from being without doubts." "I consider its success a problem," he wrote. "It is yet to be determined by experience whether it be consistent with that *stability* and *order* in Government which are essential to public strength & private security and happiness."[131]

Hamilton's letter was intended to quiet the uproar generated by his program, but neither this effort nor his earlier attempt to calm Jefferson's fears was of any avail. By the time that the New Yorker sought to clarify his views in conversation with the secretary of state, the two Virginians had conferred with Chancellor Livingston, with Aaron Burr, and with a number of the other men known to be hostile to Hamilton or distressed by his system of finance; they had even, by then, managed secretly to recruit the poet and publicist Philip Freneau to found a journal which would serve as an organ dedicated to the defense of the republican cause against the putative adherents of monarchism.[132] Nine months later, when Hamilton penned the letter explaining his views, an epic struggle was already under way: Jefferson was making a concerted effort to persuade the president to dismiss his former aide-de-camp as a conspirator against the republic, and Madison was directing the efforts of a formed opposition within the House of Representatives. From that time on, every step taken by the secretary of the treasury and virtually every decision reached or measure proposed by the administrations of George Washington and John Adams would be interpreted as an attempt to establish America's dependence on England, federal dominion over the states, and executive domination of Congress—all in subversion of America's nascent republican order.[133]

In the midst of the bitter, partisan strife that broke out in the 1790s, Thomas Jefferson consoled himself with the thought that "in every free & deliberating society there must, from the nature of man, be opposite parties & violent dissensions & discords."[134] His was a just, if melancholy, observation. It really is doubtful whether it would have been possible to avoid the great quarrel which divided the men most responsible for founding and sustaining the world's first fully modern republic. One must, nonetheless, wonder whether that quarrel had to break out as soon as it did and assume the precise shape that it so quickly assumed. There is much to be said for the judgment voiced by Gouverneur Morris some months before the Federalist party went down to ignominious defeat. "The thing, which, in my opinion has done most mischief to the federal party," he remarked, "is the ground given by some of them to believe, that they wish to establish a monarchy."[135] Alexander Hamilton was, indeed, "indiscreet." He recognized that it would be impossible to institute even a limited monarchy in the United States, and he knew that there was no point in even arguing for such a policy; yet, as Morris would ultimately observe, he "never failed on every occasion to advocate the excellence of, and avow his attachment to, monarchical government." As a result of his stubborn, public adherence to opinions offensive to his compatriots, he "singularly promoted the views of his opponents . . . and approached the evils he apprehended by his very solicitude to keep them at a distance."[136]

CHAPTER 4

Thomas Jefferson and the Spirit of Popular Resistance

If to any people it be the avowed object of policy in all its internal refinements, to secure the person and the property of the subject, without any regard to his political character, the constitution indeed may be free, but its members may likewise become unworthy of the freedom they possess, and unfit to preserve it. The effects of such a constitution may be to immerse all orders of men in their separate pursuits of pleasure, which they may now enjoy with little disturbance; or of gain, which they may preserve without any attention to the commonwealth. If this be the end of political struggles, the design, when executed, in securing to the individual his estate, and the means of subsistence, may put an end to the exercise of those very virtues that were required in conducting its execution. —Adam Ferguson

III.iv.1

The election held in the year 1800 marked a watershed in American politics. Thomas Jefferson supplanted John Adams in the presidency, and, perhaps even more important, Jefferson's Republican party swept the Federalist party from its position of predominance in the House of Representatives once and for all. Looking back on the event nearly two decades thereafter, the author of the Declaration of Independence would remark that it was "as real a revolution in the principles of our government as that of 1776 was in its form."[1] This claim—like Jefferson's fervently held conviction that the struggles of the 1790s were really "contests of principle, between the advocates of republican, and those of kingly government"—was a gross exaggeration.[2] Still, it would not be inaccurate to depict "the revolution of 1800" as a turning point in the conduct of administration. Though the Louisiana Purchase and the War of 1812 delayed its completion, Jefferson and his successors did set the nation on a course that resulted in the elimination of the national bank and the extinction of the federal debt. The initial victory of the Republicans and their success in retaining power thereafter ensured that Hamilton's system would eventually be dismantled altogether.[3]

The ascendancy of the Jeffersonian Republicans had other effects as well, and though their chief importance lay in the formation of public opinion, they were for that very reason all the more profound.[4] Sometime early in 1792, Hamilton first came to recognize that the two Virginians were not just quibbling about certain aspects of the measures he proposed, but had established a formed opposition to defeat what they took to be "some dreadful combination against State Government & republicanism; which according to them, are convertible terms." This circumstance he found extremely distressing. "In such a state of mind," he observed,

> both these Gentlemen are prepared to hazard a great deal to effect a change. Most of the important measures of every Government are connected with the Treasury. To subvert the present head of it they deem it expedient to risk rendering the Government itself odious; perhaps foolishly thinking that they can easily recover the lost affections & confidence of the people, and not appreciating as they ought to do the natural resistance to Government which in every community results from the human passions, the degree to which this is strengthened by the *organised rivality* of State Governments, & the infinite danger that the National Government once rendered odious will be kept so by these powerful & indefatigable enemies.[5]

Some forty years later, at the time of the nullification controversy, John Marshall would look back on the events of the 1790s and remark, "We are now gathering the bitter fruits of the tree . . . planted by Mr. Jefferson, and so industriously and perseveringly cultivated by Virginia."[6] Had he lived to the year 1861, he would have exercised less restraint in voicing his complaint. In the course of their struggle, the leaders of Jefferson's Republican party had fully justified Hamilton's fears by forging weapons which would eventually be turned on the Union itself.[7]

III.iv.2

John Adams and the leaders of the Federalist party bear some responsibility for provoking the Republican reaction. In 1798, while fighting an undeclared war with France on the high seas, they faced at home an opposition openly sympathetic to the French cause and prepared to believe that the administration had contrived the naval confrontation as part of a plot to extend British influence and undermine the republic. Persuaded that a declaration of war would soon be required and fearful that it would spark rebellion in the Republican heartland of Virginia, North Carolina, and Kentucky, the Federalists opted for immediate, preventive repression; and in the wake of the XYZ Affair, they imprudently approved the Alien and Sedition Acts, thereby only further embittering the partisan struggle. Hamilton was then out of office and inclined to distance himself from the political fray, but he wrote to his friends in Philadelphia to urge restraint nonetheless. He thought the first of the two bills "deficient in precautions against abuse and for the security of Citizens"; the second he considered "highly exceptionable & such as more than any thing else may endanger civil war." "Let us not establish a tyranny," he warned one member of Adams's Cabinet. "Energy is a very different thing from violence. If we make no false step we shall be essentially united; but if we push things to an extreme we shall then give to faction *body* & solidarity."[8] His warnings went largely unheeded, and the consequences predicted were not long in coming.

While masquerading as Publius, both Alexander Hamilton and James Madison had gone to considerable lengths to allay the suspicions of the Constitution's opponents by emphasizing that there was little danger to be apprehended from unconstitutional encroachments on the part of the federal government. "The State Legislatures," they explained, "will be ever ready to mark the innovation, to sound the alarm to the people, and to exert their local influence in effecting a change of federal representatives." Indeed, the more severe the crisis, the more likely it would be that "every Government would espouse the common cause. A correspondence would be opened. Plans of resistance would be concerted. One spirit would animate and conduct the whole."[9] In 1798, Jefferson and Madison thought that just such a crisis had come. With the freedom of the press seemingly at stake, the legislatures of Kentucky and Virginia resorted to the strategy which the authors of *The Federalist* had outlined. They passed resolutions secretly drafted by the two Republican leaders; they corresponded with the legislatures of the other states; and they hinted at resistance.[10] In the process, they set a precedent which would later return to haunt the author of the strategy they followed.

In *The Federalist*, Madison had remarked that the decision to ratify the Constitution was to be a federal, not a national, decision—"the act of the people as forming so many independent States, not as forming one aggregate nation."[11] Thomas Jefferson made this description of his fellow citizens' establishment of a more perfect union the foundation of his argument when he composed the Kentucky Resolutions in October 1798. He described the federal exercise of "undelegated powers" as "unauthoritative, void, and of no force." He claimed that "each party" to the federal compact possessed "an equal right to judge for itself, as well of infractions as of the mode and measure of redress." And, most important, he asserted that, where the general government has assumed undelegated powers, "a nullification of the act is the rightful remedy." As he put it, "Every State has a natural right in cases not within the compact, (casus non foederis,) to nullify of their own authority all assumptions of power by others within their limits." Indeed, each was in duty bound to "take measures of its own for providing that neither" the Alien and Sedition Laws "nor any others of the General Government not plainly and intentionally authorized by the Constitution, shall be exercised within their respective territories." In his view, the success of the American Revolution itself was at stake: the Alien and Sedition Acts "and successive acts of the same character, unless arrested at the threshold, necessarily drive these States into revolution and blood, and will furnish new calumnies against republican government, and new pretexts for those who wish it to be believed that man cannot be governed but by a rod of iron." [12] At the time that he penned these incendiary words, Jefferson was vice-president of the United States.

In this, as in other matters, James Madison was considerably more cautious and judicious than his close friend and neighbor. [13] To begin with, he made no appeal to natural right, and he nowhere attributed to each of the individual states as such "an equal right to judge for itself, as well of infractions as of the mode and measure of redress." When he drafted the Virginia Resolutions in December 1798, then entered the state assembly and wrote his famous report defending those resolutions, he made the states united the final arbiters of the Constitution. In both documents, he consistently and deliberately employed the plural form. In the resolutions, he argued that "the powers of the federal government" are derived from and limited by "the compact to which the states are parties." Where there is "a deliberate, palpable, and dangerous exercise of other powers, not granted by the said compact, the states who are parties thereto have the right, and are in duty bound, to interpose, for arresting the progress of the evil, and for maintaining, within their respective limits, the authorities, rights, and liberties appertaining to them." In defending that claim, he subsequently asserted that there was "no tribunal superior to the authority of the parties" to the compact and that "the parties themselves must" therefore "be the rightful judges, in the last resort, whether the bargain made has been pursued or violated."

To justify state interposition, the resolutions made a series of charges. The federal government was said to be attempting "to enlarge its powers by forced constructions" of the Constitution. It was deliberately ignoring the enumeration of powers and expounding "certain general phrases" within the Constitution "so as to consolidate the states, by degrees, into one sovereignty, the obvious tendency and inevitable result of which would be to transform the present republican system of the United States into an absolute, or at best a mixed monarchy." This was most clearly made evident by the Alien and Sedition Acts—the latter of which presumed a power "not delegated by the Constitution, but, on the contrary, expressly and positively forbidden" by the First Amendment. The Sedition Act was of vital importance because it was "levelled against the right of freely examining public characters and measures, and of free communication among the people thereon, which has ever been justly deemed the only effectual guardian of every other right."

Madison did not specify in the resolutions what he meant by *interposition*. Later, in his report, he mentioned the state legislature's ability to rally public opinion, its capacity to propose amendments to the Constitution, and the like.[14] To Jefferson's dismay, he chose to describe the Alien and Sedition Acts as "unconstitutional" but not to declare them "null, void, and of no force, or effect."[15] Accordingly, he nowhere endorsed "nullification" as "the rightful remedy" against federal encroachment, and he neither hinted at secession nor suggested that Virginia unilaterally take action to prevent enforcement of the two federal statutes within the state. Mindful that the crisis might become considerably more severe, he left open the question just how far the interposition of the state governments might extend.[16]

Between 1798 and 1800, the two leaders of the Republican party walked a fine line between protest and rebellion. James Madison consistently leaned toward the first of these two options without ever entirely ruling out the second; Thomas Jefferson was prepared to countenance talk of secession, particularly when the other states bluntly rejected the appeals made to them by Kentucky and Virginia. Indeed, had Madison not intervened to restrain his friend, Jefferson would have drafted for the two legislatures new resolutions explicitly threatening withdrawal from the Union.[17] In the end, however, after the Republican party proved successful in the elections of 1800, neither man was displeased that the resolutions actually introduced in and passed by the Kentucky legislature were much more moderate in tone than those which Jefferson had drafted himself.[18]

The dramatic Republican victory in 1800 and the subsequent demise of the Federalist party assured the wide acceptance of the principles which the Republicans espoused, and it reversed as well the momentum leading toward a subordination of the states to the nation. By asserting the compact theory of the Constitution and by making the parties to that compact the judges of last resort, the Republican leaders unwittingly restored to the states something of the supremacy which they had possessed under the Articles of Confederation. This would have been perilous under any circumstances; for a republic situated on an extended territory and divided by the question of slavery, it would be very nearly fatal.[19]

III.iv.3

In attacking the Alien Acts, Thomas Jefferson and James Madison made no mention of slavery. Their fellow southerners mentioned very little else. To judge from the statements they made, the planters of Virginia and the neighboring states were not much worried that these measures would place a power in the president's hands dangerous to public liberty; they feared, rather, that to accept the federal government's right to determine whether aliens would be expelled from the United States would be to accept that same government's right to expel the slaves. For similar reasons, when these Jeffersonians attacked the Sedition Act, they spoke less often of the need for a free press than of the rightful prerogatives of the states.[20] Though generally perceptive, the two great Republican leaders appear not to have noticed the link between slavery's defense and their countrymen's desire to restrict federal power.

Thomas Jefferson went to his grave utterly blind to the danger. On the way, he did what he could to keep alive the spirit and principles of 1798. In 1821, for example, he reinforced the authority of the Kentucky Resolutions by acknowledging his authorship of them. Soon thereafter, the program of internal improvements proposed by John Quincy Adams reawakened the aged statesman's fear of consolidation. In 1825, he drafted a letter of protest first denying that the general welfare clause of the Constitution sanctioned the expenditure of federal monies for internal improvements and then expressing the conviction that a dissolution of the Union was preferable to "submission to a government of unlimited powers."[21] Had it not been for James Madison, he probably would have submitted the letter to the state assembly.[22] To Virginia governor William Branch Giles, who had been a Republican stalwart in the struggle against the Federalists, Jefferson wrote of "the rapid strides with which the federal branch of our government is advancing towards the usurpation of all the rights reserved to the States, and the consolidation in itself of all powers, foreign and domestic; and that, too, by constructions which, if legitimate, leave no limits to their power." Here, too, though he knew that his correspondence would eventually find its way into print, he spoke openly of the possibility of secession.

> And what is our resource for the preservation of the constitution? Reason and argument? You might as well reason and argue with the marble columns encircling them. The representatives chosen by ourselves? They are joined in the combination, some from incorrect views of government, some from corrupt ones, sufficient voting together to out-number the

sound parts; and with majorities only of one, two, or three, bold enough to go forward in defiance. Are we then *to stand to our arms?* . . . No. That must be the last resource, not to be thought of until much longer and greater sufferings. If every infraction of a compact of so many parties is to be resisted at once, as a dissolution of it, none can ever be formed which would last one year. We must have patience and longer endurance then with our brethren while under delusion; give them time for reflection to profit by the chapter of accidents; and separate from our companions only when the sole alternatives left, are the dissolution of our Union with them, or submission to a government without limitation of powers.[23]

Despite his willingness to employ the threat of secession, the aging statesmen exercised caution in one important regard. He did not publish the original draft of the Kentucky Resolutions, and so it did not become known until 1832 that the vice-president's version had been much more radical in asserting the prerogatives of the states than the resolutions actually passed.[24] The publication of that draft, coming at the precise moment that it did, gave considerable impetus to the cause of nullification.[25] By then, however, Jefferson had been dead for six years.

In this particular, James Madison was less fortunate than his friend; he lived long enough to foresee the threat posed to the Union by the deliberate distortion and systematic misapplication of the principles propagated in 1798. He never repudiated those principles. But, when the nullification controversy broke out, he acted vigorously—first, to defend the constitutionality and propriety of the tariff then under attack; then, to denounce the doctrine of nullification expounded in South Carolina's Exposition and Protest of 1828 as incompatible with the Constitution, the Virginia Resolutions, and the sacred principle of majority rule; and finally, to refute the notion that any party to the federal compact could justly claim the legal right to withdraw unilaterally from the Union.[26] His notes indicate that Madison spent considerable time during his last four years of life preparing an extended essay refuting the claims made on nullification's behalf by men like John C. Calhoun, George McDuffie, James Hamilton, Jr., and Robert Y. Hayne. In that essay, the octogenarian statesman insisted that the interposition advocated in the Virginia Resolutions was intended to be the effort not of any individual state but rather of the states as a whole. He denied that Virginia had ever seriously considered doing anything on her own more radical than the publication of a remonstrance intended to rally public opinion, and he argued with persuasive force that Jefferson had never contemplated the possibility that a single state, acting alone, could somehow actively obstruct the enforcement of federal law and still remain secure within the Union and at peace with the United States.[27]

There can be little doubt that Madison was deeply worried. When he died in 1836, he left behind as his political testament a document intended to thwart those intent on using the principles of 1798 as a means for promoting disunion. "The advice nearest to my heart and deepest in my convictions is that the Union of the States be cherished and perpetuated," he wrote. "Let the open enemy to it be regarded as a Pandora with her box opened; and the disguised one, as the Serpent creeping with his deadly wiles into Paradise."[28] Unfortunately, Madison's political testament did not reach the public until 1850, and by then it was arguably too late. Eleven years later, Fort Sumter fell and the Civil War was under way.

One cannot help but wonder what might have transpired if the two great statesmen from Virginia had devoted the energy which went into the attack on Hamilton's system to another cause—the containment and ultimate abolition of slavery. From the beginning, they were both keenly aware that the continued existence of slavery and its expansion could give rise to tensions endangering the Union. Like many of their contemporaries, the two had read and taken to heart Montesquieu's humanitarian critique of slavery, and they both knew that the institution bred morals and manners contrary to the egalitarian spirit of modern republican liberty. In his *Notes on the State of Virginia*, Jefferson had given great weight to the "unhappy influence on the manners of our people produced by the existence of slavery among us."

> The whole commerce between master and slave is a perpetual exercise of the most boisterous passions, the most unremitting despotism on the one part, and degrading submissions on the other. Our children see this, and learn to imitate it; for man is an imitative animal. This quality is the germ of all education in him. From his cradle to his grave he is learning to do what he sees others do. If a parent could find no motive either in his philanthropy or his self-love, for restraining the intemperance of passion towards his slave, it should always be a sufficient one that his child is present. But generally it is not sufficient. The parent storms, the child looks on, catches the lineaments of wrath, puts on the same airs in the circle of smaller slaves, gives a loose to his worst of passions, and thus nursed, educated, and daily exercised in tyranny, cannot but be stamped by it with odious peculiarities. The man must be a prodigy who can retain his manners and morals undepraved by such circumstances. . . . With the morals of the people, their industry also is

destroyed. For in a warm climate, no man will labour for himself who can make another labour for him. This is so true, that of the proprietors of slaves a very small proportion indeed are ever seen to labour.[29]

In his correspondence, Jefferson elaborated on this theme. He described northerners largely in favorable terms. They might be "interested, chicaning, superstitious and hypocritical in their religion," but they were at the same time "cool, sober, laborious, persevering, independant, jealous of their own liberties, and just to those of others." His fellow southerners he depicted in a far less flattering fashion. They might be "generous, candid, independant, without attachment or pretensions to any religion but that of the heart," but they were also "fiery, Voluptuary, indolent, unsteady, zealous for their own liberties, but trampling on those of others."[30] Jefferson was concerned also with matters more fundamental than morals and manners; in particular, he was fearful that slavery might eventually have a dangerous effect on public opinion. To the readers of his book, Jefferson posed a simple question: "Can the liberties of a nation be thought secure when we have removed their only firm basis, a conviction in the minds of the people that these liberties are the gift of God? That they are not to be violated but with his wrath?"[31] In the 1780s, the Virginia planter clearly regarded the institution of slavery as a threat to the survival of republican freedom.

Madison's sentiments on the subject were no less firm. At the Philadelphia convention, he alluded to slavery in drawing attention to the insufficiency of conscience as a constraint against the establishment and maintenance of a tyranny through majority rule. "We have seen," he remarked, "the mere distinction of colour made in the most enlightened period of time a ground for the most oppressive dominion ever exercised by man over man."[32] Later, in 1791, when he was making notes in preparation for publishing a series of essays in Philip Freneau's *National Gazette*, he echoed the analysis of slavery's impact on morals and manners that had been laid out by Montesquieu and Jefferson. Slavery, he contended, causes the masters to "cherish pride, luxury, and vanity." "In proportion as slavery prevails in a State," he added, "the Government, however democratic in name, must be aristocratic in fact. The power lies in a part instead of the whole; in the hands of property, not of numbers. All the antient popular governments, were for this reason aristocracies. The majority were slaves. Of the residue a part were in the Country and did not attend the assemblies, a part were poor and tho in the city, could not spare the time to attend. The power, was exercised for the most part by the rich and easy." These notes were not a learned disquisition intended for an academic audience. In framing his historical observations,

Madison had his own region particularly in mind. As he sadly remarked, "The Southern States of America, are on the same principle aristocracies." He even alluded to the fact that Virginia was the least democratic of the states. There, the law restricting the suffrage to freeholders disenfranchised almost half of the state's free inhabitants and thereby reinforced the oligarchy of the slaveholders. "The slavery of the Southern States, throws the power much more into the hands of property, than in the Northern States," he observed. "Hence the people of property in the former are much more contented with their establishd. Governments, than the people of property in the latter." [33]

Madison was quite forceful on this subject. But his remarks were never read by his fellow planters in the South. Focusing instead on the danger purportedly posed by Hamilton's funding program and the class of speculators whom it enriched, the distinguished congressman from Virginia put aside his notes on slavery and never completed the essay he had outlined. In the same period, Thomas Jefferson fell silent as well. The two Republican leaders knew that they could hardly rally support against Hamilton if they were campaigning against the institution which was the chief source of southern wealth and political power; therefore, to stop a nonexistent conspiracy against the republic, they acquiesced in the tyranny exercised by the white southern majority over the region's black minority. To be sure, neither man ever lent his name to the cause of slavery. To the end of their days, when canvassed or otherwise given the opportunity to state their opinions in private, they both politely advocated gradual abolition and colonization. [34] But, especially after 1791, neither was willing to press for immediate action on the question of abolition, and neither was prepared to risk antagonizing his friends and neighbors in the South by bringing home to them the enormity of their continuing to profit from "the most oppressive dominion ever exercised by man over man." In fact, neither man was even willing to set an example for his fellow slaveholders by subjecting himself and his heirs to the financial disabilities involved in his freeing the slaves whom he owned.

What the two men did in their years of retirement was perhaps even more damaging than what they failed to do. At the time of the Missouri crisis, when the opponents of slavery in the North sought to halt its spread to the West, Jefferson denounced their attempt as a Federalist plot. [35] Convinced straightaway that "the speck in our horizon" would "burst on us as a tornado, sooner or later" and persuaded that "the line of division lately marked out between different portions of our confederacy, is such as will never . . . be obliterated," he vigorously opposed as a "canker . . . eating on the vitals of our existence" the penchant of his fellow Virginians for sending their sons "to the northern seminaries" where they were destined to imbibe "opinions and principles in discord with those of their country."[36] The thought is not pleasant, but it must be faced: if Jefferson had still been alive in 1861, he might well have followed his native Virginia in reluctantly siding with the secessionist states of the Deep South.[37] Madison was always more cautious than his old friend, and he would certainly have opposed secession to the very end. But he had always managed, at least in some measure, to accommodate his views to those of his neighbors, and one may wonder whether he would have been willing, for the sake of the Union, to turn his back on his beloved state once its decision had been made.[38] The two former presidents both argued that the interests of the nation and the states would best be served by a diffusion of the slave population over the Union as a whole, and Madison added to his remarks on the matter a claim more ominous still. Nearly four decades before Judge Taney was to hand down his fateful decision in the case of Dred Scott, this eloquent defender of the American Constitution vigorously denied that the federal government possessed the constitutional right to exclude slavery from any of the territories entrusted to its care.[39] Whatever the intentions and expectations of the two Virginians, the practical consequence of their efforts in the 1790s and thereafter was a strengthening of the slaveholder aristocracy.

In retrospect, then, one may justly regret that the two great statesmen from Virginia bitterly opposed Alexander Hamilton's system and chose at the same time to champion the cause of states' rights. But it is only fair to note that the defense of local prerogative, which united the Anti-Federalists of the late 1780s with the Republicans of the 1790s, had a certain justification as well. If Jefferson and Madison can be faulted for failing to grasp—or for choosing to avert their gaze from—the fact that slavery was a far more serious threat to America's great republican experiment than Hamilton's plan of consolidation, they seem nonetheless to have understood one aspect of the republican project more fully than their chosen antagonist. When pondering the great quarrel between the Founders, one may sometimes be reminded of Madison's observation that the "propensity of mankind to fall into mutual animosities" is so strong "that where no substantial occasion presents itself the most frivolous and fanciful distinctions have been sufficient to kindle their unfriendly passions and to excite their most violent conflicts."[40] To the Republican depiction of the Federalist program, Madison's remark can in large measure be aptly applied. But even with this point granted, it would still be a grave error to suppose that nothing of substantive importance was at stake in the struggle which Hamilton's most distinguished detractors initiated in the early national period. It all turned on the conviction, which Jefferson and his supporters shared with Machiavelli, Locke, Sidney, Trenchard and Gordon, and Bolingbroke, that a new species of demotic virtue—unrecognized as such in antiquity, but essential to the maintenance of the liberty peculiar to the modern free state—could and must be fashioned from the popular penchant for resistance to authority.[41]

III.iv.4

Shays's Rebellion, which broke out in western Massachusetts some months before the Constitutional Convention met in Philadelphia, stirred fears which contributed much to the calling of that convention, to its ultimate success, and to the eventual acceptance by the states of the constitution which it proposed.[42] As a consequence, the Anti-Federalists were particularly sensitive to the influence exerted by that uprising. Shortly after the Bay State voted for ratification, one prominent Pennsylvanian sadly observed, "The new constitution was viewed in Massachusetts through the medium of a SHAYS, the terrors of HIS insurrection had not subsided; a government that would have been execrated at another time was embraced by many as a refuge from anarchy, and thus liberty deformed by mad riot and dissention, lost her ablest advocates."[43] This Pennsylvanian was typical of the men one would think most likely to have been sympathetic to the rebels. But nowhere in America, not even among the Anti-Federalists, could one find a respected public figure willing to say a kind word about the uprising or to make excuses for the men implicated in it.[44]

The nearly universal dearth of sympathy for the Shaysites makes the attitude of Thomas Jefferson, then serving as an American envoy in Paris, seem all the more perplexing. The expatriate planter may, in fact, have been alone in being unperturbed by the insurrection; he was almost certainly unique in greeting the news of the event with a measure of jubilation. "I like a little rebellion now and then," the Virginian wrote to Abigail Adams. "It is like a storm in the Atmosphere. . . . The spirit of resistance to government is so valuable on certain occasions, that I wish it to be always kept alive."[45]

This arresting remark cannot be dismissed as a passing, thoughtless, idle observation; nor is it an example of the rhetorical excess to which Jefferson was prone. Throughout the year 1787, the fledgling diplomat reiterated his opinion again and again when writing to his friends back home. To Edward Carrington, he observed that, in Europe, "under pretence of governing they have divided their nations into two classes, wolves and sheep." The same could only too easily happen in the infant American republics. "Cherish therefore the spirit of our people, and keep alive their attention," he urged his correspondent. "Do not be too severe upon their errors, but reclaim them by enlightening them. If once they become inattentive to the public affairs, you and I, and Congress and Assemblies, judges and governors shall all become wolves."[46] In his correspondence with James Madison, Jefferson was prepared to acknowledge as an evil "the turbulence" to which popular government is "subject." But he soon added, "Even this evil is productive of good. It prevents the degeneracy of government, and nourishes a general attention to the public affairs. I hold it that a little rebellion now and then is a good thing, and as necessary in the political world as storms in the physical. . . . It is a medecine necessary for the sound health of government."[47]

To yet another correspondent, Jefferson wrote in much the same vein: "God forbid we should ever be 20. & years without such a rebellion." He had little fear of the ignorance of the people; it was easy enough to make them aware of their errors. The real danger was that they would "remain quiet under" their "misconceptions." In this, he spied "a lethargy, the forerunner of death to the public liberty." The Virginian drove the point home by posing a simple question. "What country," he asked, "can preserve it's liberties if their rulers are not warned from time to time that their people preserve the spirit of resistance?" As long as that spirit remained alive, he would be sanguine. "Let them take arms," he thundered. "The remedy is to set them right as to facts, pardon and pacify them. What signify a few lives lost in a century or two? The tree of liberty must be refreshed from time to time with the blood of patriots and tyrants. It is it's natural manure."[48] Here—in his fear that the people would become inured to acquiescence and thus gently fall prey to servitude—lies the theoretical foundation of Jefferson's opposition to Hamilton and his program. Where the New Yorker leaned toward Hobbes and followed the dictates of the political architecture pioneered by Harrington and further developed by Hume, Montesquieu, Blackstone, Lolme, and the Court Whigs, the Virginian inclined toward Machiavelli and espoused the political jealousy and watchfulness advocated by Locke and given powerful reinforcement by Sidney, Trenchard and Gordon, Bolingbroke, and England's Country opposition.

The New Yorker seems not to have considered popular lethargy and slavishness a real danger at all. At the Philadelphia convention, when he intervened to oppose the constitutional provision barring placemen from serving in Congress, he denounced the notion that patronage and corruption would somehow undermine the regime. "Hume's opinion of the British constitution confirms the remark," he contended, "that there is always a body of firm patriots, who often shake a corrupt administration."[49] Five years later, when he wrote to Edward Carrington to charge that his opponents from Virginia were arming the states against the nation, he spoke of "the natural resistance to Government which in every community results from the human passions."[50] In his opinion, it was that natural resistance which had to be curbed if disorder was not to be endemic; and to that end, he was persuaded, "'Tis essential there should be a permanent will in a community."[51]

Short of tyranny, there were various ways to encourage permanence and stability in public policy, and Alexander Hamilton suggested more than one. He praised Britain's hereditary monarchy and its House of Lords; he advocated the institution of a president elected for life and a senate chosen to serve during good behavior; and, as secretary of the treasury, he tried to establish a stable, national interest grounded on a system of public finance and energetic federal intervention to encourage economic development. These institutions and measures all served the same political end, but each threatened as well to create what Madison had condemned in *The Federalist* as "a will in the community independent of the majority, that is, of the society itself."[52] The problem was insuperable. No will dependent on the majority could possess the permanence and stability which Hamilton thought requisite; and—unless the New York was, in fact, correct in supposing that there was always "a body of firm patriots" sufficient to "shake a corrupt administration"—a government emancipated in large part from popular control might well tend gradually over time to become a regime of savage wolves ruling over docile sheep. It is no wonder, then, that Jefferson wrote, "I own I am not a friend to a very energetic government. It is always oppressive."[53] Nor is it surprising that he heartily disliked the aspect of the Constitution which gave Hamilton the most hope—the absence of any provision limiting the number of terms which a man could serve as president of the United States.[54]

The same concerns dictated Jefferson's other objection to the new constitution—the failure to include a bill of rights within the document.[55] Jefferson had no illusions regarding the strength of parchment barriers as a bulwark against the tyrannical rule of a popular majority, but he was in fact much less prone than Madison to worry about that possibility. He feared the evil intentions of those wielding power far more than the selfishness and folly of the great mass of ordinary men. Before he read *The Federalist*, he was inclined to regard the proposed constitution as suspect. "Our Convention has been too much impressed by the insurrection of Massachusetts," he wrote after perusing the text for the first time, "and in the spur of the moment they are setting up a kite to keep the hen yard in order."[56] Though he eventually supported ratification of that Constitution, Jefferson never really changed his mind on the more fundamental question. In 1816, he wrote to John Taylor that if . . . the control of the people over the organs of their government be the measure of its republicanism, and I confess I know no other measure, it must be agreed that our governments have much less of republicanism than ought to have been expected; in other words, that the people have less regular control over their agents, than their rights and their interests require. And this I ascribe, not to any want of republican dispositions in those who formed these constitutions, but to a submission of true principle to European authorities, to speculators on government, whose fears of the people have been inspired by the populace of their own great cities, and were unjustly entertained against the independent, the happy, and therefore orderly citizens of the United States.[57]

Jefferson was not at all averse to institutional safeguards, but he placed far more trust in the efficacy of popular enlightenment. "Above all things," he wrote, "I hope the education of the common people will be attended to; convinced that on their good sense we may rely with the most security for the preservation of a due degree of liberty."[58] For the Virginian, this was a central, lifelong concern. The need for popular enlightenment as a bulwark against tyrannical rule dictated his support for the adoption of the Bill of Rights, and it caused him to devote much of his time in the last years of his life to the foundation of the University of Virginia.

III.iv.5

Jefferson's commitment to education deserves particular attention. Although he was passionate, he was by no means doctrinaire in his commitment to democratic rule. Indeed, by the standards of classical antiquity, he was not a democrat at all. He thought "little edification" could "be obtained from" the "writings" of the ancients "on the subject of government," chiefly because he judged that "the introduction of" the "new principle of representative democracy" had "rendered useless almost everything written before on the structure of government."[59] In his view, that principle made it possible to create within the United States a new type of mixed regime comparable to Harrington's *Oceana* in that it reserved a special place for men of intellect like Jefferson himself.[60]

The Virginian's most revealing discussion of this fundamental question was occasioned by John Adams's suggestion that "you and I ought not to die, before we have explained ourselves to each other."[61] Noting that Adams had alluded in several letters to the existence of a natural aristocracy, Jefferson replied that he, too, believed that there was "a natural aristocracy among men"—one founded on "virtue and talents" which set them apart from ordinary men. He observed that the invention of gunpowder had rendered "bodily strength, like beauty, good humor, politeness and other accomplishments, . . . but an auxiliary ground of distinction," and he denied that "wealth and birth" could be the foundation for anything but "an artificial aristocracy" bereft of any real claim to distinction. He foresaw the day when "rank, and birth, and tinsel-aristocracy" would "finally shrink into insignificance," even in Europe. He contended that "science had liberated the ideas of those who read and reflect" and that "the American example had kindled feelings of right in the people." "An insurrection has consequently begun," he observed, "of science, talents and courage against rank and birth, which have fallen into contempt." In the future, nature's noblemen were destined to rule: "The natural aristocracy I consider as the most precious gift of nature for the instruction, the trusts, and government of society. And indeed it would have been inconsistent in creation to have formed man for the social state, and not to have provided virtue and wisdom enough to manage the concerns of society. May we not even say that form of government is the best which provides the most effectually for a pure selection of these natural aristoi into the offices of government?" The form of government that Jefferson had in mind was that which already existed within the United States. He thought "the best remedy" to be "exactly that provided by all our constitutions." These left "to the citizens the free election and separation of the aristoi from the pseudo-aristoi, of the wheat from the chaff." He was confident that "in general they will elect the real good and wise." "In some instances," he acknowledged, "wealth may corrupt, and birth blind them; but not in sufficient degree to endanger the society." It was the peculiar merit of the representative principle that it made possible the establishment, on democratic foundations, of government by the best men.[62]

Jefferson did not suppose that it would be easy to establish or maintain such a regime. He was perfectly willing to concede that abject poverty, superstition, and ignorance rendered some peoples at least temporarily unfit for self-government of any kind.[63] He feared that this might be the case even in America. In his later years, he actually wondered whether it might not be prudent to deny citizenship to Virginians over the age of fifteen but unable to pass a simple literacy test.[64] Though the cure that he then contemplated was new, the concerns were long-standing. Early in his career, Jefferson had proposed that the state assembly adopt a comprehensive program of legislation designed to prepare the state's citizens—"the laboring" as well as "the learned"—for the daunting task before them.[65] To understand that program, one must see its most important elements in terms of the whole.[66]

The young statesman first sought to clear the way for his natural aristocracy by removing the artificial supports which had long enabled those outside the Republic of Letters to hold sway among men. To lessen the likelihood that superstition would enable the clergy to exercise a tyranny over the minds of his fellow citizens, Jefferson introduced a bill disestablishing the Episcopalian church. As drafted, this bill attacked "the impious presumption of legislators and rulers, civil as well as ecclesiastical, who, being themselves but fallible and uninspired men, have assumed dominion over the faith of others." It contended "that our civil rights have no dependance on our religious opinions, any more than our opinions in physics or geometry," and it declared "that the opinions of men are not the object of civil government, nor under its jurisdiction." [67] In this fashion, Jefferson disposed of clerical pretensions. He then aimed his second blow at the rich and wellborn. Their defeat was easily and painlessly accomplished in a fashion suggested by Montesquieu.[68] To reduce the chance that wealth would corrupt and birth blind his compatriots, Jefferson simply "laid the axe to the root of Pseudo-aristocracy" by persuading the Virginia general assembly to abolish entails and outlaw primogeniture.[69] Bereft of legal props, with their property being gradually dispersed, the great families would soon enough wither away.

After eliminating the privileges buttressing the natural aristocracy's rivals, Jefferson concerned himself with promoting the fortunes of those men of genius who were truly worthy of high office. To encourage the emergence of a class of virtuous and talented individuals fit for leadership in the state, and to prepare the common people to select nature's noblemen from among the pretenders, he proposed "a systematical plan of general education." [70] From 1779 on, he pressed the Virginia general assembly to pass his Bill for the More General Diffusion of Knowledge and institute throughout the state a system of publicly supported elementary schools.[71] Over the course of three years, these would teach all of the state's young residents (boys and girls alike) not just reading, writing, and arithmetic, but also the history of Greece, Rome, England, and America. These schools were to be under the supervision of a visitor who would each year choose from among the children of those parents too poor to provide for their son's further education "the boy, of best genius in the school" and send him on at public expense to study Greek, Latin, geography, and mathematics at one of the twenty grammar schools to be erected within the state. After a year or two, "the best genius" was to be selected from among the scholarship students within each class at each of the grammar schools. The others would then be dismissed, and the boy chosen would continue his studies until he had completed a term of six years. "By this means," Jefferson observed, "twenty of the best geniusses will be raked from the rubbish annually, and be instructed, at the public expence, so far as the grammar schools go." Half of these would then receive public support to go on to study "all the useful sciences" at the university level. "By that part of our plan which prescribes the selection of the youths of genius from among the classes of the poor," Jefferson concluded, "we hope to avail the state of those talents which nature has sown as liberally among the poor as the rich, but which perish without use, if not sought for and cultivated."[72]

The proprietor of Monticello drafted this proposal decades before he had even thought of founding a university in central Virginia.[73] At the time, the only institution of higher education in Virginia was the College of William and Mary, which Jefferson had himself attended. Persuaded that this college was inadequate as constituted, he urged a thorough reform of its bylaws and of its curriculum "to aid and improve that seminary, in which those who are to be the future guardians of the rights and liberties of their country may be endowed with science and virtue, to watch and preserve the sacred deposit." From the time of its founding, the college had been—like virtually every other institution of higher learning in the world—a religious establishment chiefly designed to educate the clergy of a particular sect. Jefferson sought to transform what had been an Anglican institution into a wholly secular establishment with a thoroughly modern curriculum including mathematics and both political and natural science. To accomplish this, he proposed abolishing the professorships in theology and oriental languages altogether. After the reform, there would be eight professorships—one to give instruction in moral philosophy, the laws of nature and of nations, and the fine arts; and others to teach law and police, history, mathematics, anatomy and medicine, natural philosophy and natural history, ancient languages, and modern languages. Mindful of the religious purposes of those who had originally endowed the college, Jefferson was willing to empower the board of professors to appoint a missionary to the Indians; but, characteristically, he stipulated that this individual devote a portion of his time to investigating and reporting on the laws, customs, religions, traditions, and languages of those with whose welfare he was charged. Jefferson was far less interested in encouraging the Indians to convert to Christianity than in fostering progress in science and scholarship in general.[74]

To that end, Jefferson advanced a third proposal: that the general assembly appropriate every year two thousand pounds "to be laid out in such books and maps as may be proper to be preserved in a public library." This library, to be established in Richmond, was not to lend its books and maps out, and it was apparently not intended for use by ordinary citizens of the commonwealth. It was, rather, an institute for advanced study established to indulge "the researches of the learned and curious."[75] It can hardly be fortuitous that he sought to locate this center of research in the city where the state legislature was to meet. There, the men entrusted with governing the state could consult the library and seek enlightenment from the learned individuals attracted by its presence.

Unfortunately, despite persistent effort on Jefferson's part, his "systematical plan of general education" was never enacted. The state assembly did make some provision to encourage the establishment of local elementary schools, and Jefferson was able to effect a partial reform of the College of William and Mary in 1779 when he served as a Visitor to that venerable institution.[76] But these halfhearted efforts left him unsatisfied.[77] To Adams, he lamented that his "system" was incomplete. "The law for religious freedom . . . having put down the aristocracy of the clergy and restored to the citizen the freedom of the mind, and those of entails and descents nurturing an equality of condition among them, this on Education would have raised the mass of the people to the high ground of moral respectability necessary to their own safety and to orderly government; and would have completed the great object of qualifying them to select the veritable aristoi for the trusts of government, to the exclusion of the Pseudalists."[78] Though splendid in conception, Jefferson's plan never attracted the requisite popular support.

In the end, the aging statesman had to settle for the foundation at Charlottesville of the University of Virginia on lines closely akin to those specified in his bill to reform the College of William and Mary.[79] Had he been given the opportunity to choose, he would have preferred the general education of the many to the higher education of the few, but he was denied the luxury of choice.[80] He could console himself with the thought that, by establishing a great university, he could at least see to it that the future leaders of the state received a proper political education by studying with care the second of John Locke's *Two Treatises of Government*, Algernon Sidney's *Discourses of Government*, *The Declaration of Independence*, *The Federalist*, the Virginia Resolutions of 1799, and Washington's "Farewell Address"—all under the guidance of an orthodox Whig.[81] That feature of his plan and the provisions he made for religious instruction merit careful consideration.

III.iv.6

In defending freedom of conscience, Jefferson once shocked his compatriots by writing, "It does me no injury for my neighbor to say there are twenty gods, or no god. It neither picks my pocket nor breaks my leg." The great statesman had assimilated John Locke's sly reduction of faith to opinion, and he recognized the implications thereof. In general, he was persuaded that "he is less remote from the truth who believes nothing than he who believes what is wrong," and he rejoiced in the fact that the Virginia statute for religious freedom was "meant to comprehend, within the mantle of its protection, the Jew and the Gentile, the Christian and Mahometan, the Hindoo, and Infidel of every denomination." In fact, Jefferson openly argued that "difference of opinion is advantageous in religion," and he clearly intimated that, in physics and geometry, such differences are harmless.[82] But he said nothing of the sort regarding political opinion—and for good reason. He knew better. He knew that, in defense of differing political opinions, men would do far more than pick pockets and break legs. After all, he had himself watched a dispute over questions of fundamental principle develop in Britain's North American colonies, bitterly divide the colonists, and finally erupt into a revolutionary war. He recognized that it would never be possible "to perfect the principles of society" so fully that "political opinions" would be rendered "as inoffensive as those of philosophy" and "mechanics." Like James Madison, he suspected "political difference" to be "inseparable from the different constitutions of the human mind, & that degree of freedom which permits unrestrained expression." But he never for a moment doubted that "political dissension" was "a great evil," and he thought it "as worthy the efforts of the patriot as of the philosopher, to exclude it's influence, if possible, from social life."[83]

To this end, Jefferson sought to encourage religious diversity and a measure of political homogeneity. On the question of religion, he was fully in agreement with James Madison and Adam Smith. Where all sects were in the minority, all would have an interest in defending religious toleration; and in such a situation, the competition between sects would favor an amalgamation of doctrine and a moderation of the religious passions which had all too often in the past given rise to political dissension. In his view, "The way to silence religious disputes, is to take no notice of them."[84] Accordingly, Jefferson initiated a revolutionary departure from all precedent and decided to eliminate all but natural theology from the curriculum of the University of Virginia; and when this stirred opposition in religious circles, he added an amendment to his plan, inviting the various sects to establish schools of divinity on the confines of the university so that the candidates for the clergy could mingle with one another and draw sustenance from a secular curriculum informed by the precepts of the Enlightenment.[85] As he put it in a letter to a prominent advocate of Unitarianism, "By bringing the sects together, and mixing them with the mass of other students, we shall soften their asperities, liberalize and neutralize their prejudices, and make the general religion a religion of peace, reason, and morality."[86]

In this connection, Jefferson proposed setting aside a time each day when the students would be both "free . . . to attend religious worship at the establishment of their respective sects" and "expected" to do so.[87] Jefferson's later admirers might wonder whether a state institution should deliberately encourage religious observance, but the great statesman never evidenced any doubts himself. As a measure for separating church and state, his Bill for Establishing Religious Freedom was far more rigorous than the First Amendment. It not only barred the establishment of religion and protected its free exercise: it asserted that "to compel a man to furnish contributions of money for the propagation of opinions which he disbelieves and abhors, is sinful and tyrannical," and it specified "that no man shall be compelled to frequent or support any religious worship, place, or ministry whatsoever." It even stipulated "that all men shall be free to profess, and by argument to maintain, their opinions in matters of religion, and that the same shall in no wise diminish, enlarge, or affect their civil capacities." Jefferson's rhetoric is utterly uncompromising. And yet he saw nothing unlawful or improper in having elementary students in the public schools he proposed establishing in Virginia devote a certain amount of time to religious pursuits so long as "no religious reading, instruction, or exercise shall be prescribed or practiced inconsistent with the tenets of any religious sect or denomination."[88]

Jefferson advanced these suggestions regarding education quite late in his life, but they in no way marked a break from the outlook he evidenced four decades before. It is important to attend to a fact generally ignored by scholars: the Bill for Establishing Religious Freedom was but one of the four statutes regulating the relations between church and state that were included in the general Revisal of the Laws which Jefferson, with Edmund Pendleton and George Wythe, had been commissioned in 1776 to prepare for consideration by the Virginia assembly. The system of legislation which they presented in 1779 also included A Bill for Punishing Disturbers of Religious Worship and Sabbath Breakers and A Bill for Appointing Days of Public Fasting and Thanksgiving. The former enforced public respect for religion: it stipulated that no minister of the gospel be arrested while preaching or performing religious worship; it specified that citizens who interrupt or otherwise disrupt religious services be imprisoned or fined; and, most important, it exacted a penalty of ten shillings from anyone found working or employing his apprentices, servants, or slaves in labor or other business on the Sabbath. The second piece of legislation enlisted religion as a handmaiden of public policy:

it authorized the chief magistrate of the Commonwealth of Virginia to declare days of thanksgiving and days of public fasting and humiliation, and it
inflicted a fine of fifty pounds on every minister in the state who neglected
to perform divine service and preach a sermon suited to the occasion. In
late October 1785, when James Madison introduced Jefferson's Bill for Establishing Religious Freedom, he introduced the two other bills as well. The
legislature that passed the Virginia statute of religious freedom passed the
first of the two other bills the following October.[89]

The appearance of contradiction disappears upon close examination. The
author of the Declaration of Independence and of the Statute of Virginia for
Religious Freedom never lost sight of what contemporary civil libertarians
tend all too often to forget: that the case for political and religious liberty presupposes the existence of a "Creator," an "Almighty God" capable of endow-
ing men with "inalienable rights" and of creating "the mind free."[90] Jefferson
asserted that the First Amendment had built "a wall of separation between
church and State," and he celebrated the fact.[91] He taught his compatriots
that "the way to silence religious disputes, is to take no notice of them,"
and he encouraged doctrinal diversity. But he never claimed that America's
governments should take no notice of the contest between atheism, agnosticism, and religious belief, and neither he nor Madison ever supposed that
the existence of "a wall of separation between church and State" precluded
governmental encouragement of belief in God.[92] True to his principles as a
strict constructionist of the federal constitution and as a defender of state prerogatives, Jefferson, while president, carefully sidestepped any public action
that might seem to smack of sectarian bias. For this reason, he broke with
precedent and refrained altogether from prescribing for his countrymen religious exercises such as days of fasting and prayer.[93] And yet, in his second
inaugural address, the great defender of religious liberty did not hesitate to
invoke "the favor of that Being in whose hands we are, who led our fore-
fathers, as Israel of old, from their native land, and planted them in a country
flowing with all the necessaries and comforts of life."[94] If he lent his authority
as president to the cause of religious faith, it was because he had good reason to welcome the influence of religion once it was somehow deprived of
theocratic ambition and rendered benign. The public authority had a perfectly legitimate interest in fostering faith if it was, in fact, true (as Jefferson
supposed it was) that the "only firm basis" for "the liberties of a nation" is
"a conviction in the minds of the people that these liberties are of the gift of
God" and "that they are not to be violated but with his wrath."[95]

For precisely the same reason, the public authority had an interest in promoting the political principles on which it was founded. Jefferson never

advocated political persecution.[96] From studying John Locke,[97] he came to believe that "the opinions and belief of men depend not on their own will, but follow involuntarily the evidence proposed to their minds." He therefore denied that "the opinions of men" can properly be "the object of civil government" and "under its jurisdiction," and he contended "that truth is great and will prevail if left to herself; that she is the proper and sufficient antagonist to error, and has nothing to fear from the conflict unless by human interposition disarmed of her natural weapons, free argument and debate; errors ceasing to be dangerous when it is permitted freely to contradict them."[98] In his first inaugural address, the new president made his stand perfectly clear. "Having banished from our land that religious intolerance under which mankind so long bled and suffered," he remarked, "we have yet gained little if we countenance a political intolerance as despotic, as wicked, and capable of as bitter and bloody persecutions." From this, he drew the logical conclusion. "If there be any among us who would wish to dissolve this Union or to change its republican form," he urged the nation, "let them stand undisturbed as monuments of the safety with which error of opinion may be tolerated where reason is left to combat it."[99] And yet, in extremis, when time or circumstance threatened to prevent truth from holding its natural sway, Jefferson was as prepared as his Federalist opponents to enforce the law of criminal libel against writers and editors whose attacks on public officials appeared to endanger the new republican order. He merely insisted that the laws enforced be state laws enforced in state courts. In denouncing the Sedition Act, he and his followers cited the First Amendment, not to argue that the press should be free from all regulation, but to insist that the Constitution, as amended, quite properly relegated all such regulation to the states. Though prepared to defend the freedom of the press, they did not think it impossible to distinguish liberty from license.[100]

Jefferson could favor freedom of the press and its regulation for the same reason that he allowed the professors teaching physics and geometry to choose their textbooks but denied this privilege to the individual giving instruction in political science.[101] He was a firm believer in the progress of the sciences and the arts, and he was convinced that political experimentation would yield progress as well.[102] "When I contemplate the immense advances in science and discoveries in the arts which have been made within the period of my life," he told one correspondent, "I look forward with confidence to equal advances by the present generation, and have no doubt they will consequently be as much wiser than we have been as we than our fathers were, and they than the burners of witches."[103] Thus, where the ancient Greek would have turned back to the *pátrios politeía* and his Roman

counterpart would have consulted the *mos maiorum*, the American statesman marched blithely ahead. He never embraced James Madison's argument
on behalf of the utility of prejudice and the salutary effects of veneration
for the Constitution. He explicitly rejected the classical republican notion
"that to secure ourselves where we are, we must tread with awful reverence
in the footsteps of our fathers." In fact, he attributed the "barbarism and
wretchedness" of America's indigenous peoples to their "bigotted veneration for the supposed superlative wisdom of their fathers." But, though he
was committed to the notion that there was no "term" that one could "fix and
foresee" to man's advancement in "knowledge and well-being," [104] Jefferson
denied that first principles were subject to change. He regarded some truths
as "self-evident," and these he proposed to "establish" as surely as he had
disestablished the Episcopalian church.[105] The author of the Declaration of
Independence appears to have recognized what his successors have all too
often forgotten: that, without a fixed standard by which to judge what is
right and what is wrong, it is impossible to distinguish a nation's progress
from its decay.[106]

In principle, Jefferson would have been willing to see *The Federalist*, the
Virginia Resolutions of 1799, and Washington's "Farewell Address" dropped
from the curriculum when rendered obsolete by the advancement of knowledge. Indeed, in principle, he would have been willing to add Hamilton's
Report on the Subject of Manufactures to the list of prescribed texts if it could
be shown that he had himself been wrong and that his opponent's system
actually served the cause of republican government. This far Jefferson would
in principle go. But one may justly doubt whether he would ever voluntarily
have sanctioned abandoning Locke, Sidney, and the Declaration of Independence: for these texts dealt primarily with "the laws of nature and of nature's
God." As he put it, "Nothing . . . is unchangeable but the inherent and unalienable rights of man." Because he believed that the truth, if given fair play,
would rout error, Jefferson was prepared to tolerate the advocacy of contrary
principles—but not by a man employed by the state to profess government
and law at the University of Virginia. The "principles of government" taught
in that (and, for that matter, in every public) institution were to be "founded
in the rights of man." [107] James Madison, who succeeded Jefferson as the university's rector, rightly linked the prescription of texts with the "framing" of
"a political creed." He thought the matter delicate "as in the case of religion,"
but neither he nor Jefferson had any doubt that "the public right" was "very
different in the two cases." [108] What Madison said of his deceased colleague
was true for both. From the outset, they intended to make the University of

Virginia "a temple dedicated to science & Liberty" and therefore "a nursery of Republican patriots as well as genuine scholars." [109]

It is a measure of the importance he accorded education that Jefferson had it engraved on his tombstone that he most wanted to be remembered not just as "Author of The Declaration of Independence" and "of the Statute of Virginia for Religious Freedom" but also as "Father of the University of Virginia." [110] Had he succeeded in securing the passage of his Bill for the More General Diffusion of Knowledge, Thomas Jefferson would certainly have added that accomplishment to his list. He once remarked that his educational plan was the most important of the legal reforms embedded in the famous report presented in June 1779 by the Committee of Revisors appointed by the general assembly of Virginia just three years before. [111]

III.iv.7

Thomas Jefferson was not alone in recognizing that the new regime's dependence upon the principle of representation introduced a measure of aristocracy within the various governments composing it. In fact, he was not even the first to praise America's republican regime for making it possible for a "natural aristocracy" of those men most noted for their "virtue and talents" to govern. The distinction between those variously dubbed "princes," "*generous spirits*," or "natural aristocrats" and those termed "the people," "*the vulgar sort*," or "the natural democrats" is fundamental to early modern political thought. It was initiated by Machiavelli, and as we have seen, it was taken up by Sir Francis Bacon, René Descartes, and Thomas Hobbes. John Adams lifted the phrase "natural aristocrats" from James Harrington's *Oceana*; he elaborated the notion in light of the arguments of John Locke and Lord Bolingbroke; and he introduced them both into public discourse in America on the eve of the Constitutional Convention, when he published the first volume of his *Defence of the Constitutions of Government of the United States of America*. He called America's natural aristocracy "the brightest ornament and glory of the nation" and argued that it could "always be made the greatest blessing of society, if it be judiciously managed in the constitution." [112] Others had their doubts. By the time that the ratifying conventions met in the various states, Americans were debating whether a distant government with institutions designed to encourage the election to high office of "men who possess the most attractive merit, and the most diffusive and established characters" might not in due course be fatal to democratic rule. [113]

The leading members of the revolutionary generation recognized that democracy and representation are incompatible,[114] and they were mindful of the ancient Greek dictum that election, even popular election, is an aristocratic mode for choosing magistrates.[115] In drafting the Articles of Confederation and in framing most of the state constitutions, they had sought to mitigate the danger by introducing James Harrington's principle of rotation, and everywhere they had tried to render elected officials accountable to their constituents by requiring frequent elections.[116] Similar concerns guided the framers of the federal constitution. As James Madison put it in the course of defending that document, "The elective mode of obtaining rulers is the characteristic policy of republican government. The means relied on in this form of government for preventing their degeneracy are numerous and various. The most effectual one is such a limitation of the term of appointments, as will maintain a proper responsibility to the people."[117] If Federalists, Anti-Federalists, and the Republican successors of the latter were united in refusing even to consider the possibility that their various representatives should be selected by lot, it was at least in part because they shared the Whig conviction, initially stated by Montesquieu and then taken up by Thomas Jefferson, that ordinary men were "unqualified for the management of affairs requiring intelligence above the common level, yet competent judges of human character." Like the Virginia planter, they believed that "experience" had "proved it safer, for the mass of individuals composing the society, to reserve to themselves personally the exercise of all rightful powers to which they are competent, and to delegate those to which they are not competent to deputies named, and removable for unfaithful conduct, by themselves immediately."[118]

The framers of the federal constitution were especially sensitive to the fact that the new nation could not in the long run safely and properly function if denied the service of an aristocracy of knowledgeable and prudent men. For this reason, they embedded within the Constitution, in the very passage that secured the patent of monopoly for inventors, a phrase guaranteeing copyright protection for authors.[119] Like Jefferson, they were determined to do what they could to reward and encourage those among their countrymen endowed with intellectual gifts. James Madison, Charles Pinckney, and George Washington were among the most vigorous proponents of such a policy.

At the Philadelphia convention, Madison and Pinckney sought to include within the Constitution's enumeration of powers a clause explicitly conferring on the new government the right "to establish an University" and thereby implying that it should do so. No one objected to the idea itself, but Gouverneur Morris apparently spoke for the majority of his colleagues when he dismissed the stipulation as "not necessary" because redundant, explaining that "the exclusive power" given Congress "at the Seat of Government" was already sufficient sanction for such an establishment.[120] Washington took his cue from Morris's assertion. In his first annual message to Congress and, again, in his last, the nation's first president proposed that the federal government establish in Washington, D.C., a national university the "primary object" of which "should be the education of our youth in the science of *government.*" "In a republic," he asked, "what species of knowledge can be equally important and what duty more pressing on its legislature than to patronize a plan for communicating it to those who are to be the future guardians of the liberties of the country?"[121] The arguments which Washington advanced while president differed little from those employed by Jefferson in Virginia. "There is nothing which can better deserve your patronage than the promotion of science and literature," he told the First Congress.

> Knowledge is in every country the surest basis of public happiness. In one in which the measures of government receive their impressions so immediately from the sense of the community as in ours it is proportionably essential. To the security of a free constitution it contributes in various ways—by convincing those who are intrusted with the public administration that every valuable end of government is best answered by the enlightened confidence of the people, and by teaching the people themselves to know and to value their rights: to discern and provide against invasions of them; to distinguish between oppression and the necessary exercise of lawful authority; between burthens proceeding from a disregard to their convenience and those resulting from the inevitable exigencies of society; to discriminate the spirit of liberty from that of licentiousness—cherishing the first, avoiding the last—and uniting a speedy but temperate vigilance against encroachments, with an inviolable respect to the laws.[122]

In his farewell address, Washington returned to this theme, exhorting his countrymen to "promote, . . . as an object of primary importance, institutions for the general diffusion of knowledge." As he put it, "In proportion as the structure of a government gives force to public opinion, it is essential that public opinion should be enlightened."[123] The great Federalist president was no more persuaded than his Republican opponent that political heresy could work no harm. When he once again urged Congress to establish a national university, he argued that "the assimilation of the principles, opinions, and manners of our countrymen by the common education of a portion of our

youth from every quarter well deserves attention. The more homogeneous
our citizens can be made in these particulars the greater will be our prospect
of permanent union."[124]

Washington's request was not met. To this day, there is no national university constructed on the lines which he had in mind. This fact, though striking,
should not be taken as an indication that he stood alone. In his inaugural
address, John Adams echoed the sentiments of Washington's farewell address, and Presidents Thomas Jefferson, James Madison, James Monroe, and
John Quincy Adams all renewed their great predecessor's request that Congress take up the matter.[125] Other concerns may have seemed more pressing
at the time, and partisan resentments and fears proved to be insuperable
obstacles; but there was no lack of interest and desire on the part of the
leading statesmen of the revolutionary generation. Though James Madison
and his colleagues had designed the Constitution with an eye to human vice
and folly, they never seriously doubted that the United States of America
was—like ancient Sparta, though in a radically different fashion—a mixed
regime to a substantial degree dependent for its survival on the prudence of
those selected to hold the public trust and on the enlightened vigilance of
the divers citizens who made that selection.

Some frankly doubted that the best men would really be chosen. Alexander Hamilton conceded that so long as a relative equality reigned, "the
tendency of the people's suffrages will be to elevate merit even from obscurity." But, he suggested, as wealth increases and becomes concentrated in
a few hands, as luxury prevails, "virtue will be in a greater degree considered as only a graceful appendage of wealth, and the tendency of things
will be to depart from the Republican standard."[126] John Adams entertained
similar fears. Like Aristotle, he saw importance in the fact that it is much
easier to discern excellences of the body than excellences of the soul. Even
before Jefferson spelled out his theory, the elder man drew attention to its
weakness. "Now, my Friend, who are the *aristoi*?" he asked. "Philosophy
may Answer 'The Wise and Good.' But the World, Mankind, have by their
practice always answered, 'the rich the beautiful and well born.' . . . What
chance have Talents and Virtues in competition, with Wealth and Birth? and
Beauty?"[127]

Like many of the Anti-Federalists,[128] Adams also wondered just how often
genuine civic virtue would be attached to talent. He had pored over Machiavelli, Bacon, and Descartes; he had reflected on the arguments advanced
by Hobbes, Harrington, and Locke; and he was therefore inclined to associate erudition and intellectual acuity with a heightening rather than with a
diminution of the force of the passions.[129] Moreover, neither he nor Jefferson

nor, for that matter, any of the American founders was prepared to acknowledge that the natural aristocracy had any legitimate claim to rule in its own right. They hoped, rather, that "the learned" could be persuaded to serve "the laboring"—to govern or, rather, to administer the government with the consent of the common people and on their behalf. Thus, when George Mason composed the Virginia Declaration of Rights, he included an article stipulating that "no man, or set of men, are entitled to exclusive or separate emoluments or privileges from the community, but in consideration of public services." In its constitution, North Carolina employed the same wording, and the article can be found, in slightly altered form, in the declaration of rights John Adams penned for Massachusetts. Similar provisions, specifying that all magistrates are trustees or servants accountable to the people for their conduct in office, were prefixed to the constitutions adopted in Pennsylvania, Maryland, Vermont, New Hampshire, Delaware, and Connecticut. Not one of the states that adopted a bill of rights failed to follow suit. Everyone agreed with Hamilton that "the prohibition of titles of nobility . . . may truly be denominated the corner stone of republican government."[130]

Despite the public consensus on this question, Adams shared Harrington's fear that the natural aristocracy of the learned would inevitably overstep the limits and establish a tyrannical dominion over the laboring. He had long suspected that, in America, "the rich, the well-born, and the able" would soon come to "acquire an influence among the people that will soon be too much for simple honesty and plain sense, in a house of representatives," and he had concluded that this influence could be reduced only by banishing the members of this aristocracy to a senate constituted on the model of Britain's House of Lords.[131] Much the same argument was advanced by Alexander Hamilton and Gouverneur Morris at the Philadelphia convention.[132] If these same three American statesmen also looked on hereditary monarchy with considerable favor, it was chiefly because, like Jean Louis de Lolme, they thought a strong, unitary executive necessary within an extended commercial republic as a check not only to popular distemper but also to aristocratic pretense and power.[133]

There was more to this scheme than a mere system of sociopolitical checks and balances. In the 1780s, when Adams gave up not only the hope but even the desire that America's new republican regime form a citizenry imbued with "a positive Passion for the public good, the public Interest, Honour, Power, and Glory," he began casting about for something more firmly grounded in the selfish passions that might serve as a substitute for disinterested virtue. He knew—as all of the Founders knew—that, even if one might dispense with disinterestedness in the general citizen body, the republic could not long survive and prosper if deprived of public-spirited statesmen. In the wake of the new constitution's ratification, he was particularly fearful that America's ablest men would prefer the pleasures of private life to involvement in public affairs and that men driven by avarice or the mere ambition for power and high office would soon come to rule the infant republic. Like Gouverneur Morris and Alexander Hamilton, he hoped that the love of lasting fame might attract the talented into public service and induce them to sacrifice temporary, private, material advantage for the common good; and so, just three days after he took up his duties as vice-president in late April 1789, Adams launched a vigorous campaign to confer grand titles on the leading magistrates and legislators of the new republic.[134]

Even when that campaign failed and he found himself dubbed "His Rotundity" and treated as a laughingstock in circles where he had once inspired affection, consideration, and respect, Adams persisted in making a case for pomp and circumstance. In his notorious *Discourses on Davila*, he explored in detail the various political consequences of the *"passion for distinction."* This desire Adams considered the "great leading passion of the soul"; in it he found "the great spring of social activity." "By this destination of their natures," he explained, "men of all sorts, even those who have the least of reason, virtue or benevolence, are chained down to an incessant servitude to their fellow creatures; laboring without intermission to produce something which shall contribute to the comfort, convenience, pleasure, profit, or utility of some or other of the species, they are really thus constituted by their own vanity, slaves to mankind." In consequence, the true "province of policy" is "not to eradicate" but "to regulate" the passions so that "they should be gratified, encouraged, and arranged on the side of virtue." Above all else, the legislator must aim at increasing the size of "the tribe out of which proceed your patriots and heroes, and most of the great benefactors to mankind"; and he must devise means for attracting into public service those who "aim at approbation as well as attention; at esteem as well as consideration; and at admiration and gratitude, as well as congratulation."

Adams argued that the statesman intent on this achievement must study and imitate the ancients. "Has there ever been a nation who understood the human heart better than the Romans, or made a better use of the passion for consideration, congratulation, and distinction?" he asked.

> They considered that, as reason is the guide of life, the senses, the imagination and the affections are the springs of activity. Reason holds the helm, but passions are the gales. And as the direct road to these is

through the senses, the languages of signs was employed by Roman wisdom to excite the emulation and active virtue of the citizens. *Distinctions* of *conditions*, as well as of ages, were made by difference of clothing. The laticlave or large flowing robe, studded with broad spots of purple, the ancient distinction of their kings, was, after the establishment of the consulate, worn by the senators through the whole period of the republic and the empire. The tribunes of the people were, after their institution, admitted to wear the same venerable signal of sanctity and authority. The angusticlave, or the smaller robe, with narrower studs of purple, was the distinguishing habit of Roman knights. The golden ring was also peculiar to senators and knights, and was not permitted to be worn by any other citizens. The prætext, or long white robe, reaching down to the ancles, bordered with purple, which was worn by the principal magistrates, such as consuls, prætors, censors, and sometimes on solemn festivals by senators. The chairs of ivory; the lictors; the rods; the axes; the crowns of gold; of ivory; of flowers; of herbs; of laurel branches; and of oak leaves; the civil and the mural crowns; their ovations; and their triumphs; every thing in religion, government, and common life, among the Romans, was parade, representation, and ceremony. Every thing was addressed to the emulation of the citizens, and every thing was calculated to attract the attention, to allure the consideration and excite the congratulations of the people; to attach their hearts to individual citizens according to their merit; and to their lawgivers, magistrates, and judges, according to their rank, station, and importance in the state. And this was in the true spirit of republics, in which form of government there is no other consistent method of preserving order, or procuring submission to the laws.[135]

His compatriots' failure to appreciate the point of his argument left Adams dismayed. In the end, he was no more able than Hamilton and Gouverneur Morris to reconcile himself fully to living in a wholly democratic republic. In 1812, the old revolutionary looked back to the Stamp Act and the struggle that followed and remarked, "From the year 1761, now more than Fifty years, I have constantly lived in an enemies Country."[136] In 1826, he was invited to Washington, D.C., to participate in the celebrations marking the fiftieth anniversary of the signing of the Declaration of Independence. Like Thomas Jefferson, he was too infirm to travel; and like the Virginian, he took the opportunity to pen a memorable letter declining the invitation. "A memorable epoch in the annals of the human race," he called the event of 1776, "destined in future history to form the brightest or the blackest page, according to the use or the abuse of those political institutions by which they shall in time to come be shaped by the *human mind.*"[137]

III.iv.8

Thomas Jefferson was considerably more sanguine than his Federalist opponents. But, though he seems not to have worried greatly that America's best men would forsake public affairs, he was no more willing than Hamilton, Morris, and Adams to rely on the public-spiritedness of the citizens of ability and intellect; he was, in fact, perfectly prepared to acknowledge that his "natural aristocracy of virtue and talent," if left unwatched, could and would turn into a pack of wolves. To prevent the able from combining with the rich, the beautiful, and the wellborn to prey on his sheep, he looked not to a monarch, but to the sheep themselves. In the ancient democracies, as Jefferson knew, there had been no need to foster popular resistance to the abuses of authority; the people had ruled directly themselves. Representative democracy was another matter entirely. By placing the government at a certain distance from the people, it avoided the danger of mob rule but at the risk of subjecting the citizens to the arbitrary whim of those holding power; it was, in short, an uneasy compromise between classical democracy and the absolute monarchy espoused by Thomas Hobbes.[138] If the delicate balance was to be maintained, those holding office would have to be kept under constant surveillance. For Jefferson, as for Locke, Sidney, Trenchard and Gordon, Bolingbroke, and the like, this was the crux of the matter.[139]

To this end, the great statesman sought from the outset to use his educational program to instill the requisite vigilance in the citizenry. In the preamble to his Bill for the More General Diffusion of Knowledge, he acknowledged that "certain forms of government are better calculated than others to protect individuals in the free exercise of their natural rights, and are at the same time themselves better guarded against degeneracy." But he immediately qualified this observation by noting that "experience hath shewn, that even under the best forms, those entrusted with power have, in time, and by slow operations, perverted it into tyranny; and it is believed that the most effectual means of preventing this would be, to illuminate, as far as practicable, the minds of the people at large, and more especially to give them knowledge of those facts, which history exhibiteth, that, possessed thereby of the experience of other ages and countries, they may be enabled to know ambition under all its shapes, and prompt to exert their natural powers to defeat its purposes."[140] In his *Notes on the State of Virginia*, Jefferson emphasized the vital importance of this proposal. The study of Greek, Roman, English, and American history would apprise the citizens "of the past" and thereby "enable them to judge of the future." In this fashion, "it will avail them of the experience of other times and other nations; it will qualify them as judges of the actions and designs of men; it will enable them to know ambition under every disguise it may assume; and knowing it, to defeat its views." Jefferson deemed this a task of greater moment than the education of the natural aristocracy. "Of all views of this law," Jefferson concluded, "none is more important, none more legitimate, than that of rendering the people the safe, as they are the ultimate guardians of their own liberty." [141] That was the purpose of the comprehensive system of legislation which the young statesman first presented in June 1779.

Thirty-one years later, after observing the manner in which his opponents in New England had been able to mobilize the populace of the region against his embargo by means of the town meetings, Jefferson added an amendment to his collection of proposals. For the purpose of establishing elementary schools, he had advocated dividing the counties into "hundreds" or "wards." Now, he sought the establishment of wards for another reason as well: they were, he thought, the perfect instruments for local self-government. They would inevitably focus popular attention on public affairs, and they would function as "a regularly organized power" enabling the people "to crush, regularly and peaceably, the usurpations of their unfaithful agents," free "from the dreadful necessity of doing it insurrectionally." [142] "By making every citizen an acting member of the government, and in the offices nearest and most interesting to him," Jefferson hoped to "attach him by his strongest feelings to the independence of his country, and its republican constitution." [143] As he put it, "Where every man is a sharer in the direction of his ward-republic, or of some of the higher ones, and feels that he is a participator in the government of affairs not merely at an election one day in the year, but every day; when there shall not be a man in the State who will not be a member of some one of its councils, great or small, he will let the heart be torn out of his body sooner than his power be wrested from him by a Caesar or a Bonaparte. . . . As Cato, then, concluded every speech with the words, '*Carthago delenda est*,' so do I every opinion, with the injunction, 'divide the counties into wards.' " [144]

It is important to stress that Jefferson did not give primacy to political participation as an end in itself. [145] His ultimate desire to foster local government had the same roots as his long-standing commitment to states' rights. Like the Anti-Federalists, he sought to minimize the responsibilities of those governments set at a distance from the people and to maximize popular vigilance by fostering popular control of local affairs. Precisely the same concerns dictated the desire, which he shared with the Anti-Federalists and with many a Federalist as well, that the individual citizens of the United States be armed and that they be organized locally under their own officers as a militia. Those responsible for proposing the pertinent provisions in the various state bills of rights, for enacting the relevant state laws, and for requesting, framing, and ratifying what we now know as the Second Amendment to the federal constitution took for granted William Blackstone's exposition of the parallel passage in the English bill of rights. In America, as in England, the individual's right to bear arms was an "auxiliary right" much like freedom of speech and freedom of the press. It was conceded as a legal or even constitutional right because it was thought essential to the protection of the more fundamental, natural rights to life, personal liberty, and private property. To be precise, the right to keep and bear arms was "a public allowance, under due restrictions, of the natural right of resistance and self-preservation, when the sanctions of society and laws are found insufficient to restrain the violence of oppression."[146] If American sheep were not to become prey to a pack of wolves, it was because they were not to be sheeplike at all.[147]

In 1787 and 1788, these same hopes and fears had dictated Jefferson's more general demand for the passage of a bill of rights. His eagerness that this be done at the first possible opportunity after the federal constitution's ratification had been intimately linked with his desire to foster public education and to direct the healthy spirit of popular resistance into the proper channels. In the late 1780s, the Virginian was already nursing suspicions regarding the federal executive—but that department was not then "the sole, it" was, in fact, "scarcely the principal object" of his "jealousy." At that time, he was at one with Madison in supposing "the tyranny of the legislatures . . . the most formidable dread." In combating the danger, he thought, the passage of a bill of rights would serve two critical functions: it would arm the judiciary and make judicial review a check on legislative and executive abuse alike, and it would both educate the public with regard to its rights and provide a rallying point for popular resistance against unjust and tyrannical measures. "The jealousy of the subordinate governments is a precious reliance," he conceded in a letter to Madison. "But observe that those governments are only agents. They must have principles furnished them whereon to found their opposition. The declaration of rights will be the text whereby they will try all the acts of the federal government." These were the very arguments which James Madison would advance just a few months later when he proposed to the First Congress that a bill of rights be drafted for submission to the states.[148]

III.iv.9

James Madison taught his compatriots that "it is proper to take alarm at the first experiment on our liberties." "This prudent jealousy" he held "to be the first duty of Citizens, and one of the noblest characteristics of the late Revolution."[149] There is, however, little in *The Federalist* to suggest that Madison had himself beforehand given much thought to the danger posed to the regime by public lethargy. His correspondence with Jefferson and their subsequent conversations, when coupled with the evident tendency of Hamilton's system to strengthen the central administration in its contest with state and local government, seem to have caused Madison, in the early 1790s, to reconsider the foundations of public liberty and to place a much greater emphasis on the need for popular vigilance than he had ever done before. Once again, as in *The Federalist*, he began his reflections by considering the influence exerted by geographical extension on the conduct of the government. In making notes for the brief, unsigned essays which he later submitted to the *National Gazette*, he wrote, "The larger a community, the more respectable the whole & the less the share of importance felt by each member—the more submissive consequently each individual to the general will."[150] In one of the first of these essays to be published, he linked this phenomenon with the problem of sustaining the regime. "The larger a country," he observed, "the less easy for its real opinion to be ascertained, and the less difficult to be counterfeited; [and yet] when ascertained or presumed, the more respectable it is in the eyes of individuals. This is favorable to the authority of government." "For the same reason," he added, "the more extensive a country, the more insignificant is each individual in his own eyes. This may be unfavorable to liberty."[151] There lay the problem, and it would only be aggravated by a general consolidation of the nation under a single, centralized government.

Madison now firmly opposed such a consolidation because he believed that it would render it virtually impossible to sustain the requisite popular vigilance. Because "one Legislature" would be incompetent "to regulate all the various objects belonging to the local governments," it would be necessary to transfer "many of them to the executive department," and "the encreasing splendour and number of its prerogatives supplied by this source, might prove excitements to ambition too powerful for a sober execution of the executive plan, and consequently strengthen the pretexts for an hereditary designation of the magistrate." Even more important, however, the abolition of the state governments "would prevent that controul on the Legislative, which is essential to a faithful discharge of its trust," since neither the voice nor the sense of ten or twenty millions of people, spread through so many latitudes as are comprehended within the United States, could ever be combined or called into effect, if deprived of those local organs, through which both can now be conveyed. In such a state of things, the impossibility of acting together, might be succeeded by the inefficacy of partial expressions of the public mind, and this at length by a universal silence and insensibility, leaving the whole government to that *self directed course*, which, it must be owned, is the natural propensity of every government.[152]

By the end of 1791, Madison's thinking with respect to the importance of "the *federal* principle" had advanced a great distance. In the process, his commitment to nationalism had waned, and he had gained a new appreciation for the virtues of state and local initiative.

Madison thought political consolidation a great threat, but he did not consider it the most immediate danger. The desire to encourage popular attentiveness to public affairs and to safeguard popular control dictated the Virginian's opposition to Hamilton's general system of administration as well. Montesquieu had argued that there were three forms of government—pure despotisms founded on fear, regular monarchies animated by honor, and republics maintained by aristocratic moderation or by democratic virtue.[153] As a corrective, Madison offered an alternative schema. Some governments, he noted, operate by means of "a permanent military force, which at once maintains the government, and is maintained by it; which is at once the cause of burdens on the people, and of submission in the people to their burdens." These are the regimes most commonly evident on the continent of Europe. Other governments derive their "energy from the will of society" and operate "by the reason of its measures, on the understanding and interest of society." These are "the republican governments which it is the glory of America to have invented, and her unrivalled happiness to possess." Unfortunately, there is a third form of government as well: "A government operating by corrupt influence; substituting the motive of private interest in place of public duty; converting its pecuniary dispensations into bounties to favorites, or bribes to opponents; accommodating its measures to the avidity of a part of the nation instead of the benefit of the whole: in a word, enlisting an army of interested partizans, whose tongues, whose pens, whose intrigues, and whose active combinations, by supplying the terror of the sword, may support a real domination of the few, under an apparent liberty of the many." This government is "an imposter." Luckily, Madison added, it is not to be found "on the west side of the Atlantic." But he hinted that such a disguised oligarchy might emerge in that locale if the "happiness" of America's republican governments is not "perpetuated by a system of administration corresponding with the purity of the theory." [154]

The establishment of a corrupt government on the English model would have been reprehensible in itself; the prospect was made even less palatable by the fact that such a government would over time tend to shed its disguise and develop into a military regime comparable in character to those found on the continent of Europe. Like Thomas Paine, Madison believed that there was a symbiotic relationship between monarchy and war. On the one hand, armed conflict arose more often than not from the ambition, revenge, avidity, and caprice so evident where there was "a will in the government independent of the will of the people." On the other hand, when war did break out, it inevitably fostered a concentration of power in the hands of the few men responsible for its conduct. One could therefore quite effectively reduce the likelihood of war "by subjecting the will of the government to the will of the society," and this reform would be even more successful in achieving its object if one could somehow at the same time subject "the will of society to the reason of society." It would, however, be impossible to make reason predominant if the Hamiltonian system were to prevail: by saddling future generations with the price for adventures foolishly undertaken today, the funding of a national debt in the English fashion was virtually an incentive to war. "Here," Madison remarked,

> our republican philosopher might have proposed as a model to lawgivers, that war should not only be declared by the authority of the people, whose toils and treasures are to support its burdens, instead of the government which is to reap its fruits: but that each generation should be made to bear the burden of its own wars, instead of carrying them on, at the expence of other generations. And to give the fullest energy to his plan, he might have added, that each generation should not only bear its own burdens, but that the taxes composing them, should include a due proportion of such as by their direct operation keep the people awake, along with those, which being wrapped up in other payments, may leave them asleep, to misapplications of their money.

"Were a nation to impose such restraints on itself," the congressman concluded, "avarice would be sure to calculate the expense of ambition; in the equipoise of these passions, reason would be free to decide for the public good; and an ample reward would accrue to the state, first, from the avoidance of all its wars of folly, secondly, from the vigor of its unwasted resources for wars of necessity and defence." In the best of all possible circumstances, an even greater consummation might be expected. "Were all nations to follow the example," Madison added, "the reward would be doubled to each; and the temple of Janus might be shut, never to be opened more."[155]

With these dangers and this prospect in mind, Madison devoted much of his free time to reflection on the circumstances best suited for focusing popular attention on public affairs and for fostering the spirit of resistance to public malfeasance and tyrannical measures. He favored Jefferson's overall educational program,[156] but that was not all that he had in mind. "Whatever facilitates a general intercourse of sentiments," he observed, such "as good roads, domestic commerce, a free press, and particularly a *circulation of newspapers through the entire body of the people*, and *Representatives going from, and returning among every part of them*, is equivalent to a contraction of territorial limits, and is favorable to liberty, where these may be too extensive."[157] The consolidation of public sentiment was, in fact, the glue binding the Union together. That much Madison had recognized all along. Though he argued in *The Federalist* that the community of passion and interest naturally fostered in a small republic was a threat both to justice and to the maintenance of republican liberty, he never for a moment doubted the need for a measure of unanimity regarding fundamental political principles.[158] Even when anxious chiefly for the maintenance of public order, he had thought it essential that the Constitution become an object of reverence.[159] Later, when he had first contemplated proposing a bill of rights, he had remarked, in passing, on the fashion in which "the political truths declared in that solemn manner acquire by degrees the character of fundamental maxims of free Government, and as they become incorporated with the National sentiment, counteract the impulses of interest and passion."[160] By the end of 1791, he feared the collapse of liberty and was prepared to take radical measures; by then, he thought the arguments presented in *The Federalist* seriously inadequate; and so, by then, he was ready to cooperate with Thomas Jefferson in founding a political party as a temporary expedient aimed at transforming veneration for the Constitution and the Bill of Rights into something akin to a secular civil religion.

"All power has been traced up to opinion," the Virginian observed. "The stability of all government and security of all rights may be traced to the same source."

> How devoutly is it to be wished, then, that the public opinion of the United States should be enlightened; that it should attach itself to their governments as delineated in the *great charters*, derived not from the usurped power of kings, but from the legitimate authority of the people;

and that it should guarantee, with a holy zeal, these political scriptures from every attempt to add to or diminish from them. Liberty and order will never be *perfectly* safe, until a trespass on the constitutional provisions for either, shall be felt with the same keenness that resents an invasion of the dearest rights; until every citizen shall be an ARGUS to espy, and an AEGEON to avenge, the unhallowed deed.[161]

Under the pressure of circumstances and renewed reflection, the man who had once thought a bill of rights unnecessary and almost superfluous had radically reversed his course. In the 1790s, James Madison took up the very themes which the Anti-Federalists had emphasized in opposing ratification of the Constitution just a few years before. He, too, could now assert that "whatever the refinement of modern politics may inculcate, it is still certain that some degree of virtue must exist, or freedom cannot live." He, too, could now express doubts whether "the progress of commercial society" would not so alter "the opinions and manners of the people of America" that these would no longer be "capable to resist and prevent an extension of prerogative or oppression."[162]

In the decades that followed the framing of the American Constitution, its ratification, and the successful establishment of the new government, the convictions and fears once voiced by men like Pennsylvania's Federal Republican and New York's Cato became the central concerns of Thomas Jefferson and James Madison. These convictions and fears account for most of the public stands taken by the two statesmen in those fateful years—including their advocacy of party government, their strict construction of the Constitution, their defense of states' rights, and, of course, the vigorous and successful opposition which they mounted against Congress's acceptance of the recommendations embodied in Alexander Hamilton's controversial *Report on the Subject of Manufactures*.[163]

CHAPTER 5

A Republican Distribution of Citizens

In our North American colonies, where uncultivated land is still to be had upon easy terms, no manufactures for distant sale have ever yet been established in any of their towns. When an artificer has acquired a little more stock than is necessary for carrying on his own business in supplying the neighbouring country, he does not, in North America, attempt to establish with it a manufacture for more distant sale, but employs it in the purchase and improvement of uncultivated land. From artificer he becomes planter, and neither the large wages nor the easy subsistence which that country affords to artificers, can bribe him rather to work for other people than for himself. He feels that an artificer is the servant of his customers, from whom he derives his subsistence; but that a planter who cultivates his own land, and derives his necessary subsistence from the labour of his own family, is really a master, and independent of all the world.
—Adam Smith

III.v.1

Shortly after the author of the Declaration of Independence became president of the United States, a yellow fever epidemic swept the country. Upon learning from his old friend Benjamin Rush, the leading physician in Philadelphia, that the disease had carried off fewer victims in that great metropolis than might have been expected, he wrote back in a somewhat philosophical vein, observing, "When great evils happen, I am in the habit of looking out for what good may arise from them as consolations to us, and Providence has in fact so established the order of things, as that most evils are the means of producing some good. The yellow fever will discourage the growth of great cities in our nation, & I view great cities as pestilential to the morals, the health and the liberties of man. True, they nourish some of the elegant arts, but the useful ones can thrive elsewhere, and less perfection in the others, with more health, virtue & freedom, would be my choice."[1] This was not a passing observation; it reflected what was a settled conviction. In 1784, after disorders in Philadelphia had forced the Continental Congress to withdraw to Princeton, New Jersey, Jefferson made some notes listing considerations that should be taken into account in selecting a permanent seat for the government. One of the reasons dictating the rejection of Princeton was its proximity to Philadelphia and "the risque," if events were to require removal, "of returning under the commercial & corrupt influence of" that great city.[2]

Thomas Jefferson feared and distrusted cities because of the kind of people who resided in them. In 1797, while in the midst of his struggle with the Federalist party, he bewailed the circumstance that "the great body of what are called our merchants" were, in fact, "foreign & false citizens." These men, he contended, "fill our sea ports, are planted in every little town & district of the interior country, sway everything in the former places by their own votes, & those of their dependants, in the latter, by their insinuations & the influence of their ledgers."[3] Some twenty years thereafter, the Virginian would write from retirement to Horatio Gates that "merchants have no country. The mere spot they stand on does not constitute so strong an attachment as that from which they draw their gains."[4]

To begin to grasp the thinking which lies behind Jefferson's loathing for cities and merchants, one must turn to a book which the planter published some thirty-six years before he penned his note to Horatio Gates. In his *Notes on the State of Virginia*, the young statesman had expressed the fear that industrialization might eventually destroy America's democratic institutions. His statement, though long, deserves discussion in full, for the force of the rhetoric employed reflects the strength with which the opinion was held. Jefferson prefaced his discussion with an observation and a suggestion. He observed that the "political oeconomists of Europe have established it as a principle that every state should endeavour to manufacture for itself," and he suggested that "the difference of circumstances" between the American states and those in Europe might well "produce a difference of result." The pertinent difference in circumstances which he had in mind was the "immensity of land courting the industry of the husbandman" in America. The question which should properly be asked is whether it is best that the citizens of a country blessed with an abundance of soil as yet uncultivated "should be employed in" the improvement of the land or whether "one half should be called off from that" enterprise "to exercise manufactures and handicraft arts for the other."

In judging this question, Jefferson adopted not an economic, but a political standard. "Those who labour in the earth are the chosen people of God, if ever he had a chosen people, whose breasts he has made his peculiar deposit for substantial and genuine virtue." So the Virginia planter argued. "It is the focus in which he keeps alive that sacred fire, which otherwise might escape from the face of the earth."

Corruption of morals in the mass of cultivators is a phaenomenon of which no age nor nation has furnished an example. It is the mark set on those, who not looking up to heaven, to their own soil and industry, as does the husbandman, for their subsistance, depend for it on the casualties and caprice of customers. Dependance begets subservience and venality, suffocates the germ of virtue, and prepares fit tools for the designs of ambition. This, the natural progress and consequence of the arts, has sometimes perhaps been retarded by accidental circumstances: but, generally speaking, the proportion which the aggregate of the other classes of citizens bears in any state to that of its husbandmen, is the proportion of its unsound to its healthy parts, and is a good-enough barometer whereby to measure its degree of corruption. While we have land to labour then, let us never wish to see our citizens occupied at a work-bench, or twirling a distaff. Carpenters, masons, smiths, are wanting in husbandry: but, for the general operations of manufacture, let our work-shops remain in Europe. It is better to carry provisions and materials to workmen there, than bring them to the provisions and materials, and with them their manners and principles. The loss by the transportation of commodities across the Atlantic will be made up in happiness and permanence of government.

This explained Jefferson's aversion to urban life. "The mobs of great cities add just so much to the support of pure government, as sores do to the strength of the human body," he contended. "It is the manners and spirit of a people which preserve a republic in vigour. A degeneracy in these is a canker which soon eats to the heart of its laws and constitution."[5] It is no wonder, then, that Jefferson included in his 1776 draft of a constitution for Virginia a provision entitling landless citizens to fifty acres of state land.[6] If he had had his wish, every American would have taken up the plow.

Not long before his book was finally published in English, Jefferson had occasion to reflect once more on the manners and spirit of the American people. In a letter written in January 1786, he suggested that "good" might arise from the collapse of American credit abroad. "I see nothing else," he wrote, "which can restrain our disposition to luxury, and the loss of those manners which alone can preserve republican government."[7] A few months later, he raised the issue again and fulminated against the "extravagance" that had seized his countrymen at the end of the revolutionary struggle, describing it as "a more baneful evil than toryism was during the war." If a missionary making "frugality the basis of his religious system" were to appear on the scene and go "thro the land preaching it up as the only road to salvation," the Virginian added, "I would join his school tho' not generally disposed to seek my religion out[side] of the dictates of my own reason and feelings of my own heart." A year later, he described the war for independence as "a time of happiness and enjoiment" precisely because of "the privation of many things not essential to happiness." In the aftermath, things had somehow gotten out of hand, and Jefferson could "see no remedy . . . but an open course of law."[8]

To anyone even vaguely familiar with the classical tradition, the language used by Jefferson in expressing his distaste for merchants, in outlining his critique of manufacturing, in making his defense of agrarian life, and in launching his attack on luxury cannot but be striking. In a host of ways, the Virginian's views seem to echo those of the ancient Greeks. For one thing, he clearly shared their conviction that self-government is possible only for citizens of a certain type; and like them, he was sensitive to the manner in which occupation shapes character. It should not, then, be surprising that many scholars have succumbed to the temptation to think of Thomas Jefferson and his followers as classical republicans.[9] To determine the degree to which these scholars should be judged right or wrong, we will have to examine in greater detail the opinions of Thomas Jefferson and those of his closest associate.

III.v.2

In some measure, James Madison shared his neighbor's misgivings.[10] At the time of the Constitutional Convention and during the struggle for ratification, he seemed willing to contemplate with considerable equanimity and even a degree of favor the young republic's future as a commercial and industrial state.[11] But that equanimity was fragile and that favor, fleeting. Even in *The Federalist*, the Virginian managed discreetly to intimate that the question whether large-scale "domestic manufactures" should be given positive encouragement by the placing of "restrictions on foreign manufactures" could not ultimately be settled on the grounds of "justice" alone. There was more at stake than the inflated price which farmers would have to pay for such wares under these circumstances; "the public good" was also somehow involved.[12]

To grasp just how the public good was involved, one must first peruse a letter which Madison wrote in June 1786 in response to correspondence from Jefferson which included the latter's "reflections on the idle poor of Europe." Madison agreed with his neighbor that "the misery of the lower classes will be found to abate wherever the Government assumes a freer aspect, & the laws favor a subdivision of property." But he was persuaded that the "limited population" in the American states was as responsible for "the comparative comfort of the Mass of people . . . as the political advantages which distinguish us." The inevitable growth in the American population would pose a problem since a "certain degree of misery seems inseparable from a high degree of populousness." This was the context in which he pondered the problem of large-scale manufacturing.

> No problem in political Oeconomy has appeared to me more puzzling than that which relatest to the most proper distribution of a Country fully peopled. Let the lands be shared among them ever so wisely, & let them be supplied with labourers ever so plentifully; as there must be a great surplus of subsistence, there will also remain a great surplus of inhabitants, a greater by far than will be employed in cloathing both themselves & those who feed them, and in administering to both, every other necessary & even comfort of life. What is to be done with this surplus? Hitherto we have seen them distributed into Manufacturers of superfluities, idle proprietors of productive funds, domestics, soldiers, merchants, mariners, and a few other less numerous classes. All these classes notwithstanding have been found insufficient to absorb the redundant members of a populous society; and yet a reduction of most of these classes enters into the very reform which appears so necessary & desireable. From a more equal partition of property, must result a greater simplicity of manners, consequently a less consumption of manufactured superfluities, and a less proportion of idle proprietors & domestics. From a juster Government must result less need of soldiers either for defence agst. dangers from without or disturbances from within. The number of merchants must be inconsiderable under any modification of Society; and that of Mariners will depend more on geographical position, than on the plan of legislation. But I forget that I am writing a letter not a dissertation.[13]

At this point, Madison's discussion breaks off inconclusively, but six years later he returned to the theme in the series of brief and elegantly worded dissertations which he published in Philip Freneau's *National Gazette.*

In these later publications, Madison's focus has changed. It is no longer exclusively or even primarily social; as a consequence of his reflection on the tendency of Hamilton's system, it is now resolutely political. He is concerned chiefly not with the idle poor and their miserable lot but, rather, with the particular distribution of citizens into occupations that should be deemed most suitable for sustaining a republican regime. Off and on for the rest of their lives, Jefferson and Madison were to ponder the relationship between population increase, the existence of an agricultural surplus, the likely emergence of a glut of labor, the attendant growth of large-scale manufacturing, and the danger that all of this would ultimately pose to the American republic.[14]

In constructing the federal constitution, Madison had rejected the notion that it was reasonable "to place unlimited confidence" in those elected to Congress and to "expect nothing but the most exalted integrity and sublime virtue" from them. But he did not at any time suppose that the moral character of the citizens and their representatives was simply a matter of indifference. In *The Federalist*, as we have seen, he tried to strike a balance. "I go on this great republican principle," he later told the members of the Virginia Ratifying Convention, "that the people will have [enough] virtue and intelligence to select men of virtue and wisdom. Is there no virtue among us? If there be not, we are in a wretched situation. No theoretical checks, no form of government, can render us secure. To suppose that any form of government will secure liberty or happiness without any virtue in the people, is a chimerical idea. If there be sufficient virtue and intelligence in the community, it will be exercised in the selection of these men; so that we do not depend on their virtue, or put confidence in our rulers, but in the people who are to choose them." [15] This was the premise undergirding the arguments which Madison gradually unveiled in the pages of the *National Gazette*.

In his articles, the young congressman did not propose "any plan of legislation," and he denied that there should be any attempt to put his theory into practice "by violence on the will or property of individuals." His only concern was to establish "a monition against empirical experiments by power, and a model to which the free choice of occupations by the people, might gradually approximate the order of society." [16] That monition was clearly directed against Alexander Hamilton's proposal that the federal government deliberately foster the growth of large-scale domestic manufactures through a system of bounties. The Virginian's articles on this subject began appearing just a few months after Washington's secretary of the treasury presented to Congress his famous *Report on the Subject of Manufactures*.[17] Thereafter, Madison opposed his former ally with all the force at his command.

In the most pertinent of his articles for the *National Gazette*, Madison contended that the "best distribution" of the citizenry into occupations would be "that which would most favor *health, virtue, intelligence*, and *competency* in the *greatest number* of citizens." Madison thought it "needless" to add to his list of objects "*liberty* and *safety*" since the "first is presupposed by them" while the "last must result from them." With this as an introduction, he launched into his theme—the superiority of farming as an occupation.

The life of the husbandman is pre-eminently suited to the comfort and happiness of the individual. *Health*, the first of blessings, is an appurtenance of his property and his employment. *Virtue*, the health of the soul, is another part of his patrimony, and no less favored by his situation. *Intelligence* may be cultivated in this as well as in any other walk of life. If the mind be less susceptible of polish in retirement than in a croud, it is more capable of profound and comprehensive efforts. Is it more ignorant of some things? It has a compensation in its ignorance of others. *Competency* is more universally the lot of those who dwell in the country, when liberty is at the same time their lot. The extremes of want and of waste have other abodes.'Tis not the country that peoples either the Bridewells or the Bedlams. These mansions of wretchedness are tenanted from the distresses and vices of overgrown cities.

Madison's tone is characteristically more moderate, but his conclusions owe much to Jefferson nonetheless. He not only argues that the "class of citizens who provide at once their own food and their own raiment" are "the most truly independent and happy." He contends as well that "they are more: they are the best basis of public liberty, and the strongest bulwark of public safety." "It follows," he adds, "that the greater the proportion of this class to the whole society, the more free, the more independent, and the more happy must be society itself."[18] The agriculturalist engaged in farming and in the production of clothing and other necessities for use within his own household was the bulwark of the regime; the spread of large-scale manufacturing might someday become a threat to republican liberty.

In the next of his articles, Madison examines the alternative. He begins by drawing his readers' attention to a particularly telling example: the sad plight of the inhabitants of Birmingham and the other English towns nearby who had once made their livelihood by the manufacture of buckles. Thousands had been put out of work "in consequence of the prevailing fashion of SHOE-STRINGS & SLIPPERS." Because these men were then "without employ, almost destitute of bread, and exposed to the horrors of want in the most inclement season," they had petitioned the Prince of Wales to come to their rescue by employing the considerable influence of his own example to give "direction to the *public taste*." The story has a clear moral: occupations which depend on "mere fashion" are extremely "precarious"; they "produce the most servile dependence of one class of citizens on another class"; and they accord only too well with the spirit of monarchy. Such is not the case, however, where there is a "*mutuality* of wants." "What a contrast is here," he exclaimed, "to the independent situation and manly sentiments of American citizens, who live on their own soil, or whose labour is necessary to its cultivation, or who were occupied in supplying wants, which being founded in solid utility, in comfortable accommodation, or in settled habits, produce a reciprocity of dependence, at once ensuring subsistence, and inspiring a dignified sense of social rights." The example of the laborers formerly engaged in the making of buckles is "a lesson to nations." To the degree that "a nation consists of that description of citizens, and depends on external commerce, it is dependent on the consumption and caprice of other nations."[19] The growth of large-scale manufacturing would not only threaten freedom at home; it might ultimately make the United States an appendage of the European powers.

III. v. 3

The programmatic statements made by the two great statesmen from Virginia need to be weighed with considerable care, for there was, in fact, a chasm separating the Americans from the ancient Greeks.[20] Jefferson was aware of the difference in interests distinguishing farmers from tradesmen, and he knew that this bore on the problem of defense. That is why he emphasized that "the cultivators of the earth" possessed more *"amor patriae"* than any other class and that merchants possessed the least.[21] But war was not, in fact, his prime or even a very serious concern. Jefferson was acutely aware of the political and military advantages inherent in the new nation's distance from the quarreling states of the Old World, and, like James Madison, he took it for granted that the countries of Europe were far more dependent upon agricultural imports from the United States than the latter was on the products manufactured by the former. As a consequence, both men firmly believed that the young republic could avoid foreign entanglements, work its will abroad through a concerted policy of commercial retaliation, and thereby force the great powers to abandon all mercantilist restrictions and institute free trade. Neither seriously expected that the economic interdependence of the various states, which would then inevitably arise, would guarantee the perpetuation of peace. But they both supposed this interdependence to be conducive to that end.[22]

The emphasis which the two Virginians placed on the employment of commerce as a weapon is in itself revealing. Neither man would have quarreled with Gouverneur Morris's description of their countrymen as "the first born children of extended Commerce in modern Times."[23] The cultivators which the American advocates of westward expansion had in mind were not self-sufficient peasant proprietors; they were commercial farmers: merchants, in more than a manner of speaking, themselves.[24] "All the world is becoming commercial," Jefferson wrote to Washington. If it were "practicable to keep our new empire" free from these trends, "we might indulge ourselves in speculating whether commerce contributes to the happiness of mankind." But that was impossible. "Our citizens have had too full a taste of the comforts furnished by the arts and manufactures to be debarred the use of them. We must then in our own defence endeavor to share as large a portion as we can of this modern source of wealth and power."[25] If Jefferson favored a strategy of commercial retaliation, it was chiefly because he expected thereby to be able to force the various states of Europe to open up their markets to America's agricultural exports.

James Madison similarly acknowledged the necessity and desirability of commerce. In 1784, he endorsed American migration into the backcountry to the west of the Appalachian Mountains as a means for providing the country's growing population with employment and for delaying the otherwise inevitable onset of large-scale manufacturing in the United States. At the same time, he took it for granted that, unless the federal government could somehow guarantee that the Mississippi River would be open as an outlet for American farm production, extensive settlement of that region would be precluded.[26] Jefferson subsequently suggested that a failure on the part of the federal government to secure access to the Mississippi and to New Orleans might have another result perhaps even more dire: the secession of the regions dependent upon that outlet.[27] Thus, nearly two decades later, when President Thomas Jefferson initiated the negotiations that culminated in the Louisiana Purchase, he did so not primarily to secure an abundance of virgin land for future generations of virtuous agriculturists; like his secretary of state, James Madison, he was chiefly intent on guaranteeing to the farmers already resident in the Ohio Valley the opportunity to transport their crops for export down the Mississippi through the port of New Orleans. Indeed, the acquisition of a continental empire stretching west of that great river was an unexpected, if extremely welcome, windfall.[28] At least initially, the two statesman were more interested in securing access to markets than in purchasing land for farms.

Because the two Virginians were not much concerned with the need to form a citizenry steadfast in war, their antipathy to the growth of manufacturing in the United States was only superficially similar to that evidenced by the ancients. When Jefferson exhorted his fellow countrymen to let their workshops stay in Europe, he did so not because he feared treason or longed for *homónoia*. He was, of course, unfriendly to the notion once entertained by Madison that the polity should be composed of "a landed interest, a manufacturing interest, a mercantile interest, a moneyed interest, with many lesser interests"; in truth, he never really favored his friend's idea that "the regulation of these various and interfering interests" should form "the principal task of modern legislation" and should in this particular combination involve "the spirit of party and faction in the necessary and ordinary operations of government."[29] From the outset, Thomas Jefferson unabashedly favored agriculture at the expense of all other interests. "Is Commerce so much the basis of the existence of the U.S. as to call for a bankrupt law?" he asked. "On the contrary are we not almost merely agricultural? Should not all laws be made with a view essentially to the husbandmen?"[30]

Madison had at one time supposed that the republic would be bolstered by economic development and the resulting diversification of the means by which the citizens gained subsistence. This doctrine Jefferson firmly rejected, but he did endorse his friend's argument in its more obvious and simple geographical aspect. In fact, he warmly embraced the idea that there were great advantages to be drawn from geographical extension and the resulting multiplication of those factions rooted in the peculiarities of local agricultural production. This diversity he took to be extremely helpful in controlling the effects of *stásis*. A few years after the appearance of *The Federalist*, Jefferson wrote to a beleaguered citizen of the tiny city Geneva:

> I suspect that the doctrine, that small States alone are fitted to be republics, will be exploded by experience, with some other brilliant fallacies accredited by Montesquieu & other political writers. Perhaps it will be found, that to obtain a just republic (and it is to secure our just rights that we resort to government at all) it must be so extensive as that local egoisms may never reach it's greater part; that on every particular question, a majority may be found in it's councils free from particular interests, and giving, therefore, an uniform prevalence to the principles of justice. The smaller the societies, the more violent & more convulsive their schisms. We have chanced to live in an age which will probably be distinguished in history, for it's experiments in government on a larger scale than has yet taken place.[31]

What the Virginian suspected in 1795 he was prepared to affirm some two decades thereafter. In 1817, he wrote to the very Frenchman to whom he had addressed his *Notes on the State of Virginia* of his "confidence . . . that, contrary to the principle of Montesquieu, it will be seen that the larger the extent of country, the more firm its republican structure, if founded, not on conquest, but in principles of compact and equality."[32] From this conviction, he never deviated. Just five years before his death, he told another correspondent, "I still believe that the Western expansion of our confederacy will ensure its duration, by overruling local factions, which might shake a smaller association."[33]

Since the need to prepare for war did not figure prominently in the calculations of the two Republican statesmen, neither Jefferson nor Madison had simplicity of manners and austerity in mind when they looked with favor on those who tilled the soil. To be sure, the former's attack on large-scale manufacturing owed something to the critique of technological progress launched by Rousseau in his *Discourse on the Sciences and the Arts.* Jefferson once expressed fear regarding "the natural progress and consequence of the arts," and he was capable of writing that, "if science produces no better fruits than tyranny, murder, rapine and destitution of national morality, I would rather wish our country to be ignorant, honest and estimable as our neighboring savages are." [34] But the American was not, in fact, to be counted among those who attributed to the improvement of the arts an influence tending to the wholesale corruption of mankind. Before all else, Thomas Jefferson was an adherent of the Enlightenment. He applauded the fact that "the arts and sciences" had "advanced gradually thro' all the 16th. 17th. and 18th. centuries, softening and correcting the manners and morals of man," and he believed that "their natural effect" was, "by illuminating public opinion, to erect it into a Censor, before which the most exalted tremble for their future, as well as present fame." [35] Though cautious and wary, he was an advocate of technological progress and its contribution to human welfare, not an opponent.

Thus, it is by no means fortuitous that Jefferson wrote to John Adams in 1785, urging him to substitute "comforts" for "necessaries" in the draft of a commercial treaty with Portugal. [36] The planter from Monticello may have toyed with the idea of proposing sumptuary laws, but only because he and the other quasi-aristocratic members of his class had for generations been prone to conspicuous consumption and to debilitating debt. And the fact that those debts were owed to British merchants no doubt had much to do with the hearty dislike he evidenced for men of that profession. [37] Jefferson opposed the self-destructive extravagance of the rich, not the prosperity of ordinary men. The latter he deemed essential for the very survival of the American regime. My expectation that our republic will endure, he explained to his French correspondent, "is built much on the enlargement of the resources of life going hand in hand with the enlargement of territory, and the belief that men are disposed to live honestly, if the means of doing so are open to them." [38]

On this point, Madison was, if anything, even more enthusiastic than his neighbor and friend. He never advocated sumptuary laws—not even in an ill-considered outburst. In fact, he rejoiced at the prospect of the federal government "patronizing in every authorized mode undertakings conducive to the aggregate wealth and individual comfort of our citizens." [39] In truth, the concerns of the ancient *pólis* were never very much on the minds of the two Virginians.

III. v. 4

England and France were much closer to hand. While a colonial agent in London in 1760, Benjamin Franklin had visited the workhouses and the state-subsidized factories associated with them and had come to link large-scale manufacturing with poverty, with political corruption, and vice.[40] Jefferson made the same observation during his extended sojourn in Paris two decades later. The Virginia planter saw with his own eyes the manner in which the growth of manufactures could give rise to a new aristocracy firmly in control of those whom it employed. This was the result which Jefferson and Madison feared when they reacted so vigorously against the last of Hamilton's three great reports. As a consequence of these fears, Jefferson never ceased to hope that his fellow countrymen, by increasing their harvests, could "nourish the now perishing births of Europe, who in return would manufacture and send us in exchange our clothes and other comforts."[41] For similar reasons, Madison at one point recommended to the Philadelphia convention that the House of Representatives be chosen by "the freeholders of the Country"—men who "would be the safest depositories of Republican liberty." "In future times," he argued, "a great majority of the people will not only be without landed, but any other sort of, property." In these circumstances, they would "either combine under the influence of their common situation" and threaten "the rights of property & the public liberty . . . or which is more probable, they will become the tools of opulence & ambition."[42]

Madison's recommendation may have been in perfect accord with ancient practice, but it was, in fact, a restatement of one of the principles of traditional Whig political architecture, which was concerned with the protection of property rights far more than with the fostering of *homónoia* and the encouragement of public spirit and martial vigor. In his *Commentaries on the Laws of England*, the jurist William Blackstone stated the rationale. "The true reason of requiring any qualification, with regard to property, in voters," he explained, "is to exclude such persons as are in so mean a situation that they are esteemed to have no will of their own."

> If these persons had votes, they would be tempted to dispose of them under some undue influence or other. This would give a great, an artful, or a wealthy man, a larger share in elections than is consistent with general liberty. If it were probable that every man would give his vote freely, and without influence of any kind, then, upon the true theory and genuine principles of liberty, every member of the community, however poor, should have a vote in electing those delegates, to whose charge is com-

mitted the disposal of his property, his liberty, and his life. But, since that can hardly be expected in persons of indigent fortunes, or such as are under the immediate dominion of others, all popular states have been obliged to establish certain qualifications; whereby some, who are suspected to have no will of their own, are excluded from voting, in order to set other individuals, whose wills may be supposed independent, more thoroughly upon a level with each other.[43]

Needless to say, Madison was not the only American to recognize the force of this argument and its implications for the health of the young republic. Blackstone's views on the subject were cited with approval by James Wilson, Alexander Hamilton, John Adams, and a good many others thereafter.[44] Few, if any, among the Founding Fathers disagreed; and for this reason, they were generally inclined to prefer agriculture. Hamilton was, in fact, one among these. Even in his controversial *Report on the Subject of Manufactures*, he was prepared to concede that "the cultivation of the earth" was "a state most favourable to the freedom and independence of the human mind" and to acknowledge that it had *"intrinsically a strong claim to pre-eminence over every other kind of industry."* [45]

Hamilton's firm adherence to this opinion should give pause to those inclined to dismiss the argument for agriculture as an anachronism—the relic of an ancient prejudice. Even in our own time, the thesis that the independent farmer is the bastion of liberty and that the family farm must be preserved at all costs has powerful and persuasive advocates. Those intent on establishing totalitarian tyranny have paid silent tribute to the wisdom of the old Whig doctrine with their willingness to sacrifice economic efficiency for the sake of creating collective farms. These revolutionaries recognized more clearly than anyone else now alive that to subject those who till the soil to full political control one must reduce them to the status of hirelings as economically dependent on the state as those employed in its offices and factories. In supposing that the decline of agriculture and the spread of large-scale manufacturing would inevitably pose a grave threat to the maintenance of republican liberty in the United States, Jefferson and Madison blundered, but their argument had a point nonetheless.

The architect of the American Constitution lived to a ripe old age, but not long enough to foresee the possibility of state ownership of the means of production and all that this would entail. His fears were focused, instead, on dangers more immediately familiar to the men of his age. The Virginia planter never ceased to worry that demographic growth would eventually produce within the United States a class of "indigent laborers" bitterly opposed to the owners of property or subject to the dictates of an aristocracy of "wealthy capitalists." In time, he came to reject the conclusion reached by the great Blackstone. "*Confining* the right of suffrage to freeholders and to such as hold an equivalent property, convertible, . . . into freeholds," he argued, would violate "the vital principle of free Government, that those who are to be bound by laws ought to have a voice in making them." But through much, if not all, of his life, Madison remained an advocate of electing one branch of every state legislature on the basis of a suffrage restricted to men with property in land or the like.[46]

In 1788, when he was asked to make recommendations regarding a constitution for the new state of Kentucky, the Virginia planter took as his major premise the view that "in all populous countries, the smaller part only can be interested in preserving the rights of property." He, then, observed that "it must be foreseen that America, and Kentucky itself will by degrees arrive at this stage of Society." To prevent disaster, he concluded, Americans must take action now while land remains abundant and the majority still have an interest in protecting the rights of property. Now, when circumstances are still propitious, they must shape the constitutions of their states to meet the dangers which can be foreseen. "If *all* power be suffered to slide into hands not interested in the rights of property which must be the case whenever a majority fall under that description," he warned, "one of two things cannot fail to happen." Either the propertyless majority will unite against the rich minority and thereby "become the dupes & instruments of ambition, or their poverty & dependence will render them the mercenary instruments of wealth." Neither prospect was inviting, for in both cases liberty would "be subverted: in the first by a despotism growing out of anarchy, in the second, by an oligarchy founded on corruption."[47]

Forty years later, he still held similar views. In a memorandum circulated at the constitutional convention held by Virginia in 1829, the aged statesmen urged the other delegates to take into account "the prospective changes in the condition and composition of the society" for which they were then framing a government. He alluded to the fact that the soil, when properly cultivated, was "capable of yielding subsistence for a large surplus of consumers," and he suggested that this surplus would grow "with the increasing improvements in agriculture, and the labor-saving arts applied to it." Progress of this sort might seem a blessing, but, unfortunately, it was humanity's lot that "of this surplus a large proportion is necessarily reduced by a competition for employment to wages which afford them the bare necessaries of life." Those framing the constitution must pause to ponder "what is to be done with this unfavored class of the community." It would be "unsafe to admit them to a full share of political power." But it would be inexpedient and, in fact, dangerous to exclude a large and powerful portion of the community from participation in making its laws. "It would be happy if a State of Society could be found or framed, in which an equal voice in making the laws might be allowed to every individual bound to obey them," Madison observed. "But this is a Theory, which like most Theories, confessedly requires limitations & modifications." His own conclusion, tentatively advanced, echoed an argument made by George Mason at the federal convention more than four decades before. It might be safe, he conceded, to add to those possessed of property the heads of households, "most of whom 'having given hostages to fortune,' will have given them to their Country also."[48] Though he was prepared to make his peace with universal manhood suffrage, James Madison was decidedly reluctant, and he went to his grave convinced that the rise of large-scale manufacturing boded ill for the nation.[49]

III.v.5

In the end, of course, the wars of the French Revolution and their impact on commerce by sea forced the two statesmen from Virginia to concede that Alexander Hamilton had been at least partially right. By 1815, Madison was prepared to eat his own words and to propose to Congress "public patronage" of those branches of manufacturing able to "relieve the United States from a dependence on foreign supplies, ever subject to casual failures, for articles necessary for the public defense or connected with the primary wants of individuals." "However wise the theory may be which leaves to the sagacity and interest of individuals the application of their industry and resources," he conceded, "there are in this as in other cases exceptions to the general rule."[50] This was his settled opinion. Both then and thereafter, he favored "the policy of encouraging domestic manufactures, within certain limits, and in reference to certain articles."[51] In fact, eventually, after pondering the causes of the Panic of 1819 and of the long depression that followed, he came to see the wisdom of Alexander Hamilton's claim that agriculture would more surely prosper and that the nation would be not only stronger and more fully independent but more closely united if there were a domestic market of tradesmen, artisans, and factory workers producing items to exchange for the surplus of foodstuffs grown on the country's farms.[52]

For the proposal that he advanced in 1815, Madison had Jefferson's approval. Even in the 1790s, the two Virginians had recognized that their strategy of commercial discrimination presupposed a temporary expansion of domestic manufacturing, and they were not hesitant to welcome into their

Republican party the manufacturers, merchants, and artisans who had been alienated by Hamilton's adamant refusal to embrace a protectionist policy.[53] By 1816, they had both come to recognize that the turn to manufactures could not be a mere temporary expedient. "To be independent for the comforts of life," Jefferson reluctantly acknowledged, "we must fabricate them ourselves." In the real world of his day, those men opposed to "domestic manufacture" would have to choose between two unpalatable alternatives: reduction "to dependence" on the "foreign nation" that produced the necessary finished goods, and being "clothed in skins" and living "like wild beasts in dens and caverns." Despite grave misgivings, Jefferson was himself "not one of these" men.[54] As he had explained in a letter written to John Jay shortly after his retirement from the presidency, he now sought "an equilibrium of agriculture, manufactures, and commerce" of the sort "essential to our independence." Thus he summed up the situation: "Manufactures, sufficient for our own consumption, of what we raise the raw material (and no more). Commerce sufficient to carry the surplus produce of agriculture, beyond our own consumption, to a market for exchanging it for articles we cannot raise (and no more). These are the true limits of manufactures and commerce. To go beyond them is to increase our dependence on foreign nations, and our liability to war."[55] Though never willing to take the next step and advocate the employment of Americans in producing finished goods for export,[56] Thomas Jefferson eventually bowed to the dictates of "experience" and argued that limited industrial establishments were "now as necessary to our independence as to our comfort."[57]

This conclusion would certainly have grieved Jefferson a great deal had he not already well before that time come to be persuaded by an argument advanced by Hamilton in his *Report on the Subject of Manufactures*. The New Yorker had foreseen the objections that would be raised in response to his proposals and had dismissed them on the ground that the very abundance of virgin land within the nation's borders obviated the danger which the presence of large-scale manufacturing posed.[58] In 1805, Jefferson observed with evident satisfaction, "As yet our manufacturers are as much at their ease, as independent and moral as our agricultural inhabitants, and they will continue so as long as there are vacant lands for them to resort to; because whenever it shall be attempted by the other classes to reduce them to the minimum of subsistence, they will quit their trades and go to labouring the earth." If the industrial workers of the Old World had evidenced "a depravity of morals, a dependence and corruption" which rendered them unfit for citizenship, he noted, the cause was not their profession per se but simply "the want of food and clothing necessary to sustain life."[59] Jefferson shared

Madison's convictions. Large-scale manufacturing would be a threat to the republic, but only after the frontier had closed. In the meantime, "within certain limits, and in reference to certain articles," manufacturing was both necessary and desirable.

III.v.6

The gap separating Thomas Jefferson, James Madison, and their followers from the ancients was far greater than this analysis might thus far suggest. After the American victory in the Revolutionary War, when the two Virginians spoke of popular or demotic virtue, they almost always had independence, diligence, and frugality, not magnanimity, courage, and martial vigor, in mind. At the deepest level, their concerns were, in fact, private, not public. They were eager to instill in the citizens a jealous vigilance over their own individual rights, not the "possitive Passion for the public good, the public Interest, Honour, Power, and Glory" once called for by John Adams. The two men differed as to the advantages to be gained from fostering "a profound reverence for the laws"; but neither of them ever expected or sought to encourage "an heroic love for the publick good, . . . a contempt of riches, and a noble haughtiness of soul," for they were by no means persuaded by Mercy Otis Warren's claim that these were "the only foundations of a free government."[60]

This was, in fact, the case even during the war at the very time when Jefferson was composing the extraordinary encomium on farming that forms so striking a part of his *Notes on the State of Virginia*. With an eye to the problem of religious toleration, he then argued that

the spirit of the times may alter, will alter. Our rulers will become corrupt, our people careless. A single zealot may commence persecutor, and better men be his victims. It can never be too often repeated, that the time for fixing every essential right on a legal basis is while our rulers are honest, and ourselves united. From the conclusion of this war we shall be going down hill. It will not then be necessary to resort every moment to the people for support. They will be forgotten, therefore, and their rights disregarded. They will forget themselves, but in the sole faculty of making money, and will never think of uniting to effect a due respect for their rights. The shackles, therefore, which shall not be knocked off at the conclusion of this war, will remain on us long, will be made heavier and heavier, till our rights shall revive or expire in a convulsion.[61]

Jefferson's discussion of the dangers of corruption and the need for virtue owes far more to Machiavelli's subordination of *virtù* to the pursuit of individual security and well-being than to anything to be found in writings more ancient. The particular excellence he deemed requisite in the modern liberal republic was a species of enlightened and vigilant selfishness like that espoused by Machiavelli, Locke, Sidney, Trenchard and Gordon, and Bolingbroke and not a spirit of self-sacrifice for the sake of the community as a whole. Like Hamilton, though in a rather different fashion, the statesman from Virginia sought to extract public benefits from what had long been considered private vices.

In this regard, Noah Webster's contemporary restatement of James Harrington's endorsement of egalitarian, agrarian life deserves careful scrutiny: for, in the process, this staunch Federalist from Connecticut unveiled what the Republicans from Virginia had deliberately left hidden. "The system of the great Montesquieu will ever be erroneous," he contended, "till the words *property or lands in fee simple* are substituted for *virtue*, throughout his *Spirit of Laws*." His defense of this proposition was simple and straightforward: "*Virtue*, patriotism, or love of country, never was and never will be, till mens' natures are changed, a fixed, permanent principle and support of government. But in an agricultural country, a general possession of land in fee simple may be rendered perpetual, and the inequalities introduced by commerce are too fluctuating to endanger government. An equality of property, with a necessity of alienation, constantly operating to destroy combinations of powerful families, is the very *soul of a republic*."[62] Webster's judicious choice of words reveals what the uplifting rhetoric of the two Republican leaders obscures. In truth, neither Jefferson nor Madison was a vigorous advocate of anything which the Greeks or the Romans would have recognized as virtue. Like their opponents in the Federalist party, these two men sought to forge from self-interest a substitute for those qualities which had been the mainstay of the ancient republics; and again, like their opponents, they did so not just because they thought classical virtue insufficient. They, too, found the rigors of self-sacrifice and virtuous restraint unappealing.

The distinctively modern character of the outlook selected by Jefferson and Madison is made particularly clear in a letter which the former wrote to John Adams in December 1819. At the moment when he penned this brief missive, Jefferson had been spending a good deal of his time in retirement, amusing himself by reading the letters of Cicero. To Adams, he observed that the letters breathed "the purest effusions of an exalted patriot, while the parricide Caesar is left in odious contrast." But he felt compelled to add a disclaimer lest his correspondent mistake his attitude. "When the enthusiasm . . . kindled by Cicero's pen and principles, subsides into cool reflection," Jefferson remarked,

> I ask myself What was that government which the virtues of Cicero were so zealous to restore, and the ambition of Caesar to subvert? And if Caesar had been as virtuous as he was daring and sagacious, what could he, even in the plenitude of his usurped power, have done to lead his fellow citizens into good government? I do not say to *restore it*, because they never had it, from the rape of the Sabines to the ravages of the Caesars. If their people indeed had been, like ourselves, enlightened, peaceable, and really free, the answer would be obvious. "Restore independence to all your foreign conquests, relieve Italy from the government of the rabble of Rome, consult it as a nation entitled to self-government, and do it's will."

For the Romans, such a reform would have been inconceivable. The "whole nation" was "steeped in corruption, vice and venality," and there was nothing that "great and virtuous men" like "Cicero, Cato, and Brutus" could have done, "had it been referred to them to establish a good government for their country." The truth is that the opponents of Caesar "had no ideas of government themselves." They thought only of "their degenerate Senate." And the people were worse. They had no idea "of liberty." They thought only of "the factious opposition of their tribunes." Jefferson was even willing to deny that Rome had ever known "one single day of free and rational government."[63]

John Adams's response is also worthy of attention, for it fleshes out Jefferson's argument and throws light on what the Virginian had in mind. Of the Romans, Adams wrote, "I never could discover that they possessed much Virtue, or real Liberty there." His point was that "Pride, Strength, and Courage, were all the virtues that composed their National Characters."[64] These were, indeed, the qualities that had inspired the admiration conferred on Rome. Pride drove the Romans to attempt the conquest of an empire, and strength and courage enabled them to succeed. But men like Adams and Jefferson openly doubted whether qualities of this sort really deserved admiration, and ultimately they denied that pride, strength, and courage were virtues at all. The qualities that so distinguished the Romans might, in the end, prove inseparable from the corruption, vice, and venality which had ultimately destroyed even the pretense of liberty at Rome. Like Tyrtaeus before them, the two Americans were advocates of a revolution in ethics. The Spartan poet had denied that quickness, agility at wrestling, brute strength, physical beauty, the golden touch, regal bearing, and eloquence were of import when separated from capacity in war. His American critics denied that pride, strength, and courage deserved regard when not in service to the institution and maintenance of that free and rational government suited to an enlightened and peaceable people. Jefferson spoke for all or nearly all of his compatriots when he wrote that "the establishment of another Roman empire, spreading vassalage and depravity over the face of the globe, is not, I hope, within the purposes of heaven."[65]

Of course, there were some among Jefferson's contemporaries who denied that he had ever really broken with the ancients. At the time during his second term as president when the Virginian put the theory of commercial retaliation to the test by imposing an embargo on all American trade with the outside world, Jefferson's opponents in the Federalist party accused him of being an enemy of commerce and an admirer of ancient Lacedaemon.[66] In one regard, they had a point. In championing agriculture, as in defending states' rights and local prerogative, Jefferson and his followers reinforced the power of the slaveholding aristocracy of the South.[67] This they accomplished in two ways. First, by preventing passage of Hamilton's *Report on the Subject of Manufactures*, by gradually dismantling his system of finance, and by doing everything within their power to insure that cheap land would remain available for future generations of men willing to work it, the Republicans of the early national period certainly tried and arguably managed to put off the day when the spread of manufacturing within the agrarian states of the South would weaken, if not break, the economic and political hegemony of the planter oligarchy. In the process, they repudiated the antislavery strategy hinted at by the authors of *The Federalist* and subsequently pursued by Hamilton.[68] At the same time, by denouncing both commerce and manufacturing as professions tending to corrupt their practitioners and to endanger the republic, the Republicans bolstered the pride of all those who earned their living from the land—including the vast majority of those Americans who maintained and profited from what Madison had once termed "the most oppressive dominion ever exercised by man over man." In this fashion, they instilled in the slaveholders of the South the conviction that their domestic institutions were superior to those increasingly prevalent in the Northeast.[69]

To be sure, Jefferson had himself once argued that slavery corrupts the morals and manners of the masters; he had even been willing to suggest that slavery might eventually bring down the wrath of heaven on his countrymen.[70] But he raised no objection years later when his friend John Taylor, the chief ideologue of the Republican party, rejected his claims and endorsed the ancient Spartan notion that slavery is a school of republican virtue rather than vice. Taylor chose to confront Jefferson's argument directly; he even hinted that his fellow planter no longer entertained the convictions he had once expressed. Taylor cited the relevant passages of *Notes on the State of Virginia*, praised their author, and then dismissed his opinion. "Circumstances affect the mind," he explained, "as weather does beer, and frequently produce a sort of moral fermentation, which throws up bubbles of prismatick splendour, whilst they are played upon by the rays of some temporary effervescence, but destined to burst when the fermentation ceases." This, sadly, had been Jefferson's fate. The American Revolution and the near approach of its French successor had produced "mental fermentations and moral bubbles" which had temporarily clouded the statesman's judgment. Taylor was not about to censure his friend, but he did argue—quite cogently, in fact—that "if Mr. Jefferson's assertions are correct, it is better to run the risque of national extinction, by liberating and fighting the blacks, than to live abhorred of God, and consequently hated of men." And he added that, if his friend's claims were "erroneous, they ought not to be admitted as arguments for the emancipating policy."

In rejecting the notion that slavery corrupted the masters, Taylor first cited the example set by Jefferson himself. "Slavery was carried farther among the Greeks and Romans than among ourselves," he observed, "and yet these two nations produced more great and good patriots and citizens, than, probably, all the rest of the world." It was easy to see why this had been the case.

> Vicious and mean qualities become despicable in the eyes of freemen from their association with the character of slaves. Character, like condition, is contrasted, and as one contrast causes us to love liberty better, so the other causes us to love virtue better. Qualities odious in themselves, become more contemptible, when united with the most degraded class of men, than when seen in our equals; and pride steps in to aid the struggles of virtue. Instead therefore of fearing that children should imbibe the qualities of slaves, it is probable, that the circumstance of seeing bad qualities in slaves will contribute to their virtue.[71]

Taylor stopped short of arguing that slavery was a positive good. He did not call the institution, as South Carolina governor George McDuffie would in 1835, "the cornerstone of our republican edifice."[72] But he came very close to doing so nonetheless.

Though willing to give lip service to the notion that slavery was "a misfortune to agriculture" and even to lend his name to the cause of African colonization, the Virginia planter intimated that the maintenance of the institution might be a prerequisite for the defense of republican liberty, and he even conferred on the institution a species of divine sanction.

Virtue and vice are naturally and unavoidably coexistent in the moral world, as beauty and deformity are in the animal; one is the only mirrour in which the other can be seen, and therefore in the present state of man, one cannot be destroyed without the other. It may be thus that personal slavery has constantly reflected the strongest rays of civil liberty and patriotism. Perhaps it is suffered by the deity to perform an office without which these rays are gradually obscured and finally obliterated by characters and partial laws. Perhaps the sight of slavery and its vices may inspire the mind with an affection for liberty and virtue, just as the climates and deserts of Arabia, would make it think Italy a paradise.[73]

Thomas Jefferson's failure to answer John Taylor's challenge did him no credit. Nor did the fact that, after reading his friend's essays, he could still write that "Colonel Taylor and myself have rarely, if ever, differed in any political principles of importance."[74] It would not be unfair to conclude that the most important single practical consequence of the Republican leader's vigorous promotion of agriculture in preference to other pursuits was the strengthening of slavery.

This result could and should have been foreseen, but it seems, nonetheless, to have been unintended. It resulted from an almost grotesque failure of statesmanship on Jefferson's part—and not from any conscious desire to defend the institution he had long purported to loathe. Despite the occasion he gave for the Federalist indictment, the Virginia planter was no more an admirer of Lacedaemon than was John Adams or Alexander Hamilton. When Thomas Jefferson had the opportunity to consider the Spartan regime, he dismissed it with contempt. It was, he contended, nothing more than "the rule of military monks over the laboring class of the people, reduced to abject slavery." Athens with her empire inspired in Jefferson a similar disdain. He had no use for glory and for conquest. "These are not the doctrines of the present age," he contended. "The equal rights of man, and the happiness of every individual, are now acknowledged to be the only legitimate objects of government."[75] When Richard Price spoke of "the friends of liberty and humanity," he had men like Washington, Hamilton, Adams, Madison, and Jefferson in mind.[76] These statesmen may later have quarreled regarding the conduct of administration, but one fact should never be forgotten: it was in order to establish "the principles of humanity" that they had all joined together in the first place to initiate the American Revolution.

CHAPTER 6

Virtue in the Modern Republic

Is there a possibility that the government of nations may fall into the hands of men who teach the most disconsolate of all creeds, that men are but fireflies, and that this all is without a father? Is this the way to make man, as man, an object of respect? Or is it to make murder itself as indifferent as shooting a plover, and the extermination of the Rohilla nation as innocent as the swallowing of mites on a morsel of cheese?—John Adams

Heaven grant that it may be the glory of the United States to have established two great truths, of the highest importance to the whole human race; first, that an enlightened community is capable of self-government; and second, that the toleration of all sects does not necessarily produce indifference to religion.—Daniel Webster

III.vi.1

One must ultimately wonder whether, within a republic, a system of morals grounded solely in enlightened self-interest can really suffice. Neither war nor tyranny has disappeared from the earth, and there is no likelihood that either will do so in the foreseeable future. Spiritedness and self-sacrifice are prerequisite to the survival of even liberal democratic regimes. In the absence of martial valor, political freedom and the "principles of humanity" cannot be defended. Nor is it plausible to suppose that, in a world without tyranny and war, magnanimity could simply be dispensed with. As Cicero pointed out long, long ago, the civility required for the maintenance of civil society can hardly be sustained on a foundation of calculation alone.[1]

In the 1780s, there were many Americans who entertained doubts such as these.[2] One among them was an anonymous churchgoer who wrote a brief essay for the *Virginia Independent Chronicle* shortly after the delegates to the Philadelphia convention had disbanded. "While mankind consider the obligations to the exercise of virtue as derived from no higher source than the advantages accruing therefrom to society," he observed, "it is no difficult matter for every individual to satisfy himself, that, provided he can persuade others to the disinterested practice, his dispensing with it in his own case will be a thing of little moment."

> Hence declamations on the advantages and necessity of public and private virtue fall from the lips of every one, while their lives are stained with the most sordid and selfish practices. Though the different states

into which mankind are formed, have, generally speaking, enacted laws to restrain and punish enormities, to countenance virtue and discourage vice; yet the most approved and wisest legislators in all ages, in order to give efficacy to their civil institutions, have found it necessary to call in the aid of religion; and in no form of government whatever has the influence of religious principles been found so requisite as in that of a republic. It requires but a slight degree of observation to be convinced that mankind require the awe of some power to confine them within the line of their duty.[3]

Montaigne, Bacon, and their disciples taught men to look down, not up, and to judge themselves in light of those characteristics which make human beings most like the other members of the animal kingdom. They claimed that, by rejecting the "inhumane wisdom" of the ancients and their Christian successors, they could prepare the way for a revolution that would secure human happiness. In carrying out that revolution, the moderns largely achieved their aims, but it is quite possible that, at the same time, they sowed the seeds of their own destruction.

Sensing, if perhaps not fully apprehending, the danger, Americans of the founding generation rallied to the cause of religious faith. In New England, feeling ran particularly high. On the grounds that "the happiness of a people, and the good order and preservation of civil government, essentially depend upon piety, religion, and morality," the third article of the Massachusetts Declaration of Rights—drafted by Samuel Adams in the fall of 1779, amended, submitted to the people of the state for discussion, and eventually adopted by the delegates to the state's constitutional convention the following spring—called for the various towns and parishes to make provision at their own expense for Protestant worship and education and even authorized legislation compelling every citizen to attend the services of his own denomination.[4] Every state in the region, apart from Rhode Island, initially approved a system of religious assessments, and the constitutions adopted in Maryland, South Carolina, and Georgia were framed in the expectation that there would be plural establishments in those states as well.[5] To the very same purpose, Patrick Henry and Richard Henry Lee fought for religious assessments in Virginia.[6] Thus, while Massachusetts was alone in maintaining its Standing Order until 1833, that state was by no means peculiar.[7] Connecticut retained its plural establishment until 1818; New Hampshire held out until 1819; and the relevant article of that state's constitution remained on the books until well after the Civil War.[8]

III.vi.2

In the eighteenth century, views akin to those expressed by stalwarts of the Revolution such as Patrick Henry, Richard Henry Lee, and John and Samuel Adams were remarkably widespread. In Virginia, Edmund Pendleton, John Marshall, and, initially, even George Washington were among those inclined to favor a nondiscriminatory system of religious assessments.[9] In 1785, the Continental Congress very nearly included in the Western Lands Ordinance a provision setting aside a section within each township for the support of religion. Three-quarters of the delegates went on record in support of the measure; and a few years later, when Congress approved grants to the Ohio Company, to John Cleves Symmes, and to Royal Flint and his associates, it specified, as a matter of course, that the land be reserved.[10] By that time, the policy had been adopted by both Connecticut and New York.[11]

Thus, when the state conventions called in Virginia, New York, North Carolina, and Rhode Island for the purpose of ratifying the federal constitution demanded that the document be amended to guarantee citizens the freedom to exercise their "religion, according to the dictates of conscience," they did not intend to bar the federal government (or any other government) from promoting religion in general; they merely requested a provision stipulating that "no particular religious sect or society . . . be favored or established by [federal] law in preference to others."[12] As Madison reportedly put it on the floor of the First Congress, "The people feared [that] one sect might obtain a pre-eminence, or two combine together, and establish a religion to which they would compel others to conform." In this spirit, when the House select committee proposed that the pertinent amendment specify that "no religion shall be established by law, nor shall the equal rights of conscience be infringed," Benjamin Huntington of Connecticut rose to object to language that might be used against the collection of religious assessments in his state and that might seem to "patronize those who professed no religion at all." When a congressman from New York argued that the wording "might be thought to have a tendency to abolish religion altogether," James Madison replied that he understood the clause to mean that "Congress should not establish a religion, and enforce the legal observation of it by law, nor compel men to worship God in any manner contrary to their conscience." It is particularly telling that, although the Virginian considered his parallel proposal banning state violation of fundamental liberties such as "the equal rights of conscience" to be "the most valuable amendment on the whole list," the Senate dropped the amendment and the House ultimately concurred. As the amendment actually proposed by Congress and approved by the states was finally worded, it was specifically designed not just to preclude a federal establishment of religion but also to protect the existing state establishments from federal interference: it denied Congress the right to make any law "respecting"—i.e., either for or against—"an establishment of religion."[13]

For Supreme Court Justice Joseph Story, writing a generation later, there was no question that the framers of the Constitution and the Bill of Rights had intended to promote piety. As he put it,

> The right of a society or government to interfere in matters of religion will hardly be contested by any persons who believe that piety, religion, and morality are intimately connected with the well-being of the state, and indispensable to the administration of civil justice. The promulgation of the great doctrines of religion, the being, and attributes, and providence of one Almighty God; the responsibility to him for all our actions, founded upon moral freedom and accountability; a future state of rewards and punishments; the cultivation of all the personal, social, and benevolent virtues,—these never can be a matter of indifference in any well-ordered community. It is, indeed, difficult to conceive how any civilized society can well exist without them.

To his mind, the real difficulty faced by the Founders lay "in ascertaining the limits to which government may rightfully go in fostering and encouraging religion." They had managed to define the proper boundaries with the First Amendment, which was designed to cut off "the means of religious persecution," to prevent "the subversion of the rights of conscience in matters of religion," and to bar the institution of "any national ecclesiastical establishment which should give to a hierarchy the exclusive patronage of the national government." When the Constitution and the First Amendment were drafted and adopted, he contended, "the general if not universal sentiment in America was, that Christianity ought to receive encouragement from the State so far as was not incompatible with the private rights of conscience and the freedom of religious worship."[14]

It would be tempting to conclude that Daniel Webster was right when he told the United States Supreme Court, "All, all proclaim that Christianity, general, tolerant Christianity, Christianity independent of sects and parties, that Christianity to which the sword and the fagot are unknown, general, tolerant Christianity is the law of the land."[15] In fact, however, the leading figures in the founding generation were considerably less wedded to Christianity than Justice Story's discussion might be taken to suggest.[16] Though the celebrated jurist stoutly denied that the First Amendment was designed "to countenance, much less advance, Mahometanism, or Judaism, or infidelity, by prostrating Christianity," he was fully aware that article 6, section 3, of the original federal constitution banned religious tests for office-holding, and so even he was forced to acknowledge that the Framers intended that "the Catholic and the Protestant, the Calvinist and the Arminian, the Jew and the Infidel" be allowed to "sit down at the common table of the national councils without any inquisition into their faith or mode of worship." [17]

The full truth Story found unpalatable. It is true, of course, that, if any of the men who framed the federal constitution had any intention of "prostrating Christianity," they were too politic to make their views publicly known. But the Framers were perfectly happy to "countenance" Judaism and Islam, and this they did not seek to hide. The ban on religious tests was a considerably more radical measure than the First Amendment: it was adopted at a time when eleven of the thirteen states barred non-Christians from holding offices of public trust, and, as Edmund Randolph explained at the Virginia Ratifying Convention, it was intended to place "on the same footing" not just the Christian denominations but "all sects." [18] This point the Founders took care to drive home. George Washington spoke for all, or nearly all, of the Framers when, in his justly famous address to the Hebrew congregation of Newport, Rhode Island, he remarked,

> The citizens of the United States of America have the right to applaud themselves for having given to mankind examples of an enlarged and liberal policy—a policy worthy of imitation. All possess alike liberty of conscience and immunities of citizenship. It is now no more that toleration is spoken of as if it were the indulgence of one class of people that another enjoyed the exercise of their inherent natural rights, for, happily, the Government of the United States, which gives to bigotry no factions, to persecution no assistance, requires only that they who live under its protection should demean themselves as good citizens in giving it on all occasions their effectual support. . . . May the children of the stock of Abraham who dwell in this land continue to merit and enjoy the good will of the other inhabitants—while everyone shall sit in safety under his own vine and fig-tree and there shall be none to make him afraid. [19]

In the same spirit, Thomas Jefferson later wrote to one rabbi that the suffering of the Jews had "furnished a remarkable proof of the universal spirit of religious intolerance inherent in every sect, disclaimed by all while feeble, and practised by all when in power." "Our laws," he added, "have applied the only antidote to the vice, protecting our religious as they do our civil rights, by putting all men on an equal footing." He only regretted that "public opinion" still "erects itself into an inquisition" and that "individual dispositions" had not yet molded "themselves to the model of the law."[20] Two years later, James Madison wrote to a prominent American Jew that one of "the features peculiar to the Political system of the U. States, is the perfect equality of rights which it secures to every religious Sect," and then he remarked that "equal laws protecting equal rights, are found as they ought to be presumed, the best guarantee of loyalty & love of country; as well as best calculated to cherish that mutual respect & good will among Citizens of every religious denomination which are necessary to social harmony and most favorable to the advancement of truth."[21] By the beginning of the nineteenth century, this reading of the situation had been given the force of law.

III.vi.3

In the fall of 1796, Joel Barlow negotiated a treaty with the pasha of Tripoli on behalf of the administration of George Washington. Barlow was a radical and a Deist. He had resided in Paris for eight years; he had witnessed and was fervently devoted to the French Revolution; and he was closely connected with Thomas Paine. In the English version of the treaty, he managed to interpolate an article that has no parallel in the Arabic text and that was, one must therefore suspect, intended for American domestic consumption alone: "As the government of the United States of America is not in any sense founded on the Christian Religion,—as it has in itself no character of enmity against the laws, religion or tranquility of Musselmen,—and as the said States never have entered into any war or act of hostility against any Mehomitan nation, it is declared by the parties that no pretext arising from religious opinions shall ever produce an interruption of the harmony existing between the two countries."[22] The article in question caused distress in some quarters. In 1797, Connecticut, Massachusetts, North Carolina, New Hampshire, New Jersey, and Maryland still required that public officials be Christians.[23] The secretary of war, who had represented the last-mentioned state at both the Continental Congress and the federal convention, later compared the treaty's adoption with "trampling upon the cross"; and in 1805, when Tobias Lear negotiated a new agreement on behalf of the Jefferson administration, the first and boldest of the article's three dependent clauses was prudently dropped.[24] It is, nonetheless, striking just how little serious opposition Barlow's handiwork actually stirred when it came under consideration. The treaty was submitted to the Senate at the end of May; it was approved on the seventh of June without a single dissenting vote; and it was ratified by President John Adams just three days thereafter.[25] If the treaty had an easy passage, it was because the sentiments expressed in its most famous article accorded well with the spirit of the Revolution. Apart from John Adams, all of the early presidents deliberately and consistently employed in their public pronouncements a language compatible with any form of monotheism,[26] and Adams was made to suffer for his departures from this practice.[27] Though the Founders sought to encourage religious faith, they generally did so for secular reasons alone.

This was arguably the case even in Massachusetts. In 1807, when the Standing Order came under attack, Chief Justice Theophilus Parsons, who had served on the committee chosen to revise Samuel Adams's draft of the critical constitutional provision, issued a famous decision, in which he explained precisely why it is just to tax an individual for the support of public worship that he has no intention of ever attending. As Parsons put it,

> The object of public religious instruction is to teach, and to enforce by suitable arguments, the practice of a system of correct morals among the people, and to form and cultivate reasonable and just habits and manners; by which every man's persons and property are protected from outrage, and his personal and social enjoyments promoted and multiplied. From these effects every man derives the most important benefits, and whether he be, or be not an auditor of any public teacher, he receives more solid and permanent advantages from this public instruction, than the administration of justice in courts of law can give him. The like objection may be made by any man to the support of public schools, if he have no family who attend; and any man, who has no lawsuit may object to the support of judges and jurors on the same ground; when if there were no courts of Law, he would unfortunately find that causes for lawsuits would sufficiently abound.[28]

The chief justice's decision was in no way unusual. It is striking that the admirers of the Massachusetts establishment rarely advanced anything but secular arguments in its defense. Those who shared Samuel Adams's hope that Boston would become "a Christian Sparta" were far more deeply concerned with the preservation of the commonwealth's republican order than with the salvation of souls.[29]

What was true for the proponents of religious assessments in New England was true for their colleagues in Virginia as well. The preamble to Patrick Henry's Bill Establishing a Provision for Teachers of the Christian Religion made no mention of eternal life; it emphasized only that "the general diffusion of Christian knowledge hath a natural tendency to correct the morals of men, restrain their vices, and preserve the peace of society."[30] When Richard

Henry Lee wrote to James Madison to indicate his approval of the proposal put forward by his old rival, he justified his position on similar grounds. "Refiners may weave as fine a web of reason as they please," he contended, "but the experience of all times shows Religion to be the guardian of morals." The man whose honor it had been to move that the Continental Congress declare America's independence was perfectly happy to acknowledge that the Virginia Declaration of Rights outlawed "forcing modes of faith and forms of worship"; he was even prepared to concede that, in Virginia, "true freedom embraces the Mahomitan and the Gentoo [Hindu] as well as the Christian religion"; but he could not believe that the declaration had been intended to ban "compelling contribution for the support of religion in general." The need to foster virtue and discourage vice was overriding, and there was reason to fear that "avarice" would accomplish "the destruction of religion" and eliminate the one force capable of countering the natural human propensity to vice.[31]

Not surprisingly, the best and most influential example we have of the rhetoric which the Founders employed in defense of religion is to be found in George Washington's great farewell address. "Of all the dispositions and habits which lead to political prosperity," the new nation's first president contended,

> religion and morality are indispensable supports. In vain would that man claim the tribute of patriotism who should labor to subvert these great pillars of human happiness—these firmest props of the duties of men and citizens. The mere politician, equally with the pious man, ought to respect and cherish them. . . . Let it be simply asked, Where is the security for property, for reputation, for life, if the sense of religious obligation *desert* the oaths which are the instruments of investigation in courts of justice? And let us with caution indulge the supposition that morality can be maintained without religion. Whatever may be conceded to the influence of refined education on minds of peculiar structure, reason and experience forbid us to expect that national morality can prevail in exclusion of religious principle.[32]

In making this claim, Washington was merely stating the common sense of the matter. In October 1778, on the grounds that "true religion and good morals are the only solid foundations of public liberty and happiness," the Continental Congress called on the several states "to take the most effectual measures for the encouragement thereof, and for the suppressing of theatrical entertainments, horse racing, gaming, and such other diversions as are productive of idleness, dissipation, and a general depravity of principles and manners." At the same time, the delegates enjoined the officers of the Continental Line "to see that the good and wholesome rules provided for the discountenancing of prophaneness and vice, and the preservation of morals among the soldiers, are duly and punctually observed."[33]

The passage of time and the conclusion of the war eased circumstances but did nothing to alter opinions. The Northwest Ordinance was passed on 13 July 1787 by a unanimous vote of the delegates then present at the Continental Congress. In August 1789, the First Congress to meet under the new constitution, the very body that was then busy drafting the First Amendment, adopted an act to provide for the ordinance's enforcement. No one in either congress—not even James Madison—is recorded as having argued that it was in any way improper for one of the new nation's organic laws to justify the establishment of "schools and the means of education" within the Northwest Territory on the grounds that "religion, morality, and knowledge" are "necessary to good government and the happiness of mankind."[34]

The inclusion of this clause was not an isolated occurrence. Apparently, only one congressman deemed it incongruous that the House of Representatives—the very day after it gave the Bill of Rights its approval—should ask the president to appoint "a day of public thanksgiving and prayer, to be observed by acknowledging, with grateful hearts, the many signal favors of Almighty God";[35] and there is no contemporary evidence that, at the beginning of the legislative session, anyone had seen anything wrong with the two legislative houses appointing chaplains—as long as the two divines represented different denominations. If James Madison disapproved of the decision, as he later claimed, he failed to make a major issue of the matter, and he did not allow his misgivings to prevent him from serving on the committee instructed to nominate a chaplain for the lower chamber.[36]

The chief framer of the First Amendment considered any proposal with a potential for sectarian discrimination to be "a signal of persecution" that "degrades from the equal rank of Citizens all those whose opinions in Religion do not bend to those of the Legislative authority."[37] He therefore consistently opposed every measure that might result in direct government aid to a particular sect or sects, and he encouraged an extremely restrictive interpretation of the federal government's prerogatives in this sphere. In 1785, when the Continental Congress very nearly specified that, within each township in the national domain, a section of land be set aside for the support of religion, Madison denounced the provision as a discriminatory measure aimed at "supporting the Religion of the Majority of [local] inhabitants." It was, he said, not only "unjust in itself"; it was something "foreign to the Authority of Congs." and "smelling . . . strongly of an antiquated Bigotry."[38] Five years thereafter, in the First Federal Congress, Madison objected to census officials keeping a count of "those who are employed in teaching and inculcating the duties of religion." As he put it, "There may be some indelicacy in singling them out, as the General Government is proscribed from interfering, in any manner whatever, in matters respecting religion; and it may be thought to do this, in ascertaining who, and who are not ministers of the Gospel."[39] Years later, as president, he vetoed a bill that donated to a Baptist congregation the public land on which the church members had inadvertently constructed their meeting house. The bill was objectionable, he explained, because it "comprised a principle and precedent for the appropriation of funds of the United States for the use and support of religious societies, contrary to the article of the Constitution which declares that 'Congress shall make no law respecting a religious establishment.'"[40] If, in 1789, Madison was nonetheless prepared to have land set aside in the Northwest Territory for schools in which religious instruction could be expected to take place, it was because, like Jefferson, he recognized that the American regime presupposes the existence of a beneficent God and because he, too, thought it possible to arrange the curriculum so that "no religious reading, instruction, or exercise shall be prescribed or practiced inconsistent with the tenets of any religious sect or denomination."[41]

In 1789 and for a long time thereafter, even those Americans most fiercely opposed to anything that smacked of an establishment of religion and hostile to every vestige of a discrimination between the sects were prepared to promote religious belief; no one supposed that the federal government, much less the states, should be strictly neutral in the contest between agnosticism, atheism, and religious faith. In 1833, when the citizens of Massachusetts amended their constitution to eliminate the provision for religious assessments, they substituted for the passage expunged an article reasserting the traditional view that "the public worship of God, and instructions in piety, religion, and morality, promote the happiness and prosperity of a people, and the security of republican government" and consequently specifying that

> the several religious societies of this Commonwealth, whether corporate or unincorporate, at any meeting legally warned and holden for that purpose, shall ever have the right to elect their pastors or religious teachers, to contract with them for their support, to raise money for erecting and repairing houses for public worship, for the maintenance of religious instruction, and for the payment of necessary expenses: And all persons belonging to any religious society shall be taken and held to be members, until they shall file with the clerk of such society a written

notice, declaring the dissolution of their membership, and thenceforth shall not be liable for any grant or contract which may be thereafter made or entered into by such society.[42]

The citizens of Massachusetts were not peculiar. From the outset, at least in Virginia, the leading proponents of full disestablishment advocated the institution of a strict policy of nondiscrimination not just to head off religious strife and persecution nor simply to protect freedom of conscience but also because they genuinely believed that the separation of church and state would ignite a religious revival favorable to the cause of republican government. Though sometimes cast by the radical disestablishmentarians in doctrinaire terms, the dispute over religious assessments turned less on a matter of principle than on a question of prudence: for the American founders, the real issue was just how one might best discourage faction and encourage the particular virtues required by a modern republic. When rallying the religious dissenters of Virginia against Patrick Henry's Bill Establishing a Provision for Teachers of the Christian Religion, James Madison might denounce the civil magistrate's employing "Religion as an engine of Civil policy" and term it "an unhallowed perversion of the means of salvation"—but, in fact, that was precisely the employment of religion that he, no less than his opponents, had in mind. As Madison would later put it, when restating the argument for a separation of church and state, "a mutual independence is found most friendly to practical Religion, to social harmony, and to political prosperity."[43]

III.vi.4

In 1785, when Virginians were debating whether to impose a general assessment for the support of the state's Christian churches, the Episcopalian stalwart and future congressman John Page wrote to Thomas Jefferson to mourn the decline of the old established church, to bewail the rise of the evangelical sects, and to express the hope that Jefferson might be persuaded to support the assessment. "Nothing but a general Assessment can prevent the State from being divided between immorality, and Enthusiastic Bigottry," he contended.

> We have endeavored 8 years in vain to support the rational Sects by voluntary Contributions. I think I begin to see a Mischief arising out of the Dependence of the Teachers of the Christian Religion on their individual Followers, which may not only be destructive to Morality but to Government itself. The needy dependent Preacher not only can not boldly reprove the vicious Practices of his Friends and Benefactors, his only

Support; but he must, to keep well with them, fall into their Opinions, and support their Views and Interests: so that instead of being bound by the strongest Ties of Interest to discountenance Vice and support and strengthen the Hands of Government, they may be supporting the jarring Interests of the Enemies to all Government.[44]

As is well known, Jefferson shared his friend's overall preference for "the rational Sects."[45] If he declined nevertheless to draw a like conclusion, it was probably because here, as in the matter of disestablishment, he had learned much from the reflections of Adam Smith.

The celebrated author of *The Theory of Moral Sentiments* and *The Wealth of Nations* not only believed that "the interested and active zeal of religious teachers" would be "altogether innocent" in a society divided into a great multiplicity of sects; he was prepared to go one step further and assert that, in such circumstances, "the excessive zeal" of the various, rival denominations would be productive of "several good effects" even if "equality of treatment" should fail to instill philosophical "good temper and moderation in all, or even in the greater part of the religious sects of a particular country."

Smith prefaced his defense of zealotry with the observation that, in civilized societies marked by distinctions of rank, two different schemes of morality tend to coexist: a liberal or loose system built on "the vices which are apt to arise from great prosperity," and a strict or austere system that accords well with the needs of men short of means. Because nearly every new religious sect has originated among the common people, almost every sect preaches austerity; many have "even endeavoured to gain credit by refining upon this austere system, and by carrying it to some degree of folly and extravagance; and this excessive rigour has frequently recommended them more than any thing else to the respect and veneration of the common people."

The Scottish philosopher was willing to tolerate and even encourage a modicum of "folly and extravagance" because he believed that it was a small price to pay for the good that would accompany it. Men of rank and fortune are always in the public eye, he observed. The liberal system of morality that prevails in their sphere may open the path to "luxury, wanton and even disorderly mirth, the pursuit of pleasure to some degree of intemperance, the breach of chastity, at least in one of the two sexes," and so forth. But it does not produce "gross indecency" and "lead to falsehood or injustice" because there are limits to what society as a whole will tolerate, and these men "dare not do any thing that would disgrace or discredit" them in the eyes of their compatriots.

Men of low condition are in a different situation. They are similarly restrained only while they remain in country villages where their conduct attracts attention. In cities, the poor man is all too often "sunk in obscurity and darkness. His conduct is observed and attended to by nobody, and he is therefore very likely to neglect it himself, and to abandon himself to every sort of low profligacy and vice." Such a man can draw considerable profit from "the interested and active zeal of religious teachers," for

> he never emerges so effectually from this obscurity, his conduct never excites so much the attention of any respectable society, as by his becoming the member of a small religious sect. He from that moment acquires a degree of consideration which he never had before. All his brother sectaries are, for the credit of the sect, interested to observe his conduct, and if he gives occasion to any scandal, if he deviates very much from those austere morals which they almost always require of one another, [they are ready] to punish him by what is always a very severe punishment, even where no civil effects attend it, expulsion or excommunication from the sect. In little religious sects, accordingly, the morals of the common people have been almost always remarkably regular and orderly; generally much more so than in the established church.

In short, in an extended republic, sectarianism and religious zealotry can serve as an antidote to the anonymity of urban life. Membership in a close-knit religious association provides individuals with a sense of place, and like citizenship in the Greek *pólis*, it brings the force of shame to bear in a fashion that encourages self-restraint, decency, and a spirit of self-sacrifice. Smith was well aware of the defects inherent in the ancient city, and he acknowledges that the morals of his "little sects . . . have frequently been rather disagreeably rigorous and unsocial." But, in a commercial society blessed with religious diversity—especially if the state encourages "the study of science and philosophy" and gives "entire liberty to all those who for their own interest would attempt, without scandal or indecency, to amuse and divert the people by painting, poetry, musick, dancing; [and] by all sorts of dramatic representations and exhibitions"—he thought that no one need fear a revival of the martial fervor which had gripped the republics of antiquity or a return of the persecuting spirit which had made a slaughterhouse of Christendom.[46]

Smith's analysis had particular purchase on men dedicated to the establishment of a republic, convinced that republican government presupposes a considerable measure of virtue in the citizen body, and persuaded that urbanization is inevitable and urban life inherently corrupting. Thus, when

Thomas Jefferson contended that "difference of opinion is advantageous in religion," he justified his conclusion on the grounds that "the several Sects perform the office of a Censor morum over each other." Where there is no religious establishment, he remarked, "religion is well supported; of various kinds, indeed, but all good enough; all sufficient to preserve peace and order."[47] In his first inaugural address, Jefferson returned to the same theme and publicly celebrated the fact that his countrymen acknowledged and adored "an overruling Providence" and were "enlightened by a benign religion, professed, indeed, and practiced in various forms, yet all of them inculcating honesty, truth, temperance, gratitude, and the love of man."[48]

Like Adam Smith, Jefferson would have preferred that Christianity give way to a Socinianism exhibiting "philosophical good temper and moderation," and so, like John Page, he found the victory of the Baptists, Methodists, and Presbyterians in Virginia not entirely to his liking. Indeed, when the disciples of Calvin objected to the exclusion of theology from the curriculum of the University of Virginia, he spoke direly of "a threatening cloud of fanaticism." In Richmond, he remarked, it was "chiefly among the women" that this religious extremism was to be found. "They have their night meetings and praying parties, where, attended by their priests, and sometimes by a hen-pecked husband, they pour forth the effusions of their love to Jesus, in terms as amatory and carnal, as their modesty would permit them to use to a mere earthly lover."[49] But, while he found religious enthusiasm itself distasteful, Jefferson was inclined in general to leave his dislike for doctrine and ritual aside and to judge "the religion of others by their lives." He deemed Unitarianism far more rational than traditional Christianity; he hoped and confidently expected that, in America, the former would eventually supplant the latter;[50] but these considerations were immaterial: "Both religions I find make honest men, and that is the only point society has any authority to look to."[51]

In this regard, one fact deserves particular attention: though Jefferson shared David Hume's distrust of religious zealots, he had no admiration for clerical indolence. His Bill for Establishing Religious Freedom had been aimed in part at encouraging a religious revival in his native state and at improving the morals of the clergy. Inspired by Adam Smith's critique of Hume, Jefferson evidenced in the preamble to his bill an eagerness to confer on each citizen "the comfortable liberty of giving his contributions to the particular pastor whose morals he would make his pattern, and whose powers he feels most persuasive to righteousness." Where the faithful approved of the "personal conduct" of a cleric, the document went on, they could provide him with "temporal rewards" which would serve as "an additional incitement to earnest and unremitting labours for the instruction of mankind."[52] Where religious freedom is the rule, Jefferson elsewhere remarked, "if a sect arises, whose tenets would subvert morals, good sense has fair play, and reasons and laughs it out of doors, without suffering the state to be troubled with it."[53]

As a statesman who came under attack for his unorthodox religious beliefs, Jefferson was acutely sensitive to the least hint of a suggestion that a man's religious sentiments should be considered a test of his fitness for high office,[54] but it is striking that he never raised any objection when the evangelical opponents of Virginia's religious establishment suggested that there was one way in which the assembly could legitimately make a positive contribution to the cause of Christianity: by "supporting those Laws of Morality, which are necessary for Private and Public Happiness."[55] Few in the founding generation were inclined to take exception to the sentiments that Oliver Ellsworth expressed while defending the federal constitution's ban on test oaths: "But while I assert the right of religious liberty, I would not deny that the civil power has a right, in some cases, to interfere in matters of religion. It has a right to prohibit and punish gross immoralities and impieties because the open practice of these is of evil example and public detriment. For this reason, I heartily approve of our laws against drunkenness, profane swearing, blasphemy, and professed atheism."[56] The secular concerns which led a freethinker like Jefferson to search out nondiscriminatory means for promoting religious faith induced him as well to support the enforcement of traditional Judaeo-Christian morality within the society at large.[57] The Revisal of the Laws included measures which regulated taverns, outlawed gambling, and prohibited "all attempts to delude the people, or to abuse their understanding" whether "by pretended prophecies" or "by exercise of the pretended arts of witchcraft, conjuration, inchantment, or sorcery"; and it treated polygamy and homosexual sodomy as crimes no less serious than rape. The revisors were persuaded that capital punishment should be "the last melancholy resource against those whose existence is become inconsistent with the safety of their fellow citizens," and they contended that criminals less severely punished "would be living and long continued spectacles to deter others from committing the like offences." On these grounds, one bill composed by Jefferson and introduced by Madison specified that a man who engages in polygamy, sodomy, or rape be castrated rather than executed and that a woman guilty of a like crime have a hole at least one inch in diameter cut through the cartilage of her nose.[58]

Madison's cooperation in this venture should not occasion surprise. He shared his neighbor's anticlericalism and his distrust of religious enthusiasm. In his old age, he came to fear the concentration of property in ecclesiastical corporations and he objected to state measures exempting houses of worship from taxation; by then, he was so intent that the federal government avoid discriminating in favor of or against any sect that he doubted the propriety of appointing chaplains for Congress and for the armed forces and found fault with the practice of appointing days for solemn humiliation, fasting, and prayer.[59] He seems, however, to have regarded the victory of the evangelicals as less worrying than did his old friend. In 1819, when he contemplated the consequences for public morality, he rejoiced that "there has been an increase of religious instruction since the revolution." He shed no tears over the fact that the "old churches, built under the establish! at the public expence, have in many instances gone to ruin, or are in a very dilapidated state, owing chiefly to a . . . desertion of the flocks to other worships." Indeed, he welcomed the proliferation of "Meeting Houses . . . of the plainest and cheapest sort," and to justify his delight, he recapitulated in brief the case made forty-three years earlier by Adam Smith. "On a general comparison of the present & former times," Madison remarked,

> the balance is certainly & vastly on the side of the present, as to the number of religious teachers[,] the zeal which actuates them, the purity of their lives, and the attendance of the people on their instructions. It was the Universal opinion of the Century preceding the last, that Civil Gov! could not stand without the prop of a Religious establishment, & that the X!! religion itself, would perish if not supported by a legal provision for its Clergy. The experience of Virginia conspicuously corroborates the disproof of both opinions. The Civil Gov![,] tho' bereft of everything like an associated hierarchy[,] possesses the requisite stability and performs its functions with complete success; Whilst the number, the industry, and the morality of the Priesthood, & the devotion of the people have been manifestly increased by the total separation of the Church from the State.[60]

Four years later, he restated his conclusion. When "new sects arise with absurd opinions or overheated [i]maginations," he worried not at all. "The proper remedies lie in time, forebearance and example." The essential point, never to be forgotten, is that "rival sects, with equal rights, exercise mutual censorships in favor of good morals."[61] For its most vigorous proponents, the establishment of religious freedom was intended not only to prevent religious persecution and free the state from sectarian strife; it was designed as well to promote a healthy competition between the various preachers and sects in fostering the qualities of character most needed in a modern republic.

The moral and political concerns which united Thomas Jefferson and James Madison with advocates of religious assessments such as Patrick Henry, Richard Henry Lee, Edmund Pendleton, John Marshall, John Adams, and Samuel Adams linked them all with the great multitude of their less-exalted compatriots. In 1787 and for a long time thereafter, Americans of all persuasions considered observations like those made by George Washington in his farewell address utterly uncontroversial. When Alexis de Tocqueville visited the United States some fifty years after the British had recognized the independence of their former colonies, he found that "religion in America never involves itself directly in the government of society." He nonetheless regarded it as the preeminent American political institution: "For if it does not impart a taste for liberty, it singularly facilitates the use of it. Indeed, it is from this perspective that the inhabitants of the United States themselves consider religious belief. I do not know whether all the Americans have faith in their religion—for who can read to the bottom the human heart?—but I am certain that they believe it necessary to the maintenance of republican institutions. This opinion belongs not to a class of citizens or to a party, but to the nation entire; one encounters it in every rank of society."

Tocqueville could speak with such confidence on the matter because he had interviewed those associated with the various societies that had been organized for the propagation of the gospel in the new territories to the West. "If you interrogate these missionaries of Christian civilization," he reported, "you will be quite surprised to hear them speak so often of the goods of this world, and to meet politicians where you expected to find men of faith." In the course of the discussion, "they will tell you that 'all the American republics are intimately linked (*solidaires*) with each other; if the republics of the West were to fall into anarchy or submit to the yoke of a despot, the republican institutions which now flourish upon the shores of the Atlantic Ocean would be in great peril. It is therefore in our interest that the new states should be religious so that they may permit us to remain free.'" There was and is more to the American *politeía* than can be found in the nation's written laws.[62]

III.vi.5

At no period did this fact become more obvious than during the American Civil War. At the time of its outbreak, Abraham Lincoln tells us, "One eighth of the whole population were colored slaves, not distributed generally over the Union, but localized in the Southern part of it. These slaves constituted a peculiar and powerful interest. All knew that this interest was, somehow, the cause of the war." [63] There need be no doubt that Lincoln was right. A nation half-free, half-slave could not indefinitely endure. In 1788, few Americans would have queried Hamilton's claim that "the prohibition of titles of nobility . . . may truly be denominated the corner stone of republican government." [64] But by the mid-1830s many, if not most, of the American citizens resident in South Carolina had come to share the opinion, espoused by their governor, that slavery was "the cornerstone of our republican edifice"; [65] and in the decades that followed, the notion slowly gained ground throughout the South that Colonel Richard Rumbold and Thomas Jefferson had been wrong: that some men, distinguished by the dark color of their skins, had "been born with saddles on their backs" and that their pale-skinned brethren were a nobility which had come into the world "booted and spurred, ready to ride them legitimately, by the grace of" nature and nature's God. [66]

Shortly after his election as president, Abraham Lincoln learned that his friend and former Whig colleague Alexander H. Stephens had spoken before the Georgia assembly in opposition to secession on prudential grounds. He wrote to Stephens to request a copy of the speech, and a confidential correspondence of some interest ensued. Lincoln read the oration and wrote back to ask whether "the people of the South really entertain fears that a Republican administration would, *directly*, or *indirectly*, interfere" with slavery. "The South," he pledged, "would be in no more danger in this respect, than it was in the days of Washington." In his estimation, "the only substantial difference between us" was that "you think slavery is *right* and ought to be extended; while we think it is *wrong* and ought to be restricted." [67] Stephens thought this depiction of the situation inadequate. In his view, the critical element was the election of a president by a political party the "leading object" of which "seems to be simply, and wantonly, if you please, to put the Institutions of nearly half the States under the ban of public opinion and national condemnation." "This," he insisted, "upon general principles, is quite enough of itself to arouse a spirit not only of general indignation, but of revolt on the part of the proscribed." [68]

When the Georgia convention voted to secede from the Union, Stephens reluctantly agreed to represent his state at the gathering called to form the Confederacy. There, though decidedly unenthusiastic, he was drafted to serve as the new polity's vice-president. Upon returning home, Stephens delivered a justly famous speech to the Georgia Convention at Savannah in praise of "the new constitution," which "has put at rest, *forever*, all the agitating questions relating to our peculiar institution—African slavery as it exists amongst us—the proper *status* of the negro in our form of civilization."

This was the immediate cause of the late rupture and present revolution. Jefferson in his forecast, had anticipated this, as the "rock upon which the old Union would split." He was right. What was conjecture with him, is now a realized fact. But whether he fully comprehended the great truth upon which that rock *stood* and *stands*, may be doubted. The prevailing ideas entertained by him and most of the leading statesmen at the time of the formation of the old constitution, were that the enslavement of the African was in violation of the laws of nature; that it was wrong in *principle*, socially, morally, and politically. It was an evil they knew not well how to deal with, but the general opinion of the men of that day was that, somehow or other in the order of Providence, the institution would be evanescent and pass away. This idea, though not incorporated in the constitution, was the prevailing idea at that time. The constitution, it is true, secured every essential guarantee to the institution while it should last, and hence no argument can be justly urged against the constitutional guarantees thus secured, because of the common sentiment of the day. Those ideas, however, were fundamentally wrong. They rested upon the assumption of the equality of races. This was an error. It was a sandy foundation, and the government built upon it fell when "the storm came and the wind blew."

Our new government is founded upon exactly the opposite idea; its foundations are laid, its cornerstone rests upon the great truth, that the negro is not equal to the white man; that slavery—subordination to the superior race—is his natural and normal condition.

This, our new government, is the first in the history of the world, based upon this great physical, philosophical, and moral truth. This truth has been slow in the process of its development, like all other truths in the various departments of science. It has been so even amongst us. Many who hear me, perhaps, can recollect well, that this truth was not generally admitted, even within their day. The errors of the past generation still clung to many as late as twenty years ago. Those at the North, who still cling to these errors, with a zeal above knowledge, we justly denominate fanatics. All fanaticism springs from an aberration of the mind—from a defect in reasoning. It is a species of insanity. . . .

[Ours] is the first government ever instituted upon the principles in strict conformity to nature, and the ordination of Providence, in furnishing the materials of human society. Many governments have been founded upon the principle of the subordination and serfdom of certain classes of the same race; such were and are in violation of the laws of nature. Our system commits no such violation of nature's laws. With us, all of the white race, however high or low, rich or poor, are equal in the eye of the law. Not so the Negro. Subordination is his place. He, by nature, or by the curse against Canaan, is fitted for that condition which he occupies in our system. The architect in the construction of buildings, lays the foundation with the proper material—the granite; then comes the brick or the marble. The substratum of our society is made of the material fitted by nature for it, and by experience we know, that it is best, not only for the superior, but for the inferior race, that it should be so. It is, indeed, in conformity with the ordinance of the Creator. It is not for us to inquire into the wisdom of his ordinances, or to question them. For his own purposes, he has made one race to differ, from another, as he has made "one star to differ from another star in glory."

The great objects of humanity are best attained when there is conformity to his laws and decrees, in the formation of governments as well as in all things else. Our confederacy is founded upon principles in strict conformity with these laws. This stone which was rejected by the first builders "is become the chief of the cornet"—the real "corner-stone"— in our new edifice.[69]

What had been in 1788 an entrenched interest occasioning shame and considerable embarrassment nearly everywhere had become for many by 1861 a matter of principle and honor to be defended to the death.[70] It would not be too much to say that the secession which took place was an express repudiation of the truths declared to be self-evident in 1776 and an assertion that Negro slavery is advantageous, just, and good.

It is not difficult to see how such a transformation could come about. Jefferson had recognized that "the spirit of the people" is not "an infallible, a permanent reliance," and he had openly worried that "the spirit of the times may alter, will alter" and that the nation's rulers would "become corrupt, our people careless." In the midst of the Revolution, he had warned that from "the conclusion of this war we shall be going downhill" and that the people would "forget themselves, but in the sole faculty of making money" and neglect the defense of their own rights.[71] He was even more acutely cognizant of man's capacity for trampling upon the rights of his fellow man. On the eve of the Constitutional Convention, he had marveled at his own countrymen and perhaps at himself, "What a stupendous, what an incomprehensible machine is man! who can endure toil, famine, stripes, imprisonment & death itself in vindication of his own liberty, and the next moment be deaf to all those motives whose power supported him thro' his trial, and inflict on his fellow men a bondage, one hour of which is fraught with more misery than ages of that which he rose in rebellion to oppose."[72] And, as we have already seen, the Virginian was painfully aware of the "unhappy influence on the manners of our people produced by the existence of slavery among us." Mindful that "man is an imitative animal" who spends his live from cradle to grave "learning to do what he sees others do," he insisted that, under slavery's influence, children are so "nursed, educated, and daily exercised in tyranny" that they cannot help "but be stamped by it with odious peculiarities."[73] In classifying man as an "imitative animal," Jefferson laid bare one of the fundamental presuppositions of ancient political science. If one were to analyze the Confederacy in Aristotelian terms as a political regime (*políteía*), one would have to say that slavery was largely determinative of the "disposition of offices and honors (*táxis tôn archôn*)" within the South and that this constituted the most important part of the *paideía* that had gradually transformed the great multitude (*plêthos*) of southerners into a separate and distinct political unit capable of secession and of cooperative action (*práxis*) in war and in peace.[74]

No one did more to inhibit this transformation than Thomas Jefferson, and few did more to encourage it. By grounding the Declaration of Independence on an assertion of the rights of man, Jefferson insured that the new republican regimes in the South as well as in the North would be founded on a repudiation of slavery. Moreover, he embedded in his *Notes on the State of Virginia* an eloquent denunciation of the peculiar institution, which was to be particularly influential south of the Mason-Dixon line. But at the same time, as we have seen, Jefferson asserted the moral and political superiority of the economic sector which provided the setting for the South's most notorious domestic institution, and he devoted considerable energy to restricting the scope of the federal government and to reinforcing states' rights. Even more important, however, is a fact hitherto unmentioned in this tome. In those same *Notes on the State of Virginia*, Jefferson lent his considerable authority as a statesman and scientist to racist doctrine indistinguishable from that to which Alexander Stephens and the like would later appeal in their justifications of slavery. Of course, in advancing arguments for his "suspicion" that blacks are inferior in intelligence, Jefferson explicitly denied that even a "fixed opinion" on this subject would be pertinent to an assessment of their rights. But in suggesting the possibility that black Africans form a separate species akin to the orangutan, he made this denial seem implausible, and he thereby helped prepare the way for the South's repudiation of the universal principles underlying the Declaration of Independence.[75]

The Missouri crisis provides the first clear evidence that the South's transformation had begun. John Quincy Adams was secretary of state at the time, and he had ample opportunity to observe the debates in Congress and to contribute to those which took place in the Cabinet. He was much struck by the strength and depth of southern sentiment. The proposal that Missouri's admission to the Union be conditional upon her establishment of a program of gradual emancipation had clearly struck a vulnerable nerve. "There is a great mass of cool judgment and plain sense on the side of freedom and humanity," he observed, "but the ardent spirits and passions are on the side of oppression." One might wonder at the "fatality" by which it happened that "all the most eloquent orators" in Congress "are on its slavish side." But in the end it made perfect sense. It merely illustrated "how much more keen and powerful the impulse is of personal interest than is that of any general consideration of benevolence or humanity." After all, the slaveholders have "a deeper immediate stake in the issue than the partisans of freedom," and "their passions and interests are more profoundly agitated." For those "to the North and in the free States," the question is "merely speculative. The people do not feel it in their persons or their purses. On the slave side it comes home to the feelings and interests of every man in the community." This explained both why "the slave States have clung together in one unbroken phalanx" and why they were rendered "victorious by . . . accomplices and deserters from the ranks of freedom."[76]

After listening to the debates and discussing the question at length with his colleague John C. Calhoun and with many another southerner, Adams concluded that "this Missouri question has betrayed the secret of their souls." Of course, he observed, "in the abstract they admit that slavery is an evil, they disclaim all participation in the introduction of it, and cast it all upon the shoulders of our old Grandam Britain. But when probed to the quick upon it, they show at the bottom of their souls pride and vainglory in their condition of masterdom."

They fancy themselves more generous and noble-hearted than the plain freemen who labor for subsistence. They look down upon the simplicity of a Yankee's manners, because he has no habits of overbearing like theirs and cannot treat negroes like dogs. It is among the evils of slavery that it taints the very sources of moral principle. It established false estimates of virtue and vice; for what can be more false and heartless than this doctrine which makes the first and holiest rights of humanity to depend upon the color of the skin. It perverts human reason, and reduces man endowed with logical powers to maintain that slavery is sanctioned by the Christian religion, that slaves are happy and contented in their condition, that between master and slave there are ties of mutual attachment and affection, that the virtues of the master are refined and exalted by the degradation of the slave; while at the same time they vent execrations upon the slave-trade, curse Britain for having given them slaves, burn at the stake negroes convicted of crimes for the terror of the example, and writhe in agonies of fear at the very mention of human rights as applicable to men of color.[77]

As Adams recognized, slaveholding Americans were caught on the horns of a dilemma, and every effort on the part of northerners to encourage and help them to resolve the question and honor the principles of the Revolution by taking action to place slavery on the road to extinction had the untoward effect of forcing them to reassess their commitment to those principles. By the mid-1850s, at least in the Deep South, that process of reassessment was near completion.

There were many straws in the wind: the fissures that had developed within evangelical Christianity,[78] the ultimate refusal of courts in the North and South to give "full faith and credit" to one another's decisions in slavery's regard,[79] and the deep sectional split that had emerged first within the Whig party and eventually within the Democratic party as well.[80] But perhaps the most telling was the growing popularity throughout the South of a series of sophisticated, abstract arguments advanced on slavery's behalf by a group of ideologues, who were profoundly uneasy with commercial society, deeply hostile to the Lockean principles of the Declaration of Independence, and nostalgic for the patriarchal and quasi-patriarchal moral universe of the ancient Greeks and Romans and their Christian successors.[81] If the Civil War had resulted in the Union's permanent dismemberment, there can be little question that white supremacy and Negro slavery would have defined the distinctive "way of life" of the Confederate nation.[82] In Virginia, where Jefferson's example and that of George Washington, George Mason, Patrick Henry, James Madison, John Marshall, and the like had served to inhibit the propagation of the argument on slavery's behalf, and in North Carolina, Tennessee, and Arkansas, where slavery's economic hegemony was far from complete, the peculiar institution would eventually have become what it already was farther south: that *"something"* which was "settled, . . . permanent, and not to be called in question" because it was inseparable from the "concord regarding loved things held in common" which had turned "a multitudinous assemblage of rational beings" into "a people" possessed of "a common-wealth." [83]

To overcome the *paideía* provided by the most important of the South's domestic institutions, Jefferson could look only to the fact that the Revolution had been fought in defense of the principles enshrined in the Declaration of Independence. As we have already had occasion to note, he had the problem of slavery on his mind when he asked the readers of his *Notes on the State of Virginia* to consider whether "the liberties of a nation" can "be thought secure when we have removed their only firm basis, a conviction in the minds of the people that these liberties are the gift of God? That they are not to be violated but with his wrath?" And he posed this question at this time because he thought "a change already perceptible, since the origin of the present revolution." "The spirit of the master is abating," he wrote, "that of the slave rising from the dust, his condition mollifying, the way I hope preparing, under the auspices of heaven, for a total emancipation, and that this is disposed, in the order of events, to be with the consent of the masters, rather than by their extirpation." In the same context, however, he added another observation considerably less sanguine: "I tremble for my country when I reflect that God is just: that his justice cannot sleep for ever: that considering numbers, nature and natural means only, a revolution of the wheel of fortune, an exchange of situations, is among possible events: that it may become probable by supernatural interference! The Almighty has no attribute which can take side with us in such a contest." [84]

It is not fortuitous that Lincoln invoked this last-mentioned theme in his second inaugural address and encouraged his countrymen in both the North and the South to look on the war as a visitation of divine punishment for the sin of slavery:

> The Almighty has His own purposes. "Woe unto the world because of offences! for it must needs be that offences come; but woe to that man by whom the offence cometh!" If we shall suppose that American Slavery is one of those offences which, in the providence of God, must needs come, but which, having continued through His appointed time, He now wills to remove, and that He gives to both North and South, this terrible war, as the woe due to those by whom the offence came, shall we discern therein any departure from those divine attributes which the believers in a Living God always ascribe to Him? Fondly do we hope—fervently do we pray—that this mighty scourge of war may speedily pass away. Yet, if God wills that it continue, until all the wealth piled by the bond-man's two hundred and fifty years of unrequited toil shall be

sunk, and until every drop of blood drawn with the lash, shall be paid by another drawn with the sword, as was said three thousand years ago, so still it must be said "the judgments of the Lord are true and righteous altogether." [85]

In times of peace and prosperity, when suffering and death require comparatively little in the way of justification, it may for the most part be possible to sustain liberal democracy by attending to the dictates of political architecture, by profiting from the prudence of the nation's natural aristocracy, and by encouraging in the people a salutary political jealousy and distrust. But, as Lincoln's example suggests, no political community can long endure and none can confront a great crisis requiring sacrifice and bloodshed unless it is animated by something transcending the narrow, prosaic concern with what Machiavelli, Hobbes, and Locke had respectively dubbed "security and well-being," "commodious living," and "comfortable preservation." Despite all the best efforts of the modern political philosophers and their many and talented practical disciples, man remains ineluctably what the ancient Greeks had taken him by nature to be: a political animal whose public deliberations concerning advantage inevitably lead him on to a concern with the just and even the good. [86]

The Present Discontents

To complain of the age we live in, to murmur at the present possessors of power, to lament the past, to conceive extravagant hopes of the future, are the common dispositions of the greatest part of mankind; indeed the necessary effects of the ignorance and levity of the vulgar. Such complaints and humours have existed in all times; yet as all times have not been alike, true political sagacity manifests itself in distinguishing that complaint which only characterizes the general infirmity of human nature, from those which are symptoms of the particular distemperature of our own air and season.—Edmund Burke

For those who recognize that in our age liberal democracy has been weighed in the balance and sometimes found wanting, there is consolation in the study of the past: for the present discontents have their analogue in an earlier age. Four score and five years after the signing of the Declaration of Independence, the daring republican experiment consciously undertaken by the American Founding Fathers very nearly failed ignominiously, and it had to be revived by a man of even greater stature than Washington, Jefferson, Adams, Hamilton, and Madison—and at a cost in suffering and lives that seems staggering even in an epoch distinguished by mass murder and genocide. Abraham Lincoln's accomplishment is rendered all the more wondrous by the fact that he anticipated the renewed need for grand statesmanship a quarter-century before he delivered the Gettysburg Address.

On 27 January 1838, some fifty years after the ratification of the American Constitution, the twenty-eight-year-old state legislator delivered a lecture to the Young Men's Lyceum of Springfield, Illinois. He had evidently been reading *The Federalist*; he had apparently paused to reflect on the death of James Madison less than two years before; and he quite naturally took as his subject on that occasion "*the perpetuation of our political institutions.*" At the outset, Lincoln rejoiced that he and his compatriots found themselves "in the peaceful possession, of the fairest portion of the earth, as regards extent of territory, fertility of soil, and salubrity of climate" and that they had grown up "under the government of a system of political institutions, conducing more essentially to the ends of civil and religious liberty, than any of which the history of former times tells us." They were, he emphasized, "the legal inheritors of these fundamental blessings."

> We toiled not in the acquirement or establishment of them—they are a legacy bequeathed us, by a *once* hardy, brave, and patriotic, but *now*

lamented and departed race of ancestors. Their's was the task (and nobly they performed it) to possess themselves, and through themselves, us, of this goodly land; and to uprear upon its hills and its valleys, a political edifice of liberty and equal rights; 'tis ours only, to transmit these, the former, unprofaned by the foot of an invader; the latter undecayed by the lapse of time, and untorn by ‹usurpation—to the latest generation that fate shall permit the world to know. This task of gratitude to our fathers, justice to› ourselves, duty to posterity, and love for our species in general, all imperatively require us faithfully to perform.

He doubted whether the task of perpetuating America's political institutions would soon require resistance against an aggressor: the United States was too far distant from its potential rivals and much too strong. "If destruction be our lot," he concluded, "we must ourselves be its author and finisher."

Lincoln raised this possibility because he perceived "something of ill-omen" amongst his countrymen: "the increasing disregard for law which pervades the country." He acknowledged that the examples of vigilante justice that he cited were in their "direct consequences . . . comparatively speaking, but a small evil." But he worried that the failure to punish "the perpetrators of such acts" would encourage "the lawless in spirit . . . to become lawless in practice," and he feared lest "good men, men who love tranquility, who desire to abide by the laws, and enjoy their benefits, who would gladly spill their blood in the defence of their country; seeing their property destroyed; their families insulted, and their lives endangered; their persons injured; and seeing nothing in prospect that forebodes a change for the better; become tired of, and disgusted with, a Government that offers them no protection; and are not much averse to a change in which they imagine they have nothing to lose." In short, he foresaw that the polity might lose "the *attachment* of the People," and this he found immensely disturbing because he knew that, in such a situation, "men of sufficient tal‹ent and ambition›" would "‹not be want›ing to seize ‹the opportunity, strike the blow, and overturn that fair fabric›, which for the last half century, has been the fondest hope, of the lovers of freedom, throughout the world."

Lincoln's rhetoric in 1838, like Churchill's almost exactly a century thereafter, must have seemed to his listeners greatly exaggerated. In recognition of this fact, the future statesman argued that "there are now, and will hereafter be, many causes, dangerous in their tendency, which will not have existed heretofore; and which are not too insignificant to merit attention."

That our government should have been maintained in its original form from its establishment until now, is not much to be wondered at. It had many props to support it through that period, which now are decayed, and crumbled away. Through the period, it was felt by all, to be an un-decided experiment; now, it is understood to be a successful one. Then, all that sought celebrity and fame, and distinction expected to find them in the success of that experiment. Their *all* was staked upon it:—their destiny was *inseparably* linked with it. Their ambition aspired to dis-play before an admiring world, a practical demonstration of the truth of a proposition, which had hitherto been considered, at best not better, than problematical; namely, *the capability of a people to govern themselves.* If they succeeded, they were to be immortalized; their names were to be transferred to counties and cities, and rivers and mountains; and to be revered and sung, and toasted through all time. If they failed, they were to be called knaves and fools, and fanatics for a fleeting hour; then to sink and be forgotten. They succeeded. The experiment is successful; and thousands have won their deathless names in making it so.

The difficulty which Lincoln perceived lay, paradoxically, in the new regime's very success: "The game is caught; and I believe it is true, that with the catch-ing, end the pleasures of the chase. The field of glory is harvested, and the crop is already appropriated." The problem lay in the fact that "new reapers will arise, and *they,* too, will seek a field. It is to deny, what the history of the world tells us is true, to suppose that men of ambition and talents will not continue to spring up amongst us. And, when they do, they will as natu-rally seek the gratification of their ruling passion, as others have *so* done before them."

This led Lincoln to pose a question: "Can that gratification be found in supporting and maintaining an edifice that has been erected by others?" To this, he answered, "Most certainly it cannot." There were "many great and good men sufficiently qualified for any task they undertake, . . . whose am-bition would aspire to nothing beyond a seat in Congress, a gubernatorial or a presidential chair; *but such belong not to the family of the lion, or the tribe of the eagle.*" One could hardly expect an Alexander or a Caesar or a Napoleon to rest satisfied with ordinary office: "Towering genius disdains a beaten path. It seeks regions hitherto unexplored. It sees *no distinction* in adding story to story upon the monuments of fame, erected to the memory of others. It *denies* that it is glory enough to serve under any chief. It *scorns* to tread in the foot-steps of *any* predecessor, however illustrious. It thirsts and burns for distinc-tion; and, if possible, it will have it, whether at the expense of emancipating slaves, or enslaving freemen." Lincoln concluded this stage of his argument by asking whether it was "unreasonable then to expect, that some man pos-

sessed of the loftiest genius, coupled with ambition sufficient to push it to
its utmost stretch, will at some time, spring up among us? And when such a
one does, it will require the people to be united with each other, attached to
the government and laws, and generally intelligent, to successfully frustrate
his designs."

Lincoln brought his address to an end by drawing attention to "the powerful influence which the interesting scenes of the revolution had upon the
passions of the people as distinguished from their judgment." That influence
had in some measure smothered "the jealousy, envy, and avarice, incident
to our nature," and it had redirected "the deep rooted principles of *hate*,
and the powerful motive of *revenge*" almost "exclusively against the British
nation." In effect, it had caused "the basest principles of our nature" either
"to lie dormant, or to become the active agents in the advancement of the
noblest of cause‹s?›—that of establishing and maintaining civil and religious
liberty." But that day had passed, and as the revolutionary generation left the
stage, the memory of those scenes and the "state of feeling" accompanying
them "*must fade, is fading, has faded.*" For the pillars of revolutionary passion,
Lincoln's own contemporaries would have to substitute "other pillars, hewn
from the solid quarry of sober reason." "Passion has helped us." That he
admitted. But he insisted that in the time to come it would be the enemy.
"Reason, cold, calculating, unimpassioned reason, must furnish all the materials for our future support and defence," and these materials must be
molded "into *general intelligence,* ‹sound› *morality* and, in particular, *a reverence
for the constitution and laws.*"[1]

Lincoln's situation was in many respects quite different from our own. In
our time, mob violence and vigilante justice are comparatively rare, and the
Union no longer has anything to fear from the ambitions of abolitionists and
slaveholders. But in other respects the difficulties he described we face now.
The Revolution is no longer even a memory. Its principles are increasingly
viewed as a matter of purely antiquarian interest—even by those who sit on
the United States Supreme Court. What our ancestors fought in the distant
past to acquire or battled in more recent times to retain we now take almost
entirely for granted. More than four decades of comparative peace and prosperity have deprived us of any sense of urgency and have rendered us more
than merely complacent. That we should be presented with a truly serious
challenge from abroad or at home seems almost unthinkable, especially at a
time when our former rivals are in disarray; and if such a challenge were to
present itself, one may justly doubt whether we would be psychologically
and morally prepared to meet it. Our success is, paradoxically, the cause
of our defects. The generation now coming on the stage can hardly be said

to owe its extraordinary good fortune to its own accomplishments, and this suggests that our passions, especially the love of fame that Hamilton singled out as "the ruling passion of the noblest minds," may not be engaged and committed in liberty's defense.[2]

Something of the sort would be true for the citizens of any well-established regime. But our situation is extreme. As I have tried to show in the chapters of this and the preceding volumes, the American Founding Fathers owed a considerable debt to a group of political philosophers who regarded classical republicanism as factious and inhumane. In part because of this, in part because of their awareness of classical philosophy's contribution to the religious strife endemic to Christianity, these early modern thinkers were fearful of the consequences of flattering human pretensions to political and moral rationality; and those among them who favored republicanism were therefore intent on devising institutions which would neither presuppose any great virtue on the part of the citizens nor directly and systematically foster it in them, and which would narrowly restrict the middle ground available for public deliberation (*lógos*) and cooperative action (*práxis*) on the political community's behalf. Under the influence of these thinkers, the American founders established a regime lacking a regimen, a regime inclined to pretend that it is not a regime but something more like the "alliance (*summachía*)" described by Lycophron in which the law is merely "a covenant . . . a pledge to respect each other's rightful claims" and not an instrument "able to make the citizens good and just."[3] As a consequence, ours is and almost always has been a remarkably undemanding polity which provides little in the way of clear, direct moral guidance, and Americans have therefore generally been satisfied to live and let live and to go their own way.

Precisely because the modern republic is predicated on the notion that no one is born "booted and spurred, ready to ride" anyone else "legitimately, by the grace of" nature or nature's God, it would appear to lack a *políteuma* and a principle by which to determine its "distribution and disposition (*táxis*) of offices and honors." In that regard, it might be thought to provide its citizens with little in the way of a *paideía*, and it might be said to lack any but the most precarious sort of unity. It certainly makes little effort to give "to every citizen, the same opinions, the same passions, and the same interests," and it neither seeks to instill *homónoia* nor succeeds in doing so.[4] There is nothing surprising in the fact that such a polity should often appear to lack a sense of public purpose, that it should be inclined to drift, and that it should sometimes be vulnerable to hijacking by those resolute in the pursuit of some particular interest or trend. A truly open society would, in fact, be an empty shell: it would lack that "fixed point," that "*something* which is settled, something permanent, and not to be called in question," and it would therefore be incapable of inspiring what John Stuart Mill called "the feeling of allegiance or loyalty."[5]

To think this propensity fundamental rather than incidental to American government would, despite the considerable evidence to the contrary, be an error. The Founding Fathers owed Thomas Hobbes a great debt, but they did not establish an enlightened despotism. They embraced the principle that no one possesses a natural or God-given right to rule, but they did not thereby opt for arbitrary government. They conceded the primacy of domestic concerns and endorsed the dignity of labor and the splendor of scientific attainment. They sought the establishment of a limited government. But they did not entirely restrict their enthusiasm to the private sphere. They insisted, after all, on the people's capacity to govern themselves; they established a separation of powers designed to provide scope for statesmanship on the part of Congress, the president, and the Supreme Court; and they linked the distribution and disposition of all public offices and honors with popular consent. If they left moral police by and large in the hands of the family and church, they nonetheless conceded to state and local governments, and to the schools which these set up, considerable leeway in giving them support; and of course, at the national level, they established institutions designed indirectly to call forth the less than heroic but never entirely negligible virtues that free government requires. In short, the Founders argued for and sought to institute an enlightened republic.[6]

Thomas Jefferson caught the essential ambiguity in his first inaugural address when he asked that all "bear in mind this sacred principle, that though the will of the majority is in all cases to prevail, that will to be rightful must be reasonable."[7] The modern republic is a concerted attempt to mix wisdom with consent. If it tends to drift off course, it remains nonetheless capable of what a great many members of the founding generation at first thought frequently necessary: a more than simply Machiavellian "recurrence to fundamental principles."[8] The history of the American experiment could, in fact, be described as a dialectic between drift and return.[9] As a consequence, what Plato's Socrates tells Glaucon in *The Republic* regarding the city that they are founding in speech could properly be said with regard to the republic established by our own Founding Fathers: its health and survival require that there always be within it something possessing the same understanding (*lógos*) of the regime that the lawgiver possessed when he set down the laws.[10]

In Lincoln's day, the American republic had lost its bearings. The silent artillery of time had taken its toll, and many had unwittingly abandoned the principles of the Revolution: in the South, not a few had embraced slavery as a positive good; in the North, many had endorsed the principle of popular sovereignty, forgetting that the popular will cannot be rightful without being reasonable. This was no doubt due in part to the fact that the regime lacks a regimen and leaves individuals largely to their own devices. But it was arguably linked as well with the dismantling of Alexander Hamilton's system and with a failure to inculcate the principles of the Revolution. Jefferson was right in hoping that the University of Virginia would become "a nursery of Republican patriots as well as genuine scholars," and there is much to be said for his insistence on seeing that the students of that institution be exposed to what Madison called the new nation's "political creed."[11] If he erred in this regard, it was in neglecting to join Madison in promoting veneration for the Constitution and the Union, and he went badly wrong in sowing a distrust of the federal government, in giving centrality to states' rights, in tentatively lending his name to the cause of scientific racism, and in failing to insist that positive action be taken to honor the promise implicit in the Declaration of Independence that slavery would eventually be extinguished.

Though he deliberately refrained from criticizing the Founders, Lincoln clearly perceived their blunder. In 1838, he exhorted his listeners, "Let reverence for the laws, be breathed by every American mother, to the lisping babe, that prattles on her lap—let it be taught in schools, in seminaries, and in colleges;—let it be written in Primmers, spelling books, and in Almanacs;—let it be preached from the pulpit, proclaimed in legislative halls, and enforced in courts of justice. And, in short, let it become the *political religion* of the nation; and let the old and the young, the rich and the poor, the grave and the gay, of all sexes and tongues, and colors and conditions, sacrifice unceasingly upon its altars."[12] In his later career, he lost no opportunity to reinforce veneration for the Founding Fathers and for the principles of the Declaration of Independence. As president, he implemented a program of political and economic reform that owed much to Alexander Hamilton's original plan; and when circumstance allowed it, he freed the slaves.

Lincoln had his difficulties; we have ours. In one regard, they are the same. We spend colossal sums on education, but it cannot be said that we manage to inculcate a reverence for or even an understanding of the principles underlying our Revolution, our Constitution, and our laws. The intellectual currents of our time—utilitarianism, positivism, idealism, historicism, Marxism, pragmatism, and existentialism in all their various, multifarious, and unstable mutations—are incompatible with the conviction that all men are created equal and endowed by their creator with certain, inalienable natural rights, and it can hardly be said that what was once described as a self-evident truth commands respect in our institutions of higher learning.[13]

Equality in general may secure all but universal assent, but the content of that equality is utterly amorphous. Very few of those charged with the higher education of our young could contemplate with equanimity the notion that "the first object of Government" is to provide equal "protection" to the "different and unequal faculties of acquiring property."[14] Very few could even define what equality should mean today or will mean five years hence, for the concept is said to be evolving, and that claim is indicative of the fact that we are adrift—much as we were in Abraham Lincoln's day.

Our difficulties are reinforced by circumstances which Lincoln did not have to confront. In his time, self-government was real and tangible because it was largely local; and especially through the schools and through laws enforcing a modicum of decorum, local polities reinforced the family and church in matters of moral police. In consequence, self-government attracted the attention, it absorbed the ambitions, and it commanded the loyalty of ordinary people. In the last six decades, we have witnessed a consolidation of government and a centralization of administration which would have left even Alexander Hamilton nonplussed, and we have stood idly by while the federal courts have transformed the Constitution and the Bill of Rights into an instrument subversive of the private institutions that provide the modest, moral *paideía* needed to sustain our regime. Moreover, in quite recent times, a cozy arrangement has grown up by which the members of Congress customarily leave the most controversial and disturbing issues of public policy to the Supreme Court; then, by concentrating on constituency services, by skillfully balancing the concerns of the various lobbies, and by promoting electoral reforms that favor incumbents, our representatives manage to provide for their own permanent tenure in office. If Aristotle is right, as he surely is, in supposing that "the distribution and disposition of offices and honors" within a polity constitutes the most important element in popular education, then it could be said that our current arrangements inculcate a positive disrespect for popular consent.

The decisions of the Supreme Court, even those which flout the intentions of those who framed and ratified our Constitution and its various amendments, must no doubt be recognized as binding on the parties to any particular suit. But, as in Lincoln's day, "the candid citizen must confess that if the policy of the government, upon vital questions, affecting to the whole people, is to be irrevocably fixed by decisions of the Supreme Court, the instant they are made, . . . the people will have ceased, to be their own rulers, having, to that extent, practically resigned their government, into the hands of that eminent tribunal."[15] A legislature that sidesteps controversy and connives in judicial encroachment has sacrificed its supremacy, and elections in which eight or even nine incumbents in ten are returned to office are little more than a sham. Our government is a species of compromise between Hobbesian monarchy and classical democracy. In the wake of Jefferson's presidency, as Hamilton foresaw, it was insufficiently monarchical. In our time, the opposite is increasingly the case. Such is, I would submit, "the particular distemperature of our own air and season." [16]

There is, of course, a case to be made for consolidation and even for judicial legislation. The Founders prized self-government, as we have seen. Almost without exception, they therefore presumed that, where the meaning of the Constitution is not self-evident, the proper touchstone for interpretation is the intent evidenced by the American people in ratifying that document, in adopting subsequent amendments, and in thereby conferring on it the authority that it possesses as fundamental law.[17] Against this presumption one weighty objection can and must be raised: for, in some respects, we are arguably better governed in the administrative state than we were in earlier times. It took the Supreme Court, after all, to make us abandon a shameful and profoundly unjust public policy of racial discrimination. The will of the majority was for a great many years neither reasonable nor rightful, and we are merely harvesting the bitter fruit sown by our past sins. "Justice is the end of government," as James Madison observed. "It is the end of civil society. It ever has been, and ever will be pursued, until it be obtained, or until liberty be lost in the pursuit." Here, however, we must pause once again to reflect, for the disgraceful fact that in the past we were unequal to the task of reconciling liberty with justice in no way alters the direction in which we are tending. Nor will it change the consequences.[18]

Thomas Jefferson no doubt overreacted to the opinion issued by John Marshall in *Marbury v. Madison*. Such was his wont. He was certainly wrong in then denying the constitutionality of judicial review. As James Madison sagely observed, "The abuse of a trust does not disprove its existence." [19] But Jefferson's errors in these particulars should not blind us to the pertinence of the warning that he later issued against judicial "despotism" and "oligarchy." As recent American history proves, to accord effective, political supremacy to courts composed of men (and, now, women) appointed to office for life is to make of the Constitution "a mere thing of wax in the hands of the judiciary, which they may twist and shape into any form they please." [20] As Jefferson put it, "to consider the judges as the ultimate arbiters of all constitutional questions" is "a very dangerous doctrine indeed," for there really is "no safe depository of the ultimate powers of society but the people themselves; and if we think them not enlightened enough to exercise their control with wholesome discretion, the remedy is not to take it from them, but to inform their discretion by education." [21]

We have not yet reached the end of times. Down the road that we are now traveling, we will someday encounter a great crisis, and it remains an open question whether we will then possess sufficient democratic vigor and a sufficient "concord regarding loved things held in common" to sustain us through that crisis.[22] Indeed, one may wonder whether we do so now. The one consolation is that this has happened before and that the nation managed to pass through its difficulties, to return to its first principles, and to draw strength from the ordeal by undergoing what Lincoln called "a new birth of freedom."[23] But that can only happen if Americans pause from time to time to seriously ponder just what their first principles are and what they entail. It is with this possibility in mind that I have written this book.

Notes

ABBREVIATIONS AND BRIEF TITLES

In the notes, I have adopted the standard abbreviations for classical texts and inscriptions and for books of the Bible provided in *The Oxford Classical Dictionary*[2], ed. N. G. L. Hammond and H. H. Scullard (Oxford 1970), and in *The Chicago Manual of Style*[13] (Chicago 1982) 388–89, as well as those for journals listed in *L'Année Philologique*. Where possible, the ancient texts and medieval and modern works of similar stature are cited by the divisions and subdivisions employed by the author or introduced by subsequent editors (that is, by book, part, chapter, section number, paragraph, act, scene, line, Stephanus page, or by page and line number). In some cases, where further specification is needed to help the reader to locate a particular passage, I have included in parentheses as the last element in a particular citation the page or pages of the pertinent volume of the edition used. For fragments surviving from works of the classical period now lost, I have followed the practice now standard among classicists of citing the author's name, the fragment or line numbers, and, in parentheses following those numbers, the surname of the editor of the collection. Superscripted numerals indicate the edition of a book cited or the pertinent series of the journal. In referring the reader to earlier or later parts of my argument, I have cited volume, chapter, and section (for example, I.vii.3), indicating whether the pertinent passage appears above or below. For medieval and modern works and for journals, inscriptions, and texts not listed in the volumes cited above, the following abbreviations and short titles have been employed.

ABF
  The Autobiography of Benjamin Franklin, ed. Leonard W. Labaree et al. (New Haven 1964).
AJL
  The Adams-Jefferson Letters: The Complete Correspondence between Thomas Jefferson and Abigail and John Adams, ed. Lester J. Cappon (Chapel Hill 1959).
Alfarabi, *Aphorisms*
  Al-Fārābī, Fuṣūl Al-Madanī: Aphorisms of the Statesman, ed. and trans. D. M. Dunlop (Cambridge 1961).
———, *Opinions*
  Alfarabi, The Principles of the Opinions of the People of the Virtuous City. In Al-Farabi on the Perfect State: Abū Naṣr al-Fārābī's Mabādi' Ārā' Ahl Al-Madīna Al-Fāḍila, ed. and trans. Richard Walzer (Oxford 1985).
———, *Plato & Aristotle*
  Alfarabi's Philosophy of Plato and Aristotle[2], ed. and trans. Muhsin Mahdi (Ithaca 1969).
Annals of Congress
  Annals of Congress: The Debates and Proceedings in the Congress of the United States, ed. Joseph Gales (Washington, D.C., 1834–56).

APSR

  The American Political Science Review.

AQ

  American Quarterly.

Aquinas, *Summa theologiae*

  Thomas Aquinas, *Summa theologiae*, ed. Thomas Gilby, O.P., et al. (London 1964–76).

Aubrey, *Brief Lives* (ed. Clark)

  'Brief Lives,' chiefly of Contemporaries, set down by John Aubrey, between the Years 1669 & 1696, ed. Andrew Clark (Oxford 1898).

———, *Brief Lives* (ed. Dick)

  Aubrey's Brief Lives, ed. Oliver Lawson Dick (Harmondsworth 1982).

Averroes on Plato's Republic

  Averroes on Plato's Republic, ed. and trans. Ralph Lerner (Ithaca 1974).

Bacon, *Of the Advancement of Learning*

  In Francis Bacon, *The Advancement of Learning and New Atlantis* (London 1974).

Blackstone, *Commentaries*

  William Blackstone, *Commentaries on the Laws of England* (Oxford 1765–69).

Boccalini, *Ragguagli*

  Traiano Boccalini, *Ragguagli di Parnaso e scritti minori*, ed. Luigi Firpo (Bari 1948).

Burnet, *HMOT*

  Gilbert Burnet, *The History of My Own Time*, ed. Osmund Airy (Oxford 1897–1900).

CAF

  The Complete Anti-Federalist, ed. Herbert J. Storing (Chicago 1981).

Calvin, *Inst.*

  John Calvin, *Institutio christianae religionis* (1559). In *Joannis Calvini opera selecta*[3], ed. Peter Barth and William Niesel (Munich 1963–74) III–V.

Cato's Letters

  John Trenchard and Thomas Gordon, *Cato's Letters, or Essays on Liberty, Civil and Religious, and Other Important Subjects*[6] (London 1755).

CHJ

  Cambridge Historical Journal.

CJL

  The Correspondence of John Locke, ed. Esmond S. de Beer (Oxford 1976–   ).

CMPP

  A Compilation of the Messages and Papers of the Presidents, 1789–1897, ed. James D. Richardson (Washington, D.C., 1896).

Condorcet, *Esquisse*

  Marquis de Condorcet, *Esquisse d'un tableau historique du progrès de l'esprit humain*, ed. O. H. Prior and Yvon Belaval (Paris 1970).

DAH

  Documents of American History[7], ed. Henry Steele Commager (New York 1963).

Descartes, *Discours de la méthode*

  René Descartes, *Discours de la méthode*. In *WrRD* 125–79.

———, *Les passions de l'âme*

  René Descartes, *Les Passions de l'âme*. In *WrRD* 695–802.

DHFFC

Documentary History of the First Federal Congress of the United States of America: March 4, 1789–March 3, 1791, ed. Linda Grant De Pauw (Baltimore, 1972–).

DHRC

The Documentary History of the Ratification of the Constitution, ed. Merrill Jensen et al. (Madison, Wis., 1976–).

DSSC

*The Debates in the Several State Conventions*², ed. Jonathan Elliot (Philadelphia 1876).

EcHR

Economic History Review.

EHD

English Historical Documents, ed. David C. Douglas et al. (Oxford 1953–).

EMM

Les essais de Michel de Montaigne, ed. Pierre Villey and V.-L. Saulnier (Paris 1978).

Encyclopédie

Encyclopédie, ou dictionnaire raisonné des sciences, des arts, et des métiers, ed. Denis Diderot and Jean Le Rond d'Alembert (Paris 1751–80).

Ep.

Epistulae.

The Federalist

Alexander Hamilton, James Madison, and John Jay, *The Federalist*, ed. Jacob E. Cooke (Middletown, Conn., 1961).

Ferguson, *EHCS*

Adam Ferguson, *An Essay on the History of Civil Society*, ed. Duncan Forbes (Edinburgh 1966).

FSC

The Federal and State Constitutions, Colonial Charters, and Other Organic Laws of the States, Territories, and Colonies Now or Heretofore Forming the United States of America, ed. Francis Newton Thorpe (Washington, D.C., 1909).

GHI 1

Russell Meiggs and David Lewis, *A Selection of Greek Historical Inscriptions* (Oxford 1988).

GHI 2

Marcus N. Tod, *A Selection of Greek Historical Inscriptions* II (Oxford 1948).

GHQ

Georgia Historical Quarterly.

Grotius, *De iure belli ac pacis*

Hugo Grotius, *De iure belli ac pacis libri tres* (Amsterdam 1646). In citing the Prolegomena, I have used the paragraph numbers added by subsequent editors.

———, *De iure praedae*

Hugo Grotius, *De Jure Praedae Commentarius*, ed. James Brown Scott (Oxford 1950).

HJo

Historical Journal.

HLQ

Huntington Library Quarterly.

Hobbes, *Behemoth*

Thomas Hobbes, *Behemoth, or The Long Parliament*[2], ed. Ferdinand Tönnies (New York 1969).

——, *De cive*

Thomas Hobbes, *De Cive: The Latin Version*, ed. Howard Warrender (Oxford 1983). Because I have been unable to improve on the translation *Philosophicall Rudiments Concerning Government and Society* published by an anonymous, contemporary admirer of Hobbes, I have used it throughout when quoting *De cive*. For a critical edition of the translation, see Hobbes, *De Cive: The English Version*, ed. Howard Warrender (Oxford 1983).

——, *Dialogue*

Thomas Hobbes, *A Dialogue between a Philosopher and a Student of the Common Laws of England*, ed. Joseph Cropsey (Chicago 1971).

——, *Elements of Law*

Thomas Hobbes, *The Elements of Law Natural and Politic*[2], ed. Ferdinand Tönnies (London 1969).

——, *EW*

The English Works of Thomas Hobbes of Malmesbury, ed. Sir William Molesworth (London 1839–45).

——, *Leviathan*

Thomas Hobbes, *Leviathan*, ed. C. B. Macpherson (Harmondsworth 1968).

——, *LW*

Thomas Hobbes Malmesburiensis opera philosophica quae Latine scripsit omnia in unum corpus, ed. William Molesworth (London 1839–45).

Hooker, *Laws*

Richard Hooker, *Of the Laws of Ecclesiastical Polity*, ed. Georges Edelen, W. Speed Hill, and P. G. Stanwood (Cambridge, Mass., 1977–81).

HPT

History of Political Thought.

Hume, *EMPL*

David Hume, *Essays Moral, Political, and Literary*, ed. Eugene F. Miller (Indianapolis, 1985).

——, *EPM*

An Enquiry Concerning the Principles of Morals. In David Hume, *Enquiries Concerning the Human Understanding and Concerning the Principles of Morals*[2], ed. L. A. Selby-Bigge (Oxford 1902) 169–343.

——, *THN*

David Hume, *A Treatise of Human Nature*, ed. L. A. Selby-Bigge (Oxford 1888).

Hutcheson, *IMP*

Francis Hutcheson, *A Short Introduction to Moral Philosophy in Three Books, Containing the Elements of Ethicks and the Law of Nature* (Glascow 1747).

——, *SMP*

Francis Hutcheson, *A System of Moral Philosophy in Three Books* (London 1755).

Hyper.

Hyperides.

ICr

Inscriptiones Creticae opera et consilio Friderici Halbherr collectae, ed. Margarita Guarducci (Rome 1935–50).

JAH
Journal of American History.
JBS
Journal of British Studies.
JCC
Journals of the Continental Congress, 1774–1789, ed. Worthington Chauncey Ford et al. (Washington, D.C., 1904–37).
JChS
Journal of Church and State.
JEcH
Journal of Economic History.
Jefferson, *NSV*
Thomas Jefferson, *Notes on the State of Virginia*, ed. William Peden (New York 1972).
———, *MCPP*
The Memoirs, Correspondence, and Private Papers of Thomas Jefferson, ed. Thomas Jefferson Randolph (London 1829).
JER
Journal of the Early Republic.
JHO
James Harrington's Oceana, ed. S. B. Liljegren (Heidelberg 1924).
JMH
Journal of Modern History.
JP
Journal of Politics.
JSH
Journal of Southern History.
King, *Locke*
Peter King, *The Life of John Locke, with Extracts from his Correspondence, Journals, and Common-Place Books*[2] (London 1830).
La Rochefoucauld, *Maximes morales*
François, duc de La Rochefoucauld, *Réflexions ou sentences et maximes morales: Édition de 1678.* In *Oeuvres complètes*, ed. L. Martin-Chauffier and Jean Marchand (Paris 1964) 385–471.
———, *Maximes supprimées*
François, duc de La Rochefoucauld, *Maximes supprimées.* In *Oeuvres complètes*, ed. L. Martin-Chauffier and Jean Marchand (Paris 1964) 483–98.
LBR
Letters of Benjamin Rush, ed. L. H. Butterfield (Philadelphia 1951).
LDH
The Letters of David Hume, ed. J. Y. T. Greig (Oxford 1932).
LJL
John R. Harrison and Peter Laslett, *The Library of John Locke*[2] (Oxford 1971).
Locke, *CU*
John Locke, *Of the Conduct of the Understanding.* In *WoJL* III 203–89.
———, *ECHU*
John Locke, *An Essay Concerning Human Understanding*, ed. Peter H. Nidditch (Oxford 1979).

———, *EWrJL*

The Educational Writings of John Locke, ed. James L. Axtell (Cambridge 1968).

———, *LCT*

John Locke, *A Letter Concerning Toleration,* ed. Mario Montuori (The Hague 1963).

——— MSS

Locke MSS, Lovelace Collection, Bodleian Library.

———, *QLN*

John Locke, *Questions Concerning the Law of Nature,* ed. and trans. Robert Horwitz, Jenny Strauss Clay, and Diskin Clay (Ithaca 1990).

———, *RC*

John Locke, *The Reasonableness of Christianity as Delivered in the Scriptures,* ed. George W. Ewing (Chicago 1965).

———, *Scritti inediti*

Scritti editi e inediti sulla toleranza, ed. Carlo Augusto Viano (Turin 1961).

———, *STCE*

John Locke, *Some Thoughts Concerning Education,* ed. John W. and Jean S. Yolton (Oxford 1989).

———, *TTG*

John Locke, *Two Treatises of Government: A Critical Edition with an Introduction and Apparatus Criticus*[2], ed. Peter Laslett (Cambridge 1970)—as corrected by Nathan Tarcov, *Locke's Education for Liberty* (Chicago 1984) 229–30 n. 324, 253–54 n. 187.

———, *Two Tracts on Government*

John Locke, *Two Tracts on Government,* ed. Philip Abrams (Cambridge 1967).

LWEP

Letters Written by Eminent Persons in the Seventeenth and Eighteenth Centuries: To Which are Added, Hearne's Journeys to Reading, and to Whaddon Hall, the Seat of Browne Willis, Esq., and Lives of Eminent Men by John Aubrey, Esq., ed. Phillip Bliss and Rev. John Walker (London 1813).

Macaulay, *Essays*

Thomas Babington Macaulay, *Critical, Historical, and Miscellaneous Essays* (New York 1860).

Machiavelli, *Discorsi*

Niccolò Machiavelli, *Discorsi sopra la prima deca di Tito Livio.* In *WoNM* 73–254.

———, *Istorie fiorentine*

Niccolò Machiavelli, *Istorie fiorentine.* In *WoNM* 629–844.

———, *Il principe*

Niccolò Machiavelli, *Il principe.* In *WoNM* 255–98.

Maimonides, *Guide of the Perplexed*

Maimonides, *The Guide of the Perplexed,* trans. Shlomo Pines (Chicago 1963).

Mandeville, *Fable of the Bees*

Bernard Mandeville, *The Fable of the Bees,* ed. F. B. Kaye (London 1924).

Marsilius of Padua, *Defensor pacis*

The Defensor Pacis of Marsilius of Padua, ed. C. W. Previté-Orton (Cambridge 1928).

MJQA

Memoirs of John Quincy Adams, Comprising Portions of his Diary from 1795 to 1848, ed. Charles Francis Adams (Philadelphia 1874–76).

Montesquieu, *EL*
   Charles de Secondat, baron de La Bréde et de Montesquieu, *De l'esprit des lois.* In *WoM* II 225–995.
MPP
   Medieval Political Philosophy: A Sourcebook, ed. Ralph Lerner and Muhsin Mahdi (New York 1963).
N&Q
   Notes and Queries.
NEQ
   New England Quarterly.
PAH
   The Papers of Alexander Hamilton, ed. Harold C. Syrett (New York 1961–79).
PAmH
   Perspectives in American History.
PAR
   Pamphlets of the American Revolution, 1750–1776, ed. Bernard Bailyn (Cambridge, Mass., 1965–   ).
Pascal, *Pensées*
   Blaise Pascal, *Pensées.* In *Oeuvres complètes de Pascal*, ed. Jacques Chevalier (Paris 1954).
PBF
   The Papers of Benjamin Franklin, ed. Leonard W. Labaree et al. (New Haven 1959–   ).
PGM
   The Papers of George Mason, ed. Robert A. Rutland (Chapel Hill 1970).
PGW
   The Papers of George Washington, ed. W. W. Abbot (Charlottesville 1983).
PJA
   Papers of John Adams, ed. Robert J. Taylor (Cambridge, Mass., 1977–   ).
PJJ
   The Correspondence and Public Papers of John Jay, ed. Henry P. Johnston (New York 1890–93).
PJM
   The Papers of James Madison, ed. William T. Hutchinson, William M. E. Rachal, et al. (Chicago 1962–77; Charlottesville 1977–   ).
PJoM
   The Papers of John Marshall, ed. Herbert A. Johnson et al. (Chapel Hill 1974–   ).
PMHB
   Pennsylvania Magazine of History and Biography.
PMHS
   Proceedings of the Massachusetts Historical Society.
PrStQ
   Presidential Studies Quarterly.
PSQ
   Political Science Quarterly.
PSR
   The Political Science Reviewer.
PSt
   Political Studies.

PTh
  Political Theory.
PTJ
  The Papers of Thomas Jefferson, ed. Julian P. Boyd (Princeton 1950–   ).
RFC
  The Records of the Federal Convention of 1787, ed. Max Farrand (New Haven 1911–37).
RP
  Review of Politics.
RPM
  The Renaissance Philosophy of Man, ed. Ernst Cassirer, Paul Oskar Kristeller, and John Hermann Randall, Jr. (Chicago 1948).
SAQ
  South Atlantic Quarterly.
SDUSC
  Sources and Documents of United States Constitutions, ed. William F. Swindler (Dobbs Ferry, N.Y., 1973–79).
Shakespeare
  All references are taken from William Shakespeare, *The Complete Works*, ed. Stanley Wells and Gary Taylor (Oxford 1986).
Smith, *TMS*
  Adam Smith, *The Theory of Moral Sentiments*. In *The Glasgow Edition of the Works and Correspondence of Adam Smith* (Oxford 1976).
———, *WN*
  Adam Smith, *An Inquiry into The Nature and Causes of the Wealth of Nations*. In *The Glasgow Edition of the Works and Correspondence of Adam Smith* (Oxford 1976).
Somers Tracts
  Somers Tracts: A Collection of Scarce and Valuable Tracts, on the Most Interesting and Entertaining Subjects: But Chiefly such as Relate to the History and Constitution of These Kingdoms[2], ed. Walter Scott (London 1809–15).
Spinoza, *Opera*
  Benedict de Spinoza, *Spinoza opera*, ed. Carl Gebhardt (Heidelberg 1925). In citing particular works, I have employed the divisions introduced in *Benedicti de Spinoza opera quae supersunt omnia*, ed. Carolus Hermannus Bruder (Leipzig 1843–46), and generally used by editors since.
Sprat, *Royal-Society*
  Thomas Sprat, *The History of the Royal-Society of London, For the Improving of Natural Knowledge* (London 1667).
SRFC
  Supplement to Max Farrand's The Records of the Federal Convention of 1787, ed. James H. Hutson (New Haven 1987).
TAR
  Tracts of the American Revolution, 1763–1776, ed. Merrill Jensen (Indianapolis 1967).
Tocqueville, *DA*
  Alexis de Tocqueville, *De la démocratie en Amérique*. In *Oeuvres, papiers et correspondances*, ed. J.-P. Mayer (Paris 1951–   ) I, pts. 1–2.

Vico, *New Science*
  Giambattista Vico, *The New Science of Giambattista Vico*[2], trans. Thomas Goddard Bergin and Max Harold Fisch (Ithaca 1968).
VMHB
  Virginia Magazine of History and Biography.
WMQ
  William and Mary Quarterly[3].
WoAL
  The Collected Works of Abraham Lincoln, ed. Roy P. Basler (New Brunswick, N.J., 1953–55).
WoDS
  The Collected Works of Dugald Stewart, ed. Sir William Hamilton (Edinburgh 1854).
WoFB
  The Works of Francis Bacon, ed. James Spedding, Robert Leslie Ellis, and Douglas Denon Heath (London 1857–74).
WoFN
  Friedrich Nietzsche, *Werke*, ed. Karl Schlechta (Munich 1966).
WoGS
  The Works of George Savile, Marquis of Halifax, ed. Mark N. Brown (Oxford 1989).
WoJA
  The Works of John Adams, ed. Charles Francis Adams (Boston 1850–56).
WoJH
  James Harrington, *Works: The Oceana and Other Works of James Harrington*, ed. John Toland (London 1771).
WoJJR
  Jean Jacques Rousseau, *Oeuvres complètes*, ed. Bernard Gagnebin and Marcel Raymond (Paris 1959–69).
WoJL
  The Works of John Locke (London 1823).
WoJP
  The Theological and Miscellaneous Works of Joseph Priestley, ed. John Towill Rutt (London 1817–32).
WoJSM
  Collected Works of John Stuart Mill, ed. John M. Robson et al. (Toronto 1963–   ).
WoJW
  The Works of James Wilson, ed. Robert Green McCloskey (Cambridge, Mass., 1967).
WoLB
  The Works of Lord Bolingbroke, with a Life Prepared Expressly for this Edition, Containing Information Relative to his Personal and Public Character (London 1844).
WoM
  Charles de Secondat, baron de La Bréde et de Montesquieu, *Oeuvres complètes de Montesquieu*, ed. Roger Caillois (Paris 1949–51).
WoNM
  Niccolò Machiavelli, *Tutte le opere*, ed. Mario Martelli (Florence 1971).
WoRB
  The Works of the Honourable Robert Boyle, ed. Thomas Birch (London 1772).

WoRD

René Descartes, *Oeuvres de Descartes,* ed. Charles Adam and Paul Tannery (Paris 1964–74).

WoRF

Sir Robert Filmer, *Patriarcha and Other Writings,* ed. Johann P. Sommerville (Cambridge 1991).

WoTJ

The Works of Thomas Jefferson, ed. Paul Leicester Ford (New York 1904–5).

WPQ

Western Political Quarterly.

WrEB

The Writings and Speeches of the Right Honourable Edmund Burke (Boston 1901).

WrGW

The Writings of George Washington, ed. John C. Fitzpatrick (Washington, D.C., 1931–44).

WrJD

The Political Writings of John Dickinson, 1764–1774, ed. Paul Leicester Ford (New York 1970).

WrJM

The Writings of James Madison, ed. Gaillard Hunt (New York 1900–1910).

WrRD

René Descartes, *Oeuvres et lettres,* ed. André Bridoux (Paris 1953).

WrSA

The Writings of Samuel Adams, ed. Harry Alonzo Cushing (New York 1904–8).

WrTA

Aquinas: Selected Political Writings, ed. A. P. D'Entrèves and trans. J. G. Dawson (Oxford 1948).

WrTJ (ed. Ford)

The Writings of Thomas Jefferson, ed. Paul Leicester Ford (New York 1892–99).

WrTJ (ed. Lipscomb and Bergh)

The Writings of Thomas Jefferson, ed. Andrew A. Lipscomb and Albert Ellery Bergh (Washington, D.C., 1903).

WrTJ (ed. Peterson)

Thomas Jefferson, *Writings,* ed. Merrill D. Peterson (New York 1984).

WrTJ (ed. Washington)

The Writings of Thomas Jefferson, ed. H. A. Washington (New York 1853–55).

WrTP

The Complete Writings of Thomas Paine, ed. Philip S. Foner (New York 1945).

Introduction

1. Winston S. Churchill, *Blood, Sweat, and Tears* (New York 1941) 55–66: The Munich Agreement, 5 October 1938.

2. For an examination of this question, see Francis Fukuyama, *The End of History and the Last Man* (New York 1992).

3. On this subject, much more could be said: see Frederick W. Marks III, *Wind Over Sand: The Diplomacy of Franklin Roosevelt* (Athens, Ga., 1988). On subsequent

blunders, see Amos Perlmutter, *FDR and Stalin: A Not So Grand Alliance, 1943–1945* (Columbia, Mo., 1993).

4. See Tocqueville, *DA* 2.2.11 (139), 13, 3.19 (254), with 2.3.13, 17–19, 21.

5. Note *JHO* 174–75; see Robert Molesworth, *An Account of Denmark, As It was in the Year 1692* (London 1694) Pref.; and consider Jean Louis de Lolme, *The Constitution of England*[3] (London 1781) 4–5.

6. Carl Becker, *AHR* 30 (1924–25): 810–12. Note *PJA* II 109–10, 116–17: Letters to James Warren on 17 and 25 July 1774.

7. *The Literary Bible of Thomas Jefferson: His Commonplace Book of Philosophers and Poets*, ed. Gilbert Chinard (Baltimore 1928) 4.

8. Gilbert Chinard, "Jefferson among the Philosophers," *Ethics* 53 (1942–43): 255–68 (at 257).

9. Douglass Adair, "A Note on Certain of Hamilton's Pseudonyms," in *Fame and the Founding Fathers*, ed. Trevor Colbourn (New York 1974) 272–85 (at 278 n. 10).

10. See Charles F. Mullett, "Classical Influences on the American Revolution," *CJ* 35 (1939–40): 92–104, and "Ancient Historians and 'Enlightened' Reviewers," *RP* 21 (1959): 550–65; Robert Middlekauff, "A Persistent Tradition: The Classical Curriculum in Eighteenth-Century New England," *WMQ* 18 (1961): 54–67, and *Ancients and Axioms: Secondary Education in Eighteenth Century New England* (New Haven 1963); Gordon S. Wood, *The Creation of the American Republic, 1776–1787* (Chapel Hill 1969); J. G. A. Pocock, *The Machiavellian Moment: Florentine Political Thought and the Atlantic Republican Tradition* (Princeton 1975); and Meyer Reinhold, *Classica Americana: The Greek and Roman Heritage in the United States* (Detroit 1984).

11. Clinton Rossiter, *Seedtime of the Republic* (New York 1953) 356–59.

12. Bernard Bailyn, *The Ideological Origins of the American Revolution* (Cambridge, Mass., 1967) 23–26.

13. Hannah Arendt, *On Revolution* (New York 1963) 197, 258. One should read 111–285 (esp. 115–37, 234–85) in light of Arendt, *The Human Condition* (Chicago 1958).

14. Wood, *The Creation of the American Republic* 48–70 (esp. 49–50, 53, 58, 61, 63, 68), 418–19.

15. See J. G. A. Pocock, "Virtue and Commerce in the Eighteenth Century," *Journal of Interdisciplinary History* 3 (1972): 119–34 (esp. 120, 121 n. 6), and *The Machiavellian Moment* esp. 505–7, 545–46, 550. For a reaffirmation of the central importance of Arendt's argument for this line of thought, see Lance Banning, "Jeffersonian Ideology Revisited: Liberal and Classical Ideas in the New American Republic," *WMQ* 43 (1986): 3–19 (at 17–19).

16. For the older view, see Carl Becker, *The Declaration of Independence: A Study in the History of Political Ideas* (New York 1922); Alice M. Baldwin, *The New England Clergy and the American Revolution* (Durham, N.C., 1928); Merle Curti, "The Great Mr. Locke: America's Philosopher, 1783–1861," *Huntington Library Bulletin* 11 (1939): 107–51; and Louis Hartz, *The Liberal Tradition in America: An Interpretation of American Political Thought since the Revolution* (New York 1955). Cf. Lance Banning, "Republican Ideology and the Triumph of the Constitution, 1789 to 1793," *WMQ* 31 (1974): 167–88, Banning, *The Jeffersonian Persuasion: Evolution of a Party Ideology* (Ithaca 1978), and Drew R. McCoy, *The Elusive Republic: Political Economy in Jeffersonian America* (Chapel Hill 1980), who barely mention Locke and lay no stress on the first principles and the economic vision that he defended in his *Two*

Treatises of Government. Then, consider the following by Joyce Appleby: "What Is Still American in the Political Philosophy of Thomas Jefferson?" *WMQ* 39 (1982): 287–309; "Commercial Farming and the 'Agrarian Myth' in the Early Republic," *JAH* 68 (1982): 833–49; *Capitalism and a New Social Order: The Republican Vision of the 1790s* (New York 1984); "Republicanism and Ideology," *AQ* 37 (1985): 461–73; and "Republicanism in Old and New Contexts," *WMQ* 43 (1986): 20–34. Also consider John P. Diggins, *The Lost Soul of American Politics: Virtue, Self-Interest, and the Foundations of Liberalism* (New York 1984) 3–105; Thomas L. Pangle, *The Spirit of Modern Republicanism: The Moral Vision of the American Founders and the Philosophy of Locke* (Chicago 1988) 1–127; and Steven M. Dworetz, *The Unvarnished Doctrine: Locke, Liberalism, and the American Revolution* (Durham, N.C., 1990) 3–183. Banning's and McCoy's failure to lay emphasis on the importance of Locke's thinking owes a great deal to the doubts expressed by John Dunn and by Pocock himself regarding the influence of Locke's *Two Treatises of Government*: see Dunn, "The Politics of Locke in England and America in the Eighteenth Century," in *John Locke: Problems and Perspectives*, ed. John W. Yolton (Cambridge 1969) 45–80 (esp. 56–69); and Pocock, "Virtue and Commerce in the Eighteenth Century" 124–34, and "The Myth of John Locke and the Obsession with Liberalism," in *John Locke: Papers Read at a Clark Library Seminar, 10 December 1977*, ed. J. G. A. Pocock and Richard Ashcraft (Los Angeles 1980) 3–24. For a recent restatement of Dunn's argument as it pertains to America, see Oscar Handlin, "Learned Books and Revolutionary Action, 1776," *Harvard Library Bulletin* 34 (1986): 362–79.

17. Where Wood (*The Creation of the American Republic*) and Appleby (*Capitalism and a New Social Order*, "Republicanism and Ideology" 461–73, and "Republicanism in Old and New Contexts" 20–34) tend to see competing ideologies, Banning ("Jeffersonian Ideology Revisited" 3–19) now finds an absence of "analytical" clarity on the part of the Founders, and Isaac Kramnick discerns a great variety and confusion of "political tongues" (" 'The Great National Discussion': The Discourse of Politics in 1787," *Republicanism and Bourgeois Radicalism: Political Ideology in Late Eighteenth-Century England and America* [Ithaca 1990] 260–88). Cf. Jeffrey C. Isaac, "Republicanism vs. Liberalism? A Reconsideration," *HPT* 9 (1988): 349–77, who suggests that the republicanism adopted by the Americans was compatible with liberalism.

18. Cf. J. G. A. Pocock, "Cambridge Paradigms and Scotch Philosophers: A Study of the Relations between the Civic Humanist and the Civil Jurisprudential Interpretation of Eighteenth-Century Social Thought," in *Wealth and Virtue: The Shaping of Political Economy in the Scottish Enlightenment*, ed. Istvan Hont and Michael Ignatieff (Cambridge 1983) 235–52 (esp. 246–48, 251), with J. H. Hexter, "Republic, Virtue, Liberty, and the Political Universe of J. G. A. Pocock," in *On Historians: Reappraisals of Some of the Masters of Modern History* (Cambridge, Mass., 1979) 255–303; and see Hexter, "Personal Retrospect and Postscript," *Reappraisals in History: New Views on History and Society in Early Modern Europe*[2] (Chicago 1979) 249–78 (esp. 258–59).

19. See Pocock, "Cambridge Paradigms and Scotch Philosophers" 235, 239, 242–44. In this connection, see also Pocock, "Authority and Property: The Question of Liberal Origins" and "The Varieties of Whiggism from Exclusion to Reform: A History of Ideology and Discourse," *Virtue, Commerce, and History: Essays on Political Thought and History, Chiefly in the Eighteenth Century* (Cambridge 1985) 51–71, 215–310. Note also Pocock, "States, Republics, and Empires: The American

Founding in Early Modern Perspective," in *Conceptual Change and the Constitution*, ed. Terence Ball and J. G. A. Pocock (Lawrence, Kans., 1988) 55–77 (esp. 61–66). If Pocock's first contributions to this debate were misread, as he now insists, it was due to his insistence that "there was (it would almost appear) no alternative tradition in which to be schooled" other than the English republican tradition— which he took to be neoclassical. Cf. Pocock, " 'The Book Most Misunderstood since the Bible': John Adams and the Confusion about Aristocracy," in *Fra Toscana et Stati Uniti: il discorso politico nell'età della costituzione americana*, ed. Leo S. Olschki (Florence 1989) 181–201 (esp. 187–89, 196–201), with *The Machiavellian Moment* 507.

20. See Robert E. Shalhope, "Toward a Republican Synthesis: The Emergence of an Understanding of Republicanism in American Historiography," *WMQ* 29 (1972): 49–80, and "Republicanism and Early American Historiography," *WMQ* 39 (1982): 334–56. Note, however, the degree to which Pocock's former student Lance Banning has now jettisoned his former mentor's classical conception of American political virtue: "Some Second Thoughts on Virtue and the Course of Revolutionary Thinking," in *Conceptual Change and the Constitution* 194–212. See also Daniel T. Rodgers, "Republicanism: The Career of a Concept," *JAH* 78 (1992): 11–38.

21. In this connection, see Ralph Lerner, "Prologue: Recovering the Past," *The Thinking Revolutionary: Principle and Practice in the New Republic* (Ithaca 1987) 1–38, and Robert H. Webking, *The American Revolution and the Politics of Liberty* (Baton Rouge 1988) 1–15.

22. For a comprehensive, critical review of the pertinent literature that, perhaps too gently, makes the latter point, see Peter S. Onuf, "Reflections on the Founding: Constitutional Historiography in Bicentennial Perspective," *WMQ* 46 (1989): 341–75.

23. In evaluating the strengths and weaknesses of the recent historiography on the American Revolution, one must keep in mind its dependence on a highly dubious set of assumptions concerning the relationship between human thought and political reality: note Appleby, "Republicanism and Ideology" 461–73; read Bernard Bailyn, "The Central Themes of the American Revolution: An Interpretation," in *Essays on the American Revolution*, ed. Stephen G. Kurtz and James H. Hutson (Chapel Hill 1973) 3–31; Gordon S. Wood, "Intellectual History and the Social Sciences," in *New Directions in American Intellectual History*, ed. John Higham and Paul K. Conkin (Baltimore 1979) 27–41; and Wood, "Illusions and Disillusions in the American Revolution," in *The American Revolution: Its Character and Limits*, ed. Jack P. Greene (New York 1987) 355–61, in light of Clifford Geertz, "Ideology as a Cultural System," *The Interpretation of Cultures: Selected Essays* (New York 1973) 193–233; then, consider James Farr, "Conceptual Change and Constitutional Innovation," in *Conceptual Change and the Constitution* 13–34, in light of the material collected in II Prologue, note 7, above, and ponder James Madison's far more sensible discussion of the relationship between language and political reality: *The Federalist* 37.

24. In this connection, consider William E. Nelson, "Reason and Compromise in the Establishment of the Federal Constitution, 1787–1801," *WMQ* 44 (1987): 458–84.

25. Cf. Bernard Bailyn, *The Ordeal of Thomas Hutchinson* (Cambridge, Mass., 1974) vii–xii.

26. *WoM* II 1103: *Mes pensées* 399. See Montesquieu, *EL* 6.30.14.

27. Pl. *Tht.* 155c–d.

28. T. S. Eliot, *The Complete Poems and Plays, 1909–1950* (New York 1962) 145: "The Four Quartets, Little Gidding."

29. The foundations for such comparisons have been laid by Claude Nicolet, *The World of the Citizen in Republican Rome*, trans. P. S. Falla (Berkeley 1980), and by Peter Riesenberg, *Citizenship in the Western Tradition: Plato to Rousseau* (Chapel Hill 1992) 87–186.

30. See I Prologue, above.

31. *WoJSM* X 117–63 (at 133–34): "Coleridge." See also *WoJSM* VIII 922–23: *A System of Logic* [8] VI.x.5.

32. August. *De civ. D.* 19.24.

33. Molesworth, *An Account of Denmark, As It was in the Year 1692* Pref.

34. A number of works pertinent to the themes of this volume have appeared or come to my attention since the original edition of my book went to press.

See Pierre Manent, *Tocqueville et la nature de la démocratie* (Paris 1982); Jeffrey Leigh Sedgwick, "James Madison and the Problem of Executive Character," *Polity* 21 (1988): 5–23; Jack P. Greene, *Pursuits of Happiness: The Social Development of Early Modern British Colonies and the Formation of American Culture* (Chapel Hill 1988); *Inventing the American Presidency*, ed. Thomas E. Cronin (Lawrence, Kans., 1989); Harry V. Jaffa, *The American Founding as the Best Regime: The Bonding of Civil and Religious Liberty* (Montclair, Calif., 1990); Jack N. Rakove, *James Madison and the Creation of the American Republic* (Glenview, Ill., 1990); Robert W. Tucker and David C. Hendrickson, *Empire of Liberty: The Statecraft of Thomas Jefferson* (New York 1990); Steven C. Bullock, "The Revolutionary Transformation of American Freemasonry, 1752–1792," *WMQ* 47 (1990): 347–69; Benjamin B. Klobes, "The First Federal Congress and the First National Bank: A Case Study in Constitutional Interpretation," *JER* 10 (1990): 19–41; Greg Russell, "Jeffersonian Ethics in Foreign Affairs: John Quincy Adams and the Moral Sentiments of a Realist," *Interpretation* 18 (1990–91): 273–91; James M. McPherson, *Abraham Lincoln and the Second American Revolution* (Oxford 1991); Norman S. Grabo, "Crèvecoeur's America: Beginning the World Anew," *WMQ* 48 (1991): 159–72; Jean Yarbrough, "The Constitution and Character: The Missing Critical Principle?" in *To Form a More Perfect Union: The Critical Ideas of the Constitution*, ed. Herman Belz, Ronald Hoffman, and Peter J. Albert (Charlottesville 1992) 217–49; Colleen A. Sheehan, "The Politics of Public Opinion: James Madison's 'Notes on Government,'" *WMQ* 49 (1992): 609–27; John E. Crowley, "Commerce and the Philadelphia Constitution: Neo-Mercantilism in Federalist and Anti-Federalist Political Economy," *HPT* 13 (1992): 73–97; Donald F. Swanson and Andrew P. Trout, "Alexander Hamilton's Hidden Sinking Fund," *WMQ* 49 (1992): 108–16; Richard R. Beeman, "Deference, Republicanism, and the Emergence of Popular Politics in Eighteenth-Century America," *WMQ* 49 (1992): 401–30; Eugene R. Sheridan, "Thomas Jefferson and the Giles Resolutions," *WMQ* 49 (1992): 589–608; Knud Haakonssen, "From Natural Law to the Rights of Man: A European Perspective on American Debates," James H. Hutson, "The Bill of Rights and the American Revolutionary Experience," Jack N. Rakove, "Parchment Barriers and the Politics of Rights," and Charles L. Griswold, Jr., "Rights and Wrongs: Jefferson, Slavery, and Philosophical Quandaries," all in *A Culture of Rights: The Bill of Rights in Philosophy, Politics, and Law, 1791 and 1991*, ed. Michael J. Lacey and Knud Haakonssen (Cambridge 1992) 19–214; Richard C. Sinopoli, *The Foundations of American Citizenship: Liberalism, the Constitution, and Civic Virtue* (Oxford 1992); James R. Stoner, Jr., *Common Law and Liberal Theory: Coke, Hobbes, and the Origins of American Constitutionalism* (Lawrence, Kans., 1992); Gordon S. Wood, *The Radicalism of the American Revolution* (New York 1992); Richard J. Ellis, "Radical Lockeanism in American Political Culture," *WPQ* 45 (1992): 825–49; Eugene D. Genovese, *The Slaveholders' Dilemma: Freedom and Progress in Southern Conservative Thought, 1820–1860* (Columbia, S.C., 1992); Steven Deyle, "The Irony of Liberty: Origins of the Domestic Slave Trade," *JER* 12 (1992): 37–62; Chris Padgett, "Hearing the Antislavery Rank-and-File: The Wesleyan Methodist Schism of 1843," *JER* 12 (1992): 63–84; Simon P. Newman, "Principles or Men? George Washington and the Political Culture of National Leadership, 1776–1801," *JER* 12 (1992): 477–507; Marc W. Kruman, "The Second American Party System and the Transformation of Revolutionary Republicanism," *JER* 12 (1992): 509–37; Harvey Flaumenhaft, *The Effective Republic: Administration and Constitution in the Thought of Alexander Hamilton* (Durham, N.C., 1992); Roger H. Brown, *Redeeming the Republic: Federalists, Taxation, and the Origins of the Constitution* (Baltimore 1993); Richard P. McCormick, "The 'Ordinance' of 1784?" *WMQ* 50 (1993): 112–22; J. R. Pole, "Reflections on American Law and the American Revolution," *WMQ* 50 (1993): 123–59; T. H. Breen, "Narrative of Commercial Life: Consumption, Ideology, and Community on the Eve of the American Revolution," *WMQ* 50 (1993): 471–501; Stuart Leibiger, "James Madison and Amendments to the Constitution, 1787–1789: Parchment Barriers," *JSH* 59 (1993): 441–68; James L. Huston, "The American Revolutionaries, the Political Economy of Aristocracy, and the American Concept of the Distribution of Wealth, 1765–1900," *AHR* 98 (1993): 1079–1105; Gary L. McDowell, "Private Conscience and Public Order: Hobbes and *The Federalist*," *Polity* 25 (1993): 421–43; Lorraine Smith Pangle and Thomas L. Pangle, *The Learning of Liberty: The Educational Ideas of the American Founders* (Lawrence, Kans., 1993); Jay Fliegelman, *Declaring Independence: Jefferson, Natural Language, and the Culture of Performance* (Stanford 1993); Ralph Ketcham, *Framed for Posterity: The Enduring Philosophy of the Constitution* (Lawrence, Kans., 1993); Glenn A. Phelps, *George Washington and American Constitutionalism* (Lawrence, Kans., 1993); Samuel H. Beer, *To Make a Nation: The Rediscovery of American Federalism* (Cambridge, Mass., 1993); Peter Augustine Lawler, *The Restless Mind: Alexis de Tocqueville on the Origin and Perpetuation of Human Liberty* (Lanham, Md., 1993); *Jeffersonian Legacies*, ed. Peter S. Onuf (Charlottesville 1993); Stanley M. Elkins and Eric L. McKitrick, *The Age of Federalism* (New York 1993); Forrest McDonald, *The American Presidency: An Intellectual History* (Lawrence, Kans., 1993); and J. C. D. Clark, *The Language of Liberty, 1660–1832: Political Discourse and Social Dynamics in the Anglo-American World* (Cambridge 1994). The essays of Joyce Appleby cited above and below are now more conveniently available in Appleby, *Liberalism and Republicanism in the Historical Imagination* (Cambridge, Mass., 1992); those of Gerald Stourzh can now be found in Stourzh, *Wege zur Grundrechtsdemokratie: Studien zur Begriffs- und Institutionengeschichte des liberalen Verfassungsstaates* (Vienna 1989). Cf. Gary Wills, *Lincoln at Gettysburg: The Words That Remade America* (New York 1992), with Paul A. Rahe, "Dishonest Abe?" *Reviews in American History* 21 (1993): 218–24.

In discussing the present discontents and the breakdown of both federalism and the separation of powers (III Epilogue), I was arguably too easy on Congress: note Gary C. Jacobson, *The Electoral Origins of Divided Government: Competition in*

U.S. House Elections, 1946–1988 (Boulder, Colo., 1990); then, see John A. Marini, "Money in Politics: Campaign Finance Reform and the 1984 Election," in *The 1984 Election and the Future of American Politics*, ed. Peter W. Schramm and Dennis J. Mahoney (Durham, N.C., 1987) 183–209, and *The Politics of Budget Control: Congress, the Presidency, and the Growth of the Administrative State* (Washington, D.C., 1992); and consider R. Shep Melnick, *Between the Lines: Interpreting Welfare Rights* (Washington, D.C., 1994). See also R. Shep Melnick, *Regulation and the Courts: The Case of the Clean Air Act* (Washington, D.C., 1983); Robert S. Gilmour and Harold Seidman, *Politics, Position, and Power: From the Positive to the Regulatory State*[4] (New York 1986); Brooks Jackson, *Honest Graft: Big Money and the American Political Process* (New York 1988); John A. Rohr, "The Legitimacy of the Administrative State," John A. Marini, "Bureaucracy and Constitutionalism," and Sidney M. Milkis, "The Bureaucracy, the Constitution, and the Crisis of Republican Government," all in *Constitutionalism in Perspective: The United States Constitution in Twentieth Century Politics*, ed. Sarah Baumgartner Thurow (Lanham, Md., 1988) 95–151; Christopher H. Foreman, Jr., *Signals from the Hill: Congressional Oversight and the Challenge of Social Regulation* (New Haven 1988); *The Imperial Congress: Crisis in the Separation of Powers*, ed. Gordon S. Jones and John A. Marini (New York 1988); Richard A. Harris and Sidney M. Milkis, *The Politics of Regulatory Change: A Tale of Two Agencies* (New York 1989); Sidney M. Milkis, "The Presidency, Policy Reform, and the Rise of Administrative Politics," R. Shep Melnick, "The Courts, Congress, and Programmatic Rights," and Richard A. Harris, "Politicized Management: The Changing Face of Business in American Politics," in *Remaking American Politics*, ed. Richard A. Harris and Sidney M. Milkis (Boulder, Colo., 1989) 146–212, 261–86; *The Fettered Presidency: Legal Constraints on the Executive Branch*, ed. L. Gordon Crovitz and Jeremy A. Rabkin (Washington, D.C., 1989); Morris P. Fiorina, *Congress: Keystone of the Washington Establishment*[2] (New Haven 1989), and *Divided Government* (New York 1992); Edward J. Erler, "The Separation of Powers in the Administrative State" and "Equal Protection and Personal Rights: The Regime of the 'Discrete and Insular Minority,'" *The American Polity: Essays on the Theory and Practice of Constitutional Government* (New York 1991) 59–122; and John L. Jackley, *Hill Rat: Blowing the Lid Off Congress* (Washington, D.C., 1992).

Prologue

1. Hutcheson, *SMP* III.viii.12.

2. Cf. *JHO* 19–20 with *WoJH* 465: *A System of Politics*, where Harrington claims that "provincial government is an effect of unnatural force, or violence."

3. *Cato's Letters* IV 3–12: no. 106, 8 December 1722.

4. For an overview, laying great stress on the tensions and strains generated by the colonies' rapid development, see James A. Henretta, *The Evolution of American Society, 1700–1815: An Interdisciplinary Analysis* (Lexington, Mass., 1973) 1–156.

5. See Marc Egnal, *A Mighty Empire: The Origins of the American Revolution* (Ithaca 1988).

6. See J. R. Pole, *Political Representation in England and the Origins of the American Republic* (Berkeley 1971). Note Jack P. Greene, *The Quest for Power: The Lower Houses of Assembly in the Southern Royal Colonies, 1689–1776* (Chapel Hill 1963). In

this connection, see Charles M. Andrews, *The Colonial Background of the American Revolution* (New Haven 1924). The picture drawn by the patriot historians of the revolutionary period may be exaggerated for didactic effect: see Lester H. Cohen, "Creating a Usable Future: The Revolutionary Historians and the National Past," in *The American Revolution: Its Character and Limits,* ed. Jack P. Greene (New York 1987) 309–30. But it remains instructive nonetheless. David Ramsay's *History of the American Revolution* was, in fact, remarkably balanced and sober: see Eve Kornfeld, "From Republicanism to Liberalism: The Intellectual Journey of David Ramsay," *JER* 9 (1989): 289–313 (at 293–98).

7. See Louis Hartz, *The Liberal Tradition in America: An Interpretation of American Political Thought since the Revolution* (New York 1955), and Bernard Bailyn, "Political Experience and Enlightenment Ideas in Eighteenth-Century America," *AHR* 67 (1961–62): 339–51.

8. In the course of the Revolution, many Americans jettisoned their residual attachment to the familial model of politics and embraced the species of sturdy individualism championed by Locke and Sidney and taken up by the radical Whigs: consider Melvin Yazawa, *From Colonies to Commonwealth: Familial Ideology and the Beginnings of the American Republic* (Baltimore 1985), with an eye to II.v.12, vi.6–Epilogue, above.

9. Consider *WoFB* VI 457–59: "Of Plantations," *Essays or Counsels Civil and Moral* 33, in light of the emphasis that Bacon places on naval empire and mercantile wealth. Read *WoFB* VI 419–23, 444–52 (esp. 450–52), VII 47–64 (esp. 54–64): "Of Empire" and "Of the True Greatness of Kingdoms and Estates," *Essays or Counsels Civil and Moral* 19 and 29, and "Of the True Greatness of the Kingdom of Britain," in conjunction with Howard B. White, *Peace among the Willows: The Political Philosophy of Francis Bacon* (The Hague 1968) 29–92.

10. For the importance of demographic growth, see Joyce Appleby, "Liberalism and the American Revolution," *NEQ* 49 (1976): 3–26.

11. See Marc Egnal, "The Economic Development of the Thirteen Continental Colonies, 1720 to 1775," *WMQ* 32 (1975): 191–222, and consider James F. Shepherd, "British America and the Atlantic Economy"; James A. Henretta, "The War for Independence and American Economic Development"; Winifred B. Rothenberg, "The Emergence of a Capital Market in Rural Massachusetts, 1730–1838"; Thomas M. Doerflinger, "Farmers and Dry Goods in the Philadelphia Market Area, 1750–1800"; Joseph A. Ernst, "The Political Economy of the Chesapeake Colonies, 1760–1775: A Study in Comparative History"; Russell R. Menard, "Slavery, Economic Growth, and Revolutionary Ideology in the South Carolina Lowcountry"; and Jacob M. Price, "Reflections on the Economy of Revolutionary America," all in *The Economy of Early America: The Revolutionary Period, 1763–1790,* ed. Ronald Hoffman, John J. McCusker, Russell R. Menard, and Peter J. Albert (Charlottesville 1988) 3–87, 126–274, 303–22, in conjunction with the literature cited in Gary M. Walton's review: *WMQ* 46 (1989): 406–9. Note also Carville Earle and Ronald Hoffman, "Staple Crops and Urban Development in the Eighteenth-Century South," *PAmH* 10 (1976): 7–78, and James G. Lydon, "Philadelphia's Commercial Expansion, 1720–1739," *PMHB* 91 (1967): 401–18.

12. On this point, see Joyce Appleby, "The Social Origins of American Revolutionary Ideology," *JAH* 64 (1977–78): 935–58. Here, and elsewhere, Appleby goes astray where her argument depends upon Kramnick's and Pocock's char-

acterization of the English opposition. Note also Gary B. Nash, *The Urban Cru-cible: Social Change, Political Consciousness, and the Origins of the American Revolution* (Cambridge, Mass., 1979).

13. Of course, reactions varied: see William L. Sachse, *The Colonial American in Britain* (Madison, Wis., 1956). For a particularly striking example, see "A Penn-sylvania Farmer at the Court of King George: John Dickinson's London Letters, 1754–56," ed. H. Trevor Colbourn, *PMHB* 86 (1962): 241–86, 417–53.

14. *WrEB* II 120–23: Speech on Moving Resolutions for Conciliation with the Colonies, 22 March 1775. Consider, in this light, *WoJA* III 447–64: *A Dissertation on the Canon and Feudal Law* (1765).

15. *WrEB* II 123–24: Speech on Moving Resolutions for Conciliation with the Colonies, 22 March 1775. Burke fails to remark on one peculiarity: the fact that, when the colonists in Virginia and elsewhere embraced the Lockean argument as a defense of their own rights, they knowingly damned the institution of slavery as well. Edmund Morgan's recent attempt to explain the Virginians' fierce com-mitment to political liberty solely with an eye to the peculiar institution nicely exhibits the inadequacy of narrowly socioeconomic analysis, for he never even attempts to explain why the slaveholders of that colony should defend freedom in a fashion so dangerous to the economic foundations of their own well-being: cf. *American Slavery, American Freedom: The Ordeal of Colonial Virginia* (New York 1975) esp. 293–387.

16. For a depiction of gentry dominion in one critical colony, see Rhys Isaac, *The Transformation of Virginia, 1740–1790* (Chapel Hill 1982) esp. 58–295. Not until 1775 (if, in fact, then) did an American preacher make a systematic effort to justify divine right in the familiar Anglican terms, and then he found it impossible to get his sermon published in America: consider Jonathan Boucher, "On Civil Liberty; Passive Obedience, and Non-Resistance," *A View of the Causes and Consequences of the American Revolution; in Thirteen Discourses, Preached in North America between the Years 1763 and 1775: With an Historical Preface* (London 1797) 495–560, in light of Anne Young Zimmer and Alfred H. Kelly, "Jonathan Boucher: Constitutional Conservative," *JAH* 58 (1972): 897–922.

17. Hume, *EMPL* 73–79: "Of Superstition and Enthusiasm."

18. In this connection, consider Wilson Carey McWilliams, "The Bible in the American Political Tradition," in *Religion and Politics*, ed. Myron J. Aronoff (New Brunswick, N.J., 1984) 11–45 (esp. 21–26), in light of II Prologue, note 46, and Epilogue, note 21, above.

19. With regard to the carryover, cf. Alan Heimert, *Religion and the American Mind: From the Great Awakening to the Revolution* (Cambridge, Mass., 1966), which should be read in light of Harry S. Stout, "Religion, Communications, and the Ideological Origins of the American Revolution," *WMQ* 34 (1977): 519–41, with Ernest Lee Tuveson, *Redeemer Nation: The Idea of America's Millennial Role* (Chicago 1968), and Nathan O. Hatch, "The Origins of Civil Millennialism in America: New England Clergymen, War with France, and the Revolution," *WMQ* 31 (1974): 407–30, and *The Sacred Cause of Liberty: Republican Thought and the Millennium in Revolutionary New England* (New Haven 1977); then, see Melvin B. Endy, Jr., "Just War, Holy War, and Millennialism in Revolutionary America," *WMQ* 42 (1985): 3–25, and Patricia U. Bonomi, *Under the Cope of Heaven: Religion, Society, and Politics in Colonial America* (New York 1986). Note also Bernard Bailyn, "Reli-gion and Revolution: Three Biographical Studies," *PAmH* 4 (1970): 83–169. Bacon,

Boyle, and Locke would have found the overall results gratifying: see Edmund S. Morgan, "The Puritan Ethic and the American Revolution," *WMQ* 24 (1967): 3–43, and J. E. Crowley, *This Sheba, Self: The Conceptualization of Economic Life in Eighteenth-Century America* (Baltimore 1974). For an early and highly influential tract that throws considerable light on the political consequences of the trends alluded to in the text, see *PAR* I 203–47: Jonathan Mayhew, *A Discourse Concerning Unlimited Submission and Non-Resistance to the Higher Powers . . .* (1750). As his contemporary critics (*PAR* 208–9, 697–98) did not hesitate to point out, Mayhew had lifted a great deal from Benjamin Hoadly, from *Cato's Letters*, and from other similar sources. At the time of the Stamp Act crisis, he singled out "Sidney and Milton, Locke and Hoadly" as the great modern teachers of liberty: *PAR* 209. For a recent discussion of the long-term impact of the Great Awakening in one colony, see Isaac, *The Transformation of Virginia* 161–322.

20. Consider *WrEB* II 124–27: Speech on Moving Resolutions for Conciliation with the Colonies, 22 March 1775, in light of Gerald Stourzh, "William Blackstone: Teacher of Revolution," *Jahrbuch für Amerikastudien* 15 (1970): 184–200.

21. *DHRC* II 471–72: 4 December 1787.

22. If anything, Wilson understated that debt: in juxtaposing Blackstone and Locke, he underestimated what was owed the latter by the former, and he therefore failed to point out the revolutionary implications that Burke had quite rightly discerned beneath the conservative surface of Blackstone's argument. See *WoJW* I 76–82: Of the Study of the Law in the United States (1790).

23. Steven M. Dworetz is admirably alert to the influence of "the theistic Locke"—in part, no doubt, because he shares in the inclination of many a pious American colonist to overlook the manner in which that philosopher subverts his own repeated assertions that reason and revelation are compatible: cf. *The Unvarnished Doctrine: Locke, Liberalism, and the American Revolution* (Durham, N.C., 1990) 3–183 with II.ii.1–6, vi–vii, above, and see Alice M. Baldwin, *The New England Clergy and the American Revolution* (Durham, N.C., 1928), and Bonomi, *Under the Cope of Heaven* 189–216. For additional evidence suggesting Locke's intellectual hegemony, see David Lundberg and Henry F. May, "The Enlightened Reader in America," *AQ* 28 (1976): 262–93, and Donald S. Lutz, "The Relative Influence of European Writers on Late Eighteenth-Century American Political Thought," *APSR* 78 (1984): 189–97; and then, consult Jay Fliegelman, *Prodigals and Pilgrims: The American Revolution against Patriarchal Authority, 1750–1800* (Cambridge 1982), and Thomas L. Pangle, *The Spirit of Modern Republicanism: The Moral Vision of the American Founders and the Philosophy of Locke* (Chicago 1988) 7–127 (esp. 124–27). Cf. John Dunn, "The Politics of Locke in England and America in the Eighteenth Century," in *John Locke: Problems and Perspectives: A Collection of New Essays*, ed. John W. Yolton (Cambridge 1969) 45–80 (esp. 56–69), and Oscar Handlin, "Learned Books and Revolutionary Action, 1776," *Harvard Library Bulletin* 34 (1986): 362–79.

24. See Caroline Robbins, "Algernon Sidney's *Discourses Concerning Government*: Textbook of Revolution," *Absolute Liberty: A Selection from the Articles and Papers of Caroline Robbins*, ed. Barbara Taft (Hamden, Conn., 1982) 267–91, and Alan Craig Houston, *Algernon Sidney and the Republican Heritage in England and in America* (Princeton 1992).

25. One should adjust the argument of Bernard Bailyn, *The Ideological Origins of the American Revolution* (Cambridge, Mass., 1967) 22–159, *The Origins of Ameri-*

can Politics (New York 1968), and *Faces of Revolution: Personalities and Themes in the Struggle for American Independence* (New York 1990), in light of the understanding of the Whig canon which I have sketched in II.iv–vii, above. For some of the various elements that make up this picture, see Oscar and Mary Handlin, "James Burgh and American Revolutionary Theory," *PMHS*[2] 73 (1961): 38–57, and Isaac Kramnick, "James Burgh and 'Opposition' Ideology in England and America," in *Republicanism and Bourgeois Radicalism: Political Ideology in Late Eighteenth-Century England and America* (Ithaca 1990) 200–259; H. Trevor Colbourn, *The Lamp of Experience: Whig History and the Intellectual Origins of the American Revolution* (Chapel Hill 1965); David L. Jacobson, *The English Libertarian Heritage* (New York 1965) xvii–xix, xlviii–lxiv, and "Thomas Gordon's Works of Tacitus in Pre-Revolutionary America," *Bulletin of the New York Public Library* 69 (1965): 58–64; Pauline Maier, "John Wilkes and American Disillusionment with Britain," *WMQ* 20 (1963): 373–95; and Endy, "Just War, Holy War, and Millennialism in Revolutionary America" 3–25—along with the material cited above in notes 20, 23, and 24, and at the end of II Epilogue, note 21. See also Henry F. May, *The Enlightenment in America* (New York 1976). One can also profitably consult Forrest McDonald, "A Founding Father's Library," *Literature of Liberty* 1 (January–March 1978) 4–15.

26. The letter that John Dickinson addressed to William Pitt on 21 December 1765 sounds many of the themes touched on by Trenchard and Gordon: see *Prologue to Revolution: Sources and Documents on the Stamp Act Crisis, 1764–1766*, ed. Edmund S. Morgan (New York 1973) 118–22.

27. See Robert W. Tucker and David C. Hendrickson, *The Fall of the First British Empire: Origins of the War of American Independence* (Baltimore 1982). See also P. D. G. Thomas, *British Politics and the Stamp Act Crisis: The First Phase of the American Revolution, 1763–1767* (Oxford 1975) 1–153.

28. See Edmund S. and Helen M. Morgan, *The Stamp Act Crisis: Prologue to Revolution*[2] (New York 1962).

29. "Two Neglected Madison Letters," ed. Irving Brant, *WMQ* 3 (1946): 569–87 (at 571–72): The North American No. 1, *Pennsylvania Journal*, 17 September 1783. For his probable identity, see II.i.2, note 35, above.

30. *WrEB* II 120–21: Speech on Moving Resolutions for Conciliation with the Colonies, 22 March 1775.

31. For the speech delivered by Pitt on 14 January 1766; for The Act Repealing the Stamp Act, 18 March 1766; and for The Declaratory Act, 18 March 1766, see *Prologue to Revolution* 134–41, 155–56. In this connection, see P. D. G. Thomas, *British Politics and the Stamp Act Crisis* 154–282.

32. Note Gordon S. Wood, "Rhetoric and Reality in the American Revolution," *WMQ* 23 (1966): 3–32, and see Edwin G. Burrows and Michael Wallace, "The American Revolution: The Ideology and Psychology of National Liberation," *PAmH* 6 (1972): 167–306, and Winthrop D. Jordan, "Familial Politics: Thomas Paine and the Killing of the King, 1776," *JAH* 60 (1973): 294–308.

33. See Gordon S. Wood, "Conspiracy and the Paranoid Style: Causality and Deceit in the Eighteenth Century," *WMQ* 39 (1982): 401–41.

34. See Hiram Caton, *The Politics of Progress: The Origins and Development of the Commercial Republic, 1600–1835* (Gainesville, Fla., 1988) 381–95. Cf., however, John C. Miller, *Sam Adams: Pioneer in Propaganda* (Stanford 1936), with Pauline Maier, *The Old Revolutionaries: Political Lives in the Age of Samuel Adams* (New York 1980) 3–50.

35. On this point, despite his triumphantly Whiggish tone, Claude H. Van Tyne has much of value to say: *The Causes of the War of Independence* (Boston 1922). For a more recent and no less appreciative assessment of the arguments which the advocates of resistance advanced, see Robert H. Webking, *The American Revolution and the Politics of Liberty* (Baton Rouge 1988).

36. Consider *WrEB* II 72–73: Speech on American Taxation, 19 April 1774, in light of John Phillip Reid, *Constitutional History of the American Revolution: The Authority to Tax* (Madison, Wis., 1987).

37. See P. D. G. Thomas, *British Politics and the Stamp Act Crisis* 283–371, and *The Townshend Duties Crisis: The Second Phase of the American Revolution, 1767– 1773* (Oxford 1987); and then, consider David Ammerman, *In the Common Cause: American Response to the Coercive Acts of 1774* (Charlottesville 1974). For the deci- sive effect of British policy in one small, rural community fraught with social and psychological strains, see Robert A. Gross, *The Minutemen and Their World* (New York 1976).

38. See, for example, *PAR* 598–658: Daniel Dulany, *Considerations on the Propri- ety of Imposing Taxes in the British Colonies, For the Purpose of Raising a Revenue, by Act of Parliament* (1765).

39. See, for example, *PAR* 408–82: James Otis, *The Rights of the British Colonies Asserted and Proved* (1764), and *TAR* 108–26: Richard Bland, *An Inquiry into the Rights of the British Colonies* (1766).

40. See Pauline Maier, *From Resistance to Revolution: Colonial Radicals and the De- velopment of American Opposition to Britain, 1765–1776* (London 1973), and Ammer- man, *In the Common Cause.* Note Gross, *The Minutemen and Their World,* and see *Resistance, Politics, and the American Struggle for Independence, 1765–1775,* ed. Walter H. Conser, Jr., Ronald M. McCarthy, David J. Toscano, and Gene Sharp (Boulder, Colo., 1986).

41. See Thad W. Tate, "The Social Contract in America, 1774–1787: Revolution- ary Theory as a Conservative Instrument," *WMQ* 22 (1965): 375–91, and Webking, *The American Revolution and the Politics of Liberty.*

42. *PAH* I 47, 86–88, 122: *A Full Vindication of the Measures of the Congress, &c.,* 15 December 1774, and *The Farmer Refuted, &c.,* 23 February 1775.

43. Years later, in looking back, Jefferson would celebrate the fact that his com- patriots had "had no occasion to search into musty records, to hunt up royal parchments, or to investigate the laws and institutions of a semi-barbarous an- cestry. We appealed to those of nature, and found them engraved on our hearts." See *MCPP* IV 403–8 (at 404): Letter to Major John Cartwright on 5 June 1824.

44. See Mary Beth Norton, "The Loyalist Critique of the Revolution," in *The De- velopment of a Revolutionary Mentality* (Washington, D.C., 1972) 127–48, and Janice Potter, *The Liberty We Seek: Loyalist Ideology in Colonial New York and Massachusetts* (Cambridge, Mass., 1983). Note also Robert McCluer Calhoon, *The Loyalists in Revolutionary America, 1760–1781* (New York 1973) esp. 105–19.

45. Thomas Hutchinson, "A Dialogue between an American and a European Englishman," ed. Bernard Bailyn, *PAmH* 9 (1975): 341–410 (esp. 390–406). In this connection, see Bailyn, *The Ordeal of Thomas Hutchinson* (Cambridge, Mass., 1974).

46. Consider *TAR* 350–99 (esp. 354, 356, 362, 364, 368): Joseph Galloway, *A Candid Examination of the Mutual Claims of Great Britain and the Colonies* (February 1775), in light of Dworetz, *The Unvarnished Doctrine* 46–50.

47. Cf. *TAR* 278–86 (at 283): Massachusettensis, 19 December 1774, with *TAR*

296–304 (at 299–303): Novanglus, 23 January 1775, and see II.vi.7, above. Note *WrJD* 386–97 (esp. 389–90): *Letters from a Farmer in Pennsylvania* (1768).

48. Consider *PTJ* I 413–32 (esp. 423–32): The Declaration of Independence, 11 June to 4 July 1776, in light of Carl Becker, *The Declaration of Independence: A Study in the History of Political Ideas* (New York 1922), and Harvey C. Mansfield, Jr., "The Right of Revolution," *The Spirit of Liberalism* (Cambridge, Mass., 1978) 72–88. Cf. Garry Wills, *Inventing America: Jefferson's Declaration of Independence* (Garden City 1978), with Ronald Hamowy, "Jefferson and the Scottish Enlightenment: A Critique of Garry Wills's *Inventing America: Jefferson's Declaration of Independence*," *WMQ* 36 (1979): 503–23, and see Harry V. Jaffa, "Inventing the Past: Garry Wills's *Inventing America* and the Pathology of Ideological Scholarship," *American Conservatism and the American Founding* (Durham, N.C., 1984) 76–109.

49. See Mary Beth Norton, "The Loyalist Critique of the Revolution" 135–44, and Potter, *The Liberty We Seek* 107–80.

50. See Henry C. Van Schaack, *The Life of Peter Van Schaack, LL.D.* (New York 1842) 16–392 (esp. the manuscript material cited at 54–58, 257–63). Cf. Dunn, "The Politics of Locke in England and America in the Eighteenth Century" 77, and Handlin, "Learned Books and Revolutionary Action, 1776" 371, with Dworetz, *The Unvarnished Doctrine* 21, 28–29.

51. *PAR* 425–26: James Otis, *The Rights of the British Colonies Asserted and Proved* (1764).

52. *WrSA* I 190–91: Letter from the House of Representatives of Massachusetts to Henry Seymour Conway on 13 February 1768.

53. *PAH* I 88: *The Farmer Refuted, &c.*, 23 February 1775.

54. *FSC* VII 3813 (Virginia, 1776). For the various drafts this article went through, see *PGM* I 274–91 (esp. 277, 283, 287): The Virginia Declaration of Rights, 20 May–12 June 1776.

55. *FSC* III 1889 (Massachusetts, 1780).

56. *FSC* V 3082–83, 3099 (Pennsylvania, 1776, 1790), VI 3739–41, 3751–53, 3762–63 (Vermont, 1777, 1786, 1791), IV 2453–54, 2457, 2471–72, 2474–75 (New Hampshire, 1784, 1792).

57. *FSC* III 1688 (Maryland, 1776), V 2788 (North Carolina, 1776), VI 3264 (South Carolina, 1790).

58. *PTJ* I 429: Declaration of Independence, 4 July 1776.

59. In this connection, see Gerald Stourzh, "Fundamental Laws and Individual Rights in the 18th Century Constitution," in *The American Founding: Essays on the Formation of the Constitution*, ed. J. Jackson Barlow, Leonard W. Levy, and Ken Masugi (New York 1988) 159–94. Note Stourzh, *Vom Widerstandsrecht zur Verfassungsgerichtsbarkeit: Das Problem der Verfassungswidrigkeit im 18. Jahrhundert* (Graz 1974), and "*Constitution:* Changing Meanings of the Term from the Early Seventeenth to the Late Eighteenth Century," in *Conceptual Change and the Constitution*, ed. Terence Ball and J. G. A. Pocock (Lawrence, Kans., 1988) 35–54; consider John Phillip Reid, *Constitutional History of the American Revolution: The Authority of Rights* (Madison, Wis., 1986); and see Harvey C. Mansfield, Jr., "The Forms of Liberty," in *Democratic Capitalism? Essays in Search of a Concept*, ed. Fred E. Baumann (Charlottesville 1986) 1–21.

60. Cf. Richard K. Matthews, *The Radical Politics of Thomas Jefferson: A Revisionist View* (Lawrence, Kans., 1984), with Jean Yarbrough, "Jefferson and Property

Rights," in *Liberty, Property, and the Foundations of the American Constitution*, ed. Ellen Frankel Paul and Howard Dickman (Albany, N.Y., 1989) 65–83.

61. *PTJ* II 492–507 (at 492): The Revisal of the Laws, 18 June 1779: 64. A Bill for Proportioning Crimes and Punishments in Cases Heretofore Capital.

62. Consider *RFC* I 147, 302, 402–3, 421–23, 428, 440, 469–70, 533–34, 541–42, II 201–8: 6, 18, 25–27, 29 June, 5–6 July, and 7 August 1787, in light of Bernard H. Siegan, "One People as to Commercial Objects," in *Liberty, Property, and the Foundations of the American Constitution* 101–19, and see Marc F. Plattner, "American Democracy and the Acquisitive Spirit," in *How Capitalistic Is the Constitution?* ed. Robert A. Goldwin and William A. Schambra (Washington, D.C., 1982) 1–21.

63. See Edward J. Erler, "The Great Fence to Liberty: The Right to Property in the American Founding," in *Liberty, Property, and the Foundations of the American Constitution* 43–63.

64. Cf. Jeffrey Barnouw, "The Pursuit of Happiness in Jefferson and Its Background in Bacon and Hobbes," *Interpretation* 11 (1983): 225–48, with II.i–vii (esp. ii.1–6, vi–vii), above: Barnouw errs solely in drawing an untenable distinction between Bacon and Hobbes, on the one hand, and Locke, on the other.

65. *CMPP* I 378–82 (at 382): Thomas Jefferson, Second Inaugural Address, 4 March 1805.

66. *WrTJ* (ed. Lipscomb and Bergh) XIV 456–66 (at 466): Letter to Joseph Milligan on 8 April 1816.

67. *WoTJ* XI 519–525 (at 522–23): Letter to Pierre Samuel du Pont de Nemours on 24 April 1816.

68. Cf. *PTJ* VIII 681–83: Letter to James Madison on 28 October 1785 with *PJM* XIV 197–98: "Parties," For the *National Gazette*, ca. 23 January 1792; note *WrTJ* (ed. Lipscomb and Bergh) XIV 466: Letter to Joseph Milligan on 8 April 1816; and see *WoTJ* XI 196–204 (esp. 203): Letter to Pierre Samuel du Pont de Nemours on 15 April 1811, and *AJL* II 387–92 (at 389): Letter to John Adams on 28 October 1813. Note, in this connection, Montesquieu, *EL* 1.5.6, 8 (287), 2.13.7–8, 14, and Smith *WN* V.ii.b.

69. *PTJ* XI 251: Letter to Martha Jefferson on 28 March 1787.

70. Madison, *The Federalist* 10 (58). Note Madison's later insistence that "the rights of persons, and the rights of property . . . cannot well be separated" and the explanation he gives. See *WrJM* IX 358–64 (at 360–61): Speech in the Virginia Constitutional Convention, 2 December 1829

71. Consider *RFC* I 605: 13 July 1787 in context, and note Wilson's subsequent insistence that property is "not an end, but a means." See *WoJW* I 84: Of the Study of the Law in the United States (1790). Note also *WoJW* II 723, 730–31: *Considerations on the Nature and Extent of the Legislative Authority of the British Parliament* (1774). Cf. Forrest McDonald, *Novus Ordo Seclorum: The Intellectual Origins of the Constitution* (Lawrence, Kans., 1985) 2–4, with Pangle, *The Spirit of Modern Republicanism* 74–76.

72. Cf. *PJM* XII 196–211 (esp. 200, 203–4): Amendments to the Constitution, 8 June 1789, with *DSSC* I 334, III 657, IV 243: Ratification by Rhode Island, 29 May 1790; Virginia Ratifying Convention, 27 June 1788; and North Carolina Ratifying Convention, 1 August 1788. Note also *PJM* XII 194: Notes for a Speech in Congress, 8 June 1789. The amendment proposed by the three states reads as follows: "There are certain natural rights of which men, when they form a social compact,

cannot deprive or divest their posterity; among which are the enjoyment of life and liberty, with the means of acquiring, possessing, and protecting property, and pursuing and obtaining happiness and safety."

73. *CMPP* I 323: Thomas Jefferson, "First Inaugural Address," 4 March 1801.

74. *PAH* X 254–56: *Report on the Subject of Manufactures*, 5 December 1791.

75. *Boswell's Life of Johnson*, ed. George Birkbeck Hill (Oxford 1887) III 245: 7 April 1778. See the second of this prologue's epigraphs: Karl Marx, *Das Kapital: Kritik der politischen Ökonomie* (Frankfurt 1969–71) I 150, 289 n. 13.

76. Cf. II.i.5, 7 and iii.3, 7 with iv.9, and see vii.6–9, above.

77. If the public-spirited rhetoric of 1776 quickly gave way to a tacit acknowledgment of the primacy of the private sphere, it was because American public-spiritedness had been rooted in private interest from the start. Consider Jack P. Greene, "Introduction: The Limits of the American Revolution," in *The American Revolution* 1–13, in light of II.iii.5 (esp. note 78), above.

78. See Willi Paul Adams, " 'The Spirit of Commerce Requires that Property Be Sacred': Gouverneur Morris and the American Revolution," *Amerikastudien/American Studies* 21 (1976): 309–34 (at 327–33): Gouverneur Morris, "Political Enquiries," 1776.

79. *PGM* I 147–61 (at 159): Last Will and Testament, 20 March 1773.

80. *PTJ* VI 184–87 (esp. 185–86): Letter to James Monroe on 20 May 1782.

81. *PJM* XV 26–28 (at 26): Letter from Thomas Jefferson on 9 June 1793.

82. *Adams Family Correspondence*, ed. L. H. Butterfield (Cambridge, Mass., 1963–   ) IV 341–42: Letter from John to Abigail Adams shortly after 12 May 1780.

83. Where others touched on the subject, they did so only in passing, and they staked out a position hostile to ancient Greek practice and indistinguishable from that of Wilson. For an explicit attack on the remarks which Pericles made concerning women in his funeral oration (Thuc. 2.45.2), see *WrTP* II 34–38: "An Occasional Letter on the Female Sex." Consider also *Adams Family Correspondence* I 369–71, 381–83: Exchange of Letters between Abigail and John Adams on 31 March and 14 April 1776; *WoJA* IX 375–78 (at 376): Letter to James Sullivan on 26 May 1776; and *PTJ* XI 122–24, 391–93, 415, XIII 27–28: Exchange of Letters with Anne Willing Bingham on 7 February and 1 June 1787; "Notes of a Tour into the Southern Parts of France," 3 March 1787; and "Notes of a Tour through Holland and the Rhine Valley," 19 April 1788.

84. Consider *WoJW* I 69–96 (at 85–89): Of the Study of the Law in the United States (1790) in light of Joel Schwartz, *The Sexual Politics of Jean-Jacques Rousseau* (Chicago 1984); note Montesquieu, *EL* 5.26.8; and see *WoJW* II 721–46: *Considerations on the Nature and Extent of the Legislative Authority of the British Parliament* (1774). The case made by Wilson for an exclusion of women from the public realm was in no way peculiar, and though doomed, like Rousseau's vision of the family, it continued to hold sway for a great many years: after reviewing the material collected in note 83, above, consider Linda K. Kerber, *Women of the Republic: Intellect and Ideology in Revolutionary America* (Chapel Hill 1980), in light of Jan Lewis, "The Republican Wife: Virtue and Seduction in the Early Republic," *WMQ* 44 (1987): 689–721, and Elaine F. Crane, "Dependence in the Era of Independence: The Role of Women in a Republican Society," in *The American Revolution* 253–75; and see Rowland Berthoff, "Conventional Mentality: Free Blacks, Women, and Business Corporations as Unequal Persons, 1820–1870," *JAH* 76 (1989): 753–84.

85. Cf. *RFC* II 53: 19 July 1787 and Hamilton, *The Federalist* 72 (488), with Tac.

Hist. 4.6 (which should be read in light of *Ann.* 13.49, 14.12, 48–49, 15.20–23, 16.21–35, *Hist.* 2.91, 4.4–8, 42–43, 53, *Dial.* 5, *Agr.* 2, 42, 45; Juv. 5.33–37; Mart. 1.8; and Sen. *Ep.* 113.32), and then see Hume, *THN* II.i.11; cf. II.i.3–4 with I.i.4, above; consider Gerald Stourzh, *Alexander Hamilton and the Idea of Republican Government* (Stanford 1970) 95–106; and note III.iv.7, below.

86. *WrTP* I 4: *Common Sense* (January 1776).

87. Cf. I.i.3, ii.2–3, 6–iii.5, above, with *WoJA* V 454–60: *A Defence of the Constitutions of Government of the United States of America* (1787–88).

88. *WoJA* IV 526: *A Defence of the Constitutions of Government of the United States of America* (1787–88).

89. For much of what follows, see Douglass Adair, "Fame and the Founding Fathers," *Fame and the Founding Fathers*, ed. Trevor Colbourn (New York 1974) 3–26.

90. *WoJA* IV 200: *Thoughts on Government* (1776).

91. David Ramsay, *The History of the American Revolution* (London 1793) II 315–16. See the articles cited in III.ii.4, note 37, below.

92. Philip Freneau, *Poems of Freneau*, ed. Harry Hayden Clark (New York 1929) 13: "The Rising Glory of America," 1771.

93. *AJL* I 194–96 (at 196): Letter to John Adams on 30 August 1787.

94. *PAH* I 580–81: Publius Letter, III, 16 November 1778.

95. See "Two Neglected Madison Letters" 572: The North American No. 1, *Pennsylvania Journal*, 17 September 1783, with II.i.2, note 35, above.

96. Consider *WoJW* I 69–71: Of the Study of the Law in the United States (1790) in light of Israel Evans, *A Sermon, Delivered at Concord, Before the Hon. General Court of the State of New Hampshire, at the Annual Election, Holden on the First Wednesday in June, M. DCC. XCI* (Concord, N.H., 1791) 31–32, and DeWitt Clinton, *An Address Delivered Before Holland Lodge, December 24, 1793* (New York 1794) 8. Wilson was similarly critical of the quasi-patriarchal principles inherent in classical political thought: cf. the material cited in II.vii.2, above, with *WoJW* I 97–125 (esp. 105–9), II 585–610: Lectures on Law (1790–91).

97. Madison, *The Federalist* 38 (239–41).

98. *WoAL* I 108–15 (at 113): Address Before the Young Men's Lyceum of Springfield, Illinois, 27 January 1838.

99. Consider *TAR* 301: Novanglus, 23 January 1775, and *WrTJ* (ed. Lipscomb and Bergh) XVI 118–19: Letter to Henry Lee on 8 May 1825 in light of Charles R. Kesler, "The Founders and the Classics," in *The Revival of Constitutionalism*, ed. James W. Muller (Lincoln, Nebr., 1988) 43–68. Cf. John Zvesper, "The American Founders and Classical Political Thought," *HPT* 10 (1989): 701–18.

100. For the passages cited, see III Introduction, above.

101. Consider *WoJA* VI 219–20: *A Defence of the Constitutions of Government of the United States of America* (1787–88) in light of William E. Nelson, "Reason and Compromise in the Establishment of the Federal Constitution, 1787–1801," *WMQ* 44 (1987): 458–84. For 26 December 1787 as the date of composition, see *The Life and Correspondence of Rufus King*, ed. Charles R. King (New York 1894–1900) I 320–21: Letter to Theophilus Parsons on 20 February 1788.

102. Consider Gary Wills, *Cincinnatus: George Washington and the Enlightenment* (Garden City 1984), in light of II.v.5, above.

103. See John Phillip Reid, *The Concept of Liberty in the Age of the American Revolution* (Chicago 1988).

104. See above, II.i.1.

105. Cf. *PJJ* III 221–22: Letter to Jacob Reed on 12 December 1786 and *PJoM* I 199–201: Letter to James Wilkinson on 5 January 1787 with the first of this prologue's two epigraphs: *Diary and Autobiography of John Adams*, ed. L. H. Butterfield (Cambridge, Mass., 1961) 281–82: 30 December 1765.

106. "Liberty!" wrote one prominent American. "Thou emanation from the all-beauteous and celestial mind! To Americans thou has committed the guardianship of the darling rights of mankind, leaving the Eastern world where indolence has bowed the neck to the yoke of tyranny; in this Western hemisphere hast thou fixed thy sacred empire; whilst the sons of Europe shackled with the manacles of oppression, sigh for thy safety, and pant for thy blessings; the band of patriots who are here thy votaries, cemented by thy invisible power, will be bound to the partners of their toils and dangers by ties more close than those of kindred, more sacred than those of friendship." See "Two Neglected Madison Letters" 587: The North American No. 2, *Pennsylvania Journal*, 8 October 1783, with II.i.2, note 35, above. Consider Bertram Wyatt Brown, " 'Sacred Honor' and the American Revolution," unpublished lecture delivered at the National Humanities Center, 27 February 1990, and see III.i.1 (esp, note 10), below.

107. Consider Harvey C. Mansfield, Jr., "Constitutional Government: The Soul of Modern Democracy," *The Public Interest* 86 (Winter 1987): 53–64, and *America's Constitutional Soul* (Baltimore 1991), in light of *WoJA* IV 526, 556–58, VI 219: *A Defence of the Constitutions of Government of the United States of America* (1787–88); ponder Mansfield, *Taming the Prince: The Ambivalence of Modern Executive Power* (New York 1989) esp. 247–97; and see III.i.6–8, iii.2, iv.5–9, below.

108. *PTJ* XVI 449: Letter to Thomas Mann Randolph, Jr., on 30 May 1790.

109. For a useful discussion of the manner in which the Americans deployed the institutional political science of Machiavelli, Harrington, and their successors in an attempt to honor Lockean first principles, see David A. J. Richards, *Foundations of American Constitutionalism* (New York 1989) 18–130. Consider, however, III Epilogue, note 17, below.

Chapter 1

1. The essays of the late Martin Diamond are invaluable for understanding the intention of the Framers, and my debt to his work is substantial: see Diamond, *As Far as Republican Principles Will Admit*, ed. William Schambra (Washington, D.C., 1992). The recent publications of comparable worth include Paul Eidelberg, *The Philosophy of the American Constitution: A Reinterpretation of the Intentions of the Founding Fathers* (New York 1968); Douglass Adair, *Fame and the Founding Fathers*, ed. Trevor Colbourn (New York 1974); Alexander Landi, "Madison's Political Theory," *PSR* 6 (1976): 73–112; David F. Epstein, *The Political Theory of The Federalist* (Chicago 1984); William Kristol, "The Problem of the Separation of Powers: *Federalist* 47–51," in *Saving the Revolution: The Federalist Papers and the American Founding*, ed. Charles R. Kesler (New York 1987) 100–130; Daniel Walker Howe, "The Language of Faculty Psychology in *The Federalist Papers*," in *Conceptual Change and the Constitution*, ed. Terence Ball and J. G. A. Pocock (Lawrence, Kans., 1988) 107–36; and Harvey C. Mansfield, Jr., *Taming the Prince: The Ambivalence of Modern Executive Power* (New York 1989). I have greatly profited from consulting two recently

published tools for research: *The Founders' Constitution*, ed. Philip B. Kurland and Ralph Lerner (Chicago 1987), and *The Federalist Concordance*, ed. Thomas S. Engeman, Edward J. Erler, and Thomas B. Hofeller (Chicago 1988). Though brilliant, the dissertation of Douglass Greybill Adair is seriously flawed in a variety of ways: it depicts Hamilton in a simplistic fashion; it obscures Madison's reversal of course after 1789; and it is naive in its failure to take seriously the real difficulties which the attempt to establish a viable liberal democratic regime posed in 1787 and still poses today. But, these errors notwithstanding, Adair's account remains of considerable value. See "The Intellectual Origins of Jeffersonian Democracy: Republicanism, the Class Struggle, and the Virtuous Farmer" (Yale University 1943). Needless to say, the fact that its author never published his dissertation suggests that he may have been aware of its shortcomings.

2. The obvious care taken in composing *The Federalist* and the effort made to insure its publication in book form argues against the view—advanced by Albert Furtwangler, *The Authority of Publius: A Reading of the Federalist Papers* (Ithaca 1984)—that the authors failed to foresee that their work might have a lasting impact and neglected to prepare their arguments with this in mind.

3. For a brief sketch of Ferguson's life, see the *Dictionary of National Biography* XVIII (New York 1889) 336–40.

4. Consider Ferguson, *EHCS* 3.2 (122–23), in light of II.iv.8, note 106, above, and see Ronald Hamowy, *The Scottish Enlightenment and the Theory of Spontaneous Order* (Carbondale, Ill., 1987). Note also Ronald L. Meek, *Social Science and the Ignoble Savage* (Cambridge 1976).

5. For the import of this process of experimentation and debate, see Edward S. Corwin, "The Progress of Constitutional Theory between the Declaration of Independence and the Meeting of the Philadelphia Convention," *AHR* 30 (1925): 511–36.

6. Locke, *TTG* II.i.1. Note viii.100–104.

7. Hume, *EMPL* 465–87: "Of the Original Contract."

8. For a perceptive discussion of some of the reasons why this pamphlet had so explosive an impact, see Bernard Bailyn, "Common Sense," in *Fundamental Testaments of the American Revolution* (Washington, D.C., 1973) 7–22.

9. See Roy N. Lokken, "The Concept of Democracy in Colonial Political Thought," *WMQ* 16 (1959): 568–80; Willi Paul Adams, "Republicanism in Political Rhetoric before 1776," *PSQ* 85 (1970): 397–421; and Cecelia M. Kenyon, "Republicanism and Radicalism in the American Revolution: An Old-Fashioned Interpretation," *WMQ* 19 (1962): 153–82. In this connection, consider Robert R. Palmer, "Notes on the Use of the Word 'Democracy,' 1789–1799," *PSQ* 68 (1953): 203–26.

10. *The Federalist* 39 (250). It is uncertain whether it was Madison, Hamilton, or both who vigorously rejected the notion "that there is not sufficient virtue among men for self-government; and that nothing less than the chains of despotism can restrain them from destroying and devouring one another." See 55 (378). That the honor of Americans and even of mankind is somehow at stake in the American experiment in republicanism is a recurring theme. Note 11 (72–73), 36 (230), 39 (251), 49 (340–41), 76 (514).

11. For Thomas Lloyd's report of the famous speech with which Wilson opened the convention, see *DHRC* II 350–63 (esp. 353, 362): 24 November 1787. For the slightly different account recorded by Alexander J. Dallas, see *DHRC* II 340–50 (esp. 342).

12. *WoJA* IV 292–93: *A Defence of the Constitutions of Government of the United States of America* (1787–88).

13. Hamilton, *The Federalist* 1 (3).

14. See *WrJM* IX 70–77 (at 72): Letter to John G. Jackson on 27 December 1821. For the rebellion and its impact on the framing and ratification of the Constitution, see David P. Szatmary, *Shays' Rebellion: The Making of an Agrarian Insurrection* (Amherst, Mass., 1980), with Forrest McDonald, *Novus Ordo Seclorum: The Intellectual Origins of the Constitution* (Lawrence, Kans., 1985) 177 n. 61. For a contemporary account, see Richard D. Brown, "Shays's Rebellion and Its Aftermath: A View from Springfield, Massachusetts, 1787," *WMQ* 40 (1983): 598–615. For the view that the rebellion had little influence on the Constitution and little effect in preparing the way for the convention, see Robert A. Feer, "Shays's Rebellion and the Constitution: A Study in Causation," *NEQ* 42 (1969): 388–410. In Massachusetts, the severity employed in repressing the rebellion stirred a backlash that later endangered ratification: see Richard D. Brown, "Shays's Rebellion and the Ratification of the Federal Constitution in Massachusetts," in *Beyond Confederation: Origins of the Constitution and American National Identity*, ed. Richard Beeman, Stephen Botein, and Edward C. Carter II (Chapel Hill 1987) 113–27.

15. For the events of this eleven-year period as they affected the infant nation as a whole, see Jack N. Rakove, *The Beginnings of National Politics: An Interpretive History of the Continental Congress* (New York 1979) esp. 111–360, and McDonald, *Novus Ordo Seclorum* 143–83. Cf. Merrill Jensen, *The Articles of Confederation: An Interpretation of the Social-Constitutional History of the American Revolution, 1774–1781* (Madison, Wis., 1940), *The New Nation* (New York 1950), and *The American Revolution within America* (New York 1974) 167–220, for the utterly implausible view that the Articles of Confederation—with minor adjustments—would have been an instrument more or less adequate to the needs of a modern state. One need only ponder the severe strains produced within the United States by the wars of the French Revolution to become aware just how essential the partial consolidation which did take place actually was; without it, the Union would almost certainly have dissolved. The Anti-Federalists may have feared that ratification of the constitution proposed by the Philadelphia convention would prepare the way for tyranny, but few of them were prepared to say much in praise of the Articles of Confederation. Note also Jack N. Rakove, "The Legacy of the Articles of Confederation," *Publius* 12, no. 4 (Fall 1982): 45–66, and "The Collapse of the Articles of Confederation," in *The American Founding: Essays on the Formation of the Constitution*, ed. J. Jackson Barlow, Leonard W. Levy, and Ken Masugi (New York 1988) 225–45.

16. *WrGW* XXVI 485–86: 8 June 1783. In this connection, see Frederick W. Marks III, *Independence on Trial: Foreign Affairs and the Making of the Constitution* (Baton Rouge 1973), and "Power, Pride, and Purse: Diplomatic Origins of the Constitution," *Diplomatic History* 11 (1987): 303–19. Years later, Madison would write, "Such indeed was the aspect of things that in the eyes of all the best friends of liberty a crisis had arrived which was to decide whether the Am[n] Experiment was to be a blessing to the world, or to blast forever the hopes which the republican cause had inspired." See *WrJM* IX 72: Letter to John G. Jackson on 27 December 1821. Note Hamilton's favorable response to Washington's letter: *PAH* III 462–63: Letter to George Washington on 30 September 1783.

17. See Jerrilyn Greene Marston, *King and Congress: The Transfer of Political Legitimacy, 1774–1776* (Princeton 1987).

18. See Rakove, *The Beginnings of National Politics* 133–359.

19. See E. Wayne Carp, *To Starve the Army at Pleasure: Continental Army Administration and American Political Culture, 1775–1783* (Chapel Hill 1984). In this connection, see also E. James Ferguson, "Currency Finance: An Interpretation of Colonial Monetary Practices," *WMQ* 10 (1953): 151–80, and *The Power of the Purse: A History of American Public Finance, 1776–1790* (Chapel Hill 1961), as well as Clarence L. Ver Steeg, *Robert Morris: Revolutionary Financier* (Philadelphia 1954).

20. *PAH* III 309–10: Letter from George Washington on 31 March 1783. Two weeks later, Washington wrote again to emphasize that "no man can be more opposed to State funds & local prejudices than myself" and added that "no man perhaps has had better opportunities to *see* & to *feel* the pernicious tendency of the latter than I have." See *PAH* III 329–31: Letter from George Washington on 16 April 1783.

21. For the relationship between what was taking place in Congress and the disturbances in the army at Newburgh, see Ferguson, *The Power of the Purse* 155–71; Ver Steeg, *Robert Morris* 166–86; H. James Henderson, *Party Politics in the Continental Congress* (New York 1974) 318–49; and Richard H. Kohn, *Eagle and Sword: The Federalists and the Creation of the Military Establishment in America, 1783–1802* (New York 1975) 17–39. Kohn contends that the agitation in the camp actually culminated in a conspiracy to carry out a coup d'état and that Robert Morris, Gouverneur Morris, and Alexander Hamilton deliberately stirred up the mutineers and then arranged for Washington to quash them. This thesis has been much debated recently. For Kohn's initial presentation of this view, see "The Inside History of the Newburgh Conspiracy: America and the Coup d'Etat," *WMQ* 27 (1970): 187–220. Note the subsequent exchanges between Kohn and his critics: Paul David Nelson, "Horatio Gates at Newburgh, 1783: A Misunderstood Role," *WMQ* 29 (1972): 143–58, and C. Edward Skeen, "The Newburgh Conspiracy Reconsidered," *WMQ* 31 (1974): 273–98.

22. For the manner in which the colonial experience prepared Americans for the task they faced in the 1780s, see Andrew McLaughlin, "The Background of American Federalism," *APSR* 12 (1918): 215–40. In this connection, see also Jack P. Greene, *Peripheries and Center: Constitutional Development in the Extended Polities of the British Empire and the United States, 1607–1788* (Athens, Ga., 1986).

23. See Merrill Jensen, "The Cession of the Old Northwest," *Mississippi Valley Historical Review* 23 (1936): 27–48, and "The Creation of the National Domain, 1781–1784," *Mississippi Valley Historical Review* 26 (1939): 323–42. See, more recently, Peter S. Onuf, *The Origins of the Federal Republic: Jurisdictional Controversies in the United States, 1775–1787* (Philadelphia 1983) esp. 3–145.

24. *WrGW* XXVI 485–86: 8 June 1783.

25. See Forrest McDonald, *E Pluribus Unum: The Formation of the American Republic, 1776–1790* (Boston 1965) 133–54. See above, III.i.1, note 14.

26. See William M. Wiecek, *The Guarantee Clause of the U.S. Constitution* (Ithaca 1972) 11–77. Looking back on these events some years later, John Marshall, *The Life of George Washington* (Fredericksburg, Va., 1926) IV 368, would attribute the "great and visible improvement in the circumstances of the people" occurring around 1790 in large part to "the influence of the Constitution on habits of think-

ing and acting," which, "though silent, was considerable." As he put it, "In depriving the states of the power to impair the obligations of contracts, or to make anything but gold and silver a tender in payment of debts, the conviction was impressed on that portion of society which had looked to the government for relief from embarrassment, that personal exertion alone could free them from difficulties; and an increased degree of industry and economy was the natural consequence of this opinion." See also Marshall, IV 193–98, 288–89. The subsequent revolution in law that restricted juries to the determination of facts and then eliminated considerations of just price and just wage from the adjudication of contractual disputes was entirely in keeping with the spirit of the new constitution. It makes far more sense to interpret this revolution as an example of judicial statesmanship than to see it narrowly in terms of class analysis: cf. Morton Horwitz, *The Transformation of American Law, 1780–1860* (Cambridge, Mass., 1977) esp. 160–252, with William E. Nelson, *Americanization of the Common Law: The Impact of Legal Change on Massachusetts Society, 1760–1830* (Cambridge, Mass., 1975). The Framers intended to give every encouragement to commerce, and the sanctity of contracts would be central to the achievement of that end.

27. For the experiments in the states and the events that lead to the calling of the federal convention, see Gordon S. Wood, *The Creation of the American Republic, 1776–1787* (Chapel Hill 1969) 125–467. See also Alfred F. Young, "Conservatives, the Constitution, and the 'Spirit of Accommodation,'" in *How Democratic Is the Constitution?* ed. Robert A. Goldwin and William A. Schambra (Washington, D.C., 1980) 117–47.

28. *PJJ* III 221–22: Letter to Jacob Reed on 12 December 1786, and *PJoM* I 199–201 (at 201): Letter to James Wilkinson on 5 January 1787.

29. *PJM* X 212: 24 October 1787. On the floor of the convention, Madison emphasized "the necessity of providing more effectually for the security of private rights, and the steady dispensation of Justice." As he put it, "Interferences with these were evils which had more perhaps than anything else, produced this convention." His point was that "faction & oppression" had "prevailed in the largest as well as the smallest" of the states. See *RFC* I 134–36: Speech of James Madison on the 6th of June, 1787. "The necessity of such a Constitution was enforced," Madison would later recall, "by the gross and disreputable inequalities which had been prominent in the internal administrations of most of the States." And, when near the end of his life, he would observe that "the abuses committed within the individual States previous to the present Constitution, by interested or misguided majorities, were among the prominent causes of its adoption, and particularly led to the provision contained in it which prohibits paper emissions and the violations of contracts, and which gives an appellate supremacy to the judicial department of the U. S." See *WrJM* IX 72, 520–28 (at 522): Letter to John G. Jackson on 27 December 1821, and Letter on Majority Rule, 1833.

30. For a particularly vivid and often perceptive depiction of the delegates and their deliberations, see Clinton Rossiter, *1787: The Grand Convention* (New York 1987). Note also Lance Banning, "The Constitutional Convention," in *The Framing and Ratification of the Constitution*, ed. Leonard W. Levy and Dennis J. Mahoney (New York 1987) 112–31.

31. Consider *RFC* I 7–17: 28–29 May 1787 in light of Eidelberg, *The Philosophy of the American Constitution* 32–39, and see *RFC* III 478–79: Jared Sparks's Record of a Conversation with James Madison, 19 April 1830.

32. See *RFC* II 641–46 and *SRFC* 276: 17 September 1787. Benjamin Franklin's plea for unanimity deserves particular attention.

33. In this connection, see *PAH* IV 275–77: Conjectures about the New Constitution, 17–30 September 1787.

34. For an overview of the struggle that ensued, see Steven R. Boyd, *The Politics of Opposition: Antifederalists and the Acceptance of the Constitution* (Millwood, N.Y., 1979); Robert Allen Rutland, *The Ordeal of the Constitution: The Antifederalists and the Ratification Struggle of 1787–1788* (Boston 1983); and *Ratifying the Constitution*, ed. Michael Allen Gillespie and Michael Lienesch (Lawrence, Kans., 1989). For events in New York, where *The Federalist* was composed and first published, see Robin Brooks, "Alexander Hamilton, Melancton Smith, and the Ratification of the Constitution in New York," *WMQ* 24 (1967): 339–58; John P. Kaminski, "New York: The Reluctant Pillar," in *The Reluctant Pillar: New York and the Adoption of the Federal Constitution*, ed. Stephen L. Schechter (Troy, N.Y., 1985) 48–117; and Cecil L. Eubanks, "New York: Federalism and the Political Economy of Union," in *Ratifying the Constitution* 300–340.

35. For a comprehensive survey and assessment of the arguments which the Anti-Federalists deployed, see Herbert J. Storing, *What the Anti-Federalists Were For: The Political Thought of the Opponents of the Constitution* (Chicago 1981). Though far less inclusive, Cecilia M. Kenyon's earlier discussion remains quite useful: see "Men of Little Faith: The Anti-Federalists on the Nature of Representative Government," *WMQ* 12 (1955): 3–43. For a helpful survey of the overall debate, see Isaac Kramnick, " 'The Great National Discussion': The Discourse of Politics in 1787," in *Republicanism and Bourgeois Radicalism: Political Ideology in Late Eighteenth-Century England and America* (Ithaca 1990) 260–88. Note also Herbert J. Storing, "The 'Other' Federalist Papers: A Preliminary Sketch," *PSR* 6 (1976): 215–41; Murray Dry, "Anti-Federalism in *The Federalist*: A Founding Dialogue on the Constitution, Republican Government, and Federalism," in *Saving the Revolution* 40–60; Richard C. Sinopoli, "Liberalism, Republicanism & the Constitution," *Polity* 19 (1987): 331–52; Terence Ball, "A Republic—If You Can Keep It," in *Conceptual Change and the Constitution* 137–64; and Cathy D. Matson and Peter S. Onuf, *A Union of Interests: Political and Economic Thought in Revolutionary America* (Lawrence, Kans., 1990).

36. For the manner in which Madison's experience in practical politics, particularly what he learned while serving in the Virginia assembly, gradually gave rise to his disillusionment with classical republicanism's reliance on civic virtue, see James Conniff, "The Enlightenment and American Political Thought: A Study of the Origins of Madison's *Federalist Number 10*," *PTh* 8 (1980): 381–402.

37. Madison, *The Federalist* 14 (88).

38. *PAH* V 207: Letter from George Washington on 28 August 1788. John Marshall later echoed this opinion: see *The Life of George Washington* IV 241–42.

39. *PTJ* XIV 188: Letter to James Madison on 18 November 1788. Jefferson later included the book in the government curriculum he devised for the University of Virginia: see below, III.iv.5.

40. See *WrJM* VIII 410–11: Letter to James K. Paulding on 23 July 1818. Hamilton, who always took care in the selection of pseudonyms, had used this particular appellation before: Douglass Adair, "Fame and the Founding Fathers," and "A Note on Certain of Hamilton's Pseudonyms," *Fame and the Founding Fathers* 3–26 (esp. 15–16), 272–85. Since Hamilton also initiated the project, recruited

both Madison and Jay, and ultimately saw to the publication of their newspaper essays as a book, it seems reasonable to suspect that he was similarly responsible for selecting the pseudonym employed in the end. In any case, as a consequence of the name's employment, the authorship of some of the numbers remains disputed. In determining attribution, I have followed Douglass Adair, "The Authorship of the Disputed *Federalist* Papers," *Fame and the Founding Fathers* 27–74—an essay originally published in 1944. The statistical study of stylistic characteristics undertaken by Frederick Mosteller and David L. Wallace supports Adair's conclusion that Madison bore the primary responsibility for all of the disputed papers. See Mosteller and Wallace, *Inference and Disputed Authorship: The Federalist* (Reading, Mass., 1964). In truth, however, the question of authorship is for the most part merely academic. As a whole, the series of essays is almost as coherent as the authors intended it to be, and this fact supports Furtwangler's suggestion that there was considerable collaboration: see *The Authority of Publius*. For an exaggerated, but nonetheless valuable presentation of the opposing view, see Alpheus Thomas Mason, "The Federalist—A Split Personality," *AHR* 57 (1952): 625–43. The division of labor between Hamilton and Madison did to some extent reflect the difference in outlook which became evident in the 1790s, but the quarrel which erupted at that time had as much to do with a change of mind on Madison's part regarding a number of important questions: see below, III.ii–iv.

41. See Thomas L. Pangle, "Civic Virtue: The Founders' Conception and the Traditional Conception," in *Constitutionalism and Rights*, ed. Gary C. Bryner and Noel B. Reynolds (Provo, Utah, 1987) 105–40.

42. *The Federalist* 9 (51–52). Aristotle was considerably less friendly to what he termed "the techniques (*sophísmata*) of legislation": cf. *Pol.* 1297a14–41 with 1307b40–1308a2.

43. Forrest McDonald, *Novus Ordo Seclorum* 205–9, makes much of this fact. As he amply demonstrates (225–93), when Madison later denied that he could justly be termed "*the* writer of the Constitution of the U.S." and contended instead that the Constitution "ought to be regarded as the work of many heads and many hands," he was not guilty of false modesty. See *RFC* III 533: Letter to William Cogswell on 10 March 1834.

44. For Madison's strategy, see *PJM* IX 317–22 (esp. 317–19), 368–71, 382–87: Letters to Thomas Jefferson on 19 March and to Edmund Randolph and George Washington on 8 and 16 April 1787. On the role played by Madison before and at the convention, see *The States Rights Debate: Antifederalism and the Constitution*[2], ed. Alpheus Thomas Mason (Oxford 1972) 30–58; Rakove, *The Beginnings of National Politics* 360–99; Harold S. Schultz, "James Madison: Father of the Constitution?" *Quarterly Journal of the Library of Congress* 37 (1980): 215–22; Michael P. Zuckert, "Federalism and the Founding," *RP* 48 (1986): 166–210; and Lance Banning, "The Practicable Sphere of a Republic: James Madison, the Constitutional Convention, and the Emergence of Revolutionary Federalism," in *Beyond Confederation* 162–88. See, however, III.iii.5, note 82, below.

45. Consider Donald S. Lutz, "The Relative Influence of European Writers on Late Eighteenth-Century American Political Thought," *APSR* 78 (1984): 189–97, in conjunction with Frank H. Fletcher, *Montesquieu and English Politics, 1750–1800* (London 1939), and Paul Merrill Spurlin, *Montesquieu in America, 1760–1801* (University, La., 1940), and *The French Enlightenment in America: Essays on the Times of the Founding Fathers* (Athens, Ga., 1984) 86–98. Then, see James W. Muller,

"The American Framers' Debt to Montesquieu," in *The Revival of Constitutionalism*, ed. James W. Muller (Lincoln, Nebr., 1988) 87–102, and consider Anne M. Cohler, *Montesquieu's Comparative Politics and the Spirit of American Constitutionalism* (Lawrence, Kans., 1988).

46. Montesquieu, *EL* 1.8.16.

47. *CAF*: Robert Yates and John Lansing, "Reasons of Dissent" (2.3.7); Luther Martin, "The Genuine Information Delivered to the Legislature of the State of Maryland" (2.4.44); Letters of Cato III (2.6.10–21); Letters of Centinel I (2.7.17–19); Letters from the Federal Farmer II (2.8.15–19); Essays of an Old Whig IV (3.3.20); The Address and Reasons of Dissent of the Minority of the Convention of Pennsylvania To Their Constituents (3.11.16–17); The Fallacies of the Freeman Detected by A Farmer (3.14.7); Letters of Agrippa IV (4.6.16–17); Observations on the New Constitution, and on the Federal and State Conventions By A Columbian Patriot (4.28.4); Address by John Francis Mercer (5.5.5–6); Address by Cato Uticensis (5.7.6–9); Speeches of Patrick Henry in the Virginia State Ratifying Convention (5.16.11); Speech of George Mason in the Virginia Ratifying Convention (5.17.1, cf. 2.2.2); James Monroe, *Some Observations on the Constitution* (5.21.12–13); Speeches by Melancton Smith [in the New York Ratifying Convention] (6.12.9); Notes of Speeches Given by George Clinton before the New York State Ratifying Convention (6.13.14–18). Cf. Hamilton's retort to the Anti-Federalists' insistent citation of Montesquieu: *The Federalist* 9 (52–54).

48. *The Federalist* 10 (57), 14 (83).

49. There is less difference between the position taken by Publius here and that of Plato and Aristotle than one might initially think: consider *The Federalist* 10 (58–59, 61) in light of 31 (194–95), and see I.ii.1, above.

50. The tension can most effectively be resolved where a friendship of sorts grows up between the rich and the poor—based on the generosity of the former and the deference of the latter. This can take place because the properly educated gentleman (*kalokagathós*) longs for honor, not wealth, and is willing to sacrifice the latter in exchange for the former. One needs to ponder the political implications of Arist. *Eth. Nic.* 1159b25–1163b12, 1167a22–b16 (esp. 1163a24–b12, 1167a35–b1) in light of *Pol.* 1267a37–b7. For a fragmentary sketch of just such a regime, consider Arist. *Pol.* 1323a14–1342b34 in light of Carnes Lord, *Education and Culture in the Political Thought of Aristotle* (Ithaca 1982) esp. 180–202. For the relationship between education, the political regime, virtue, the distribution of property, and claims to rule, see *Eth. Nic.* 1179a33–1181b23, *Pol.* 1259b18–1260b24, 1263b29–40, 1266a31–1267b21, 1271a18–26, 1276a30–1276b15, 1280a9–1281a10, 1282b14–1284b34, 1289a15–25 (with *Rh.* 1365b30–1366a16), 1292b11–21, 1293b22–1294a29, 1307b19–1310a38.

51. See II.iv–vii, above, and consider Walter Berns, "The 'New' Science of Politics and Constitutional Government," in *Constitutionalism and Rights* 63–77, in light of Harvey C. Mansfield, Jr., "Modern and Medieval Representation," in *Representation*, ed. J. R. Pennock and G. Chapman, *Nomos* 11 (1968): 55–82, and "Hobbes and the Science of Indirect Government," *APSR* 65 (1971): 97–110. Then, cf. J. R. Pole, *Political Representation in England and the Origins of the American Republic* (Berkeley 1971), and Gordon S. Wood, *Representation in the American Revolution* (Charlottesville 1969), with Jean Yarbrough, "Representation and Republicanism: Two Views," *Publius* 9 (1979): 77–98, and see Edmund S. Morgan, *Inventing the People: The Rise of Popular Sovereignty in England and America* (New York 1988), and

John Phillip Reid, *The Concept of Representation in the Age of the American Revolution* (Chicago 1989). Note George Mace, *Locke, Hobbes, and the Federalist Papers: An Essay on the Genesis of the American Political Heritage* (Carbondale, Ill., 1979). In the course of denouncing the American polity as a Hobbesian regime, Frank M. Coleman testifies to Hobbes's intellectual hegemony by demonstrating an inability to project an alternative understanding of the public purpose transcending the Malmesbury philosopher's materialist vision: cf. *Hobbes and America: Exploring the Constitutional Foundations* (Toronto 1977). To escape Hobbes's clutches and reestablish politics as an autonomous and sovereign activity, one would have to find one's way back to something like Aristotle's account of man's moral and political rationality—which Rousseau, the young Marx, and those who equate political activity and choice with the exercise of collective will resolutely refuse to do: cf., for example, Benjamin R. Barber, "Against Economics: Or, Capitalism, Socialism, but Whatever Happened to Democracy?" with William Kristol, "The Friends and Enemies of Democratic Capitalism," both in *Democratic Capitalism? Essays in Search of a Concept*, ed. Fred E. Baumann (Charlottesville 1986) 22–78. In its own, peculiar, indirect way, the American regime in practice does greater justice to Aristotle's claim than its critics do in their theories.

52. Cf. [Noah Webster], *Examination into the Leading Principles of the Federal Constitution Proposed by the Late Convention Held at Philadelphia by A Citizen of America* (Philadelphia 1787) 6–9, 13, with Montesquieu, *EL* 1.2.2, 2.11.6 (399–400), 8, 3.19.27 (576). For Webster's authorship of the pertinent pamphlet, see *DHRC* XIII 405–6. His essay is conveniently reprinted in *Pamphlets on the Constitution of the United States*, ed. Paul Leicester Ford (Brooklyn 1888).

53. *DHRC* II 343–44, 353–55: 24 November 1787.

54. Consider *The Federalist* 9 (50–53) in light of II.iv.3–8 (esp. 8), above, and see this chapter's epigraph: *WoJA* VI 10: *A Defence of the Constitutions of Government of the United States of America* (1787–88).

55. After noting *PAH* I 254–56: Letter to Gouverneur Morris on 19 May 1777, consider *The Federalist* 9 (51–53) in light of Montesquieu, *EL* 2.9.1–3, and see James Wilson, *DHRC* II 358: Pennsylvania Ratifying Convention, 24 November 1787. A year before Hamilton coined the phrase "representative democracy," Jeremy Bentham spelled out in detail the inadequacy of the inherited typology of regimes for analyzing modern governmental forms: Bentham, *A Fragment on Government*, ed. J. H. Burns and H. L. A. Hart (Cambridge 1988) 3.8–18. At the Pennsylvania Ratifying Convention, James Wilson similarly alluded to Montesquieu's discussion of federalism as a means for uniting the advantages of republicanism and monarchy and asserted that he and his colleagues at the federal convention had invented the first fully federal republic. See *DHRC* II 341–43: 24 November 1787.

56. *The Federalist* 10 (61–62), 14 (84), 55 (374).

57. Cf. Madison's critique of large assemblies (*The Federalist* 58 [395–96]) with Hobbes's contention (*Elements of Law* II.ii.5) that the effectual truth of democracy is "an aristocracy of orators"; see II.iv.8, above; and then consider *The Federalist* 10 in light of Harvey C. Mansfield, Jr., "Republicanizing the Executive," in *Saving the Revolution* 168–84, and *Taming the Prince* 1–278 (esp. 247–78). In Madison's estimation, the only viable alternative to geographical extension is the creation of "a will in the community independent of the majority": *The Federalist* 51 (351–52).

58. Consider *PJM* IX 384: Letter to George Washington on 16 April 1787 in light of Michael P. Zuckert, "Federalism and the Founding" 166–210.

59. "In a large government, which is modelled with masterly skill," the Scot contended, "there is compass and room enough to refine the democracy, from the lower people, who may be admitted into the first elections or first concoctions of the commonwealth, to the higher magistrates, who direct all the movements." See Hume, *EMPL* 528: "Idea of a Perfect Commonwealth."

60. Consider Madison, *The Federalist* 10 (60, 62–63), in conjunction with Gordon S. Wood, "The Democratization of Mind in the American Revolution," in *Leadership in the American Revolution* (Washington, D.C., 1974) 63–88, and see Jay, *The Federalist* 3 (15), and Madison, *The Federalist* 6 (31), 42 (283). The last of the passages quoted is decisive against the ancient heresy recently revived by Gordon S. Wood, "Democracy and the Constitution," in *How Democratic Is the Constitution?* 1–17, and Gary Wills, *Explaining America: The Federalist* (Garden City 1981) 95–270, that Madison's solution to the problem of faction was subordinate to the promotion of rule by an aristocratic or virtuous social elite. On the eve of the Constitutional Convention, Madison sketched out his theory in a brief memorandum entitled "The Vices of the Political System of the United States." In his discussion, he made it clear that the procedures designed to encourage the election of men of character and intelligence were a relatively minor concern—an "auxiliary desideratum for the melioration of the republican form." There is no reason to believe that he ever changed his mind. When he wrote to Thomas Jefferson on 24 October 1787, shortly after the convention had completed its work, he once again outlined the theory behind the new constitution—this time without even mentioning his hope that the new system of government would encourage the election of such individuals. Cf. *PJM* IX 357 with X 206–20. Hamilton was persuaded that, as fortunes grew less equal in the new republic, wealth would overshadow true merit as an attraction for political support. See *DSSC* II 256: The New York Ratifying Convention, 21 June 1788. For the sources of Wills's error, see below, notes 63 and 67. See also David F. Epstein's review, *The Public Interest* 65 (Fall 1981) 152–56.

61. See Douglass Adair, "'THAT POLITICS MAY BE REDUCED TO A SCIENCE': David Hume, James Madison, and the Tenth Federalist," *Fame and the Founding Fathers* 93–106. Cf. Edmund S. Morgan, "Safety in Numbers: Madison, Hume, and the Tenth Federalist," *HLQ* 49 (1986): 95–112, who rightly stresses Madison's originality while nonetheless understating his debt to Hume.

62. Montesquieu, *EL* 2.11.4.

63. Cf. Hume, *EMPL* 42–43: "Of the Independency of Parliament," with Machiavelli, *Discorsi* 1.3; and see *PAH* I 94–95: *The Farmer Refuted, &c.*, 23 February 1775, and *WoJA* VI 415: Letter to Samuel Adams on 18 October 1790. "I am not often satisfied with the opinions of Hume," writes Adams, "but in this he seems well-founded, that all projects of government, founded in the supposition or expectation of extraordinary degrees of virtue, are evidently chimerical." Gary Wills's misreading of Madison (above, note 60) is at least in part founded upon a misinterpretation of Hume. Wills rightly makes much of the Framers' dependence on the latter, and he quotes the crucial passage cited here (*Explaining America* 190–91); but because he fails to recognize the decisive importance of this passage for the interpretation of Hume's *political* (as opposed to his *moral*) philosophy, he grossly underestimates Hume's skepticism regarding the possibility of virtuous rule. On this subject, the Scot was anything but sanguine.

64. In expressing his approbation of the pertinent passage in Machiavelli, John

Adams shows that similar views were held by Hobbes, Harrington, Mandeville, Montesquieu, Bolingbroke, and Lolme as well as by Joseph Priestley and Richard Price. See *WoJA* IV 408–15 (with 556–58): *A Defence of the Constitutions of Government of the United States of America* (1787–88).

65. *The Federalist* 51 (349). See also the disparagement of virtue's efficacy in Madison's memorandum "Vices of the Political System of the United States": *PJM* IX 355–57. On the floor of the federal convention, while presenting his own solution to the problem of faction, Madison repeated the gist of the argument which he had outlined in that preparatory document. See *RFC* I 134–36: 6 June 1787. Forty-two years later, he still held the same opinion. See *WrJM* IX 358–64 (at 361–62): Speech in the Virginia Constitutional Convention, 2 December 1829.

66. Hobbes, *Leviathan* II.25 (311).

67. For the distinction made by Montesquieu and its import, see Thomas L. Pangle, *Montesquieu's Philosophy of Liberalism: A Commentary on the Spirit of the Laws* (Chicago 1973) 48–160. Gary Wills (above, note 60) misinterprets the intention of Hamilton and Madison, greatly exaggerating the degree to which they thought political virtue possible in and necessary for the American republic, chiefly because he (*Explaining America* 185–92) misunderstands Montesquieu and neglects this distinction. The American regime was not modeled on the virtuous republics of antiquity; it was an adaptation of Britain's quasi-republican regime. The passages quoted from Montesquieu (*EL* 1.5.6, 19 [304]) should be interpreted in light of what he has to say elsewhere concerning England's government, the relationship between her laws and her mores and manners, the role played by commerce in modern times, and England's commercial character: *EL* 3.11.6, 19.26–27, 4.20.1–2, 4–8, 10, 12–14, 21, 23, 21.5, 7, 20, 22.2, 17–18, 23.8, 17 (695). Cf. *WoGS* I 302.26–303.2: *A Rough Draught of a New Modell at Sea*.

68. *The Federalist* 47 (324). For that constitution, Madison subsequently remarked, Montesquieu "professed an admiration bordering on idolatry." See *PJM* XV 66–74 (at 68): "Helvidius" Number 1, 24 August 1793.

69. Hume "Idea of a Perfect Commonwealth" 512–29 (esp. 525, 527–28). In part because of this assertion and in part because his multivolume history debunked Whig myths concerning the historical sources for political authority in England, many of the American founders mistakenly supposed Hume an opponent of republicanism and found his work distasteful. See, for example, *WoJA* IV 559: *A Defence of the Constitutions of Government of the United States of America* (1787–88); *WrTJ* (ed. Ford) IX 71–75: Letter to John Norvell on 14 June 1807; *AJL* II 357: Letter from John Adams to Thomas Jefferson on 15 July 1813; and Jefferson, *MCPP* IV 403–8: Letter to Major John Cartwright on 5 June 1824. It would nonetheless be an error to make much of the discreet silence James Madison maintained regarding the degree to which the tenth *Federalist* was indebted to the thinking of the Scot: cf. Theodore Draper, "Hume & Madison: The Secrets of Federalist Paper No. 10," *Encounter* 58, no. 2 (February 1982): 34–47. In the circles Madison frequented, at least some of Hume's works commanded considerable respect: though Thomas Jefferson would later denounce Hume's history as "poison," in 1790, he still thought so highly of "several of Hume's political essays" that he recommended them as reading for his young son-in-law. Cf. *WrTJ* (ed. Washington) V 532–36: Letter to William Duane on 12 August 1810 with *PTJ* XVI 448–50 (at 449): Letter to Thomas Mann Randolph, Jr., on 30 May 1790. It is doubtful that Jefferson turned bitterly against Hume prior to his encounter with the Scots

philosopher's American disciple Alexander Hamilton, and even with regard to Hume's *History of England*, Jefferson remained remarkably ambivalent to the end of his days: see Douglas L. Wilson, "Jefferson vs. Hume," *WMQ* 46 (1989): 49–70.

70. *The Federalist* 10 (64).

71. *The Federalist* 51 (351–52).

72. *PTJ* XIV 188: Letter to James Madison on 18 November 1788.

73. *The Federalist* 10 (58–59).

74. *RFC* I 135: 6 June 1787.

75. *PJM* X 213–14: Letter to Thomas Jefferson on 24 October 1787.

76. *PJM* VIII 302: Memorial and Remonstrance against Religious Assessments, 20 June 1785.

77. For an earlier statement of the argument that follows, see Paul A. Rahe, "Church and State: Jefferson, Madison, and 200 Years of Religious Freedom," *The American Spectator* 19, no. 1 (January 1986): 18–23. Consider Walter Berns, *Taking the Constitution Seriously* (New York 1987) 147–80, in light of Harvey C. Mansfield, Jr., "The Religious Issue and the Origin of Modern Constitutionalism," *America's Constitutional Soul* (Baltimore 1991) 101–14.

78. Voltaire, *Letters Concerning the English Nation* (London 1733) 44–45. In French, this work is called *Lettres Philosophiques*.

79. Montesquieu, *EL* 5.25.12.

80. Hume, *EMPL* 54–63 (esp. 60–63): "Of Parties in General."

81. Cf. Hume, *EMPL* 64–72 (esp. 65–66): "Of the Parties of Great Britain," with the observation which Edmund Burke (*WrEB* I 438) registered in 1770 in his pamphlet *Thoughts on the Cause of the Present Discontents* that "the great parties which formerly divided and agitated the kingdom are known to be in a manner entirely dissolved," and see Tocqueville, *DA* 1.2.2.

82. Hume, *EMPL* 47–53 (esp. 51): "Whether the British Government inclines more to Absolute Monarchy, or to a Republic."

83. *PJM* I 170–79: Virginia Declaration of Rights, 16 May–29 June 1776. See Irving Brant, *James Madison* (Indianapolis 1941–61) I 234–51.

84. David Hume, *The History of England* (New York 1878) III 129.

85. *PJM* I 101, 105: Letters to William Bradford on 1 December 1773 and 24 January 1774. See also *PJM* I 112–13, 160–61: Letters to William Bradford on 1 April 1774 and 28 July 1775. The notes kept by Bradford and by Madison's other classmates indicate that, in the lectures that Witherspoon delivered on moral philosophy in their senior year, he blasted Shaftesbury, Hume, and Mandeville and drummed into his charges the dictum of Aristotle and his Christian admirers that government exists not just for the preservation of mere life but also for the promotion of good and virtuous living. Though he opposed "lordly domination and sacerdotal tyranny" and therefore defended religious as well as political freedom, Witherspoon also emphasized that it was the magistrate's duty to punish profanity and impiety, and he indicated that indirect support and even direct, financial aid to religion was legitimate and perhaps even desirable as along as there was no discrimination between the various Christian sects: see Ralph Ketcham, "James Madison at Princeton," *Princeton University Library Chronicle* 28 (1966): 24–54 (at 38–40, 44–46), and James Hastings Nichols, "John Witherspoon on Church and State," *Journal of Presbyterian History* 42 (1964): 166–74.

86. See note 83, above: the original draft of Madison's amendment included the stipulation "that no man or class of men ought, on account of religion to be

invested with peculiar emoluments or privileges; nor subjected to any penalties or disabilities unless under colour of religion, any man disturb the peace, the happiness, or safety of society."

87. For a detailed history of the struggle for disestablishment, see Thomas E. Buckley, S.J., *Church and State in Revolutionary Virginia, 1776–1787* (Charlottesville 1977) 1–172. For the aftermath, see Buckley, "Evangelicals Triumphant: The Baptists' Assault on the Virginia Glebes, 1786–1801," *WMQ* 45 (1988): 33–69. For a brief account of the role played by Madison, see Brant, *James Madison* I 298–300, II 343–55. See also *PTJ* I 525–58: Notes and Proceedings on Discontinuing the Establishment of the Church of England, 11 October–9 December 1776, and *PJM* VIII 295–306, 473–74: "Memorial and Remonstrance against Religious Assessments," 20 June 1785, and Letter to Thomas Jefferson on 22 January 1786. Madison ends his discussion of religious matters in the latter with the comment that "the enacting clauses past without a single alteration, and I flatter myself have in this Country extinguished for ever the ambitious hope of making laws for the human mind."

88. Cf. *DSSC* III 330: 12 June 1788 with *The Federalist* 51 (351–52), where Madison advances the same argument.

89. *The Wealth of Nations* was first published in 1776. At some point during the decade that followed, Madison read the work with care. See *PJM* VIII 266: Letter to Thomas Jefferson on 27 April 1785.

90. Locke, *LCT* 36–37.

91. Smith, *WN* V.i.g.3–8. The remaining paragraphs of Smith's remarkably frank discussion deserve attention as well. Cf. *PJM* I 106, 109, 112: Exchange of Letters with William Bradford on 24 January, 4 March, and 1 April 1774; *PJM* VIII 301–3: "Memorial and Remonstrance against Religious Assessments," 20 June 1785, Articles 8 and 11; and *WrJM* VIII 425–33 (at 430–32): Letter to Robert Walsh on 2 March 1819. As the last item cited indicates, Madison was inclined in later years to describe the American experience with disestablishment in the very terms once employed by Smith. Note Smith's debt to Montesquieu, *EL* 3.19.27 (580–81).

92. Edmund Randolph, *History of Virginia*, ed. Arthur H. Shaffer (Charlottesville 1970) 183.

93. Thomas E. Buckley, S.J., *Church and State in Revolutionary Virginia* 173–82, rightly emphasizes the influence of the evangelical Christians. See also Rhys Isaac, " 'The Rage of Malice of the Old Serpent Devil': The Dissenters and the Making and Remaking of the Virginia Statute for Religious Freedom," in *The Virginia Statute for Religious Freedom: Its Evolution and Consequences in American History*, ed. Merrill D. Peterson and Robert C. Vaughan (Cambridge 1988) 139–69.

94. William Cabell Rives, *History of the Life and Times of James Madison* (New York 1859–68) II 220–21. For the passage quoted by Madison, see Voltaire, *Letters Concerning the English Nation* 44–45.

95. *WrJM* VIII 412–13: Letter to Mordecai M. Noah on 15 May 1818.

96. It can hardly be fortuitous that, in critical documents, both resort to the language of Deism. Cf. *PTJ* I 413–33 (esp. 423, 429): *The Declaration of Independence* with Madison, *The Federalist* 43 (297). See also *WrJM* IX 573–607 (esp. 590, 599): Notes on Nullification, 1835–36—where "the law of nature & of nature's God" turns out to be an extrapolation from Thomas Hobbes's "*natural* right of self-preservation." For another circumstance in which Madison appealed to "*nature*

and *nature's God*," see *WrJM* VI 332–40 (at 340): Address of the General Assembly to the People of the Commonwealth of Virginia, 23 January 1799. At Princeton, if Madison perused all of the books that Dr. Witherspoon assigned, he will have encountered *The Being and Attributes of God* by Newton's Dr. Clarke. His own testimony suggests that he was swayed from religious orthodoxy at about the time of the Revolution by renewed study of the work. Fifty years later, he would still endorse "reasoning from the effect to the cause, 'from Nature to Nature's God,'" and he evidently hoped that the students at the University of Virginia would learn to do the same. Note the inclusion of Clarke's work on the list that Madison drew up in 1824 of theological works appropriate for use at the university (*WrJM* IX 203–7n), and see *WrJM* IX 229–31: Letter to Frederick Beasley on 20 November 1825. Though Madison was outwardly observant, he never joined any church, and his heterodoxy was widely suspected at the time. For further discussion, see Brant, *James Madison* I 68–71, 85, 111–22, 127–31, III 268–73, and Ralph Ketcham, "James Madison and Religion—A New Hypothesis," *Journal of the Presbyterian Historical Society* 38, no. 2 (June 1960): 65–90, and *James Madison: A Biography* (New York 1971) 55–58, 61, 66, 162–68. Ketcham demonstrates Madison's interest in metaphysical questions but provides no evidence to support his assertion that the mature Madison should be considered a more or less orthodox Christian. In fact, given the political circumstances, the absence of substantive evidence suggests the opposite opinion, for it is far easier to explain the reticence of a statesman who holds unorthodox opinions than to account for the silence of a politician whose views accord well with those of his compatriots. In any case, as Madison's private correspondence indicates, his motive for entering the fray on behalf of freedom of conscience and against the establishment of religion was from the outset political and not religious. Note that, from at least one political perspective, Deism is the functional equivalent of atheism: see Hobbes, *De cive* III.xv.14, and consider II Prologue, note 46, above.

97. See J. G. A. Pocock, "Religious Freedom and the Desacralization of Politics: From the English Civil Wars to the Virginia Statute," in *The Virginia Statute for Religious Freedom* 43–73.

98. *The Federalist* 11 (71).

99. On this point, see Lance Banning, "James Madison, the Statute for Religious Freedom, and the Crisis of Republican Convictions," in *The Virginia Statute for Religious Freedom* 109–38.

100. See Martin Diamond, "Democracy and *The Federalist*: A Reconsideration of the Framers' Intent," *APSR* 53 (1959): 52–68 (esp. 64–67). In this connection, see also Adair, "The Intellectual Origins of Jeffersonian Democracy" 187–271.

101. See *PJM* X 212–13: Letter to Thomas Jefferson on 24 October 1787.

102. Hamilton, *The Federalist* 35 (218–22).

103. *PJM* X 214: 24 October 1787. At the convention, Hamilton evidenced similar misgivings. See *RFC* I 283, 287–88: 18 June 1787.

104. *PJM* X 163–64, 209–14: 6 September and 24 October 1787. For what the Virginian means by "a feudal system of republics," see Hamilton, *The Federalist* 17. As Madison's second letter indicates, the convention assigned to the courts the responsibility which he wanted to award to the federal government itself. For further discussion, see Charles F. Hobson, "The Negative on State Laws: James Madison, the Constitution, and the Crisis of Republican Government," *WMQ* 36 (1979): 215–35, and Michael P. Zuckert, "Federalism and the Founding" 166–210.

105. Consider *The Federalist* 51 (353).

106. See Willi Paul Adams, *The First American Constitutions: Republican Ideology and the Making of the State Constitutions in the Revolutionary Era*, trans. Rita and Robert Kimber (Chapel Hill 1980).

107. Consider *The Federalist* 14 (84, 89), 51 (349), in light of II.v.4–12, above; and see Locke *TTG* II.xi.138, xii.143–44, xiv.159; Hume, *EMPL* 14–31: "That Politics May be Reduced to a Science"; Montesquieu, *EL* 2.11.6; Blackstone, *Commentaries* I 150–51; and Jean Louis de Lolme, *The Constitution of England*³ (London 1781) 60–479.

108. *The Federalist* 39 (257), 51 (347–48). Consider the following by Martin Diamond: "The Federalist's View of Federalism," in *Essays in Federalism*, ed. George Benson et al. (Claremont, Calif., 1961) 21–64; "On the Relationship of Federalism and Decentralization," in *Cooperation and Conflict: Readings in American Federalism*, ed. Daniel J. Elazar et al. (Itasca, Ill., 1969) 72–81; "The Ends of Federalism," *Publius* 3, no. 2 (1973): 129–52; "What the Framers Meant by Federalism," in *A Nation of States: Essays on the American Federal System*², ed. Robert A. Goldwin (Chicago 1974) 25–42; and "*The Federalist* on Federalism: 'Neither a National Nor a Federal Constitution, But a Composition of Both,'" *Yale Law Journal* 86 (1977): 1273–85.

109. Cf. *The Federalist* 47 (324–26), 78 (523), with Montesquieu, *EL* 2.11.6 (397).

110. Jefferson, *NSV* 13 (120–21).

111. Note the use which Madison makes of Jefferson's discussion: *The Federalist* 48 (335–36).

112. *The Federalist* 51 (349).

113. *The Federalist* 60 (405).

114. Consider *The Federalist* 57 (386), 58 (395), in light of *WoJA* VI 219: *A Defence of the Constitutions of Government of the United States of America* (1787–88); cf. Montesquieu, *EL* 2.11.9 with 1.3.5–7; and see Cohler, *Montesquieu's Comparative Politics and the Spirit of American Constitutionalism* 34–169.

115. Cf. Martin Diamond, "The Separation of Powers and the Mixed Regime," *Publius* 8, no. 3 (1978): 33–43, with Harvey C. Mansfield, Jr., "Separation of Powers in the American Constitution," *America's Constitutional Soul* 115–27, and see Kristol, "The Problem of the Separation of Powers" 100–130.

116. *RFC* III 539–51 (at 539): Preface to Debates in the Convention of 1787.

117. See Diamond, "The Separation of Powers and the Mixed Regime" 33–43, and John Agresto, "'A System Without a Precedent'—James Madison and the Revolution in Republican Liberty," *SAQ* 82 (1983): 129–44.

118. After noting I.vi.5, above, cf. Eidelberg, *The Philosophy of the American Constitution* 40–260, with Harvey C. Mansfield, Jr., "Liberal Democracy as a Mixed Regime," *The Spirit of Liberalism* (Cambridge, Mass., 1978) 1–15, and see Kristol, "The Problem of the Separation of Powers" 100–130.

119. See *The Federalist* 1 (4–5), 3 (16–17), 5 (25–27), 6 (29–32), 10, 13 (81), 15 (94–98), 16, 17 (105), 20 (128), 22 (144), 24 (155), 27 (173–74), 31 (194–95), 34 (212), 37 (231–32), 41 (268–69, 275), 42 (283), 48 (333–34), 49, 50 (346), 55 (374, 378), 58 (395–96), 63 (423–425), 70 (475), 71 (481–83), 72 (491–92), 73 (495–96), 76 (510–11), 85 (589–90).

120. Cf. Howe, "The Language of Faculty Psychology in *The Federalist Papers*" 107–36, with the evidence presented in II.i.3–7, ii.2–6, iv.3–8, v.4–7, 10–11, vi.4–7, vii.4–8, above.

121. Cf. *The Federalist* 51 (349) with 49 (343).

122. Consider Polyb. 6.3–18 in light of Mansfield, *Taming the Prince* 75–85.

123. Cf. Madison, *The Federalist* 56 (378), 57 (384), with Hamilton, *The Federalist* 75 (505–6), 76 (513–14).

124. Consider John Quincy Adams, *The Jubilee of the Constitution* (New York 1839) 54, in light of Madison, *The Federalist* 49; then see Arist. *Pol.* 1284a3–b33, 1286a7–1288a5, and note Hamilton, *The Federalist* 25 (163).

125. Cf. *WoAL* IV 168–69: Fragment on the Constitution and Union, January 1861, with Maimonides, *Guide of the Perplexed* I Introduction (11–12), and see Prov. 25:11; then, note *The Federalist* 49, and see *WoAL* I 108–15: Address Before the Young Men's Lyceum of Springfield, Illinois, 27 January 1838.

126. *The Federalist* 51 (352).

127. See Harvey C. Mansfield, Jr., "Social Science and the Constitution," in *Confronting the Constitution: The Challenge to Locke, Montesquieu, Jefferson, and the Federalists from Utilitarianism, Historicism, Marxism, Freudianism, Pragmatism, and Existentialism . . .* , ed. Allan Bloom (Washington, D.C., 1990) 411–36.

128. Cf. Arist. *Pol.* 1263b36–37 with 1276a8–b15, and see 1278b6–15; then, consider August. *De civ. D.* 19.24; Johann Peter Eckermann, *Gespräche mit Goethe* (Jena 1905) II 298–99: Conversation held 1 April 1827; and *WoJSM* X 117–63 (at 133–34): "Coleridge," in light of I Prologue, iv.2–6, and v.3, above; and see *The Federalist* 49. For an attempt to read the Constitution in this light, see George Anastaplo, *The Constitution of 1787: A Commentary* (Baltimore 1989).

129. Consider *The Constitution of the United States of America*, article 2, section 1.

130. Consider *The Federalist* 49 and 63 (esp. 427–28) in light of 71 (esp. 482–83); note *The Federalist* 10 and 51; and see Charles R. Kesler, "*Federalist* 10 and American Republicanism," in *Saving the Revolution* 13–39: as Madison's treatment of religious opinions suggests, the unanimity of opinion expected regarding the inalienable rights of man is, at least in part, derivative from a healthy respect for the self-assertive human tendency to disagree.

131. *The Federalist* 28 (179), 35 (218–21), 57 (384–87), 71 (482).

132. *The Federalist* 48 (333–34), 58 (395–96), 62 (418–19), 63 (422–25), 64 (433–34), 75 (506–7), 76 (512–14).

133. Cf. *The Federalist* 67 with 70 (471–73) and 77 (520–21); consider 37 and 41 (270); and cf. Anastaplo, *The Constitution of 1787* 26–73, 89–123, with Mansfield, *Taming the Prince* 1–278 (esp. 247–78). See III.iii.2 (at note 26), below.

134. *The Federalist* 48 (333–34), 68 (460–61), 70–71, 73 (495–96), 76 (510–13). In this connection, see Ralph Ketcham, *Presidents above Party: The First American Presidency, 1789–1829* (Chapel Hill 1984).

135. Consider *RFC* II 53: 19 July 1787 and *The Federalist* 68 (461), 72, 76 (509), in light of Eidelberg, *The Philosophy of the American Constitution* 166–201, and see Jeremy Rabkin, "Bureaucratic Idealism and Executive Power: A Perspective on *The Federalist*'s View of Public Administration," in *Saving the Revolution* 185–202.

136. Consider Pl. *Leg.* 6.769a–771a (with 772b–d), 12.949e–953e, 957a–e, 960b–969d, in light of *Resp.* 6.497c–d, and see Ralph Lerner, "The Supreme Court as Republican Schoolmaster," *The Thinking Revolutionary: Principle and Practice in the New Republic* (Ithaca 1987) 91–136.

137. Cf. *The Federalist* 51 (351) with 49 (341).

138. *The Constitution of the United States of America*, article 3, section 2.

139. *CAF*: Letters from the Federal Farmer XV–XVI (2.8.185, 195).

140. *CAF*: Essays of Brutus XI–XV (2.9.130–96, esp. 130–44, 186–96).

141. See Ann Stuart Diamond, "The Anti-Federalist 'Brutus,'" *PSR* 6 (1976): 249–81.

142. *The Federalist* 78.

143. *The Federalist* 78 (522–23), 81 (545–46).

144. *The Federalist* 78 (526), 80 (534–39), 82 (553–57).

145. Cf. *The Federalist* 78 (529–30) and 81 (543–44) with 51 (348).

146. See Don E. Fehrenbacher, *The Dred Scott Case: Its Significance in American Law and Politics* (New York 1978).

147. Cf. *The Federalist* 22 (139) and 58 (397) with 47 (esp. 323–26, 331), and see 48 (332), 66 (445–46), 81 (543), with II.v.12, above, and *WoJA* V 37: *A Defence of the Constitutions of Government of the United States of America* (1787–88).

148. Consider *DHRC* II 348–49, 362–63: Pennsylvania Ratifying Convention, 24 November 1787, in light of Arist. *Pol.* 1309b14–1310a35, and see 1308b20–1309a31.

149. Consider *The Federalist* 63 (425), 71 (482–83), and 73 (495–96) in light of 1 (3) and 51 (349).

150. *The Federalist* 47 (323–24), 51 (349), 63 (425).

151. *The Federalist* 73 (493).

152. *The Federalist* 51 (351, 353), 57 (386).

153. *The Federalist* 10. See the exhaustive discussion of this point in Epstein, *The Political Theory of The Federalist* 59–110. Cf. Kesler, "*Federalist* 10 and American Republicanism" 13–39, who seems strangely reluctant to acknowledge the restricted, Lockean character of the American understanding of "justice and the public good."

154. *The Federalist* 51 (353), 57 (386).

155. Cf. Pl. *Leg.* 1.650b; Arist. *Pol.* 1252b27–1253a39, 1278b15–30, 1280a25–1281a10, 1283b42–1284a3, *Eth. Nic.* 1097a15–1098b8, 1169b16–18; and Hooker, *Laws* V.i.1–2, VIII.iii.5, with *WrTJ* (ed. Ford) X 390–92: Letter to Roger C. Weightman on 24 June 1826; consider Martin Diamond, "Ethics and Politics: The American Way," in *The Moral Foundations of the American Republic*[3], ed. Robert H. Horwitz (Charlottesville 1986) 75–108; and see Mansfield, "Liberal Democracy as a Mixed Regime" 1–15.

156. *The Federalist* 49. Note Hamilton, *The Federalist* 25 (163).

Chapter 2

1. *CAF*: James Monroe, *Some Observations on the Constitution* (5.21.12).

2. *CAF*: Letters of Cato III (2.6.12). Cf. *WoAL* II 461–69: "A House Divided": Speech at Springfield, Illinois, 16 June 1858.

3. Although it would be an exaggeration to speak of regional parties, sectional tension did come to exert considerable influence over the deliberations of Congress: see H. James Henderson, *Party Politics in the Continental Congress* (New York 1974). In this connection, note also Joseph L. Davis, *Sectionalism in American Politics, 1774–1787* (Madison, Wis., 1977).

4. *PJM* IX 371: Letter to Edmund Randolph on 8 April 1787. See also *PJM* IX 291–92: Notes on [the Congressional] Debates of 21 February 1787.

5. *RFC* I 135: 6 June 1787. To support his overall point, Madison gives seven examples. This is the fourth.

6. See William M. Wiecek, "The Statutory Law of Slavery and Race in the Thirteen Mainland Colonies of British America," *WMQ* 34 (1977): 258–80.

7. *PJJ* III 342: Letter to Granville Sharp of the English Anti-Slavery Society in June (?) 1788. For the details, see Arthur Zilversmit, *The First Emancipation: The Abolition of Slavery in the North* (Chicago 1967). In supposing that, at the time of the Philadelphia convention, there were already eight northern and only five southern states, Madison was counting Delaware as part of the North. See *RFC* II 10: 14 July 1787. His fellow Virginian George Mason held the same opinion. See *RFC* II 362: 21 August 1787. Madison's subsequent suggestion to the delegates at the Virginia Ratifying Convention that New York and New Jersey "would, probably oppose any attempts to annihilate this species of property" should be discounted: the argument was advanced at a time when Madison was making a spirited attempt to still the alarm inspired by Patrick Henry and George Mason; and, in any case, his was an observation made with regard to the short run. See *DSSC* III 459: Virginia Ratifying Convention, 15 June 1788.

8. Jefferson, *NSV* 14 (138). After considering William W. Freehling, "The Founding Fathers and Slavery," *AHR* 77 (1982): 81–93, and Alison Goodyear Freehling, *Drift toward Dissolution: The Virginia Slavery Debate of 1831–1832* (Baton Rouge 1982) 96–109, see III.vi.5 (with the literature cited in note 75), below.

9. For Jefferson's proposal and Madison's effort, see *PTJ* II 470–73: "Report of the Committee of Revisors, submitted 18 June 1779," with Jefferson, *NSV* 14 (137–43). In this connection, see also *PJM* VIII 403–5: Letter to George Washington on 11 November 1785; *PTJ* VI 298: Jefferson's Proposed Revision of the Virginia Constitution, May–June 1783; and *WrTJ* (ed. Ford) I 67–68: Autobiography.

10. George S. Brookes, *Friend Anthony Benezet* (Philadelphia 1937) 443–44: Letter from Patrick Henry to Robert Pleasants on 18 January 1773.

11. See *JCC* VI 1091–98 (esp. 1093, 1096): 28 June–4 July 1776.

12. For the details, see Pete Maslowski, "National Policy toward the Use of Black Troops in the Revolution," *South Carolina Historical Magazine* 73 (January 1972): 1–17. For a brief discussion of John Laurens's character, see Richard J. Hargrove, "Portrait of a Southern Patriot: The Life and Death of John Laurens," in *The Revolutionary War in the South: Power, Conflict, and Leadership: Essays in Honor of John Richard Alden*, ed. W. Robert Higgins (Durham, N.C., 1979) 182–202. See also the articles cited in III.ii.4, note 37, below. For the development of slavery in South Carolina, see Peter H. Wood, *Black Majority: Negroes in Colonial South Carolina from 1670 through the Stono Rebellion* (New York 1974). For its impact on morals, manners, and opinions, see Jack P. Greene, " 'Slavery or Independence': Some Reflections on the Relationship among Liberty, Black Bondage, and Equality in Revolutionary South Carolina," *South Carolina Historical Magazine* 80 (July 1979): 193–214. For the war in the South, see John S. Pancake, *This Destructive War: The British Campaign in the Carolinas, 1780–1782* (University, Ala., 1985). See, as well, *An Uncivil War: The Southern Backcountry during the American Revolution*, ed. Ronald Hoffman, Thad W. Tate, and Peter J. Albert (Charlottesville 1985).

13. In his letter, Hamilton argued that "the negroes will make very excellent soldiers, with proper management" and suggested that "their want of cultivation (for their natural faculties are probably as good as ours) joined to that habit of subordination which they acquire from a life of servitude, will make them sooner became soldiers than our White inhabitants." The fact that the endeavor might open "a door to their emancipation" had "no small weight in inducing"

him "to wish the success of the project; for the dictates of humanity and true policy equally interest" him "in favour of this unfortunate class of men." For the passages quoted, see *PAH* II 17–19, III 120–21: Letter to John Jay on 14 March 1779, and Letter from Lieutenant Colonel John Laurens in July 1782. Soon after writing, Laurens was killed in a skirmish. For the hopes fostered by the Laurens family, see the reflective letter Henry Laurens later sent Hamilton: *PAH* III 605–8: 19 April 1785.

14. For Georgia's rather peculiar early history as a charity colony with an agrarian law and a ban on alcoholic spirits, Roman Catholicism, and the legal profession, in addition to slavery, see Kenneth Coleman, "The Founding of Georgia"; Milton L. Ready, "Philanthropy and the Origins of Georgia"; Phinizy Spalding, "James Edward Oglethorpe's Quest for an American Zion"; and Betty Wood, "The Earl of Egmont and the Georgia Colony," all in *Forty Years of Diversity: Essays on Colonial Georgia*, ed. Harvey H. Jackson and Phinizy Spalding (Athens, Ga., 1986) 4–20, 46–96. For the actual prohibition of slavery, see *The Colonial Records of the State of Georgia*, ed. Allen D. Candler (Atlanta, Ga., 1904–16) I 49–52: Act of 9 January 1734. In this connection, see Betty Wood, "Thomas Stephens and the Introduction of Slavery in Georgia," *GHQ* 58 (1974): 24–40, and *Slavery in Colonial Georgia* (Athens, Ga., 1984) 1–87. Wood's denial that the trustees were hostile to slavery per se is at least partially belied by the evidence she presents for James Oglethorpe's attitude in 1739.

15. See *The Colonial Records of the State of Georgia* XVIII 7–47 (at 42–44) and XIX, pt. 1, 291–332 (at 324–29): Acts of 24 January 1755 and 29 September 1773.

16. For the Scots' response, which seems to have been composed by the father of Lachlan McIntosh, see *The Clamorous Malcontents: Criticism and Defenses of the Colony of Georgia, 1741–1743*, ed. Trevor R. Reese (Savannah 1973) 169–70 (with 249–50): 3 January 1738–39. Cf. Montesquieu, *EL* 3.15.1–19 (esp. 1 [490]), and III.iv.3, below. For the circumstances which occasioned its dispatch, see Harvey H. Jackson, "The Darien Antislavery Petition of 1739 and the Georgia Plan," *WMQ* 34 (1977): 618–31.

17. See *The Revolutionary Records of the State of Georgia*, ed. Allen D. Candler (Atlanta, Ga., 1908) I 38–43 (at 41–42): 12 January 1775. For Lachlan McIntosh's relations with Henry Laurens and for the role he played in the deliberations at Darien, see Harvey H. Jackson, *Lachlan McIntosh and the Politics of Revolutionary Georgia* (Athens, Ga., 1979) 1–34 (with 164 n. 14).

18. For the later situation and outlook of Lachlan McIntosh, see III.ii.5, note 74, and III.ii.7, note 113, below. I find implausible the suggestion that the Darien resolution was merely a cynical attempt to persuade the restive slaves of St. Andrew's Parish that "their freedom . . . was conditioned on the success of the Whig cause, which they could best support . . . by remaining slaves." Cf. Harvey H. Jackson, " 'American Slavery, American Freedom' and the Revolution in the Lower South: The Case of Lachlan McIntosh," *Southern Studies* 19 (1980): 81–93. Like many historians in recent years, Jackson is too apt to discount the moral anguish felt—especially in the first flush of revolutionary idealism—by slaveholders caught between injustice and financial ruin.

19. For the development of slavery in Georgia after 1750, see Betty Wood, *Slavery in Colonial Georgia* 88–206. For the central importance it had achieved by the end of the colonial period, see Jack P. Greene, "Travails of an Infant Colony:

The Search for Viability, Coherence, and Identity in Colonial Georgia," in *Forty Years of Diversity* 278–309.

20. *PTJ* VIII 258–59, 356–57: Exchange of Letters with Richard Price on 2 July and 7 August 1785. For the passage which offended Price's readers in South Carolina, see Richard Price, *Observations on the Importance of the American Revolution, and the Means of Making it a Benefit to the World* (Philadelphia 1785) 47. Price's pamphlet is reprinted in *Richard Price and the Ethical Foundations of the American Revolution*, ed. Bernard Peach (Durham, N.C., 1979) 177–224. If one excludes Thomas Paine from consideration, Price was at this time the best-known English admirer of the Revolution. His earlier pamphlet *Observations on the Nature of Civil Liberty, the Principles of Government and the Justice and Policy of the War with America*, which was first published in London in February 1776, was certainly the most famous British tract on the subject. It went through nearly twenty editions and was translated into German, French, and Dutch. For some of those whom Price has in mind when he speaks of "the friends of liberty and humanity," see Nicholas Hans, "Franklin, Jefferson, and the English Radicals at the End of the Eighteenth Century," *PAPhS* 98 (1954): 406–26.

21. See William W. Freehling, *The Road to Disunion* I 131–43.

22. *PTJ* XV 71–72: Letter from Francis Kinloch on 26 April 1789. In this connection, see Jefferson, *NSV* 14 (137–43), 18 (162–63). Slavery had defenders even in Virginia: see Fredrika Teute Schmidt and Barbara Ripel Wilhelm, "Early Pro-slavery Petitions in Virginia," *WMQ* 30 (1973): 133–46, and David W. Robson, "'An Important Question Answered': William Graham's Defense of Slavery in Post-Revolutionary Virginia," *WMQ* 37 (1980): 644–52.

23. For the background to this dispute, which was more than merely a struggle for power and which turned on the question of corporate versus individual representation, see Rosemarie Zagarri, *The Politics of Size: Representation in the United States, 1776–1850* (Ithaca 1987) 1–104. For its resolution, see Herbert J. Storing, "The Constitutional Convention: Toward a More Perfect Union," in *American Political Thought: The Philosophic Dimensions of American Statesmanship*[3], ed. Morton J. Frisch and Richard G. Stevens (Itasca, Ill., 1983) 51–68, and see the article cited in III.ii.3, note 25, below. In some spheres, the dispute persisted well into the nineteenth century. As one would expect, there were battles over apportionment. Moreover, to the annoyance of those representing the more populous states, the less populous states sought to maximize their corporate influence by electing congressmen and presidential electors at large. Eventually, Congress outlawed at-large elections for the House of Representatives, and the large states fell in line with small-state practice in the selection of presidential electors. See Zagarri, *The Politics of Size* 105–44.

24. *RFC* I 486, II 10: 30 June and 14 July 1787. See also the account given by Robert Yates of New York, who mistakenly attributes Madison's initial remark to 29 July: *RFC* I 476. Madison returned to the same theme on more than one occasion. See *RFC* I 601–2, II 81, 111: 13, 21, and 25 July 1787. Soon after Madison first broached the issue, Rufus King of Massachusetts chimed in, stating that he "was fully convinced that the question concerning a difference of interests did not lie where it had hitherto been discussed, between the great & small States; but between Southern & Eastern." In similar fashion, Hugh Williamson of North Carolina would later remark on the "essential difference of interests

between the N. & S. States, particularly in the carrying trade"; George Mason of Virginia would describe the two sections as being in "interest different"; and Charles Pinckney of South Carolina would speak of "the two great divisions" as the "Northern & Southern Interests." See *RFC* I 510, 516, 566, II 100–101, 362–63, 450: 2, 10, and 24 July, and 21 and 29 August 1787. When Hamilton later spoke of "causes, as well physical as moral, which may, in a greater or less degree, permanently nourish different propensities and inclinations" within "the different parts of the union," he had slavery and the great divide between North and South in mind: cf. *The Federalist* 60 (404–5) with 13 (80–82), and consider Hamilton's doubts about the prudence of westward expansion (III.iii.2, note 24, below) in light of the quarrels that occasioned the Civil War.

25. Madison hoped by his intervention to deflect the attention of the delegates from the debate then under way. But, by drawing attention to the danger to which the extended republic would, in fact, be exposed, he inadvertently provided a rationale for giving each state equal representation in one of the two houses of the national legislature. Only then could one expect the North, a section purportedly destined to have a smaller population articulated into a larger number of states, to have the leverage to protect its various interests: see Jack Rakove, "The Great Compromise: Ideas, Interests, and the Politics of Constitution Making," *WMQ* 44 (1987): 424–57.

26. See *RFC* I 486–87, II 9–10, 111: 30 June and 14 and 25 July 1787, and *PJM* IX 371, 383: Letters to Edmund Randolph and to George Washington on 8 and 16 April 1787: Madison counted five southern and eight northern states, but in the long run, he expected the former to be much more populous than the latter. For the time being, he knew that George Mason of Virginia was right in supposing that the southern representation would be "the *minority* in both Houses." See *RFC* II 362–63, 451: 21 and 29 August 1787.

27. For the confused fashion in which the rule emerged, see Howard A. Ohline, "Republicanism and Slavery: Origins of the Three-Fifths Clause in the United States Constitution," *WMQ* 28 (1971): 563–84.

28. For a thorough account of this dimension of the structure of American politics, see Drew R. McCoy, "James Madison and Visions of American Nationality in the Confederation Period: A Regional Perspective," in *Beyond Confederation: Origins of the Constitution and American National Identity*, ed. Richard Beeman, Stephen Botein, and Edward C. Carter II (Chapel Hill 1987) 226–58. In this connection, see *DHRC* XIII 149–58: The United States, Spain, and the Navigation of the Mississippi River.

29. For Paterson's speech, see *RFC* I 561: 9 July 1787. For the remarks made by Wilson, Morris, and King, see *RFC* I 581–83, 586–88, 593, 603–4: 11–13 July 1787. For the quite similar opinion sketched out on paper by John Dickinson, see *SRFC* 158: 9 July 1787. Note, however, the conciliatory attitude evidenced by Rufus King and James Wilson. See *RFC* I 562, 595: 9 and 12 July 1787. Elbridge Gerry voiced his objections only after deciding to oppose ratification: *RFC* II 633: 15 September 1787. In this connection, see *SRFC* 234, 241–42, 247, 254: Letters from Elbridge to Ann Gerry on 21, 26, and 29 August and 1 September 1787.

30. See *RFC* I 562: 9 July 1787.

31. Cf. *RFC* I 533 and *SRFC* 149: 5 July 1787 with *RFC* II 221–23: 8 August 1787. Note, however, *RFC* II 106: 24 July 1787.

32. *RFC* I 585–86: 11 July 1787.

33. Harrison's motion was defeated on a straight sectional vote. For the debate and its eventual resolution, see *JCC* VI 1079–81, 1098–1102, IX 800–802: 30 July–1 August 1776, 13–14 October 1777. In this connection, see *Letters of Delegates to Congress, 1774–1789*, ed. Paul H. Smith (Washington, D.C., 1976–) VIII 299: Letter from Nathaniel Folsom to Meschech Weare on 21 November 1777.

34. For the proposal and the debate, see *JCC* XXIV 214–16, 223–24, XXV 948–49, 952: 27–28 March and 1 April 1783. For further evidence, see *PJM* VI 35–39, 148–49, 215, 402, 407–8, 425, 435: Notes of Debates, 14 and 28 January, 11 February, 27–28 March, and 1 and 7 April 1783. See also *PJM* VI 311–16 (esp. 313–14), 406–7, 439–41, 487–98 (esp. 492): Report on Restoring Public Credit, 6 March 1783; Amendment to Report on Restoring Public Credit, 28 March 1783; Letter to Edmund Randolph on 8 April 1783; Report on Address to the States, 25 April 1783. In the last document, Madison remarked of the new rule for apportioning requisitions that "the only material difficulty which attended it in the deliberations of Congress, was to fix the proper difference between the labor and industry of free inhabitants, and of all other inhabitants." For the amendment proposed, see *DHRC* I 148–50: Amendment to Share Expenses According to Population, 18 April 1783. Use of the three-fifths rule in apportioning representation appears to have been part of the plan Charles Pinckney drew up for consideration by the federal convention. See *DHRC* I 245–47: Charles Pinckney's Plan, 29 May 1787. In general, northerners were prepared to believe that slaves were not much inclined to work. See, for example, *DSSC* II 38: Massachusetts Ratifying Convention, 17 January 1788.

35. See *RFC* I 580–81, 596: 11–12 July 1787. Note, in this connection, *RFC* I 562: 9 July 1787.

36. There is no logical inconsistency between this observation and Pinckney's subsequent claim that he and his colleagues "obtained a representation for our property," for within the Lockean dispensation, the ownership of productive labor is the ultimate source of all other property: consider *DSSC* IV 282–83: South Carolina Legislature, 17 January 1788, in light of Locke, *TTG* II.v.25–45. As the French vice-consul resident in Wilmington, North Carolina, put it in a dispatch to his superiors, "The new constitution calculates the wealth of a state only by the *work* of its inhabitants." See *DHRC* XVI 11–16 (at 12): Letter from Gaspard Joseph Amand Ducher to Comte de la Luzerne on 2 February 1788. James Madison's attempt to make sense of the formula for determining representation solely on the grounds of "the personal rights of the people" resulted in a rationale that was, as even he was forced to acknowledge, "a little strained in some points." See *The Federalist* 54. In explaining the clause, Hamilton stressed the link between "representation and taxation." See *PAH* V 23–24, 30, 33: Speech at the New York Ratifying Convention on 20 June 1788. He, in fact, suspected that "the different degrees of industry and improvement in different" places would render population "a precarious measure of wealth." See *RFC* I 286: 18 June 1787. In Gouverneur Morris's opinion, direct taxation was mentioned in the critical clause "in order to exclude the appearance of counting the Negroes in *the Representation*" so that "the including of them may now be referred to the object of direct taxes, and incidentally only to that of Representation." See *RFC* II 607–8: 13 September 1787.

37. In time, Ramsay would mute the sentiments that so isolated him in Charleston, and in some measure, he would even accommodate himself to the institution that he so loathed: see Arthur H. Shaffer, "Between Two Worlds: David Ramsay

and the Politics of Slavery," *JSH* 50 (1984): 175–96, and Eve Kornfeld, "From Republicanism to Liberalism: The Intellectual Journey of David Ramsay," *JER* 9 (1989): 289–313. One could perhaps describe Ramsay's intellectual odyssey as the transformation of a Country Whig into a Court Whig, but there is no reason to suppose that he was ever anything but a liberal republican.

38. *RFC* I 592, 605: 12–13 July 1787.

39. *RFC* II 95, 443, 446, 453–54: 23 July and 28–29 August 1787. Madison would later refer to the concession which Pinckney secured as a "clause which secures to us that property which we now possess." See *DSSC* III 453–54: Virginia Ratifying Convention, 15 June 1788.

40. *RFC* II 183: "Report of the Committee of Detail," 6 August 1787. The committee had five members: Rutledge, Edmund Randolph of Virginia, Nathaniel Gorham of Massachusetts, Oliver Ellsworth of Connecticut, and James Wilson of Pennsylvania.

41. See the exchange between Rawlins Lowndes and Pinckney: *DSSC* IV 272, 285: South Carolina Legislature, 16–17 January 1788.

42. *RFC* II 417: 25 August 1787. The widespread character of this conviction is evident in a last-minute change which the Framers made in the fugitive-slave clause. Originally, as reported by the Committee of Style, it began, "No person legally held to service or labour in one state." In the version finally approved, this phrase was altered to read, "No person held to service or labour in one state, under the laws thereof." The amendment was made, Madison reports, "in compliance with the wish of some who thought the term (legal) equivocal, and favoring the idea that slavery was legal in a moral view." See *RFC* II 601, 628: 12 and 15 September 1787. In this fashion, the Framers acknowledged the existence of the relevant state laws without in any way conceding their justice and propriety.

43. In notes that he drew up for a speech never delivered at the convention, John Dickinson expressed the fear that "omitting the *Word* will be regarded as an Endeavour to conceal a principle of which we are ashamed." See *SRFC* 158: 9 July 1787. That fear was justified soon thereafter, when the Anti-Federalist Samuel Bryan charged that the delegates chose "words" that "are dark and ambiguous" in order "to conceal from Europe, that in this enlightened country, the practice of slavery has its advocates among men in the highest stations." See *CAF*: Letters of Centinel III (2.7.76). As even Luther Martin was prepared to acknowledge, the Framers guarded "against the word '*slaves*' [because] they anxiously sought to avoid the admission of expressions which might be odious in the ears of Americans, although they were willing to admit into their system those *things* which the *expressions* signified." See *CAF*: Luther Martin, "The Genuine Information Delivered to the Legislature of the State of Maryland" (2.4.64). Note the comments made in Philadelphia by William Paterson of New Jersey and James Wilson of Pennsylvania. See *RFC* I 561, 595: 9 and 12 July 1787. See also *WrJM* IX 1–13 (esp. 1–3): Letter to Robert Walsh on 27 November 1819. As Benjamin Rush had occasion to note, "No mention was made of *Negroes* or *slaves* in this Constitution only because it was thought the very words would contaminate the glorious fabric of American liberty and government." See *LBR* I 441–44 (at 442): Letter to John Coakley Lettsom on 28 September 1787. In a brief moment of pique, Gouverneur Morris suggested that the most offensive clause refer explicitly to the "importation of slaves into N. Carolina,—Carolina & Georgia"; he wanted

"it to be known . . . that this part of the Constitution was a compliance with those States." See *RFC* II 415–16: 25 August 1787. It would be hard to improve on Lord Acton's observation that "slavery was deplored, was denounced, and was retained." See Lord Acton, *Lectures on Modern History* (London 1906) 314.

44. The manuscript evidence adequately disproves the claim, advanced in various quarters, that Madison subsequently reworked his notes to a partisan end: see James H. Hutson, "Introduction," *SRFC* xx–xxv.

45. *RFC* II 220–22: 8 August 1787. For the decision on representation, see *RFC* I 592–97: 12 July 1787. The discussion took place on the days immediately preceding the vote.

46. *RFC* II 364: 21 August 1787.

47. *RFC* II 370: 22 August 1787. Note *RFC* II 640: 15 September 1787. By this time, Mason had evidently read Jefferson, *NSV* 18 (162–63), if not also his principal source: Montesquieu, *EL* 3.15.1–19.

48. In this connection, see *CAF*: Luther Martin, "The Genuine Information Delivered to the Legislature of the State of Maryland" (2.4.68–71).

49. *DSSC* III 269–73, 452–54: Virginia Ratifying Convention on 11 and 15 June 1788.

50. The debate at the federal convention would no doubt have taken on a different character had anyone at the time drawn the attention of the delegates from the South to the fact that—although the compromise eventually reached temporarily limited the federal government's power to prevent the existing states' import of slaves—there was no provision within the Constitution explicitly barring the central administration from eventually exercising the authority given it under the interstate commerce clause to stop the interstate as well as the international traffic in slaves. Disagreement over the import of this fact would later cause much consternation: see Walter Berns, "The Constitution and the Migration of Slaves," *Yale Law Review* 78 (1968): 198–228. It deserves notice that, in 1807, when Congress voted to abolish the transatlantic slave trade, it acted also to regulate the domestic coastal slave trade: *United States Statutes at Large* II 429–30.

51. *RFC* II 364: 21 August 1787.

52. Cf. *JCC* XXV 948: 28 March 1783 with *RFC* II 415–16: 25 August 1787. Apart from Jefferson himself, Williamson was the only southern delegate to the Continental Congress to vote for the Virginian's proposal that slavery be barred altogether from the western territories: see III.ii.5, note 84, below.

53. *RFC* II 373: 22 August 1787.

54. *RFC* II 372–73: 22 August 1787. For a summary of the case made by the delegates from the Deep South, see the notes kept by James McHenry of Maryland: *RFC* II 378: 22 August 1787.

55. *RFC* II 374: 22 August 1787. As Randolph predicted, the clause was a lightning rod for criticism during the ratification struggle. See *CAF*: Letters of Centinel III (2.7.76); Essays of Brutus III (2.9.39); Essay by Deliberator (3.13.5); A Letter from a Gentleman in a Neighboring State to a Gentleman in this City (4.2.9); A Friend to the Rights of the People (4.23.3.5); Consider Arms, Malichi Maynard, and Samuel Field, *Reasons for Dissent* (4.26.8–15); Essay by Phileleutheros (4.27.3–5); Essays by Republicus (5.13.14); Letters from a Countryman from Duchess County (6.6.2–4, 9–14); Letters from a Countryman (6.7.6). See also *DHRC* III 424–25, XIV 254, 503–30: Speech by Benjamin Gale of Connecticut, 12 November 1787; Philadelphiensis II, *Philadelphia Freeman's Journal*, 28 Novem-

ber 1787; and Various Letters Illustrating Quaker Opposition to the Protection of Slavery in the Constitution. In reply, Federalists tended to argue that the clause was virtually a promise that the evil traffic would soon come to an end, and they celebrated this as an important concession made by the states of the lower South. See *DHRC* II 539–40, III 160–61, XIII 253, 432, XIV 514–15, XVI 427–28: Thomas McKean, Debates at the Pennsylvania Ratifying Convention, 10 December 1787; Reply to George Mason's Objections to the Constitution, *New Jersey Journal*, 26 December 1787; *Pennsylvania Gazette*, 26 September 1787; Tench Coxe, "An American Citizen IV: On the Federal Government," Philadelphia, 21 October 1787; Plain Truth to Timothy Meanwell, *Philadelphia Independent Gazetteer*, 30 October 1787; James Iredell, "Marcus V," *Norfolk and Portsmouth Journal*, Norfolk, Virginia, 19 March 1788. Only one Anti-Federalist conceded the point. See *CAF*: Letters from The Federal Farmer XVIII (2.8.229). See also the various exchanges at the Massachusetts Ratifying Convention: *DSSC* II 41, 107–8, 120, 149–50: 18, 25–26, 30 January and 4 February 1788.

56. For the first hint that the delegates from New England might be willing to cut such a deal, see the remarks of Rufus King at *RFC* I 562: 9 July 1787. With regard to the bargain actually made, see *CAF*: Luther Martin, "The Genuine Information Delivered to the Legislature of the State of Maryland" (2.4.65–67). "I found the *eastern* States, notwithstanding their *aversion to slavery*, were very willing to indulge the southern States at least with a temporary liberty to prosecute the *slave trade*, provided the southern States would in their turn gratify them, by laying no *restriction* on *navigation acts*." So Martin reported after his return to Annapolis. Note, as well, *PTJ* XIII 205: Letter from George Mason on 26 May 1788.

57. *RFC* II 364, 371–73: 21 and 22 August 1787.

58. *RFC* II 375: 22 August 1787.

59. For the details, see Robert Allen Rutland, *The Ordeal of the Constitution: The Antifederalists and the Ratification Struggle of 1787–1788* (Boston 1983) esp. 162–69, 182–253, 282–83, 302–3; and Lance Banning, "Virginia: Sectionalism and the General Good," and Michael Lienesch, "North Carolina: Preserving Rights," in *Ratifying the Constitution*, ed. Michael Allen Gillespie and Michael Lienesch (Lawrence, Kans., 1989) 261–99, 343–67. The fact that the delegates to the Georgia Ratifying Convention voted as one to join the proposed Union says much about the pressure they were under from the Spaniards in Florida and the Indians on the frontier and nothing as to what would have happened if it had been clear that their immediate neighbors to the north were intent on forming a separate confederation: see Rutland, *The Ordeal of the Constitution* 87–88; consider the letter quoted in III.ii.5, note 74, below; and see John P. Kaminski, "Controversy amid Consensus: The Adoption of the Federal Constitution in Georgia," *GHQ* 58 (1974): 244–61, and Edward J. Cashin, "Georgia: Searching for Security," in *Ratifying the Constitution* 93–116.

60. See Robert M. Weir, "South Carolina: Slavery and the Structure of the Union," in *Ratifying the Constitution* 201–34. The wealthy men who owned rice plantations in the lowcountry were considerably less hungry for slaves than the residents of the upcountry to the west: see Patrick S. Brady, "The Slave Trade and Sectionalism in South Carolina, 1787–1808," *JSH* 38 (1972): 601–20.

61. In defending the Constitution in South Carolina's House of Representatives, Pinckney was prepared to argue that "the Southern States . . . are so weak that by ourselves we could not form a union strong enough for the purpose of

effectually protecting each other." See *DSSC* IV 283–84: 17 January 1788. In this connection, see *RFC* II 449–50, 452: 29 August 1787.

62. For the ethos that governed their conduct, see Bertram Wyatt-Brown, *Southern Honor: Ethics and Behavior in the Old South* (New York 1982).

63. *Prigg v. Pennsylvania*, 16 Peters 539, 611 (1842). The fundamental importance of the fugitive-slave clause for the South as a whole is obscured by the fact that it was easily adopted once the compromise regarding the slave trade had been made: the absence of opposition precluded the necessity for assertiveness on the part of the southern delegates.

64. *RFC* II 369–71: 22 August 1787.

65. Nonetheless, some scholars manage: for a provocative restatement of the neo-abolitionist interpretation of the events at the federal convention, see Paul Finkelman, "Slavery and the Constitutional Convention: Making a Covenant with Death," in *Beyond Confederation* 188–225.

66. See *DHRC* III 389–92 (at 390): Letter from New York, *Connecticut Journal*, New Haven, 31 October 1787.

67. Cf. *WrTJ* (ed. Ford) X 157–58: Letter to John Holmes on 22 April 1820 with Ter. *Phorm.* 506, Suet. *Tib.* 24.1–25.1, and Thuc. 2.63.2. Jefferson was steeped in the classics: see Carl J. Richard, "A Dialogue with the Ancients: Thomas Jefferson and Classical Philosophy and History," *JER* 9 (1989): 431–55.

68. *The Belknap Papers* (Boston 1877–91) II 405–12: Letter from St. George Tucker to Jeremy Belknap on 29 June 1795.

69. In this connection, see Jefferson, *NSV* 14 (137–43); *WrTJ* (ed. Ford) IX 477–79, X 45n–46n, 157–58, 289–93: Letters to Edward Coles on 25 August 1814, to Samuel Kercheval on 5 September 1816, to John Holmes on 22 April 1820, and to Jared Sparks on 4 February 1824; *WrTJ* (ed. Peterson) 1447–50: Letter to Albert Gallatin on 26 December 1820; Henry S. Randall, *The Life of Thomas Jefferson* (New York 1857) III 539: Letter to James Heaton on 20 May 1826; *PJM* XII 437–38: "Memorandum on an African Colony for Freed Slaves," ca. 20 October 1789; and *WrJM* VIII 439–47, IX 130–34 (esp. 134), 224–29, 261–66 (at 265–66), 306–12 (at 310–11), 468–70, 498–502: Letter to Robert J. Evans on 15 June 1819; "Answers to Questions Concerning Slavery," 1823; and Letters to Frances Wright on 1 September 1825, to the Marquis de Lafayette in November 1826 and on 20 February 1828, to R. R. Gurley on 28 December 1831, and to Thomas R. Dew on 23 February 1833.

70. *The Belknap Papers* II 412–16: Letters from James Sullivan and John Adams to Jeremy Belknap on 30 July and 22 October 1795. For subsequent discussion, see II 417–23, 425–28: Letters from St. George Tucker to Jeremy Belknap on 27 November 1795 and 3 April and 13 August 1797.

71. [Noah Webster], *Examination into the Leading Principles of the Federal Constitution Proposed by the Late Convention Held at Philadelphia by A Citizen of America* (Philadelphia 1787) 39–40.

72. See *DSSC* II 41, 149–50: 18 January and 4 February 1788. For the Federalist argument, see III.ii.4, note 55, above.

73. James Wilson, the only Pennsylvanian to attend both the federal convention and the state ratifying convention, was probably the man responsible for propagating this view. In speaking to the delegates at the latter, he said, "I consider this as laying the foundation for banishing slavery out of this country; and though the period is more distant than I could wish, yet it will produce the same kind, gradual change, which was pursued in Pennsylvania. . . . And in the mean-

time, the new states which are to be formed will be under the control of Congress in this particular; and slaves will never be introduced amongst them." The following afternoon, he added, "Yet the lapse of a few years and Congress will have power to exterminate slavery from within our borders." See *DHRC* II 462–63, 499–500: 3–4 December 1787. Note the similar remarks of Thomas McKean. See *DHRC* II 539–40: 10 December 1787. Something of the sort was suggested at the New Hampshire Ratifying Convention. See *DSSC* II 203. Note, in addition, the material collected by Walter Berns, "The Constitution and the Migration of Slaves" 201–5.

74. To a friend chosen to preside over the Georgia Ratifying Convention, McIntosh justified his opposition, writing, "It is known to have been the intention of the Eastern and Northern States to abolish slavery altogether when in their power, which, however just, may not be convenient for us so soon as for them, especially in a new country and hot climate such as Georgia. Let us therefore keep the proper time for it in our power while we have it. This Constitution prolongs the time for 20 years more." See *DHRC* III 259–61: Letter from Lachlan McIntosh to John Wereat on 17 December 1787. By this time, McIntosh had done service as a general in the Continental Army, had become president of the Georgia Society of the Cincinnati, and was in desperate financial straits as a consequence of his loss of property in the war; Wereat had been chief justice of the Georgia Supreme Court and was then serving as state auditor. Both men were from St. Andrew's Parish, and their relations had long been close. See Harvey H. Jackson, *Lachlan McIntosh and the Politics of Revolutionary Georgia* 24–151, and George R. Lamplugh, " 'To Check and Discourage the Wicked and Designing': John Wereat and the Revolution in Georgia," *GHQ* 61 (1977): 295–307.

75. See *The Papers of Daniel Webster*, ed. Charles M. Wiltse et al. (Hanover, N.H., 1974–89) IV, pt. 2, 513–51 (at 523–26): The Constitution and the Union, 7 March 1850.

76. For the demographic evidence, see Philip D. Curtin, *The Atlantic Slave Trade: A Census* (Madison, Wis., 1969) 72–75. Note also Gerald W. Mullin, *Flight and Rebellion: Slave Resistance in 18th Century Virginia* (New York 1974) 15–16. One prominent South Carolina Anti-Federalist believed that the climate of the South in general and of his own state in particular was so injurious to health—with its "excessive heats" and "the baneful effects of [its] fogs and swamps"—that, "from our limitation of importing negroes after the term of twenty years, instead of rising in representation we should gradually degenerate." See *CAF*: Speech of Rawlins Lowndes in the South Carolina Legislature, 18 January 1788 (5.12.3).

77. Here the exception proves the rule. There was, in fact, at least one northerner who noted what had happened in Virginia and grasped in some measure its political import. At the federal convention, Oliver Ellsworth remarked that the "slaves . . . multiply so fast in Virginia & Maryland that it is cheaper to raise than import them." See *RFC* II 371: 22 August 1787. In defending the Constitution against the objections raised by George Mason, he carried the logic of this observation one step further: "Mr. Mason has himself about three hundred slaves and lives in Virginia where it is found by prudent management they can breed and raise slaves faster than they want them for their own use, and could supply the deficiency in Georgia and South Carolina; and perhaps Colonel Mason may suppose it more humane to breed than import slaves." See *DHRC* III 489–90: A Landholder VI, *Connecticut Courant*, Hartford, 10 December 1787. But, though

Ellsworth foresaw this eventuality, even he failed to consider the possibility that slavery might spread in this fashion to the western territories as well. In South Carolina, David Ramsay similarly recognized that "the importations of the ensuing 20 years, added to the natural increase of those we already have, and the influx from our northern neighbours, who are desirous of getting rid of their slaves, will afford a sufficient number for cultivating all the lands in this state," but he, too, failed to take the next logical step. See *DHRC* XVI 25: Civis—To the Citizens of South Carolina, *Charleston Columbian Herald*, 4 February 1788.

78. Jefferson, *NSV* 8 (87). In claiming that the treatment of slaves in Virginia was relatively mild, Jefferson was probably correct, but other practices may also help explain the remarkable fertility of the American slave population. See Herbert S. Klein and Stanley L. Engerman, "Fertility Differentials between Slaves in the United States and the British West Indies: A Note on Lactation Practices and Their Possible Implications," *WMQ* 35 (1978): 357–74; and Robert W. Fogel and Stanley L. Engerman, "Recent Findings in the Study of Slave Demography and Family Structure," *Sociology and Social Research* 63 (1979): 566–89.

79. For the statistical evidence, see Robert William Fogel and Stanley L. Engerman, *Time on the Cross: The Economics of American Negro Slavery* (Boston 1974) 13–58. In this connection, see also Curtin, *The Atlantic Slave Trade* 51–93.

80. *CAF*: Luther Martin, "The Genuine Information Delivered to the Legislature of the State of Maryland" (2.4.71). Note the similarity of the argument later advanced by Lincoln: *WoAL* I 114–15: The Perpetuation of Our Political Institutions, Address Before the Young Men's Lyceum of Springfield, Illinois, on 27 January 1838. A number of Anti-Federalists similarly anticipated Lincoln's argument that no principle could be found to justify African slavery that might not also serve to justify the enslavement of its original proponents. Cf. *WoAL* II 222–23: Fragment on Slavery, 1 July 1854, with *CAF*: A Gentleman in a Neighboring State (4.2.9); Consider Arms, Malichi Maynard, and Samuel Field, *Reasons for Dissent* (4.26.8); Essays by Republicus (5.13.14).

81. The Anti-Federalists certainly did: at the New Hampshire Ratifying Convention, Joshua Atherton is said to have objected that "we become *consenters to*, and *partakers in*, the sin and guilt of this abominable traffic, at least for a certain period, without any positive stipulation that it should even then be brought to an end." See *DSSC* II 203–4 with Jean Yarbrough, "New Hampshire: Puritanism and the Moral Foundations of America," in *Ratifying the Constitution* 235–58 (esp. 245–49). See also *CAF*: Consider Arms, Malichi Maynard, and Samuel Field, *Reasons for Dissent* (4.26.12). In similar fashion, when Charles Cotesworth Pinckney and Robert Barnwell defended the Constitution in South Carolina's House of Representatives, they argued the likelihood that the trade would be left open after 1808. See *DSSC* IV 285–86, 296–97: 17 January 1788. David Ramsay soon echoed their claim. See *DHRC* XVI 21–27 (at 25): Civis—To the Citizens of South Carolina, *Charleston Columbian Herald*, 4 February 1788. The fact that the federal government abolished the trade at the earliest possible moment and did so by an almost unanimous vote in both houses of Congress is not decisive against Luther Martin's argument. In 1807, the senators and congressmen from the lower South had the rebellion of Toussaint L'Ouverture in Santo Domingo and the Gabriel Prosser conspiracy to consider, and they were cognizant that human beings reared as slaves were far less likely to rebel than those born in Africa. On the former event, see C. L. R. James, *The Black Jacobins: Toussaint L'Ouverture and the San Domingo*

Revolution[2] (New York 1963); on the latter event, see Mullin, *Flight and Rebellion* esp. 140–63. To be sure, Congress passed three more laws against the slave trade during the first term of James Monroe's presidency; one of these even declared it to be piracy punishable by death: see *United States Statutes at Large* III 450–53, 532–34, 600–601. This action was, however, not much more than a moral gesture: for the American navy, the enforcement of these laws was never a paramount concern, and Congress was not willing to sanction the British navy's boarding of slave ships flying the American flag until 1862. See Hugh G. Soulsby, *The Right of Search and the Slave Trade in Anglo-American Relations, 1814–1862* (Baltimore 1933).

82. *RFC* II 415: 25 August 1787.

83. Ibid.

84. *JCC* XXVI 247: 19 April 1784. The ban was proposed again by Rufus King in 1785, but to no effect: *JCC* XXVIII 164–65, 239: 16 March and 6 April 1785. In this connection, see *PTJ* VI 604, 608, 611–12 (with n. 21), VII 118: Plan for Government of the Western Territory, 3 February–23 April 1784; and Letter to James Madison on 25 April 1784. See also Donald L. Robinson, *Slavery in the Structure of American Politics, 1765–1820* (New York 1971).

85. *PTJ* X 58: The Article on the United States in the *Encyclopédie Méthodique*, Jefferson's Observations on Démeunier's Manuscript, 22 June 1786.

86. The ban was absent from the initial drafts and even the penultimate draft. It was added by amendment on the day the bill was adopted, apparently as an afterthought and without any great difficulty, and the Northwest Ordinance was itself passed by a unanimous vote of the delegates present: *JCC* XXX 251–55, 402–6, XXXI 669–73, XXXII 281–83, 313–20, 333, 334–43 (esp. 343): 9 May, 13 July, and 19 September 1786, 9 May and 11–13 July 1787. See Jay A. Barrett, *Evolution of the Ordinance of 1787* (New York 1891); Robert F. Berkhofer, Jr., "Jefferson, the Ordinance of 1784, and the Origins of the American Territorial System," *WMQ* 29 (1972): 231–62; Arthur Bestor, "Constitutionalism and the Settlement of the West: The Attainment of Consensus, 1754–1784," in *The American Territorial System*, ed. John Porter Bloom (Athens, Ohio, 1973) 13–44; and Peter S. Onuf, *Statehood and Union: A History of the Northwest Ordinance* (Bloomington, Ind., 1987) esp. 109–52. Staughton Lynd argues that the passage of the Northwest Ordinance at this time was a part of a grand compromise involving the Continental Congress and the federal convention; though intriguing, this contention is unsupported by any positive evidence and seems implausible as well: see "The Compromise of 1787," *Class Conflict, Slavery, and the United States Constitution* (Indianapolis 1967) 185–213. Like most nineteenth-century Americans, I have trouble seeing Congress's halting attempt to limit slavery's expansion as anything other than a sign of the founding generation's desire to signal its principled hostility to the peculiar institution while prudently accommodating the slaveholding interest: cf. Paul Finkelman, "Slavery and the Northwest Ordinance: A Study in Ambiguity," *JER* 6 (1986): 343–70, and "Evading the Ordinance: The Persistence of Bondage in Indiana and Illinois," *JER* 9 (1989): 21–51, with the sensible remarks of Bernard Bailyn, "The Central Themes of the American Revolution," in *Essays on the American Revolution*, ed. Stephen G. Kurtz and James H. Hutson (Chapel Hill 1973) 3–31 (at 27–31), and William W. Freehling, "The Founding Fathers and Slavery" 81–93.

87. See *DHRC* II 462–63: James Wilson, Pennsylvania Ratifying Convention on 3 December 1787.

88. For the offer which North Carolina made on 2 June and rescinded on 20 November 1784, see *The State Records of North Carolina*, ed. Walter Clark (Goldsboro, N.C., 1886–1907) XXIV 561–63, 678–79. The cession took place in December 1789 on the condition specified, and soon thereafter the First Congress organized as the Southwest Territory what would in 1796 become the state of Tennessee. Except in its omission of the ban on slavery, the territorial charter resembled the Northwest Ordinance. For the terms of the cession, see *Annals of Congress* II 2208–12. For the act providing for the organization of the Southwest Territory, see *Annals of Congress* II 2226–27: 26 May 1790. In this connection, see *DHFFC* I 233–34, 244, 252–53, 283, 285–86, 297, 301, 303–5, 322–23: Senate Legislative Journal, 1 and 18 February, 4–5 March, 12–14 and 30 April, and 4, 6, 10, and 26 May 1790; and *DHFFC* III 345–46, 386, 388, 397, 403, 423, 427: House of Representatives Journal, 26 and 29 March, 28–29 April, and 5, 10, and 26–27 May 1790.

89. *RFC* II 415: 25 August 1787.

90. See *RFC* II 559: 10 September 1787. When Madison proposed a modification in the procedure for amending the Constitution to simplify and ease the process and John Rutledge responded by insisting that the clause protecting the slave trade be made unamendable, Madison appears to have incorporated Rutledge's stipulation into his own proposal.

91. *DSSC* III 454: Virginia Ratifying Convention, 15 June 1788. At about the same time, John Jay wrote in much the same vein: "The Convention which formed and recommended the new Constitution had an arduous task to perform, especially as local interests, and in some measure local prejudices, were to be accommodated. Several of the States conceived that restraints on slavery might be too rapid to consist with their particular circumstances; and the importance of union rendered it necessary that their wishes on that head should, in some degree, be gratified." See *PJJ* III 342: Letter to Granville Sharp of the English Anti-Slavery Society in June (?) 1788.

92. On these grounds, Madison argued the necessity for a constitutional provision guaranteeing to every state a republican government: see *The Federalist* 43 (291–92).

93. *The Federalist* 11 (66), 12 (73–74).

94. *The Federalist* 14 (83), 56 (379).

95. Hume, *EMPL* 273–74, 277–78: "Of Refinement in the Arts."

96. Note the arguments that Madison advanced in a polemical piece that he wrote for the party press. See *PJM* XIV 206–9: "Universal Peace," for *The National Gazette*, 31 January 1792.

97. See Ralph Lerner, "Commerce and Character," *The Thinking Revolutionary: Principle and Practice in the New Republic* (Ithaca 1987) 195–221, and Albert O. Hirschman, *The Passions and the Interests: Political Arguments for Capitalism before Its Triumph* (Princeton 1977) 9–113.

98. Cf. *AJL* II 458–61 (at 458): Letter from Thomas Jefferson to John Adams on 11 January 1816 with *PAH* XIX 329–47 (at 332): *To Defence* no. XX, 23–24 October 1795. In this connection, see *AJL* II 331–33, 387–92: Letters from Thomas Jefferson to John Adams on 15 June and 28 October 1813; *WrTJ* (ed. Washington) VII 377–78: Letter to William Ludlow on 6 September 1824. Note the emphasis which Jefferson placed on the need to soften men. See *WrTJ* (ed. Ford) VII 98–100: Letter to James Madison on 1 January 1797.

99. See *WoAL* III 356–63: Second Lecture on Discoveries and Inventions, 11 February 1859. Note also II 437–42: First Lecture on Discoveries and Inventions, 6 April 1858.

100. See the passing remarks of Martin Diamond, "Conservatives, Liberals, and the Constitution," in *Essays on Liberalism and Conservatism in the United States*[2], ed. Robert A. Goldwin (Chicago 1967) 76–78.

101. *The Federalist* 56 (382).

102. For the situation in 1776, see Gary Wills, *Inventing America: Jefferson's Declaration of Independence* (Garden City 1978) 34–48.

103. I cite the fourth edition: Thomas Pownall, *The Administration of the Colonies* (London 1768) 34, 93–94. The first was published in 1764.

104. *Letters of Members of the Continental Congress*, ed. Edmund Cody Burnett (Washington, D.C., 1921–36) I 60: Letter from John Adams to William Tudor on 29 September 1774.

105. *PBF* IX 90: "The Interest of Great Britain With Regard to her Colonies."

106. *The Belknap Papers* I 309: Letter from Jeremy Belknap to Ebenezer Hazard on 8 March 1784.

107. For further discussion, see Jack P. Greene, "The Background of the Articles of Confederation," *Publius* 12, no. 4 (Fall 1982): 15–44. In this connection, see also Jack N. Rakove, *The Beginnings of National Politics: An Interpretive History of the Continental Congress* (New York 1979) 333–99. For a case study illustrating the distinctive character of two of the most important states, see H. James Henderson, "Taxation and Political Culture: Massachusetts and Virginia, 1760–1800," *WMQ* 47 (1990): 90–114.

108. *The Federalist* 53 (362–63), 56 (381).

109. *The Federalist* 53 (363–64), 56 (381–82).

110. *PJM* XI 125–26: Speech to the Virginia Ratifying Convention on 12 June 1788. See also *PJM* VIII 107–8: Letter to Thomas Jefferson on 20 August 1784. The passage cited from Madison's speech at the Virginia gathering is fatal to the claim, advanced by Douglass Adair in his unpublished dissertation, that the Framers— and Madison in particular—designed the Constitution for a nation of virtuous farmers and deemed it inadequate from the start to meet the needs of a modern, industrial state: "The Intellectual Origins of Jeffersonian Democracy: Republicanism, the Class Struggle, and the Virtuous Farmer" (Yale University 1943) 272–95. At the Philadelphia convention, when Edmund Randolph introduced Madison's Virginia Plan, he included internal improvements and the promotion of "manufactures" among the objects to be pursued by the new government. See *RFC* I 18, 25–26: 29 May 1787. Madison later opposed attempts to make the possession of land a prerequisite for election to public office on the grounds that commerce and manufacturing would need protection against the agricultural interest, and he subsequently advanced the need to promote domestic manufactures as one of his arguments in favor of conferring on Congress the right to tax exports. See *RFC* II 123–24, 361–63: 26 July and 21 August 1787. In *The Federalist*, he looked forward to the day when Congress would have to substitute bounties for tariffs on the import of "raw materials" destined to "be wrought into articles for exportation." See *The Federalist* 41 (276–77). Madison's views on the relationship between population density, poverty, and the growth of manufacturing were commonplace in the eighteenth century: see Drew R. McCoy, "Jefferson and Madison on Malthus: Population Growth in Jeffersonian Political Economy," *VMHB* 88 (1980):

259–76, and *The Elusive Republic: Political Economy in Jeffersonian America* (Chapel Hill 1980). For the misgivings regarding manufactures that Madison expressed subsequent to 1787, see below, III.v.2–6.

111. See George Tucker, *The Laws of Wages, Profits and Rent, Investigated* (Philadelphia 1837) 46–50, and *Political Economy for the People* (Philadelphia 1859) 83–93. Tucker publicly opposed slavery from the time he reached his early twenties; in 1820, in a speech delivered in Congress in connection with the Missouri Compromise, he began advancing arguments strikingly similar (though not quite identical) to those which Madison hinted at in *The Federalist* and in the debates at the Virginia Ratifying Convention. Whether the delivery of this speech had anything to do with the decision to offer him a professorship at the University of Virginia remains unclear. See Tipton R. Snavely, *George Tucker as Political Economist* (Charlottesville 1964) 134–53. As applied to Virginia in particular, the thesis hinted at by Madison and developed by Tucker had a long and vigorous life: see Alison Goodyear Freehling, *Drift toward Dissolution* 122–69, 202–15, 241–49. In time, it stirred a response from those who had come to think slavery a positive good: see Joseph J. Spengler, "Malthusianism and the Debate on Slavery," *SAQ* 34 (1935): 170–89, and "Population Theory in the Ante-Bellum South," *JSH* 2 (1936): 360–89.

112. I omit sugar because Louisiana was not part of the Union in 1787 and, in any case, did not introduce the commercial production of that crop until 1795: see Fogel and Engerman, *Time on the Cross* 20.

113. For the outlook of the Founding Fathers and for that of nearly all Americans prior to the nullification struggle, see Herbert J. Storing, "Slavery and the Moral Foundations of the American Republic," in *The Moral Foundations of the American Republic*[3], ed. Robert H. Horwitz (Charlottesville 1986) 313–32. Even when Lachlan McIntosh opposed an unconditional ratification of the Constitution on the ground that it might force his fellow citizens to abandon slavery before it was "convenient," he took it for granted that abolition was "just" and that it would eventually come to pass. See *DHRC* III 259–61: Letter from Lachlan McIntosh to John Wereat on 17 December 1787.

114. Jefferson, *NSV* 18 (163).

115. *WrJM* VIII 439–47, IX 85n, 468–70, 498–502: Letters to Robert J. Evans on 15 June 1819, to the Marquis de Lafayette on an Unspecified Date, to R. R. Gurley on 28 December 1831, and to Thomas R. Dew on 23 February 1833. See *WrJM* IX 77–85: Parable of Jonathan Bull & Mary Bull (1821), and consider Drew R. McCoy, *The Last of the Fathers: James Madison and the Republican Legacy* (Cambridge 1989) 217–322. Note also Irving Brant, *James Madison* (Indianapolis 1941–61) VI 431, 509–10, 517, and Ralph Ketcham, *James Madison: A Biography* (New York 1971) 625–30.

116. *The Federalist* 60 (404–5).

117. In this they were by no means alone: see Ralph Ketcham, *Presidents above Party: The First American Presidency, 1789–1829* (Chapel Hill 1984).

118. To a close friend, Washington's secretary of the treasury wrote, "When I accepted the Office, I now hold, it was under a full persuasion, that from similarity of thinking, conspiring with personal goodwill, I should have the firm support of Mr. Madison, in the *general course* of my administration. Aware of the intrinsic difficulties of the situation and of the powers of Mr. Madison, I do not believe I should have accepted under a different supposition." See *PAH* XI 426–45 (esp. 427, 432): Letter to Edward Carrington on 26 May 1792.

119. To the very end, however, Madison still expected that Virginia would soon become a center for manufactures. See *WrJM* IX 520–28 (at 525–26): Letter on Majority Rule, 1833.

120. *WrTJ* (ed. Lipscomb and Bergh) XV 248–50: Letter to John Holmes on 22 April 1820.

121. *WrJM* IX 12: Letter to Robert Walsh on 27 November 1819.

122. As Walter Berns, *The First Amendment and the Future of American Democracy* (New York 1976) 112–19, points out, the opposition which the two men mounted against Alexander Hamilton's entire program—above all else, his plan to promote manufactures—may have contributed significantly to the failure of the strategy outlined by Madison in *The Federalist*: see below, III.iii.1–7, iv.1–3, v.1–6.

123. See *WrTJ* (ed. Lipscomb and Bergh) XV 248–50: Letter to John Holmes on 22 April 1820, and *WrJM* IX 1–13: Letter to Robert Walsh on 27 November 1819. The case for diffusion was neither new nor peculiar to Jefferson and Madison; Virginians had begun employing this argument in Congress as early as 1798: see Robert McColley, *Slavery and Jeffersonian Virginia* (Urbana, Ill., 1964) 173–81 (esp. 173–74).

124. Consider *MJQA* IV 528–29: 20 February 1820 in light of *MJQA* IV 502–3, 530–31: 10 January and 24 February 1820.

125. *MJQA* V 11–12: 3 March 1820.

126. See Harry V. Jaffa, "The Nature and Origin of the American Party System," *Equality and Liberty: Theory and Practice in American Politics* (New York 1965) 3–41, and John Zvesper, *Political Philosophy and Rhetoric: A Study of the Origins of American Party Politics* (Cambridge 1977).

127. *The Federalist* 10 (59).

Chapter 3

1. *CAF: A Review of the Constitution Proposed by the Late Convention* by A Federal Republican (3.6.21), 28 October 1787.

2. *CAF*: Letters of Cato V (2.6.34).

3. *CAF*: Mercy Otis Warren, *Observations on the New Constitution, and on the Federal and State Conventions. by a Columbian Patriot*, Boston, 1788 (4.28.2). For Warren's authorship of this pamphlet, see Charles Warren, "Elbridge Gerry, James Warren, Mercy Warren, and the Ratification of the Federal Constitution in Massachusetts," *PMHS* 64 (1932): 143–64.

4. *CAF*: Mercy Otis Warren, *History of the Rise, Progress and Termination of the American Revolution*, 1805 (6.14.14–15).

5. *CAF*: Mercy Otis Warren, *History of the Rise, Progress and Termination of the American Revolution*, 1805 (6.14.67).

6. As Alfred F. Young, *The Democratic Republicans of New York: The Origins, 1763–1797* (Chapel Hill 1967), and Norman K. Risjord, "The Evolution of Political Parties in Virginia, 1782–1800," *JAH* 60 (1974): 961–84, have shown, all but a handful of the original Anti-Federalists eventually became Republicans in the course of the 1790s. The exceptions can generally be explained in terms of personal rivalries and friendships or in terms of state and sectional loyalties. Contempo-

raries recognized that there was a connection between the debate over ratification and the dispute that erupted in 1791–92. When he came under attack, Hamilton sadly alluded to this link. "It is much to be wished," he remarked, "that the true state of the case may not have been, that the Antifoederal Champions have been encouraged in their activity, by the countenance which has been given to their principles, by certain foederalists, who in an envious and ambitious struggle for power influence and preeminence have imbraced as auxiliaries the numerous party originally disaffected to the Government in the hope that these united with the factious and feeble minded foederalists whom they can detach will give them the proedominancy." See *PAH* XII 228–58 (at 258): Letter of 18 August 1792 to George Washington with Objections and Answers respecting the Administration of the Government. In this connection, see also *Works of Fisher Ames*, ed. W. B. Allen (Indianapolis 1983) 877–83 (esp. 882): Letter to George Richards Minot on 30 November 1791, and *PJoM* III 516: Letter to Timothy Pickering on 15 October 1798. In general, see Richard E. Ellis, "The Persistence of Antifederalism after 1789," in *Beyond Confederation: Origins of the Constitution and American National Identity*, ed. Richard Beeman, Stephen Botein, and Edward C. Carter II (Chapel Hill 1987) 295–314.

7. See Lance Banning, "Republican Ideology and the Triumph of the Constitution, 1789 to 1793," *WMQ* 31 (1974): 167–88.

8. See Mandeville, *Fable of the Bees* I 145, 369. Note also I 6–7, 208–9.

9. In this century, Hamilton has rarely received sympathetic treatment; even his biographers have tended to take at face value many of the charges propagated by his enemies. For a detailed analysis of one striking example of the bias and carelessness that continue to characterize much of the literature on the subject, see Thomas P. Govan, "Alexander Hamilton and Julius Caesar: A Note on the Use of Historical Evidence," *WMQ* 32 (1975): 475–80. For an important exception to the general pattern, see Forrest McDonald, *Alexander Hamilton: A Biography* (New York 1979). See also Gerald Stourzh, *Alexander Hamilton and the Idea of Republican Government* (Stanford 1970). I have profited considerably from reading both books. Note also Douglass Adair, "Fame and the Founding Fathers," *Fame and the Founding Fathers*, ed. Trevor Colbourn (New York 1974) 3–26 (esp. 13–21), and Ralph Ketcham, *Presidents above Party: The First American Presidency, 1789–1829* (Chapel Hill 1984) 188–214.

10. See Franklin H. Head, "Alexander Hamilton As a Constitutional Statesman," in *Alexander Hamilton*, ed. Melvin Gilbert Dodge (New York 1896) 7–8.

11. See *Life, Letters, and Journals of George Ticknor*[10], ed. George S. Hillard (Boston 1880) I 261. Talleyrand's admiration was apparently reciprocated by Hamilton: II 113–14.

12. See Charles Warren, *The Supreme Court in United States History*[2] (Boston 1926) I 149 n. 1. For the opinion of Chancellor Kent, see *Memoirs and Letters of James Kent*, ed. William Kent (Boston 1898) 281–331: Letter to Mrs. Elizabeth Hamilton on 10 December 1832. See, as well, *Memoirs and Letters of James Kent* 31–32.

13. See *The Spur of Fame: Dialogues of John Adams and Benjamin Rush, 1805–1813*, ed. John A. Schutz and Douglass Adair (San Marino, Calif., 1966) 47–48: Letter to Benjamin Rush on 25 January 1806.

14. *WrTJ* (ed. Lipscomb and Bergh) IX 309–11: Letter to James Madison on 21 September 1795. Years later, Jefferson would refer to Hamilton as "a man

whose mind was really powerful, but chained by native partialities to everything English." See *WrTJ* (ed. Ford) 34–37 (at 34): Letter to William H. Crawford on 20 June 1816.

15. Hamilton published *A Full Vindication of the Measures of Congress* in mid-December 1774. According to his son, the statesman was born on 11 January 1757. See John Church Hamilton, *The Life of Alexander Hamilton* (New York 1834) I 1. Those who suppose that he was born two years earlier cite the report of the probate clerk who dealt with the estate of Hamilton's mother when she died in 1768 and who recorded that the boy was then thirteen. See *PAH* I 1–3: Probate Court Transaction on Estate of Rachel Lavien, 19 February 1768. Hamilton had no reason to lie to the members of his family, and the probate clerk is far more likely to have slipped up than Hamilton's son.

16. For this document, see *RFC* III 234.

17. Jared Sparks, *The Life of Gouverneur Morris with Selections from his Correspondence* (Boston 1832) III 262: Letter to Robert Walsh on 5 February 1811.

18. Hamilton first suggested this stratagem in 1780 when, at the request of James Duane, he wrote a long letter detailing the causes of the federal government's weakness and suggesting an antidote. See *PAH* II 400–418: Letter to James Duane on 3 September 1780. In 1782, Hamilton persuaded the New York legislature to issue a call for just such a convention: *PAH* III 110–13: Resolution of the New York Legislature Calling for a Convention of the States to Revise and Amend the Articles of the Confederation, 20 July 1782. Note also the proposal which Hamilton drafted for submission to the Continental Congress but in the end deemed premature. See *PAH* III 420–26: Continental Congress. Unsubmitted Resolution Calling for a Convention to Amend the Articles of Confederation, July 1783. For Hamilton's agitation to this end, see *PAH* II 649–52, 654–57, 660–65, 669–74, III 75–82, 99–106: *The Continentalist* I (12 July 1781), II (19 July 1781), III (9 August 1781), IV (30 August 1781), V (18 April 1782), VI 4 (July 1782). When the time was ripe, Hamilton was not behindhand. He was a delegate to the Annapolis Convention in 1786 and drafted the address calling for a federal convention to amend the Articles of Confederation. See *PAH* III 686–89: Address of the Annapolis Convention, 14 September 1786.

19. "Mine is an odd destiny," Hamilton wrote, in a moment of despair not many months before his fatal duel with Aaron Burr. "Perhaps no man in the UStates has sacrificed or done more for the present Constitution than myself—and contrary to all my anticipations of its fate . . . I am still labouring to prop the frail and worthless fabric." See *PAH* XXV 544: Letter to Gouverneur Morris on 29 February 1802. In assessing the last five words of this passage, one should keep in mind Hamilton's contention that a "new government, constructed on free principles, is always weak, and must stand in need of the props of a firm and good administration; till time shall have rendered its authority venerable, and fortified it by habits of obedience." See *PAH* XXV 233: Letter Concerning the Public Character and Conduct of John Adams, 24 October 1800.

20. For Washington's desire that Hamilton return, see *PAH* IV 225: Letter from George Washington on 10 July 1787.

21. *RFC* II 645–46: 17 September 1787. Note also *RFC* II 524: 6 September 1787.

22. For the notes, the various summaries of the speech, and the draft of a constitution which Hamilton read, see *RFC* I 282–311 and *SRFC* 82–84, 91–93: 18 June 1787. At the end of the convention, Hamilton submitted a more detailed plan to

Madison: *RFC* III 617–30. For a detailed analysis of what the young statesman had in mind, see Paul Eidelberg, *The Philosophy of the American Constitution: A Reinterpretation of the Intentions of the Founding Fathers* (New York 1968) 106–36.

23. *RFC* I 284–86: 18 June 1787. In the notes which he made for his great speech, Hamilton wrote, "The government must be so constituted as to offer strong motives. In short, to interest all the *passions* of individuals. And turn them into that channel." See *RFC* I 311. Almost immediately after delivering his speech, Hamilton retracted his suggestion that outright abolition might be appropriate: "He had not been understood yesterday. . . . *As States*, he thought they ought to be abolished. But he admitted the necessity of leaving in them, subordinate jurisdictions." See *RFC* I 323, 328: 19 June 1787. In urging ratification, he incurred a charge of inconsistency and disingenuousness by taking a much more sanguine view of the states: *PAH* V 99–104, 107–8, 111–12, 135–40: Speeches at the New York Ratifying Convention on 27–28 and 30 June 1788.

24. *RFC* I 287–88: 18 June 1787. For the notes which Hamilton made while listening to Madison's discussion of geographical extension and the problem of faction, see *RFC* I 72, 146–47: 1 and 6 June 1787. In *The Federalist*, Hamilton for the most part suppressed his misgivings regarding the size of the new polity; but it is worth noting that, where Madison emphasized that "the increased intercourse among those of different States . . . will contribute to a general assimilation of their manners and laws," Hamilton sounded a note of caution, observing that "there are causes, as well physical as moral, which may, in a greater or less degree, permanently nourish different propensities and inclinations in this particular." Cf. *The Federalist* 53 (363–64) with 60 (404–5); see 56 (381–82) and consider III.ii.2, note 24, above. In this connection, see also *CMPP* I 213–24 (esp. 216–19): George Washington, Farewell Address, 17 September 1796. Consistent with his reasoning in this matter, Hamilton later expressed doubts regarding the advantages thought to be attendant on the vast acquisitions west of the Mississippi River which Jefferson as president and Madison as secretary of state secured from Napoleon. See *PAH* XXVI 129–36 (esp. 133): "Purchase of Louisiana," *New-York Evening Post*, 5 July 1803. Note, in this connection, Douglass Adair, "Hamilton on the Louisiana Purchase: A Newly Identified Editorial from the *New-York Evening Post*," *Fame and the Founding Fathers* 260–71.

25. *RFC* I 288: 18 June 1787. For the passage which Hamilton quotes, see Jacques Necker, *A Treatise on the Administration of the Finances of France*, trans. Thomas Mortimer (London 1785) I 60.

26. Here I follow Hamilton's notes: *RFC* I 309–10. His point was that "there ought to be a principle in government capable of resisting the popular current." But he was eager at the same time to ensure that the popular branch represented popular interests. In this connection, one should consider the arguments he later advanced in favor of increasing the number in the House of Representatives. See *RFC* II 553–54: 8 September 1787. Cf. Jean Louis de Lolme, *The Constitution of England*³ (London 1781) 195–290, 324–479.

27. *RFC* I 288–90, 299, 309–10: 18 June 1787. Here, I have drawn both on the records kept by those who listened to Hamilton and on his notes for the speech. In this connection, one should also consult the plan of government that Hamilton submitted to James Madison at the close of the convention: *RFC* III 617–30.

28. *RFC* I 376, 381–82: 22 June 1787.

29. Hume, *EMPL* 42–46 (at 44–45): "On the Independency of Parliament."

30. *RFC* I 301: 18 June 1787. See also *RFC* I 293 n. 9.

31. See *The Federalist* 1 (6–7), 85 (590). Hamilton's initial remark he later repeated. Madison then echoed the faint praise his colleague had bestowed on the Constitution. See *The Federalist* 23 (146), 37 (237).

32. *PAH* IV 275–77: Conjectures about the New Constitution, 17–30 September 1787. While at the convention, though he knew that his own plan had no chance of being adopted, Hamilton nonetheless remained hopeful that matters could be managed so that "the Genl. Govt. shd. maintain itself" and "the State Govts. might gradually dwindle into nothing." See *RFC* I 358–59: 21 June 1787.

33. Perhaps most important: in assessing political questions, the two men spoke precisely the same language. Compare what Hamilton had to say in his one great speech at the Philadelphia convention (quoted above) with what Washington wrote in the midst of the Revolutionary War to one of the Virginia delegates to the Continental Congress: *WrGW* XI 286–90: Letter to John Bannister on 21 April 1778.

34. In the relationship, Washington was clearly the suitor; and, especially when still quite young, Hamilton feared and resented his dependence on the man—much in the way that a son just come of age will resent any sign of dependence on his father. See *PAH* II 563–69, 575–77: Exchange of Letters with Philip Schuyler on 18 and 25 February 1781. In subsequent years, the relationship was far less troubled, and the two became extremely close. When Washington's private secretary wrote to report that the general had died on 14 December 1799, Hamilton included in his reply the observation that he had himself "been much indebted to the kindness of the General," adding that the man had been "an Aegis very essential to me." See *PAH* XXIV 100–101, 155, 198–200: Exchange of Letters with Tobias Lear on 15 December 1799, 2 and 16 January 1800. To the former president's widow, he then wrote, "There can be few, who equally with me participate in the loss you deplore. In expressing this sentiment, I may without impropriety allude to the numerous and distinguished marks of confidence and friendship, of which you have yourself been a Witness; but I cannot say in how many ways the continuance of that confidence and friendship was necessary to me in future relations." See *PAH* XXIV 184–85: Letter to Martha Washington on 12 January 1800. See also *PAH* XXIV 111–13: General Orders, 21 December 1799—where Hamilton refers to "the irreparable loss of a kind and venerated Patron and father!" Note, as well, *PAH* XXIV 116: Letter to Charles Cotesworth Pinckney on [22] December 1779.

35. Hamilton came to have a healthy respect for the political wisdom and empirical knowledge required of anyone entrusted with designing a system of taxation: see *The Federalist* 36 (221–22). For his first halting attempt to grapple with financial affairs, see *PAH* II 234–51: Letter to an Unknown Recipient, December 1779–March 1780. For his subsequent efforts, see *PAH* II 400–418, 604–35: Letters to James Duane and Robert Morris on 3 September 1780 and 30 April 1781.

36. See P. G. M. Dickson, *The Financial Revolution in England: A Study in the Development of Public Credit, 1688–1756* (London 1967), and John Brewer, *The Sinews of Power: War, Money, and the English State, 1688–1783* (New York 1989).

37. See *The Law Practice of Alexander Hamilton: Documents and Commentary*, ed. Julius Goebel (New York 1964–81) I 616–17: Western Lands Brief, 1786.

38. See *PAH* IV 95: New York Assembly. Remarks on an Act for Raising Certain Yearly Taxes Within This State, 17 February 1787.

39. For Hamilton's course of studies, see McDonald, *Alexander Hamilton* 27–94. See also Forrest McDonald, *Novus Ordo Seclorum: The Intellectual Origins of the Constitution* (Lawrence, Kans., 1985) 97–142 (with particular reference to 136 n. 66), and Donald F. Swanson and Andrew P. Trout, "Alexander Hamilton, 'the Celebrated Mr. Neckar,' and Public Credit," *WMQ* 47 (1990): 422–30. McDonald goes astray only in supposing that Hamilton ultimately followed Hume in jettisoning Locke's social contract theory: *Alexander Hamilton* 31–32, 97 (with 384–85 n. 1). If the New Yorker makes no mention of the social contract when he lists "the great & essential principles necessary for the support of Government" on the floor of the federal convention, it is because he is discussing the dictates of political architecture and not first principles: *RFC* I 284–86: 18 June 1787. Elsewhere, he makes it clear that he still adheres to the doctrine of self-evident political and moral truths that underlies Locke's theory and that he links the "original right of self-defence" with the right to revolution in a thoroughly Lockean fashion: *The Federalist* 23 (147), 28 (178–80), 31 (193–95). After 1776, Hamilton is comparatively reticent regarding the natural rights of mankind, but only because he follows Blackstone, rather than Machiavelli, Algernon Sidney, and the authors of *Cato's Letters*, in supposing that a frequent recurrence to first principles undercuts the political stability and the habit of unthinking obedience to the law he deemed prerequisite to the protection of men's rights in civil society: see Mackubin Thomas Owens, Jr., "Alexander Hamilton on Natural Rights and Prudence," *Interpretation* 14 (1986): 331–51, with II Epilogue, above. McDonald, *Alexander Hamilton* 51, 57–62, 378 n. 17, greatly underestimates Hamilton's debt to the English jurist: see, as a corrective, Stourzh, *Alexander Hamilton and the Idea of Republican Government* 9–37.

40. *PAH* I 155–58: *The Farmer Refuted, &c.*, 23 February 1775.

41. See *PAH* II 234–51, 400–418: Letter to an Unknown Recipient, December 1779–March 1780, and Letter to James Duane on 3 September 1780.

42. See *PAH* II 604–35 (esp. 618 and 635): Letter to Robert Morris on 30 April 1781.

43. *PAH* VI 51–168 (esp. 70, 106): *Report Relative to a Provision for the Support of Public Credit*, 9 January 1790.

44. *PAH* III 105–6: *The Continentalist* no. VI, 4 July 1782.

45. This was the argument which Rufus King made in favor of assumption at the Philadelphia convention with Hamilton in attendance: see *RFC* II 327–28: 18 August 1787.

46. *PAH* VII 236–342: *Second Report on the Further Provision Necessary for Establishing Public Credit* (Report on a National Bank), 13 December 1790. For Hamilton's debt to the English example, see Charles F. Dunbar, "Some Precedents Followed by Alexander Hamilton," in *Economic Essays*, ed. O. M. W. Sprague (New York 1904) 91–93. In making the bank a profit-making institution governed by private stockholders, the New Yorker was expanding on a suggestion advanced by Necker, *A Treatise on the Administration of the Finances of France* III 348–51. The French minister had learned from sad experience that publicly controlled institutions are almost inevitably subject to a political manipulation which tends to render them fiscally unsound. For further discussion of the actual operations of Hamilton's system and his departure from the British model, see Donald F. Swanson, *The Origins of Hamilton's Fiscal Policies* (Gainesville, Fla., 1963).

47. *PAH* VIII 217–23 (esp. 223): Notes on the Advantages of a National Bank,

enclosed with a Letter to George Washington on 27 March 1791. The material quoted comes from the final paragraph of the memorandum.

48. *PAH* XIX 40–42: *The Defence of the Funding System,* July 1795. Hamilton's attempt to downplay these considerations should be discounted. In public, he always asserted that his program was designed to extinguish the debt. He believed that this was an illusion essential to the maintenance of public credit, and to sustain this illusion, he created the sinking fund. But, in practice, that fund was used chiefly to intervene in the market in order to stabilize the value of the debt. If the debt was a national blessing, actually paying it off would be a curse. It would eliminate the economic as well as the political advantages which, Hamilton asserted, arise from the debt's existence.

49. The program developed by Morris and his associates (Hamilton included) foreshadows in a number of respects the plan outlined in the first two of Hamilton's three great reports: cf. E. James Ferguson, "The Nationalists of 1781–1783 and the Economic Interpretation of the Constitution," *JAH* 56 (1969–70): 241–61, with Jack N. Rakove, *The Beginnings of National Politics: An Interpretive History of the Continental Congress* (New York 1979) 296–329 (esp. 298–306). See also Janet A. Riesman, "Money, Credit, and Federalist Political Economy," in *Beyond Confederation* 128–61.

50. *PAH* I 56: *A Full Vindication of the Measures of the Congress, &c.,* 15 December 1774.

51. *PAH* III 423: Continental Congress. Unsubmitted Resolution Calling for a Convention to Amend the Articles of Confederation, July 1783.

52. *DHFFC* III 265: House of Representatives Journal, 15 January 1790.

53. See *WrGW* XXX 491–92: First Annual Address to Congress, 8 January 1790.

54. *PAH* XXI 436: *The Stand* no. VI, 19 April 1798.

55. Hamilton's summary of the commonly held view is both accurate and succinct: cf. *The Federalist* 6 (31) with Montesquieu, *EL* 4.20.1–2. For the opinions propagated by Thomas Paine, see *WrTP* I 9–10, 20, 27, 46, 400–404: *Common Sense* and *The Rights of Man* 2.5.

56. See *PJM* XIV 206–9: "Universal Peace," *National Gazette,* 31 January 1792. For an earlier analysis of the martial propensities of absolute monarchies and for a partial correction of the view later advanced by Madison that republics will be less prone to war, see John Jay, *The Federalist* 4 (18–23).

57. See *The Federalist* 6. The likelihood of war, the requirement that the Union be trusted with the extensive prerogatives necessary for meeting that eventuality, and the need for a powerful executive capable of conducting foreign policy with secrecy and dispatch—these are themes to which Hamilton gives great emphasis. See *The Federalist* 24–36, 70–71, 74–75. Note also Madison, *The Federalist* 41, 46, and Jay, *The Federalist* 64.

58. See *PAH* X 1–342 (esp. 258–66, 291–94): *Report on the Subject of Manufactures,* 5 December 1791.

59. *PAH* X 266–67: *Report on the Subject of Manufactures,* 5 December 1791.

60. See, in particular, *PAH* II 234–51: Letter to an Unknown Recipient, December 1779–March 1780.

61. From the outset, he cast about for means by which to reduce the principal: see Robert M. Jennings, Donald F. Swanson, and Andrew P. Trout, "Alexander Hamilton's Tontine Proposal," *WMQ* 45 (1988): 107–15.

62. Scholars who fail to appreciate fully the dire consequences of a collapse of

credit for the new regime, for its manufacturing concerns, and for the economy as a whole will find it easy to credit the charge, advanced by the more passionate advocates of protectionism, that Hamilton was not seriously interested in promoting manufactures: see, for example, John R. Nelson, Jr., "Alexander Hamilton and American Manufacturing: A Reexamination," *JAH* 65 (1978–79): 971–95, and *Liberty and Property: Political Economy and Policymaking in the New Nation, 1789–1812* (Baltimore 1987) 22–51. There is no indication in his text or notes that Nelson bothered to consult the preeminent discussion of Hamilton's political economy: see McDonald, *Alexander Hamilton* 117–236.

63. *PAH* II 417: Letter to James Duane on 3 September 1780.

64. See Hamilton, *The Federalist* 27 (esp. 173). Above all else, the Union had "to attract to its support, those passions, which have the strongest influence upon the human heart." See *The Federalist* 16 (102–3).

65. *PAH* XXV 366: An Address to the Electors of the State of New York, 21 March 1801.

66. See III Prologue, above.

67. See *DSSC* I 322–23, 325–26, 329, 336: Ratification by the Commonwealth of Massachusetts, 7 February 1788; the State of South Carolina, 23 May 1788; the State of New Hampshire, 21 June 1788; the State of New York, 26 July 1788; and the State of Rhode Island, 29 May 1790. In this connection, see *DSSC* II 545: Proceedings of the Meeting at Harrisburg, in Pennsylvania, 3 September 1788. Note, as well, *DHRC* II 624: The Address and Reasons of Dissent of the Minority of the Convention of the State of Pennsylvania to their Constituents, 18 December 1787. An amendment to this effect was considered by the First Congress and defeated in the House by a vote of thirty-nine to nine: see *DHFFC* III 163–64: House of Representatives Journal, 22 August 1789. For subsequent developments, see William D. Barber, " 'Among the Most *Techy Articles of Civil Police'*: Federal Taxation and the Adoption of the Whiskey Excise," *WMQ* 25 (1968): 58–84. The willingness of the delegates to the Philadelphia convention and of the members of the First Congress to ignore public sentiment on this matter was rooted in their awareness of the degree to which the radical Whig critique of direct taxation had contributed to the financial crisis that nearly crippled the efforts of the United States in the Revolutionary War. In this connection, see E. Wayne Carp, *To Starve the Army at Pleasure: Continental Army Administration and American Political Culture, 1775–1783* (Chapel Hill 1984).

68. See Lance Banning, *The Jeffersonian Persuasion: Evolution of a Party Ideology* (Ithaca 1978) 21–125, and E. James Ferguson, "Political Economy, Public Liberty, and the Formation of the Constitution," *WMQ* 40 (1983): 389–412. Note John M. Murrin, "The Great Inversion, or Court versus Country: A Comparison of the Revolution Settlements in England (1688–1721) and America (1776–1816)," in *Three British Revolutions: 1641, 1688, 1776*, ed. J. G. A. Pocock (Princeton 1980) 368–453. In this connection, one may also wish to consult Ruth Bogin, " 'Measures So Glaringly unjust': A Response to Hamilton's Funding Plan by William Manning," *WMQ* 46 (1989): 315–31.

69. See *PAH* I 50, 75–76, 94, 144–45: *A Full Vindication of the Measures of the Congress, &c.*, 15 December 1774, and *The Farmer Refuted, &c.*, 23 February 1775.

70. See Hamilton, *The Federalist* 27, 31.

71. *RFC* I 464–65: 29 June 1787. Madison had long been persuaded and never ceased to doubt that the dismemberment of the Union would result in petty wars,

the creation of a host of standing armies, the growth of public indebtedness, and, as a consequence of all these, the demise of republicanism. Cf. *PJM* VIII 431–32: Notes for Debate on Commercial Regulations by Congress, 30 November–1 December 1785, with *The Federalist* 41 (270–72), 274. By 1787, he thought the dismemberment of the Union imminent: *PJM* IX 294–95, 299, 371: Letters to Edmund Pendleton on 24 February 1787 and to Edmund Randolph on 25 February and 8 April 1787.

72. See *PJM* IX 383: Letter to George Washington on 16 April 1787, and *RFC* I 355–58, 499–500: 21 and 30 June 1787. See also *PJM* IX 368–71: Letter to Edmund Randolph on 8 April 1787. Madison was particularly eager to avoid being tarred with the brush of consolidation, and he made it a point of honor that George Mason expressly exempt him from the charge he lodged during the Virginia Ratifying Convention when he said, "There are many gentlemen in the United States who think it right that we should have one great, national, consolidated government, and that it was better to bring it about slowly and imperceptibly rather than all at once." Consider *DSSC* III 522: 18 June 1788 in light of the oral tradition: Hugh Blair Grigsby, *The History of the Virginia Federal Convention of 1788, with Some Account of Eminent Virginians of that Era Who Were Members of that Body* (Richmond 1890–91) I 97.

73. From the moment it was suggested to the moment it was adopted, Madison fought this concession to the states: see *RFC* I 461–64, 470–79, 485–87, 496–97, 499–500, 515, 519, 522–23, 527–29, 535, 551, 554, 562, II 5, 8–10, 12: 29–30 June, 2–3, 5, 7, 9, 14–15 July 1787. Later, when he was called on to justify the Connecticut Compromise, Madison could manage at best a tepid defense. See *The Federalist* 62 (416–19)

74. Cf. *RFC* II 19–20: 16 July 1787 with *PJM* X 4–5.

75. Consider *PJM* X 163–64, 209–14: Letters to Thomas Jefferson on 6 September and 24 October 1787 in light of Charles F. Hobson, "The Negative on State Laws: James Madison, the Constitution, and the Crisis of Republican Government," *WMQ* 36 (1979): 215–35, and Michael P. Zuckert, "Federalism and the Founding," *RP* 48 (1986): 166–210.

76. *RFC* I 356–58, 446–49: 21 and 28 June 1787. See *RFC* I 463–65: 29 June 1787. It is worth noting that Madison's account of these speeches appears to understate the radical character of his assault on the states. His notes should be compared with the records kept by Robert Yates of New York (*RFC* I 363–64, 455–57, 471–72), by Rufus King of Massachusetts (367, 458, 477), and by William Paterson of New Jersey (459, 479). As edited by Edmond C. Genet, Yates's account is occasionally tendentious: see James H. Hutson, "Robert Yates's Notes on the Constitutional Convention of 1787: Citizen Genet's Edition," *Quarterly Journal of the Library of Congress* 35 (1978): 173–82, and "Introduction," *SRFC* xxv–xxvi. Nonetheless, the records kept by King and Paterson confirm the accuracy of Yates's summary of these particular speeches in sufficient detail to mitigate the truth of the charge, lodged by the Virginian many years later, that the published version of Yates's notes was, with regard to the question at issue, extremely misleading. Cf. *RFC* III 410–16: Extracts from Yates's Secret Proceedings (1808) with *RFC* III 446–47, 516–18, 521–31: Letters of James Madison to Joseph Gales on 26 August 1821, to Nicholas P. Trist in December 1831, to W. C. Rives on 21 October 1833, and to John Tyler at an unspecified date subsequent to 6 February 1833. Note Madison's willingness, later in the convention, to speak of the states becoming

"consolidated into one nation." See *RFC* II 386–87: 23 August 1787. It deserves notice that, according to Yates, when Edmund Randolph presented the Virginia Plan (which was in large part Madison's handiwork), the governor "candidly confessed" that the resolutions composing that plan "were not intended for a federal government" and intimated that "he meant a strong *consolidated* union, in which the idea of states should be nearly annihilated." Consider *RFC* I 24 and *SRFC* 26: 29 May 1787 in light of Hutson, "Introduction," *SRFC* xxv–xvi. If Randolph later flirted with Anti-Federalism, it was largely because his enthusiasm for consolidation was considerably dampened by the adoption of the Connecticut Compromise and by his recognition that the concession made to the small states would render the Constitution unpopular in Virginia. If Madison's memory later played tricks on him, it was presumably because he knew that he had never actually pressed for or even favored full consolidation and because he soon changed his mind about the potential for tyranny posed by the federal government and became a principled defender of states' rights. At the time of the convention, the Virginian was no doubt sincere in claiming that he considered the annihilation of the states "inexpedient" as well as "unattainable." But this was solely because he saw no harm in leaving "the local authorities" intact to the extent that they could be "subordinately useful." See *PJM* IX 369, 383: Letters to Edmund Randolph and George Washington on 8 and 16 April 1787. Only later did he come to appreciate the virtues of leaving to the states a capacity for insubordination.

77. See *PJM* VI 487–98: Report on Address to the States by Congress, 26 April 1783.

78. For a detailed examination of Madison's attitude at the time of the convention, see above, III.ii. In the debates held in Philadelphia, Madison had echoed the arguments of those who advanced the need to promote domestic manufactures as a justification for conferring on Congress the right to tax exports. See *RFC* II 361–63: 21 August 1787.

79. See Madison, *The Federalist* 41 (276–77).

80. See *PAH* XI 426–45 (esp. 427, 432): Letter to Edward Carrington on 26 May 1792.

81. For this document, see *RFC* III 237.

82. For the manner in which Madison's activities in the Continental Congress foreshadow his later opposition to Hamilton's funding program, see Lance Banning, "James Madison and the Nationalists, 1780–1783," *WMQ* 40 (1983): 227–55. Banning goes too far when he attempts to find consistency in Madison's every twist and turn: "The Hamiltonian Madison," *VMHB* 92 (1984): 3–28. Though the Virginian never wavered in his commitment to republicanism and to the principles outlined in the Declaration of Independence, he did change his mind more than once with regard to the means best suited to securing the Revolution. More recently, Banning has come to emphasize just how much prolonged reflection on the debates at the federal convention altered Madison's opinions, but—in what is otherwise a valuable article—he still overestimates the Virginian's consistency and underestimates the degree to which his disappointment with the republican experiments in the states prior to the opening of the convention had temporarily instilled in him a deep distrust of the states and an instinctive desire for consolidation: see "The Practicable Sphere of a Republic: James Madison, the Constitutional Convention, and the Emergence of Revolutionary Federalism," in *Beyond Confederation* 162–87. Even if one rejects the reports of Yates, King, and Paterson,

it is clear from Madison's own account of the speeches he delivered at the convention on 21, 28, and 29 June 1787 (above, note 76) that the Virginian's commitment to the maintenance of the states' prerogatives was not then grounded in anything more weighty than his recognition that a complete consolidation was both unnecessary and deemed repugnant by the majority of the citizens in every state. For similarly sympathetic accounts that do greater justice to Madison's change of opinion in the years following the federal convention, see Paul C. Peterson, "The Problem of Consistency in the Statesmanship of James Madison: The Case of the Virginia Report," in *The American Founding: Politics, Statesmanship, and the Constitution*, ed. Ralph A. Rossum and Gary L. McDowell (Port Washington, N.Y., 1981) 122–34, and Jack N. Rakove, "The Madisonian Moment," *University of Chicago Law Review* 55 (1988): 473–505. Note, however, Colleen A. Sheehan, "Madison's Party Press Essays," *Interpretation* 17 (1990): 355–77.

83. *PAH* XI 441–42: Letter to Edward Carrington on 26 May 1792.

84. See *PTJ* XIV 16–21 (at 18): Letter from James Madison on 17 October 1788.

85. Cf. Drew R. McCoy, *The Last of the Fathers: James Madison and the Republican Legacy* (Cambridge 1989) 39–73, who is insufficiently sensitive to the gap separating Burke from Hume, and Madison from both. For a more balanced and accurate depiction of the American statesman's position, see Marvin Meyers, "Revolution and Founding: On Publius-Madison and the American Genesis," *Quarterly Journal of the Library of Congress* 37 (1980): 192–200.

86. Cf. Madison, *The Federalist* 49, with Jefferson, *NSV* 221: Draught of a Fundamental Constitution for the Commonwealth of Virginia (Appendix 2), and consider the pertinent exchange of letters between the two men. Cf. *PTJ* XV 392–97: Letter to James Madison on 6 September 1789 with *PJM* XIII 18–26: Letter to Thomas Jefferson on 4 February 1790, and see Adrienne Koch, *Jefferson and Madison: The Great Collaboration* (New York 1950) 62–96. Note Hamilton, *The Federalist* 25 (163).

87. For the situation in Virginia, see *The Documentary History of the First Federal Elections, 1788–1790*, ed. Merrill Jensen et al. (Madison, Wis., 1976–   ) II 251–97, 317–49, 363, 366–409. See also Richard R. Beeman, *The Old Dominion and the New Nation, 1788–1801* (Lexington, Ky., 1972) 1–27.

88. In his later years, when queried concerning the break with Hamilton, Madison is reported to have remarked, "I deserted Colonel Hamilton, or rather, Colonel Hamilton deserted me; in a word, the divergence between us took place—from his wishing to *administration*, or rather to administer the government (these were Mr. M.'s very words), into what he thought it ought to be; while, on my part, I endeavored to make it conform to the Constitution as understood by the Convention that produced and recommended it, and particularly by the State conventions that *adopted* it." See *RFC* III 533–34: Interview with Nicholas P. Trist on 27 September 1834. Cf., however, III.iii.7, note 126, below. After the Philadelphia convention, Madison made it a point to dissociate himself from those thought to be planning to use the institutions of the new regime to accomplish a gradual and imperceptible reduction of the states: see above, note 72.

89. For Jefferson's views on this question, see *PTJ* XII 438–43, 570–72, XIV 649–51, 659–63: Letters to James Madison on 20 December 1787, to Alexander Donald on 7 February 1788, to Francis Hopkinson on 13 March 1789, and to James Madison on 15 March 1789.

90. *PTJ* XIV 16–21 (at 18–20): Letter from James Madison on 17 October 1788.

91. For the emphasis which the Anti-Federalists placed on the educational effect of including a bill of rights in the Constitution, see *CAF*: Letters from The Federal Farmer XVI (2.8.196), Essays of an Old Whig IV (3.3.22), Essays by the Impartial Examiner (5.14.10), Letter from a Delegate Who Has Catched Cold (5.19.16).

92. *PTJ* XIV 16–21 (at 20): Letter from James Madison on 17 October 1788.

93. *PJM* XII 196–210: Amendments to the Constitution, 8 June 1789. For a half-hearted defense of what Madison calls "the nauseous project of amendments," see *PJM* XII 346–48: Letter to Richard Peters on 19 August 1789.

94. See *The Federalist* 39 (256–57), 44 (302–5), 51 (353), 62 (416–17), and *DSSC* III 96–97, 408–9: Virginia Ratifying Convention, 6 and 14 June 1788. See above, III.i.

95. *PJM* X 214: Letter to Thomas Jefferson on 24 October 1787.

96. See *The Federalist* 45.

97. See, for example, *DSSC* IV 546–80: Madison's Report on the Virginia Resolutions, 1799–1800.

98. For the speculation in the public debt, see E. James Ferguson, *The Power of the Purse: A History of American Public Finance, 1776–1790* (Chapel Hill 1961) 251–86; for the results, see Ferguson, "The Nationalists of 1781–1783 and the Economic Interpretation of the Constitution" 254 (esp. n. 38). For the economic problems of the Virginia planters, see Timothy H. Breen, *Tobacco Culture: The Mentality of the Great Tidewater Planters on the Eve of Revolution* (Princeton 1985).

99. North Carolina and Virginia contrived to tax the state certificates out of existence. See Adelaide L. Fries, "North Carolina Certificates of the Revolutionary War Period," *North Carolina Historical Review* 9 (1932): 229–42, and E. James Ferguson, *The Power of the Purse* 222, 230, 233. Rhode Island—the last state to ratify the Constitution—adopted a scheme designed to achieve the same end: see Forrest McDonald, *We the People: The Economic Origins of the Constitution* (Chicago 1958) 326–38.

100. At the Philadelphia convention, with Hamilton in attendance, Elbridge Gerry drew attention to this problem and predicted that the wholesale assumption of state debts would occasion precisely the trouble that it eventually caused: *RFC* II 356: 21 August 1787.

101. *The Federalist* 62 (421). Not surprisingly, then, Madison was later particularly annoyed to discover "the members of the Legislature who were most active in pushing" Hamilton's plan for a national bank "openly grasping its emoluments." See *PJM* XIV 42–43: Letter to Thomas Jefferson on 10 July 1791.

102. Of the thirteen congressmen who supported Madison's program of discrimination, nine were Virginians. For the vote, see *Annals of Congress* II 1298: 22 February 1790; for the overall reaction in Virginia, see Beeman, *The Old Dominion and the New Nation* 67–89. Not long after the struggle in Congress began, Edmund Randolph wrote to Madison that "the people of Virginia are, I believe, almost unanimous against the assumption of the state-debts. Some of the strongest antifoederalists here are high in their eulogiums on all of you, who have opposed the measure." See *PJM* XIII 224–25: Letter from Edmund Randolph on 20 May 1790. In this context, one should pay particular attention to the resolutions passed by the Virginia general assembly in October and December 1790. See *The Statutes at Large; Being a Collection of All the Laws of Virginia, from the First Session of the Legislature, in the Year 1619*, ed. William Waller Hening (Richmond 1809–23) XIII 234, 237–39. Madison would later cite Virginia's protest against the

federal measures providing for assumption and funding. See *PJM* XIV 275–76: Speech on the Public Debt, 31 March 1792.

103. For the proposal and the arguments made in its favor, see *PJM* XIII 24–39, 47–59: Discrimination between Present and Original Holders of the Public Debt, 11, 18–19 February 1790.

104. For the arguments he advanced, see *PJM* XIII 60–63, 65–66, 72–73, 80–85: Assumption of the States Debts, 24 and 26 February, 1–3 March 1790, and *PJM* XIII 99–102: Public Debt, 10–12 March 1790.

105. Thus far, no evidence has been presented to justify the suspicion sometimes voiced that Madison was himself involved in land speculation along the Potomac: cf. *PTJ* XIX 3–73 (at 9–16): Locating the Federal District, and *PJM* XII 59–62 (at 61). For additional information, see *PJM* XIV 1: Creation of the *National Capital*, 6 April 1791.

106. First, see Jacob E. Cooke, "The Compromise of 1790," *WMQ* 27 (1970): 523–45; then, consider Kenneth Russell Bowling, "Dinner at Jefferson's: A Note on Jacob E. Cooke's 'The Compromise of 1790,'" *WMQ* 28 (1971): 629–40, along with Cooke's response (640–48); and, finally, read McDonald, *Alexander Hamilton* 163–88 (with the notes).

107. See Kenneth R. Bowling, "The Bank Bill, the Capital City, and President Washington," *Capitol Studies* 1 (1972): 59–71, and McDonald, *Alexander Hamilton* 198–210 (with the notes). For a contemporary (and partisan) account, see [William Loughton Smith], *The Politicks and Views of a Certain Party, Displayed* (n.p. 1792). Cf. *PJM* XIV 396–402 (at 400): Notes on William Loughton Smith's *Politicks and Views*, ca. 4 November 1792.

108. For the arguments which the two men advanced, see *PJM* XIII 372–88, 395–96: The Bank Bill, 2 and 8 February 1791, and Draft Veto of the Bank Bill, 21 February 1791; and *PTJ* XIX 275–82: "Opinion on the Constitutionality of the Bill for Establishing a National Bank," 15 February 1791. See also *PJM* XIII 364–70: Notes on Banks (ca. 1 February 1791) and Notes on the Bank of England (ca. 1 February 1791).

109. *The Statutes at Large* XIII 237–39. The only Virginian of note to oppose the resolution was John Marshall: see Albert J. Beveridge, *Life of John Marshall* (New York 1916–19) II 65–68. In general, see Harry Ammon, "The Formation of the Republican Party in Virginia, 1789–1796," *JSH* 19 (1953): 283–310. Hamilton was reportedly quite distressed that, when the national bank was established some months later, almost no one from Virginia or North Carolina chose to subscribe to its stock: see *PTJ* XX 615–16: Letter to James Madison on 10 July 1791.

110. Consider *PJM* XIII 380–81: The Bank Bill, 2 February 1791, in light of *PJM* XVI 290–301 (at 295–96): Jay's Treaty, 6 April 1796, and *WrJM* IX 70–77 (esp. 71–72n, 74–75), 190–92 (esp. 191), 218–21 (at 219), 370–75: Letters to Thomas Ritchie on 15 September 1821, to John G. Jackson on 27 December 1821, to Henry Lee on 25 June 1824, to Thomas Jefferson on 8 February 1825, and to M. L. Hurlbert in May 1830. For early indications of Madison's commitment to strict construction, see the penultimate paragraph of *PJM* XIV 179–80: Letter to Henry Lee on 1 January 1792, and see *PJM* XIV 193–94, 220–24: Letter to Henry Lee on 21 January 1792, and Speech on Bounty Payments for Cod-Fisheries, 6 February 1792. See McCoy, *The Last of the Fathers* 73–83. Jefferson was similarly opposed to allowing the Constitution to become "a mere thing of wax in the hands of the judiciary." After being elected president, he pledged that he would administer the Con-

stitution "according to the safe and honest meaning contemplated by the plain understanding of the people of the United States, at the time of its adoption,—a meaning to be found in the explanations of those who advocated . . . it." Cf. *WoTJ* XII 135–40 (esp. 137): Letter to Spencer Roane on 6 September 1819, with *WrTJ* (ed. Lipscomb and Bergh) X 248–49: Letter to Messrs. Eddy, Russel, Thurber, Wheaton, and Smith on 27 March 1801. See also *WrTJ* (ed. Lipscomb and Bergh) X 417–20 (esp. 419): Letter to Wilson Cary Nicholas on 7 September 1803. This understanding of the canons for constitutional interpretation was in no way controversial: see III Epilogue, note 17, below. Although, from the outset, Madison firmly supported federal judicial review of state action as prerequisite for sustaining the supremacy of the Union, he feared that judicial review of federal legislation might render "the Judiciary Dept paramount in fact to the Legislature, which was never intended, and can never be proper." See *PJM* XI 281–95 (esp. 293 [with 284–85]): Observations on the "Draught of a Constitution for Virginia," ca. 15 October 1788.

111. *PJM* XIII 384, 386–87: The Bank Bill, 8 February 1791.

112. See Merrill D. Peterson, "Thomas Jefferson and Commercial Policy, 1783–1793," *WMQ* 22 (1965): 584–610; Drew R. McCoy, "Republicanism and American Foreign Policy: James Madison and the Political Economy of Commercial Discrimination, 1789 to 1794," *WMQ* 31 (1974): 633–46; and McCoy, *The Elusive Republic: Political Economy in Jeffersonian America* (Chapel Hill 1980) 136–65. For Madison's earlier efforts along these lines within his native state, see McCoy, "The Virginia Port Bill of 1784," *VMHB* 83 (1975): 288–303.

113. See Hamilton, *The Federalist* 11 (66–68).

114. Cf. *PAH* VII 426: Letter to Thomas Jefferson on 13 January 1791, with *PTJ* XX 234–36: Letter to James Monroe on 17 April 1791. Scholars who join Jefferson, Madison, and their allies in underestimating the vulnerability of the new nation's economy and in failing to give adequate stress to the necessity of establishing public credit on a proper foundation quite naturally tend to charge Hamilton with unnecessarily fostering American subservience to Great Britain: see John R. Nelson, Jr., *Liberty and Property* 52–79, 173–75.

115. If the two men came to see the foreign and domestic policies advocated by Hamilton as separate parts of a single conspiracy, it may largely have been because substantial extracts from a British document fell into Jefferson's hands late in the summer of 1791, indicating that, by the end of 1790, England's leaders perceived in Congress and in the Senate in particular *"a party . . . already formed in favor of a connection with Great Britain."* See *PTJ* XVII 267–72: Report of a Committee of the Lords of the Privy Council for Trade and Plantations, 28 January 1791.

116. Note, in particular, the cordial tone of the correspondence between Jefferson and Hamilton. See *PTJ* XVIII 68, 459–60, 562–64: Letters exchanged with Alexander Hamilton on 24 November and 29 December 1790, 11, 13, and 24 January 1791. In this connection, see also *PAH* VII 440–42: Conversations with George Beckwith, 19–20 January 1791. One other event is relevant. Jefferson was at this time vice-president of the American Philosophical Society; his close friend David Rittenhouse was president. On 21 January the society conferred on Hamilton the privilege of membership. See *PAH* VIII 29: Election to American Philosophical Society, 14 February 1791. By March, the tone of Jefferson's letters has become less warm. See *PTJ* XIX 536, 642: Letters to Alexander Hamilton on 12 and 31 March 1791.

117. *WrTJ* (ed. Ford) I 165–66: "The Anas." See also IX 446–51: Letter to Dr. Walter Jones on 2 January 1814.

118. On the development of Adams's thinking, see Gordon S. Wood, *The Creation of the American Republic, 1776–1787* (Chapel Hill 1969) 567–92, and Ralph Lerner, "Recovering the Revolution," *The Thinking Revolutionary: Principle and Practice in the New Republic* (Ithaca 1987) 1–38 (esp. 16–29).

119. See Joyce Appleby, "The Jefferson-Adams Rupture and the First French Translation of John Adams' *Defense*," *AHR* 73 (1968): 1084–91.

120. See *WoJA* VI 221–403: *Discourses on Davila*. Jefferson was also quite painfully aware that his old friend had initially been eager that the president of the United States be addressed in quasi-royal fashion as "His Highness" or "His High Majesty." See *PTJ* XV 147–48, 315–16: Exchange of Letters with James Madison on 23 May and 29 July 1789. See below, III.iv.7, note 134 and context.

121. *PTJ* XIX 241–42: Letter to George Mason on 4 February 1791. A mere six days before he submitted his own opinion that the federal government had no constitutional right to establish a national bank, Jefferson wrote to a friend that Congress had "passed . . . a bill for establishing a ban[k] to which it is objected that they have transcended their powers"—but he carefully refrained from endorsing this view himself. "There are certainly persons in all the departments who are for driving too fast," he noted. "Government is founded on opinion, [and] the opinion of the public, even when it is wrong, ought to be respected to a certain degree." See *PTJ* XIX 263: Letter to Nicholas Lewis on 9 February 1791.

122. It is not certain precisely when Madison reached this conclusion, but by the beginning of May he could speak of "speculators & Tories" as if the two were one. See *PJM* XIV 16: Letter to Thomas Jefferson on 1 May 1791. By early July, he could write, "It pretty clearly appears also in what proportions the public debt lies in the Country—What sort of hands hold it, and by whom the people of the U.S. are to be governed." With regard to the national bank, he added that Hamilton's father-in-law Philip John "Schuyler is to be put at the Head of the Directors if the weight of the N.Y. subscribers can effect it." See *PJM* XIV 43: Letter to Thomas Jefferson on 10 July 1791. Before summer's end, he was writing that "the stock-jobbers will become the pretorian band of the Government—at once its tool & its tyrant; bribed by its largesses, & overawing it by clamours & combinations." See *PJM* XIV 69: Letter to Thomas Jefferson on 8 August 1791. Madison would eventually favor a constitutional amendment requiring each congressman to "state on oath, the amount of his property in public and Bank Stock of every Kind" and to "swear that during the term of his continuing a member, he will not purchase or deal in any such paper, or any public lands, or any another public property whatever." See *PJM* XIV 470: Notes on Proposed Constitutional Amendments, ca. 3 March 1793.

123. Jefferson had employed the phrase "political heresies" in a letter welcoming the publication in America of the first volume of Thomas Paine's *Rights of Man*; the controversy arose when the printer published the critical section of Jefferson's note as a preface to the book. For the event, the controversy, and the various letters subsequently exchanged, see *PTJ* XX 268–313: *Rights of Man*: The "Contest of Burke and Paine in America." See, in particular, *PTJ* XX 290, 302–3, 305–6: Letter to Jonathan B. Smith on 26 April 1791 and Exchange of Letters with John Adams on 17 and 29 July 1791. Well before these events, James Madison had evidenced a low opinion of John Adams. In coming to his old friend's defense, Jefferson ac-

knowledged that "*he is vain, irritable, and a bad calculator of* the force and probable effects of the motives which govern men." Then, he added that "this is *all* the *ill* which can possibly be *said of* him. He is as disinterested as the being which made him: he is profound in his views: and accurate in his judgment *except where knowledge of the world* is necessary to form a judgment. He is so amiable, that I pronounce you will love him if you ever become acquainted with him. He would be, as he was, a great man in *Congress*." Soon thereafter, Madison would attack Adams for the "*political principles avowed in his book*," for "*his extravagant self importance*," and for his "*impatient ambition.*" See *PTJ* XI 94–95, XIV 17–18: Letters to James Madison on 30 January 1787 and from James Madison on 17 October 1788.

124. *PAH* VIII 33–34: Conversation with Thomas Jefferson, 13 August 1791.

125. John Marshall, *The Life of George Washington* (Fredericksburg, Va., 1926) V 202–5 (esp. 203–4).

126. Near the end of his life, however, even Jefferson seemed willing to concede the point. To Martin Van Buren, he wrote, "Hamilton frankly avowed that he considered the British Constitution, with all the corruptions of its administration, as the most perfect model of government which had ever been devised by the wit of man; professing however, at the same time, that the spirit of this country was so fundamentally republican, that it would be visionary to think of introducing monarchy here, and that, therefore, it was the duty of its administrators to conduct it on the principles their constituents had elected." See *WrTJ* (ed. Lipscomb and Bergh) XVI 66: Letter to Martin Van Buren on 29 June 1824. Note *RFC* III 480–81: Jared Sparks's Report of a Conversation with James Madison, 25 April 1830. In his correspondence, Madison was similarly circumspect: "Of Mr. Hamilton, I ought perhaps to speak with some restraint, though my feelings assure me, that no recollection of political collisions, could control the justice due to his memory. That he possessed intellectual powers of the first order, and the moral qualifications of integrity & honor in a captivating degree, has been decreed to him by a suffrage now universal. If his Theory of Gov! deviated from the Republican Standard, he had the candor to avow it, and the greater merit of cooperating faithfully in maturing & supporting a system which was not his choice. The criticism to which his share in the administration of it, was most liable was, that it had the aspect of an effort to give to the instrument a constructive & practical bearing not warranted by its true & intended character." See *WrJM* IX 451–56 (at 454): Letter to James K. Paulding on 1 April 1831.

127. Nor is there any reason to suppose that the other adherents of the Federalist party were monarchists in disguise: cf. Richard Buel, Jr., *Securing the Revolution: Ideology in American Politics, 1789–1815* (Ithaca 1972), with James M. Banner, *To the Hartford Convention: The Federalists and the Origins of Party Politics in Massachusetts, 1789–1815* (New York 1970), and Linda K. Kerber, *Federalists in Dissent: Imagery and Ideology in Jeffersonian America*[2] (Ithaca 1980).

128. See Morton J. Frisch, "Power and Responsibility: The Republican Statesmanship of Alexander Hamilton," in *The American Founding* 46–61. Thus, in the course of trying to persuade his fellow New Yorkers to ratify the Constitution, Hamilton is said to have remarked, "We have been told, that the spirit of patriotism and love of liberty are almost extinguished among the people; and that it has become a prevailing doctrine, that republican principles ought to be hooted out the world. . . . There have been, undoubtedly, some men who have had speculative doubts on the subject of government; but the principles of republicanism

are founded on too firm a basis to be shaken by a few speculative and sceptical reasoners." He is also said to have contended that "all men agree that Republican Principles & govt. are the most Noble." See *PAH* V 44–45, 49, 51: Speech to the New York Ratifying Convention, 21 June 1788.

129. *RFC* I 424: 26 June 1787. In the notes which he made in preparation for the speech in which he lavished praise on the British monarchy, he wrote, "Here I shall give my sentiments of the best form of government—not as a thing attainable by us, but as a model which we ought to approach as near as possible." See *RFC* I 308. In this connection, see also *PAH* XXV 536–39, XXVI 147–49: To the *New-York Evening Post*, 24 February 1802, and Letter to Timothy Pickering on 16 September 1803.

130. *PAH* XI 443: Letter to Edward Carrington on 26 May 1792.

131. *PAH* XI 443–44: Letter to Edward Carrington on 26 May 1792. A few months later, Hamilton provided Washington with a similar testimonial designed to quiet the fears which Jefferson, Madison, and their friends were stirring up. At the federal convention, he observed, "No man, that I know of, contemplated the introducing into this country of a monarchy. A very small number (not more than three or four) manifested theoretical opinions favourable in the abstract to a constitution like that of Great Britain, but every one agreed that such a constitution except as to the general distribution of departments and powers was out of the Question in reference to this Country. The Member who was most explicit on this point (a Member from New York) declared in strong terms that the republican theory ought to be adhered to in this Country as long as there was any chance of its success—that the idea of a perfect equality of political rights among the citizens, exclusive of all permanent or hereditary distinctions, was of a nature to engage the good wishes of every good man, whatever might be his theoretic doubts—that it merited his best efforts to give success to it in practice— that hitherto from an incompetent structure of the Government it had not had a fair trial, and that the endeavour ought then to be to secure to it a better chance of success by a government more capable of energy and order." See *PAH* XII 228– 58 (at 253): Letter of 18 August 1792 to George Washington with Objections and Answers respecting the Administration of the Government. The notes taken by Madison and by others who attended the convention do not confirm Hamilton's claim concerning his own public statements, but they do not disprove it either. Those notes are too abbreviated to be all-inclusive. Washington could, in any case, consult his own memory of the proceedings.

132. For the details and the relevant evidence, see *PTJ* XX 718–59: Jefferson, Freneau, and the Founding of the *National Gazette* and *PTJ* XX 434–73: The Northern Journey of Jefferson and Madison. See also *PJM* XIV 56–57: The Origins of Freneau's *National Gazette*, 25 July 1791. I see no reason to play down the political import of the trip which Jefferson and Madison took through New York and New England in May and June 1791. The simple fact that the two used it as an opportunity to enlist Freneau is a sign that they had decided to form an opposition, and for that effort they would inevitably require other help as well. If the evidence that their trip had a political purpose is limited, it is merely an indication that the two men conducted their business with unusual discretion. Hamilton's friends certainly recognized that something was afoot. See *PAH* VIII 478–79, IX 529–37 (at 534): Letters from Robert Troup and Nathaniel Hazard on 15 June and 25 November 1791. We know that the trip afforded the two men an occasion

for pondering the political events of the preceding year: *WrJM* IX 403–7 (at 405): Letter to Margaret B. Smith in September 1830.

133. See Banning, *The Jeffersonian Persuasion* 126–302. See also Noble E. Cunningham, Jr., *The Jeffersonian Republicans: The Formation of Party Organization, 1789–1801* (Chapel Hill 1957). In this connection, see *WrTJ* (ed. Ford) I 174–78, 198–210, 202–5, 214–16, 256–61, VI 1–6, 149–52: "The Anas" and Letters to George Washington on 23 May and 9 September 1792. Madison made an attempt to persuade Washington also. See *PJM* XIV 299–304 (at 301–3): Memorandum on a Discussion of the President's Retirement, 5 and 9 May 1792.

134. *Massachusetts Historical Society Collections*[7] 1 (1900): 61–64: Letter from Thomas Jefferson to John Taylor on 4 June 1798.

135. Sparks, *The Life of Gouverneur Morris with Selections from his Correspondence* III 128: Letter to Rufus King on 4 June 1800. Hamilton's observations support Morris's conclusion. "Sympathy with the French Revolution acts in a much narrower circle than formerly," he observed, "but the jealousy of monarchy, which is as active as ever, still furnishes a hand by which the factious mislead well meaning persons." See *PAH* XXIV 167–71 (at 168): Letter to Rufus King on 5 January 1800.

136. Sparks, *The Life of Gouverneur Morris with Selections from his Correspondence* III 262: Letter to Robert Walsh on 5 February 1811.

Chapter 4

1. *WrTJ* (ed. Ford) XII 136: Letter to Spencer Roane on 6 September 1819.

2. *WrTJ* (ed. Ford) I 156–57: "The Anas."

3. For this point, see Lance Banning, *The Jeffersonian Persuasion: Evolution of a Party Ideology* (Ithaca 1978) 273–302. With considerable justice, John M. Murrin, "The Great Inversion, or Court versus Country," in *Three British Revolutions: 1641, 1688, 1776*, ed. J. G. A. Pocock (Princeton 1980) 368–453, suggests that the American Revolution differed from the Glorious Revolution chiefly in the fact that, in the United States, the country party rather than the court party came to dominate public administration.

4. See John Zvesper, *Political Philosophy and Rhetoric: A Study of the Origins of American Party Politics* (Cambridge 1977).

5. *PAH* XI 441–42: Letter to Edward Carrington on 26 May 1792.

6. *PMHS*[2] 14 (1900): 353–54: Letter from John Marshall to Joseph Story on 25 December 1832.

7. This was already evident in 1832 when Andrew Jackson found it impossible to rally his own states' rights supporters behind his Nullification Proclamation: see Richard E. Ellis, *The Union at Risk: Jacksonian Democracy, States' Rights, and the Nullification Crisis* (Oxford 1987).

8. For the passages quoted, see *PAH* XXI 522, XXII 453: Letters to Oliver Wolcott on 29 June 1798 and to Theodore Sedgwick on 2 February 1799. For Hamilton's eagerness that the Alien Acts not be "cruel and violent," see *PAH* XXI 495: Letter to Timothy Pickering on 7 June 1798. John Marshall held a similar opinion. See *PJoM* III 485, 505–6, IV 3–4: Letter to Timothy Pickering on 11 August 1798; Letter to a Freeholder, *Virginia Herald*, 2 October 1798; Letter to George Washington on 8 January 1799. See also *PJoM* III 520, 530: Letters to Timothy Pickering

on 22 October 1798 and to George Washington on 30 December 1798. In this connection, see also the relevant discussion in the editorial note at *PJoM* IV 37.

9. See *The Federalist* 26 (168–69), 28 (178–80), 44 (305), 46 (320), 60 (404), 84 (582–83), 85 (593).

10. For the evidence regarding the origin, purpose, composition, and ultimate amendment of the resolutions, see Adrienne Koch and Harry Ammon, "The Virginia and Kentucky Resolutions: An Episode in Jefferson's and Madison's Defense of Civil Liberties," *WMQ* 5 (1948): 145–76. See also James Morton Smith, "The Grass Roots Origins of the Kentucky Resolutions," *WMQ* 22 (1970): 221–45.

11. See Madison, *The Federalist* 39 (254).

12. *WrTJ* (ed. Ford) VII 289–309: Drafts of the Kentucky Resolutions of 1798, October 1798.

13. For the nature of the disagreement underlying the differences between the Kentucky and Virginia resolutions, see Harry V. Jaffa, "Partly Federal, Partly National: On the Political Theory of the American Civil War," *The Conditions of Freedom: Essays in Political Philosophy* (Baltimore 1975) 161–83. For a discussion of the difference between nullification and interposition, see Joseph McGraw, "Virginia Republicans on the Strategies of Political Opposition, 1788–1800," *VMHB* 91 (1983): 54–72 (at 56–60). Note also Drew R. McCoy, *The Last of the Fathers: James Madison and the Republican Legacy* (Cambridge 1989) 9–37, 119–170.

14. *DSSC* IV 546–80: Madison's Report on the Virginia Resolutions, 1799–1800. See *PJM* XVII 303–51: The Report of 1800.

15. For Jefferson's efforts to have the excluded phrase included in the resolutions, see *WoTJ* VIII 483: Letter to Wilson Cary Nicholas on 29 November 1798. The phrase was added to Madison's draft before it was presented to the Virginia assembly, then excised by subsequent amendment.

16. Jefferson had urged him to keep his options open. See *PJM* XVII 175–81: Letter from Thomas Jefferson on 17 November 1798. See also *WrTJ* (ed. Lipscomb and Bergh) X 65: Letter to John Taylor on 26 November 1798.

17. For the critical piece of evidence, see *PJM* XVII 257–59: Letter from Thomas Jefferson on 23 August 1799. For Madison's effectiveness in restraining his friend the vice-president, see Koch and Ammon, "The Virginia and Kentucky Resolutions" 166–74.

18. For the resolutions actually passed in Kentucky, see *WrTJ* (ed. Ford) VII 288–89: Kentucky Resolutions, 10 November 1798.

19. In this context, the observations of Alexis de Tocqueville deserve careful attention: for, apart from failing to detect the changes then taking place in southern sentiment and to foresee their import, the French traveler came closer to accurately diagnosing the danger when he toured the new nation in 1831 and 1832 than anyone alive at the time: *DA* 1.2.10 (380–412).

20. For the relevant evidence and its import, see Walter Berns, "Freedom of the Press and the Alien and Sedition Laws: A Reappraisal," *The Supreme Court Review* (1970): 135–42, and *The First Amendment and the Future of American Democracy* (New York 1976) 80–146.

21. See *WrTJ* (ed. Lipscomb and Bergh) XVII 442–48: Draft Declaration and Protest of the Commonwealth of Virginia, on the Principles of the Constitution of the United States of America, and on the Violations of them, December 1825.

22. See *WrTJ* (ed. Lipscomb and Bergh) XVI 140–42: Letter to James Madison on 24 December 1825.

23. See *WrTJ* (ed. Ford) X 354–57: Letter to William Branch Giles on 26 December 1825. In this connection, see the penultimate paragraph of X 222–26: Letter to Justice William Johnson on 27 October 1822. See also X 358–59: Letter to William F. Gordon on 1 January 1826. For Jefferson's awareness that, after his death, his correspondence would be published, see X 246–49: Letter to Judge William Johnson on 4 March 1823.

24. For Jefferson's eagerness to keep secret the role he had played, see *WrTJ* (ed. Ford) VII 290n–291n: Letter to John Cabel Breckinridge on 11 December 1821.

25. See Merrill D. Peterson, *The Jefferson Image in the American Mind* (New York 1960) 17–66, and William W. Freehling, *Prelude to Civil War: The Nullification Controversy in South Carolina, 1816–1836* (New York 1968) esp. 207–10.

26. See *WrJM* IX 316–40, 317–26n, 354–58n, 383–403: Letters to Joseph C. Cabell on 18 September and 30 October 1828, to Nicholas P. Trist on 15 February 1830, and to Edward Everett on 28 August 1830. In this connection, one should also note *Letters and Other Writings of James Madison* (Philadelphia 1865) IV 183–87: Letter to Charles Jared Ingersoll on 25 June 1831.

27. For his mature reflections on this subject, see *WrJM* IX 573–607: Notes on Nullification, 1835–36. For an extraordinarily careful exposition of the Kentucky and Virginia resolutions and of the doctrines underlying the subsequent dispute concerning nullification, see Jaffa, "Partly Federal, Partly National" 161–83. See also McCoy, *The Last of the Fathers* 85–170.

28. See *The Mind of the Founder: Sources of the Political Thought of James Madison*[2], ed. Marvin Meyers (Hanover, N.H., 1981) 443: "Advice to My Country." Madison appears to have drafted this testament in October 1834. See also *WrJM* IX 351–57: Outline, September 1829.

29. Cf. Jefferson, *NSV* 18 (162–63), with Montesquieu, *EL* 3.15.1–19, and see III.ii.2, 4, above. Cf. Pl. *Leg.* 6.777d–e.

30. See *PTJ* VIII 467–70: Letter to Chastellux on 2 September 1785, with Enclosure.

31. Jefferson, *NSV* 18 (163).

32. *RFC* I 135: 6 June 1787.

33. *PJM* XIV 163–64: Madison's *National Gazette* Essays, 19 November 1791–20 December 1792.

34. See, for example, *WrTJ* (ed. Ford) IX 477–79, X 45n–46n, 157–58, 289–93: Letters to Edward Coles on 25 August 1814, to Samuel Kercheval on 5 September 1816, to John Holmes on 22 April 1820, and to Jared Sparks on 4 February 1824; *WrTJ* (ed. Peterson) 1447–50: Letter to Albert Gallatin on 26 December 1820; Henry S. Randall, *The Life of Thomas Jefferson* (New York 1857) III 539: Letter to James Heaton on 20 May 1826; and *WrJM* VIII 439–47, IX 224–29, 498–502: Letters to Robert J. Evans on 15 June 1819, to Frances Wright on 1 September 1825, and to Thomas R. Dew on 23 February 1833.

35. See *WrTJ* (ed. Peterson) 1447–50: Letter to Albert Gallatin on 26 December 1820. See also *WrTJ* (ed. Ford) X 179–81, 279–83: Letters to the Marquis de Lafayette on 26 December 1820 and 4 November 1823, and *WrTJ* (ed. Lipscomb and Bergh) 279–81: Letter to Charles Pinckney on 30 September 1820.

36. See Jefferson, *MCPP* IV 350–52: Letter to General James Breckinridge on 15 February 1821.

37. For Jefferson's contribution to the developments which eventually gave rise

to civil war, see Robert E. Shalhope, "Thomas Jefferson's Republicanism and Antebellum Southern Thought," *JSH* 42 (1976): 529–56.

38. One might want to ponder the difficulties that Madison had in wrestling with the question of slavery in light of the sad fate of a public figure who was a disciple of Jefferson, then Madison, and who eventually penned the first biography of the latter: consider McCoy, *The Last of the Fathers* 217–322, in light of Patrick Sowle, "The Trials of a Virginia Unionist: William Cabell Rives and the Secession Crisis, 1860–1861," *VMHB* 80 (1972): 3–20, and see McCoy, *The Last of the Fathers* 323–369. Note, however, Ralph L. Ketcham, "The Dictates of Conscience: Edward Coles and Slavery," *Virginia Quarterly Review* 36 (1960): 46–62.

39. See *WrTJ* (ed. Lipscomb and Bergh) XV 248–50: Letter to John Holmes on 22 April 1820, and *WrJM* IX 1–13: Letter to Robert Walsh on 27 November 1819.

40. *The Federalist* 10 (59).

41. Note II.vi.6–7 and Epilogue, above; then, consider Lance Banning, "Some Second Thoughts on Virtue and the Course of Revolutionary Thinking," in *Conceptual Change and the Constitution*, ed. Terence Ball and J. G. A. Pocock (Lawrence, Kans., 1988) 194–212, in light of III.iv.4–v.6, below; and see Russell L. Hanson, "'Commons' and 'Commonwealth' at the American Founding: Democratic Republicanism as the New American Hybrid," in ibid., 165–93.

42. For a contemporary discussion of this point, see *CAF*: Mercy Otis Warren, *History of the Rise, Progress and Termination of the American Revolution*, 1805 (6.14.24–37). For a more recent assessment, see David P. Szatmary, *Shays' Rebellion: The Making of an Agrarian Insurrection* (Amherst, Mass., 1980) 120–34.

43. See *CAF*: Letters of Centinel XVIII (2.7.182)

44. The Anti-Federalists do not often mention the event. Shays's rebellion was, as they knew, grist for the Federalist mill, but it is nonetheless striking that, when the Anti-Federalists do advert to the insurrection, they never suggest or even hint that it was harmless or an occurrence giving rise to little danger. See *CAF*: Letters of Cato III (2.6.16); Letters of Centinel XVIII (2.7.182); Essays of Brutus X, XIV (2.9.127, 176); Essays by Vox Populi (4.4.30); Essays by Candidus II (4.9.38); Mercy Otis Warren, *History of the Rise, Progress and Termination of the American Revolution*, 1805 (6.14.24–37).

45. *AJL* I 172–73: Letter from Thomas Jefferson to Abigail Adams on 22 February 1787. Cf. I 168–69: Letter from Abigail Adams to Thomas Jefferson on 29 January 1787. For similar expressions of opinion, see *PTJ* X 621, 629: Letters to Abigail Adams on 21 December and to Ezra Stiles on 24 December 1786.

46. *PTJ* XI 48–50: Letter to Edward Carrington on 16 January 1787.

47. *PTJ* XI 92–97: Letter to James Madison on 30 January 1787. Eleven months later, Jefferson returned to this theme once again. See also XII 438–43 (at 442): Letter to James Madison on 20 December 1787.

48. *PTJ* XII 355–57: Letter to William Stephens Smith on 13 November 1787.

49. Alexander Hamilton, *RFC* I 381–82: 22 June 1787. See Hamilton, *The Federalist* 76 (513–14). Note, in this connection, *CMPP* I 218–19: George Washington, Farewell Address, 17 September 1796. "Within certain limits," the nation's first president was prepared to concede the probable truth of the "opinion that parties in free countries are useful checks upon the administration of the government, and serve to keep alive the spirit of liberty." "But," he argued, "in those of the popular character, in governments purely elective, it is a spirit not to be encouraged. From their natural tendency it is certain there will always be enough of

that spirit for every salutary purpose; and there being constant danger of excess, the effort ought to be by force of public opinion to mitigate and assuage it. A fire not to be quenched, it demands a uniform vigilance to prevent its bursting into a flame, lest, instead of warming, it should consume."

50. *PAH* XI 441–42: Letter to Edward Carrington on 26 May 1792.

51. Here I draw on the notes which Hamilton made in preparation for delivering his great speech at the Philadelphia convention. See *RFC* I 309: 18 June 1787.

52. *The Federalist* 51 (351).

53. *PTJ* XII 442: Letter to James Madison on 20 December 1787.

54. See *PTJ* XII 349–51, 355–57, 438–43, 570–72, XIV 649–51: Letters to John Adams and William Stephens Smith on 13 November 1787, to James Madison on 20 December 1787, to Alexander Donald on 7 February 1788, and to Francis Hopkinson on 13 March 1789. On this point, John Adams was in agreement with Hamilton. See *AJL* I 213–14: Letter from John Adams to Thomas Jefferson on 6 December 1787.

55. See *PTJ* XII 438–43, 570–72, XIV 328–32 (at 328), 649–51, 659–63: Letters to James Madison on 20 December 1787, to Alexander Donald on 7 February 1788, to George Washington on 4 December 1788, to Francis Hopkinson on 13 March 1789, and, again, to James Madison on 15 March 1789.

56. See *PTJ* XII 355–57: Letter to William Stephens Smith on 13 November 1787. In this connection, see also *AJL* I 211–12: Letter from Thomas Jefferson to John Adams on 13 November 1787.

57. *WrTJ* (ed. Ford) X 27–31 (at 30–31): Letter to John Taylor on 28 May 1816.

58. *PTJ* XII 438–43 (at 442): Letter to James Madison on 20 December 1787.

59. *WrTJ* (ed. Washington) VII 31–32: Letter to Isaac H. Tiffany on 26 August 1816.

60. See Harvey C. Mansfield, Jr., "Thomas Jefferson," in *American Political Thought: The Philosophic Dimensions of American Statesmanship*³, ed. Morton J. Frisch and Richard G. Stevens (Itasca, Ill., 1983) 23–50. For a more detailed account of what this mixture of principles involves, see Mansfield, *The Spirit of Liberalism* (Cambridge, Mass., 1978) esp. 1–16, 37–38, 65–71, 94.

61. Cf. *AJL* II 358 with 391: Letter from John Adams to Thomas Jefferson on 15 July 1813 and Jefferson's reply on 28 October 1813.

62. *AJL* II 387–92: Letter from Thomas Jefferson to John Adams on 28 October 1813. For Adams's prior discussion of the problem posed by aristocracy and for his response to Jefferson, see *AJL* II 350–52, 365–66, 370–72, 376–77, 397–402, 406–9: Letters from John Adams to Thomas Jefferson on 9 July, 14 August, 2 and 15 September, 15 November, and 19 December 1813.

63. In this regard, one should pay particular attention to Jefferson's doubts regarding the viability of republicanism in Spanish America. See *WrTJ* (ed. Washington) V 580–81: Letter to Alexander von Humboldt on 14 April 1811; *WrTJ* (ed. Ford) IX 430–33, X 22–25, 82–86, 185–87: Letters to Alexander von Humboldt on 6 December 1813, to Pierre Samuel Dupont de Nemours on 24 April 1816, to the Marquis de Lafayette on 14 May 1817, and to John Adams on 22 January 1821. Note also Jefferson's reflections on the causes for the failure of the French Revolution. See *WrTJ* (ed. Ford) IX 504–11, X 279–83 (at 280): Letters to the Marquis de Lafayette on 14 February 1815 and 4 November 1823, and *AJL* II 387–92 (at 391), 596–97: Letters from Thomas Jefferson to John Adams on 28 October 1813 and 4 September 1823.

64. See *WrTJ* (ed. Lipscomb and Bergh) XVII 417–41 (at 424): Letter to Joseph C. Cabell on 9 September 1817, with draft of "An Act for Establishing Elementary Schools." He first began toying with this possibility when he read the constitution proposed by the Cortes in Spain. See *WrTJ* (ed. Ford) X 22–25: Letter to Pierre Samuel Dupont de Nemours on 11 January 1816.

65. For the legislative program as a whole, see *PTJ* II 303–665 (esp. 336–657): The Revisal of the Laws, 18 June 1779. For Jefferson's division of the world into "the laboring" and "the learned" and for the connection between this distinction and the shape taken by his educational program, see *WrTJ* (ed. Lipscomb and Bergh) XIX 485–88: Letter to Peter Carr on 7 September 1814.

66. See Ralph Lerner, *Making Republicans: Jefferson's Experiment in Virginia* (Claremont, Calif., 1984), and "Jefferson's Pulse of Republican Reformation," *The Thinking Revolutionary: Principle and Practice in the New Republic* (Ithaca 1987) 60–90.

67. See *PTJ* II 545–53: The Revisal of the Laws, 18 June 1779: 82. A Bill for Establishing Religious Freedom. The Virginia general assembly deleted the last of the passages quoted before passing the law in January 1786.

68. Cf. Montesquieu, *EL* 1.5.6 with 8 (287), and see 1.5.3, 5, 9.

69. For the phrase quoted, see *AJL* II 387–92: Letter from Thomas Jefferson to John Adams on 28 October 1813. For similar sentiments, see James Wilson, *RFC* I 159: 7 June 1787, and [Noah Webster], *Examination into the Leading Principles of the Federal Constitution Proposed by the Late Convention Held at Philadelphia by A Citizen of America* (Philadelphia 1787) 46–49. For the law abolishing entails, see *PTJ* I 560–62: Bill to Enable Tenants in Fee Tail to Convey Their Lands in Fee Simple, 14 October 1776; for that eliminating primogeniture, see *PTJ* II 391–93: The Revisal of the Laws, 18 June 1779: 20. A Bill Directing the Course of Descents. If Jefferson's reforms were easily passed, it was largely because the abundance of land in Virginia had prevented entail and primogeniture from having any great and lasting effect on colonial society: see C. Ray Keim, "Primogeniture and Entail in Colonial Virginia," *WMQ* 25 (1968): 545–86. For the long-term political import of the abolition of entail and primogeniture that took place throughout the new nation, see Tocqueville, *DA* 1.1.3. For a somewhat confused, if nonetheless useful, account of the overall context in which Jefferson developed his argument, see Stanley N. Katz, "Republicanism and the Law of Inheritance in the American Revolutionary Era," *Michigan Law Review* 76 (1977): 1–29.

70. See *WrTJ* (ed. Ford) I 66: Autobiography.

71. See *PTJ* II 526–35: The Revisal of the Laws, 18 June 1779: 79. A Bill for the More General Diffusion of Knowledge. For a later version, see *WrTJ* (ed. Lipscomb and Bergh) XVII 417–41: Letter to Joseph C. Cabell on 9 September 1817, with draft of "An Act for Establishing Elementary Schools."

72. Jefferson, *NSV* 14 (146–49).

73. For the history of Jefferson's efforts on behalf of education, see Merrill D. Peterson, *Thomas Jefferson and the New Nation: A Biography* (Oxford 1970) 145–52, 961–88.

74. See *PTJ* II 535–43: The Revisal of the Laws, 18 June 1779: 80. A Bill for Amending the Constitution of the College of William and Mary, and Substituting More Certain Revenues for Its Support.

75. See *PTJ* II 544–45: The Revisal of the Laws, 18 June 1779: 81. A Bill for Establishing a Public Library.

76. See *WrTJ* (ed. Ford) I 66–70: Autobiography.

77. See *WrTJ* (ed. Ford) VII 413–16, 475–77: Letter to Dr. Joseph Priestley on 27 January 1800, and A Memorandum (Service to My Country).

78. *AJL* II 387–92: Letter from Thomas Jefferson to John Adams on 28 October 1813.

79. For the overall plan as it developed, see *Early History of the University of Virginia As Contained in the Letters of Thomas Jefferson and Joseph C. Cabell*, ed. Nathaniel F. Cabell (Richmond 1856) 432–47: Report of the Commissioners for the University of Virginia (Rockfish Gap Report), 4 August 1818, and *WrTJ* (ed. Lipscomb and Bergh) XIX 361–499 (esp. 407–8, 413–16, 433–51, 454–61): An Exact Transcript of the Minutes of the Board of Visitors of the University of Virginia during the Rectorship of Thomas Jefferson, 5 May 1817 to 7 April 1826. In the mid-1790s, Jefferson toyed with the idea of shifting the Academy of Geneva to Virginia; in 1800, he began talking of establishing a new, thoroughly modern university in the piedmont. See *WrTJ* (ed. Ford) VII 2–6, 406–10, 413–16: Letters to François d'Ivernois on 6 February 1795 and to Dr. Joseph Priestley on 18 and 27 January 1800; *WrTJ* (ed. Peterson) 1149–53: Letter to Littleton Waller Tazewell on 5 January 1805; and *WrTJ* (ed. Lipscomb and Bergh) XVII 417–41: Letter to Joseph C. Cabell on 9 September 1817, with draft of "An Act for Establishing Elementary Schools." In this connection, see *WrTJ* (ed. Washington) V 520–22: Letter to Messrs. Hugh L. White and Others on 6 May 1810. To this project, he turned his attention a few years after he left the presidency. At first, he focused on the establishment of an academy in Albemarle County. See *WrTJ* (ed. Lipscomb and Bergh) XIX 211–21: Letter to Peter Carr on 7 September 1814. Perhaps the clearest testimony of the degree to which Jefferson was dedicated to this project is the fact that, though very nearly bankrupt, he nonetheless kept his promise and left his library to the university. See *WrTJ* (ed. Lipscomb and Bergh) XVII 465–70 (at 469), XIX x: Thomas Jefferson's Will. See also Merrill D. Peterson, *Thomas Jefferson and the New Nation* 961–88, 989–92, 1006–7.

80. To one close collaborator, Jefferson wrote, "Were it necessary to give up either the Primaries or the University, I would rather abandon the last, because it is safer to have a whole people respectably enlightened, than a few in a high state of science, and the many in ignorance. This last is the most dangerous state in which a nation can be. The nations and governments of Europe are so many proofs of it." See *Early History of the University of Virginia* 266–68: Letter to Joseph C. Cabell on 13 January 1823.

81. See *WrTJ* (ed. Lipscomb and Bergh) XIX 460–61: An Exact Transcript of the Minutes of the Board of Visitors of the University of Virginia during the Rectorship of Thomas Jefferson, 4 March 1825. "In the selection of our Law Professor, we must be rigorously attentive to his political principles," Jefferson observed. Before the Revolution, this would have been easy, he explained. "Our lawyers were then all Whigs. Even now, they suppose themselves, indeed, to be Whigs, because they no longer know what Whigism or republicanism means. It is in our seminary that that vestal flame is to be kept alive." See *WrTJ* (ed. Lipscomb and Bergh) XVI 155–59 (at 156–57): Letter to James Madison on 17 February 1826. See also III.iv.6, note 101, below.

82. Cf. Jefferson, *NSV* 6 (33), 17 (159–60), with *PTJ* II 545–53: The Revisal of the Laws, 18 June 1779: 82. A Bill for Establishing Religious Freedom; note *WrTJ* (ed. Ford) I 62: Autobiography; and see J. G. A. Pocock, "Religious Freedom and the Desacralization of Politics: From the English Civil Wars to the Virginia Statute," in

The Virginia Statute for Religious Freedom: Its Evolution and Consequences in American History, ed. Merrill D. Peterson and Robert C. Vaughan (Cambridge 1988) 43–73.

83. See *WrTJ* (ed. Ford) VII 127–30: Letter to Thomas Pinckney on 29 May 1797. With these concerns in mind, Jefferson betrayed considerable interest in the university's history curriculum. See *WrTJ* (ed. Lipscomb and Bergh) XVI 124–29: Letter to an Unknown Recipient on 25 October 1825.

84. Jefferson, *NSV* 17 (161). For Madison and Adam Smith on this question, see above, III.i.5.

85. See *WrTJ* (ed. Lipscomb and Bergh) XIX 414–16: An Exact Transcript of the Minutes of the Board of Visitors of the University of Virginia during the Rectorship of Thomas Jefferson, 7 October 1822. In an anonymous review of the Rockfish Gap Report, Edward Everett initially remarked that "this is probably the first instance in the world, of a university without any . . . provision" for "instruction" in "divinity." Later, he added, "The result of this hazardous experiment it is not for us to anticipate." See [Edward Everett], "University of Virginia," *North American Review* 10 (1820): 115–37 (at 130–31). "A University with sectarian professorships," Madison responded, "becomes, of course, a Sectarian Monopoly: with professorships of rival sects, it would be an Arena of Theological Gladiators. Without any such professorships, it may incur for a time at least, the imputation of irreligious tendencies, if not designs. The last difficulty was thought more manageable than either of the others." See *WrJM* IX 124–30 (at 126): Letter to Edward Everett on 19 March 1823.

86. See *WrTJ* (ed. Ford) X 242–44: Letter to Thomas Cooper on 2 November 1822. The offer to Cooper of one of the university's eight professorships caused Virginia's Presbyterians to suspect that Jefferson intended to make his university a hotbed of Socinianism; had they known that he had sounded out two other Unitarians as well, they would undoubtedly have caused a greater fuss. See *Early History of the University of Virginia* 164–72, 215–16, 223–27, 229–37 (with note): Letters Exchanged Between Thomas Jefferson and Joseph C. Cabell on 19 and 22 February and 1 and 8 March 1819, on 5 August 1821, and on 3, 7, and 14 January 1822. In this connection, note their earlier fears: *Early History of the University of Virginia* 128–29, 155–59: 26 February 1818, 4 February 1819. For Jefferson's enthusiasm for Unitarianism and for his hope that it would, in due course, sweep the country, see below, III.vi.4, note 50.

87. See *WrTJ* (ed. Lipscomb and Bergh) XIX 449: An Exact Transcript of the Minutes of the Board of Visitors of the University of Virginia during the Rectorship of Thomas Jefferson, 4 October 1824.

88. Cf. *PTJ* II 545–53: The Revisal of the Laws, 18 June 1779: 82. A Bill for Establishing Religious Freedom, with *WrTJ* (ed. Lipscomb and Bergh) XVII 417–41 (at 425): Letter to Joseph C. Cabell on 9 September 1817, with draft of "An Act for Establishing Elementary Schools." By the late 1790s, Jefferson's interpretation of the First Amendment and of the doctrine of enumerated powers would perhaps have left him less than happy to see the federal government take on such responsibilities. See *WrTJ* (ed. Ford) IX 174–76: Letter to Rev. Samuel Miller on 23 January 1808. Jefferson's caution in this regard had far more to do with his having embraced the cause of states' rights than with any squeamishness about government support for religion.

89. See *PTJ* II 555–56: The Revisal of the Laws, 18 June 1779: 84. A Bill for Pun-

ishing Disturbers of Religious Worship and Sabbath Breakers, and 85. A Bill for Appointing Days of Public Fasting and Thanksgiving. See below, note 93.

90. Cf. *PTJ* I 413–33: *The Declaration of Independence*, with *PTJ* II 545–53: The Revisal of the Laws, 18 June 1779: 82. A Bill for Establishing Religious Freedom, and see Thomas E. Buckley, S.J., "The Political Theology of Thomas Jefferson," in *The Virginia Statute for Religious Freedom* 75–107.

91. See *WrTJ* (ed. Washington) VIII 113–14: Letter to Messrs. Nehemiah Dodge and Others, A Committee of the Danbury Baptist Association, in the State of Connecticut, 1 January 1802.

92. For further discussion, see below, III.vi.1–4.

93. For the logic behind his stance, see *CMPP* I 378–82 (at 379–80): Thomas Jefferson, Second Inaugural Address, 4 March 1805, and *WrTJ* (ed. Ford) IX 174–76: Letter to Rev. Samuel Miller on 23 January 1808. It deserves notice that, as governor of Virginia, Jefferson did not hesitate to proclaim days of fasting and prayer: *WrTJ* (ed. Ford) III 178: 11 November 1779.

94. *WrTJ* (ed. Ford) VIII 341–48: Thomas Jefferson, "Second Inaugural Address," 4 March 1805.

95. Jefferson, *NSV* 18 (163).

96. Nor did he argue for outlawing immigration from abroad. But, because he feared that immigrants from the monarchies of Europe would "bring with them the principles of the governments they leave," pass these on "to their children," and "infuse" into American legislation "their spirit, warp and bias its direction, and render it a heterogeneous, incoherent, distracted mass," Jefferson doubted "the expediency of inviting them by extraordinary encouragements." See Jefferson, *NSV* 8 (84–85); then, consider *CMPP* I 326–32 (at 331): Thomas Jefferson, First Annual Message, 8 December 1801.

97. For Jefferson's adaption of Locke's argument, see S. Gerald Sandler, "Lockean Ideas in Thomas Jefferson's *Bill for Establishing Religious Freedom*," *JHI* 21 (1960): 110–16.

98. *PTJ* II 545–46: The Revisal of the Laws, 18 June 1779: 82. A Bill for Establishing Religious Freedom. Accordingly, he promised one prospective instructor that, at the University of Virginia, he could look forward to "illimitable freedom of the human mind. For here we are not afraid to follow truth wherever it may lead, nor to tolerate any error so long as reason is free to combat it." See *WrTJ* (ed. Lipscomb and Bergh) XV 302–4 (at 303): Letter to William Roscoe on 27 December 1820.

99. *CMPP* I 321–24 (at 322): Thomas Jefferson, "First Inaugural Address," 4 March 1801.

100. See Leonard W. Levy, *Emergence of a Free Press* (Oxford 1985) and *Jefferson and Civil Liberties: The Darker Side* (New York 1973); then, Harry V. Jaffa, "On the Nature of Civil and Religious Liberty," *Equality and Liberty: Theory and Practice in American Politics* (New York 1965) 169–89; and, finally, Berns, "Freedom of the Press and the Alien and Sedition Laws" 135–42 and *The First Amendment and the Future of American Democracy* 80–146. One should also keep in mind that the state laws were generally less liberal than the Sedition Act. In particular, they tended to accord with the common law, which, in refusing to acknowledge that the truth of a charge could be a proper defense against its prosecution as a seditious libel, was far less protective of the right freely to examine public characters and public

measures than the controversial Federalist act. Characteristically, it was Alexander Hamilton, rather than Thomas Jefferson, who was the great champion of the view that, in matters affecting the common weal of a republic, the truth of a charge could legitimately be made a proper defense against its prosecution as libel. The reasoning he advanced in *People v. Croswell* was echoed in the opinion of James (later, Chancellor) Kent, and it was subsequently embodied in legislation in New York and elsewhere. See *The Law Practice of Alexander Hamilton: Documents and Commentary*, ed. Julius Goebel (New York 1964–81) I 775–848: Freedom of the Press: *People v. Croswell*, and *Memoirs and Letters of James Kent*, ed. William Kent (Boston 1898) 323–26: Letter to Mrs. Elizabeth Hamilton on 10 December 1832.

101. In most fields, Jefferson explained, the university's professors would be more expert and therefore better prepared to select textbooks than its Visitors. But, he added, "There is one branch in which we are the best judges, in which heresies may be taught, of so interesting a character to our own State, and to the United States, as to make it a duty in us to lay down the principles which shall be taught. It is that of government. Mr. Gilmer being withdrawn, we know not who his successor may be. He may be a Richmond lawyer, or one of that school of quondam federalism, now consolidation. It is our duty to guard against the dissemination of such principles among our youth, and the diffusion of that poison, by a previous prescription of the texts to be followed in their discourses." See *Early History of the University of Virginia* 339–41: Letter to Joseph C. Cabell on 3 February 1825.

102. See, for example, *WrTJ* (ed. Peterson) 1063–66, 1149–53: Letters to William Green Munford on 18 June 1799 and to Littleton Waller Tazewell on 5 January 1805; *WrTJ* (ed. Ford) VII 413–16: Letter to Dr. Joseph Priestley on 27 January 1800; and *AJL* II 331–33: Letter from Thomas Jefferson to John Adams on 15 June 1813.

103. See *WrTJ* (ed. Washington) VII 101: Letter to Dr. Benjamin Waterhouse on 3 March 1818.

104. For the material quoted, see *Early History of the University of Virginia* 435–37: Report of the Commissioners for the University of Virginia (Rockfish Gap Report), 4 August 1818. On the American Indian, see also *WrTJ* (ed. Ford) VIII 341–48: Second Inaugural Address, with "Notes of a Draft," 4 March 1805. Cf. Madison's defense of veneration: III.iii.5, above.

105. In this connection, one should pay careful attention both to the title and to the last paragraph of Jefferson's Bill for Establishing Religious Freedom. See *PTJ* II 545–47: The Revisal of the Laws, 18 June 1779: 82. A Bill for Establishing Religious Freedom.

106. In this connection, see Charles R. Kesler, "Woodrow Wilson and the Statesmanship of Progress," in *Natural Right and Political Right: Essays in Honor of Harry V. Jaffa*, ed. Thomas B. Silver and Peter W. Schramm (Durham, N.C., 1984) 103–27, and Robert Eden, *Political Leadership & Nihilism: A Study of Weber & Nietzsche* (Tampa, Fla., 1983). As a consequence of the general abandonment of the notion that some truths are self-evident and of the prevalence of a blind trust in progress, most scholars fail to appreciate the force of Jefferson's argument for civic education: see, most recently, David P. Peeler, "Thomas Jefferson's Nursery of Republican Patriots: The University of Virginia," *JChS* 28 (1986): 79–93.

107. Jefferson, *MCPP* IV 403–8 (at 406, 408): Letter to Major John Cartwright on 5 June 1824.

108. Cf. Letter from Thomas Jefferson to James Madison on 1 February 1825 (Manuscripts Division, Library of Congress) with *WrJM* IX 218–20: Letter to Thomas Jefferson on 8 February 1825, and see Hamilton, *The Federalist* 23 (151), 26 (165). Madison wondered whether the inclusion of the Virginia Resolutions in Jefferson's canon might not give it a partisan character and suggested that his friend add Washington's "Inaugural Address" and his "Farewell Address" to the list of prescribed texts. In his first inaugural address, Jefferson spoke of the "principles" that form "the creed of our political faith, the text of civic instruction, the touchstone by which to try the services of those we trust." See *CMPP* I 324: Thomas Jefferson, First Inaugural Address, 4 March 1801.

109. See *WrJM* IX 256–66 (at 258–59): Letter to Samuel Harrison Smith on 4 November 1826. For further evidence of Jefferson's intentions, see *WrTJ* (ed. Washington) VII 204–6: Letter to General James Breckinridge on 15 February 1821, and *WrTJ* (ed. Lipscomb and Bergh) XVI 146–51 (esp. 151): Letter to William Branch Giles on 26 December 1825.

110. See *WrTJ* (ed. Peterson) 706: Epitaph [1826].

111. See *PTJ* X 243–45: Letter to George Wythe on 13 August 1786.

112. Cf. *WoJA* IV 390–98 (esp. 397), 406–15 (esp. 410–15): *A Defence of the Constitutions of Government of the United States of America* (1787–88), with II.v.7, vi.7, and Epilogue, above, and see II.i.3, 5, 7, iv.6, above.

113. See Herbert J. Storing, *What the Anti-Federalists Were For: The Political Thought of the Opponents of the Constitution* (Chicago 1981) 48–52, and Saul Cornell, "Aristocracy Assailed: The Ideology of Backcountry Anti-Federalism," *JAH* 76 (1990): 1148–72. For the phrase quoted, see Madison, *The Federalist* 10 (63). For an early defense of the fact that United States "senators will generally be taken from that class of citizens, that form what some call a natural aristocracy," see Philadelphia's *Independent Gazetteer*, 23 October 1787: "A Supplement to the Essay on Federal Sentiments." See also *DHRC* XIV 75–76: Letter from James Kent to Nathaniel Lawrence on 9 November 1787. For the fears expressed by the Anti-Federalists concerning this natural aristocracy, see below, note 128. At the Pennsylvania Ratifying Convention, an Anti-Federalist delegate argued that the proposed constitution created congressional districts that were much too large; he feared that a "natural aristocracy" of the rich, the wellborn, and the able would come to dominate the country if that constitution were adopted. In reply, James Wilson argued that a "natural aristocracy" should, in fact, govern—"that men should be employed that are most noted for their virtue and talents." As he put it later the same day, "The meaning of a natural aristocracy—trace it to the original, and it is the men most noted for *virtue* and *abilities*. It is only in little remote corners where demagogues arise. In large districts the man of abilities and virtue can only be appointed." See *DHRC* II 465–66, 488–501 (esp. 488–89, 501), 505: Debates on 3–4 December 1787. Note also *DHRC* XVI 504–5: Letter from James Freeman to Theophilus Lindsey on 29 March 1788. A very similar debate took place six months later at the New York Ratifying Convention between Melancton Smith, Alexander Hamilton, and Chancellor Robert R. Livingston. See *DSSC* II 245–51, 256–57, 260, 275–78, 280–81: 20 and 23 June 1788.

114. Cf. *RFC* II 284–85: 14 August 1787 with *CAF*: Letters from the Federal Farmer IX (2.8.113), Essays by a Farmer (5.1.29), and see *WoJA* VI 462: Letters to John Taylor on and after 15 April 1814.

115. By Montesquieu, they had been reminded that the ancient democracies customarily employed the lottery to fill offices not requiring special talents and skills: consider *EL* 1.2.2 (242) in light of I.vii.2, note 16, above.

116. See *DHRC* I 86–94 (at 87): Act of Confederation of the United States of America, 15 November 1777, and Willi Paul Adams, *The First American Constitutions: Republican Ideology and the Making of the State Constitutions in the Revolutionary Era*, trans. Rita and Robert Kimber (Chapel Hill 1980) 230–55 (esp. 243–45, 251–53), 308–11. The New England states were exceptional in not employing rotation. Note the inclusion of rotation and recall in the provisions of the Virginia Plan designed to govern the operations of the more democratic branch of the national legislature. See *RFC* I 20: 29 May 1787.

117. Madison, *The Federalist* 57 (384).

118. Cf. *WrTJ* (ed. Ford) X 22–25: Letter to Pierre Samuel Dupont de Nemours on 24 April 1816 with Montesquieu, *EL* 2.11.6 (399–400).

119. *The Constitution of the United States of America*, article 1, section 8, [clause 8]: "The Congress shall have the power . . . to promote the progress of science and useful arts, by securing for limited times to authors and inventors the exclusive right to their respective writings and discoveries."

120. See *RFC* II 321–22, 616: 18 August and 14 September 1787. In this connection, note *LBR* I 525: 491–94: "To Friends of the Federal Government, A Plan for a Federal University," 29 October 1788.

121. *CMPP* I 199–204 (at 202): George Washington, "Eighth Annual Message to Congress," 7 December 1796.

122. *CMPP* I 65–67 (at 66): George Washington, "First Annual Message to Congress," 8 January 1790.

123. *CMPP* I 220: George Washington, "Farewell Address," 17 September 1796.

124. *CMPP* I 202: George Washington, "Eighth Annual Message to Congress," 7 December 1796.

125. *CMPP* I 228–32 (at 231), 405–10 (at 410), 482–87 (at 485), 562–69 (at 568), 573–80 (at 576), II 11–20 (at 18), 311–17: John Adams, "Inaugural Address," 4 March 1797; Thomas Jefferson, "Sixth Annual Message to Congress," 2 December 1806; James Madison, "Second Annual Message to Congress," 5 December 1810, "Seventh Annual Message to Congress," 5 December 1815, and "Eighth Annual Message to Congress," 3 December 1816; James Monroe, "First Annual Message to Congress," 2 December 1817; and John Quincy Adams, "First Annual Message to Congress," 6 December 1825. For the attempt to establish such a university during Jefferson's second administration, see Merrill D. Peterson, *Thomas Jefferson and the New Nation* 855–60.

126. Hamilton, *DSSC* II 256: New York Ratifying Convention, 21 June 1788.

127. Cf. *AJL* II 370–72 (at 371): Letter from John Adams to Thomas Jefferson on 2 September 1813 with Arist. *Pol.* 1245b39. Though he does not cite its author, there is reason to suspect that the aged statesman may be commenting on this very passage from Aristotle's *Politics*. Again and again, he returns not just to the distorting effects of wealth and birth but also—and more emphatically—to the remarkable influence of physical beauty. By the emphasis he gives to the last-mentioned quality, Adams reveals his understanding of the roots of the problem. The beauty of the body is visible in a fashion that the beauty of the soul is not. See *AJL* II 350–52, 365–66, 376–77, 397–402, 406–9: Letters from John

Adams to Thomas Jefferson on 9 July, 14 August, 15 September, 15 November, and 19 December 1813. See above, II.i.4, note 92.

128. See, for example, *CAF*: Letters of Cato VI (2.6.43), Letters from the Federal Farmer III, VII, IX (2.8.25, 97, 113), Essays of Brutus III (2.9.42). See also note 113, above.

129. Consider *WoJA* VI 274–76: *Discourses on Davila* XIII (1790–91) in light of II.i.3, 5, 7, iv.6, v.7, and vi.7, above.

130. Cf. *FSC* VII 3813 (Virginia, 1776) with V 2787 (North Carolina, 1776) and III 1890 (Massachusetts, 1780); then see I 537–38 (Connecticut, 1818); I 568, 570 (Delaware, 1792); III 1687, 1690 (Maryland, 1776); IV 2454–55, 2472 (New Hampshire, 1784, 1792); V 3082–83 (Pennsylvania, 1776); VI 3740, 3752, 3762–63 (Vermont, 1777, 1786, 1793); and *The Federalist* 84 (577–78). See also *SDUSC* II 198 (Delaware, 1776: Declaration of Rights and Fundamental Rules).

131. *WoJA* IV 288–91, 391–401, 411–15, 444–48: *A Defence of the Constitutions of Government of the United States of America* (1787–88). Though he considered the Continental Congress "only a diplomatic assembly," Adams took note of the fact that it "will always be composed of members from the natural and artificial aristocratical body in every state" and argued that it was therefore necessary "to give negatives to the governors" of the various states "to defend the executive against the influence of this body." See *WoJA* IV 579–80: *A Defence of the Constitutions of Government of the United States of America* (1787–88). For the tension between "the laboring" and "the learned," and for the need to establish a political balance between the two groups, see *WoJA* VI 279–81, 341, 365, 392–99: *Discourses on Davila* XIII, XXIII, XXXI, Postscript (1790–91). For what separated the Federalists from their Republican opponents, see *WoJA* VI 411–26, 447–521: Exchange of Letters between John and Samuel Adams, 12 September–20 November 1790, and Letters to John Taylor on and after 15 April 1814.

132. For the speeches made by Hamilton and Morris, see *RFC* I 288–91, 299–301, 303–4, 308–10, 511–14, 517–19: 18 June and 2 July 1787.

133. For Hamilton and Adams, see III.iii.2 and 6–7, above; for Morris, see *RFC* II 52–54, 68–69, 75–76, 103–5, 112–13, 120, 299–300, 479: 19–21 and 24–26 July and 15 and 31 August 1787. Note *RFC* II 284–85: 14 August 1787. Cf. Jean Louis de Lolme, *The Constitution of England*[3] (London 1781) 195–290, 324–479. For the influence exercised by Lolme on Adams and others, see Robert R. Palmer, *The Age of the Democratic Revolution: A Political History of Europe and America, 1760–1800* (Princeton 1959) I 145–48, 271–76. His thesis had purchase even in Anti-Federalist circles. See *CAF*: Essays by a Farmer II (5.1.26–32).

134. See James H. Hutson, "John Adams' Title Campaign," *NEQ* 41 (1968): 30–39, and Bruce Miroff, "John Adams: Merit, Fame, and Political Leadership," *JP* 48 (1986): 116–32. For a more comprehensive account of Adams's overall outlook, see John Paynter, "John Adams: On the Principles of a Political Science," *PSR* 6 (1976): 35–72. The rapid turnover in both the House and the Senate during their first century of existence is eloquent testimony to the justice of Adams's fear that, under normal conditions, government service would not be sufficiently attractive to America's natural aristocracy: see Jack N. Rakove, "The Structure of Politics at the Accession of George Washington," in *Beyond Confederation: Origins of the Constitution and American National Identity*, ed. Richard Beeman, Stephen Botein, and Edward C. Carter II (Chapel Hill 1987) 261–94. It is not fortuitous

that, when Morris and Hamilton singled out "the love of fame" as a motive which might lead a man to pursue the public good, they had the executive in mind: see III.i.7, above.

135. See *WoJA* VI 232–52 (esp. 232, 243, 245–46, 248): *Discourses on Davila* IV–VI (1790–91). Cf. Hamilton, *RFC* I 381–82: 22 June 1787. Where Hamilton looks to David Hume, Adams relies on Adam Smith: see above, III.iii.2–3, and compare *WoJA* VI 248–62: *Discourses on Davila* VI–VIII (1790–91), with Smith, *TMS* I.iii.2.

136. *Old Family Letters: Copied from the Originals*, ed. Alexander Biddle, Ser. A (Philadelphia 1892) 369: Letter to Benjamin Rush on 8 January 1812.

137. *WoJA* X 416–17: Letter to John Whitney on 7 June 1826.

138. On this point, see *PJM* IX 355–57 (at 357): "The Vices of the Political System of the United States." The central importance accorded the executive was an essential element of this scheme. In 1788, when William V of Orange read the proposal designed by the federal convention, he remarked to John Adams, "Sir, you have given yourselves a king, under the title of president." He was not far wrong. See *WoJA* VI 470: Letters to John Taylor on and after 15 April 1814.

139. Jefferson acknowledged that "morality, compassion, generosity, are innate elements of the human constitution," but he feared a government "farther and farther removed from the control of society" because he believed that "the human character . . . requires in general constant and immediate control, to prevent its being biased from right by the seductions of self-love." See *WrTJ* (ed. Ford) X 22–25: Letter to Pierre Samuel Dupont de Nemours on 24 April 1816.

140. See *PTJ* II 526–35: The Revisal of the Laws, 18 June 1779: 79. A Bill for the More General Diffusion of Knowledge.

141. Jefferson, *NSV* 14 (148). Jefferson never lost interest in this project. See *WrTJ* (ed. Ford) IX 276–78: Letter to John Tyler on 26 May 1810; *AJL* II 387–92: Letter from Thomas Jefferson to John Adams on 28 October 1813; *WrTJ* (ed. Lipscomb and Bergh) XIX 485–88: Letter to Peter Carr on 7 September 1814; *WrTJ* (ed. Washington) VI 540–44: Letter to Joseph C. Cabell on 2 February 1816; *WrTJ* (ed. Ford) X 50–55: Letter to John Taylor on 21 July 1816; *WrTJ* (ed. Lipscomb and Bergh) XVII 417–41: Letter to Joseph C. Cabell on 9 September 1817, with draft of "An Act for Establishing Elementary Schools"; Jefferson, *MCPP* IV 405: Letter to Major John Cartwright on 5 June 1824; *WrTJ* (ed. Lipscomb and Bergh) XVI 84–89: Letter to an Unknown Recipient on 22 December 1824.

142. See *WrTJ* (ed. Ford) IX 276–78, X 37–45, 45n–46n, 50–55: Letters to John Tyler on 26 May 1810, to Samuel Kercheval on 12 July and 5 September 1816, and to John Taylor on 21 July 1816; *AJL* II 387–92: Letter from Thomas Jefferson to John Adams on 28 October 1813; *WrTJ* (ed. Washington) VI 540–44: Letter to Joseph C. Cabell on 2 February 1816; Jefferson, *MCPP* IV 405: Letter to Major John Cartwright on 5 June 1824. See also *Early History of the University of Virginia* 184–88: Letter to Joseph C. Cabell on 28 November 1820. As this and the letter to Cabell cited above make clear, the ward proposal was closely linked with Jefferson's campaign to establish primary schools. The passage quoted in the text comes from the second of the two letters to Samuel Kercheval.

143. *WrTJ* (ed. Ford) X 37–45 (at 40–41): Letter to Samuel Kercheval on 12 July 1816.

144. *WrTJ* (ed. Washington) VI 540–44: Letter to Joseph C. Cabell on 2 February 1816.

145. As should be clear from the evidence presented thus far, Jefferson's commitment to the establishment of the ward-republic will not bear the heavy weight which Hannah Arendt places upon it. Neither the stated intentions nor the deeds of the Founding Fathers justify her supposition that "the ultimate end of revolution was [public, participatory] freedom and the constitution of a public space where freedom would appear." Jefferson would certainly have been taken aback by her assertion that "the elementary republics of the wards, the only tangible place where everyone could be free, actually were the end of the great republic whose chief purpose in domestic affairs should have been to provide the people with such places of freedom and to protect them." His writings confirm the conventional view that the "chief goals" of the American Revolution were what Arendt calls "public welfare and private happiness." She fails to link Jefferson's proposal of reform with his discussion of representative democracy's need for a natural aristocracy and with the dangers which, he thought, that aristocracy's existence would inevitably pose; accordingly, she misses the point of the reform altogether. Cf. Arendt, *On Revolution* (New York 1963) 111–285 (esp. 115–37, 234–85) with II.iv–vii, above, and see Jean Yarbrough, "Republicanism Reconsidered: Some Thoughts on the Foundation and Preservation of the American Republic," *RP* 41 (1979): 61–95 (esp. 84–92), who errs in attributing the "North-American" letters to Madison: II.i.2, note 35, above.

146. The evidence—collected, presented, and variously interpreted by Robert E. Shalhope, "The Ideological Origins of the Second Amendment," *JAH* 69 (1982): 599–614; Lawrence Delbert Cress, "An Armed Community: The Origins and Meaning of the Right to Bear Arms," *JAH* 71 (1984): 22–42; and David T. Hardy, "The Second Amendment and the Historiography of the Bill of Rights," *Journal of Law and Politics* 4 (1987): 1–62—should be understood in terms of Blackstone, *Commentaries* I 119–41 (with special attention to 139). If I am correct in asserting (II.i.2, ii.8–10, iii.5, v.4–III.iv.7, above, and III.iv.9–v.6, below) that Whigs of all stripes, in America as well as in Britain, were united in accepting Blackstone's dictum (*Commentaries* I 135) that "the public good is in nothing more essentially interested, than in the protection of every individual's private rights," the current dispute between those who interpret the Second Amendment in terms of individual rights and those who stress communal duties is an artifact of contemporary scholarship grounded on a dichotomy than would have made little, if any sense to anyone in the eighteenth century. The revolutionary generation disliked standing armies and saw them as a threat to liberty. Even when they conceded the necessity of such an army, they wanted to see the individual citizens armed and organized as a militia in such a way as to help provide for the common defense while safeguarding the right to revolution.

147. For Tocqueville's development and transformation of Jefferson's case for local administration of local affairs, see *DA* 1.1.5, 2.3–4, 8, 2.2.1–8. In this connection, see Harvey C. Mansfield, Jr., "Tocqueville and the Future of the American Constitution," *America's Constitutional Soul* (Baltimore 1991) 177–92.

148. Cf. *PTJ* XIV 659–63 (at 659–61) with 16–21: Letter to James Madison on 15 March 1789 and Letter from James Madison on 17 October 1788, and then note the arguments added in *PJM* XII 196–210: Amendments to the Constitution, 8 June 1789.

149. *PJM* VIII 300: Memorial and Remonstrance against Religious Assessments, 20 June 1785.

150. *PJM* XIV 159: Notes for the *National Gazette* Essays, ca. 19 December 1791–3 March 1792.

151. *PJM* XIV 170: "Public Opinion," *National Gazette*, 19 December 1791.

152. *PJM* XIV 137–39: "Consolidation," *National Gazette*, 3 December 1791.

153. Montesquieu, *EL* 1.3.1–11.

154. *PJM* XIV 233–34: "Spirit of Governments," *National Gazette*, 18 February 1792. In this connection, see Robert J. Morgan, "Madison's Analysis of the Sources of Political Authority," *APSR* 75 (1981): 613–25.

155. *PJM* XIV 206–9: "Universal Peace," *National Gazette*, 31 January 1792. In a similar spirit, Jefferson later suggested the passage of a constitutional amendment barring the federal government from borrowing funds. See *WoTJ* VIII 479–83 (at 481): Letter to John Taylor on 26 November 1798.

156. See *WrJM* IX 103–9: Letter to William T. Barry on 4 August 1822.

157. *PJM* XIV 170: "Public Opinion," *National Gazette*, 19 December 1791.

158. In the tenth *Federalist*, Madison praised geographical extension because it helped prevent groups of men "united and actuated by some common impulse of passion, or of interest" from securing dominion; it is not fortuitous that he raised no objection to there being a unanimity based on political (as opposed to religious) opinion. See Madison, *The Federalist* 10 (esp. 57, 61). From the outset, at least in this one regard, if not in others, Madison was aware that his argument for the superior viability of extended republics is flawed: see John Zvesper, "The Madisonian Systems," *WPQ* 37 (1984): 236–56.

159. See Madison, *The Federalist* 49–50. This famous discussion is a critique of Jefferson's notion that constitutions should be subject to revision at regular intervals. Cf. Jefferson, *NSV* 221: Draught of a Fundamental Constitution for the Commonwealth of Virginia (Appendix 2).

160. *PTJ* XIV 16–21 (at 20): Letter from James Madison on 17 October 1788.

161. *PJM* XIV 191–92: "Charters," *National Gazette*, 18 January 1792.

162. See *CAF*: *A Review of the Constitution Proposed by the Late Convention* by A Federal Republican (3.6.21), 28 October 1787, and Letters of Cato V (2.6.34).

163. For the importance which the two Virginians placed on preventing the acceptance of Hamilton's report, see *PJM* XIV 183–85, 193–96: Exchange of Letters with Henry Lee on 8 and 21 January 1792 and Letter to Edmund Pendleton on 21 January 1792, and *WrTJ* (ed. Ford) I 174–78: "The Anas."

Chapter 5

1. *WoTJ* IX 147: Letter to Benjamin Rush on 23 September 1800.

2. *WoTJ* IV 314–15: Notes on the Permanent Seat of Congress, 13 April 1784.

3. *WrTJ* (ed. Ford) VII 119–24 (at 121): Letter to Elbridge Gerry on 13 May 1797.

4. *PTJ* XIV 221: Letter to Horatio Gates on 17 March 1817.

5. Jefferson, *NSV* 19 (164–65). For Jefferson's continuing hostility to urban life, see *WrTJ* (ed. Lipscomb and Bergh) XIII 203: Letter to Henry Middleton on 8 January 1813, and *AJL* II 391: Letter from Thomas Jefferson to John Adams on 28 October 1813. In this connection, note also *PTJ* VIII 426–27, 633, XII 438–42 (at 442): Letters to John Jay on 23 August 1785, to G. K. van Hogendorp on 13 October 1785, and to James Madison on 20 December 1787. In one letter, Jefferson wrote, "New York, . . . like London, seems to be a Cloacina of all the depravities of

human nature." See *WrTJ* (ed. Lipscomb and Bergh) XV 467–70 (at 469): Letter to William Short on 8 September 1823. In this connection, see Harry V. Jaffa, "The Virtue of a Nation of Cities: On the Jeffersonian Paradoxes," *The Conditions of Freedom: Essays in Political Philosophy* (Baltimore 1975) 99–110 (esp. 99–105).

6. See *PTJ* I 362: The Virginia Constitution: III. Third Draft by Jefferson, 1776.

7. *PTJ* IX 217–19: Letter to Archibald Stuart on 25 January 1786.

8. *PTJ* IX 445–46, XI 636: Letters to John Page on 4 May 1786 and to Henry Skipwith on 28 July 1787.

9. The locus classicus for this view is the unpublished dissertation of Douglass Adair: see "The Intellectual Origins of Jeffersonian Democracy: Republicanism, the Class Struggle, and the Virtuous Farmer" (Yale University 1943) esp. 27–151, 272–95. See, more recently, J. G. A. Pocock, *The Machiavellian Moment: Florentine Political Thought and the Atlantic Republican Tradition* (Princeton 1975) esp. 506–52, and Douglas L. Wilson, "The American *agricola*: Jefferson's Agrarianism and the Classical Tradition," *SAQ* 80 (1981): 339–54. Traces of this conviction can be seen also in Forrest McDonald, *The Presidency of Thomas Jefferson* (Lawrence, Kans., 1976); Lance Banning, *The Jeffersonian Persuasion: Evolution of a Party Ideology* (Ithaca 1978); and Drew R. McCoy, *The Elusive Republic: Political Economy in Jeffersonian America* (Chapel Hill 1980).

10. With regard to the economic underpinnings of republicanism, Jefferson, Madison, and Adams shared a number of assumptions: see Joseph J. Spengler, "The Political Economy of Jefferson, Madison, and Adams," in *American Studies in Honor of William Kenneth Boyd*, ed. David Kelly Jackson (Durham, N.C., 1940) 3–59.

11. See above, III.ii.6–7.

12. *The Federalist* 10 (60).

13. *PJM* IX 76–77: Letter to Thomas Jefferson on 19 June 1786. For the letter which occasioned these reflections, see *PTJ* VIII 681–82: Letter to James Madison on 28 October 1785.

14. See Drew R. McCoy, "Jefferson and Madison on Malthus: Population Growth in Jeffersonian Political Economy," *VMHB* 88 (1980): 259–76. For the historical background which serves as a context for their reflection, see Edmund S. Morgan, "Slavery and Freedom: The American Paradox," *JAH* 59 (1972): 5–29.

15. Cf. Madison, *The Federalist* 55 (378), with Madison, *DSSC* III 536–37: Virginia Ratifying Convention, 20 June 1788, and see III.i.3–8, above.

16. *PJM* XIV 245–46: "Republican Distribution of Citizens," *National Gazette*, 3 March 1792.

17. For Hamilton's report and the various drafts it went through, see *PAH* X 1–340: *Report on the Subject of Manufactures*, 5 December 1791. For the contributions of Tench Coxe to its argument and to the foundation in New Jersey of Hamilton's Society for Establishing Useful Manufactures, see Jacob Cooke, "Tench Coxe, Alexander Hamilton, and the Encouragement of American Manufactures," *WMQ* 32 (1975): 369–92.

18. *PJM* XIV 245–46: "Republican Distribution of Citizens," *National Gazette*, 3 March 1792.

19. *PJM* XIV 257–59: "Fashion," *National Gazette*, 20 March 1792.

20. In general, the recent work of Joyce Appleby is a useful corrective to the tendency to see in Jefferson an ancient Greek redivivus. Note, especially, "What Is Still American in the Political Philosophy of Thomas Jefferson?" *WMQ* 39 (1982):

287–309. See "Commercial Farming and the 'Agrarian Myth' in the Early Republic," *JAH* 68 (1982): 833–49, and *Capitalism and a New Social Order: The Republican Vision of the 1790s* (New York 1984). One may also wish to consult "Republicanism and Ideology," *AQ* 37 (1985): 461–73; "Republicanism in Old and New Contexts," *WMQ* 43 (1986): 20–34; and Michael Durey, "Thomas Paine's Apostles: Radical Emigrés and the Triumph of Jeffersonian Republicanism," *WMQ* 44 (1987): 661–88. Appleby goes astray only where she follows Pocock's *The Machiavellian Moment*: Harrington's appropriation of Venetian institutions and Montesquieu's admiration for Augustan England were grounded in a repudiation, not in an acceptance of the principles of classical republicanism, and John Adams was no more deeply indebted to the ancients than Jefferson himself. John P. Diggins's treatment of Adams and of the adherents of the Federalist party in general is superior to that found in Appleby, but he too errs in assuming that Pocock's discussion of non-American thinkers is more or less correct. Cf. *The Lost Soul of American Politics: Virtue, Self-Interest, and the Foundations of Liberalism* (New York 1984) 3–105 with II.iv–v and Epilogue, above. A scholar intent on reassessing Pocock's argument would do well to begin by considering the importance for James Harrington and his later admirers of Thomas Hobbes's conviction that country people make better subjects than city folk: II.iv.8, v.5, above.

21. *PTJ* X 16: "Answers to Démeunier's First Queries (24 January 1786)."

22. To grasp the full import of this issue, one should read Merrill D. Peterson, "Thomas Jefferson and Commercial Policy, 1783–1793," *WMQ* 22 (1965): 584–610, in tandem with Drew R. McCoy, "Republicanism and American Foreign Policy: James Madison and the Political Economy of Commercial Discrimination, 1789 to 1794," *WMQ* 31 (1974): 633–46, and McCoy, *The Elusive Republic* 136–65. For a related, partisan, but nonetheless useful discussion, see *PTJ* XVIII 516–76: Representation by France against the Tonnage Acts.

23. See Clarence L. Ver Steeg, *Robert Morris: Revolutionary Financier* (Philadelphia 1954) 166–67: Letter of Gouverneur Morris to Matthew Ridley on 6 August 1782. Copies of this letter can be found in the Ridley Papers at the Massachusetts Historical Society and in the Chamberlain Collection of the Boston Public Library.

24. See Peter S. Onuf, *Statehood and Union: A History of the Northwest Ordinance* (Bloomington, Ind., 1987) 1–66.

25. *PTJ* VII 25–26: Letter to George Washington on 15 March 1784.

26. See *PJM* VIII 107–8: Letter to Thomas Jefferson on 30 August 1784.

27. See *PTJ* XI 92–97 (at 93–94): Letter to James Madison on 30 January 1787. Jefferson knew whereof he spoke. At the time that he wrote these words, the Mississippi had already been closed to the American settlers for more than two years; it would not be opened again until 1788; and some Kentuckians were talking of leaving the Union. For an earlier expression of interest in this question, see *PTJ* III 168: Letter to Bernardo de Galvez on 8 November 1779. Southerners deemed the Mississippi question a central concern: see above, III.ii.3 (esp. note 28).

28. The original American purpose in initiating the negotiations with Napoleonic France is most clearly evident in the instructions which Madison issued to the two American ministers plenipotentiary. It was then taken for granted that France would retain all of its possessions west of the Mississippi River. See *WrJM* VII 9–19: Instruction to Robert R. Livingston and James Monroe, 2 March 1803. Regarding the emphasis which Madison gave to the question of commercial out-

lets, see Walter LaFeber, "Foreign Policies of a New Nation: Franklin, Madison, and the 'Dream of a new Land to Fulfill with People in Self-Control,'" in *From Colony to Empire: Essays in the History of American Foreign Relations*, ed. William Appleman Williams (New York 1972) 10–37. In other respects, this essay is less satisfactory: LaFeber gives an almost exclusive emphasis to the elements of continuity in Madison's thinking and consequently understates the change of course which Madison made in the early 1790s; in the process, he neglects the import of Madison's attack on Hamilton's *Report on the Subject of Manufactures* and the depth of his newfound commitment to states' rights. See also Alexander DeConde, *The Affair of Louisiana* (New York 1976).

29. Madison, *The Federalist* 10 (59).

30. *PJM* XIV 423–24 (at 424): Letter from Thomas Jefferson on 12 December 1792.

31. *WrTJ* (ed. Ford) VII 2–6: Letter to François d'Ivernois on 6 February 1795.

32. *WrTJ* (ed. Lipscomb and Bergh) XV 129–31: Letter to Barré de Marbois on 14 June 1817.

33. See *WoTJ* XII 205–6: Letter to Henry Dearborn on 17 August 1821.

34. Jefferson, *NSV* 19 (164–65), and *AJL* II 291: Letter from Thomas Jefferson to John Adams on 21 January 1812.

35. *AJL* II 458–61 (at 458): Letter from Thomas Jefferson to John Adams on 11 January 1816. In this connection, see *AJL* II 331–33, 387–92: Letters from Thomas Jefferson to John Adams on 15 June and 28 October 1813, and *WrTJ* (ed. Washington) VII 377–78: Letter to William Ludlow on 6 September 1824. Note the emphasis which he placed on the need to soften men. See *WrTJ* (ed. Ford) VII 98–100: Letter to James Madison on 1 January 1797. John Adams was similarly persuaded that "the Sciences and Arts have vastly and immensely ameliorated the condition of Man, and even improved his Morals." See *Statesman and Friend: Correspondence of John Adams with Benjamin Waterhouse, 1784–1822*, ed. Worthington Chauncey Ford (Boston 1927) 122–25: Letter to Benjamin Waterhouse on 26 February 1817.

36. *PTJ* IX 64: Letter to John Adams on 27 November 1785.

37. Jefferson's flirtation with the notion of sumptuary laws should be considered in light of Timothy H. Breen, *Tobacco Culture: The Mentality of the Great Tidewater Planters on the Eve of Revolution* (Princeton 1985). In the very letter in which he raises the question of legislation, Jefferson describes the war years "as a time of happiness and enjoiment" precisely because "amidst the privation of many things not essential to happiness, we could not run in debt because no body would trust us." See *PTJ* XI 636: Letter to Henry Skipwith on 28 July 1787.

38. See *WrTJ* (ed. Lipscomb and Bergh) XV 129–31: Letter to Barré de Marbois on 14 June 1817. Note also the concluding paragraphs of XIII 13–21: Letter to Destutt de Tracy on 26 January 1811.

39. See *CMPP* I 568: James Madison, "Seventh Annual Message to Congress," 5 December 1815.

40. See Drew R. McCoy, "Benjamin Franklin's Vision of a Republican Political Economy for America," *WMQ* 35 (1978): 605–28, and *The Elusive Republic* 49–67. In most respects, Franklin's outlook foreshadows that of Jefferson and Madison.

41. *WrTJ* (ed. Lipscomb and Bergh) XI 1–3: Letter to Jean Baptiste Say on 1 February 1804.

42. For the discussion to which Madison contributed, see *RFC* II 201–6 (esp. 203–4): 7 August 1787.

43. Blackstone, *Commentaries* I 165–66. Blackstone's argument is a paraphrase of Montesquieu's earlier summation and endorsement of Whig doctrine: see *EL* 2.11.6 (400). The view defended by Montesquieu and Blackstone goes back at least as far as the Putney Debates: *Puritanism and Liberty: Being the Army Debates (1647–9) from the Clarke Manuscripts with Supplementary Documents,* ed. A. S. P. Woodhouse (London 1938) 63–64, 82–83. It remained predominant in England to the end of the eighteenth century and beyond: see H. T. Dickinson, *Liberty and Property: Political Ideology in Eighteenth-Century Britain* (London 1977) 69, 88–89, 116–18, 127–28, 162, 191, 214, 217–29, 237–40, 250–53, 279–81, 284, 303.

44. See *WoJW* II 725–26: *Considerations on the Authority of Parliament,* 17 August 1774; *PAH* I 106: *The Farmer Refuted, &c.,* 23 February 1775; *WoJA* IX 375–78: Letter from John Adams to James Sullivan on 26 May 1776; and the material collected in Chilton Williamson, "American Suffrage and Sir William Blackstone," *PSQ* 68 (1953): 552–57, and Rowland Berthoff, "Conventional Mentality: Free Blacks, Women, and Business Corporations as Unequal Persons, 1820–1870," *JAH* 76 (1989): 753–84.

45. *PAH* X 236: *Report on the Subject of Manufactures,* 5 December 1791.

46. For his mature reflections on the matter, one should consult the notes which Madison made on the subject subsequent to his retirement. See *Letters and Other Writings of James Madison* (Philadelphia 1865) IV 21–30: Notes on Suffrage. See also *WrJM* IX 358–64: Speech in the Virginia Constitutional Convention, 2 December 1829. And note *WrJM* IX 520–28: Letter on Majority Government, 1833.

47. *PJM* XI 280–95 (esp. 287–88): Letter to John Brown on 12 October 1788 and "Observations on Jefferson's Draft of a Constitution for Virginia" dated 15 October 1788. See also *PJM* VIII 350–57: Letter to Caleb Wallace on 23 August 1785.

48. Cf. *WrJM* IX 358–360n.: Note During the Convention for Amending the Constitution of Virginia, 1829, with George Mason, *RFC* II 203, 207–8: 7 August 1787.

49. See Drew R. McCoy, *The Last of the Fathers: James Madison and the Republican Legacy* (Cambridge 1989) 192–207. Note 240–52.

50. *CMPP* I 567: James Madison, "Seventh Annual Message to Congress," 5 December 1815. See also *CMPP* I 534–40 (at 539–40), 574: James Madison, "Fifth Annual Message to Congress," 7 December 1813, and "Eighth Annual Message to Congress," 3 December 1816.

51. *WrJM* VIII 392–93: Letter to D. Lynch, Jr., on 27 June 1817. See also *WrJM* IX 316–40 (with notes): Letters to Joseph C. Cabell on 18 September and 30 October 1828. Madison's position was adopted by James Monroe. See *CMPP* II 4–10 (at 8–9), 18, 54–62 (at 61): James Monroe, "First Inaugural Address," 4 March 1817; "First Annual Message to Congress," 2 December 1817; and "Third Annual Message to Congress," 7 December 1819.

52. Consider McCoy, *The Last of the Fathers* 171–92, in light of III.iii.4, above.

53. Led by Albert Gallatin, these interests retained considerable influence within Republican councils up to the moment when Andrew Jackson wrested the presidency from John Quincy Adams, and they profited greatly from Jefferson's embargo and Madison's war. It is essential, however, to keep in mind that the advocates of manufacturing were marginal figures in a largely agrarian coalition, that their ability to affect actual public policy was always restricted, and

that Jefferson and Madison were never more than halfhearted in the support they gave the manufacturing interests: John R. Nelson, Jr., *Liberty and Property: Political Economy and Policymaking in the New Nation, 1789–1812* (Baltimore 1987) 80–161, exaggerates the importance of this element within the Republican coalition to the point of misrepresenting the outlook of the party's two principal leaders. Andrew Jackson was a much more plausible heir to Thomas Jefferson than Henry Clay.

54. *WrTJ* (ed. Lipscomb and Bergh) XIV 387–93: Letter to Benjamin Austin on 9 January 1816. In this connection, see XIV 258–67: Letter to Jean Baptiste Say on 2 March 1815.

55. *WrTJ* (ed. Lipscomb and Bergh) XII 270–71: Letter to John Jay on 7 April 1809.

56. In Jefferson, the fear that the need to find foreign markets for America's manufactured goods would drive the nation to war ran deep. In the midst of the War of 1812, he wrote to an old friend, "Our enemy has indeed the consolation of Satan, on removing our first parents from Paradise: from a peaceful agricultural nation he makes us a military and manufacturing one." See *WrTJ* (ed. Washington) VI 398–402 (at 400): Letter to William Short on 28 November 1814. Two years later, he vented his resentment against "ephemeral and pseudo-citizens . . . infected with the mania of rambling and gambling" which give rise to "eternal war." He preferred to "exclude them from our territory, as we do persons infected with disease," and he was perfectly prepared to see Virginia separate from the states "which are for unlimited commerce and war, and confederate with those alone which are for peace and agriculture." See *WrTJ* (ed. Ford) X 34–37 (at 34–35): Letter to William H. Crawford on 20 June 1816. It is a mistake to attribute to Jefferson a real change of heart: cf., for example, William D. Grampp, "A Re-examination of Jeffersonian Economics," *Southern Economic Journal* 12 (1946): 263–82.

57. *WrTJ* (ed. Lipscomb and Bergh) XIV 387–93: Letter to Benjamin Austin on 9 January 1816. Note *WrTJ* (ed. Ford) IX 373–77: Letter to John Melish on 13 January 1813. In the 1790s, when Jefferson expresses similar views, he does so only in his capacity as secretary of state in the Washington administration: see *PTJ* XX 563, 565–66: Letters to William Carmichael and David Humphreys on 23 June 1791. At the time, he was much less friendly than the president to the prospect of a dramatic increase in American manufacturing.

58. Cf. *PAH* X 254, 265–66: *Report on the Subject of Manufactures*, 5 December 1791, with this chapter's epigraph: Smith, *WN* III.i.5.

59. *WrTJ* (ed. Lipscomb and Bergh) XI 55–56: Letter to Mr. Lithson on 4 January 1805.

60. For the passages quoted, see *PJA* IV 124–25: Letter to Mercy Otis Warren on 16 April 1776, and *CAF*: Mercy Otis Warren, *Observations on the New Constitution, and on the Federal and State Conventions. by a Columbian Patriot*, Boston, 1788 (4.28.2). For the difference in outlook evidenced by the two Virginians, cf. Madison, *The Federalist* 49, with Jefferson, *NSV* 221: Draught of a Fundamental Constitution for the Commonwealth of Virginia (Appendix 2), and *WrTJ* (ed. Ford) X 37–45: Letter to Samuel Kercheval on 12 July 1816.

61. Jefferson, *NSV* 17 (161).

62. Cf. [Noah Webster], *An Examination into the Leading Principles of the Federal Constitution Proposed by the Late Convention Held at Philadelphia by A Citizen of America* (Philadelphia 1787) 46–49 (at 47), with *JHO* 186–87, and note Montesquieu, *EL* 1.5.5 (278).

63. *AJL* II 548–50: Letter from Thomas Jefferson to John Adams on 10 December 1819.

64. *AJL* II 550–51: Letter from John Adams to Thomas Jefferson on 21 December 1819.

65. *WoTJ* XI 476: Letter to Thomas Leiper on 12 June 1815.

66. See McCoy, *The Elusive Republic* 219, and Linda K. Kerber, *Federalists in Dissent: Imagery and Ideology in Jeffersonian America*² (Ithaca 1980) 23–66.

67. My discussion of the manner in which Jefferson unwittingly strengthened the institution of slavery owes much to Harry V. Jaffa, "Agrarian Virtue and Republican Freedom: An Historical Perspective," *Equality and Liberty: Theory and Practice in American Politics* (New York 1965) 42–66. See also Robert E. Shalhope, "Thomas Jefferson's Republicanism and Antebellum Southern Thought," *JSH* 42 (1976): 529–56.

68. Consider the likely, long-term political effect of Jefferson's claim that, "in proportion as commercial avarice and corruption advance on us from the north and east, the principles of free government are to retire to the agricultural States of the south and west, as their last asylum and bulwark." See *WrTJ* (ed. Lipscomb and Bergh) XIII 203: Letter to Henry Middleton on 8 January 1813. In this connection, see *WrTJ* (ed. Ford) IX 419–21: Letter to James Martin on 20 September 1813.

69. See above, III.ii.1–5.

70. Jefferson, *NSV* 18 (162–63).

71. John Taylor, *Arator: Being a Series of Agricultural Essays, Practical and Moral*³ (Baltimore 1817) 14 (43–46). In this connection, see also 13 (40–42). The first of Taylor's essays appeared in the popular press on 25 December 1810. See Freda F. Stohrer, "*Arator*: A Publishing History," *VMHB* 88 (1980): 442–45.

72. *Camden Journal*, 28 November 1835.

73. John Taylor, *Arator* 13 (40), 14 (46–47).

74. *WrTJ* (ed. Ford) X 169–71: Letter to Thomas Ritchie on 25 December 1820.

75. *WrTJ* (ed. Lipscomb and Bergh) XV 482: Letter to Monsieur A. Coray on 31 October 1823.

76. *PTJ* VIII 258–59: Letter from Richard Price on 2 July 1785.

Chapter 6

1. Cic. *Leg.* 1.14.40–15.43.

2. For a useful survey of the evidence, see William G. McLoughlin, "The Role of Religion in the Revolution: Liberty of Conscience and Cultural Cohesion in the New Nation," in *Essays on the American Revolution*, ed. Stephen G. Kurtz and James H. Hutson (Chapel Hill 1973) 197–255.

3. *CAF*: "A Proposal for Reviving Christian Conviction," *Virginia Independent Chronicle*, 31 October 1787 (5.8.2).

4. For the article, see *FSC* III 1889–90 (Massachusetts, 1780). For its origins, see William G. McLoughlin, *New England Dissent, 1630–1833: The Baptists and the Separation of Church and State* (Cambridge, Mass., 1971) I 602–4. This provision was controversial from the outset. The original draft did not restrict support to Protestants or even Christians and did not include the clause specifying that "every denomination of Christians, demeaning themselves peaceably and as good subjects of the commonwealth, shall be equally under the protection of the law; and

no subordination of any one sect or denomination to another shall ever be established by law." See *Journal of the Convention for Framing a Constitution of Government for the State of Massachusetts Bay* (Boston 1832) 191–215 (at 193): The Report of a Constitution, or Form of Government, for the Commonwealth of Massachusetts, 28 October 1779. The convention devoted considerable time to its discussion: in this connection, it suspended the rule prescribing that no member could speak more than twice on a question without special leave, and it eventually appointed a committee to rewrite the article: 38–42, 45–47, 179–80: 1–6, 10 November 1779, 15 June 1780. In the town meetings called to discuss the constitution, article 3 incurred more opposition than any other provision: some opposed religious assessments on principle; others objected to guaranteeing Catholics equal protection under the law. As a result, though the majority of those attending the meetings apparently gave their consent to ratification, there is considerable doubt whether the article had the requisite two-thirds support: see Samuel Eliot Morison, "The Struggle over the Adoption of the Constitution of Massachusetts, 1780," *PMHS* 50 (1917): 353–411, and Robert J. Taylor, "Construction of the Massachusetts Constitution," *Proceedings of the American Antiquarian Society* 90 (1980): 317–46. For the returns from the town meetings, see *The Popular Sources of Political Authority: Documents on the Massachusetts Constitution of 1780*, ed. Oscar and Mary Handlin (Cambridge, Mass., 1966) 475–930. Later, at the Massachusetts Constitutional Convention of 1820, John Adams sought, unsuccessfully, to have the phrase "all men, of all religions" substituted for the phrase "every denomination of Christians." See *WoJA* IV 222–24 n. 7. The convention proposed eliminating the state's power to compel church attendance and sought to include non-Protestant Christians within the system of assessments, but the citizens in attendance at the town meetings rejected the amendment: McLoughlin, *New England Dissent* II 1160–85. Finally, in 1833, when religious assessments were eliminated, Massachusetts extended equal protection of the law to "all religious sects and denominations." See *FSC* III 1914 (Massachusetts).

5. For the evolution that took place in each of the former colonies, see Chester James Antieau, Arthur T. Downey, and Edward C. Roberts, *Freedom from Federal Establishment: Formation and Early History of the First Amendment Religion Clauses* (Milwaukee 1964) 1–110, and Thomas J. Curry, *The First Freedoms: Church and State in America to the Passage of the First Amendment* (New York 1986) 1–192. See also Leonard W. Levy, "The Original Meaning of the Establishment Clause," *Constitutional Opinions: Aspects of the Bill of Rights* (Oxford 1986) 135–61 (esp. 153–61), and *The Establishment Clause: Religion and the First Amendment* (New York 1986) 1–62.

6. For the details, see Thomas E. Buckley, S.J., *Church and State in Revolutionary Virginia, 1776–1787* (Charlottesville 1977) 71–143.

7. For the history of Massachusetts's establishment, see John D. Cushing, "Notes on Disestablishment in Massachusetts, 1780–1833," *WMQ* 26 (1969): 169–90. Note also John T. Noonan, Jr., " 'Quota of Imps,' " in *The Virginia Statute for Religious Freedom: Its Evolution and Consequences in American History*, ed. Merrill D. Peterson and Robert C. Vaughan (Cambridge 1988) 171–99.

8. See *FSC* I 544–45 (Connecticut, 1818) and IV 2454, 2471–72, 2493–95, 2510 (New Hampshire, 1784, 1792, 1902). For the process by which full disestablishment took place, see William G. McLoughlin, *New England Dissent* esp. I 591–II 1262. See also Charles B. Kinney, *Church and State: The Struggle for Separation in New Hampshire, 1630–1900* (New York 1955).

9. See *The Letters and Papers of Edmund Pendleton*, ed. David John Mays (Charlottesville 1974) II 474–75: Letter to Richard Henry Lee on 28 February 1785. When Patrick Henry's bill stirred adamant opposition, Washington regretted that it had ever been proposed: see *WrGW* XXVIII 285: Letter to George Mason on 3 October 1785.

10. For the land ordinance, see *JCC* XXVIII 251–56, 290–96, 309–10, 316–17, 322–23, 326–29, 339–40, 342–43, 370–73, 375–81 (esp. 293–96, 378): 12, 22–23, and 27–28 April, 2–3, 5–6, and 19–20 May 1785. For the actual grants, see *JCC* XXXII 276, 311–13, 345–46, 350–51, 376–77, XXXIII 399–401, 427–30, 448, 512, 593–94, 697–98, XXXIV 100–101 (with n. 1), 181–82, 564–66 (esp. XXXII 276, 312, XXXIII 400, 512, 697–98, XXXIV 181–82, 566): 9 May, 10, 14, 17, 20, 23, and 27 July, 1 August, 21 September, and 2 and 22 October 1787, 19 March, 26 May, and 30 September 1788. In this connection, see also *The Territorial Papers of the United States*, ed. Clarence Edwin Carter et al. (Washington, D.C., 1934–75) II: *The Territory Northwest of the River Ohio, 1787–1803* 52–56, 70–72, 74–77, 80–88 (esp. 54–55, 70, 71 n. 84, 77, 81, 83, 86): Proposals of S. H. Parsons and Others for Purchase of Lands, 21 July 1787; Committee Report on the Sale of Lands, 23 July 1787; Petition of John Cleves Symmes for a Grant of Land, 29 August 1787; Letter from William Grayson to James Madison on 31 August 1787; Proposal of Royal Flint and Associates for a Purchase of Land, 18 October 1787; Report of the Board of Treasury: Proposal of Royal Flint and Joseph Parker, 22 October 1787; Indenture Between the Board of Treasury and the Agents of the Ohio Company, 27 October 1787; and Indenture Between the Board of Treasury and Manassah Cutler and Winthrop Sargent, 27 October 1787. For further discussion, see Ronald A. Smith, "Freedom of Religion and the Land Ordinance of 1785," *JChS* 24 (1982): 589–602, and III.vi.3, note 38, below.

11. See M. Louise Greene, *The Development of Religious Liberty in Connecticut* (New York 1905) 360–61 (with 380–92), and see *Laws of New York* (5 May 1786) c. 67.

12. See *DSSC* I 328, 334, III 659, IV 244: Ratification by New York, 26 July 1788; Ratification by Rhode Island, 29 May 1790; Virginia Ratifying Convention, 27 June 1788; North Carolina Ratifying Convention, 1 August 1788. See also *DSSC* I 326, II 549–55 (at 553): Ratification by New Hampshire, 21 June 1788; Maryland Ratifying Convention, 26–28 April 1788. For the arguments advanced during the ratification debates, see Antieau, Downey, and Roberts, *Freedom from Federal Establishment* 111–22, and Leonard W. Levy, "The Original Meaning of the Establishment Clause" 138–42, and *The Establishment Clause* 85–89.

13. See *Annals of Congress* I 433–35, 440–41, 729–31, 755, 766, 779, 913: 8 June, 15, 17, 20, and 24 August, and 24 September 1789. For the amendment's legislative history in the Senate, see *DHFFC* I 151, 166, 181, 186, 189, 192: Senate Legislative Journal, 3, 9, 21, 24–25 September 1789. On the amendments suggested by the House, the changes effected by the Senate, and the consequences of ratification as understood at the time, see Antieau, Downey, and Roberts, *Freedom from Federal Establishment* 123–209; Michael J. Malbin, *Religion and Politics: The Intentions of the Authors of the First Amendment* (Washington, D.C., 1978); Curry, *The First Freedoms* 193–222; and Levy, "The Original Meaning of the Establishment Clause" 143–61, and *The Establishment Clause* 63–119. For the canons by which the Constitution is to be interpreted, see above, III.iii.6 (esp. note 110). The superintendence of religion was not among the federal government's enu-

merated powers, and the advocates of ratification insisted that Congress had no jurisdiction in the matter; of course, by explicitly banning religious tests for federal office, the Constitution acknowledged that, in the exercise of those enumerated powers within its legitimate sphere (e.g., in enacting regulations for the District of Columbia, the national domain, and the armed forces), Congress was otherwise free to do what seemed necessary and proper: see *PJM* XI 18–19: Letter to Edmund Randolph on 10 April 1788. The First Amendment was intended to conciliate those who feared federal usurpation, and it, in fact, limited the federal government's prerogatives in exercising its enumerated powers. Beyond question, it barred the exercise of those powers in a fashion giving preference to any one sect or any restricted group of sects. Some certainly believed that it ruled out the enactment within the District of Columbia and the national domain of a system of religious assessments comparable to those found in New England and authorized by the constitutions of Maryland, Georgia, and South Carolina. But it is clear from the First Congress's election of chaplains, its endorsement of the Northwest Ordinance, and its passage of a resolution calling for "a day of public thanksgiving and prayer, to be observed by acknowledging, with grateful hearts, the many signal favors of Almighty God," that the ban on passing laws "respecting an establishment of religion" was not seen by the great majority of those responsible for the proposal as barring indirect, strictly nondiscriminatory, moral and material support for religion in general. See Michael W. McConnell, "Accommodation of Religion," *The Supreme Court Review* (1985): 1–59.

14. Joseph Story, *Commentaries on the Constitution of the United States*[5], ed. Melville M. Bigelow (Boston 1891–1905) II sec. 1871–72, 1874–79.

15. *The Writings and Speeches of Daniel Webster* (Boston 1903) XI 135–77 (at 176): The Girard Will Case: The Christian Ministry and the Religious Instruction of the Young, 20 February 1844.

16. Story's account gibes better with the outlook predominant among evangelical Christians of that generation: see William G. McLoughlin, "Isaac Backus and the Separation of Church and State in America," *AHR* 73 (1968): 1392–1413.

17. Story, *Commentaries on the Constitution of the United States*[5] II sec. 1877, 1879.

18. *DSSC* III 204: 10 June 1788. See Morton Borden, "Federalists, Antifederalists, and Religious Freedom," *JChS* 21 (1979): 469–82.

19. See *George Washington: A Collection*, ed. W. B. Allen (Indianapolis 1988) 547–48: 7 August 1790. For the original, see Papers of George Washington CCCXXXV 19–20, Library of Congress, Washington, D.C. For Washington's outlook and record, see Paul F. Boller, Jr., "George Washington and Religious Liberty," *WMQ* 17 (1960): 486–506.

20. See Anson Phelps Stokes, *Church and State in the United States* (New York 1950) I 862–63: Letter from Thomas Jefferson to Rabbi Mordecai M. Noah on 28 May 1818.

21. See *WrJM* IX 29–30: Letter to Jacob de la Motta in August 1820.

22. See *Treaties and Other International Agreements of the United States of America, 1776–1949*, ed. Charles I. Bevans (Washington, D.C., 1968–76) XI 1070–80 (at 1072): Tripoli. For the Arabic text and an accurate English translation, see *Treaties and Other International Acts of the United States of America*, ed. Hunter Miller (Washington, D.C., 1931–48) II 349–85: Tripoli, 4 November 1796 and 3 January 1797. Students of Barlow's brief career as a diplomat have neglected the problem posed by the discrepancy between the treaty's Arabic and its English text: see, for ex-

ample, James Woodress, *A Yankee's Odyssey: The Life of Joel Barlow* (Philadelphia 1958) 153–86, and Milton Cantor, "Joel Barlow's Mission to Algiers," *The Historian* 25 (1963): 172–94.

23. See *FSC* III 1690, 1700, 1702, 1715 (Maryland, 1776, 1795, 1798, 1851); III 1908, 1912–13 (Massachusetts, 1780, 1821); IV 2460–63, 2477, 2479, 2492 (New Hampshire, 1784, 1792, 1877); V 2597–99 (New Jersey, 1776, 1844); V 2793, 2798–99, 2806, 2815 (North Carolina, 1776, 1835, 1868). Until 1833, at least in principle, the Massachusetts constitution denied Jews equal protection of the law: above, III.vi.1, note 4. As late as 1818, Connecticut was unwilling to extend a guarantee of equal treatment to non-Christian denominations: *FSC* I 537, 544–45 (1818). Maryland finally guaranteed religious liberty to all in 1836 and added a provision to that effect to the state constitution in 1851: consider *FSC* 1689–90, 1715 (1776, 1851), in light of Benjamin H. Hartogensis, "Unequal Rights in Maryland since 1776," *American Jewish Historical Society Publications* 25 (1917): 93–107, and E. Milton Altfeld, *The Jew's Struggle for Religious and Civil Liberty in Maryland* (Baltimore 1924).

24. See Bernard Steiner, *Life and Correspondence of James McHenry* (Cleveland 1907) 470: Letter to Oliver Wolcott on 26 September 1800, and see *Treaties and Other International Agreements* XI 1081–87 (at 1084): Tripoli. This time, the article appeared in the Arabic text: *Treaties and Other International Acts* II 529–56: Tripoli, 4 June 1805. Circumspection was required of an administration headed by an individual suspected of being an infidel: see below, III.vi.4, note 54.

25. For the Senate vote, see *The Journal of the Senate, John Adams Administration, 1797–1801*, ed. Martin P. Claussen (Wilmington, Del., 1977) I 157, 160: 26 and 30 May and 7 June 1797 (Fifth Congress, First Session).

26. Adams began his presidency by emphasizing his "veneration for the religion of a people who profess and call themselves Christians" and his "fixed resolution to consider a decent respect for Christianity among the best recommendations for public service." See *CMPP* I 232: Inaugural Address, 4 March 1797. When he proclaimed days of "solemn humiliation, fasting, and prayer," he tended to speak in Trinitarian terms. See *CMPP* I 268–70 (at 269), 284–86 (at 285): 23 March 1798 and 6 March 1799. Washington consistently avoided such language, rarely used the word *God*, and tended to speak of "that Almighty Being who rules over the universe," of "the Great Author of every public and private good," of "the Invisible Hand which conducts the affairs of men," and of "the great Lord and Ruler of Nations." See *CMPP* I 51–54, 64–66, 162–67 (at 162), 179–80, 182–84 (at 182), 199–204 (at 199), 213–24 (at 214, 221, 224): First Inaugural Address, 30 April 1789; Proclamation of Day of Thanksgiving, 3 October 1789; First Annual Address, 8 January 1790; Sixth Annual Address, 19 November 1794; Proclamation of a Day of Thanksgiving, 1 January 1795; Seventh Annual Address, 8 December 1795; Eighth Annual Address, 7 December 1796; Farewell Address, 17 September 1796. Jefferson followed his example: *CMPP* I 321–24 (at 323–24), 326–32 (at 326), 342–46 (at 342), 378–82 (at 380), 451–56 (at 456): First Inaugural Address, 4 March 1801; First Annual Message, 8 December 1801; Second Annual Message, 15 December 1802; Second Inaugural Address, 4 March 1805; Eighth Annual Message, 8 November 1808. So did Madison: *CMPP* I 466–68 (at 468), 473–77 (at 477), 487, 491–96 (at 496), 513–21 (at 513, 520–21), 526–30 (at 530), 532–40 (at 532–33, 540), 547–54 (at 551, 554), 558, 560–69 (at 560–61, 568): First Inaugural Address, 4 March 1809; First Annual Message, 29 November 1809; Second Annual Mes-

sage, 5 December 1810; Third Annual Message, 5 November 1811; Proclamation of Day of Thanksgiving, 9 July 1812; Fourth Annual Message, 4 November 1812; Special Session Message, 25 May 1813; Proclamation of Day of Thanksgiving, 23 July 1813; Fifth Annual Message, 7 December 1813; Sixth Annual Message, 20 September 1814; Message to Senate and House of Representatives, 18 February 1815; Proclamation of a Day of Thanksgiving, 16 November 1814; Proclamation of Day of Thanksgiving, 4 March 1815; Seventh Annual Message, 5 December 1815.

27. In the highly charged atmosphere of the late 1790s, Adams's proclamations sparked controversy. The more scurrilous among his opponents contended that the proclamations were connected with the calling of a general assembly of the Presbyterian church; Adams was charged with aiming at its establishment as a national church, and the suspicion he incurred cost him critical political support. "The national fast recommended by me turned me out of office," Adams later concluded. "Nothing is more dreaded than the national government meddling with religion." See *The Spur of Fame: Dialogues of John Adams and Benjamin Rush, 1805–1813*, ed. John A. Schutz and Douglass Adair (San Marino, Calif., 1966) 224–26 (at 224): Letter to Benjamin Rush on 12 June 1812, and *Statesman and Friend: Correspondence of John Adams with Benjamin Waterhouse, 1784–1822*, ed. Worthington Chauncey Ford (Boston 1927) 68–71: Letter to Benjamin Waterhouse on 3 December 1811.

28. *Barnes v. First Parish*, 6 Mass. 401.

29. See *WrSA* IV 236, 238: Letter to John Scollay on 30 December 1780. For a perceptive discussion of the logic underlying the Standing Order, see Conrad Wright, "Piety, Morality, and the Commonwealth," *Crane Review* 9, no. 2 (Winter 1967): 90–106.

30. *A Bill Establishing a Provision for Teachers of the Christian Religion* (Richmond 1784).

31. See *PJM* VIII 149–52: Letter from Richard Henry Lee on 26 November 1784.

32. *CMPP* I 220: George Washington, Farewell Address, 17 September 1796.

33. *JCC* XII 1001–3: 12 October 1778.

34. See *JCC* XXXII 334–43 (esp. 340, 343): 13 July 1787, and *United States Statutes at Large* I 50: Act of 7 August 1789. In 1789, there was so little controversy that the final vote went unrecorded in both houses: see *DHFFC* III 116–17, 133–35, 137, 139: House of Representatives Journal, 21 July and 5–7 August 1789, and *DHFFC* I 105–6, 108, 110, 114: Senate Legislative Journal, 4–7 August 1789. The fact that the pertinent article of the original ordinance was amended at the bill's third reading deserves attention. Originally, it had read: "Institutions for the promotion of religion and morality, schools and the means of education shall forever be encouraged, and all persons while young shall be taught some useful Occupation." See *JCC* XXXII 314–20 (at 318): 11 July 1787. See above, III.ii.5, note 86.

35. See *Annals of Congress* I 914–15: 25 September 1789. The Senate added its support the following day: *DHFFC* I 197: Senate Legislative Journal, 26 September 1789.

36. See *DHFFC* I 12, 16, 23, 25: Senate Legislative Journal, 7, 15, 22, and 25 April 1789, and *DHFFC* III 17, 25–26, 33–34, 44: House of Representatives Journal, 9, 17, 25, and 27 April and 1 May 1789. See below, III.vi.4, note 59.

37. See *PJM* VIII 294–306 (at 302): Memorial and Remonstrance against Religious Assessments, 20 June 1785.

38. *PJM* VIII 285–86: Letter to James Monroe on 29 May 1785. The land grants

to the Ohio Company and to John Cleves Symmes took place while Madison was absent at the Philadelphia convention; after the statesman returned to New York, the Board of Treasury approved the grant to Royal Flint, Joseph Parker, et al. on the terms extended to the Ohio Company and Symmes: above, III.vi.2, note 10. Madison was no doubt pleased one day later when the Continental Congress voted that, in the future, "no gift of land be made for seminarys of learning or other purpose than those contained in the Ordinance of the 20th of May [17]85." See *JCC* XXXIII 701–2 (with 701 n. 1): 23 October 1787, and see *Territorial Papers* II 78: Congress—The Sale of Lands, 23 October 1787.

39. See *Annals of Congress* I 1108: 2 February 1790.

40. *CMPP* I 490: James Madison, Veto Message, 28 February 1811. See also *CMPP* I 489–90: James Madison, Veto Message, 21 February 1811.

41. See *WrTJ* (ed. Lipscomb and Bergh) XVII 417–41 (at 425): Letter to Joseph C. Cabell on 9 September 1817, with draft of "An Act for Establishing Elementary Schools."

42. See *FSC* III 1914 (Massachusetts, 1833). Note also *FSC* I 544–55 (Connecticut, 1818).

43. Cf. *PJM* VIII 301: Memorial and Remonstrance against Religious Assessments, 20 June 1785, with *James Madison on Religious Liberty*, ed. Robert S. Alley (Buffalo, N.Y., 1985) 82: Letter to F. L. Schaeffer on 3 December 1821.

44. See *PTJ* VIII 428–31: Letter from John Page on 23 August 1785.

45. For an overview, see Eugene R. Sheridan, "Introduction," in *Jefferson's Extracts from the Gospels*, ed. Dickinson W. Adams et al. (Princeton 1983) 3–42. For Jefferson's interest in Unitarianism, see the material collected in note 50, below.

46. Smith, *WN* V.i.g.8–15.

47. Jefferson, *NSV* 17 (160–61).

48. *CMPP* I 323: Thomas Jefferson, First Inaugural Address, 4 March 1801.

49. See *WrTJ* (ed. Ford) X 242–44: Letter to Thomas Cooper on 2 November 1822. For Jefferson's dislike of Calvin, whom he identified quite rightly as a proponent of religious persecution, see *Jefferson's Extracts from the Gospels* 385–86, 391–94 (at 392–93), 401–2, 405–7, 410–15: Letters to Thomas B. Parker on 15 May 1819, to William Short on 13 April 1820, to Jared Sparks on 4 November 1820, to Benjamin Waterhouse on 26 June and 19 July 1822, to John Adams on 11 April 1823, and to George Thacher on 26 January 1824.

50. See *Thomas Jefferson Correspondence, Printed from the Originals in the Collection of William K. Bixby*, ed. Worthington Chauncey Ford (Boston 1915) 238–39: Letter to Wells and Lilly on 1 April 1818; *WrTJ* (ed. Ford) X 242–44: Letter to Thomas Cooper on 2 November 1822; and *Jefferson's Extracts from the Gospels* 331–36, 385, 401–10, 413–15: Letters to Benjamin Rush on 21 April 1803 (with Syllabus of an Estimate of the merit of the doctrines of Jesus, compared with those of others), to Salma Hale on 26 July 1818, to Jared Sparks on 4 November 1820, to Timothy Pickering on 27 February 1821, to Thomas Whittemore on 5 June 1822, to Dr. Benjamin Waterhouse on 26 June and 19 July 1822, to James Smith on 8 December 1822, to John Davis on 18 January 1824, and to George Thacher on 26 January 1824.

51. See *Jefferson's Extracts from the Gospels* 375–77, 408–9: Letters to Margaret Bayard Smith on 6 August 1816 and to James Smith on 8 December 1822.

52. See *PTJ* II 545: The Revisal of the Laws, 18 June 1779: 82. A Bill for Establishing Religious Freedom.

53. Jefferson, *NSV* 17 (161).

54. In this connection, see Charles O. Lerche, Jr., "Jefferson and the Election of 1800: A Case Study in the Political Smear," *WMQ* 5 (1948): 467–91, and Constance B. Schulz, " 'Of Bigotry in Politics and Religion': Jefferson's Religion, the Federalist Press, and the Syllabus," *VMHB* 91 (1983): 73–91. Jefferson would almost certainly have been opposed to the de facto Protestant establishment that typified America in the era after his death. See Robert T. Handy, *A Christian America: Protestant Hopes and Historical Realities* (New York 1971), and Elwyn A. Smith, "The Voluntary Establishment of Religion," in *The Religion of the Republic*, ed. Elwyn A. Smith (Philadelphia 1971) 154–82.

55. See Thomas E. Buckley, S.J., *Church and State in Revolutionary Virginia* 140: Petition dated 3 November 1785.

56. See *DHRC* III 500: A Landholder VII, *Connecticut Courant*, 17 December 1787.

57. Cf. Thomas E. Buckley, S.J., *Church and State in Revolutionary Virginia* 180–82, who reads the concerns of twentieth-century libertarians back into the thinking of Jefferson and Madison and therefore makes the mistake of holding the evangelicals responsible for the Bill for Punishing Disturbers of Religious Worship and Sabbath Breakers.

58. See *PTJ* II 447–48, 492–507 (esp. 493, 497, 502), 559–61: The Revisal of the Laws, 18 June 1779: 45. A Bill for Licensing and Regulating Taverns; 64. A Bill for Proportioning Crimes and Punishments in Cases Heretofore Capital; and 88. A Bill to Prevent Gaming.

59. See "Madison's 'Detached Memoranda,' " ed. Elizabeth Fleet, *WMQ* 3 (1946): 534–68 (at 551–62), with Leo Pfeffer, "Madison's 'Detached Memoranda': Then and Now," in *The Virginia Statute for Religious Freedom* 283–312. Though Madison served on the committee in the First Congress that selected a chaplain and determined his remuneration, he later claimed that the deed was done "not with my approbation." On at least four occasions while president, he proclaimed days of humiliation and prayer: see above, III.vi.3, note 26 (near the end). Later he remarked, "There has been another deviation from the strict principle in the Executive Proclamations of fasts & festivals, so far, at least, as they have spoken the language of *injunction*, or have lost sight of the equality of *all* religious sects in the eye of the Constitution." See *WrJM* IX 98–103: Letter to Edward Livingston on 10 July 1822.

60. *WrJM* VIII 425–33 (at 430–32): Letter to Robert Walsh on 2 March 1819.

61. *WrJM* IX 124–34 (at 127): Letter to Edward Everett on 19 March 1823.

62. Tocqueville, *DA* I.ii.9 (301–15, esp. 304–8). See II.i.5–7, ii.9–17. If the modern republic presupposes the disestablishment of religion, it nonetheless relies upon the religion it displaces: see Harvey C. Mansfield, Jr., "The Religious Issue and the Origin of Modern Constitutionalism," *America's Constitutional Soul* (Baltimore 1991) 101–14 (esp. 101–4).

63. *WoAL* VIII 332–33: Second Inaugural Address, 4 March 1865.

64. *The Federalist* 84 (577–78). See III.iv.7, above.

65. *Camden Journal*, 28 November 1835. See III.v.6, above.

66. Consider *WrTJ* (ed. Ford) X 390–92: Letter to Roger C. Weightman on 24 June 1826 in light of Douglass Adair, "Rumbold's Dying Speech, 1685, and Jefferson's Last Words on Democracy, 1826," *Fame and the Founding Fathers*, ed. Trevor Colbourn (New York 1974) 192–202, and see William W. Freehling's depic-

tion of the political and ideological struggle that took place between "conditional terminators" of the Jeffersonian persuasion and "perpetualists" such as Calhoun: *The Road to Disunion: Secessionists at Bay, 1776–1854* (New York 1990).

67. *WoAL* IV 146, 160–61: Letters to Alexander H. Stephens on 30 November and 22 December 1860.

68. For the entire correspondence and the pertinent speech, see Alexander H. Stephens, *A Constitutional View of the Late War Between the States; its Causes, Character, Conduct and Results Presented in a Series of Colloquies at Liberty Hall* (Philadelphia 1868–70) II 265–300.

69. Henry Cleveland, *Alexander H. Stephens in Public and Private: With Letters and Speeches, Before, During, and Since the War* (Philadelphia 1866) 717–29 (esp. 721–23): The Cornerstone Speech, 21 March 1861. In this connection, see Thomas E. Schott, *Alexander H. Stephens of Georgia* (Baton Rouge 1988) esp. 291–335.

70. See Bertram Wyatt Brown, "Honor and Secession," *Yankee Saints and Southern Sinners* (Baton Rouge 1985) 183–213, and Kenneth S. Greenberg, *Masters and Statesmen: The Political Culture of American Slavery* (Baltimore 1985).

71. Jefferson, *NSV* 17 (161).

72. *WrTJ* (ed. Ford) IV 185: Letter to Jean Nicolas Démeunier on 26 June 1786.

73. Jefferson, *NSV* 18 (162–63).

74. After noting Arist. *Poet.* 1448b4–20, cf. *Pol.* 1263b36–37 with 1276a8–b15; see 1278b6–15; and consider I Prologue, above.

75. Consider Jefferson, *NSV* 14 (137–43), in light of Jean Yarbrough, "Race and the Moral Foundation of the American Republic: Another Look at the Declaration and the *Notes on Virginia*," *JP* 53 (1991): 90–105. As a consequence of the fact that Jefferson espoused a variety of opinions that are difficult, if not impossible, to reconcile, scholars have advanced a variety of arguments concerning his position on the question of slavery. For a survey of the pertinent evidence, see William W. Freehling, "The Founding Fathers and Slavery," *AHR* 77 (1982): 81–93, and Alison Goodyear Freehling, *Drift toward Dissolution: The Virginia Slavery Debate of 1831–1832* (Baton Rouge 1982) 96–109. Cf. William Cohen, "Thomas Jefferson and the Problem of Slavery," *JAH* 56 (1969): 503–26, and John Chester Miller, *The Wolf by the Ears: Thomas Jefferson and Slavery* (New York 1977). In this connection, see David Brion Davis, *The Problem of Slavery in the Age of Revolution, 1770–1823* (Ithaca 1975) 169–84. See also William W. Freehling, *The Road to Disunion* I: *Secessionists at Bay, 1776–1854* (New York 1990) 121–31.

76. *MJQA* IV 506–7, 524–25, 533, V 3–4, 15: 16 January, 11 and 27 February, and 1–3 and 7 March 1820. See *MJQA* IV 496, 522, 528–29, 532–33, V 12–15, 199: 5 January, 11, 20, and 26–27 February, 4–6 March, and 12 November 1820.

77. *MJQA* V 4–12 (esp. 10–11): 3 March 1820. In this connection, consider Kenneth S. Greenberg, "The Nose, the Lie, and the Duel in the Antebellum South," *AHR* 95 (1990): 57–74.

78. See Mary B. Putnam, *The Baptists and Slavery, 1840–1845* (Ann Arbor 1913); C. Bruce Staiger, "Abolitionism and the Presbyterian Schism of 1837–1838," *Mississippi Valley Historical Review* 36 (1949): 391–414; and Donald G. Mathews, *Slavery and Methodism: A Chapter in American Morality, 1780–1845* (Princeton 1965).

79. See Paul Finkelman, *An Imperfect Union: Slavery, Federalism, and Comity* (Chapel Hill 1981).

80. See Roy Franklin Nichols, *The Disruption of American Democracy* (New York 1948). For an enlightening, if unpersuasive, attempt to make sense of the collapse

of the party system and of secession without giving central place to slavery, cf. Michael F. Holt, *The Political Crisis of the 1850s* (New York 1978). Holt's refusal to concede slavery's central importance is rooted in his failure to appreciate the profound difference made by the change of opinion throughout the South as to whether the peculiar institution was advantageous, just, and good. For useful correctives, see Robert F. Durden, *The Self-Inflicted Wound: Southern Politics in the Nineteenth Century* (Lexington, Ky., 1985), and Richard H. Sewell, *A House Divided: Sectionalism and Civil War, 1848–1865* (Baltimore 1988).

81. For a representative selection, see *The Ideology of Slavery: Proslavery Thought in the Antebellum South, 1830–1860*, ed. Drew Gilpin Faust (Baton Rouge 1981). See William Sumner Jenkins, *Pro-Slavery Thought in the Old South* (Chapel Hill 1935). The most interesting and radical of these writers was George Fitzhugh. Though he was by no means representative of mainstream proslavery thought, he deserves close attention, for he pressed the argument on slavery's behalf to its logical conclusion by focusing his attack directly against Adam Smith, John Locke, Thomas Hobbes, and the commercial society of the North; and in the process, he arguably foreshadowed the position to which an independent slaveholders' republic would eventually have been driven. Consider *Ante-Bellum: Writings of George Fitzhugh and Hinton Rowan Helper on Slavery*, ed. Harvey Wish (New York 1960) 41–156: *Sociology for the South, or the Failure of Free Society* (1854) and *Cannibals All! or, Slaves Without Masters* (1857), in light of Eugene D. Genovese, *The World the Slaveholders Made: Two Essays in Interpretation* (New York 1969). For a discussion of the chief precursor of the ideologues of the 1850s, see Genovese, *Western Civilization through Slaveholding Eyes: The Social and Historical Thought of Thomas Roderick Dew* (New Orleans 1986). That one can find antecedents for the proslavery argument in the rhetoric of the extreme Federalists and that this argument retained purchase in some circles in the North in no way alters the fact that the comparatively successful propagation of the proslavery argument in the South was a political phenomenon of profound importance distinguishing that region from the North: cf. Larry E. Tise, *Proslavery: A History of the Defense of Slavery in America, 1701–1840* (Athens, Ga., 1987), with Eugene D. Genovese's review: *GHQ* 72 (1988): 671–83.

82. See Emory M. Thomas, *The Confederate Nation: 1861–1865* (New York 1979). States' rights became the creed of the South only when it became evident that the slaveholders might someday lose control of the federal government. Those who framed the constitution of the Confederacy acted in the same spirit, for they betrayed remarkably little interest in writing states' rights into that document— except, of course, in prohibiting interference with slavery in the states: see Don E. Fehrenbacher, *Constitutions and Constitutionalism in the Slaveholding South* (Athens, Ga., 1989) 33–81.

83. Cf. *WoJSM* X 117–63 (at 133–34): "Coleridge" with August. *De civ. D.* 19.24. As one would expect, there was a close correlation between slaveholding and secessionist sentiment in states such as Virginia, North Carolina, and Tennessee: see Daniel W. Crofts, *Reluctant Confederates: Upper South Unionists in the Secession Crisis* (Chapel Hill 1989) esp. 361–81. There was a similar link between the absence of slaveholding and armed southern resistance to the Confederacy: see Eric Foner, "The South's Inner Civil War," *American Heritage* 40, no. 2 (March 1989): 46–56.

84. Jefferson, *NSV* 18 (163).

85. *WoAL* VIII 333: Second Inaugural Address, 4 March 1865.

86. See Hor. *Epist.* 1.10.24.

Epilogue

1. *WoAL* I 108–15: Address Before the Young Men's Lyceum of Springfield, Illinois, 27 January 1838. In citing the text, I have used angle brackets to indicate the passages which the editor has marked off as illegible. My reading of Lincoln's speech owes much to Harry V. Jaffa, *Crisis of the House Divided: An Interpretation of the Issues in the Lincoln-Douglas Debates* (Chicago 1982) 183–272.

2. *The Federalist* 72 (488).

3. Arist. *Pol.* 1280b10–12. See I.i.5, above.

4. Cf. Arist. *Pol.* 1263b36–37 with 1276a8–b15, and see 1278b6–15; then, consider *The Federalist* 10 in light of *WrTJ* (ed. Ford) X 390–92: Letter to Roger C. Weightman on 24 June 1826.

5. *WoJSM* X 117–63 (at 133–34): "Coleridge."

6. Cf. Joseph Cropsey, "The United States as a Regime and the Sources of the American Way of Life" and "Modernization: United States Policy and the Meaning of Modernity," *Political Philosophy and the Issues of Politics* (Chicago 1977) 1–15, 157–71, with "The Moral Basis of International Action," ibid., 172–88, and see Harvey C. Mansfield, Jr., *America's Constitutional Soul* (Baltimore 1991).

7. *CMPP* I 322: First Inaugural Address, 4 March 1801.

8. Their attitude is especially visible in the bills of rights added to or included within the various state constitutions: *FSC* VII 3814 (Virginia, 1776); V 2788 (North Carolina, 1776); V 3083–84 (Pennsylvania, 1776); VI 3741, 3754, 3764 (Vermont, 1777, 1786, 1793); III 1892 (Massachusetts, 1780); IV 2457, 2475 (New Hampshire, 1784, 1792). Cf. *WrJD* 386–97 (at 386): *Letters from a Farmer in Pennsylvania* (1768); *WoJW* II 721–46 (at 727): *Considerations on the Nature and Extent of the Legislative Authority of the British Parliament* (1774); *American Political Writing during the Founding Era, 1760–1805*, ed. Charles S. Hyneman and Donald S. Lutz (Indianapolis 1983) I 480–522 (at 499–500): [Theophilus Parsons], "The Essex Result," 1778; and Jefferson, *NSV* 221: Draught of a Fundamental Constitution for the Commonwealth of Virginia (Appendix 2), with Madison, *The Federalist* 49–50. Note, however, *RFC* II 476–77: 31 August 1787 and *The Federalist* 43 (297–98) with 41 (270).

9. One implication of the "conceptual" history now fashionable would be that every such return is illusory and that all historical change is really drift: see Terence Ball and J. G. A. Pocock, "Introduction," in *Conceptual Change and the Constitution*, ed. Terence Ball and J. G. A. Pocock (Lawrence, Kans., 1988) 1–13 (esp. 7–11).

10. Pl. *Resp.* 6.497c–d. Note *Leg.* 6.769a–771a (with 772b–d), 12.949e–953e, 957a–e, 960b–969d.

11. Note *WrJM* IX 256–66 (at 258–59): Letter to Samuel Harrison Smith on 4 November 1826; cf. Letter from Thomas Jefferson to James Madison on 1 February 1825 (Manuscripts Division, Library of Congress) with *WrJM* IX 218–20: Letter to Thomas Jefferson on 8 February 1825, and see Hamilton, *The Federalist* 23 (151), 26 (165), and Madison, *The Federalist* 49; then, consider III.i.6–8 and iv.6, above.

12. *WoAL* I 112: Address Before the Young Men's Lyceum of Springfield, Illinois, 27 January 1838.

13. Consider the essays collected in *Confronting the Constitution: The Challenge to Locke, Montesquieu, Jefferson, and the Federalists from Utilitarianism, Historicism, Marxism, Freudianism, Pragmatism, and Existentialism* . . . , ed. Allan Bloom (Washington, D.C., 1990), and see Harvey C. Mansfield, Jr., *The Spirit of Liberalism* (Cambridge, Mass., 1978) 16–71, 89–114, and *America's Constitutional Soul* esp. 1–17, 73–162. For a defense of what now passes as academic orthodoxy, cf. Richard Rorty, "The Priority of Democracy to Philosophy," in *The Virginia Statute for Religious Freedom: Its Evolution and Consequences in American History*, ed. Merrill D. Peterson and Robert C. Vaughan (Cambridge 1988) 257–82. Rorty's complacency in the face of nihilism is rooted in his failure to appreciate the degree to which political practice is guided by the fundamental principles which inform public opinion.

14. Madison, *The Federalist* 10 (58). Consider, in particular, the evidence collected by Marc F. Plattner, "Natural Rights and the Moral Presuppositions of Political Economy," in *From Political Economy to Economics and Back?* ed. James H. Nichols, Jr., and Colin Wright (San Francisco 1990) 35–56.

15. *WoAL* IV 262–71 (at 268): First Inaugural Address-Final Text, 4 March 1861.

16. For this epilogue's epigraph, see *WrEB* I 437: *Thoughts on the Present Discontents* (1770). See John Agresto, *The Supreme Court and Constitutional Democracy* (Ithaca 1984).

17. After considering the testimony of James Madison and Thomas Jefferson (III.iii.6, note 110, above), cf. H. Jefferson Powell, "The Original Understanding of Original Intent," *Harvard Law Review* 98 (1985): 885–948, with Charles A. Lofgren, "The Original Understanding of Original Intent?" *Constitutional Commentary* 5 (1988): 77–113. The most impressive, recent attempt to demonstrate that judicial supremacy was intended by the Founders provides ample evidence for a refutation of that very position: cf. David A. J. Richards, *Foundations of American Constitutionalism* (New York 1989) 131–299, with 18–130. Cf. also Richards, *Toleration and the Constitution* (New York 1986).

18. Consider Walter Berns, *Taking the Constitution Seriously* (New York 1987) esp. 181–241, in light of Madison, *The Federalist* 51 (352).

19. *WrJM* IX 137–44 (at 143): Letter to Thomas Jefferson on 27 June 1823.

20. *WrTJ* (ed. Ford) X 140–43: Letter to Spencer Roane on 6 September 1819.

21. *WoTJ* XII 161–64: Letter to William Charles Jarvis on 28 September 1820.

22. August. *De civ. D.* 19.24.

23. *WoAL* VII 17–23 (at 23): Address Delivered at the Dedication of the Cemetery at Gettysburg, 19 November 1863.

Index

Abraham, 54, 210
Absolute monarchy, 176
Accident and force, government based on, 34–35, 47, 71
Act of Settlement, 56–57
Acton, Lord, 288–89 (n. 43)
Adair, Douglass, xxiii, 266–67 (n. 1)
Adams, Abigail, 21, 156
Adams, John, 194, 201, 231; fascinated by classical republican example but does not embrace, xxiii, 331–32 (n. 20); interest in political architecture, 1; on tendency of compatriots to link safeguarding liberty with glory, 3; inclined to see conspiracy where carelessness lies, 13; disputes with Daniel Leonard whether British rule oppressive, 15; espouses revolution principles of Sidney, Harrington, and Locke, 15; echoes Locke on natural freedom and equality of man, 17; argues for subordination of public to domestic life, 21–24; castigates Aristotle for excluding merchants and artisans from public life, 24; author of *A Defence of the Constitutions of Government of the United States*, 24, 29, 169; traces revolution principles to Aristotle, Plato, Livy, and Cicero as well as to Sidney, Harrington, and Locke, 27; assumes that some men are able to apply *lógos* to moral and political issues, 28–29; convinced that well-ordered constitution can call forth capable men, 30; fears majority tyranny, 31; celebrates American accomplishment in establishing without pretense of divine intervention first governments grounded in principles of nature, 33–34; admires political maxim that every man must be considered a knave, 45, 275–76 (nn. 63–64); on obstacles to abolition of slavery, 95; on American diversity, 102; on likelihood of formation of Court and Country parties in America, 109; contemptuous description of Hamilton, 112; author of *Discourses on Davila*, 140–41, 174; dispute with Jefferson over virtues of British Constitution, 140–44, 312–13 (n. 123); loss of presidency to Jefferson, 145; helps provoke overreaction of Jeffersonian Republicans, 146–47; discusses republic's need for and dangers inherent in

natural aristocracy, 159–60, 163, 169, 172–76, 319 (n. 62), 326–28 (nn. 127, 131, 134); calls for national university, 172; with an eye to Aristotle concedes that it is easier to discern excellences of body than excellences of soul, 172, 326–27 (n. 127); at first thinks passion for public good necessary in modern republic, 173, 200; seeks substitute for virtue in love of fame, 173–75, 327–28 (nn. 133–35); wishes to exploit for the common good the passion for distinction and to confer grand titles on leading magistrates, 174–75, 312 (n. 120), 327–28 (nn. 133–38); bitterness in old age, 175; doubts about future of republic, 175–76; approves of Blackstone's argument for denying suffrage to dependent poor, 195–96; comes to doubt whether classical virtue is salutary and desirable, 201–5; partisan of modern virtue of humanity, 205; fears that atheism may endanger republican government, 206, 208; ratifies treaty denying that American republic was founded on Christian religion, 211–12; suffers for use of Christian language in presidential pronouncements, 212, 340–41 (nn. 26–27); advocates religious assessments in Massachusetts, 222; Madison dislikes, 312–13 (n. 123); debt to Adam Smith, 328 (n. 135); friendly to spirit of commerce and progress in the arts and thinks they improve morals, 333 (n. 35)
Adams, John Quincy, 334–35 (n. 53); on Jefferson, Declaration of Independence, and slavery, 1–2; on Constitution and Declaration of Independence, 61; on slavery as threat to Union, 107; program of internal improvements, 150; proposes national university, 172; on southern adherence to slavery, 227–28
Adams, Samuel: conspiratorial frame of mind, 13; on man's right to fruits of his labor, 16; desire to make Boston a Christian Sparta, 39, 108, 212; supports establishment of religion in Massachusetts, 207–8, 212, 222
Africa, African: and slavery, 78, 89–90, 204, 224; and colonization, 204
Agriculture, 34; modern republics devoted to improvement of, 22, 205; and manu-

mankind for self-government, 33; on inadequacy of old confederation, on mutability and injustice of state laws, and on origins of Constitutional Convention, 37, 270 (n. 29), 305–8 (nn. 71, 76, 82); critique of classical republicanism and case for geographical extension, 39–48, 54–55, 65, 114, 271 (n. 36), 330 (n. 158), 332–33 (n. 28); preeminence at Constitutional Convention, 40, 49, 272 (n. 44), 288 (n. 42); on attempt by *pólis* to use moral training and superstition to give "to every citizen the same opinions, the same passions, and the same interests," 41–42; on capacity of frivolous and fanciful distinctions to give rise to civil strife, 41–42, 48; on origins of faction, 41–42, 164; sees in geographical extension, economic differentiation, and multiplication of religious sects an antidote to faction, 41–55 passim, 63, 76, 108, 114, 192–93; exhibits respect for the capacity of political architecture to shape civil society and social and class groupings within it, 41–74 passim; on threat posed within community by gap between the propertied and the propertyless, 42; on incompatibility of direct democracy with personal security and rights of property, 44; embraces indirect rule and "the great principle of representation," 44, 56; makes quasi-Hobbesian case that a large, popular assembly made up of men like Socrates would still be a mob, 44, 65, 274 (n. 57); eager to encourage officeholding by the best men, 44–45, 170; conviction that enlightened statesmen will not always be at helm, 45, 275 (n. 60); on man's limited capacity for virtue, 45–46, 276 (n. 65); indebted in part to Montesquieu and Hume for his discussion of faction, 45–47; on religion as motive for persecution, 48–49; favors tepid piety, 48–54; indebted to Locke, Voltaire, Montesquieu, Hume, and Adam Smith for his understanding of religious factionalism, 49–54, 278 (n. 91); seems to have been skeptical of revealed religion and inclined to rational religion, 53, 278–79 (n. 96); fears failure to give federal government a veto, 55–56; on structure of federal government, 55–72 passim; and federal principle, 56–58, 133–34, 147–49, 178–83; and separation of powers, 57–72 passim; seeks intermediate ground between ancient and modern political science, aiming to use institutions of limited government to liberate "the reason of the public," 58–72 passim; concedes human depravity while arguing human

capacity for virtue in some measure, 60, 267 (n. 10); attempts to reconcile wisdom and virtue with popular consent, 61; on justice as end of government to which, if necessary, liberty will be sacrificed, 62, 239; recognizes political utility of veneration for Constitution, 62–63, 130–32, 168, 182–83, 237, 330 (n. 159); advocates exclusion of the people in their collective capacity from administration of government, 63; in accepting Supreme Court comes close to accepting will in community independent of majority, 67; on majority rule, 71; on need for frequent elections, 72–73, 170; concedes distinction between "public good" and "private rights," 73; on injustice of slavery and slave trade, 76, 88–89, 97–98, 153–54, 203, 228; fears slavery will divide Union, 76–77, 82–84, 283 (n. 7); proposes gradual emancipation in conjunction with colonization, 78, 95, 104–5; expects southern to outstrip northern population growth, 84; and three-fifths rule, 85–87; on labor as primary source of wealth, 86–87; among many at Constitutional Convention unwilling to admit in Constitution that there can be property in men, 88–89, 288–89 (nn. 42–43); keeps notes of constitutional debates, 89–93, 113, 141; accepts compromise on slave trade, 97–99; on commercial character of Union, on its diversity, on likelihood that manufacturing would soon be widespread, and on likelihood of gradual assimilation of manners, mores, and institutions, 99–104, 128, 296–97 (n. 110), 298 (n. 119), 307 (n. 78); expectation that slavery's importance in the South would decline, 103–5; fails to foresee need for party system, 105–6; foresees Civil War at time of Missouri crisis, 106; long insensitive to danger posed to Union by slavery, 106–8, 148–55, 203–5, 226–27, 317–18 (nn. 37–38), 336 (nn. 67–68), 343–44 (n. 66); turns to diffusion throughout Union as antidote, 107, 155; on perpetual peace and penchant for war where will in government is independent of the people, 122, 181–82, 304 (n. 56); evolution of his attitudes regarding the relationship between federal and state governments, 127–30, 133–34, 147–51, 178–83, 305–8 (nn. 71–73, 76, 78, 82); origins of breach with Hamilton, 127–44 passim, 307–15 passim; turnabout on question of discriminating between original holders of debts incurred during Revolutionary War and speculators who later purchased certificates, 128, 134–36, 309–